THE INDIAN NATIONAL CONGRESS
Centenary Hindsights

THE INDIAN NATIONAL CONGRESS

Centenary Hindsights

edited by

D. A. LOW

DELHI
OXFORD UNIVERSITY PRESS
BOMBAY CALCUTTA MADRAS
1988

Oxford University Press, Walton Street, Oxford OX2 6DP

New York Toronto
Delhi Bombay Calcutta Madras Karachi
Petaling Jaya Singapore Hong Kong Tokyo
Nairobi Dar es Salaam
Melbourne Auckland

and associates in
Berlin Ibadan

Phototypeset by Spantech Publishers Pvt Ltd, New Delhi 110008
Printed by Rekha Printers (P) Ltd, New Delhi 110020
and published by S.K. Mookerjee, Oxford University Press
YMCA Library Building, Jai Singh Road, New Delhi 110001

FOREWORD

During 1985 a number of international conferences of historians and political scientists were held in various parts of the world in association with the centenary of the founding of the Indian National Congress. One of these conferences was held at St Antony's College, Oxford, and was jointly sponsored by the Centre of Indian Studies in the University of Oxford, and the Centre of South Asian Studies in the University of Cambridge. The object of the conference was to review the current state of knowledge, and it focused upon the ongoing debates concerning the history of Indian nationalism and a number of related themes. Amongst the fifty and more participants were scholars from elsewhere in Britain, Europe, the United States, Australia, and Pakistan. A distinguished contingent was present from India. Warm thanks are due to the Government of India, the British Academy, the Charles Wallace Fund, and the British Economic and Social Research Council for generous grants towards the Conference expenses.

The principal animator and organiser was Dr Tapan Raychaudhuri, Reader in South Asian History in the University of Oxford. The participants would all wish to express their very warm thanks to him for all the very considerable efforts he expended to bring the conference together and make it so enjoyable and stimulating an experience.

As a small part of the division of labour, the present editor undertook to see some of the papers through the press and we are grateful to the Oxford University Press for agreeing to publish this selection. It does not purport to provide a comprehensive survey. It is hoped, however, that it will stand alongside the other volumes of conference proceedings from the Centenary Year 1985 as part of a larger effort to enhance our understanding of a remarkable story.

Clare Hall, Cambridge   D. A. Low

CONTENTS

CONGRESS AND THE RISORGIMENTO: A COMPARATIVE STUDY OF NATIONALISM

ANTONY COPLEY

More than any other nationalist movement the Italian Risorgimento captured the imagination of contemporary Europe and through the writings of historians, especially of such English historians as G. M. Trevelyan, continued to do so amongst succeeding generations. The Indian freedom struggle under the direction of the Indian National Congress cast an analogous spell over the twentieth century, especially in the Third World. In the centenary year of the founding of Congress, and partly in an endeavour to find something new to say on so thoroughly debated a movement, it seemed promising to put Congress and the Risorgimento alongside one another and ask some comparative questions. In what way, for example, was Congress to borrow from the Risorgimento? How similar were their strategies, both in the pursuit of national unification and in their quest for an authentic popular nationalism? In many ways Congress had as much to learn from the failures of the Risorgimento as from its successes.

Manifold obstacles stand in the way of such comparative

history and it may be as well at the outset to show that these are
appreciated: a recognition of the limited gains to be made from
such a comparative exercise may be the best way of indicating
its positive advantages. There are self-evident massive differences of population (Italy's was but 27 million in 1870, India's
at the time of independence, over 300 million) and of land-mass.
Another problematic is that of chronology. That of the Risorgimento covers the decades 1790–1870; that of the Indian nationalist
movement under Congress 1885–1947. How meaningful are
comparisons between societies at different moments of time?
This essay, however, argues from the premise that there is a
more meaningful comparison to be drawn between the histories of
India and Italy from the beginning of the nineteenth century down
to the mid twentieth: throughout this period both countries
were struggling towards a sense of national self-consciousness.
Arguably the history of a more authentic, if hardly more admirable, Italian nationalism begins after 1870: its expression lay in
late nineteenth century imperialism, especially under Crispi in
the 1890s, and in Mussolini's Fascism. There is a well-known
dichotomy applied to Italian history: a period of poetry during
the Risorgimento is succeeded by a period of prose. In fact the
rhetoric and romanticism surrounding the Risorgimento are
highly misleading. Congress politicians had as much to learn
from the painful working out of economic, social and political
questions in the so-called period of prose as from the period of
unification. There was, above all, the horrible warning of the
emergence of Fascism out of Italy's continuing quest for an
integral nationalism. Clearly India's own quest for a national
identity did not begin in 1885. If historians are hesitant at establishing any links between India's traditional culture and the
centralized empires of ancient India and modern Indian nationalism, and continue to wonder if the idea of nationalism is not
acquired through contact with Europe, something in this context
has to be said on such pre-1885 phenomena as the Bengal Renaissance and the Great Rebellion of 1857–8. One might also wonder
at the outset whether very precise comparisons are of value.
Should one attempt comparisons between leaders, between say
Mazzini and Aurobindo Ghose, Garibaldi and Gandhi, Cavour

and Patel? Could a case be made for comparing Italian irreden-
tism, particularly over the Alto Adige, and India's concern for
its frontiers, especially in the North East Frontier Agency?
There is an interesting case to be made for comparing the kind
of parliamentary politics pursued in Italy after 1870 (though in
fact introduced by Cavour in Piedmont in the 1850s), known as
transformismo, with the factional politics of independent India.
Such comparisons are certainly tempting. They lead in endless
directions, some telling, some gratuitous. This essay will restrict
itself to two main lines of enquiry: a comparison of the political
strategies both nationalist movements were to pursue for unification, and an examination of the way both sought some kind of
integral nationalism within their highly pluralist societies.

It is interesting to open out the discussion at this stage by
looking at the commentaries of three outstanding twentieth-
century leaders on the Italian story: Gandhi, Jawaharlal Nehru
and Subhas Bose. They reveal a very interesting diversity of
response.

Gandhi's highly perceptive, if not wholly accurate, insights are
to be found in *Hind Swaraj*, that seminal text in his affirmation of
Indian nationalism. It was first published in Gujarati in 1909. One
of the texts cited amongst the 'authorities and testimonies' of *Hind
Swaraj* was Mazzini's *The Duties of Man*. Gandhi was replying to an
argument that India should throw off imperial rule in the same
manner as Italians had liberated themselves—by force of arms—
from Austrian control. He may be unfair in bracketing Garibaldi
with Cavour and Victor Emmanuel II and seeing him as a mere
protagonist of the ambitions of the Savoyard dynasty. But he is
almost 'modern' in supporting Mazzini's argument that Italy had
not in fact achieved freedom, not only because Italians had failed
to achieve a republic but because the masses, above all the peasantry, had gained nothing from unification. Gandhi was, of course,
equally concerned to argue that a violent struggle would be self-
defeating, not just because of the superior military power of the
Raj but because violent means could not lead to any happy end.
He observed of Italy: 'Mazzini has shown in his writings on
duty that every man must learn how to rule himself. This has
not happened in Italy.'[1] Gandhi's commentary seemingly anti-

cipates some of the findings of that most sophisticated of modern interpreters of the Risorgimento, Denis Mack Smith. In his pioneering monograph *Cavour and Garibaldi, 1860: A Study in Political Conflict* (1954) he blows apart the Trevelyan thesis of an Italy united under the conjoint leadership of Cavour, Garibaldi and Mazzini, and shows that Italy had not been united in the cause of Italian patriotism but in the interests of the Piedmontese monarchy. Gandhi's comments on the Italian peasantry may have been a lucky by-product of his own growing concern with the plight of the Indian peasant, but again they anticipate Mack Smith's view that the peasantry were bypassed by the Risorgimento. Gandhi raises the fundamental question which concerns modern historians: what was the extent of popular involvement in the Risorgimento? Gandhi was to visit Italy but once, on his return journey to India from the second Round Table Conference. Pope Pius XI would not agree to see him, though we gather from Madeleine Slade's memoir that Gandhi was transfixed by a life-size crucifix he saw in the Sistine Chapel on his visit to the Vatican. Mussolini, on the other hand, sought him out, though the dictator left a less favourable impression: to his question, what did Gandhi make of the Fascist state, Gandhi replied, 'You are building a house of cards.' Mussolini apparently paid Gandhi a compliment by rising to greet him during the ten-minute interview. He usually sat throughout such meetings. Gandhi may have been impressed by the maternity and children's welfare centres he was to visit, but certainly not by the display of the Balilla (the Fascist youth organization) on one of their military exercises.[2]

Jawaharlal Nehru's comments are drawn from his *Glimpses of World History*, itself an absolutely engrossing and often brilliant exercise in comparative history. The work is a compilation of letters which Nehru wrote to his daughter, Indira, on and off, during his detention in the years 1931 to 1933. In the space devoted to the history of Europe Italy does not loom large, and its history does not seem to be such as to endear Italy to Nehru. In many ways the rise of Mussolini and Fascism to power seems to overshadow and condition his response. His hostile account of Roman civilization owes much to his re-reading of Gibbon's ironic *Decline and Fall*. He sees Roman civilization as one of rich men, 'a rather commonplace and dull crowd'.[3] He is appalled by their conspicuous consumption, their dependence on slavery and their surrender to military dictatorship. Nehru's interpretation reveals rather interesting features in his attitude to tradition and his ambiguous regard for India's past. In a spirit of cultural pride he contrasts continuity in the history of Indian and Chinese tradition with the way Roman civilization was destroyed by the barbarian invasions. He denies any real continuity between ancient Rome and the neo-classical imperial ideal of the medieval Holy Roman empire and the Papacy, though no doubt this is also inspired by a wish to ridicule the Roman posturings of Mussolini. Nehru also emphasizes how much more advanced Asian states were than those of medieval Europe; yet his was a critical pride in India's past, for he was keenly aware that the continuing hold of tradition was a brake on India's way forward to modernization. He recognized that such medieval comparisons were misleading, for within medieval Europe new liberating forces were at work, with the rise of cities, a new middle class, printing, and maybe above all a new curiosity about science. He acknowledged the contribution of Venice and Genoa as commercial cities and the cultural achievements of the north Italian cities. Yet Italy does not emerge any too favourably from his account of the Renaissance. Maybe the agnostic Nehru was too alienated by the history of the medieval Papacy and the Counter-Reformation. He does, however, have favourable things to say about the Florentine Renaissance, especially of Leonardo da Vinci, 'a favourite of mine'. 'Much may be forgiven Florence', he says—

we may excuse her even her money-lenders because of the great men she has produced. The shadow of these great sons of hers lies on her still and as you pass the streets of this beautiful city or look at the lovely Arno as it flows by under the medieval bridges, an enchantment seems to come over you and the past becomes vivid and alive. Dante goes by, and Beatrice, the lady he loved, passes, leaving faint perfume trailing behind her. And Leonardo seems to march along the narrow streets, lost in thought, pondering over the mysteries of life and Nature.[4]

Yet the Renaissance in Italy is seen quickly to founder. Nehru is particularly scathing of the political theory of Macchiavelli. Italy is written off as a backwater by the late sixteenth century. Nehru seems unaware of the writings of Vico and Beccaria in the eighteenth century and would no doubt have been surprised at the claims made by the likes of Benedetto Croce for Italy's contribution to the Enlightenment.

Yet the stirrings of revival (and Risorgimento means rebirth) came with the idea of Italia: Nehru compares this to Indian reverence for Bharat Mata, or Mother India. Nehru's enthusiasm is to be far more engaged by the French Revolution, and his account of the industrial revolution and the rise of socialism overshadows his handling of nineteenth-century nationalism. He recognizes Napoleon's unwitting contribution to the rise of nationalism and is perceptive in his grasp of the way Napoleon was subsequently to manufacture the myth of his consciously contributing to the rise of new European states. Nehru attacks the settlement of the Congress of Vienna but goes on to expose serious flaws in the character of the nationalist response to its constraints. He seemingly looks at nineteenth century nationalism through the socialist eyes of the Second International. He sees it as tainted with a chauvinism which led to imperialism. 'A narrow spirit of nationalism', he claims, 'was whipped up in each western country, so that the masses might be misled and made to hate their neighbours in other countries and thus be kept ready for war.'[5] He likewise emphasizes that the people at large had gained little from nationalism and would not do so unless a national revolution was accompanied by a social.

But Nehru's was a romantic temperament and he could not fail to be moved in part by the trilogy of G. M. Trevelyan on the Risorgimento. Clearly Trevelyan's enthusiasm for the Roman Republic of 1848–9 had rubbed off on Nehru, and he is more subject to that myth of a Risorgimento triumvirate of Cavour, Garibaldi and Mazzini. However, he is alert to Cavour's opportunism in harnessing the influence of the radicals to be rid of dynastic rivals to Piedmont and to Mazzini's disappointment, as a republican, with the new Italy. He is very scathing of Italy's opportunist changing of sides in the First World War: 'this attitude of offering her services to the highest bidder was not a very edifying one but nations are quite callous and have a way of behaving in a manner which would shame any private individual."[6] At this point in the history Nehru's attention is dominated by the Russian Revolution, and when he comes to describe the rise of Fascism he does so in Marxist terms. Italy is seen to be the most exhausted of the European belligerent states, and as the sit-in strikes of 1920 'fizzled out'[7] Mussolini was able to capitalize on the fears of the ruling classes, above all the capitalists, whilst at the same time borrowing the slogans of the left to appeal to the people in a bid for power. Nehru struggles in vain to make sense of such a radical right movement. He can see no consistent ideology in Fascism, denies that it has one, and sees it simply as acting as part of the establishment. He scoffs at the Roman trappings of Fascism. But Nehru's attempt to understand Fascism through Marxist spectacles leaves him blind to the way Fascism was a desperate and dreadfully misguided attempt to fill the vacuum left by the failure of the Risorgimento to engender any real all-embracing sense of national identity. Nehru's blindness to the appeal of nationalism in its Fascist form is curiously akin to his failure to read the appeal of communalism.

Subhas Bose, on the contrary, was very aware of this element in Mussolini's Italy. Like Nehru Bose was a radical nationalist but in his case this was to lead him into a flirtation with Fascism. From childhood Bose had displayed a penchant for military parades and was to make a fool of himself by trying to introduce a para-military element into the Congress Volunteers at the Calcutta Congress of 1928. In the Italian Fascist party Bose was to find a brand of militant nationalism which answered his psychological needs. He first visited Italy in 1934; he met Mussolini three times on that occasion and subsequently twice. Gina Sculpa at the Italian Foreign Office, whom Bose had earlier met as the Italian Consul-General in Calcutta, made sure of a warm welcome. Bose's relationship with the Fascists was always to be more friendly than those with the Nazis. It was in response to Fascism that Bose worked out by 1934 his weird hybrid of Fascism and Communism, his Samyavadi Sangha, which was to achieve a lurid and mercifully brief fulfilment in the Nazi-Soviet pact of

1939–41. Bose was later to claim that he could not have anticipated the imperialist ambitions of Fascist Italy and its assault on Abyssinia. Could one argue that what Bose really saw in Fascism was a discipline and militancy that he believed necessary for the attainment of Indian independence and that he was not a true convert to Fascism? It seems difficult to deny, with his expression of contempt for democracy and his cult of the party, that he had not gone a long way down the road to Fascism. During the War it was his meeting with Mussolini on 29 May 1941 that did most to raise his status in the eyes of suspicious officials of the German Foreign Office and the Nazis. But it was to be another Indian exile, the Muslim Schedai, who persuaded the Italians to encourage, through the Centro Militare India, Indian participation in the Axis war effort, with the revival of the Friends of India society (Amici dell'India) and the publication of a journal, *Italia e India*—though all this was to fizzle out by late 1942. Bose put his efforts into raising an Indian Legion under the auspices of the Nazi party but in the end concluded that his best prospects lay with the Japanese.[8]

But to turn back to the Risorgimento of the nineteenth century and to its political background, it makes most sense to comment on the political pluralism of Italy by portraying the peninsula as it was in the early nineteenth century. This is not to underestimate the influence of Napoleonic rule on the course of the Risorgimento, but most historians see the emergence of Italian nationalism as a post-Napoleonic phenomenon.[9] Regionalism within the peninsula was as old as the barbarian invasions of the fifth century and there is a strong case for arguing that such pluralism was truer to the spirit of the Italian people than unity: *campanilismo*, loyalty to one's local city or state, was the most meaningful of the political loyalties of the peoples of the peninsula. It is hardly surprising that there are interpreters and historians of the Risorgimento who see unification as a disaster and bemoan the passing of the historic principalities (one thinks particularly of Harold Acton's writings on the Kingdom of Naples and Sicily). This has also encouraged a school of thought that a federal rather than a unitary solution would have better served the aspirations of Italians to nationhood. In 1815 only the most idealistic of nationalists would have made much of a case for the unification of such diverse states. In the north there was feudal Piedmont, ruled by a military, aristocratic élite, as much French as Italian in outlook (the court language was French), and indeed whose mainland territories had been absorbed within metropolitan France during the Napoleonic period. However, the acquisition of Genoa in the Congress settlement of 1815 both strengthened the commercial middle-class element in the state and slanted its interests more towards Italy. Its minor but ambitious dynasty was well poised to exploit the great-power rivalries of France and Austria, providing it was not, in the process, devoured by their greater military might. Direct Austrian influence in Italy was drastically extended by Habsburg acquisition of Lombardy and Venetia: to this was added indirect influence through its dynastic links with Modena, Parma and Tuscany. Then came the Papal states, an enclave of highly reactionary, clerical rule, a theocracy governed by an ecclesiastical and aristocratic élite with a craven and subservient middle class. The papacy had also experienced direct French rule and part of its territories, the Legations (now restored to them), had been hived off to form part of Napoleon's Kingdom of Italy. It has been claimed that as one left the Papal states for the kingdom of Naples and Sicily one left Europe for Africa; certainly here again was a region of marked contrast, itself sub-divided, under the highly autocratic Spanish Bourbons, a society that had undergone some social changes in the Neapolitan half of the kingdom under the government of Napoleon's son-in-law, Joachim Murat, and in the Sicilian half under the guidance of Bentinck (a former Governor of Madras and Governor-General to be) during the British presence, but which remained an area of appalling social backwardness. The idea of nationalism was to join the even greater intellectual tide of Romanticism which swept over Europe, and it was inevitable that something in the nature of the Risorgimento would acquire some kind of a hold on the peninsula. Yet, even so, one might reasonably argue that its dynamic came less from any positive sense of Italia and more from xenophobic hatred of Austrian rule. The Austrian presence was to be increasingly felt as it took on the task of imposing the Congress system on the peninsula, contributing to the suppression of the armed uprisings of 1820 in Sicily, 1822 in Turin, 1831 in the Central Duchies and of 1848 throughout the peninsula. The Austrians were most hated for their rule in Lombardy-Venetia during the Metternich era. Paradoxically it has become almost an orthodoxy amongst historians that the economy and government of that province was the most progressive in Italy. Might not the future of the Lombards have been better served, indeed, by absorption within the Habsburg, Danubian economy? But here the Habsburgs betrayed their lack of economic finesse, for it was the very constraints imposed on the ambitious Lombard entrepreneurial class that bred their greater susceptibility to the appeal of nationalism. There are interesting comparisons to be drawn between their support for the Risorgimento and the Swadeshi movement in late-nineteenth-century India.

It will already be obvious that beneath the political fragmentation of the peninsula lay even deeper social divisions. It is a truism of the Risorgimento that it only recruited a following from the élites. Maybe its greatest paradox is that a movement claiming to speak on behalf of the Italian people only really mobilized the active engagement of a landowning, liberal conservative élite. Throughout the peninsula, though most strongly in the north, such a class existed and came to see some rationale in unification, perhaps out of class self-interest, more probably out of a genuine patriotic awareness that only in this way could Italians participate in the new, more industrialized, more aggressive Europe rapidly emerging by mid-century. If Italy was still largely a pre-modern economy, in the old capitalist cities of northern Italy a more modern capitalism was taking shape, above all in the textile industry and in the great cities of Turin and Milan. This has led one outstanding interpreter of modern Italian history, Antonio Gramsci, to see in the Risorgimento a conspiracy by northern industrialists to turn the south into a captive agrarian economy and a safe outlet for northern manufacture. The losers in this story were the great majority of the population, the peasantry. Stuart Woolf has persuasively argued that during the critical period of the 1820s to the 1870s there was a failure in the modernization of Italian agriculture: 'the final stage of a structural crisis.'[10] Apart from limited areas of peasant farming in the Po valley, elsewhere the share-cropping peasantry or *mezzadria* in the centre and north, even more the peasantry on the great estates or *latifundia* of the south, were to experience decline. An increasingly large percentage became landless. By 1881 out of every 1000 inhabitants there were 46 *mezzadri*, 59 peasant proprietors and a majority of simple labourers.[11] Mack Smith interprets the Risorgimento as a whole series of civil wars, both regional and class. Old and new élites fought for ascendancy; the peasantry were excluded. No social revolution accompanied the political, and the Italian state that emerged by 1870 had almost totally failed to incorporate the peasant masses. More Italians were to die in the peasant uprisings, or brigandage, that greeted the new Piedmontese administration in the south than in all the other civil wars of the Risorgimento put together.

There was a further failure of integration, maybe not so serious, but relevant here, and that lay in the profound hostility that grew up between church and state in the course of the Risorgimento. The Vatican refused to recognize the new state; its creators were excommunicated, and good catholics—in theory anyway— were to abstain from all participation in the new political dispensation. This was a further serious limitation on a new sense of corporate identity amongst Italians. Crispi was often quoted as saying that the greatest Italian would be he who settled the quarrel between church and state: Mussolini was to do so with the Concordat of 1929, though the totalitarian ambitions of Fascism led to but an uneasy truce.

In a sense a comparison with the political background to Indian nationalism has to be made twice over: firstly, contemporary with the Risorgimento, down to 1857; secondly, with the political system that was to prevail under the Raj. How was that multiplicity of states that was to emerge after the death of Aurangzeb and the disintegration of the Mughal empire, in the so-called Black Century, to achieve any kind of all-India structure? Wherein lay the natural political outcome for such dynastic rivalries? Did it lie with the Maratha bid to replace the Mughals as the ruling dynastic state? What natural ties linked such diverse states as Tipu Sultan's Mysore, the various satellite Mughal states of Arcot, Hyderabad, Oudh, Bengal, etc., the Hindu Rajput states, and the Maratha states? Did 1857 indeed represent a 'nationalist' endeavour by princely India to unite against the common challenge of the Company? But there were here analogous civil wars to those of Italy, for Sikh and Gurkha turned against Muslim, Hyderabad and Maratha turned against Mughal, and such divisions, as they had in the past, were to cripple Indian resistance. In this context it also becomes clear that the Company, far from playing an Austrian role of divide and rule, was taking on a quasi-Napoleonic role of conquest and bringing more and more of the states under its own paramount control. It was of course this aspect of its rule that led some Indians to see in the Company a progressive force for change. This, however, became less and less the case after 1858. With the decision of the Raj to freeze the political status quo of the subcontinent princely India was shored up by the Raj as a major barrier to political unification.

So how should one characterize the task of political integration after 1857? Should one emphasize the competing interests of the different provinces or regions, north versus south, the advanced provinces of Bengal, Bombay and Madras against the backward but up and coming areas of Gujarat, the UP, Andhradesa? The deepest quarrel, as was to become increasingly apparent in the twentieth century, lay between Indian Muslims and Hindus. It was this division that encouraged the belief that India's best way forward lay in a federal rather than a unitary structure. The Raj saw itself as mediating between such competing interests. But again, as with Austria in Italy, arguably it was hostility to the British as an oppressive colonial presence that did most to inspire a sense of common Indian political selfconsciousness.

The social divisions, as in Italy, were arguably even stronger. Here they do not need to be described: they are all those divisions of caste and community that had increasingly put Indian unity at risk since the medieval period. There is a similar story of competing élites, class divisions and the alienation of the peasantry. In 1857 there was an astonishing rallying of the peasantry, above all in the former territories of the kingdom of Oudh, to the traditional gentry élite, and this has encouraged some historians to see in 1857 the beginnings of a modern, radical and democratic nationalism. Maybe, at the least, it alerted the new élite, the new-style nationalists, to the supreme necessity of politicizing the peasantry and rallying them to the nationalist movement. Maybe the first to think along such lines was the first president of the INC, Allan Octavian Hume. But the man who, above all, was to put such a concern to the test was Gandhi.

Let us now turn to the whole question of strategy and compare the ways in which Italian nationalists between 1815 and 1870 and Indian nationalists, particularly during the early years of Congress, 1885 to 1907, faced the challenge of political unification. The parallel between on the one hand the radicals and the moderates in Italy and on the other the extremists and the moderates in India is strikingly close. Maybe all nationalist movements develop such tensions and polarize along such lines, but the similarities of policy and social cleavage suggest some special relationship between the Italian and the Indian story. This essay was approached in the expectation that Mazzini would emerge as a direct formative influence in both movements, but he has not quite emerged as the anticipated common factor. If the Italian radicals are rightly identified as exponents of a unitary solution to unification, it should be stated at the outset that some radicals saw greater wisdom in a federal solution. The distinguished Lombard intellectual Cattaneo was of this opinion and, under the duress of 1848, the Leghorn radical Guerrazzi shifted his sympathies from Mazzini's Roman republic to defending the interests of Tuscany. Mazzini's radicalism lay as much in his political style, his belief in action, in the need for constant insurrection if the cause of Italy was to catch on amongst Italians. He had embarked on his radical career as a Carbonarist but came to distrust them, with their secret societies, as political amateurs, though, ironically, the Young Italy movement which he set up in 1831 in rivalry was to take on many of the same clandestine, cloak-and-dagger characteristics. The radicals looked for popular support and were branded as subversives, but Mazzini's message was in fact ambiguous. He sought the reconciliation and transcendence of class conflict in the nationalist movement. It was this kind of populism that has led some critics to see in Mazzini a forerunner of the demagogic nationalism and the corporate state of Mussolini's Italy. Some Mazzinians had a clearer sense of the need to rally the peasantry and one, Pisacane, was to embark on a forlorn mission to the south in 1857 in the belief that the solution to Italian unification lay in the support of the southern peasantry. He was to be murdered by those very peasants whose support he sought. Mazzini was less aware of the key role of the peasantry. Maybe his supreme contribution to the Risorgimento lay in his moral leadership, in the extraordinary integrity of his personality, in the unstinting sacrifice he was ready to make for his ideals. Maybe he did look to Italy's past, to the civilization of ancient Rome, to the medieval period and to Dante, but, however theocratic, his was also a forward-looking vision, a generous ideal of nationalism in which Italian nationalism would become the initiator for a new federal structure of European states.

The moderates on the other hand were appalled by the insurrectionary tactics and clandestine methods of the radicals. Broadly speaking, they represented the interests of an Italian enlightened conservative élite, though a few of their outstanding spokesmen, e.g. the priest Gioberti, came from a humbler social background. Theirs, above all, was a federal programme and they looked, in the case of Gioberti, to the papacy—and in the case of D'Azeglio and Cesare Balbo to the Piedmontese monarchy—to assume the role of leading the different regions into some all-Italian federal structure. D'Azeglio emphasized the role of enlightened public opinion in contrast to that of the Mazzinian underground for spreading nationalist ideas: his was an ideal of a 'kind of non-secret daylight conspiracy'.[12] They sought political unification without social revolution. In the end the moderates were forced to settle for a very different solution, the imposition of a Piedmontese controlled unitary state, the outcome of Cavour's dominant intervention in the story between 1848 and 1861. Maybe this was not all along Cavour's intention: in 1858, in the treaty he drew up with the Emperor Napoleon III at Plombières, he would have settled for a loose federal structure in which Piedmont, by acquiring Lombardy, Venice and the

Legations, would be the dominant partner in a new northern state of Upper Italy; the Duchies, together with the papal Romagna, would form a kingdom of Central Italy; the Pope would be left with but a small state, known as the Patrimony; and the kingdom of Naples and Sicily would remain outside this new structure. It was Garibaldi's expedition to the south that rewrote the rules of the game and forced Cavour into exceptional moves both to incorporate the south and impose the Piedmontese monarchy on a unitary state so as to thwart the republican ambitions of the radicals.

If we now turn to India it is interesting at this point to interject Italian commentary on the rebellion of 1857.[13] The radicals were sympathetic. Carlo Cattaneo, author of *L'India Antica e Moderna* (India, Ancient and Modern) had already branded the Company as exploitative and oppressive. During 1857 the Mazzinian republican journal *Italia del Popolo* (People's Italy) rejected the view of the uprising as merely military and saw it as authentically popular and national. Another radical journal, *La Ragione* (Reason), emphasized the inhumanity of Company rule, attributing famine to its policies and drawing attention to its destruction of native industries. The moderates on the other hand, anxious to retain the support of England for the Risorgimento, always more alert to diplomatic factors, saw no legitimizing nationalism. To quote one such opinion, Joseph Maccari in the *Rivista Contemporanea* (Contemporary Review) wrote: 'the sepoy rebellion is purely an act of military sedition, kindled by the religious fanatics of the Brahmins; the desire for independence and liberty has got nothing to do with it.'[14]

The impact of Mazzini on Indian nationalism would make a fascinating subject for research. Evidence of direct influence may be hard to come by; analogous ideas, however, may prove abundant. One would like to claim that the Young Bengal movement of the 1830s, under the inspirational leadership of Derozio, was directly inspired by Mazzini but one can only really point to their obvious parallel as a generational conflict. At one stage Mazzini was going to restrict membership of Young Italy to the under-40s. The Derozians are better seen, anyway, as a secularizing anti-traditionalist response to European values rather than as nationalists, and maybe a closer link between Mazzini and India lies in those elements of the Bengal Renaissance which sought to revitalize the Bengali language and engender Bengali patriotism. If we move on to the early Congress it is a little frustrating to find that the one Congress leader who consciously identified himself with Mazzini was a moderate, Surendranath Bannerjea.[15] Yet there are obvious similarities between the attitudes of Italian radicals and those of the Congress extremists. There is a good case for a comparison between Aurobindo Ghose and Mazzini. Aurobindo looked to the Italian revolutionaries as one example for the Indian nationalists. He emphasized the need to develop an underground movement and was not afraid of violence. (Did Mazzini himself support terrorism? He knew nothing of the attempt by a Mazzinian, Orsini, to assassinate Emperor Napoleon III.) Aurobindo saw India as having some exemplary role to play in spreading to the world the cult of the Mother goddess; in much the same way Mazzini believed Italy should be the initiator for other new nationalisms. Aurobindo saw in nationalism a new religion which would transcend social divisions; this is strikingly similar to Mazzini's social philosophy of class integration. Just as Mazzini's Party of Action, so the extremists, for all their pursuit of popular support, were to remain an élite movement. Aurobindo was to experience a prolonged period of 'internal' exile at Pondicherry; Mazzini was to be in virtual life-long exile from Italy after 1831, apart from the year as Triumvir in the Roman republic and his returning, if but to die, in Pisa, on 10 March 1872. It would be fascinating to explore similarities in their psychology: both were brought up by mentally disturbed mothers; maybe their idealism reflects some compensatory response for such early childhood disturbance.[16] Another extremist, V. D. Savarkar, was quite explicitly an admirer of Mazzini. As a student in London in the 1900s he translated a biography of Mazzini into Marathi. Mazzini was admired as a man who had inspired national unity. Savarkar went on to become an advocate of terrorism and violence.

A parallel can be drawn between the Italian and the Congress moderates as an élite. The Congress moderates were an anglicized élite, anxious to defend their privileged status both from an increasingly hostile Raj and upward-mobilizing groups within Indian society. They were 'moderates' in the sense that they sought to bargain with the Raj rather than seek out confrontation: the extremists were to brand their style as the politics of mendicancy. In this sense there is no real parallel with the Italian moderates. Their convergence lies in their common stress on open politics; open discussion in the press, open debate in the councils. They shared D'Azeglio's aristocratic and élitist distaste for the tactics of the political underground. The moderates represented the high castes, especially the Brahmins, and the educationally privileged; they dominated the new European professions of law and medicine and Indian representation within the administration. Yet they were increasingly aware of the way such privilege alienated them from the main mass of the Indian people and put at risk their claim to speak on behalf of Indian nationalism. Both moderates and extremists sought ways out of what historians have called the 'politics of limitation.' If Italian Fascism can in part be seen as the distorted pursuit of that very nationalism which had eluded the Risorgimento, how similar was the risk that India's quest for a popular nationalism would follow along the same misguided path?

Clearly not all the conditioning factors which bred Italian Fascism existed in India. It became fashionable in the India of the 1970s to draw analogies between the India of Indira Gandhi and the Marxist regime in Chile under Allende, and to claim that her government was threatened by the same Fascist forces that brought General Pinochet to power. The savage irony of such fears lay in their justifying the Emergency regime, the closest India has in fact yet come to an experience of a Fascist dictatorship. It is a confusion of categories to see in the Raj of the 1920s a Fascist government (it was merely an authoritarian one), though some of its conduct, as at Amritsar in 1919 and in its suppression of the August 1942 uprising, showed some of the characteristics of Fascist brutality. Italian Fascism was to emerge out of the social unrest and disillusionment which followed from the exhaustions of war. Disaffected ex-soldiers, déraciné intellectuals and criminal elements, were to find a satisfactory outlet for their violence and mindless nihilism in the

Fascist party, set up in 1919. The ruling classes, industrialists and landowners, terrified at social unrest amongst workers and peasants, saw in such a movement the means of containing revolutionary socialism. It was this collusion between the establishment and a politically criminal movement that led to Mussolini's appointment as Prime Minister in 1922.

But there was also a spurious radicalism within Fascism which was used to seek out a popular backing, and with Fascism in power pursuing quasi-totalitarian ambitions it sought to camouflage the hollowness of its social reform programme with an appeal to a chauvinistic, imperialistic nationalism. Within India a not dissimilar movement was taking shape, also claiming, maybe more legitimately, to be a social reform movement, likewise expressing a chauvinistic, Indian nationalism. Its roots lay in the nineteenth century Arya Samaj movement. It took on a more overtly political complexion with the setting up of the Hindu Mahasabha in 1916. It took on an openly Fascist character in the breakaway para-military organization, the RSS. There are clear parallels to be drawn between Fascism and Hindu communalism. Muslim communalism was developing along similar lines. The Muslim League became increasingly an overtly communal movement. Its para-military organization, the Khaksars, was evidently Fascist in style. Within the Indian subcontinent the impact of the Depression, the growing inpoverishment of the peasantry and the worsening prospects of employment for disaffected graduates were all creating the social and intellectual conditions for the rise of Fascism. Did the Congress party see these dangers?

Accusations of Fascism were very much in the air in inter-War India. Congress branded the Raj as Fascist. The Muslim League and the Raj branded Congress as totalitarian and Fascist. Arguably Congress saw the dangers of the political virus of Fascism, and one quarantine measure was to forbid joint membership of Congress and the Hindu Mahasabha. Should Gandhi take the credit for steering Congress itself away from the siren attractions of Fascism and containing its spread within the subcontinent? It was Gandhi who led Congress away from that militant nationalism, with its strong Hindu communal content,

which Tilak had inspired. Nehru stressed that Gandhi had introduced a 'peaceful nationalism' into the Congress programme.
There was, of course, no church-state quarrel in India analogous
to that in Italy: Hinduism has no religious establishment. But
there was a continually awkward choice on the link to be made
between religion and politics. The moderates had tried to keep
them apart: theirs was an agnostic, secular style, which deepened
their isolation from the Indian masses. The extremists had
brought them together, but in such a way as to encourage Hindu
communalism. Gandhi also sought to bring them together, but in
such a way that Hindu-Muslim differences would be trans-
cended in a common nationalist movement. Did he succeed or did
he unwittingly contribute to the spread of communalism?
Maybe a more critical analysis has to be undertaken on the
similarities between Fascism and communalism, but it does
raise a very awkward question about Gandhi's leadership and its
impact.

Perhaps this is a jarring note on which to end this comparison,
and it is not intended to suggest that Gandhi was in the least
a Fascist; it is simply to comment on the way any political
movement with a religious idiom is in danger of arousing a
religious and communal response within India's religiously
pluralist society. I have in no way exhausted the possibilities of
this comparative approach. It would be fascinating, for example,
to compare the roles which Manzoni and Verdi played in the
Risorgimento with the contribution of Bankim Chandra Chatterjee and Rabindranath Tagore to Indian nationalism. If there
are virtues in such a comparative approach it raises the possibility of other such exercises. One could compare the whole
debate over the political structure of the pluralist Habsburg
monarchy with that over the Indian subcontinent. Tsarist Russia
and the Raj and the plight of the peasantry in both those auto-
cracies cries out for some comparative analysis.

One of the most difficult questions that faced nationalists in
both Italy and India was whether their countries should be
unified along federal, confederal or unitary lines. Italy, at the
very last moment, opted for a unitary state. In India the debate
always really oscillated between forms of federation: the ques-

tion was whether the centre or the regions should have the upper hand. Here likewise the decision was postponed till the eve of independence. In 1946 there was still the possibility of a loose federation incorporating the Indian Muslims. In 1947 Congress opted for a more centralized state at the cost of Pakistan. Might other arrangements have been better suited to the needs of two such politically pluralist communities or were these the right decisions?

NOTES

1. Quoted in James D. Hunt, *Gandhi in London* (New Delhi, 1978). For *Hind Swaraj* see Gandhi, *Collected Works*, vol. x (Ahmedabad, 1963).
2. See Mira Behn, *The Spirit's Pilgrimage* (London, 1960), pp. 150–1; Geoffrey Ashe, *Gandhi: A Study in Revolution* (London, 1968), p. 312.
3. Jawaharlal Nehru, *Glimpses of World History* (1934; rpt. London 1949), p. 89.
4. Ibid., pp. 278–9.
5. Ibid., p. 400.
6. Ibid., p. 813.
7. Ibid., p. 814.
8. I have drawn this information from S. C. Bose, *The Indian Struggle 1920–1934* (Calcutta, 1948), and Mihir Bose, *The Lost Hero* (London, 1982).
9. The most useful introductory books to the history of the Risorgimento and modern Italy are Stuart Woolf, *A History of Italy 1700–1860* (London, 1979); this is particularly good on economic and social history; Harry Hearder, *Italy in the Age of the Risorgimento 1790–1870* (London, 1983); Denis Mack Smith, *Italy: A Modern History* (Ann Arbor, 1959).
10. Stuart Woolf, pp. 282–3.
11. Mack Smith, p. 149.
12. M. D'Azeglio *Things I Remember*, trans. by E. R. Vincent (Oxford, 1966), p. 343.
13. See Lilliana Dalle Nogare, 'Echoes of 1857 in Italy', in P. C. Joshi, ed., *Rebellion 1857* (New Delhi, 1957).
14. Ibid., p. 325.

15. Leonard A. Gordon, *Bengal: The Nationalist Movement 1876–1940* (New York, 1974), p. 30.
16. For Aurobindo Ghose see Leonard Gordon, chapter 4; Sri Aurobindo, *On Himself* (Pondicherry, 1972); A. B. Purani, *The Life of Sri Aurobindo* (Pondicherry, 1978).

THE EARLY CONGRESS AND THE BRITISH RADICAL CONNECTION

EDWARD C. MOULTON

The founding generation of the Indian National Congress consisted primarily of western-educated lawyers, journalists and other modern professionals familiar with the evolution of constitutional government in the British metropolis and its white-settler colonies. They were anxious that these models should be followed in India, despite the obvious difficulties of applying a governing system developed in an individualistic, industrializing society such as Britain to a more group-oriented society, overwhelmingly dependent on a backward agricultural system and heavily immersed in its ancient cultural traditions. India was, moreover, a society where modern education was just beginning to take root and where the new urban middle class, which Congress represented, constituted only a tiny fraction of the total population. To these basic problems the early Congress leaders devoted little attention. Instead they concentrated on the more immediate obstacle, the overriding presence of a British imperial Raj which was still confident in its moral, racial and material superiority, and backed with the largest and best equipped army in Asia. While a sense of realism obviously dictated against any overt challenge to the British presence in India, most early Congressmen in fact undoubtedly believed that there were benefits to be gained through a continuing association with Britain. Rather than challenging the British connection, early Congress leaders looked to Britain for allies in their pursuit of political reform and greater autonomy. They hoped that these allies would help to neutralize what they regarded as the core of the opposition to the liberalization of the Raj, the hardened English bureaucrats who manned the civil and military administration in India.

It is probable that at whatever date Congress had come into existence, British sympathizers would have been drawn largely from segments of the political spectrum that were most committed to socio-political reform or most influenced by internationalist sentiment. The fact that the establishment of the Congress occurred in 1885, a time which coincided with a strong resurgent tide of imperialism in Britain and the Western world generally, made it practically certain that active Indian nationalist sympathizers would be confined to the left of the British political spectrum. While no British political faction remained untainted by the 'new imperialism', on the whole its influence was most pervasive in the Conservative Party and the centre-right of the Liberal Party, including the Unionists who split with Gladstone over greater autonomy for Ireland. It is not my contention that British radicals—a term used here to include the left of the Liberal Party and the various socialist and labour groups that emerged after 1884—had a general or sustained interest in Congress or Indian nationalist issues. I do contend, however, that from the time of the founding of the Congress till around 1920 the only real committed and sustained British support for Congress came from a small core of individuals who were either radicals or socialists of one kind or another. On high-profile Indian issues of repression and reform these Congress sympathizers were sometimes able to influence a wider spectrum of their particular political constituencies to condemn the autocracy of the Raj and press the regime in a more progressive direction.

Moving to more specific issues, I maintain that the tendency of much Indian nationalist and leftist historiography to dismiss Radical British Congress activists, such as Allan O. Hume and his two closest radical and dissident former Indian Civil Service colleagues, William Wedderburn and Henry J. S.

Cotton, as fifth-column agents for the Raj, seriously over-simplifies the complexity of their role and is not sustainable on the basis of a balanced interpretation of their long-term contributions to the movement.¹ Hume's role, as a founder and full-time general secretary of the Congress for its first decade, is pivotal, while the others were mainly involved in the activities of the British Congress Committee. The origins of this Committee, its role in trying to mobilize support in Britain and the controversy over its impact on Congress policy are important themes in this essay. This Committee, as we shall see, stimulated a considerable number of Liberal and Labour MPs to take a somewhat greater interest in India, though only a handful ever identified closely with the nationalist cause. The star British metropolitan recruit in the early days of the Congress was the prominent radical MP and free thinker Charles Bradlaugh, while in the post-1905 period V. H. Rutherford probably ranked as the most thoroughgoing and long-term radical supporter of Congress.

In addition to the above radicals, two socialist leaders, in particular, stood out in their sympathies for Indian nationalism. These were James Keir Hardie, leader of the Independent Labour Party, and Henry M. Hyndman, founder and long-time leader of the Marxist-oriented Social Democratic Federation. Stimulated by the British Committee and the political momentum in the subcontinent, Hardie took a major interest in Indian issues from 1905 till his death in 1915. Hyndman's special interest in India pre-dated the formation of Congress by a decade and was sustained until he died in 1921. Unlike the Liberal radicals, who identified almost exclusively with the Indian constitutional reformers who dominated the Congress organization until 1917, both Hardie and Hyndman maintained some contact with militant nationalists. Hyndman also openly courted the support of young Indian revolutionaries who were active in London and Paris during the pre-1914 decade.

The historiography of the Congress and early Indian nationalism has given comparatively little attention either to the above individuals, who took a special interest in India, or to the more general theme of Congress and British radicalism. Scholarly writing on the leading Liberal radicals involved in the early Congress has been rather sparse. One partial exception is the case of Hume, whose role in helping to establish the Congress has been the subject of considerable debate and controversy. He has not generally, however, been treated either kindly or fairly. As I have indicated elsewhere, Hume has been condemned out of hand by various leftist and nationalist historians as a fifth-column agent of British imperialism, or denigrated by more liberal, middle-of-the-road scholars as a cantankerous, deceitful, self-serving and autocratic individual.[2] Even the more sympathetic and balanced assessments of Hume's role in the Congress, such as those provided by S. R. Mehrotra and John R. McLane, have tended to focus too narrowly upon his role in the founding and early days of the Congress.[3] McLane has not viewed Hume's activities in the context of his long-term and thoroughgoing radicalism, and Mehrotra has not developed this theme, though he is obviously conscious of its importance. The result, as I argue below, is that important dimensions of Hume's contributions have been overlooked or misinterpreted.

As for other leading British radical Congressmen, they have been even more neglected than Hume. Henry J. S. Cotton, an open sympathizer of Congress during his Indian Civil Service years and a leading member of its British Committee from 1903 till his death in 1915, has received practically no scholarly attention, except for my own recent article, which attempts to provide a critical overview of his support for Congress and its programmes of constitutional agitation.[4] Neglected too have been the positive contributions to the early Congress of the radical political organizer and India-returned journalist William Digby, who was appointed secretary of the British Congress Committee on its creation in 1889 and became first editor of its monthly journal, *India*, established in 1890. While McLane has briefly highlighted Digby's difficulties with the Congress over his indiscriminate personal promotion of the interests of various princely states on a mere fee-for-service basis, he neglects altogether Digby's sustained efforts, until he resigned from the Committee in 1892 to promote Indian political reform and publicize the Congress

programme in Britain.[5] Somewhat less ignored in recent scholarship has been William Wedderburn, who served as chairman of
the British Congress Committee from its foundation until his
death in 1917 and had the unique distinction of being the only
Briton to be elected president of Congress on two occasions. A
number of studies dealing with the early nationalist period,
notably B. R. Nanda's *Gokhale:The Indian Moderates and the
British Raj* (OUP, 1977) and Margot D. Morrow's 'The Origin
and Early Years of the British Committee of the Indian National
Congress, 1885–1907' (London Ph.D. thesis, 1977), have given
considerable and generally sympathetic attention to Wedderburn's role in the early Congress. Stimulated in part by their
work I have attempted in a recent essay on Wedderburn to
provide an integrated assessment of his long-term involvement
in Indian politics, seen against the context of his lifelong commitment to liberal radicalism.[6] Finally, few of the radical MPs
whom the British Congress Committee motivated to take a special
interest in India have received any meaningful notice in nationalist
or Congress historiography. Passing reference has often been
made to Charles Bradlaugh's sponsorship of a Congress-drafted
Indian Reform Bill in the British Parliament, or to the occasional
support from Irish Home Rulers, but other radical sympathizers,
such as V.H. Rutherford and Frederic C. Mackarness, who were
especially active in the period 1906–10, have been almost
completely ignored.[7]

Nor has significant scholarly attention been accorded to the
activities of the socialists Hyndman and Hardie, and their
respective parties in support of Indian nationalist objectives.
For example, the most recent general scholarly examination of
nationalism in the subcontinent, R. Suntharalingam's *Indian
Nationalism: an Historical Analysis* (New Delhi, 1983), does not
contain even a single passing reference to Hardie or Hyndman.
Even R. C. Majumdar's vast tome, *Struggle for Freedom* (Bombay,
1969), contains only one brief incidental reference to Hyndman
and little more than that to Keir Hardie's involvement in Indian
issues. A more specialized recent work, M. N. Das's *Indian National
Congress versus the British, 1885–1918* (New Delhi, 1978), while
dedicated to four British radicals who were actively involved in
the early Congress, makes only cursory references to their two

fellow socialist leaders.[8] An exception to the above pattern is the recent study by the East German scholar Horst Krüger, entitled *Indische Nationalisten und Weltproletariat* (Berlin, 1984). Krüger devotes some fifty pages to the activities of Hyndman and Hardie in support of Indian nationalism and credits them with considerable influence. One limitation of his analysis, however, is that it is circumscribed by the intellectual straitjacket of orthodox Marxism. It is worth noting as well that the general neglect in Indian historiography of the pro-India activities of Hyndman and Hardie is also characteristic of British historiography. C. Tsuzuki's very fine biographic study, *H. M. Hyndman and British Socialism* (Oxford, 1961), gives scant attention to Hyndman's involvement in Indian affairs. Much the same is true of the various biographies of Keir Hardie.[9]

No single study exists on the general theme of the Indian National Congress and British radicalism. The closest work, and the most analytical and perceptive, is that of Margot Morrow on the British Congress Committee.[10] She accepts as a basic premise that the British supporters of Congress were mainly radicals and Irish nationalists, and carefully examines such issues as their motives for assisting the movement, the interest groups to which they belonged, the ideological tensions among them and the biases underlying their Congress collaboration.[11] A less probing but informative overview of the organization and activities of the British Committee over its entire period of existence is Harish Kaushik's brief monograph, *The Indian National Congress in England, 1885–1920* (Delhi, 1972). Kaushik does not emphasize the British radical context of the Congress support in Britain, though the many sympathetic individuals to whom he refers in his monograph were all of that political persuasion. On the post-1900 period there is one study that deals with the British Labour Party and India, namely the French scholar, Georges Fischer's, *Le parti travailliste et la décolonisation de l'inde* (Paris, 1966). Fischer's work is based almost exclusively on secondary sources and pays little attention either to Labour's links with Congress or to the Indian political context. A more general and penetrating analysis of Labour's attitude to empire, including India, is provided in P. S. Gupta's *Imperialism and the British Labour Movement, 1914–1964* (London, 1975). Useful as this study is in assessing Labour attitudes and policies towards India in the period after World War I, it does not, as the title indicates, deal with relations with the subcontinent during the early Congress era.

In the ensuing discussion of the major themes and issues pertinent to an examination of relations between the early Congress and British radicalism reference will be made, where appropriate, to the above scholarship relating to this subject.

A close connection between Congress and British radicalism was embodied, in the first instance, in the person of Allan O. Hume, a far more consistent and thoroughgoing radical than has usually been recognized. As the son of Joseph Hume, one of Britain's most prominent radical MPs during the second quarter of the nineteenth century, Hume was nurtured in radical politics. A career in the Indian Civil Service from 1849 to 1882 failed to dampen his radicalism. Though well known for his fiery temperament it was primarily political differences with his superiors during Lytton's Conservative viceroyalty which led to his demotion from the central secretariat in 1879 and his premature resignation from the ICS in 1882.[12] A combination of enthusiasm over Ripon's local self-government initiative and indignation over the European racist outcry against the Ilbert Bill drew Hume out of his reclusive retirement in Simla and prompted him to take the initiative in helping to mobilize Western-educated Indians to form a national political organization.

Hume obviously realized that such an organization would not be welcomed by the autocratic, British-Indian bureaucracy and initially envisaged the first public session of the Congress as a rather tame affair. He privately informed the Viceroy, Dufferin, of plans for a Congress and considered approaching the Liberal Governor of Bombay, Reay, to preside, a notion which Dufferin disliked and which was promptly abandoned.[13] However, Hume's real plans for the Congress, as articulated in his speeches and writings over the next few years, were both radical and far-reaching, and, it should be noted, shaped more by his reading of British and French socio-political history than India's readiness for modern politics. On two important occasions a combination of Hume's radicalism and outspokenness was to get him into serious trouble with the more cautious Indian leadership of the Congress.

The principal Indian founding fathers of Congress such as Dadabhai Naoroji, W. C. Bonnerjee and P. N. Mehta undoubtedly had a far more integrated view of the objectives of the movement than one would deduce from the series of diverse resolutions approved at the various annual sessions. For Hume, in particular, the primary objectives of Congress were the promotion of national unity and the achievement of representative and responsible government, along the lines of what had been achieved in Canada and other white-settler colonies of the empire. In his well-known Allahabad speech of 1888 Hume emphasized that the first objective of Congress was 'the fusion into one national whole of all the different... elements that constitute the population of India.'[14] In elaboration he stressed the desire of the Congress founders, first 'to eliminate provincial jealousies, prejudices and misconceptions,' and second 'to exorcise sectarian and class antipathies by associating in one common work, for the common good... leading members of all sects and classes.' During his years as full-time general secretary Hume put considerable effort into reducing regional misunderstanding among the Indian leaders. His genuine concern over Hindu-Muslim relations and his serious but relatively unsuccessful efforts to enlist greater Muslim participation in the early Congress have been well documented by McLane.[15]

While Hume considered the development of Indian nationhood as the very *raison d'être* of Congress, the policy objectives to which he attached overriding importance were representative government and, concomitantly, Indianization of the civil and military services. His deep convictions about the fundamental importance of representative government were cogently articulated in response to criticisms about Congress neglect of socio-cultural reform. Hume admitted that on general philosophic grounds he attached primary importance to the 'elevation' of moral values and, secondly, the 'diffusion' of intellectual enlightenment.[16] He continued:

Only third in importance ... is political enfranchisement, but I throw my energies into this latter, firstly, because I have read history ... and I have come to see that neither moral elevation nor mental culture are nationally possible without some considerable political enfranchisement. There have been periods of intellectual culture as in the Augustan age, accompanied ... by political serfdom, but that culture was but the fruit of seed sown ... in an antecedent era of political freedom. You may create the grandest academies. You may found the purest religious sects, but without the infinitely varied inducements to mental exertion and moral restraint afforded by political freedom, your nature will never be either cultured or virtuous.

These were the sentiments of a real democrat and that is exactly what Hume was. During the first five years of his general secretaryship Hume was intimately involved in the development of Congress proposals for a substantial measure of constitutional reform, including a significant enlargement of the membership and functions of legislative councils and public election of fifty per cent of council members.[17]

While Hume attached top priority to political reform, he regarded Indianization of the administration as a crucial feature of that process. However much Europeans might moralize about their trusteeship or modernizing roles, Hume was convinced that their vehement opposition to extensive Indian employment was really motivated by racist and mercenary considerations.[18] He had no sympathy for either of the latter positions. In testimony to the Public Service Commission in 1887 Hume maintained that concepts of fundamental justice dictated that Indians should 'have a preferential right to all posts in the administration of their own country provided they are competent' to fill them.[19] For him this was no empty platitude for he believed that the growth of modern education meant that large numbers of Indians were indeed competent to hold high-level administrative positions. His advanced views on civil and military Indianization were most cogently stated in one of his anonymously published pamphlets of 1886.

As speedily as may be, without needless expense and without injustice to individuals, 90 percent of the *non*-Indian agency employed in the Government in all its multifarious branches should be replaced by Indians. Instead of increasing the European army, as has just been done by 10,000 men, it should have been diminished by at least an equal number, and as time went on further and further reduced, any loss of military strength being made up by the encouragement of Indian volunteers and the organization of an Indian militia. . . .[20]

Speaking before the Public Service Commission he amplified his ultimate vision as follows:

I look forward to the time, . . . when every appointment in the country, except that of the Viceroy, will be held by residents of India. . . . This is the case at the present day in the Dominion of Canada, why should it not be so here?[21]

The Canadian analogy implied that the Viceroy would be the ceremonial head of state, not the leader of the government. Indian leaders of Congress may have shared these sentiments, but in the early years none articulated more advanced views than Hume on the Indianization issue.

The prime importance which Hume attached to political and administrative reform was intimately connected with his profound concerns about India's poverty. As a long-time district officer of Etawah in present-day Uttar Pradesh, Hume had extensive first-hand knowledge of Indian agrarian conditions. Concerned over the country's economic backwardness Hume had attempted, at the outset of his appointment as secretary of the newly created central government Department of Agriculture, Revenue and Commerce in 1871, to forge that department into a dynamic engine of agricultural modernization. He advocated such boldly reformist initiatives as the extensive employment of agricultural experts; the establishment of agricultural colleges; the creation of at least 'one large Government model farm in every district of the country'; the foundation of agricultural associations; and the publication of a journal of agriculture.[22] But all this was far too radically interventionist and expensive for most of the governing establishment even to contemplate seriously, and Hume's hopes for a concerted developmental thrust in agriculture were crushed. Instead, the Secretary of State insisted that the department focus primarily on revenue matters and ordered that the word 'revenue' not 'agriculture' come first in the title of the department.[23] In 1879 the Indian government abolished the department altgether, an action designed by John Strachey and Lytton in large part as a device for getting rid of Hume, who had become a 'very troublesome Secretary'.[24] Hume's response was to publish a detailed exposé on the ill-fated department, *Agricultural Reform in India* (London, 1879), in which he argued that the failure to promote basic agricultural development was the 'most conspicuous blot' on the British Indian administration and a prime cause of the 'serious...internal troubles' besetting the country, namely 'debt, famine and discontent'.[25]

Hume's concerns about the poverty of the Indian masses were articulated even more strongly after he became secretary of the Congress. In the mean time Hume had undoubtedly been influenced by Hyndman's much publicized articles of the late 1870s indicting the financial and economic policies of the Raj and popularizing, for the first time, Dadabhai Naoroji's hitherto little-noticed 'economic drain' theory.[26] Whereas Hume had previously condemned the British for neglecting agricultural development and saddling the country with an overly-expensive administrative system, he now added the effects of the economic drain to his critique. Like Hyndman and Naoroji he argued that India was not only poor but that it was getting poorer, all as a direct consequence of British rule. His views were cogently summed up in one of his anonymous pamphlets of 1886:

> Here and here only, is the source of the trouble: year by year a large and ... increasing share of the profits of the industry of the country is being drawn out of [India], where it ought to remain to increase our working capital, and is being permanently transferred to another country [Britain] which alone thereafter benefits by it, and the consequence is that year by year the country is growing poorer, and year by year that squalid penury which is everywhere swallowing up our lower classes like a rising swamp, is deepening, widening, blackening![27]

Though basically bourgeois in outlook, Hume's interpretation of the forces responsible for this process was essentially socialistic; 'the gigantic machine of British commerce', in the interest of 'dividends to British investors', was devouring the 'entire earnings' of India. This line of argument was in fact similar to that used by Hyndman in his writings following his formal conversion to Marxist-oriented socialism in 1881, namely in *England for All* (London, 1881) and *The Bankruptcy of India* (London, 1886).

Hume further believed that India's grave financial and economic problems could only be solved by genuinely representative government. In his view there were clear parallels between India's economic plight and that of Britain before the Reform Bill of 1832 or of Canada before the introduction of responsible government in the wake of the rebellions of 1837. Hume drove this message home in this second anonymously published pamphlet of 1886:

We have no chance of getting rid of those odious fiscal arrangements which are ruining India, and starving our people, until we are really, and not merely nominally, represented in the governing body of the country, and possess that direct share in the administration of our own country, which is the birthright of every free citizen. ....[28]

Hume not only had advanced and integrated views on India's political and economic reform needs but a radical prescription for achieving these goals. That prescription, as he explained in 1886, was mass political mobilization along the lines of Richard Cobden's Anti-Corn Law League. Hume, who had first-hand familiarity with that pioneering movement of middle-class agitation, emphasized that the League had been scorned by the authorities when formed in 1839, but with well-organized and popular agitation had triumphed completely in only seven years. He speculated that Congress might take 'as long or longer' than Cobden's 'noble band' to achieve its goal of replacing 'the existing despotism . . . by a more or less representative form of Government.'[29] He was on firmer ground when he went on to assert his confidence in 'ultimate success', as long as 'every Indian . . . of this our motherland' were prepared to join 'the great war . . . for justice . . . liberties and rights'.

Hume's convictions about the crucial role of mass agitation explain his sustained efforts during 1887–8 to enlist support for Congress among Indian peasant proprietors, a theme which has been briefly explored for the first time in McLane's recent study of the early Congress.[30] On Hume's initiative the Congress issued two vernacular pamphlets which explained in simple, colloquial language the evils of the existing arbitrary administration and the need for more popular government. Hume himself wrote one of the pamphlets. While he contended that the pamphlet contained 'no fireworks, only common sense, pleasantly put',[31] in fact it graphically depicted the image of a wasteful, uncaring and despotic '*sirkar*', callously raising land revenue and taxes, shamelessly promoting 'abkari shops', and generally treating villagers like 'cattle'.[32] It was moreover a regime under which agrarian conditions were deteriorating, people were 'growing poorer and poorer', and discontent was becoming widespread. These pamphlets were published in ten or more vernacular languages and, according to Hume, some 300,000 copies were circulated.[33] The pamphlet campaign was supplemented by a vigorous programme of public meetings in smaller towns in the major regions of the country. Hume himself addressed a number of such town meetings in north India, at which, according to one first-hand report, he urged involvement of the 'masses ... in political questions', and a 'fair share' for them in their own government.[34]

Designed to pressurize the government in a reformist direction, the sharp tone and the mass thrust of the campaign instead created an administrative backlash against Congress. The development and tangible manifestations of this rising government hostility to Congress and to Hume's activism have been extensively documented.[35] The important point to note here is that while Hume responded by publicly defending the general Congress programme and the mass campaign, the leadership of the movement did not back him up.[36] Even though Hume had evidently submitted proofs of his vernacular pamphlet to at least seven Congress leaders, the high command acted by late 1888 to halt the mass campaign.[37] Congress, it is true, did not formally repudiate the two vernacular pamphlets. However, the Allahabad Congress of 1888 disclaimed responsibility for the activities of its officers between sessions and asserted that it was responsible 'for the formal resolutions passed at its sittings and for nothing else'.[38] This was a calculated rebuff to Hume, a clear warning of the leadership's concern over his radicalism. It is highly significant that it was only in 1889, following the failure of his mass mobilization strategy, that Hume turned his attention to the urgency of establishing an effective Congress organization in Britain.[39]

Disappointed over the failure of his mass campaign and the

lack of parliamentary support for Bradlaugh's Indian reform bill, Hume made one last desperate effort to stir the Congress into action by articulating the potential revolutionary implications of rising mass poverty. He undoubtedly had a hand in the formulation of a strongly-worded poverty resolution at the 1891 Congress session. In his introduction to that year's annual report Hume maintained that the 'dominant note' of the session was 'solicitude for the masses', and that remedying the 'increasing suffering of the people' must take 'precedence [over] every other subject'.[40] The concern that educated Indians were not sufficiently serious about the economic plight of the masses, rather than any concrete evidence of an impending popular uprising, accounts for Hume's well-known confidential circular of 1892 to all Congress committees. In his most outspoken language to date Hume warned 'the rich and well-to-do' members of Congress that the existing autocratic administration was 'ill-adapted to the wants of the country, ... pauperizing the people, ... [and] inevitably preparing the way for one of the most terrible cataclysms in the history of the world'.[41] Hume compared the situation of the Indian people to that of the French masses before the Revolution and gave the following dire warning:

All history shows that, however peaceful a population, a time comes when starvation, injustice and despair instil into them a new nature and drives them into violence and crime.

The cup of ... misery of scores of millions of our masses is well nigh full, and ... day by day Poverty, the mother of Anarchy, is pressing with a heavier and heavier hand upon an ever-growing portion of our population.

As surely as night follows day, must a terrible rising evolve ... unless we can remedy existing evils and redress the more prominent of our paupers' grievances.

Intended to arouse a sagging Congress to a greater sense of purpose, Hume's alarmist warnings had the opposite effect. Only a few extremists, such as Hyndman in Britain and Tilak in India, openly supported him.[42] The Congress high command, together with the British Committee, publicly repudiated this circular. D. E. Wacha undoubtedly summed up their positions when he contended that Hume's 'inflammatory' language 'border[ed] on the seditious', and that he was 'cutting the throat of the Congress by his own ill-advised and precipitate action.'[43]

It is usually overlooked that even the stern Congress censure failed to silence Hume. Instead, he openly criticized Congress for its public posture of 'lukewarmness', its general paralysis and its 'timidity'.[44] A year later he publicly warned British officialdom of the 'certainty' of the 'speedy' violent overthrow of the existing regime, 'unless at once we broaden its base by associating with it the intelligence, the energy, and the local knowledge of the people themselves'.[45] For Hume the failure to achieve significant political or socio-economic reform was intimately connected with his inability to develop Congress into a broad-based movement, committed to thoroughgoing change. This in turn explains Hume's highly significant confession of 'failure' in his Congress work as he retired from effective full-time general secretaryship in 1894 and left India for the last time.[46] On that occasion he sadly acknowledged that he had 'not succeeded in securing...any appreciable fraction' of the boldly reformist programme he had mapped out for Congress in its early years. Far from being a restraint on Congress, Hume had a consistently radical vision and a sense of urgency which the movement as a whole did not appear to share.

Once the Congress Committee was formed in London in 1889, and especially after Hume joined it upon leaving India in 1894, it became the focal point of efforts to mobilize British radical and more general Liberal support for the Indian National Congress. In their studies of the British Congress Committee Kaushik and Morrow give extensive coverage to the general political and publicity activities of the Committee, but do not specially highlight its role in attracting radical adherents to the Indian nationalist cause. In fact, except for Hyndman and William Digby, whose keen interest in Indian affairs pre-dated the formation of Congress, practically all other radicals and Labourites who were enlisted in the Indian nationalist cause from 1889 to 1920 owed their recruitment to the activities of the British Committee. Even before the Committee was formally constituted W. C. Bonnerjee and Dadabhai·Naoroji, as the nucleus of a semi-independent Indian Political Agency managed by Digby, achieved the great coup of enlisting the prominent radical MP Charles Bradlaugh to take up Indian issues in Parliament.[47] Bradlaugh's much heralded participation in the Bombay Congress session of 1889 and his subsequent introduction of Congress's India Reform Bill in Parliament are well known. It was a tragedy for the early Congress that Bradlaugh died in early 1891 just as he was beginning to develop a reputation as an informed and powerful defender of Indian nationalist interests in the House of Commons. Other valuable parliamentary adherents from the earliest days of the Committee were the advanced Liberals W. D. Caine and Samuel Smith, both of whom were keen temperance enthusiasts and promoted that movement in India.[48] They were however, less dynamic and radical than Bradlaugh and no substitute for his loss.

Despite the valiant efforts of the Committee's chairman, Wedderburn, and key members such as Naoroji and Hume, the rising imperialist tide around the turn of the century took its toll. Anticipating electoral defeat over his pro-Indian and pro-Boer activities Wedderburn himself decided not to run for re-election to Parliament in 1900, thus ending a Commons career which had lasted since 1893. For the next five years there were so few Congress supporters in the Commons that the Indian Parliamentary Committee, which Wedderburn and Naoroji had organized in 1893 and had been very active in for a number of years, fell into abeyance.

The British Committee itself, which Wedderburn continued to lead, also became rather moribund in these discouraging years of Conservative dominance in Britain and Curzonian imperial rule in India. In fact the British Committee and its journal, India, were so short of funds between 1901 and 1903 that both would probably have collapsed had it not been for a last-minute financial rescue mounted by Naoroji, Wedderburn, Hume, Bonnerjee and other prominent Congress leaders.[49] In 1903 as well, the Committee was strengthened by the addition to its ranks of Henry Cotton, a positivist and political radical, whom Curzon had forced into premature retirement from the chief commissionership of Assam because of his vigorous public efforts to secure more equitable judicial treatment and better economic conditions for the deprived tea plantation labourers.[50] However, it was only with the Liberal triumph and Labour upsurge in the general election of 1906 that the British Committee, and its parliamentary wing in particular, entered on a renewed and vigorous phase of activity which lasted for approximately a decade. Cotton, the new MP for East Nottingham, became the *de facto* leader of a small but dedicated band of pro-India radical and Labour members who formed the vital core of the Indian Parliamentary Committee, and whose nominal membership briefly climbed to as high as 190 MPs.[51] Among the most committed of the new radical-cum-Liberal supporters of Indian nationalism were V. H. Rutherford, Frederic Mackarness, T. Hart-Davies, C. J. O'Donnell and J. Herbert Roberts.

Of these five, Mackarness and Rutherford proved to be particularly devoted to India's cause. Mackarness, who was an experienced and highly principled lawyer, distinguished himself by his concerted opposition to the arbitrary deportations and other violations of basic liberties promulgated by the Indian government during the troubled years 1907–10. To better mobilize opposition in Britain to these despotic measures he took the lead in establishing an Indian Civil Rights Committee in 1908, and two years later a pamphlet of his documenting the abuses and corruption of the Indian police was banned from circulation in the subcontinent.[52] While Mackarness left politics in 1911 to take up a judicial appointment, his more radical associate Rutherford became a dedicated and lifelong advocate of the developing Indian nationalist movement. In order to strengthen his 'service to India in Parliament', Rutherford, who was partially sponsored by the British Committee, visited India in late 1907, associating himself with Congress militants as well as moderates during his tour of leading northern cities and participating in the tempestuous Surat Congress of that year.[53] From then until his election defeat in January 1910 he vigorously used his position in the Commons to advocate Home Rule for India and to denounce the repressive measures implemented by Minto's administration.

Even more significant politically than the support of the radical activists was the adhesion of Keir Hardie and some nineteen members of his Labour Party to the Indian Parliamentary Committee.[54] Hardie, as the charismatic working-class leader of the Independent Labour Party, had an interest in India which dated back to 1886 when, on his first visit to London, he had chaired a public lecture by Dadabhai Naoroji.[55] During his first term in Parliament, 1892–5, the years in which Naoroji was also an MP, Hardie joined the Indian Parliamentary Commitee, though it was only after 1905 that he became heavily involved in Indian issues in the Commons. Hardie collaborated closely with Cotton and the radical activists with whom his party seemed to have no fundamental policy differences on Indian issues.[56] Both groups were united by a common reformist sentiment and a desire to end the iniquities and injustices of an arbitrary and increasingly despotic regime in India. Hardie appointed one of his party members, James O'Grady, as a special spokesman on Indian affairs. In July 1906, after careful coaching by the visiting Congress leader G. K. Gokhale, Hardie made his first major Commons speech on India, deploring its poverty and criticizing the unrepresentative nature of British administration.

The following year Hardie won the hearts of Indian nationalists as no MP since Bradlaugh had done by his controversial visit to India to see first hand the 'actual condition of the people', and 'to get at the truth' regarding the troubled political situation in partitioned Bengal and other parts of the country.[57] Hardie's India tour was organized and managed by Congress, but he made a deliberate point of not associating merely with moderates such as Banerjea and Gokhale, and had meetings with leading militants such as Aurobindo Ghose and B. G. Tilak. He was greeted with particular enthusiasm in partitioned Bengal and created a storm of protest in Britain over his assertions that official efforts to break the Swadeshi movement 'savoured more of Russian than British methods'.[58] The British authorities would have welcomed a convincing pretext for deporting Hardie from India, but the kind of 'violent public disorder' which would have given grounds for such action did not occur.[59] Even so, the Viceroy concluded that Hardie's visit 'tended to stimulate unrest, to promote sedition in the press, to give fresh life to the boycott and to encourage agitators to hope that their most extreme claims will receive support from an organized party in Parliament'.[60] Hardie's detailed account of his Indian visit was published first in a series of articles in the Independent Labour Party newspaper *Labour Leader*, and then brought out in a book, *India: Impressions and Suggestions* (London, 1909). His considered conclusion was that the unrest in India was British-induced and would never be allayed 'until the people ... have some effective form of self-government'.[61] Hardie continued his active involvement on Indian issues in the Commons until 1910, and the following year Labour formalized its relations with the British Committee by appointing O'Grady to membership of that body. In the mean time Hardie's heir apparent, Ramsay MacDonald, showed an increasing interest in India, undertook a fact-finding visit there in 1909, and would have been elected President of Congress two years later had not his wife's severe illness intervened to prevent it.

During the War years, as the British Committee continued under Wedderburn's ageing and failing leadership, political momentum in India and Britain shifted from the moderate-dominated Congress organization to the new Home Rule leagues organized by Annie Besant and Tilak. Besant, as a former socialist, had continuing ties with British leftists, and the Independent Labour Party activist George Lansbury became the leader of her Home Rule League Committee in England. Two other Labourites, Graham Pole and John Scurr, were founding members of the Committee. Lansbury's Committee deliberately associated itself with Indian militants and pitched its message to 'the British masses' who were no longer being reached by the British Congress Committee.[62] As for the latter Committee, an open rift occurred between it and the movement in India following Wedderburn's death in early 1918 and the rise of Tilak to a dominant position in the reunited Congress.[63] During his pro-longed visit to Britain in 1919 Tilak and his Congress deputation reorganized the British Committee and the editorship of its journal, *India*, to bring both into line with changing Congress policies in India. Former Committee members H. V. Rutherford and (acting chairman) G. B. Clark, and J. M. Parikh, long-term associates of Wedderburn and Naoroji respectively, favoured the policy reorientations and remained on the restructured Committee. Among the new recruits to the Committee the most significant were Labour MPs Josiah C. Wedgwood and Ben Spoor, both of whom attended the Nagpur Session of the Indian National Congress in 1920 but declined to endorse the Party's new non-co-operation policy. Also, the journal *India*, in the final two years of its existence, had the editorial assistance of three well-known leftists—B. G. Horniman, Helena Normanton and Fenner Brockway. Of these, Brockway supported Gandhi's programme, as did Rutherford, who had recently shifted his allegiance from the Liberals to Labour.[64]

At the institutional level the British radical association with Congress ceased in early 1921 when, on Gandhi's rise to leadership, the focus on political mobilization within India led to the dissolution of the British Committee and the closure of the journal *India*. However, personal contacts between interested British leftists and Congress persisted until the last days of the Raj. These relationships, as well as a more detailed study of the British Committee and its recruitment of sympathizers over its thirty-year history, warrant further examination. Similar attention needs to be given to the Committee's role in promoting inter-country visits of political leaders and journalists and its furtherance of informal personal contacts between Indian nationalists and British leftist sympathizers.

In the foregoing sketch of the Congress Committee's recruitment of and collaboration with British radicals Hyndman has been omitted because he does not quite fit that pattern. Hyndman's interest in India and his first questioning of the beneficence of the Raj were aroused by the stinging financial and economic indictment of British rule published in the early 1870s by James C. Geddes, a brilliant young ICS officer and a zealous new convert to positivism.[65] Later that decade, as famine, press censorship, cotton tariff controversy and an expansionist frontier policy brought Indian affairs into the limelight of publicity in Britain, Hyndman undertook his own independent investigation of India's economic conditions. Still under the influence of his bourgeois Conservative upbringing, he was alarmed to discover that British rule was leading the country towards bankruptcy rather than economic prosperity. Just before publishing his conclusions in a number of high-profile articles in the prestigious journal *Nineteenth Century*, Hyndman happened to come upon Naoroji's recent publication, *The Poverty of India* (London 1877), in which he articulated his now famous 'economic drain' theory.[66] Hyndman accepted Naoroji's arguments concerning the drain and, with appropriate acknowlegement to Naoroji, employed that thesis and utilized some of his statistical data in his first article, 'The Bankruptcy of India'.[67] Though scathingly denounced by *The Times* for relying on a mere Indian for his statistical data, Hyndman stuck to his guns.[68] It was hardly surprising therefore that Hyndman and Naoroji soon developed a close and lasting personal relationship.[69] The former's articles received extensive and highly favourable attention in the Indian press, but when he became an avowed socialist and an exponent of class war in the early 1880s public opinion towards him in India appears to have cooled.[70] The Congress was basically capitalist in its orientation and it is significant that although Hyndman continued to show an unflagging interest in Indian affairs and constantly publicized the economic exploitation of India inherent in British rule, he was never invited to participate in any of the Congress institutional organizations in Britain.[71]

Under the influence of Marxist thought Hyndman became increasingly convinced that radical change could not be achieved by peaceful means. As early as 1884 he warned in the columns of *Justice*, the Social Democratic Federation's weekly of which he was editor, that 'insurrection . . . of a ruined people' was looming in India and that 'insurrection is the only 'way out' from [the] . . . unbearable tyranny' of British imperialism.[72] More than a decade later, as western India was disturbed by famine, bubonic plague and political assassinations in Puna, Hyndman used the columns of *Justice* to encourage and justify rebellion in India.[73] His stand caused considerable alarm among governing authorities in Britain and India. It also frightened Naoroji, who informed Hyndman that he could no longer work with him and 'the S.D.F. on Indian matters'.[74] To the chagrin of

Naoroji and the British Committee Hyndman responded by forthrightly criticizing the whole moderate, constitutional approach of Congress. In 1898 he wrote to Naoroji:

> What do you judicious people gain by your moderation? What does your journal *India* gain by its dullness ... ? To the naked eye, and even to the microscope, nothing! They [the governing classes] just kick you and pass seditious acts over you and lie about you, even more than they do with us. We, at least, have the satisfaction of chasing them, deriding them, making them look ridiculous and driving them into furious anger. Moreover, we are getting ready for the inevitable crash which is coming—not in India alone.[75]

Hyndman was thus anticipating by nearly a decade the criticism which the militants in India were to raise against the methods of the moderate leadership of Congress. As a result he became something of a 'hot potato' to the organization Congress. This was well illustrated by the reaction of the Bombay Presidency Association when the question of endorsing Hyndman's candidature for Parliament was put before it in 1904. After 'weighing pros and cons' the Association declined its support.[76] Explaining the decision Wacha wrote:

> We all know how Mr. H. has fought for India, yet it is considered that his extreme views and the manner of placing them, though they can pass unchallenged in the free atmosphere of England, are liable to be misinterpreted here, and we do not want that our Association should in any way be linked with his extreme views.

Wedderburn too felt pressurized by Hyndman's extremism and complained in 1905 that the work of the British Committee was being adversely affected by the socialist leader's denunciation of them as 'useless and even mischievous Moderates'.[77]

Under these circumstances it was only natural that Hyndman gravitated towards the open support of young Indian militants and revolutionaries who became increasingly active in London from around 1905. During 1904 he established contact with Shyamji Krishnavarma, who had been educated at Oxford and called to the Bar in 1884 but whose subsequent experiences in India had turned him against the Raj and the cautious Congress leadership. Encouraged by Hyndman Krishnavarma established an Indian Home Rule Society in London in 1905 and launched a revolutionary journal, the *Indian Sociologist*.[78] Later that year Hyndman formally opened India House, Krishnavarma's London hostel for student activists. Hyndman not only patronized the revolutionaries in London, among them Virendranath Chatto-padhyaya, a future founder of the Communist Party of India, but in 1907 was instrumental in securing an opportunity for Madam B. T. Cama, a Paris-based Indian revolutionary, to speak at the International Socialist Congress at Stuttgart. While she paid formal tribute to 'Comrade' Hyndman's thirty-five years of work for India, his own special contribution to the Congress was an SDF report entitled 'The Ruin of India by British Rule'. This was such a stinging indictment of the Raj that the Indian government placed a temporary ban on the pamphlet, as well as on *Justice*. In 1909 Minto persuaded Morley to make the ban on Hyndman's India-related publications permanent on the following grounds:

Hyndman has for many years exercised a marked influence among natives who hold extreme views about the British connection. [His] opinions and his manner of expressing them are scarcely less violent than those of Shyamji Krishnavarma himself, and their propagation is the more harmful inasmuch as the author is an Englishman and believed by the ignorant in this country to be a leader of English public opinion.[79]

On the outbreak of World War I Hyndman split with the main body of the newly formed British Socialist Party, supported the War effort and, in the process, became less attached to violent revolution.[80] He continued to give some attention to India and threw his support, for example, behind the Congress-Muslim League constitutional reform proposals of 1918, detailing a scheme for full self-government within the empire.[81] Following the War he pressurized his small socialist party to go one step further and endorse a resolution demanding the 'emancipation of India from British rule at an early date'.[82] To the Indian govern-ment this was tantamount to treason and it retained the ban on Hyndman's publications until after his death in 1921. In fact Hyndman had the unique distinction of having more publica-tions banned by the British than any other Englishman.

This brief overview of Hyndman's more than forty years' involvement in the affairs of India suggests that there are numerous important questions still to be investigated. Among these are the influence of his economic analysis of the effects of British rule and the dynamics of his relations with Congress 'moderates' before 1897 and with militants and extremists after that date.

One aspect of the British Committee's activities which has been well analysed is that of the Indian Parliamentary Committee between 1893 and 1907. This is the focal point of Morrow's study referred to earlier. She provides a meticulous examination of the composition and membership of the Indian Parliamentary Committee during its initial period, 1893 to 1900, and again during its revived existence from 1906 to 1908. Particularly valuable is her probing analysis of the major interest groups which associated themselves with the work of the Committee. The major groups which she identifies are the temperance advocates, the anti-opium lobby, the social purity movement and the Irish nationalists. She demonstrates conclusively that each of these interest groups had their own particular priorities, and that these frequently did not coincide with the policies and priorities of the Indian National Congress.[83] One result, as she shows conclusively by an analysis of eleven major Commons division votes on Indian issues in the later 1890s, was that on average less than fifty per cent of the nominal membership of the Committee supported these resolutions.[84] On at least one important issue, that of a Liberal opposition motion to disallow the protective Indian Sugar Duty Act passed by Lord Curzon's government in 1899, all of the Congress's principal parliamentary sympathizers ignored the Indian nationalist desire for protection and voted for disallowance.[85] It is this kind of negativism, combined with the minority support from the nominal membership of the Parliamentary Committee for most of the Indian resolutions debated in the Commons, which induces Morrow to the logical conclusion that the Committee was by no means wholehearted in its support for Congress. On the contrary, she concludes that much of the Congress support in Britain was tainted with imperialist attitudes. This, coupled with the obvious bias of the British Committee for the 'moderates' as opposed to the rising generations of 'extremists' or militant nationalists, leads her to the further conclusion that the British Committee basically operated as a 'restraining and moderating influence ... [on] the politics of the Indian National Congress'.[86]

These are surely valid conclusions, yet they do not provide the full story on the multi-faceted influence and impact of British radicalism on the Congress during this early period. As my own research on some of the most prominent British radicals involved in the early Congress has demonstrated, and as I have suggested here, there were particular individuals, most notably Hume and Hyndman, who tried to influence Congress in more advanced political and socio-economic directions. Other key supporters such as Wedderburn and Cotton fitted into the same category on at least some important issues. Examples of this include Wedderburn's pioneering and tireless promotion of agricultural banks as a device to increase agrarian development and improve the conditions of peasant proprietors, and his efforts during his second presidency of Congress in 1910 to promote reconciliation between the 'moderates' and 'extremists' and between Hindu and Muslim political leaders.[87] As for Cotton, his single-handed and courageous efforts to improve the harsh lot of Assam's tea-plantation workers have already been noted. Interestingly, Congress followed up Cotton's initiative for increased coolie wages with a supporting resolution at its 1901 session. Congress did not follow through with a similar resoulution on the even more sensitive issue of Cotton's efforts to secure greater equity within the judicial system for Assam's coolies. Congress did, however, clearly signal its general high regard for Cotton by electing him as its president in 1904. Then too, other active sympathizers such as Keir Hardie and Rutherford, if they did not encourage Congress into new directions, certainly supported some of the more militant tendencies in the movement.

On the basis of my wider research a number of generalizations can be made concerning the areas in which the committed core of British radical supporters of Congress had a positive or reinforcing influence on nationalist developments in India. These areas included support for far-reaching political reform and

Indianization of the administration, resistance to frontier expansionism and militarism, and sustained opposition to arbitrary detention and deportation of political prisoners as well as to repressive legislation which undermined freedom of the press and civil liberties. On economic issues many of them basically shared the nationalist analysis of the negative impact of British rule. On the other hand their ideological commitment to free trade was so strong that they could rarely bring themselves to support even limited protectionism in India. In this respect they were imperialist. In a political sense too they favoured a continuing connection between India and Britain—not one based on force and exploitation but on a recognition of mutual interest which they believed would emerge in India if the country had the kind of autonomy enjoyed by dominions such as Canada.

It is worth noting that the commitment and dedication of the leading British radical supporters was frequently and in some instances fulsomely acknowledged by their contemporary Indian associates. Congress paid laudatory formal tribute to supporters such as Bradlaugh, Cotton, Hume, Keir Hardie and Wedderburn, while some of the individual Indian 'moderates' came close to idolatry in their praise of some of these leaders. Nor did the tributes come only from moderates. For example, Tilak on occasion lauded to the skies Hume's general contributions to Indian nationalism, notwithstanding the profound differences between them on the issue of social reform.[88] Gandhi too recognized the value of Hume's contributions, as witnessed by the following rhetorical question in his *Hind Swaraj*: 'How can we forget what ... Hume has written, how he lashed us into action, and with what effort he has awakened us, in order to achieve the objects of Congress?'[89] A similar kind of tribute was paid by Lajpat Rai to Henry Cotton. In a letter to the family upon learning of Cotton's death Lajpat Rai wrote: 'We have lost one of our greatest benefactors, kindest friends and devoted supporters. Young India can never forget the services of Sir Henry Cotton'.[90] A third example is the following glowing tribute which Tilak paid to Hyndman in 1919:

I ... deplore my inability to adequately acknowledge your kindness, to my country and to me personally. You have laboured hard for the last forty years, and your latest book, *The Awakening of Asia*, is a fitting

coping-stone to the magnificent edifice of your life-long work, and
the chapters in it about India are being already circulated in the form
of a booklet, and will in future be admitted as a masterpiece of political
vision. To myself personally you have always kindly and freely given
advice during my prolonged stay of over a year in the country, and
helped the cause of Home Rule for India by your powerful advocacy
of her complete emancipation from foreign domination.[91]

One further comment of a revisionist nature is, I think,
warranted with respect to the notion that the British Committee,
by its persistent requests to Congress for funding to support the
publication of the journal *India* and its other activities, created a
distortion in the overall movement. Instead of being a complement
to the movement in India, the British Committee seemed at
times to become the centre of Congress activity. That was clearly
not the intention of Hume when he initiated the committee, and
if moderates in India put too much 'faith in the eventual effectiveness of British agitation', Hume at least never shared that
view.[92] His attitude was lucidly expressed in the verses of a
poem which he penned in 1886 to promote notionalist mobilization. The first verse reads as follows:

> Sons of Ind, why sit ye idle
> Wait ye for some Deva's aid?
> Buckle to, be up and doing!
> Nations by themselves are made;[93]

Significantly, the last line formed a refrain which was repeated
in each of the seven verses. Nearly a decade after his retirement
to Britain Hume repeated that message in a special written
address to the Congress entitled 'A Call to Arms.' On that
occasion he reminded the Congress that nations were created
only by struggle and 'self-sacrifice' and reminded them of the
example of the Irish, 'who have been fighting tooth and nail . . .
for nearly a century'.[94] He went on to chide Indian leaders for
naively assuming that 'any despotic Government . . . *will willingly*
yield you . . . political privileges' and appealed to them to

be in earnest; disregard all threats—spurn all coercion—prove to the
British nation that you are really determined to be fairly dealt
with . . . that you are resolved never to give them a day's peace till you
are so dealt with; that you will spend your time, your money, your
lives, if need be, in bringing this about.

The problem was not, I would argue, that the British Committee was too politically active, but that Congress in India was not doing enough to build a broad-based nationalist movement. In a similar vein a few years later Hume revealed that he did not really believe that the British would be induced to make far-reaching changes in India until Congress could rally to its cause at least three or four hundred thousand dedicated and committed supporters.[95] Not till Gandhi arrived on the scene was this level of national mobilization achieved.

While this essay has touched only upon some of the major facets of the British radical connection with Congress, it demonstrates that there was much that was positive and reinforcing in the relationship. It is certainly an oversimplification and a distortion to view the connection merely as a negative and restraining factor on the development of the early Congress. While the pro-India radicals were too small a minority in British politics ever to shape government policy in India, they did at times have an ameliorating influence on the autocracy of the Raj. They were also of some influence in pressurizing the regime in a more reformist direction. At times when the heavy hand of repression made life in India especially difficult for political activists, such as during the pre-World War I decade, British radical sympathizers were a source of encouragement to many nationalists in India. Indeed, it is not too far-fetched to suggest that British radical and Congress linkages developed in this early period left a legacy which had its impact on the later generation of Indian social democratic leaders such as Krishna Menon and Jawaharlal Nehru.

NOTES

Research for this paper was made possible by grants from the Shastri Indo-Canadian Institute, the Social Sciences and Humanities Research Council of Canada, and The Research Board of the University of Manitoba.

1. See, for example B. L. Grover, *A Documentary Study of British Policy Towards Indian Nationalism, 1885–1909* (Delhi, 1967), who concludes that Hume rendered 'incalculable' services to 'the cause of British imperialism' (p. 28). See also, R. C. Majumdar, *History of the Freedom Movement in India*, vol. i (Calcutta, 1962),

pp. 388–92; and N. Ray, *Nationalism in India* (Aligarh, 1973), p. 89.

2. Moulton, 'Allan O. Hume and the Indian National Congress: A Reassessment.' *South Asia* 8 (1985).

3. S. R. Mehrotra, *Towards India's Freedom and Partition* (New Delhi, 1979), pp. 44–62; and J. R. McLane, *Indian Nationalism and the Early Congress* (Princeton, 1977), pp. 89–129.

4. Moulton, 'Early Indian Nationalism: Henry Cotton and the British Positivist and Radical Connection, 1870–1915', *Journal of Indian History* 60 (1982), pp. 125–59. Geraldine H. Forbes, in her book *Positivism in Bengal* (Colombia, Mo., 1975), devotes several pages to Cotton's activities as a proponent of religious positivism in Bengal but does not discuss his political activities.

5. McLane, pp. 125–7.

6. Moulton, 'William Wedderburn and Early Indian Nationalism, 1870–1917', in *Changing South Asia: Politics and Government*, edited by K. Ballhatchet and D. Taylor (Hong Kong, 1984), pp. 37–54.

7 For Bradlaugh's pro-Congress activities, see M. N. Das, *Indian National Congress versus the British* (Delhi, 1978). A succinct discussion of Irish linkages is provided in H. V. Brasted's 'The Irish Connection: The Irish Outlook on Indian Nationalism, 1870–1906', in *Changing South Asia: Politics and Government*, pp. 67–78. For brief references to the India-related activities of Rutherford and Mackarness, see Moulton, 'British Radicals and India in the Early Twentieth Century', in *Edwardian Radicalism, 1900–1914*, edited by A. J. A. Morris (London, 1974), pp. 26–46.

8. The book is dedicated to Hume, Bradlaugh, Wedderburn and Cotton.

9. See, for example, Iain McLean, *Keir Hardie* (London, 1975); Kenneth O. Morgan, *Keir Hardie: Radical and Socialist* (London, 1975); and Emrys Hughes, *Keir Hardie* (London, 1956).

10. See also, Morrow, 'The British Committee of the Indian National Congress as an Issue in and an Influence upon Nationalist Politics, 1889–1901', in *Changing South Asia*, pp. 55–66.

11. Morrow, 'Origin and Early Years of the British Committee of the Indian National Congress, 1885–1907' (London, Ph.D. thesis, 1977), p. 16.

12. Moulton, 'Allan O. Hume', pp. 6–7.

13. Ibid.; and Hume to Ripon, 13 Jan. 1889, Ripon Papers, Add. MS. 43616 (British Library).

14. Hume, *The Indian National Congress: Its Origins, Aims and Objects* (Calcutta, 1888), p. 4.

15. McLane, pp. 104–14.

16. Hume to Tyabji, 13 Sept. 1888, Tyabji Papers (Indian National Archives).

17. Moulton, 'Allan O. Hume', pp. 12–16.

18. *Public Service Commission*, vol. 8 (Calcutta, 1887), p. 112.

19. Ibid.

20. [Hume], *The Old Man's Hope* (Calcutta, 1886), p. 7.

21. *Public Service Commission*, p. 314f.

22. Hume, Minute, 25 Aug. 1871. Govt. of India, Revenue Dept., Papers on Agriculture, 1868–79, L/E/5/63 (India Office Library).

23. Secretary of State to Governor-General in Council, no. 27, 3 Aug. 1871, Revenue, Agriculture and Commerce Dept., L/E/3/491.

24. Lytton to Eden, 10 May 1879, Lytton Papers, 518/4 (India Office Library).

25. Hume, *Agricultural Reform in India* (London, 1879), p. 31.

26. H. M. Hyndman, 'The Bankruptcy of India', *Nineteenth Century* 4 (1878), pp. 585–608; and 5 (1879), pp. 443–62. See also, Horst Krüger, *Indische Nationalisten und Weltproletariat* (Berlin, 1984), p. 313.

27. [Hume], *The Old Man's Hope*, p. 6.

28. Ibid., p. 9.

29. Ibid.

30. McLane, pp. 114–18.

31. Hume to Ripon, [c. June 1887], Ripon Papers.

32. [Hume], *A Conversation between Moulvi Farid-ud-din...and Rambaksh ...*, appendix (in English translation), INC Report (1887).

33. Hume to Ripon, 13 Jan. 1889, Ripon Papers, Add. MS. 43616.

34. 'Mr. A. O. Hume at Jubbulpore', enclosed in Colvin to Dufferin 25 Apr. 1888, Dufferin Papers, F130/64d (India Office Library).

35. B. Martin, *New India, 1885* (Bombay, 1970): McLane; and Moulton, 'Allan O. Hume'.

36. See especially Hume's letter to Colvin, published in *Audi Alteram Partem* (Simla, 1888).

37. Hume to Ripon, 13 Jan. 1889, Ripon Papers, Add.MS 43616.

38. Quoted in Anil Seal, *The Emergence of Indian Nationalism* (Cambridge, 1968), p. 294.

39. H. P. Kaushik, *The Indian National Congress in England (1885–1920)*, (Delhi, 1972), app. 1, iii.

40. Report, INC, 1891; reprinted in A.M. and S. Zaida (eds.), *The Encyclopaedia of Indian National Congress*, vol. 2, 1891–1895 (New Delhi, 1977), p. 23.

41. Hume to Every Member of the Congress Party, 16 Feb. 1892, *India*, 13 May 1892.

42. *India*, 13 May 1892; and *Mahratta*, 3 Apr. 1892.
43. Wacha to Dadabhoy, 19 Mar. and 2 Apr. 1892, *Dadabhai Naoroji Correspondence*, II, 1 (Bombay, 1977), pp. 281–4.
44. Hume to B. N. Pandit, 24 Feb. 1892, *India*, 13 May 1892.
45. Hume, 'The Truth about India', *India*, 1 Sept. 1893.
46. *Mr. A. O. Hume's Farewell to India* (London, 1894).
47. David Tribe, *President Charles Bradlaugh, M. P.* (London, 1971), p. 275.
48. Morrow, 'Origin and Eary Years of the British Committee', pp. 137–8.
49. Morrow, 'The British Committee of the Indian National Congress', pp. 59–62.
50. Moulton, 'Early Indian Nationalism: Henry Cotton', pp. 140–4.
51. *India*, 2 Mar. 1906.
52. G. P. Gooch, *Frederic Mackarness: A Brief Memoir* (London, 1922), pp. 37–56.
53. Moulton, 'British Radicals and India', pp. 37–8.
54. Morrow, 'Origin and Early Years of the British Committee', p. 381.
55. Hardie Speech, Poona, Oct. 1907, Govt. of India, Home Dept. Proc., Pub., Pol. A (Feb. 1908), p. 63.
56. Moulton, 'British Radicals and India', pp. 33–45.
57. Hardie to Gokhale, 9 July 1907, Gokhale Papers, 224/12 (National Archives of India).
58. Hardie, *India: Impressions and Suggestions* (London, 1909), pp. 24–5 and 112–14.
59. Morley to Minto, 3 Oct. 1907, Govt. of India, Home Dept. Proc., Pol. A (Feb. 1908), p. 50.
60. Minto to Morley, 6 Oct. 1907, ibid.
61. Hardie, *India*, p. 117.
62. Weekly Report, C.I.D., 5 Oct. 1915. Govt. of India, Home Dept. Proc., Pol. B (Oct. 1915), p. 629.
63. *India*, 8 Nov. 1918.
64. See, for example, Rutherford's, *Modern India: Its Problems and their Solution* (London, 1927), pp. 1–54.
65. R. T. Hyndman, *The Last Years of H. M. Hyndman* (London, 1923), p. 312; and James Geddes, *The Logic of the Indian Deficit* (London, 1871).
66. R. T. Hyndman, ibid.
67. *Nineteenth Century*, 4, 20 (Oct. 1878).
68. *The Times*, 8 Oct. 1878.
69. R. P. Masani, *Dadabhai Naoroji* (London, 1939), pp. 197–202 and 410–12.

70. See, for example, the *Indian Mirror*, 9, 12, 15, 16, 20 Nov. 1878; and the *Bengalee*, 23 Nov. 1878.
71. See, for example, Hyndman, *The Ruin of India by British Rule* (London, 1907).
72. *Justice*, 23 Aug. and 11 Oct. 1884.
73. Ibid., 20 Mar. and 10 and 17 July 1897.
74. Quoted in Masani, p. 400.
75. Ibid.
76. Wacha to Naoroji, 20 Feb. 1904, *Dadabhai Naoroji Correspondence*, II, 2 (Bombay, 1977), p. 857.
77. Wedderburn to Gokhale, 14 Jan. 1905, Gokhale Papers 579/17.
78. J.C. Ker, *Political Troubles in India, 1907–1917* [Confidential C.I.D. Report] (Calcutta, 1917), pp. 170–1.
79. Viceroy to Secretary of State, 27 May 1909, Govt. of India, Home Dept. Proc., Pol.A (June 1909), p. 36.
80. C. Tsuzuki, *H. M. Hyndman and British Socialism* (London, 1961), pp. 218–35.
81. Hyndman, *The Awakening of Asia* (London, 1919), pp. 262–70.
82. *Justice*, 21 Aug. 1919. Quoted in P. S. Gupta, *Imperialism and the British Labour Movement, 1914–1964* (London, 1975), p. 41.
83. Morrow, 'Origin and Early Years of the British Committee', pp. 136–64.
84. Ibid., p. 197.
85. Morrow, 'The British Committee of the Indian National Congress', p. 57.
86. Ibid., p. 63.
87. Moulton, 'William Wedderburn and Early Indian Nationalism, 1870–1917', in *Changing South Asia*, pp. 37–54.
88. *The Mahratta*, 23 Dec. 1894.
89. Printed in *Collected Works of Mahatma Gandhi*, vol. 10, 1910–11 (Delhi, 1963), p. 8.
90. Lajpat Rai to [H.E.A.] Cotton, 3 Nov. 1915, Cotton Collection, microfilm 1619 (India Office Library).
91. Quoted in F. J. Gould, *Hyndman: Prophet of Socialism, 1842–1921* (London, 1928), pp. 265–6.
92. Morrow, 'The British Committee of the Indian National Congress', p. 61.
93. Quoted in Mehrotra, p. 59.
94. [Hume] *A Call to Arms* (London, 1903).
95. Mehrotra, p. 56.

THE POLITICS
OF RESPECTABILITY:
INDIAN WOMEN AND THE
INDIAN NATIONAL CONGRESS

GERALDINE FORBES

INTRODUCTION

Historians whose work focuses on gender in twentieth-century India are frequently asked why women, much lauded for their participation in the movement for independence, are not more visible in politics today and have not been able to significantly improve their socio-economic position generally. These questions assume that participation led to politicization and naturally to continued political participation. One of the ways of answering these questions is to examine the interaction between those women who participated in the independence struggle and the Indian National Congress. Specifically, I intend to consider the role of women in the early Congress, Gandhi's programme and his role in mobilizing women, and the institutions developed to bring women of the cities of Calcutta and Bombay into the agitational politics of 1920–2 and 1930–2. My purpose is to establish a clearer understanding of the complex interrelationship that developed between the Indian National Congress, Gandhi and women. My central argument is that the structures developed to

mobilize women for the protest movement proved inadequate
to the tasks of politicizing women, ensuring continued participation, or acting as channels for the expression of their interests.
That these institutions developed as they did, with all their
limitations, can best be understood as a function of the limited
autonomy allowed women in a society which valued modesty
and practised sex segregation.

WOMEN AND THE EARLY CONGRESS

The early Indian National Congress, because it claimed to
speak for all groups and all classes in India, decided to avoid
issues which would foster antagonism. This meant that topics
associated with women's status—education, child marriage,
polygamy, purdah and widowhood—were delegated to the
National Social Conference.[1] Following Gandhi's rise to power
in Congress, social issues were made an integral part of the
party's platform. Although it was not until the twentieth century
that Congress eagerly sought the help of women in carrying out
its programmes, Indian women played a role in the meetings from
the beginning. Attitudes towards social reform, the development
of educational institutions for women, women's journalism, and
clubs for women had all contributed to the development of a new
group of women in India. Although this was a small group and its
members not representative of Indian women as a whole, their
numbers were growing, as was their interest in women's issues
and in political and social change. The earliest women's organizations all had some connection, either through their members or
their parent organization, to Congress, and it is this connection
that has bequeathed to history the notion of the inseparability of
the women's movement and the Indian National Congress.

Unfortunately, many of those who have written on this period
have opted for one of two simplistic views of the relationship
between Congress and women. Either they are laudatory:
Congress, particularly Gandhi, transformed Indian women;[2] or
they condemn Congress and Gandhi for manipulating women
for political ends.[3] The reality of the interaction was extremely
complicated; the most active women worked with the support
of husbands and families and frequently the women in the
women's movement were also those involved with politics. To

see them as puppets (led out of purdah into political agitation) or dupes (tricked or coerced into abandoning feminism for nationalism) ignores the legacy of the nineteenth century and denies both the intelligence of these women as well as the complexity of their relationship with Congress. It also overlooks the way in which consciousness and ideology developed: for many women political involvement spurred their feminism, while commitment to improving the status of women encouraged their involvement in the freedom struggle.

When Congress met in Bombay in 1889 there were ten women in attendance. These included Swarnakumari Devi, a well-known Bengali writer and editor of *Bharati*; Kadambini Ganguli, Bengal's first woman doctor; Pandita Ramabai, a social reformer, educationalist and noted Sanskrit scholar; and a number of Bombay women who were educated but less well known than these three. The following year, when Congress met in Calcutta, both Swarnakumari Devi and Kadambini Ganguli attended as delegates.[4] In 1901 a song, 'Hindustan', written by Swarnakumari's younger daughter Saraladevi, was performed by a chorus of fifty-six girls representing all regions of India. The following year the National Congress anthem was sung in Gujarati by Lady Vidyagauri Nilkanth and her sister Sharda Mehta.[5] This remained the Congress anthem until 1905 when Saraladevi sang Bankim Chandra Chatterjee's 'Bande Mataram' at the Benares session.

In addition to providing Congress with a few observers and delegates and the spirit of song, a number of Bengali women organized meetings and social events to further encourage women's interest in political and social issues. Saraladevi introduced festivals and rituals to celebrate Bengali heroes and arranged a *swadeshi* exhibition for the Bombay Congress in 1904. Kadambini Ganguli arranged a Mahila Sammelan (Women's Conference) in Calcutta for the wives of Congress members gathered at the Annual Session in 1906. In 1908 she organized a women's committee to support Gandhi's efforts in the Transvaal.[6]

Apart from attending Congress sessions and arranging women's meetings that coincided with Congress; women were beginning to demonstrate their interest in political issues in other forums. In June 1899 the *Indian Social Reformer* reported that government representatives had received a telegram from B. Rama Bai and a memorial signed by B. Amma Bai and other ladies protesting the proposed abolition of the hospital in Manjeshwar. The article reported that the 'ladies got their own way'; the government vetoed the proposal to close the hospital and approved its budget.[7]

On a larger scale the protest movement against Lord Curzon's partition of Bengal gained the support of many women. The boycott agitation, begun earlier, finally received Congress approval at the Benares session of 1905. While some of the Swadeshi movement actions fit the traditional pattern of meetings, speeches and petitions, the press and the platform were used 'to preach the new creed the radical nationalism' and reach an audience previously untouched by political action.[8] And this new audience included Bengali housewives who were neither formally educated nor had the autonomy or leisure to attend political gatherings with any regularity.

The wedding of swadeshi activities (such as spinning and weaving) to popular religious observances (such as Durga Puja) made it possible to involve large numbers of women. For example, when Lilavati Devi, Hemangini Das and Nirmala Sarkar introduced spinning wheels and looms into the homes of their neighbourhood they urged women to spin enough every day to make their Durga Puja saris. Other women were encouraged to take the vow of Meyer Konta (Mother's Chest) to be observed by daily setting aside a handful of rice for the motherland. Thus women would be reminded of their duty to the nation, children would learn patriotism first-hand, and a storehouse of rice would be created.[9]

In another effort to modify traditional institutions to serve political ends Ramendra Sundar Trivedi composed the Banga Lakshmi Vratakatha (the tale of the vow for the Goddess Lakshmi of Bengal). Meant to be read to a group of women gathered to hear the story of Lakshmi and renew their vow to the Goddess of Fortune, this particular version explained the boycott and swadeshi in religious terms. The Vratakatha was read by Trivedi's daughter at the Vishnu temple (at Trivedi's mother's home) in the village Jemokandir, Murshidabad district, to 1000 women on 16 October 1903.[10] This Vrata relates how the Goddess of Fortune came to reside in Bengal and focuses on critical periods in Bengal's history. These were periods when the people neglected their duty and Lakshmi threatened to leave. Her threats always recalled people to their senses and reminded them of their duty to religion and society. When the British came, they made fools of the Bengalis by giving them cheap and shoddy products in exchange for items of value. The Goddess was furious and she decided to abandon Bengal forever. Upon hearing her decision Bengalis wept and begged her to stay. This commotion annoyed the governor (a puffed-up fellow) who decided to separate brother from brother and Hindu from Muslim. Hoping to convince Lakshmi to stay Bengalis took the vow of Swadeshi promising to no longer lust after the products of the foreigner and instead learn to live comfortably with the things they could make themselves. Hearing their vow Lakshmi agreed to stay in Bengal.[11]

On the day declared 'Partition Day', 16 October 1905, the women of Bengal were asked to observe *arandhan* rites, i.e. to observe a day without lighting the hearth and cooking food. That it was widely observed is borne out in women's accounts: Shudha Mazumdar recalled:

My first introduction to politics was in 1905 when I was seven years old and Mother served us with *phalahar* (fruit meal) when it was neither a fast-day nor a *puja* day. It was not a holy day nor did I hear of any holy purpose, so I was somewhat puzzled to notice the unusual silence in the kitchen and find that no fires were burning at all. On inquiry I learnt it was associated with the Swadeshi movement.[12]

Generally women were neither accustomed nor encouraged to attend public meetings. Not only were women of the 'respectable classes' required to spend most of their time in the vicinities of their homes, the demands of food preparation meant they had little time to do other things. A non-cooking day made it possible for women to be part of the political movement without overtly neglecting the household. Nevertheless, there were a few occasions when women demonstrated publicly and when they did so they made a great impression. Following the August 1907 sentencing of Bhupendranath Dutta to one year's rigorous imprisonment for preaching revolution in the newspaper *Jugantor* 200 women gathered at the home of Dr Nilratan Sarkar to congratulate Bhupendranath's mother. Equally impressive was the appearance of Hemangini Das and a few other women at Nimtola Ghat to witness the cremation of the patriot Brahmobandhah Uppadhyay. Before the pyre was lit Hemangini made a short speech about Brahmobandhah Uppadhyay's ability to evoke the patriotism of women.[13]

These activities occurred in Bengal because it was the centre of the Swadeshi protest. However, there were a few sympathy protests by women in other areas, particularly UP and the Punjab. Although the action was localized, the forces which made possible this degree of participation by women were not. Education, journalism, women's organizations and a 'new spirit' all contributed to the notion that women had a role to play in politics. Before World War I their role was supportive. There were no women leaders, no women's political organization and no formalized integration of women into political institutions.

Our information about how many women were involved in ceremonies and demonstrations is highly subjective. We know that 200 women were at the meetings to congratulate Bhupendranath Dutta's mother, that 1000 ladies gathered to hear the Vratakatha at Trivedi's mother's temple, that two women were delegates to the Indian National Congress in 1890, and that fifty-six girls sang at the Congress session in 1901; but beyond this there is very little data. Some authors have looked to British accounts for verification of women's participation in the Swadeshi movement. J. C. Bagal cites an article by Mrs James MacDanald, wife of the then Prime Minister, which claimed that women had been meeting in each other's homes and collectively vowing to buy only Swadeshi products. Even though zenana women do not always know how to read and write, she wrote, the Swadeshi movement speaks to them and has an impact on their lives.[14] The journalist Valentine Chirol supported this view. He wrote in *Indian Unrest*: 'the revolt seems to have obtained a firm hold in the zenana....'[15] While it is possible to take these as indicators that the movement among women was widespread, English people were terribly suspicious of the zenana simply because it was a part of the empire they did not control. Just as conspiracies were thought to be hatched in dark narrow lanes, so the inhabitants of the impenetrable zenanas were suspected of nurturing dangerous political notions.[16]

The impact of these activities was primarily symbolic—both for the British and for Indians. To both groups the involvement of women signalled the depth of the patriotic movement. For the British it was a danger signal; for Indians it added a new and poignant dimension to their cause. Children would be nurtured on patriotism, meals would be spiced with patriotism, the gods and goddesses would be worshipped with patriotic fervour. The emotional impact was great even if the numbers were small. In *Gharey Bairey* (the Home and the World) Rabindranath Tagore has emphasized the danger associated with women's involvement in politics and ascribed that danger to women's lack of experience and knowledge of the larger world. Although Tagore may have exaggerated, this story underlines women's derivative status and limited impact. While women were powerful inspirational figures, they did not have the political power necessary to influence Congress policy or tactics.

WOMEN ENTER THE POLITICAL ARENA

It was only after World War I that an infrastructure (leaders, women's organizations, the integration of women into existing political organizations) was created that made possible women's entry into agitational politics as part of the Congress programme. In the early years of the twentieth century there were three women who attained the status of national leaders and became models for future generations of women. Two of these women were Indian: Madame Bhikhaiji Rustom K.R. Cama and Sarojini Naidu, and the other was English: Annie Besant.

Madame Cama, born in 1875, was educated at Alexandra Parsi Girls School in Bombay, married a Parsi reformer and began her residence in Europe in 1907. She was soon noticed making the rounds of various radical congresses accompanied by a well-known seditionist, and by August had created an Indian national flag of green, yellow and red bearing the words 'Bande

Mataram'. In her speeches Madame Cama urged the 'dumb millions of Hindus who are undergoing tyranny under the English capitalists and the British government' to imitate the Russians and overthrow their foreign rulers. The dumb millions, in Madame Cama's speeches, always included both men and women and she frequently referred to the treatment of Indian women by the British rulers as a reason to overthrow the tyrants. It is not clear how many Indians in India were aware of her speeches and activities at this time but she did make an impression on Indians studying and living in Europe. Perin Naoroji, one of Dadabhai Naoroji's granddaughters studying in England, travelled to Paris to meet her and became her travelling companion in 1910. In the 1930s Perin Naoroji Captain became a stalwart member of the Bombay Congress. By this time Indian women had elevated Madame Cama to the level of heroine and invoked her name, along with that of the Rani of Jhansi, in the their recitation of a list of brave and politically active Indian women.[17]

Annie Besant was born in London in 1847 and had an extensive career behind her when she arrived in India to attend the 1893 Annual Conference of the Theosophical Society. Connected with a number of radical causes in England, she had written in 1874 that women should be represented in the law-making process because they were expected to adhere to the law.[18] In India she was overcome for a time by what the *Indian Social Reformer* called 'a fit of spirituality', but then rallied and returned to some of the topics that had interested her in England.[19] When Hindu College opened in Benares in 1901 Besant wrote about her plans to open a college for girls as one of the first steps in the process of regenerating Indian women. A few months later she wrote an article urging that ancient India's segregation of the sexes be preserved in modern institutions. Do not follow the West, Besant cautioned her readers, rather look to your own past for models. 'The ancient and wise way was training, educating and raising the women, putting her more and more on a high level, and then giving her a reasonable and dignified liberty.'[20] The *Indian Social Reformer* chided her for her romantic view of ancient India. Hinduism, one journalist reminded her, did not look to the lives of gods and goddesses for models but rather took its rules of social behaviour from the law codes. The practical question, the *Reformer* concluded, was how to get women educated.[21]

By 1914 Besant had broken her vow of 1894 not to enter politics and in the next few years practically everything she touched turned to politics. In 1915 she unveiled her plan to establish a Home Rule League and by 1 September 1916 the League was a fact. By speaking publicly and writing for her paper *New India*, she was deemed a threat by the government and asked to leave the country. When she refused she was interned. Widespread protests gained her release and by August 1917 Besant had been elected President of the Indian National Congress. When the 1917 session of Congress met in Calcutta there were 400 women present. Unfortunately the Annie Besant who spoke at this session was exhausted by her recent experiences and her speech lacked the fire of her earlier appearances.[22] In the same year she was named President of the Women's Indian Association and in her own person joined Congress and this newly formed organization dedicated itself to female franchise and social reforms.

The youngest of these three women was Sarojini Naidu, born Sarojini Chattopadhyay in Hyderabad in 1879. She had travelled to England in 1895 to study at King's College, London, and Girton College, Cambridge. While in England she wrote poetry and attracted the attention of a few literary figures who were charmed by the English poetry of this delicate Indian girl. She returned to India in 1898, married Captain M. Govinderajalu Naidu, Principal Medical Officer of the Gokinda Brigade with HH the Nizam's forces, and bore him four children.[23]

Sarojini Naidu attended her first session of Congress in 1904 when it met in Bombay. Because her father had established a Congress branch in Hyderabad Sarojini was nurtured on the writings of India's great patriots. At Bombay she was finally able to meet some of the well-known nationalist leaders and one of the veterans of women's educational work, Ramabai Ranade. And, she was invited to recite her poem, 'Ode to India', before Congress. When Congress met in Calcutta in 1906 Sarojini's fiery speech so impressed Gokhale that he urged her to dedicate her life to the country. The next year she again spoke at Congress and at the twenty-second session of the

Indian National Social Congress (1908) she moved a resolution for the amelioration of the condition of Hindu widows. She spoke in favour of Karve's home and school as model institutions that could make widows into useful and respected members of society. How could there be political freedom she asked, when the country continued to suffer from this degrading 'cancer'?[24] By this time she was clearly established as a forceful public speaker who linked the cause of India's freedom with the need to improve women's status.

Her first meeting with Gandhi occurred in London in 1914. Sarojini had heard much about his campaign in South Africa and had looked forward to an opportunity to meet him. Returning to India in 1915 she attended the Congress session at Bombay and recited a poem for communal harmony: 'Awake', dedicated to Muhammad Ali Jinnah, concludes with voices representing all the Indian religions pledging their loyalty to the motherland.[25] By 1917 her political activities paralleled those of Annie Besant. In that year she spoke to the Congress presided over by Besant, supported the formation of the Women's Indian Association and led the women's franchise delegation that met Edwin Montagu. At the 1918 Congress in Bombay Sarojini moved the resolution that women and men be given the same tests to determine their eligibility to vote.[26]

By the end of World War I Indian women had been introduced to politics. An ideology evoking the 'golden age' legitimized their political roles, and the political tacticians had devised political activities for women that violated neither the ideology nor the norms of sex segregation. Perhaps most important, a few women leaders had emerged as inspirational figures. These women, particularly Besant and Naidu, made felt women's presence as initiators and leaders in Congress, inspired other women to consider political involvement, and linked improvement in women's status with nationalist aspirations. However, neither developed a programme for women nor carved for women a place in the Indian National Congress. At this point Gandhi appeared on the scene and forged the lasting connection between the Indian National Congress and women.

It is difficult to pinpoint the origins of Gandhi's views on women for he was a pragmatic man rather than a systematic thinker. In an essay on the traditional influences on Gandhi A. L. Basham claims that he got from his parents morality, from his nurse the habit of calling on Rama; and from Hinduism the belief that *tapas* (asceticism) generates an immense power which is able to influence even the gods. But his view of women and his insistence on the dignity of labour, Basham insists, came from Western sources. Basham contends that Gandhi first wrote about women as 'helpmates' in 1898 during the first phase of the struggle in South Africa.[27] And it was also in South Africa that Gandhi decided to take the vow of *brahmacharya* [celibacy] in 1906. He argued that this vow was an essential step in his effort to understand and respect, first, his wife, and second, all women. When he came to England in that same year to petition for the rights of Transvaal Indians he became aware of the Suffragettes. And when the eleven women arrested for demonstrating in front of the House of Commons refused to pay their fines and were awarded prison sentences, Gandhi was moved to write an article for *Indian Opinion*. In 'Deeds Better than Words' Gandhi wrote that he was impressed that women from respectable families were willing to brave the insults of the streets and the brutality of the police. During the next year he continued to follow and write about the Suffragette struggle. On one occasion he discussed the propriety of men adopting 'women's tactics'. Gandhi concluded that the Suffragettes were demonstrating 'manliness' and Indian men who imitated them would not appear 'effeminate', rather they would make it clear that they had finally refused to accept oppression. It was only when the Suffragettes turned to violence that he lost sympathy with the movement and wrote articles condemning their tactics.[28]

Gandhi's first long and well-developed speech on women in India was made in 1918 to the Bhagini Samaj.[29] Founded in 1916 in memory of G. K. Gokhale, this organization drew its membership from the Gujarati community. In this speech Gandhi reminded his middle-class audience that 85 per cent of Indian women lived in poverty and ignorance. The role of the Bhagini Samaj would be to produce leaders who could work for social reform, female education and new laws to give women their natural rights. These women leaders needed to be 'pure, firm and self-controlled', like the ancient heroines Sita, Damayanti and Draupadi. They would be able to awaken women to their essential equality with men, their right to freedom and liberty, and their right to a supreme place in their own sphere of activity.[30] Equality did not mean that women would perform the same tasks as men: in Gandhi's ideal world men and women would 'follow different vocations suitable to their different physical and emotional temperaments.'[31]

NON-CO-OPERATION, 1920–2

The Rowlatt Acts and the Amritsar massacre set the stage for the Non-Co-operation movement of 1920–2. Gandhi first called for a hartal on 30 March 1919 and then changed the date to 6 April. It was on this day that he addressed a meeting of 'ladies of all classes and communities' and asked women to join the satyagraha movement so that men could be fully involved.[32] In subsequent speeches he suggested specific activities for women. Gandhi urged women to take the swadeshi vow: the promise to relinquish foreign goods and spend a certain amount of time each day spinning thread. He explained the need for this work in terms that women would understand but which also revealed his perception of women's proper role in society and the struggle for independence from British rule. India's poverty, according to Gandhi, was a direct result of abandoning indigenous crafts and becoming dependent on foreign-made items. And women, home-makers and nurturers, the key figures in India's regeneration, were ignorant of the causes of poverty. To be able to save India women must understand and be integrated into the world so that they could play an equal role with men. In answer to the question of how to accomplish this in as brief a time as possible Gandhi proposed that rich and cultured women take the vow to spin and act as models for the masses of women. His suggestion was acted upon in Bombay where a number of prominent women, including Lady Dorab Tata, Lady Petit, Ramabai Ranade, Lilavati Banker and Mrs Jerbanu Merwanji Kothawala, all agreed to learn to spin.[33]

In urging women to become involved in political activities

Gandhi reminded them of Sita's sacrifice for the state. In a series of articles and speeches on the atrocities in the Punjab, and particularly Amritsar, Gandhi explained to women that the British rulers were the equivalent of the demon Ravana. It was in the Punjab, the land of the rishis, that Indians had been humiliated, in fact made to crawl on their stomachs 'like serpents'. It was clear that under Ravanaraja the people were enslaved and were slowly losing all sense of dharma. Under these circumstances women had both a religious and civic duty to become like Sita. Just as Sita refused to adorn herself for Ravana or forsake her husband, no matter how great her suffering, Indian women would have to prepare for sacrifice. Only then, when women had joined men in the fight against this immoral government, could Ramaraja be re-established.[34]

This was a powerful message and different in content, although not in texture, from the earlier Bengali attempt to combine the swadeshi vow with the story of Lakshmi leaving Bengal. The difficulty with the Rama–Sita analogy was Ravana's abduction and attempted rape of Sita. Fathers and husbands who accepted the identification of the British Raj with Ravana might have been led to become more protective of their womenfolk. Gandhi understood that he was wielding a two-edged sword. He told his male audience to remember Sita's bravery when she was abducted and her ability to remain chaste even while a prisoner of Ravana. God, he reminded them, protects the honour of chaste women just as he protected Draupadi in the epic Mahabharata.[35]

Because Gandhi and other leaders sought to unite Hindus and Muslims in this movement, references to Hindu legends were not always appropriate. Appearing with Maulana Shaukat Ali at a meeting in Patna the appeal to women was significantly modified. Gone were references to Rama, Sita, Ravana and Draupadi; women were urged to work harmoniously with one another and to support the movement by spinning and urging their husbands to join.[36] But on other occasions Gandhi's speeches to Muslim women paralleled those to Hindu women; he denounced British rule as the rule of Satan and urged women to give up foreign cloth and learn to spin to save Islam. Spinning, he told an audience of women in Bombay, was the duty of every religious woman.[37] Reflecting on the impact of Gandhi's message Smt Ambujammal said he 'touched the hearts of women'. Gandhi, she said, told them that their involvement was essential, that they had a role to play, that it was a legitimate role (like that played by goddesses and heroines), and that they had the courage to do it. It was not essential to abandon home and family to work in the movement; in fact Gandhi urged women to 'do what you can' even from the home.[38] He made women believe that they counted.

But had Gandhi not also paid attention to the attitudes of their guardians, it is unlikely he would have been successful. Sucheta Kripalani has credited his ability to mobilize women to his special attention to male attitudes: 'Gandhi's personality was such that it inspired confidence not only in women but in the guardians of women, their husbands, fathers and brothers.' Since his moral stature was high, 'when women came out and worked in the political field, their family members knew that they were quite secure, they were protected.'[39]

As the Non-Co-operation movement inaugurated at the special session of Congress in 1920 moved forward, it became clear that there were a number of women willing to play a more active role in the protest movement than had been suggested in Gandhi's speeches about the swadeshi vow. Congress had declared 6 to 13 April 1921 Satyagraha week and during that week Sarojini Naidu addressed a number of meetings in Bombay. The last one she addressed was attended by over 500 women. Those present decided to form the Rashtriya Stree Sangha, a women's political organization that would be independent but work closely with Congress. Members of the RSS would become members of the District Congress Committee, collect money for the Tilak Swaraj Fund and assist in introducing the spinning wheel. By August the group had been formed and when Urmila Devi, the widowed sister of the Bengali leader C. R. Das, addressed them she urged the women to leave their homes and serve the country. In November 1000 Bombay women demonstrated against the visit of the Prince of Wales.[40]

However, the situation was somewhat different in Bengal. C. R. Das decided that Congress volunteers should appear on the streets of Calcutta to sell khaddar and test the government's ban on Congress volunteers. Das' son was among the first batch of volunteers to be arrested. His wife, Basanti Devi, his sister, Urmila Devi, and his niece, Suniti Devi, were among the second. Subhas Bose, one of Das' greatest admirers, had been shocked by this plan. He and a number of other young men protested that 'no lady should be permitted to go out as long as there was a single man left.'[41] But he became a convert. When word of this arrest spread a huge crowd composed of 'Marwaris, Muslims, Bhattias, Sikhs, coolies, mill-hands and school boys' formed and milled around until the ladies were released. One observer explained it was as if all the womenfolk had been arrested. The next day, 8 December 1921, the whole city was in commotion. As for the women from the Das family, 'they resumed picketing cloth shops and selling khaddar joined by numerous other lady volunteers, especially Sikh ladies; Calcutta students came out in hundreds, joined the prohibited volunteers corps, and marched out with khaddar on, seeking imprisonment. On that day, 170 were arrested.'[42]

Hearing about the Calcutta events Gandhi immediately recognized the potential of women's involvement in picketing. Writing in *Young India* he suggested that women in other parts of the country follow this model.[43] It was clear that the arrest of a few prominent and well-respected women was sufficient to shame large numbers of men into joining the struggle. But it was not only men who were affected. There were 6000 ladies at the All-Indian Ladies Conference in Ahmedabad where Bi Amma, the mother of Mohammad Ali and Shaukat Ali, spoke from the Congress pandal. She told those gathered that they had patriotic duties. They must enlist as Congress volunteers and when their men had been sent to jail for protesting, fearlessly begin picketing to keep 'the flag flying'.[44] By January the women of Lahore, led by the principal of the Kanya Mahavidyalaya (Girls' School) of Jullundar, were picketing.[45] Sporadic demonstrations by women occurred in other cities, but it was clear that Bombay and Calcutta were the main arenas for women's activism. Yet even in these cities the women who protested and took part in political activities did so to inspire men or 'to keep the flag flying.'

It was only in Bombay that a fledgling women's political organization existed.

At this time the relationship between the few brave women who joined the Non-Co-operation movement and Congress leaders was very good. Gandhi's message: be like Sita and spin, was being followed by a handful of dedicated women who acted with the support of their male guardians. One of the problems which disturbed women activists was how to differentiate themselves from 'women of the street'. As C.S. Lakshmi has observed, 'in the 1921 movement in the Tamil region, the women who stood in the forefront in meetings were prostitutes who could face the public boldly.'[46] This was an extremely touchy subject. Élite women appearing in public for the first time were terribly afraid of being confused with prostitutes. At the same time, prostitutes were coming forward to join Congress. In Barisal, East Bengal, 350 'fallen sisters' decided to join Congress, contribute from their earnings to the Tilak fund, and engage in Congress work. Gandhi wanted them to find another occupation and although most of them expressed their willingness to do so neither Gandhi nor other Congress leaders could suggest alternatives. When he suggested they take up spinning they replied that they would not be able to earn a living and only eleven volunteered to try the experiment. Actually, Gandhi had no answer. Unable to present a viable alternative he reiterated his platitudes about the spinning wheel: 'The wheel is a kind of wall for the protection of women. I cannot think of any other thing which may serve as a support for such sisters in India.'[47] But this was no solution for either the women engaged in prostitution or for those newly active women who wanted the freedom to move without opprobrium. For reasons closely related to his personal belief in the necessity of sexual restraint as a precondition to social and political reform, Gandhi wanted the 'right kind' of woman to join the movement. Moreover, the participation of women from 'respectable families' was possible only if it could be demonstrated that involvement in these protests could be accomplished without scandal. As he had said in his earliest speeches, he wanted women from the higher classes to take the swadeshi vow because they would be emulated by other women.

Following Gandhi's suspension of the Non-Co-operation movement in 1922 he devoted himself to reconstruction. During those years he travelled extensively, spoke to numerous groups and refined his position on women's role in public life. Speaking frequently to women's groups he repeated two messages: the best role model was Sita and spinning was an essential aspect of women's work.

Sita was a strong woman, Gandhi told his audiences. To call such a woman weak was to 'murder language and violate dharma' for she had demonstrated her ability to withstand all assaults on her chastity.[48] As a young bride she had followed her husband into the forest, donned clothing made of tree bark and given up all luxuries; later, as a prisoner of Ravana, she had resisted his attempts to seduce her. Sita had not recognized untouchability, he told women, nor had she been regional in her outlook. Gradually, mention of other heroines and goddesses receded from his speeches as he dwelt on Sita's virtues as appropriate for the Indian women he hoped to influence.

Spinning could solve all India's problems. Unemployment would disappear when people began spinning and created the need for ancillary occupations such as carding and weaving. Spinning would bring discipline; discipline would make women pure in their hearts and souls and closer to the model woman Sita. In the wearing of homespun cloth, urban women would identify with their poor village sisters. But the benefits envisioned by Gandhi went far beyond changes which would result from the physical acts of spinning and wearing homespun cloth. Somehow spinning would break down regional prejudice and would even help eradicate a host of social customs which kept women backward—child marriage, enforced widowhood and prostitution. Essential to the success of this programme was gaining the support of women from the higher classes who would devote their lives to this work and, in turn, influence other women.

Women's involvement would uplift women at the same time as it would help solve India's problems. As women worked for swaraj their own problems would disappear. Even though Gandhi recognized the existence of a set of problems unique to women he saw no reason for conflict between a women's movement and a nationalist movement.

THE CIVIL DISOBEDIENCE MOVEMENT

When Gandhi returned to politics in 1928 he launched a movement in which women's involvement differed both quantitatively and qualitatively from the early years of the 1920s. Women's participation in the Civil Disobedience movement of 1930–2 won them a place in history, but the groundwork for their tremendous response to Gandhi's call had been laid in the period between 1925 and 1930. It was during this period that women's organizations and networks were formed, enabling them to respond to Gandhi's call.

The response of Bombay women received the most attention from the press, and rightly so since their demonstrations were the largest and their picketings the best organized. The explanation for this must be sought in a number of factors, including the cosmopolitan nature of the city, its transportation system, the presence of Parsis and Christians which had accustomed people to the public movement of 'respectable women', and Gandhi's special appeal to Gujaratis.[49] The Rashtriya Stree Sangha had been formed in 1921 in response to Gandhi's appeal for a women's organization dedicated to swaraj. Sarojini Naidu served as its president with Goshiben Naoroji Captain and Avantikabai Gokhale as vice-presidents and Perin Naoroji Captain and Mrs Ratten Behn Mehta as secretaries. The RSS had two aims: swaraj and the emancipation of Indian women. Their goals were closely related; swaraj was to be achieved through peaceful means including spinning. Women's emancipation would be achieved through women's political activities—learning about the condition of the country, helping in their country's 'uplift', and learning organizational skills through running the RSS without male help. When the Tilak Swaraj Fund was organized these women collected Rs 44,519 which Gandhi then handed back to them for women's work. They used the money to set up the Khadi Vasthra Bhandar, where 300 poor girls worked embroidering homespun cloth. They organized khaddar exhibitions, began a school for the 'depressed classes' and sold khaddar in the street.[50] While the reports comment on 'hundreds of meetings for women' where lectures were given about the condition of the country, neither membership lists, exact dates of the meetings nor copies of the lectures have been preserved. Nevertheless, the leadership and structure of the RSS were sufficiently developed for the RSS to spawn a new organization in 1930 and claim a membership of 700 women ready for action.

Following the Lahore Congress Conference of 1929 efforts were made to mobilize women for another assault on the British government. The Rashtriya Stree Sangha leaders, realizing that not all their members would be prepared to demonstrate, called for the formation of a separate volunteer corps for day-to-day work. These women formed the Desh Sevika Sangh. Each woman took an oath that she would spin and wear khaddar, in this case a saffron (*kesari*) sari with a white blouse. The kesari saris were designed to evoke images of Rajput women who sent their men to battle and then donned such saris before performing *johor* (suicide by fire) to avoid capture.[51]

Gandhi had opened the Civil Disobedience campaign in March 1930 with his 240-mile march from Ahmedabad to Dandi to make salt in defiance of the British monopoly. Women had asked to be included in this march[52] but Gandhi refused on the grounds that the British would call Indians cowards for hiding behind women.[53] Nevertheless, at every stop large numbers of women gathered to hear him speak. Police reports include accounts of meetings of 1000, 2000 and even 10,000. To what extent the audiences were able to hear Gandhi's speeches is questionable for reports indicate that these were very noisy meetings. Gandhi spoke to them about their duties: picketing liquor and toddy shops, boycotting taxed salt, and spinning and wearing khaddar.[54] Once the opening stage of satyagraha—the march to Dandi—was over women were fully incorporated into the movement. As satyagraha spread to other parts of India local Congress leaders placed no ban on women's participation.

Upon reaching Dandi Gandhi convened a women's conference and unveiled his programme for women.[55] Women were to have a programme organized by women and suited to their special talents. Their special areas of concern were to be the boycott of foreign cloth and liquor shops. Gandhi had decided to put women in charge of these activities because he feared the potential violence of his male followers. On the basis of past experience he concluded that only women had the patience necessary to perform these tasks. Women, according to Gandhi, could enter the hearts of men and transform them. As soon as he presented this programme those women present formed an organization for work in Gujarat. Mrs Tyabji became the president and Mithubehn Petit the secretary of a new organization dedicated to picketing liquor and toddy shops and making personal appeals to shop owners to close their doors.[56]

Soon after this meeting Gandhi published a pamphlet entitled 'How to do the Picketing'. The picketing team was to be composed of nine women and a leader. Prior to any actual picketing the team was to elect a delegation to meet the owner and request he either close his shop, if it were a liquor shop, or restrict sales, if it were a shop which sold foreign cloth. Only if he refused this request were the women to begin appealing to potential customers. Throughout the exercise Gandhi required that they be dressed in a recognizable 'uniform', carry banners, and whenever possible sing *bhajans*. In keeping with his concern that the picketers present themselves as 'respectable' women Gandhi prohibited obstructing customers and the use of abusive language. Men were to absent themselves, thereby reducing the potential for violence. And those women who were unable to picket could form a behind-the-scenes network: encouraging their neighbours to spin and wear khaddar and distributing propaganda. Finally, there should be a careful handling of all accounts and receipts. Gandhi concluded this list with the statement: 'The whole scheme presupposes on the part of men a genuine respect for women and sincere desire for their rise.'[57]

With these speeches and publications Gandhi presented women with a clear and specific programme of action, and women responded very quickly. The *Bombay Chronicle* reported that 'thousands of Gujarati women' demonstrated at the Chowpatty Sea Face and collected sea water in their brass and copper jugs.[58] Women volunteers picketed toddy shops, asking the owners to close and the patrons to leave,[59] while other women sold salt and carried on an intensive house-to-house campaign for swadeshi.[60]

Much of this activity had been organized by the Desh Sevika Sangh which took over the task of designing and supervising the picketing campaign. At first picketing seemed an exciting activity and DSS membership rose to 560. Before long it became clear that this inflated number included many 'ornamental sevikas' and membership dropped, remaining stable at about 300. Members were asked to place themselves in one of four categories: A—prepared to picket toddy shops, face public insult and go to jail; B—prepared to picket cloth shops and be arrested but unwilling to face assault or go to jail; C—prepared to go house-to-house to preach swadeshi (this was considered especially appropriate for women with young children); and D—willing to go house-to-house to teach spinning.[61]

While the Desh Sevika Sangh found the ornamental sevikas something of a nuisance, the 'wrong kind' of woman posed a more serious problem. Having been approached by 'undesirable women', DSS leaders made it clear that they wanted to recruit only from the 'good classes'. According to Goshibehn Captain this was necessary if the picketers were to demand respect from the public. Women picketers must preserve their 'dignity and innate modesty', she insisted, and this would be impossible if they were marching side-by-side with women of 'undesirable' character or even 'leftists' who had suggested tactics such as lying in the doorways of foreign cloth shops. Theoretically the DSS was open to all who were willing to take the vow and follow orders: actually the conditions of entry to membership were very strict. Females over the age of eighteen were eligible to apply but the committee could 'refuse to admit any person without disclosing the reason to the applicant'.[62] Goshibehn, like so many other women leaders of the time, was more concerned with modesty than sisterhood. Sentenced to prison for three months in 1935 Goshibehn was horrified to find a prostitute as her cell-mate. Characterizing these women as 'low-class' and diseased, she reported that she and her fellow sevikas judiciously avoided association with them.[63]

By May the sevikas had begun picketing and Sarojini Naidu

had been nominated to lead the raid on the Dharasna Salt Works. She led the protest on 15 May 1930, was arrested and released. On 21 May she led the second batch of raiders, was arrested and this time jailed for almost a year. Sarojini's presence at the Dharasna Salt Works and the picketing carried on in the city attracted considerable attention. Those who witnessed their actions were inspired. Kamaladevi Chattopadhyay, who watched the 21 May scene, tried to capture the magic of that day:

But they (the satyagrahis) were brave. They watched their leader sitting with an unfailing smile on her lips, occasionally breaking into rippling humour, giving an encouraging glance here and a sweet look there. They watched her with amazement as she cheered and heartened them.... She was a delicate poetess who had spent her days rhyming tender verse. Yet here Sarojini Naidu sat, at perfect ease, as much a queen of this burning sandy world as she had been of her luxurious mansion.[64]

Equally impressive were the picketing and the processions organized by the Desh Sevikas. Many foreign-cloth merchants, faced with the reality of lady picketers, had signed a pledge not to sell foreign cloth until an honourable peace had been arranged for the country.[65] Processions, often including 1000 to 2000 women, amazed the country. The demonstration arranged to celebrate Gandhi's birthday and ask for the release of Lilavati Munshi, Perin Captain and Mrs Lukanji was a mile-long chain of women led by saffron-clad sevikas carrying placards. It was estimated that the procession itself included more than 5000 women and that at either end a crowd of over 10,000 assembled. Both the placards carried and the speeches delivered emphasized a number of themes that had come to be associated with women's participation in the movement: communal harmony, Gandhi's undisputed leadership, loyalty to Congress and the identification of swaraj with female emancipation.[66] As a result of these activities Bombay made headlines all over the country and the Congress organizers in other areas were encouraged to emulate their model. The participation of women suggested a successful movement with 'firm public support', and gave a significant boost to morale in the days following Gandhi's arrest.

But Gandhi's view of women's participation and of their right to determine their own actions was not shared by other Congress leaders. When he asked Sarojini to lead the raid at Dharasna some of his colleagues argued that the situation was too dangerous and her presence was more urgently needed elsewhere. But Gandhi was adamant and Sarojini herself declared 'that the time had come when women must share equally the sufferings and sacrifice of their men comrades in the struggle for the liberation of their country.'[67] In asking women to participate Gandhi had told them to plan their own work and not let men tell them what to do.[68] However, less than one year after their spectacular processions, leaders of the DSS were shocked to hear that Congress planned to form another organization to carry on women's work. At this time the INC was revamping its constitution to increase control over volunteers. Nehru wanted the DSS to seek formal recognition but he was also interested in the formation of a women's department within Congress. While this would have represented a significant step forward in terms of the integration of women and women's issues into the Congress structure, the DSS jealously guarded its independence.

Goshibehn immediately wrote to Sardar Patel, Joint Honorary Secretary of the Bombay Provincial Congress Committee, arguing that there was no need for a new organization since the DSS had been formed for this purpose and had always consulted with the BPCC about its work. She concluded by asking for a 'clear mandate' regarding DSS work and Patel agreed to place her letter before the Council. At this point Nariman, the Bombay Congress leader, played the role of mediator and proposed that the DSS be recognized as a Congress organization. Nehru replied that this would be possible only if its organizational structure conformed to certain rules and the training of volunteers be taken more seriously. In the end Nariman won and the DSS was accorded the recognition of the Working Committee as a 'Corps within the meaning of the Hindustan Seva Dal'. However, it was decided that rule number 14, that picketers had to be given special training, did not apply.[69]

The reorganization scheme had been designed to curb unruly elements within Congress and, while some leaders would have liked more control over the DSS, women did not constitute a major threat to Congress rule. On another level the reorganization scheme aimed at closer integration of the various constituencies which made up Congress. The leaders of the DSS failed to see the advantages associated with closer involvement with Congress. They successfully blocked the formation of a viable women's department but retained control of their own informal sex-segregated political organization.

After the DSS had been given its mandate the issue of who made decisions continued to surface. Since it was impossible to picket only foreign-cloth shops and picket all markets equally, picketing hurt some innocent businesses. By the summer of 1931 a number of 'patriotic merchants' were complaining to Congress. Sardar Patel spoke to DSS leaders about the problem and suggested they devote more attention to swadeshi activities and less to closing shops. They assured him they would do their best but when Patel spoke with a body of merchants he felt it necessary to ask the merchants to be patient.[70] Gandhi's plan of action for women had been bold and exciting and women had been successful in carrying out a programme termed uniquely suited to their temperaments and talents. But instead of using their new power to demand representation at various levels in the Indian National Congress, they remained independent and continued to co-operate, despite minor tensions, with Congress.

The end of December 1931 brought Gandhi's return from the Round Table Conference in London and his immediate arrest. Congress was declared illegal and so were the RSS and DSS. Both the RSS and DSS were dissolved by their leaders and their funds and records were given over to the 'First Sevika' who was to pass them to the next in line if she were arrested. Meanwhile vigorous picketing of the market was resumed, public meetings were called and a flood of pamphlets was distributed. As predicted the leaders were arrested and jailed and leadership was passed to the next in line. Even with dwindling numbers and increasingly dangerous conditions the women continued to picket. The accounts of these days reveal that violence was just below the surface and that communal tensions were high. On some occasions the crowd protected the women from the police,

but on other occasions it was the police who protected the women
from the crowd. With the Hindu-Muslim riots of 1932 the work of
the DSS was suspended. Following Gandhi's fast against the
untouchable award in 1932 members of the old RSS and DSS
formed yet another organization. With many of the old members
present the Gandhi Seva Sena appeared in 1932 to work for
communal harmony and Harijan uplift.[71]

Bengal, like Bombay, was an active province in terms of
women's protest during the Civil Disobedience movement of
1930–2. As was true in Bombay, the foundation of women's
participation in the 1930s had been laid in the 1920s. In Bengal
decision-making was clearly shared between women leaders
and Congress leaders, there were more 'feeder organizations',
and a thinner line between violence and non-violence. The difference between women's participation in the two cities can be
explained in terms of the differences in leadership and politics,
as well as the physical layout of the cities and socio-economic and
cultural factors. What was similar was the way in which the
women of Bengal were touched by Gandhi's words and programme, the formation of women's political groups and the lack
of integration with Congress policies and institutions.

The Mahila Rashtriya Sangha, the first organization to mobilize
women for political work, was begun in 1928. Subhas Chandra
Bose had approached Latika Bose (Ghosh) after she successfully
organized a women's demonstration against the Simon Commission and asked her to take the responsibility of forming a new
organization. At first she was reluctant to accept the offer. A
graduate of Oxford University, she knew that joining Congress
would destroy whatever chance she might have of securing a
position in the Educational Service. In the end Subhas prevailed
and Latika agreed to join Congress and form the MRS.[72]

When the Mahila Rashtriya Sangha was formed Subhas'
mother, Probhavati Bose, was named president and his sister-
in-law, Bivabati, vice-president. Subhas had wanted Basanti
Devi, veteran of the Non-Co-operation movement, to become
president. But Latika disagreed, arguing that Basanti Devi was
considered too westernized by most Bengali women. Not only
was Probhavati orthodox, she could be introduced as 'Ma', the
mother of Bengal's most popular nationalist leader, Subhas

Chandra Bose. With Probhavati's consent Latika used ten neighbourhood educational groups to form the nucleus of the organization.[73]

The Mahila Rashtriya Sangha, much like the RSS in Bombay, wanted to achieve both swaraj and the improvement of women's status. These two goals were inseparable: MRS leaders argued that unless women's lives improved the nation could never be free, and that improving women's lives depended on freedom from foreign domination. The first step toward swaraj involved educating women to the realities of their country's condition and their condition as women. But in articles designed to mobilize women Latika's explanation of India's poverty and the appropriate remedies was closer to Gandhi's message and Trivedi's special Vratakatha than to feminism. Latika ordered women to wake up and take a good look at their country. It was a poor country but it had not always been poor. At one time India had been renowned for its arts and crafts, revered for the scholarship of its universities and famous for its great leaders. Now, under foreign domination, its people were poor, its crafts replaced by foreign-made items, its leaders weaklings. Meanwhile women stayed indoors and closed their eyes to its poverty. What was to be done, she asked. Was there any power left in the people? Remember the tales our grandmother told us, wrote Latika, the tales of the devas and the asuras. Just as the devas were losing, Durga appeared as Shakti. Women needed to remember that they were the Shaktis of the nation. And they needed to remember the stories of the brave Rajput queens who sent their husbands and sons into battle and then prepared for their own death. Like the heroines of old, modern women had to realize the Shakti within themselves and, like sparks, ignite the fires that would leave people purified and ready to serve the motherland.[74]

In recruiting for the MRS Latika sought the names of likely members from male Congress leaders. Because family approval and support for women's activities was essential for the success of this venture, Latika sought to recruit women whose fathers, brothers or husbands were involved with Congress or the revolutionary movement.[75] Through a network of shakti mandirs women would be taught about the need for independence. But at the same time, the mandirs would teach literacy, mothercraft, first aid and self-defence. Latika and other women involved in building women's political organizations recognized that women were totally isolated from the affairs of the country.[76] They concluded that unless ordinary women began to see themselves within the larger context of the nation they would be unwilling to make the personal sacrifices the political movement would demand.[77] One of the most dramatic acts by Bengali women occurred well in advance of the Civil Disobedience movement. In 1928 Subhas Bose decided that female volunteers, like males, must march in military fashion, in uniforms, at the opening of the Congress session in Calcutta. Colonel Latika was placed in charge of recruiting and leading the girls. She managed to collect 300 young women from Bethune College and Victoria Institution, and from among the Calcutta Corporation teachers. Their 'uniforms' consisted of dark green saris with red borders worn over white blouses—the colours of the Congress flag. All through the planning and organizing there were various issues to be considered—whether or not the young women would wear trousers, whether or not they would stay in the camp at night or return to their homes, and whether or not they should be allowed to march in the regular procession or simply serve at tea stalls and do other work to make the session run smoothly. Latika always argued for the trappings of modesty—saris instead of trousers, no females in camp at night, etc., but she stood her ground on the issue of women marching in the regular procession. Although she confessed she made a poor Colonel, failing to stay in step and salute correctly, she wanted female volunteers to appear as the equals of men in the struggle for freedom.[78] And the marching girls had an electric effect. According to one press report:

It was in itself a sufficient indication that henceforward whenever the clarion call for National Service would go forth—there would come as spontaneous and enthusiastic a response from the mothers and sisters as from the manhood of this country. The ladies of Bengal are no longer content with applauding their fighting brethren from afar but are determined to render what they can in the active service of the Motherland. They want to be in the thick of the fight. As the ladies clad in their saris marched past to the sound of the bugle and the beating of the drum, there could traced not a touch of all the frailties that are so commonly attributed to them. No faltering, no hesitancy, no softness associated in popular minds with the womanhood of Bengal but chivalry written on every face and manifest in every movement.[79]

During this Congress session women were very visible. They manned the tea-stalls, helped with local arrangements and held an All-India Women's Social Conference in conjunction with the regular Congress session. The Conference was presided over by Her Highness the Maharani (Jr) of Travancore and considered resolutions on dowry, female education, and divorce. All those present agreed that dowry created humiliating conditions for girls and that it had not been a custom during India's Golden Age. Discussing female education, they lamented that so little was being done and urged government to allocate more funds for schools. Then came the most controversial of issues—divorce. Although she had been asked not to mention this topic, Mrs Renuka Ray denounced the existing system and demanded equal rights for men and women in marital life. Her resolution, urging support for Sir Hari Singh Gour's divorce bill, was passed. In deference to the conservative elements of the conference most newspapers decided not to report this part of the meeting.[80]

Despite the discomfort of some Congress leaders the 1928 session of Congress set a precedent for the involvement of Bengali women in political activities. Not only were they determined to march side-by-side with men in demonstrations, they also demanded the right to speak about women's issues. Unfortunately the volatile political situation made it difficult to gain support for women's issues.[81]

In response to the Congress call in 1929 for groups of women ready to serve, a number of Calcutta women formed the Nari Satyagraha Samiti. Urmila Devi was named president, Jyotimoyee Ganguli vice-president, Santi Das secretary and Bimal Protiba Devi joint-secretary. Urmila Devi had been named president because of her long association with Gandhi and her galvanizing arrest in 1921. However, she was not very active and was more representative of an earlier generation than of the women who marched and picketed in 1930–1. About fifteen to twenty women, able to picket regularly and risk jail-going, formed the core of this group. They were all educated, from professional families and had, until this time, observed a form of modified purdah. In terms of marital status they were diverse; among the group were single women, married women and widows. The early NSS was composed entirely of Bengali women (of the Brahmin, Kayastha and Boidya castes) but they were later joined by women from other communities. They chose white khaddar saris as their picketing uniform.[82]

An extremely important member of the NSS was the secretary Santi Das. She had inherited her daring from her mother. Asokalata, the daughter of one of Keshub Chunder Sen's missionaries was among the first women to pass the Bethune College entrance examination. Asokalata's advanced notions on female education were not shared by her husband. When he opposed sending their daughters to Calcutta University Asokalata left him and educated her daughters herself. Santi took her MA at Calcutta University and then opened a school (Deepali Siksha Mandir) in their home with the help of her mother and sister.[83]

Santi recruited women for picketing from amongst her students and Calcutta Corporation schoolteachers. She found a number of women who wanted to join because they were convinced the movement really needed them. Having watched the police beating male protesters the women believed their femininity would protect them from violence.[84] In 1930 the Calcutta newspapers reported many incidents involving women but the numbers involved were few in comparison with Bombay. Sometimes 200 to 300 women were mobilized but more frequently demonstrations were held with 15 to 25 women present. But numbers are not always a good indicator of impact. Whereas in Bombay Gandhi had insisted that men stay away from picketing women, this was rarely the case in Calcutta. When twenty-two ladies of the Calcutta NSS were arrested in July 1930 the shopkeepers of Burrabazar immediately closed their shops because they feared the violence of the crowd.[85] A few days later four ladies sitting on some bales of foreign cloth deterred coolies from moving the bales.[86] All those picketing were considered 'respectable women' and the watching crowds would have exploded in violence had the police molested them. Sensing this the police learned to treat the women with respect while they lathi-charged the crowd.

In these demonstrations the threat of violence was never far below the surface. By May and June the Civil Disobedience campaign had unleashed some very un-Gandhian ways of fighting the British. And by October the British had applied special ordinances which made it possible for them to search and detain without reasonable suspicion. Magistrates were given special powers and it became more and more dangerous to be involved with any political movement. As the police ordinances were rigorously applied, fewer women demonstrated and more women became active revolutionaries. Bina Das and others have suggested there was a cause-effect relationship; they joined the revolutionaries because they wanted to advance the cause of independence and because other channels were closed to them. By 1931 Bengal was declining as a centre for non-violent political activity while women revolutionaries became famous for assassinations, daring raids and political dacoity.[87]

The intensity of the times, the activities of women, and the difficulty of garnering any attention for women's issues gave rise to a demand for a separate women's Congress in Bengal. In the first week of May 1931 Santi Das, acting as convener for the Congress, requested women to send ten delegates from each district. In preparation for the Calcutta meeting district meetings were held where Congress women discussed the need for social reform.[88] When they arrived at the Calcutta Congress the delegates were met by young volunteers wearing crimson khaddar saris, ushered to their seats and treated to a speech by the grand old lady of politics and feminism, Saraladevi Chaudhurani. If some of the district conferences had seemed full of platitudes about Indian womanhood and their great awakening during the Civil Disobedience movement, Saraladevi's speech hit hard.

Saraladevi explained that a separate Congress for women was necessary because women, from their earliest childhood (when they were denied the sweets which were given to their brothers) had been treated as separate and inferior. The sexes were interdependent but,

men had exploited women far more for their own purposes than helped them in realizing their needs. The woman's feeling has never been the man's, neither the woman's point of view his. In giving expression to this deep seated conviction at last and asserting themselves, the women of Bengal have come on a line with the women of other countries....[89]

Discussing the entry of women into political affairs, Saraladevi acknowledged that it was men who had encouraged them to join. However, there were few among these men who cared about improving the lives of women. Women who had participated in the movement could expect flowery speeches but not appointment to subcommittees and councils. Summing up women's experience with politics she said that Congress had 'assigned to women the position of law-breakers only and not law-makers.'[90] To change the situation women needed to demand equal treatment and equal status. They needed to join together so that leaders like Nehru, who concerned themselves with peasants and workers, would begin to foucs on 'teeming womenfolk'. If women were to demand fair and equal treatment from Congress then Congress might well have an anti-brothel campaign. Congress regarded drinking liquor harmful to men and asked that toddy shops be picketed and boycotted. Why wasn't the same done to brothels, Saraladevi asked. Weren't brothels as harmful and destructive to women?[91] Saraladevi concluded what was certainly the most forceful feminist speech of the 1930s with a list of women's demands. Women's ten 'Fundamental Rights' included: equal inheritance, equal right to guardianship, no sex discrimination, fair wages, punishment for sex-related crimes, closing brothels, compulsory primary education, adult education, female teachers in co-educational institutions and adult franchise. At the end of the speech she urged women to also remember the message of the Gita, and seek purification through political work. While engaged in political work and efforts to improve women's status it was women's responsibility to conserve India's civilization.[92]

Neither Saraladevi's feminism nor her suggestions as to the best plan of action were shared by all present. Saraladevi was in favour of adult franchise but other women preferred separate electorates. Some women wanted separate electorates to preserve their 'special' sex-segregated status, but others, like Santi Das, believed that separate electorates would allow women to express their needs. It had been her 'bitter experience', she said, that when men and women worked together 'the former invariably dominated the show with the result that the latter could not get proper facilities to contribute their share.' But support for separate electorates never gained sufficient support and the women present passed a resolution in favour of adult franchise. Other resolutions requested the release of detenus, commutation of death sentences given to Bengali and Punjabi revolutionaries, and the organization of Desh Sevikas to work in the *mofussil*. These final resolutions were neither exciting nor feminist. Resolutions in support of allowing inter-caste, inter-racial marriage, birth control and equal treatment of women in insurance plans never gained sufficient support to pass.[93] Nor did the plans to form a Women's Congress bear fruit. In the highly charged political environment of Bengal women's issues were swept aside and women gained neither a voice in the political institutions which existed nor a political organization of their own.

CONCLUSIONS

To look at the involvement of women in the struggle for independence by looking only at the activities of élite women in these two cities leaves much to be desired. However, I would argue that the data from other Indian cities is similar to what exists for a study of Calcutta and Bombay. Thus, while women played a significant role in agitational politics, they did not develop their own political organizations nor were they integrated into decision-making bodies in Congress.

But what happens when one attempts to move beyond élites and élite data? First, there is the difficulty of trying to learn about the women who participated.[94] We know how many Indian women were convicted (see Table 1), but that only confirms that their numbers were small. A two-volume work on UP freedom fighters includes the names of 192 women convicted in the period 1921–42. Of these, one was convicted in 1921; 21 in the period 1930–1; 152 between 1932–4; and 30 in the period 1940–2. The shortest sentence was for one month, the longest for two years. Twenty-four women, 12.5 per cent, were convicted more than once. The full names of a few women are given but most are simply listed as Kamla Devi, Maya Devi, Kanti Devi, etc. In most cases the name of the husband or father is included. 104

women, mostly from Varanansi, are identified as 'the daughter of ...'; 73 women as 'the wife of ...'. There is no indication whether the remaining 15 were widowed or the victims of careless record-keeping. One hunts through these records for details that would make it possible to 'flesh out' the names. Only one woman was listed as an official leader of women. Prem Mai Devi of Jalaun district, wife of Ram Shankar Saksena, was President of the Urai Mahila Congress Committee and a member of the District Congress. In 1941 she was sentenced to three months in prison and fined Rs 400. Obviously this is not enough information to construct even a short biography but it is far more information than we have on the other women listed. We are left with the impression that many of these women joined the movement with their male guardians. Their participation undoubtably helped rally others to the cause, but it is clear that they neither formed political organizations nor gained positions of power in Congress.[95]

Gail Pearson has done a masterful job of obtaining detailed information on the Bombay women who participated in the nationalist protests but even here there is much more we would like to know. Pearson argues that most writing on the independence struggle includes the 'myth of participation' and that the figures of actual participants are often very small. Using police records, documents of associations, newspaper accounts and the few extant records from the organizations formed to carry out political demonstrations, Pearson notes that many of the women came from 'D' ward. This she has described as a respectable residential area where middle-class women could move about safely, thereby remaining in what Pearson terms 'the extended female space'. The women who participated exhibited complete loyalty to Gandhi:

The nation was characterized as the Motherland and women completely indentified with the nation. The National Movement was not some object to which women contributed, it was 'our hour of supreme need'. . . . This ideology of nationalism was exhibited by women when they wove and wore the flag sari.[96]

Pearson concludes that men in the political movement wanted women to contribute to an effective civil disobedience campaign while women wanted to participate because of their commitment to Gandhi and nationalist ideology. Neither men nor women were interested in social questions.[97]

In another attempt to gain some understanding of the rank and file I interviewed four women from Udipi, Karnataka, who were convicted and served prison sentences between 1931 and 1942. The data that emerged from these interviews illustrates that these women were differentially motivated, and further that political considerations played only a small role in their decisions to take action. The two stories which follow illustrate this point.

Kamala Adhikari said that her husband had read about the Salt satyagraha in high school but was not able to join Congress until 1936. In 1938 he became Chairman of Taluk Congress and after hearing Gandhi say that women would have to take part in the struggle he 'told' his wife to join the movement. She did individual satyagraha and was sentenced to Cuddalore Central Gaol for six months. Kamala felt a religious duty to fight to free the country from slavery (her religious model was Harishachandra) and a duty to obey her husband (he had taken the marriage *mandala* from her neck when he went to prison in 1940). Unused to leaving the house, she simply went and stood in front of the Jaina temple until she was arrested. When she returned from prison she resumed her household duties and neither went to meetings nor participated in constructive work. She reported that the experience of offering satyagraha and going to prison had not effected much change in her life.[98]

Ambabai had been married at age twelve and gone to live in Bombay in 1920. In Bombay her next-door neighbour, a member of the Bhagini Samaj, taught her how to spin and told her about Gandhi, Tilak and swaraj. Widowed at age sixteen, Ambabai returned to Udipi to live in her father's house and 'sit in the God's room'. As she remembers this time it seems as if she spent five years doing nothing but praying. She became bored and disgusted with life and suffered from irregular menses. It was at this time she dreamed that Krishna came to her, ran his hands over her body and said, 'Do not be afraid, as long as I am here I will take care of you.' Taking this as a sign she joined those picketing foreign-cloth shops and toddy shops. With others she made and sold salt. The first time she was arrested the magistrate released her but when she was arrested the next day she was sentenced to four months in prison. Instead of finding imprisonment a dreadful experience Ambabai enjoyed it and gained weight. Following her release Congress leaders asked her to make speeches about the importance of spinning and wearing khaddar, to teach people how to spin, and to speak at the annual car festival about the evils of alcohol. She happily carried out these activities and for three months led prabhat pheries (singing processions) every morning. Ambabai regards these as the happiest days of her life.[99]

What do we learn from this evidence? First, I think they make it clear that there is much we do not know about women's participation in the nationalist movement once we move outside the major urban areas. We have records (scanty as they are) of the women's organizations of Bombay and Calcutta but no records, save those preserved in memories, of many of the women in towns and villages who were convicted and went to prison. In fact we know very little about 'women' and the Indian National Congress, and only something about those women who became leaders of associations and organizations during the nationalist period. The tendency to focus on women as a collectivity rather than on a specific group of women is one of the legacies of the independence struggle. In an effort to transform the nationalist movement into a mass movement it was necessary to require the support of diverse groups. Gail Pearson has argued that nationalist leaders consciously manipulated the word 'women' to suggest the 'participation of a united social universe'.[100] For contemporary historians this generalized category operates against the construction of a coherent picture of the relationships of different groups of women with Congress. It is apparent that a vast gap existed between well-educated women from families which had begun their experiments with women's modernization in the nineteenth century and less-educated women who responded to their 'dual duty'—to their beloved Gandhi who told them to rise up to free their enslaved country, and to their guardians who invited them (or ordered them) to join. The less-educated women generally followed men, and the data suggests that if participation had a long-range impact on their lives it was not in the realm of politics.

It was only in urban areas that there were organizations able to blend feminism and nationalism. Since the early years of the twentieth century there were a few women who had argued that associations dominated by men overlooked women's concerns. To counter this situation they formed their own women's organizations—led by women—to discuss women's problems. Faced with the need for disciplined action during the nationalist movement they borrowed from this model and formed women's political organizations. There were many advantages in doing so: women retained leadership positions, there were adequate opportunities for women to learn how to run organizations. They were safe havens for women newly emerged from purdah and they operated in harmony with the society's conventions for female modesty. On the other hand this structure made close co-operation with the Indian National Congress difficult. Consequently few of these women came to understand the realities of political power. Since their stated goal was independence they did not develop organizations that would continue beyond the duration of the struggle for independence.

Conservative elements in society approved of separate organizations for women. And because the leaders of these organizations were dependent on the goodwill of conservatives, they were committed to upholding a standard of modest behaviour which worked against the development of a strong women's movement. They only admitted women classified as 'respectable', thereby undermining the claim that they spoke for all women. To see this as a male or Congress plot to 'control' women is naive; the women leaders were themselves concerned with image. In a society not yet used to women of the upper and middle classes participating in life outside the home, the entry of women into political life could have posed serious problems. But this did not happen because women participated in politics either with their guardians—fathers, brothers or husbands—or under the protection of a women's organization.

The evidence makes it clear that a strong connection was never forged between the women who joined the nationalist

movement and the Indian National Congress. The women of
Bombay and Calcutta were moved by Gandhi's words. He had
made them feel important, fired them with enthusiasm to help
the country and promised that they would be rewarded for their
efforts. Since he had told women to 'do what you can', many of
them felt they were fully participating in the nationalist movement by spinning at home. And the women leaders believed
Gandhi when he told them that women would be fully integrated
into the country's political bodies. But there were other leaders—
on both a national and local level—who did not share Gandhi's
vision for Indian women. It was not until the elections of 1937
that confrontation occurred. Activist women expected to run for
safe seats but few of them had gained positions of power and
influence in the party. In the eyes of party leaders women's
evasion of back-room politics in favour of a respectable image
meant they were ill-prepared to run for office.

Finally, I think we have to ask whether or not the various
ideologies which co-existed were compatible and could have fitted
together in either a women's department or women's platform
acceptable to Congress. Gandhi's view of women's equality
was certainly compelling and in harmony with his social ideals,
but he could not accept women's sexuality. To transmit his
ideas he used a simplistic, religious model. In the end it was the
religious model which was remembered and the modernist aspects
of his message which were lost. The urban women leaders were
educated and influenced by an ideology of women's rights and
even feminism. Yet few of them dared to speak of what they
believed: many, like Latika Ghosh, returned to simple religious
messages when they spoke to women. They were successful in
mobilizing women but at significant cost to the ideological
position which linked political independence and women's
emancipation.

It is extremely difficult to measure or even describe the
inspirational role of women at this time. What this meant in
terms of rewards for women might be answered by looking at
the constitution and its promise of equality. But what women's
involvement did not accomplish was either a strong women's
department within Congress or a separate women's political

organization. Attitudes towards women's proper place were too widely shared and strongly held at this time for the emergence of a women's movement unsheltered by the umbrella of respectability.

TABLE I

	Total convicted	Convicts as percentage of population	Women	Women as percentage of total convicts
Madras	3,490	0.007	291	8.34
Bombay	14,101	0.064	939	6.66
Bengal	12,791	0.026	776	6.07
UP	14,659	0.030	656	4.48
Punjab	1,774	0.008	121	6.82
B & O	14,903	0.040	370	2.48
CP	4,014	0.026	299	7.45
Assam	1,271	0.015	93	7.32
NWFP	6,053	0.250	0	0
Delhi	1,048	0.165	66	6.29
Coorg	269	0.165	9	3.35
Ajmer-Merwara	298	0.053	9	3.02
Totals	74,671		4859	4.86[101]

NOTES

1. Gordon Johnson, *Provincial Politics and Indian Nationalism: Bombay and the Indian National Congress, 1880–1915* (London, Cambridge University Press, 1973).
2. See, for example, Tara Ali Baig, *India's Woman Power* (New Delhi, S. Chand and Co., 1976) and Radha Krishna Sharma, *Nationalism, Social Reform and Indian Women* (Patna, Janaki Prakashan, 1981).
3. For example, see Vijay Agnew, *Elite Women in Indian Politics* (New Delhi, Vikas, 1979) and Gail Pearson, 'Women in Public Life in Bombay City with Special Reference to the Civil Disobedience Movement,' Ph.D. Thesis, JNU Centre for Historical Studies, 1979.
4. Aparna Basu, 'The Role of Women in the Indian Struggle for Freedom', B. R. Nanda, ed., *Indian Women: From Purdah to Modernity* (New Delhi, Vikas, 1976), p. 17.

5. Bimanbehari Majumdar and Bhakat Prasad Mazumdar, *Congress and Congressmen in the pre-Gandhian Era, 1885–1917* (Calcutta: Firma K. L. Mukhopadhyay, 1967), pp. 128–9. Majumdar and Mazumdar refer to the two ladies in terms of their husbands: Mrs Ramanibhai Mahipatram, BA (Lady Nilkanth) and Mrs Sumant Batukram, BA (Sharada Mehta). They have explained that the Congress anthem was listed in the report of 1902 without an author. However, it was very similar to a Bengali song composed by Satyendranath Tagore to be sung at the Hindu Mela in Calcutta in 1868. Also see A. M. Zaidi and S. Zaidi, ed., *The Encyclopedia of the Indian National Congress*, vol. 4, 1901–1905 (New Delhi, S. Chand and Co., 1978), p. 320.

6. J. C. Bagal, *Jattiya Andolane Bangla Nari* (Calcutta, Vishva-Bharati, Bhadra 1361 B.S. (1954), p. 15.

7. *The Indian Social Reformer*, 4 June 1899, p. 310.

8. Sumit Sarkar, *The Swadeshi Movement in Bengal, 1903–1908* (New Delhi, 1973), p. 253.

9. The various notes on women's participation come from J.C. Bagal.

10. From Ramendra Sundar Trivedi's 'Banga Laxsmir Vrata Katha'. In *Ramendra Rachcna Sangraha*, selected and edited by Suniti Kumar Chattopadhyaya (Calcutta, Bangiya Sahitiya Parisad, 1371). Translated by Tridib Ghosh.

11. Ibid.

12. Shudha Mazumdar, *A Pattern of Life, the Memoirs of an Indian Woman*, ed. Geraldine Forbes (New Delhi, Manohar, 1977), p. 58.

13. Bagal, ibid.

14. Bagal, pp. 15–16.

15. Valentine Chirol, *Indian Unrest* (London, 1910), p. 103.

16. See Veena T. Oldenburg, *The Making of Colonial Lucknow, 1856–1877* (Princeton, N. J., Princeton University Press, 1984).

17. Goshiben Captain, 16–5–1970, S-22. Cambridge University Transcripts: 'History Sheet on Madame Cama, prepared by the Criminal Intelligence Office', Confidential Home Dept, 1913. Political Dept. B. Proceedings, August 1913, no. 61.

18. Annie Besant, 'The Political Status of Women', 2nd. ed. Pamphlet (London, C. Watts, 1885).

19. *Indian Social Reformer* (hereafter *ISR*), 17 Mar. 1901.

20. 'Mrs. Besant on Indian Womanhood', *Indian Ladies Magazine* (hereafter *ILM*), vol. I, no. 7, Jan. 1902, pp. 195–7.

21. 'Mrs. Besant on Womanhood', *ISR*, 17 Mar. 1901.

22. Arthur H. Nethercot, *The Last Four Lives of Annie Besant* (London,

1963), pp. 232–72; 'Annie Besant', *Dictionary of National Biography* (hereafter *DNB*), India, vol. I, pp. 151–4.

23. 'Sarojini Naidu', *DNB*, vol. 3, pp. 194–7; V. S. Naravane, *Sarojini Naidu* (New Delhi, 1980), pp. 15–19; P. A. Subrahmanya Ayyar, *Sarojini Naidu* (Madras, Cultural Books, 1957), p. 221.

24. 'Mrs. Sarojini Naidu', *Forward*, Congress Number, 1925, p. 9; 'Sarojini Naidu', *DNB*, vol. 3, pp. 194–7; Naravane, Sarojini Naidu Exhibit, Delhi Archives, Dec. 1980.

25. Naravane, pp. 28–31.

26. Dr Sitaramayya Pattabhi, *The History of the Indian National Congress*, vol. I, (1885–1935) (Bombay, Padma Publications Ltd., 1935, reprint 1946), p. 52.

27. A. L. Basham, 'Traditional Influences on the Thought of Mahatma Gandhi', R. Kumar. ed., *Essays on Gandhian Politics* (Oxford, Clarendon Press, 1971), pp. 26–41. For an excellent article on Gandhi see Madhu Kishwar, 'Gandhi on Women', *Economic and Political Weekly*, vol. xx, no. 40, 5 Oct. 1985, pp. 1691–1701 and vol. xx, no. 41, 12 Oct. 1985, pp. 1753–7.

28. Quoted in James D. Hunt's article, 'Suffragettes and Satyagraha: Gandhi and the British Women's Suffrage Movement', presented to Annual Meeting of the American Academy of Religion. St Louis, Missouri, Oct. 1976.

29. The Bhagini Samaj was founded on 19 Feb. 1916 in memory of the late Shri Gopal Krishna Gokhale. His disciple Shri Karsondas Chitalia, a member of the Servants of India Society, established the organization. The first president was Smt Jaijee Petit, a Parsi, who was assisted in the early organization by another well-known social worker of Bombay—Lady Lakshmibai Jagmohandas. From *Bhagini Samaj*, a pamphlet (Bombay, no date).

30. Interview with Jaisree Raiji, Bombay, 2 May 1976; M. K. Gandhi, *Women and Social Injustice* (Ahmedabad, Navajivan Publishing House, 1st. ed. 1942, 4th ed. 1954), pp. 4–5.

31. Barbara Southard, 'The Feminism of Mahatma Gandhi', *Gandhi Marg*, vol. III, no. 7. Oct. 1981, pp. 404–21.

32. Gandhi, 'Speech at Ladies Protest Meeting, Bombay', *CWMG*, vol. xv, p. 89.

33. Gandhi, 'Speech at Women's Meeting, Godhra', *CWMG*, xvi, p. 168; 'Speech at Women's Meeting, Dohad', *CWMG*, xvi, pp. 79–80; 'Speech at Women's Meeting Rajket', *CWMG*, 25 Sept 1919, p. 168; 'Speech at Women's Meeting, Surat', *CWMG*, xv, pp. 322–6; 'Speech at Women's Meeting, Bombay, *CWMG*, xv, pp. 290–2.

34. 'Speech at Women's Meeting, Bombay', *CWMG*, xviii, 'Duty of Women', *CWMG*, xviii, pp. 57–8; 'Speech at Women's Meeting, Dakor', *CWMG*, pp. 391–5.
35. Articles in *Young India*, 15 December 1921, in Gandhi, *Women and Social Injustice* (1942), p. 155; 'Women of Gujarat', *CWMG*, xxii, pp. 181–2.
36. 'Speech at Women's Meeting, Patna', *CWMG*, xix, 1966, pp. 67–86.
37. 'Speech at Meeting of Muslim Women', *CWMG*, xx, 19 July 1921, p. 397.
38. Interview with S. Ambujammal, Madras, 19 Jan. 1976.
39. Smt. Sucheta Kripalani, Nehru Memorial Museum and Library (hereafter NMML), Oral History Transcripts.
40. Pearson, 'Women in Public Life', pp. 175–84.
41. *The Indian Annual Register* (hereafter *IAR*), ii, 1922, p. 320.
42. *IAR*, i, 192, pp. 44–5.
43. 'Women's Part', *Young India*, 15 Dec. 1921.
44. Gail Minault, 'Purdah Politics: The Role of Muslim Women in Indian Nationalism, 1911–1924,' in G. Minault and H. Papanek, ed., *Separate Worlds, Studies of Purdah in South Asia* (Columbia, Mo. South Asia Books, 1982), p. 254: *IAR*, i, 1922, p. 454.
45. *IAR*, i, 1922, p. 55.
46. C. S. Lakshmi, *The Face Behind the Mask: Women in Tamil Literature* (Delhi, Vikas, 1984), p. 8.
47. Gandhi, 'Fallen Sisters', *CWMG*, xxi, pp. 92–5.
48. Gandhi, 'Reply to Women's Address, Noakali', *CWMG*, xxvii, 14 May 1925, p. 999. Madhu Kishwar argues that Sita and Draupadi were symbols that Gandhi sometimes 'overburdened' with the qualities he wished them to carry. Kishwar, 'Gandhi on Women', *EPW*, xx, no. 40, p. 1691.
49. For a discussion of this topic see Pearson, 'Women in Public Life'.
50. 'Awakened Womanhood of India,' *Bombay Chronicle*, (hereafter *BC*), 23 July 1930; Booklet from Gandhi Seva Sena, Bombay (cover page is missing), pp. 1–3.
51. 'Victory or Death Must be Woman's Slogan in the Fight', *BC*, 17 Mar. 1931.
52. 'Women Satyagrahis', *BC*, 11 Mar. 1930; 'Dadabhai Naoroji's Granddaughter Pleads with Mahatma', *BC*, 31 Nov. 1930, p. 1.
53. Agnew, *Elite Women*, p. 39; Secret-camp Jalalpur, 11 Apr. 1931, Home Political Dept., 247/II/1930, Reports ii, Bombay.

54. Home Political Dept., 247/II/1930, Reports II, Bombay. Secret and Confidential Reports from Gandhi's March.

55. This programme had already been published in *Young India* entitled 'To the Women of India'. In it Gandhi told women to take up two tasks: boycotting and spinning. He said men could join women in these activities but since women would run the show, men should be subordinate. 'Women's Part in National Struggle', *BC*, 10 Apr. 1930, p. 1.

56. 'Speech at Gujarati Women's Conference, Dandi', *CWMG*, 13 Apr. 1930, XLIII, 1971, pp. 251–2; 'Special Task Before Women', *CWMG*, XLIII, pp. 271–5.

57. Gandhi, 'How to Do the Picketing', *Young India*, 24 Apr. 1930, p. 144.

58. *BC*, 14 Apr. 1930.

59. 'Women Picket Liquor Shops in Surat', *BC*, 16 Apr. 1930, p. 1; 'Gandhiji Confers with Women,' *BC*, 17 Apr. 1930, p. 1; 'Women's Response', *BC*, 17 Apr. 1930; 'Gandhiji Confers with Women on Picketing', *BC*, 18 Apr. 1930, p. 1.

60. 'Satyagraha Activities in Bombay', *BC*, 30 Apr. 1930, p. 1.

61. 'Awakened Womanhood of India', *BC*, 23 Jul. 1930; Booklet from Gandhi Seva Sangh, p. 5.

62. Appendix 6, The Constitution of the Desh Sevika Sangh as amended in May 1931, All-India Congress Committee (hereafter AICC) Files, G-8/1929; Goshiben Captain, Interview.

63. Captain, Interview.

64. Kamaladevi Chattopadhyay, 'The Struggle for Freedom', *Women's Forum*, no. 4, Jul-Aug. 1972.

65. Booklet from Gandhi Seva Sena, p. 7.

66. 'Bombay Celebrates Gandhi Birthday', *BC*, 4 Oct. 1930, p. 1; 'Women's Activities in G Ward', *BC*, 1 July. 1930; 'Desh Sevika Sangh', *BC*, 2 Jul. 1930, p. 1; 'Women Picketers Bar Voters Way to Polling Booth', *BC*, 19 Sep. 1930.

67. 'Women Must Share Sacrifice with Men', *BC*, 15 May 1930, p. 1.

68. G. Captain.

69. Appendix 14, Desh Sevika Sangh, AICC Files, G-8, 1929, pts 1 & 22, letters Apr-Oct 1931.

70. Appendix 9, 'A Synopsis of Sardar Vallabhbhai's Advice to the Merchants and the Sevikas on 24th June, 1931', AICC Files, G-8, 1929, pts 1 & 23.

71. 'Report of the Desh Sevika Sangh, 1931–1934', and 'Report of the Gandhi Seva Sena', AICC Files, G-8/1929, pts 1 & 2.

72. Interview with Latika Ghosh, 29 Feb. 1976, Calcutta. Latika Ghosh was the daughter of Manmohan Ghosh and niece of Sri Aurobindo. She took the name Bose when she married in 1924. When the marriage was annulled in 1935, she resumed using the name Ghosh.

73. Ibid.

74. Latika Bose, 'Mahila Rashtriya Sangha', *Banglar Katha,* 11 Ashwin 1335 (1928), np.; Latika Bose, *Banglar Katha,* 22 Jaistha 1335 (1928), p. 7.

75. Tanika Sarkar has argued that in India women rarely make totally independent decisions to become politically involved but more frequently act as 'a sum and product of diverse relationships within the family and kinship nexus'. Tanika Sarkar, 'Politics and Women in Bengal—the Conditions and Meaning of Participation', *The Indian Economic and Social History Review*, vol. xxi, no. 1, Jan.-Mar. 1984, p. 91.

76. Bose, *Banglar Katha,* 11 Ashwin 1335.

77. Latika Ghosh, Interview, 29 Feb. 1976 and 10 Mar. 1976, Calcutta.

78. Ibid.

79. 'Rally of Lady Volunteers', *Forward,* 20 Dec. 1928. p. 7.

80. 'All India Social Conference', *Forward,* 20 Dec. 1928, p. 8; Interview with Renuka Ray, Calcutta, 22 Apr. 1980.

81. Barbara Southard, 'Bengal Women's Education League: Pressure Group and Professional Association', *Modern Asian Studies*, 18, 1 (1984), pp. 55–88, (p. 88).

82. Interview with Santi Das Kabir, New Delhi, 25 Mar. 1976.

83. Ibid.

84. Ibid.

85. 'Lively Scene in Burrabazar', *Amrita Bazar Patrika* (hereafter *ABP*), 24 July 1930, p. 3.

86. 'Lady Satyagrahis Pass Night in the Street', *ABP*, 26 July 1930, p. 5.

87. See Forbes, 'Goddesses or Rebels? The Women Revolutionaries of Bengal', *The Oracle*, vol. ii, no. 2, April 1980, reprinted in *Women, Politics and Literature in Bengal*, ed. C. B. Seely (Michigan State University, Asian Studies Center), 1981.

88. 'Future of Indian Womanhood', *ABP*, 29 Apr. 1931, p. 6.

89. 'Srimati Saraladevi Chaudhurani's Speech at the Bengal Women's Congress', *Stri-Dharma*, vol. 14, Aug. 1931, pp. 508–10; 'Women's Congress', *ABP*, 2 May, 1931, p. 7.

90. Ibid.
91. Ibid.
92. Ibid.
93. 'Bengal Women's Conference', *The Hindu*, 3 May 1931, p. 3. 'Women's Congress', *ABP*, 3 May 1931, p. 7.
94. Tanika Sarkar'a article, 'Politics and Women in Bengal—the Conditions and Meaning of Participation', which comments on the involvement of women in Bankura, Midnapur, Comilla and Noakali and Jogesh C. Bagal's 'Women in India's Freedom Movement', *The Modern Review*, vol. 94, Jan.-Jun. 1953, pp. 467–80 and vol. 94, July 1953, pp. 53–61, are both extremely useful for understanding Bengal, but there is less detailed information for other areas of India. There are a number of studies now in progress which will shed a great deal of light on this question in the next few years.
95. *Fighters for Freedom*, vols 1 & 2 (Lucknow: Information Service, UP, 1963, 1964).
96. Pearson, 'Women in Public Life', p. 374.
97. Pearson, 'Women in Public Life'.
98. Interview with Kamala Adhikari, South Canara Dist., 27 May 1976, trans. M. Ashton and L. Bhat.
99. Interview with Ambabai, Udipi, 24 May 1976, trans Ashton and Bhat.
100. Gail Pearson, 'Nationalism, Universalization and the Extended Female Space', in Gail Minault, ed., *The Extended Family: Women and Political Participation in India and Pakistan* (Delhi, Chanakya Publications, 1981), pp. 176–7.
101. From Table 8, 'Convictions for Civil Disobedience, 1932–1933', in Judith Brown, *Gandhi and Civil Disobedience: the Mahatma in Indian Politics, 1928–1934* (Cambridge, Cambridge University Press, 1977), pp. 284–6.

AGRARIAN BASES OF NATIONALIST AGITATIONS IN INDIA: AN HISTORIOGRAPHICAL SURVEY

The last fifteen years have seen a considerable advance at various levels in our understanding of peasant movements and their relationship with the Congress and nationalist politics, especially during the 1920s and 1930s.[1] Over the years the Indian state has brought out collections of official documents on the freedom struggle in various provinces as well as short notices on some freedom fighters, preceded by a synoptic history of various relevant districts.[2] These documents allow one to follow nationalist agitations in the countryside in far greater detail than was possible earlier, and the writings of David Hardiman and Hites Sanyal have forcefully shown what wealth of information awaits those willing to talk to peasants instead of just contemplating the Home Political Files.

A certain amount of the local history of Congress and peasants is also being written by the *mufassil* intelligentsia and in the History Departments of regional universities. Amar Bahadur Singh Amresh's *Ek Aur Jalianwala*, a popular account by a local resident of Unchahar of police firings on the *kisans* of Awadh at

Fursatganj and Munshiganj in Rae Bareli in 1921, is something like a piece representative of a broadly nationalist discourse.[3] Writings such as this are characterized by a reaction against the scant attention paid to local peasant and nationalist agitations in the standard accounts of Tara Chand and Sitaramaiya: the urgency of hinterland prose-writers derives from a desire to have local experiences inscribed into the authorized texts of nationalism in the subcontinent. In accounts such as Amresh's any disjunction between autonomous peasant movements and the Congress is quickly assimilated to the career of Gandhian nationalism, and in true nationalist fashion the politics of an undifferentiated peasantry is seen to be fired by the fuel of generalized oppression:

Indian historians have done injustice to the peasant movement of Awadh, nor have they tried to understand its basic causes. It seems to me that had Pt. Jawaharlal Nehru not referred to it in his *Autobiography* no one would be even mentioning it today. Even if the power of Congress and its leaders may not have been behind this movement, one would have to accept at least this much, that this movement was fully Gandhian. The leaders of this movement had faith (*shradha*) in Gandhiji and they were conducting it in a non-violent fashion. Even if no force was exercised there was a fire in the movement which later got transformed into a volcano. That fire was the oppression of the peasants by taluqdars.[4]

In similar fashion a whole crop of doctoral dissertations is being written in regional universities recounting a particular district or region's *yogdaan* (contribution) to a growing nationalist movement. The local development of Congress organization, the response of the locality to the 'nation's call', the mobilization of the *janta* by district functionaries, the impact of the visit of prominent Congressmen, the dissemination of the nationalist message by the vernacular press—these are the moulds within which most such descriptive accounts of the freedom struggle are cast.[5] Firmly nationalist in orientation, this historiography has little room for the questions being asked about mass nationalism in Cambridge and Oxford, Calcutta and Delhi.

In contrast to the placid mufassil the world of national and international scholarship on Indian nationalism is now full of articles, monographs and broad surveys on peasant movements or nationalist politics. However, comparatively little work has been addressed directly to the investigation of peasant political activity *within* nationalist agitations; the tendency has rather been to concentrate on the relationship between the two.[6] This has also led to an excessive preoccupation with 'movements', to the exclusion of 'events' which could yield meaningful insights into the modalities of peasant politics during the course of nationalist agitations.

I am not setting myself the difficult task of offering a causal explanation of nationalist agitations in the countryside, nor do I intend to dwell at any length on the differences and angularities in their regional profile. I do not subscribe either to the notion of accretions to a unilinear flow of a 'mainstream' Indian nationalism—the yogdaan perspective referred to earlier. However, in common with such writings I shall limit myself to the major nationalist agitations of 1919–22 and 1930–2.

I propose first to locate and interrogate the notion of 'agrarian base/s' in some representative writings on nationalism in the countryside.[7] I shall then argue that a further advance in our understanding of the characteristics of nationalism in rural India would not necessarily come about by a keener appreciation of its agrarian bases; instead of seeking to establish, as it were, a 'fit' between the base and its politics, it would be far better to begin by posing a 'lack of fit' between these two. This methodological procedure is required not only to steer clear of the reflective view of politics, it is also necessitated by the particular problem faced by all historians of mass nationalism in India: how to account for the intrusion of, shall we say, 'base-less' people on to the political stage, and what sense to make of the actions and beliefs of such people which so often run counter to the scripted nationalist scenario of the time.

Thus the base/agitation dichotomy has a correspondence in the split within the domain of politics itself.[8] This way of posing the issues opens up the field for investigating two sets of rather important questions—first, the disjunction between organization and movement, and second, the disjunction between pronouncements by leaders and the popular understanding of nationalist messages, including the call for action or participation in agitations.

A considerable body of recent literature on Indian nationalism has been organized around the theme of vertical mobilization through and by the 'village élite'.[9] In such writings the agrarian base of the Congress is located within a stratum of 'dominant' or 'rich' peasants; the mechanics of nationalist agitations are shown, in turn, to have worked according to the local and supra-local political designs of this 'village élite.' There are of course variations on this theme, and it may seem a bit unfair to group D. A. Low, Chris Baker, Robin Jeffrey, David Washbrook, Jacques Pouchepadass, Rajat Ray, Walter Hauser and Stephen Henningham together.[10] However, the differences among these authors are more with regard to causal explanations of the phenomenon of dominant peasant participation in nationalist politics rather than to how nationalist agitations worked (or rather were made to work) in the Indian countryside.

In D. A. Low's well-known account Congress-led agitations got under way in various regions of India as and when 'dominant peasants', power-wielders at the village level from Mughal days, interested themselves in the nationalist organization; concomitantly, 'Congress actions [in the conduct of these agitations] were very evidently determined by dominant peasant interests'.[11] The crucial variable for Low in this game is the 'swinging to the Congress' from 1918 onwards of some elements from the 'dominant peasant communities':[12]

Certain Patidar and Bhuinhars from Gujarat and Bihar seem to have led the way, followed very soon by some Rajus, Kammas and Reddis from the Andhra delta ... together with some Ahirs, Kurmis and Rajputs from several of the eastern UP districts, some Mahishyas from West Bengal, Muslim 'Jotedars' from East Bengal, Nayars from Malabar, and others besides.[13]

After 1919, when the Congress was looking for an agrarian base, 'upwardly mobile' western-educated men, involved in commercial agriculture and sucked into the vortex of local institutionalized politics generated by the administrative structure of the Raj, came forward of their own accord to don the mantle of countryside nationalists. 'In such circumstances', argues Low, 'many leading individuals, not least from among the dominant peasant communities, began to look to Congress as the appropriate vehicle for their rising political aspirations'.[14]

The highlighting by Low of this facet of the struggle between Congress and the Raj has provoked much discussion and debate.[15] An interest-based political analysis, it must be pointed out, leaves very little room for the interplay of dominance and resistance in colonial society. Did the distant attitude of the sahib in the Civil Lines not have any influence in converting collaborators into nationalists, as Prem Chand so poignantly portrayed in his short story 'Vichitra Holi' (c. 1920)?[16] Were campaigns against providing *rasad* and *begar* to the sahib on tour no evidence of the breakdown of deference to the Raj in the countryside?[17] Questions will continue to be asked, with justification, on this and similar issues.

That nationalist ideology and agitations operated at various levels in a premise with which one cannot disagree. However, a point which has not been as well debated is the attempt (by Low, among others) to explain the diversity of political occurrences during the great nationalist agitations in terms of the 'national/local' dialectic.[18] Low, after pointing out that twentieth-century conditions 'ensured that all the major (and most minor) political events were not only reported but widely discussed as well', says:

It must nevertheless be underlined (though this should not now need much labouring) that the great national agitations were always patchy occurrences....

A central issue here affecting the operations of the movement concerns the part played by local agitations within the larger national agitations. As Seal has neatly put it, the former often ran upon their own clock...There can be no doubt that there were a great many agitations that to the participants at least had a quite localised significance, and that many of these originally unfolded quite regardless of the Congress. But as Congress became stronger, more particularly from the First World War onwards, its leaders had increasingly to decide whether they would 'nationalise' local agitations—weld them, that is into a nationalist programme of action...There was the obverse here too in the 'localisation' of nationalist agitations.[19]

There can be no a priori objections to keeping an eye on 'local agitations' against the superordinate classes or the state and apprehending nationalism through its manifestations at the local level, howsoever this is defined.[20] Only a blindly nationalist view would abolish 'locality' in its quest for the onward march of a monolithic nationalist anti-imperialism. But what is most noteworthy in Low's analysis is that it is propped up by his concern to analyse 'local agitations' and their tie up with the nationalist movement in terms of the interests and activities of the local élite.[21] The local/national distinction therefore has very little on offer for the study of popular protest during the great nationalist agitations. 'Strategy' was no doubt worked out by the Congress 'high command' which decided, as Low and Judith Brown have pointed out, what issues to choose in different areas for maximum impact.[22] But it is doubtful whether linkages provided by and through the local élites can account for all the differences at the various levels of the 'local', or at the same local level. How does one explain the absence of an 'authorised' version of the message of Gandhi or non-co-operation on the one hand and the quite radical interpretations (in belief and action) of these along identifiable grids in markedly different localities on the other?[23] It seems to me that the groundswell and modalities of popular protest—which were not external nor just linked to but an essential part of nationalist agitations—are too crucial and complex to be caught in the loose mesh of 'nationalisation/localisation'; they cannot adequately be dissected by a 'clinical examination' of Gandhi's charismatic appeal.[24]

My argument is not, however, that local popular protests which did not originate in nationalist master-plans were more important than the authorised enactments of nationalist scenarios. The point is to conceptualize one essential characteristic of nationalist agitations as the intermixture and tension between these two forms. It follows that while investigation over a manageably small area can produce some splendid results, for example in the writings of Hites Sanyal, Majid Siddiqi, Kapil Kumar and David Hardiman, a 'grass-root' perspective by itself does not achieve a methodological breakthrough.[25] If the quest in such work is for rich-peasant politics, the result may even be 'the study of the little seeds which sent up their shoots to the heavens of state politics'.[26]

The local/national dichotomy is missing from Jacques

Pouchepadass' survey of agrarian movements in twentieth-century India, but not so the dominant peasantry, which once again appears as the author of all rural politics worth the name.[27] Pouchepadass subjects Hamza Alavi's notion of the politically significant role of the 'middle peasants' to a number of theoretical and empirical tests and arrives at the more satisfactory category of 'dominant peasants'.[28] It is these peasants that dominate the agrarian movements which they initiate, and they essentially convert these movements into broad-based multi-class affairs by virtue of their political claims on the poor and the landless, or by virtue of support from their numerous caste fellows.[29] He argues that both during the Gandhian and the Kisan Sabha movements organizational authority was actually passed on to dominant-peasant caste councils which were in any case more suited than lower-caste panchayats to deliberate and deal with supra-village affairs. 'As is inevitable in such cases', suggests Pouchepadass, 'the political leaders at the head of the movement make speeches; it is the castes [caste panchayats] of dominant peasants which manage everything at the base'.[30]

Pouchepadass' dominant peasants are not confined to 'the class of genuinely rich peasants'; in terms of economic relations they do not hire themselves out. More importantly for the character of politics

the dominant peasantry is nothing other than the group of peasants who, in each village, are *spontaneously* considered by the villagers as their chiefs, their *maliks* ... together with their caste-fellows and *all those who, more generally, are identified with them*. That is why movements launched by the dominant peasantry often develop along lines of class collaboration; poor peasants and the landless, either of their own will or under constraint, following in the agitation *their usual masters*, as in Champaran, Bardoli and many other movements.[31]

Sometimes during the course of the movement a second wave, led by poor peasants and the landless, may roll forward, only to be pushed back by the leadership and government repression. As the leadership of the dominant peasants is against such waves, these movements were able to develop only in the form of 'primitive revolts with insufficient organized support'.[32]

The command of the dominant peasants over political movements initiated by them against an 'enemy [which] is always exterior to the peasantry'—planters, state or landlords—is quite nearly total. However, Pouchepadass does not dwell on the relationship of his dominant peasants to the feelings of community solidarity that may, and indeed were, generated during such confrontations; in fact his stress on dominant-peasant caste councils militates against any detailed consideration of village-based solidarities.[33] A discussion of nationalist agitations in the countryside is not the main issue for Pouchepadass, but it can be reasonably argued that in terms of his model the role of his chosen category of peasants would be even more marked in such agitations. The difficulty with Pouchepadass' analysis, and one which is common to most variants of patron/client theories of mobilization, is first, that it tends to subsume the dominated within the ranks of the dominant. 'Domination', Partha Chatterjee has pointed out, 'must exist within a relationship. The dominant groups, in their exercise of domination do not consume and destroy the dominated classes, for then there would be no relation of power, and hence no domination.'[34] Second, the view propounded by Pouchepadass would come under some strain in its attempts to explain nationalist agitations in the country-side, for, faced with the broad appeal and varied reception of the message of nationalism by the peasants, it would have to maintain the thesis of authorized dissemination of the *sandesh* of the Mahatma and the Congress at the village level.[35] Such a view would be consistent with Pouchepadass' understanding of dominant peasants, who in this instance would be the local authors of the message of nationalism, and naturally of the agitation itself. The trouble with such views is that they are not really based on any detailed analysis of the consciousness of the subordinated. A priori formulations in such matters often turn out, on closer scrutiny, to be based on ignorance of the complex relationship between popular culture, religiosity and inchoate political consciousness.[36] The analysis of popular participation in nationalist agitation should, therefore, leave some room for the thoughts, feelings and aspirations of the subordinated, even if they appear only to follow their 'usual masters'.

A third problem crops up with Pouchepadass' emphasis on the organizational role of the caste panchayats of Kammas,

Rajus, Ahirs, Kurmis etc. This is very close to Dumont's view that village solidarity is the solidarity of the dominant caste.[37] Such a view can be questioned by pointing out instances of disease, famine, outside threats from dacoits, etc., which generate solidarities in the village as a whole. Pouchepadass seems to be on weak ground when he suggests that the only solidarities generated during an agrarian movement are those within and around the caste panchayats of the dominant peasantry. The reasons offered for the importance of these panchayats relative to others are not entirely convincing:

The mobilizing role of the dominant castes is naturally facilitated by the fact that they are usually represented by experienced and respected caste councils, which are used to dealing with practical questions for the whole of the caste at the regional level. The councils of the lower castes, by contrast, ordinarily confine their activities to ritual matters and to conflicts between individuals in a single village.[38]

The organizational role of caste, clan and kinship organizations in peasant political activities is of course well accepted.[39] There is evidence that as late as the 1930s caste panchayats *in general* were, to quote E. A. H. Blunt, continuing to 'engineer resistance to oppression.'[40] The problem lies more with Pouchepadass' treatment of the subject. First, there is a great deal of evidence of lower-caste councils operating beyond the village, and of lower castes taking political action and organizing this over a fairly large number of villages. Second, the attempts of the Congress activists (even if they belonged to the 'dominant peasantry') to communicate the message of nationalism to the lower castes served to widen the influence and role of their panchayats. To give one example from the period of non-co-operation: a gathering of 500 Chamars of *tahsil* Bansgaon of Gorakhpur district, UP, was held at the tahsil headquarters on 20 February 1921, where Babu Guru Prasad Singh, a non-co-operator of Bansgaon, conveyed the message of Gandhi (who asked that peace be maintained), which the Mahatma had personally delivered at the district town a few weeks earlier. The meeting no doubt passed a series of resolutions to regulate the professional and social conduct of the Chamars of the tahsil, but it also resolved to establish Chamar panchayats (presumably different from the ones which existed before) in sixty-six villages and sought to enforce novel dietary taboos. 'Everybody should give up liquor, ganja, toddy, bhang. Those persisting should be outcasted for twelve years or fined Rs 12'.[41] Similar examples can no doubt be found for other parts of the country. What is interesting is that, in eastern UP at least, this was part of a broad movement by low-caste panchayats of Dhobis, Bhangis, Chamars, Hajjams and Bhars not only to abstain from liquor and *ganja* but also meat and fish. As I have argued elsewhere, this particular emphasis on purity in the spring of 1921 can be seen as an extension of the Gandhian idea of self-purification (through abstinence from ganja and liquor) to a context where prohibition enlarged its scope to include meat and fish and became regarded as an indication of religiosity and lower-caste assertion at the same time. Inasmuch as elements of the nationalist programme were internalized by the lower castes through their panchayats, and the triumph of the *pratap* of Gandhi was broadcast in terms of a supernatural view of the suffering of those breaking the interdiction, the confinement of these panchayats to interpersonal village matters and rituals ceases to be politically immaterial, as Pouchepadass would lead us to believe.[42]

Of course Gandhi panchayats were established as units of nationalist organization at the village level, and there is a good deal of evidence to suggest that these were not necessarily controlled by the 'dominant peasants' or even subordinated to their panchayats. Let us take the example of village Pokharbhinda (140 houses) in the Sadr tahsil of Gorakhpur, nextdoor to the notorious site of Chauri Chaura. A Gandhi panchayat was formed in the village in the spring of 1921. Among its early victims was Bhawani Prasad Tiwari, mukhiya and zamindar with a 4-anna share in the village. Bhawani Prasad, belonging to the powerful Tiwari brotherhood which in the late nineteenth century 'owned' 75 per cent of the village, had been asked to resign his mukhiyaship and obey the orders of the panchayat. Of the leaders prosecuted on Bhawani Prasad's complaint one was an Upadhyay Brahmin, one Kewat and two Pasis. In retaliation 40 'houses' refused to provide their services for the repair of Bhawani's house, Prag Pasi refused him *begar*, Kunj Bihari

Ahir did not supply milk for the *shradh* of the zamindar's wife, Gobind Pasi and others decided to withhold rent, and after another round of proceedings under Section 107 agreed to send it by money order (an act widely regarded as a gesture of defiance).[43] This is a far cry from the dominant caste panchayats 'managing everything at the base of' political movements in the countryside.

Any theory which seeks to ground nationalist agitations into agrarian bases among the dominant section of the rural population runs the risk of over-emphasizing solidarities generated by, in and around superordinate groups. Solidarities generated by the 'communal form of labour' were certainly very important in insurgencies among the Santhals and Kols in nineteenth-century India.[44] The scope for the 'communal form of labour' is necessarily limited in areas of peasant agriculture, but even here the co-sharing of ploughs, sugarcane presses (or membership of *mandal* Congress Committees) generated solidarities that provided the backdrop of deliberation, preparation and communication behind so-called spontaneous happenings like Chauri Chaura.[45] This example is cited deliberately because it is so well documented, but there are innumerable other examples of picketing, defying the police, etc.—the real stuff of nationalist agitations—which were similarly organized at a distance from the 'real' agrarian base of the Congress, or of a particular movement.

Within another variant of the dominant-peasant mobilization story concerned with searching for and highlighting popular involvement, a distinction is often made between the 'political' response of the 'village élite' and the 'economic rebellion' of the non-élite. In fact, this distinction appears to provide the analytical space for studying popular movements within an all-encompassing conceptual field occupied by the familiar 'dominant peasants'. In Stephen Henningham's study of rural north Bihar the politics of nationalism is not considered a short-term response to price conjunctures and government revenue policies and is readily granted to the high-caste 'village élite'—the base—primarily because these persons were the real actors in every 'open conflict'.[46] This is no doubt an advance over the view which at first finds no tangible reason for any economic *and therefore* political conflict between village élites and the state in view of the declining burden of land revenue from the late nineteenth century.[47] However, this advance is in Henningham only partial, for while politics is granted to the village élite it is kept away from the rest of the peasant population. Demographic growth and the oscillations of price-graphs are the only factors that thrust dominated peasants intermittently into the political arena, when they are seen to make an 'effort to advance their interests and express their discontents'. The rules of the game had, however, disqualified them from playing any normal part in Bihari politics. This disjunction comes out most clearly in Henningham's account of the upsurge of 1942, where it is argued that while the 'village élite' thought and acted out its politics ('nationalist revolt'), the lower classes, prey to economic hardship, could do no better than indulge in a 'rebellion of desperation'.[48] A whole gamut of explanations for the Quit India movement—popular perceptions of the weakness of the state coupled with a resentment caused by its greater direct intervention in civil society, a sense of the 'anticipation of power' or the crisis of authority of functionaries within the state post-1937[49]—which seek not so much to devalue economic factors as to place them in a political context, are sacrificed in the bargain. Our understanding of the character of popular participation in nationalist agitations therefore remains incomplete.

This problem is highlighted in those writings of the so-called Cambridge school which, in setting out to study the behaviour of political agents, concentrate on the conditioning role of the 'machinery of political power', i.e. the 'political institutions of colonial India'. What is illuminated is not so much the base of nationalist agitations as 'the obscure underside of Indian political history'.[50] 'The character of the Congress Non-Co-operation campaign', David Washbrook notes in an introductory statement on south Indian politics some years ago, was 'closely related to the meaning given to it by the conventions of institutional politics…'.[51] Looked at from such an angle nationalist agitations appear as haphazard local affairs brought into being by the political ambitions of leaders responding to the institutional initiatives of the British Raj. In his monograph, *The Politics of South India*, Chris Baker maintains that Non-Co-operation in the Madras presidency was 'nothing more than a few attacks on liquor shops by zealous advocates of temperance, and some scuffles involving the police with forest tribesmen'.[52] In his detailed article on the subject the emphasis is squarely on establishing linkages and dissensions between the interest groups in various localities.[53] According to Baker the basis for local élite activity, which donned the mantle of nationalist agitation, really lay in the actions of the government. As 'government could never reward as many as it irritated, accommodate as many as it attracted', its attempt to keep the loyalists on its side by granting them favours only 'exacerbated local rivalries and propelled more men towards provincial as well as local discontent'.[54]

Arguably, this summary is unfair. Baker, it could be pointed out, does have a notion of 'agrarian base' which is borrowed from the 'dry' and 'wet' village model of David Washbrook.[55] Let us look at its application to nationalist agitations in the Madras presidency. For 1921–2 Baker explains the differential location of the temperance and village officials (resignation) movement in terms of the dry/wet dichotomy. In dry areas where the 'village boss' was also the hooch-king the base of the temperance movement lay in attempts, by out-groups unable to get liquor contracts, to make things difficult for their rivals. In wet areas the salient economic position of the 'village boss' had been eroded with the coming of irrigation and generalized economic development. Here the only props left with former 'bosses' were the administrative power and prestige attached to the positions of village officers. These were being curtailed by fresh legislation; the large-scale resignations of village officials in coastal Andhra, an important aspect of the Non-Co-operation movement, were a response of the élite of wet villages to the curtailment of their privileges.[56]

However, it is Baker's specific location of the village officials' resignation movement that shows his rigid approach to the question of agrarian bases. Most resignations, we are told, took place in Kistna and Godavari, in the wet areas, especially in those proprietary estates which formed a part of the immediate hinterland of towns. In Guntur the difficulty of the village officers 'was particularly acute in 1921/22 since the first efficient survey and settlement had only just been completed'. The district's village officer association had called for militant action even before this, in 1919, and in August 1920 the officers of forty villages in Guntur went on strike.[57] But it so turns out that the agitation was pretty strong in the dry areas of the district. As Baker puts it: 'In fact some of the most troublesome areas in Guntur during Non-cooperation did not fall within the 'wet' area; even so, their credit and marketing arrangements, and thus the pattern of their local politics, had been distorted along the lines of the adjacent deltaic area.'[58] This amounts to offering a reflective view of rural political activity during the Non-Co-operation movement. I am not questioning the empirical basis of Baker's observation; perhaps the dry Guntur villages were indeed 'wet-like' in their economic arrangements. That is not the point at issue: the interesting thing about the observation quoted above is that, faced with an anomaly, Baker does not seek to explain it with reference to the politics of others in the village, or beyond, in the strength of the district village officer association.[59] Having located the basis of temperance and village officers' movement in the position of the dry and wet village élites respectively, no disjunction (which may well be explainable) between the base and the modality of the movement is countenanced.

Such a view entails that politics, or a movement—such as non-payment of revenue during the calamitous years of the Depression—is the sole concern of village élites. Thus the entire discussion of the impact of the Depression on south Indian villages by Baker is in terms of the hardships faced by village officers:

The freezing of credit during the depression cut into the village officers' ability to control their rural neighbours through the power of debt. In such a situation the burden of collecting revenue during the depression became, in some areas, impossible or at least intolerable. In the 'wet' areas where ... the position of the village officers vis-à-vis their neighbours was already difficult, the problems were particularly acute. Many decided, or were forced to decide, to lead the village against the government rather than carry out government orders over the village.... Many other village officers were dismissed for taking active part in campaigns which aimed to force the government to reduce revenue rates, and some were dismissed for urging their village to withhold payment of revenue.[60]

There is surprisingly little here about the bulk of the village population and its experiences during the Depression;[61] it is the village officers who feel the adverse effects, they who decide, even when forced into doing so by peasants no longer under their immediate economic control. This is like writing the history of the *nasbandi* campaign during the Emergency in terms of the hardships faced by 'motivators' rather than those vasectomized.

The issue of the agrarian bases of nationalist agitations is not central to Judith Brown's writings on Gandhi and Indian politics.[62] In her book covering the period 1928–34 she surveys 'the continental and local effects of the civil disobedience movement' in order to demonstrate 'the nature of Gandhi's political position and the repercussions of the movement on it'.[63] The focus on Gandhi has the effect of pushing the nationalist campaigns of the 1920s and 1930s into the background. However, it is not this emphasis on Gandhi but her views on the politics of the 'lowly folk' (or rather the lack of it), and the nature of the Mahatma's mass appeal, that concern us here.

In Brown's landscape of Indian politics Non-Co-operation appears as a 'chameleon campaign', taking colour from the ambitions and calculations of Gandhi's men in the localities who, after serving a 'remote apprenticeship under [him] ... tended to become contractors in their own right for their particular groups or interests ...'.[64] The *thekedars* naturally came dyed in sundry hues, and if one were to equate their support for Gandhi with that for Non-Co-operation the movement's base would then aggregate to that 'wide band in public life—men educated either in the vernacular or in English, small town lawyers, traders, moneylenders, village officials, village priests and ulema, prosperous cultivators, men typified by the Marwaris of Calcutta and Bihar, and the Patidars of Gujarat.'[65]

This constituted India's 'new' 'political nation'. Beneath 'this wide middle sector of public life were the real "masses" of India, the illiterate, low-paid workers and the unemployed of town and countryside'. The involvement of the masses in Non-Co-operation, however, does not call for systematic analysis. This is because

Non-cooperation as an integrated political weapon never reached this far: it was manifest only in diverse local forms, when leaders found an exploitable local grievance among such lowly folk, when agitators offered the excitement and scanty monetary rewards of the Volunteer organization, and when caste aspirations or economic hardship fitted the call for temperance.[66]

Nor was Gandhi's charismatic appeal among the masses of any real political import:

From the 'lower class people' Gandhi in fact elicited no truly political response, if that is taken to mean a willingness to plan, organize and be subject to discipline for the sake of gaining power. They reacted to him with a mixture of religious adulation and millenary anticipation.[67]

I would argue that Brown here offers a rather restricted view of both 'power' and the 'political'. It can be shown, for example, that the Mahatma was appropriated politically by countless peasants who proceeded to challenge landlords and the functionaries of state, and that 'religiosity,' 'organization' and 'discipline' were not rigidly separated in popular consciousness.[68] To say this would, from Brown's point view, be to fall short of her definition of a 'truly political response'. A great many 'events', part of the major nationalist agitations, would consequently have to be either classified as 'criminal', or, following Brown, margina-lized as non-political.[69] This would restrict discussion of nationalist agitations to the confines of organized politics: the question of an 'other' domain of politics lying outside the 'legal-political framework' of formal politics could not even be posed.[70] One response to the historiography which frames agitations in the countryside within the administrative structure of the Raj is to argue for its non-applicability in the native states. Anil Seal's 'clues' of administrative structures are not universally helpful, because the structures which created networks of colla-boration (and also the base of agitational politics) did not cross over into princely India. But this exception, it has been argued, may just prove the rule.[71]

There has recently been a conscious attempt to break out of the frame of élite politics generated within administrative structures and institutions in town and countryside. The picture of nationalist agitations is seen, rather, in terms of the appeal of nationalism, and of different perceptions and patterns of political activity at a remove from what Sumit Sarkar, in a recent survey, calls 'the sanctified forms of Gandhian agitations.'[2] Such writings reveal differences in emphasis. Thus, Hites Sanyal and Alok Sheel in their studies of Midnapur (1921–31) and UP (1931–2) have shown how the emerging Congress as a 'parallel organisation'— 'embryonic state' in Sheel's terminology—was able to ride the tension between its 'real' base and the poorer kisans and sharecroppers, especially during and immediately after the Civil Disobedience movement. Gyan Pandey, in his monograph on UP, 1926–34, and in a recent article on the Kisan Sabha movement in Awadh, 1919–22, has shown how the Congress organization at the district and provincial levels consciously failed to link up with agrarian movements once they began to spill outside nationalist boundaries. David Hardiman has chosen to concentrate on the Patidar's political tradition of revenue refusal and how this overdetermined the character of nationalist agitations in the Charotar tract of Kheda district. Sumit Sarkar, in his wide-ranging survey, has touched among other things on the relationship between nationalist organization and 'popular' movements during 1917–47. Substantial peasants, protagonists of so many other accounts of nationalism in the countryside, are to be found in these writings as well. The perspective, however, is rather different; either their 'economic' struggle against the colonial state (revenue refusal) is accorded a political specific gravity, as in Hardiman, or, as with Pandey, the 'lack of fit' between 'base' and 'agitation' is underscored by positing an inverse relationship between the strength of Congress organization and the militancy of agrarian movements.

Hardiman locates the organizational base of the Congress Party among the Patidars of Kheda and explains the strength of the principal modality (revenue refusal) of nationalist agitation in the Charotar tract with reference to the specific features of the Patidar peasantry: their economic strength; their caste solidarity at the village level and kinship circles beyond the village;

their political tradition pre-dating 'the nationalist awakening' of refusing to pay unjust revenue demands; and their ability, in many cases, to resist attachment of property, successfully prevent the sale of confiscated land to third parties, or migrate to kinsmen in neighbouring princely states. The absence of these characteristics among the non-Patidar peasants of Kheda and their subordination as landless labourers and debtor-peasants to the Patidars (as in the case of Baraiyas) had significant repercussions for the modality, growth and spread of nationalist agitations.

In Baraiya-dominated villages Civil Disobedience was confined to support for salt satyagraha and resignations by a few village headmen, but could not embrace revenue refusal. In Patidar-dominated villages there was very little Baraiya support for the movement. On the contrary, they either openly opposed the Patidars, burning and looting the deserted houses of *muhajareen* peasants, or acquired lands confiscated for revenue refusal at throwaway prices. The Gandhi-Irwin pact and the inability of the Mahatma to get these lands back for the Patidars ensured the Baraiyas possession of these plots for a good seven years. Faced with this anomalous situation the Congress-in-government had to legislate in 1938 the official transfer of these lands from the Baraiyas to the 'peasant nationalists of Gujarat'.[73] 'This convinced the Baraiyas', says Hardiman, 'that Congress was essentially a Patidar Party'. The Baraiyas, along with the Patanavadiyas (both of these had been claiming Kshatriya status), organized themselves in 1937 into a Kshatriya Association in opposition to the Patidar-dominated Kheda DCC. In August 1942 they sharply opposed the Patidar-dominated movement in Kheda.[74]

Hardiman's analysis raises two important issues, both related to the unfolding of the relationship of dominance and subordination in the Kheda countryside. The Baraiyas were agricultural labourers and poor peasants in the Charotar and not very prosperous tenants and impecunious landlords outside this tract. They had the additional stigma of being notified as a 'criminal tribe' and subjected to the usual system of surveillance. They thus had an ambivalent relationship to the agitations that were mounted by the Patidars of Kheda. One of the important sequels of the satyagraha of 1918 was a spate of 'organized lootings of the grain stores of rich peasants and merchants'.[75] This was an enactment on an enlarged scale of a traditional 'crime of scarcity', *dadh* in the local parlance. In the summer of 1918 scarcity had combined with other factors, notably resentment against the state and a perceived weakening of its power and authority, to create a new political conjuncture. Rumours of the British being routed in battle by the Germans, a reduced police control in villages during the Kheda satyagraha, criticisms of the government by the Home Rulers—all suggested to the Baraiyas that 'there was no need to obey the Sarkar'.[76] This perceived break-down of authority, coupled with the failure of the monsoons and the depletion of food reserves, resulted in the 'criminal' Baraiyas attacking Patidars and Vaniyas of their own villages.[77] The articulation of anti-state sentiments by the dominated took place within the structure of dominance of village society—this meant at the base of a recently accomplished peasant satyagraha.[78] The headquarters itself had been bombarded!

The vicissitudes of the 'constructive programme' among the Baraiyas suggest once again that the base of Congress agitations could with difficulty be widened to touch non-Patidar tracts but not deepened in villages where the Patidars themselves were dominant.[79] Attempts by committed Gandhians to 'uplift' the Baraiyas, by asking them to forsake both crime and liquor and generally reform themselves, were opposed by Patidars in their own villages. Such attempts were seen as an unnecessary frater-nization with the lowly which bridged the distance that was the site for the exercise of power, as well as for the limitations that the upliftment programme imposed on Patidar exploitation of poor peasants. Baraiya reform was therefore restricted to villages in which Muslims or 'talukdars' were dominant. This meant that whatever little favour Civil Disobedience gained among the Baraiyas (salt satyagraha, resignation by village officers) was limited to non-Patidar areas. The 'constructive programme' really failed to build a nationalist base among Baraiyas in Patidar-dominated villages—the stronghold of nationalism in Gujarat. Baraiyas could not in any case have (because of their weak economic and political position) participated in the principal modality of Civil Disobedience (revenue refusal, and even resignation from headmanship) in Patidar villages. The result was the contradiction alluded to between the two principal groups in the 'key villages' of nationalist agitation. The grid of dominance and subordination had been superimposed on the base of anti-state action in the countryside.[80]

Gyanendra Pandey's discussion of the 'rural base for Congress' in UP in the early thirties was a pioneering attempt at studying the relationship between Congress organization and nationalist agitation in the countryside. Although Pandey analysed the broadcasting of nationalist 'propaganda' in considerable detail, the question of its decoding, assimilation and appropriation was not expressly posed.[81] In his discussion of 'mass mobilization', which focuses on the differential nature of the Civil Disobedience campaign in Agra and Rae Bareli districts, Pandey splits into two the notion of agrarian base. Shorn of detail his argument is that where the *organizational* base of the Congress was strong its *agrarian* base was narrow; nationalist agitation was consequently marked by control, restraint and low militancy. (The Congress, as it gained in popularity and strengthened its agrarian base during the 1920s and 1930s, became less militant.) The situation was more or less the opposite of this in areas where the potential base of the Congress was wide. These were regions where the bulk of the peasantry was 'dependent', i.e. it had very little legal rights in the occupancy of land, was relatively undifferentiated, and dominated by a small number of landlords who could transfer a disproportionate share of price dips on to this peasantry. From Pandey's account it appears that in such areas the organizational base of the Congress was weak, and a narrow nationalist framing of agrarian agitation not feasible in the first instance. As local leaders launched the peasants of these areas into militant anti-landlord campaigns, provincial personalities like J. L. Nehru curbed these intitiatives by direct intervention. Simultaneously, the district Congress organization recovered its base by purging local Congress militants. These had risen to gain control on the crest-wave of a sudden widening of the organizational base which had been caused by an influx of peasant membership.[82]

Sumit Sarkar has raised a question to this model. Why was

the Congress organizational base stronger in Agra than in Rae Bareli, and why were Congress controls operative from the beginning of the Civil Disobedience movement in Agra (and eventually so even in Rae Bareli), he asks.[83] If we were to engage in a dialogue with this line of reasoning, and subject Pandey's analysis to a close scrutiny we might be better able to pose some central issues about the relationship between agrarian base and nationalist agitation, as it was mediated by organization, ideology and consciousness.

It is tempting to reply to Sarkar that the organizational base of the Congress was not strong in areas lacking a substantial peasantry, as in Rae Bareli. Various arguments could be proferred, but I suspect that the most popular one would be that the Congress really represented the interests of substantial peasants, and so except during the upswing of the agrarian movement the poorer peasants could not be represented in the organization. However, most explanations of *why* certain agrarian classes supported the Congress, and by implication why nationalist agitations in the countryside were controlled by or were free of Congress controls, ultimately rest on an analytical distinction between the 'agrarian' and the 'national' which is difficult to sustain. This is not only because these categories were jumbled up by the Congress, and in the minds of the peasants. It is also so for the simple reason that we seem to know more about the interests than about the consciousness of the subordinated. The question of *why* the Congress organizational base was stronger in one area rather than in another may then turn out to be not the most important question after all.

In his account of nationalist agitation in Rae Bareli Pandey emphasizes the militant leadership of local activists like Kalka Prasad and their being censored by the Congress organization on the one hand, and instances of independent action by the peasants—mass relinquishment of holdings and forced grazing of cattle on taluqdars' lands—on the other.[84] This is to unfold an important plot but not quite the whole story, for it does not tell us about the interpenetration of the two kinds of politics, of local 'kangresi' militants like Kalka Prasad and of the 'independent' political actions of peasants. What solidarities were activated during such actions, what were the boundaries of 'us' and 'them' being drawn and redrawn?[85] Where and how did nationalism, and what kind of an 'understanding' (or 'misunderstanding') of nationalism, figure in all this? These are important questions for a fuller understanding of how the 'brakes' were applied in Rae Bareli. It may have been in the interest of the 'agrarian base', the local Congress organization and the 'freedom struggle' to put a stop to the class struggle in the UP countryside in 1931–2, but for that to successfully happen there must have been a nationalist aspect to that struggle.[86] To pose the problem in this way is not to subscribe to the 'nationalist' (of the first or the second half of this century) view of politics being brought to the peasantry. It is an attempt to give up the idiom of 'interests' and investigate much more systematically the contours of peasant consciousness in its imbrications with 'official' nationalism at different levels.

Sarkar's explanation of the 'acceptance of the brakes imposed by the leader without major disillusionment' in terms of 'the social composition and nature of the movement led by Gandhi' also needs some questioning.[87] This opinion, though voiced in the context of the relationship between the Mahatma and the people, can be read with justification as a comment on the relationship between 'organization' and 'movement'. Sarkar, who has recently highlighted popular struggles during nationalist agitations,[88] is here subscribing to a widespread tendency which reads off the character of a movement from an understanding of the group or class interests served by it.[89] Important as such an examination may be for characterizing the 'end product', it often militates against an analysis of the tensions and contradictions that are an essential aspect of the process of mass movements. This certainly holds true for nationalist agitations in the countryside. Without mustering an empirical case, I wish to suggest that if 'agrarian base' is not the *only* significant determinant of nationalist agitations, and if these agitations also derive their thrust and tension from the participation of those who do not necessarily form a part of their base and who are not its beneficiaries, then Sarkar's argument may seem an effort to force the complexities of 'agitations' into the confines of its palpable 'base'. This, in my opinion, is an important issue raised by the historiography of nationalism in India, and Sarkar has himself underlined it:

'History from below' has to face the problem of the ultimate relative *failure* of mass initiative in colonial India, if the justly abandoned stereotype of the eternally passive Indian peasant is not to be replaced by an opposite romantic stereotype of perennial rural rebelliousness. For an essential fact surely is that the 'subaltern' classes have remained subaltern, often surprisingly dormant despite abject misery and ample provocation, and subordinate in the end to their social 'betters' even when they do become politically active.[90]

I wish to suggest that 'the relative failure of mass initiative' was not, as Sarkar puts it, because popular struggles remained 'outside the ambit of mainstream nationalism'.[91] Sarkar gives the specific instance of *haat*-looting in north Bihar and eastern UP in the winter of 1920–1, arguing that these incidents 'coincided with…without being intrinsically a part' of 'mainstream nationalism'. The problem with such a view is not only that it flies in the face of deeply held beliefs at that time: the parties involved—the landlords and haat-managers, the state, and even the 'looters'—thought that this was all a part of the then existent Non-Co-operation movement. The problem is rather more general. The only way that haat-looting in north Bihar can be kept well out of the field of nationalist agitation is by either sticking close to the self-image of nationalism—perceiving it as a centrally articulated, authored and closed discourse, or by subsuming the diverse strands of politics during these agitations into an invariant end-product: 'class interests served by nationalism'. Such a procedure may give us certain criteria of 'relevance' and 'irrelevance' for the ordering of particular movements and events as 'more' or 'less' nationalistic, but it is a procedure which, by its exclusions, will not contribute significantly to our understanding of the characteristics of nationalist agitation and its problematic relationship to a given agrarian base.

It is now time to raise issues other than those of 'initiative', 'radical potential,' 'betrayal', 'disaffiliation', 'brakes', etc., which have been central to most serious analyses of nationalism in the countryside. Here I wish to do no more than allude to one such shift of focus. Parallel to the history of dominance and subordination in the quotidian existence of the subaltern, there is also a history of dominance, resistance, subordination, and appropriation within nationalist agitation itself. It is here that standard stories of Indian nationalism, whether Marxist or Nationalist, in their preoccupation either with betrayal or triumph, lose out. And it is here that the notion of 'subalternity'—'the composite culture of resistance to an acceptance of domination and hierarchy'—comes into play.[92] 'Agrarian bases of nationalist agitations' can be an interesting starting point, but it no longer needs to preoccupy us.[93]

NOTES

1. For bibliographic details of recent research work in this area, see Sumit Sarkar, *'Popular' Movements and 'Middle Class' Leadership: Perspectives and Problems of a 'History from Below'*, S. G. Deuskar Lectures on Indian History, 1980 (Calcutta, 1983).

2. The volumes on Maharashtra and Andhra Pradesh have been published and are well known to scholars. See *Source Material for a History of Freedom Movement in India* (Collected from Bombay Government Records, 1958), and M. Venkatrangaiya, ed., *The Freedom Struggle in Andhra Pradesh* (Hyderabad, 1965). 'Freedom Movement Papers' for Bihar are available at the Bihar State Archives and the National Archives of India. The Information Department of UP has brought out a district-wise set of *Swatantrata Sangram Ke Sainik (Sanshipt Parichay)* (Lucknow c. 1972), which is based primarily on conviction registers maintained as a part of the Defence of India Rules *bastas* at the district headquarters. In the very process of providing a Directory of accredited nationalists this series also gives clues about actions and events officially accepted by the early 1970s as a part of the Freedom Struggle. Thus while the OSD, Political Pensions, could not, in 1957, make up his mind whether 'the Chauri Chaura case was purely of a political nature', the 1972 Handbook on Gorakhpur opens with a list of the Chauri Chaura martyrs who were hanged in 1923.

3. Amar Bahadur Singh 'Amresh', *Ek Aur Jalianwala* (Uttar Pradesh Sarkar dwara Puraskrit) (Rashtriya Prakashan Mandir, Lucknow, 1981). To this must be added the considerable regional and all-

India literature on the 'Revolution of 1942'. For tracts published in the 1940s, see Dina Nath Vyas 'Kavyalankar', *Agast San '42 Ka Mahan Viplav Kranti Ka Pramanik, Romanchak evam Sampurn Advitiya Itihas* (Vinod Pustak Mandir, Agra, Samvat 2003), and *1942 ki Kranti*, by 'Jai Hind' aur 'Netaji' aadi pustak ke yashasvi lekhak, Sri Sri Ram (Bhartiya Pustak Mandir, Gwalior, 1946). These two contemporary tracts give district-wise accounts of action and police brutalities, interspersed with photographs of damage done to government establishments from official publicity material, and an artist's stylized impressions of individual instances of police torture and rape. An important tract for western India is P. P. Gokhle's *Jagrut Satara*, cited by Gail Omvedt.

4. Amresh, p. 6

5. I am basing myself largely on eastern UP. Comparable work can no doubt be cited from other regions as well. See, *inter alia*, Ram Murat Upadhyay, 'Gorakhpur Janpad Mein Swatantrata Sangharsh, (1857–1947)' (Ph.D. thesis, Gorakhpur University, 1975); Arjun Tiwari, 'Poorvi Uttar Pradesh mein Hindi Patrakarita ka Udbhav aur Vikas' (Ph.D. thesis, Gorakhpur University, 1978), now published as *Swatantrata Andolan aur Hindi Patrakarita*; Amodnath Tripathi, 'Poorvi Uttar Pradesh Ke Jan-jeevan mein Baba Raghav Das Ka Yogdaan' (Ph.D. thesis, Allahabad University, 1981).

6. At one level this is true of the works of Majid Siddiqi on the Awadh Kisan movement and of Gyanendra Pandey and David Hardiman on UP and Gujarat in the 1920s and 1930s.

7. This has resulted, in the present case, in the organisation of this essay around authors rather than themes, which may be criticised on account of the textual flabbiness, which seems visible. My defence is as follows. First, since the theme of 'agrarian bases of nationalist agitations' is not explicitly present in all the writings under review, a certain amount of discussion of the overall argument of particular authors seemed necessary. Second, the transition, or jump if you will, from one author to another has been determined by certain broad groupings of approaches to 'country politics'.

8. See Ranajit Guha, 'On some Aspects of the Historiography of Colonial India', in Guha, ed., *Subaltern Studies I: Writings on South Asian History and Society* (Delhi, 1982), and more particularly Partha Chatterjee, *Bengal, 1920–1947: vol.* I: *The Land Question*, Preface, (Calcutta, 1984), esp. pp. xxxviii–xlviii.

9. Of course terms other than 'village élite' have been used in the literature to designate what is regarded as the 'real' agrarian base

of Indian nationalism. 'Dominant peasants', village-level members of the 'new' political nation, post 1917, or 'village bosses' before this significant date, are some of the other appellations that have been recently employed.

10. D. A. Low, 'Introduction: the climactic years, 1917–47', in Low, ed., *Congress and the Raj: Facets of the Indian Struggle, 1917–47* (Delhi, 1977); Judith Brown, *Gandhi's Rise to Power, Indian Politics, 1915–1922* (Cambridge, 1974); *Gandhi and Civil Disobedience: The Mahatma in Indian Politics 1928–34* (Cambridge, 1977); Christopher John Baker, *The Politics of South India, 1920–37* (Cambridge, 1976); Robin Jeffrey, 'India: Independence and the Rich Peasant', in Jeffrey, ed., *Asia—the Winning of Independence* (London, 1981); David Washbrook, *The Emergence of Provincial Politics: The Madras Presidency 1870–1920* (Cambridge, 1976); Jacques Pouchepadass, 'Peasant Classes in Twentieth Century Agrarian Movements in India', in E. J. Hobsbawm *et al.*, eds., *Peasants in History: Essays in Honour of Daniel Thorner* (Delhi, 1980); Stephen Henningham, *Peasant Movements in India: North Bihar, 1917–1942* (Canberra, 1982); Walter Hauser and James R. Hagen, 'Princes and Peasants; Comments on the Nature of Agrarian Movements in South Asia', in Peter Robb, ed., *Rural India: A study of Land, Power and Society under British Rule* (London, 1983); Rajat Ray's article on Mewar in Robin Jeffrey, ed., *People, Princes and Paramount Power* (Delhi, 1978). See also A. Yang, 'The Agrarian Origins of Crime: A Study of Riots in Saran District, India, 1886–1920', *Journal of Social History*, 13:2, 1979.

11. Low, p. 23.

12. It may be noted that Low uses the word 'community' in a descriptive fashion, without attributing any particular role to it in moulding and ordering peasant participation in nationalist agitations.

13. Low, p. 20.

14. Ibid., pp. 22–3.

15. *Indian Historical Review*, 4:2 (Jan. 1978); *Modern Asian Studies*, 16 (1982), esp., pp. 346–7.

16. First published in the 'Holi Visheshank' of *Swadesh* (Gorakhpur), 20 March 1920, reprinted in *Mansarowar* (Allahabad, 1968).

17. Unfortunately in the historiography of Non-Co-operation in UP this theme has not received the attention it deserves.

18. Low, p. 14ff. Hugh Owen, 'Interaction between the National and the Local in Modern South Asia', *South Asia*, December 1975.

19. Low, pp. 16–17.

20. Owen has suggested that the local be construed as a 'kind of

short-hand for a number of levels—provincial, regional, district, city, suburb and mohalla'. *South Asia*, December 1975, p. 2.

21. See especially C. Baker, 'Non-cooperation in South India', in Baker and Washbrook, *South India: Political Institution and Political Change, 1880–1940* (Delhi, 1975), to which Low refers.

22. Low, p. 17; Judith Brown, *Gandhi and Civil Disobedience*.

23. See Shahid Amin, 'Gandhi as Mahatma: Gorakhpur District, Eastern UP, 1921–2'; David Hardiman, 'Adivasi Assertion in South Gujarat: the Devi Movement, 1922–3', and Sumit Sarkar, 'The Conditions and Nature of Subaltern Militancy: Bengal from Swadeshi to Non-cooperation, c., 1905–22', all in Ranajit Guha, ed., *Subaltern Studies III* (Delhi, 1984).

24. Judith Brown, *Gandhi's Rise to Power*, pp. 343ff.

25. Majid Hayat Siddiqi, *Agrarian Unrest in North India: The United Provinces, 1918–1922* (Delhi, 1981); Hitesranjan Sanyal, 'Congress Movements in the Villages of Eastern Midnapore', *Asie du Sud: traditions et changements* (Paris, 1979); Kapil Kumar, *Peasants in Revolt: Tenants, Landlords, Congress and the Raj in Oudh, 1886–1922* (Delhi, 1984); David Hardiman, *Peasant Nationalists of Gujarat: Kheda District, 1917–34* (Delhi, 1981).

26. Hardiman, p. 12.

27. Jacques Pouchepadass, 'Peasant Classes in Twentieth Century Agrarian Movements', pp. 136–55.

28. D. N. Dhanagare has dismissed Alavi's middle-peasant thesis as a myth, especially contesting the notion of the economic independence of the middle peasants. See his *Peasant Movements in India, 1920–1950* (Delhi, 1983), esp., p. 223. See also Neil Charlesworth, 'The Middle Peasant Thesis and the Roots of Rural Agitation in India, 1917–47', *Journal of Peasant Studies*. 8: 3 (April 1981). Two recent studies of peasant movements in princely India (Hauser & Hagen and Rajat Ray, cited in note 10 above) tend to support Eric Wolf's notion of the importance of marginal peasants.

29. As Pouchepadass puts it, 'It is within this relatively large category that the moving spirits of the Champaran movement were recruited in 1917.... The same in all likelihood appears to have been the case in the Kheda movements of 1918, in the Andhra delta from the 1920s onwards, in the United Provinces in 1930–2, and in the initial phase of the Telengana movement' (p. 147).

30. Ibid., p. 149.

31. Ibid., p. 148, Emphasis mine.

32. Ibid., p. 149.

33. For an argument which emphasizes community solidarity as one of the basic characteristics of peasant political activity in its various articulations with nationalism and communalism, see Partha Chatterjee, *Bengal, 1920–1947*.

34. Partha Chatterjee, 'Peasants, Politics and Historiography: a Response', *Social Scientist*, no. 120, 1983.

35. Pouchepadass, 'Local Leaders and the intelligentsia in the Champaran Satyagraha (1917): a Study in Peasant Mobilization', *Contributions to Indian Sociology* (NS) 8: 1974.

36. For a brief discussion see pp. 106–7. For a systematic critique, see Ranajit Guha, *Elementary Aspects of Peasant Insurgency in Colonial India* (Delhi, 1983).

37. *Homo Hierarchicus: The Caste System and its Implications* (London, 1972).

38. Pouchepadass, 'Peasant Classes', p. 148.

39. See Eric Stokes, *The Peasant and the Raj: Studies in Agrarian Society and Peasant Rebellion in Colonial India* (Cambridge, 1978), p. 274; David Hardiman, *Peasant Nationalists*, pp. 252–3 and *passim*.

40. 'The Structure of the Indian People', in E. A. H. Blunt, ed., *Social Service in India. An Introduction to some Social and Economic Problems of the Indian People* (London, HMSO, 1938), p. 63.

41. *Swadesh*, 27 February 1921.

42. The evidence on which this argument is based is discussed in Shahid Amin, 'Gandhi as Mahatma'.

43. Evidence of Bhawani Prasad Tiwari, Zamindar of Pokharbhinda, Chauri Chaura Trials, II, pp. 185–203; Village Papers, 1885 Settlement.

44. Ranajit Guha, *Elementary Aspects*, chapter 4.

45. Chauri Chaura Trials, District Records Room, Gorakhpur.

46. *Peasant Movements in Colonial India, North Bihar, 1917–42*, esp., pp. 14–15 and *passim*. Henningham here refers to Anand Yang's, 'Agrarian Origins of Crime', wherein it is argued that 'at the fundamental level of agrarian society, also the immediate arena of action for any peasant, the village-level controller was the key to both control and conflict'.

47. Charlesworth, in *Journal of Peasant Studies*, April 1980; Tomlinson, in *Modern Asian Studies*, 1982.

48. Henningham, chapter 7.

49. See Indivar Kamtekar, 'What Caused the Quit India Movement?', unpublished paper, Cambridge, 1983; Gyan Pandey, 'Anticipation of Power: the Bhojpuri Region in 1942', and Chandan Mitra,

'The Lion in Retreat . . . Eastern Uttar Pradesh in 1942', papers read at a Conference on the Quit India Movement, Calcutta, 1983.

50. David Washbrook, 'Introduction' in Baker and Washbrook, *South India*, p. 4.

51. Ibid., p. 4.

52. Baker, *The Politics of South India*, p. 87.

53. Baker, 'Non-cooperation in South India'.

54. Ibid., p. 138.

55. David Washbrook, 'Country Politics: Madras, 1800 to 1930', in John Gallagher *et al.*, eds., *Locality, Province and Nation: Essays on Indian Politics* (Cambridge, 1973).

56. Baker, 'Non-cooperation', pp. 103–14.

57. Ibid., p. 113.

58. Ibid., p. 144, footnote 66.

59. Both Hardiman and Sheel dwell at some length on the pressure brought to bear on village officers in Gujarat to relinquish their posts during nationalist agitations. For Sheel, see footnote 72 below.

60. Baker, *The Politics of South India*, pp. 208–9.

61. Baker has recently touched upon this problem in his book, *An Indian Rural Economy, 1880–1955: The Tamilnad Countryside* (Delhi, 1984).

62. *Gandhi's Rise to Power* and *Gandhi and Civil Disobedience*.

63. *Gandhi and Civil Disobedience*, p. 103. In her conclusion Brown emphasizes the importance of British administrative and political structure in shaping the contours of Indian politics, enabling Gandhi to play his pivotal role. India did not have a unified 'well-defined political system in which Indians encountered their compatriots and their rulers, but a cluster of intermeshing systems in each of which ideals, strategies and alliances were being created'. Gandhi functioned as a 'lubricant' to smoothen the functioning of this clanking machine of Indian politics (see p. 382).

64. *Gandhi's Rise to Power*, pp. 322, 327.

65. Ibid., p. 344.

66. Ibid., p. 345.

67. Ibid., p. 345.

68. I have tried to argue this case in 'Gandhi as Mahatma'.

69. For a preliminary discussion of one such violent 'event', see my 'Approver's Testimony, Judicial Discourse: The Case of Chauri Chaura', in Ranajit Guha, ed., *Subaltern Studies V* (Delhi, 1987).

70. I take this idea from Partha Chaterjee, *Bengal, 1920–1947*, vol. I.

71. See Rajat Ray, and Robert Stern in Robin Jeffrey, ed., *People, Princes and Paramount Power*.

72. See Hardiman, and Gyan Pandey, cited in footnote 81; Alok Sheel, 'The Congress and the Raiyat: A Study of Three Agrarian Movements, 1928–40' (M.Phil. thesis, Jawaharlal Nehru University, New Delhi, 1980); Hitesranjan Sanyal, 'Congress Movements in Eastern Midnapore'; Sumit Sarkar, *'Popular' Movements'*, p. 47.

73. *Peasant Nationalists of Gujarat*. See also Hardiman, 'The Quit India Movement in Gujarat' (mimeo, Calcutta, 1983).

74. 'Quit India Movement in Gujarat'.

75. *Peasant Nationalists of Gujarat*, p. 111.

76. Ibid., pp. 110–11.

77. For a discussion of 'breakdown', perceived or real, and its role in extending nationalist agitations beyond the 'real' base, see Sumit Sarkar's contribution to Ranajit Guha, ed., *Subaltern Studies III*.

78. The other sequels to the Kheda satyagraha bring out the disjunction between agrarian base and agitation in sharp relief. The *talatis*, the hated lower-level revenue functionaries, suffering under the inflation and retaliating against the abuse to which they had been subjected during the satyagraha, struck work in June 1918 and also appealed to Gandhi for support. Gandhi declined while the other nationalists ignored the strike. 'They could', writes Hardiman, 'hardly do otherwise after their criticism of these petty officials' (p. 109). Strikes, threatened or actual, by the Patwaris of UP during the Non-Co-operation movement were supported by the nationalists of the United Provinces. In the Kheda of 1918 the success of the no-revenue satyagraha was partly responsible for the militancy of the talatis as well as the refusal of the nationalists to recognize its anti-state potential—an interesting example of the ambiguous relationship between the agrarian base and anti-state agitations in the countryside. The failure of Gandhi's recruitment drive among the Kheda peasants is a different instance of the base recoiling on itself in opposing the arch nationalist's pro-British activities. For details, see Hardiman, pp. 108–11.

79. Sumit Sarkar, basing himself on the writings of Hardiman, Pandey and Sanyal, has emphasized the role of 'devoted Gandhian constructive workers in creating and sustaining stable political bases in the countryside'. *'Popular' Movements*, p. 42.

80. *Peasant Nationalists of Gujarat*, chapters 8 and 9.

81. Gyanendra Pandey, 'A Rural Base for Congress: the United Provinces, 1920–40', in Low, ed., *Congress and the Raj*; 'Mobilization

in a Mass Movement: Congress 'Propaganda' in the United Provinces (India), 1930–34', *Modern Asian Studies*, 9:2 (1975); *The Ascendancy of the Congress in Uttar Pradesh, 1926–34* (Delhi, 1978).

82. *Ascendancy of the Congress*, chapters 4 and 6.

83. Sarkar, *'Popular' Movements*, p. 3.

84. *Ascendancy of the Congress*, chapter 8, esp. p. 181.

85. Partha Chatterjee assigns a crucial importance to such questions in his *Bengal, 1920–1947, The Land Question*.

86. Alok Sheel distances himself from Pandey on the basis of a similar kind of reasoning, but in my opinion overemphasizes the 'hegemony' of the Congress.

87. *'Popular' Movements*, p. 67.

88. See his 'Primitive Rebellion and Modern Nationalism: a Note on the Forest Satyagraha . . .', in K. N. Pannikar, ed., *National and Left Movements in India* (New Delhi, 1980); *'Popular' Movements*, etc.; *Modern India, 1885–1947* (Delhi, 1983).

89. Thus, to quote Sarkar: 'It may be argued, finally, that irrespective of the precise social composition of the movement in a particular area, the general thrust, ideology and style of Gandhian nationalism was geared objectively to the interests of landholding intermediate-caste peasant proprietors or tenants. . . .'. But the base was also adequately aligned to the 'objective' interests of the protagonists of the movement, for as he writes on the previous page, 'Gandhian peasant movements . . . seem to have been most effective where the rural scene was not too sharply polarized, and where there existed a fairly broad stratum of small holders preferably more or less homogeneous in caste composition'. *'Popular' Movements*, pp. 66 and 65.

90. *'Popular' Movements*, p. 3.

91. Ibid., p. 52.

92. Dipesh Chakrabarty, 'Invitation to a Dialogue', in Ranajit Guha, ed., *Subaltern Studies IV* (New Delhi, 1985).

93. This essay was written in response to Dr T. Raychaudhuri's suggestion that I address myself to the theme of 'The Agrarian Bases of Nationalist Agitations in India' for the conference on the INC in Oxford in December 1985. I am grateful to Dr Raychaudhuri and David Hardiman for critical comments on an earlier draft of this essay, and to the ICSSR for a travel grant.

THE FORGOTTEN BANIA:
MERCHANT COMMUNITIES
AND THE INDIAN
NATIONAL CONGRESS

D. A. LOW

In studies of the history of the Indian National Congress a good deal of attention has been given to the manner in which different categories of India's population became, or did not become (or ceased to be) in association with it. This is, no doubt, a blunt approach that allows far too little for all the innumerable nuances that characterized the Congress' support (or shortfalls in support) that close, detailed, investigations reveal. Yet the broad brush was the fairly regular instrument of those who described these matters whilst the struggle with the British *raj* was on. When, for example, in 1936 Rajendra Prasad wrote of the support which Congress enjoyed by that time, he specified 'those who had been to school and college' and 'peasants and cultivators' as its principal adherents, whilst listing 'industrial and field workers' as not as yet having come into its ranks in any significant numbers.[1] The British similarly employed very broad categories when they came to identify both their principal supporters (e.g. 'landlords') and their opponents (e.g. 'the student and teacher class').[2] As we shall see, it is noteworthy that in his listing in 1936 of supporters of the Congress Prasad did not specifically mention 'the commercial communities', whereas in the lists the British made these figured very largely. For in neglecting the commercial communities Prasad was anticipating the short shrift they have received from the majority of the modern generation of Indian historians—the present author amongst them.[3]

A great deal of research has been devoted to the processes by which there came to be enlisted in the Congress and in its support those who, in Prasad's phrase, had 'been to school and college'— the 'western educated'. The participation of goodly numbers of them in the various Associations which sprang up, particularly in the major cities of India, through the middle of the nineteenth century and prior to the founding of the Congress in 1885, is now well known.[4] The role of such people in the foundation of Congress has been extensively explored,[5] and the part they played in its first twenty-five years as well.[6] There have been particular studies too of the activities before and after the First World War of the largest concentrations of them in Bengal,[7] and in Bombay,[8] while their counterparts in Madras have had their historians for these years as well.[9] Their activities during the First World War have then been variously recounted,[10] and the considerable part they played between the two World Wars figures very largely in most standard accounts of the major agitations which Gandhi led in those years.[11] Their participation, moreover, in nationalist politics at provincial level have been extensively recounted for that later period, in Madras particularly.[12] If detailed studies are not quite so abundant for other areas, there is nevertheless considerable information on the part they played in UP,[13] CP,[14] Bihar,[15] and even Orissa[16] and Assam.[17] We have been given a clear picture as well of the various stances of the many 'western educated' who were not fully-fledged members of the Congress but who nevertheless periodically gave it much support—strong when its actions tallied with their interests, weak, sometimes in the extreme, when it did not: a characteristic of all such categories, as we must note.[18]

Latterly much attention has also been given to the progressive accretion of support to the Congress of well-to-do peasant communities across most—though not all parts—of India from around the end of the First World War to the end of the Second.[19] Broadly this seems to have begun in parts of Bihar.[20] That was soon paralleled in Gujarat[21] and in West Bengal.[22] Similar support then came dramatically from the Khudai Khitmatgars in the Muslim-majority Frontier Province around 1930 (a story which still seems to lack its professional historian), and around that time too or shortly afterwards in places as far flung as UP,[23] CP,[24] Madras,[25] Maharashtra[26]—though not, importantly, from the Punjab.[27] There were then later such accretions in the princely states as these came to be absorbed in the mainstream of Indian and Congress politics as well.[28]

The two principal sources of support for Congress which Rajendra Prasad identified in 1936 have now therefore been extensively studied—though clearly there are many deeper studies to be made than the first generation of scholars who have worked on these subjects could reasonably have been expected to cover.

Congress, of course, at the end of the First World War and through the Gandhi-led Rowlatt satyagraha and Non-Co-operation movements also enjoyed the powerful co-operation of a great many Indian Muslims who were intent on pursuing their contemporaneous Khilafat movement.[29] One of the major facts of South Asian history in the subsequent period is, of course, that Congress lost that support.[30]

This was not the only category of Indian society, however, that came to be much dissociated from the Congress. The 'subaltern' school, as well as others, has begun to elucidate one of the dimensions to the story here.[31] The disjunctions between the separately propelled concerns and agitations of various UP peasants and those of the principal Congress leaders and their supporters in that province have been recounted,[32] and likewise those in Bihar.[33] These disjunctions were clearly very much more widespread than traditional accounts have allowed. They were present in CP, Gujarat, Maharashtra, and West Bengal,[34] quite apart from those areas where the Communist Party was to become very influential, such as Kerala.[35]

There were corresponding disjunctions between the strikes and agitations of urban workers and the campaigns of the

Congress. This was particularly the case in Bombay in the late 1920s and early 1930s;[36] but it was also the case in Madras.[37] These divergencies tallied very closely with Rajendra Prasad's acknowledgement in 1936 that Congress had by then only managed to secure support from 'a sprinkling of industrial and field workers'.

One further category of supporters of the Congress has also now been closely studied—India's commercial and industrial capitalists.[38] They became increasingly important to it in the last decade or so before independence, as they distanced themselves the more steadily from the British, and allied themselves the more closely with the Congress 'Right'. Like the 'western-educated', and like the richer peasantry, they numbered amongst them those who could not be relied upon to support Congress wholeheartedly when the going was difficult;[39] but they were very clearly a powerful addition to the Congress, as its struggle with the British reached its climax.

In these studies of the involvement of India's capitalists in Congress politics there is frequent reference to the fact that they themselves arose out of, and maintained close connections with, India's merchant communities. It is freely acknowledged too that the generality of these merchant communities were ordinarily much more staunch in their support for the Congress than the wealthier, increasingly distinguishable, capitalists. But it is upon the activities of the latter that such studies are ordinarily focused, and it is hard to find any study that discusses to the degree that acknowledgment would seem to call for (or much evidence would seem to demand) the support for the Congress of the generality of the merchant communities themselves. There are important studies of them in the period prior to their extensive involvement in Congress politics,[40] but the most we seem to have at the moment for the later period is one study of them in Bombay,[41] which usefully distinguishes between 'marketeers' and 'industrialists', and gives as much space to the political activities of the former as of the latter. This present account cannot hope to make up for these shortcomings. All it can attempt to do is to draw attention to them, and reinforce its admonition by presenting one corpus of evidence of a very broad-brush kind, and another that reinforces a developing explanation.

In 1929 the Indian National Congress at its Lahore Congress committed itself to a campaign of Civil Disobedience against the British under Gandhi's leadership. This was launched early in the next year by his Dandi march. There followed the largest agitation against the British since the combined Khilafat/Non-Co-operation movement of 1920–2. It extended through the rest of 1930.[42] But early in 1931 it was called off, partly under pressure from the merchant communities who had originally participated strongly but were now seeing their trade endangered, and partly as a consequence of some marginally hopeful signs that were emanating from the first Round Table Conference in London.[43] The upshot was the Gandhi-Irwin Pact of March 1931. But that did not hold. During the Pact's currency a great many British officials came to feel very deeply that their previously dominant position was being seriously undermined, and by expressing their concerns to successive Viceroys, Irwin and Willingdon, they secured their agreement to the proposition that if there was any renewal of Civil Disobedience British repression would be swift and comprehensive. Following the Gandhi-Irwin Pact Gandhi had agreed to go to London and attend the second Round Table Conference. But on his return at the end of 1931 Civil Disobedience was erupting spontaneously in more than one part of India, and early in January 1932 the Government of India held to its word to its principal officials, declared a countrywide state of emergency, and swiftly incarcerated the Congress leaders and many of their chief supporters. It was to be some months before the back of the renewed campaign was broken, but in due course such was its fate even so.[44]

Before that had happened the Government of India had become increasingly concerned at the suggestions that were being made, chiefly in Britain, that all they had managed to do was to generate an immense 'sullen resentment' against British rule in India. They accordingly decided to enquire of their principal subordinates whether such was the case. 'It will be very valuable to have at this time', so the Home Member of the Government of India, Sir Harry Haig, ordered in March 1932, 'an authoritative appreciation of the state of public opinion'; and in a way that was entirely characteristic of the procedures of the British Government of India a circular letter was thereupon despatched to its provincial governments in which they were asked to report whether or not India was 'sullen'. The replies to this enquiry prove on investigation to provide a great deal more information than this rather banal question might on its own have evoked. For, most importantly for our present purposes, the provincial governments were also asked not only to report on a number of other matters too, but in particular on 'the classes of the people which are (a) sympathetic with and (b) opposed to the civil disobedience movement'[45]

It cannot be very often that an imperial power has attempted such a systematic survey of those who support it and those who oppose it, but this enquiry had essentially that purpose. It needs no emphasizing that imperialists' views of who may or may not be their supporters can be all too frequently myopic. But there would seem to be less reason to be quite so sceptical when they have counted their opponents. It is not particularly gratifying to have to acknowledge that one has opponents. It is important that they should be precisely identified; and as nationalist movements became very active they could usually be fairly easily discerned. Our present interest lies in noting that in the replies to the Government of India's circular a great many British officers gave far more prominence to the range, strength and importance of the support for the Congress and its cause among the merchant communities of India than is ordinarily specified in later accounts. They placed this fully on a par with that of 'the teacher and lawyer' class and significantly ahead of that of well-to-do peasants (upon whose support for the Congress at this time they were interestingly equivocal).

The nature of the replies to the questionnaire from the Government of India was principally determined by the great relief amongst its principal officers that the anguish they had felt whilst the Gandhi-Irwin Pact was in operation was a thing of the past. Interestingly some British officers clearly believed that whilst the short-term value to their position of the subsequent repression was not to be denied, it would soon be necessary to effect some significant measure of constitutional reform in India, if only to retain upon their side numbers of those who for the time being at least continued to lend them their support. Other officers, however, the majority perhaps, were prone to give vent to some rather more stereotypical feelings. Sometimes indeed in colourful language.

All were in no doubt that there were important figures in the country, and in many cases large parts of the population, who stood firmly on their side in being directly opposed to Civil Disobedience and its Congress architects. The characteristic list of such supporters included landlords, retired military and civil officers, and (to a notable degree considering the number of times they were specifically mentioned) 'Mussalmans'. This evidence confirms indeed that Muslim support for the Congress and its works was by the early 1930s near to minimal, and that the close alliance between the Congress and very large numbers of India's Muslims of a decade previously had now essentially disappeared. The detailed evidence upon this score which the returns provide will not be set out here. It is, however, both abundant and emphatic.

British calculations as revealed by the returns concerning the attitudes towards the Congress and its agitations of India's huge rural populations were, as we have remarked, decidedly and interestingly equivocal, and since the evidence they provide about these make an important contrast to that which they offer concerning the support for them from the merchant communities, it will be illuminating to canvass it.

Some British officers seemed in no doubt early in 1932 that they had their rural area firmly under control. To the District Magistrate of Muttra, for example, the issue of whether Congress enjoyed widespread support in his area hardly arose. 'Villagers as a whole', he reported, 'want nothing more than peace and order. They have no proper appreciation of what the meaning of *swaraj* is'. His Muslim colleague writing from Mainpuri was equally assured. 'So far as these provinces are concerned,' he remarked, 'the policy of Government in granting liberal remissions of rents and land revenue to tenants and zamindars, respectively . . . has gone a long way to allay agrarian discontent and to induce feelings favourable to the Government among the rural population'. From Sitapur came a similar story. 'The position in the rural areas', so the Deputy Commissioner put it, was 'excellent'. The District Magistrate in Kolaba was supremely confident as well. 'The masses as a whole', he reported, 'particularly the agriculturists, are loyal'. Whilst his counterpart in Thana put it differently, the substance of his report was the same: 'in rural areas people are so backward and poor that the vast majority do not understand politics'. Elsewhere hereabouts their colleagues wrote very similarly and merely added some particular details. In Ahmednagar, for example, 'the majority of the classes', the District Magistrate averred, were indifferent to the Congress agitation; 'under this head come the agricultural classes in general, such as the Marathas, Wanjaris, and Dhangars'. And his Sub-Divisional Magistrate concurred: 'the Maratha agriculturists...are not only loyal but are indifferent to any agitation against Government'. The UP government summed up the position in the rural areas as it saw this by including 'the better class villagers' in the list of those whom it reckoned were 'strongly opposed to the civil disobedience movement'; while the Government of Madras was still more olympian. 'The first point on which this Government would wish to lay special emphasis', it declaimed, 'is that in this Presidency the vast majority of the rural population, probably 95 per cent, take little or no interest in the civil disobedience movement.... This is particularly true of poor and backward areas which at no time have given any trouble'.

All the same the Madras government had to qualify this. 'The one important exception', it was obliged to state, 'is the rich deltaic area included in the Telugu districts of east and west Godaveri, Kistna and Guntur.... One mainly agricultural caste, the Kamma, has been specially prominent in its hostility to the Government.... Taking the Presidency as a whole it may be said that civil disobedience has been an active force in four Telugu districts, five Tamil districts...and the two West Coast districts.' There was likewise some frank reporting from Kaira district, in Bombay presidency. Here, as the District Magistrate reported, 'high caste Hindus and most of all the Patidar cultivators from which class hail the Patel brothers who also have their home in

this District are generally' supportive of the Congress; 'even
the elderly Patidar folk seem to be very largely disaffected'. The
Government of the Frontier Province felt it necessary to be candid
too: 'in the rural areas of the Peshawar District', it wrote, '...the
bulk of the menial non-landowning classes and non-occupancy
tenants together with a number of the smaller land owners' were
prominent among those supporting the Congress. In Peshawar
district the villain of the piece was, of course, the 'Frontier
Gandhi', Abdul Ghaffar Khan. In the Pali sub-division of Almora
district, so the Deputy Commissioner reported, the ring-leader
was Har Govind Pant. 'Here I must admit', he wrote, 'that there is
a considerable amount of Congress feeling.. [in] certain villages
mostly in the Ramganga valley and the salt pattis, but a good
many in other pattis as well.'

On closer investigation the pervasive impression is in truth
that many British officers were finding it extremely difficult to
judge their standing in the rural areas at all correctly. For example,
while the seemingly very confident District Magistrate in West
Khandesh emphasized more than once that 'Khandesh is rightly
described as a very loyal, contented and prosperous part of the
Presidency', he also stated: 'I cannot help feeling that the Congress
preaching has permeated deep down in the rural state. .... There
is of course no open defiance but the cultivators are prepared to
show their annoyance when it can be quietly and safely done'.
And the Government of Bihar and Orissa reflected this view: 'if
restrictions are removed', it wrote, 'and the Congress party begins
to function again, as it will do, the people, generally, will support
them for the same reason as before, because they are organized
and can reach the villages and can make active opponents
uncomfortable, and because any other party cannot and will not
do so'. From Rae Bareli there then came a report from a young
Deputy Commissioner which his Commissioner called 'by far
and away the best appreciation' he had seen. This stated:

I now come to a class which I am not prepared to include unreservedly
either amongst those sympathetic with or opposed to the civil disobedience movement. This is the cultivating class, mostly Hindu, and
forms of course the greater part of the population of this district.
I would say that in the case of 90 per cent or over of the individuals of

this class, there is no outward sign of opposition to Government.... The *kashtkar* and agricultural labourer, and with these may be included the petty proprietor, does not oppose the civil disobedience movement, nor unless he be actively stirred up by some agitator, does he actively support the movement. If he does actively support it, his motive is economic rather than national or political. He feels that times are hard, and if some one, such as the trained literate Congress agitator, promises him some pecuniary or material advantage, he is prepared to support civil disobedience. To some extent also an appeal to his religious feelings may win his support on either side. There is no doubt that there is a latent respect for Gandhi in his mind—whether he looks upon him as a saint or practically as a deity.

This degree of uncertainty imbues almost all of the more thoughtful accounts which British officers produced of peasant support for Congress in the early 1930s. Nevertheless it seems a reasonable conclusion that while there were clearly places where the Congress could claim a very substantial measure of support in the rural areas—for example, in parts of Madras and Bombay presidencies, and in the North West Frontier Province—and while the British position was clearly in doubt in a much larger number of other such places, nevertheless, whatever their apprehensions, the British were still by no means fully convinced in the early 1930s that they had lost the acquiescence in their rule of the vast rural expanses of India taken as a whole, and felt indeed that, by and large at all events, they just about still had the situation there under control.

This picture is worth portraying since although it is possible to find some similar equivocation in the reporting by British officers in early 1932 of their impressions of the attitudes of the merchant communities towards the Congress and its activities, the general impression which the returns provide on this score is strikingly different. Throughout the merchant communities were ordinarily placed very firmly amongst those who supported and/or sympathized with the Congress and its activities. It is important to note in this connection that the assessments which British officers provided in 1932 were given of a period when the Congress leaders were all in jail and when the Congress movement was suffering from one of its gravest setbacks. In these circumstances the pervasiveness of the support for the Congress from the merchant communities, as perceived by India's British administrators, becomes all the more notable.

In a good number of the responses to the questionnaire the merchant communities appear as a matter of course with the professional classes amongst those who were most sympathetic towards the Congress and its works. Those who were 'openly so', wrote the District Magistrate from Poona, comprised 'Konknastha Brahmins (mostly Chitpawans), Gujaratis, Marwaris'. In Belgaum, the District Magistrate put it: 'Generally speaking the professional and trading classes and educated persons in general', were all staunch Congress supporters; 'the distribution being of course very much more urban than rural'. And the general picture as seen by the British was depicted by the Government of Bombay when it declared that the Congress 'naturally appeals most to the professional and educated classes and to the Hindu commercial communities'. To this the UP government simply added a few elaborated details. Those supportive of the Congress movement were, it said: '(a) the student and teacher class; (b) the petty intelligentsia of the towns; (c) the Hindu shopkeepers, moneylenders and businessmen; (d) the better educated middle class population, such as lawyers and politicians; and (e) the unemployed and loafer class both in town and country'. For the most part other respondents generally aggregated similarly.

Given the fact that the extent of the support for the Congress is not often detailed—at all events to the extent that such testimony suggests can occasionally be done—it is permissible perhaps to set out at some length some of the specifics which these returns contain. Fortuitously two sets of district officers' responses to the Government of India's questionnaire that were sent on to it are readily to hand, and it is from these that the more detailed testimony can be drawn. One of these came from UP.

From this a remarkably consistent picture emerges. L. M. Stubb, the Commissioner of Kumaon, for example, expressed himself as being in no doubt that 'the educated or professional classes and the mercantile community' in his division were strong in their support for the Congress. And he went on:

There can, I think, be no doubt that the state of the world's trade has
given great strength to the movement of discontent, and that if trade
had been good one would have heard less of civil disobedience. The
commercial community feel as do the educated unemployed that things
could hardly be worse and that any change must be for the better....The
next consideration may not seem at first sight to be a strong one but I
really think it has importance. Gandhi is a Bania and the commercial
class is predominantly ruled by Banias.... Propaganda on the side of
Congress has been extraordinarily astute and it has not I think been
generally recognized how deep that propaganda has penetrated. It is
at least three years ago that I was told by the late Nawab of Rampur
that the jewellers of Delhi with whom he had an extensive acquaintance
had assured him that they were prepared to face any risk or loss of
business in the event of a real *swaraj*. That they should express an
opinion of this kind in the face of so confirmed a reactionary as His
Highness was, I think, a remarkable illustration of the depth of their
feeling.

Stubbs's colleagues had reached very much the same conclusions. The Deputy Commissioner of Naini Tal put the matter
curtly: 'the lawyers, educated and Bania classes' seemed to
him 'all pro-Congress in sympathy'. His counterpart in Almora
detailed a similar impression; 'the shopkeepers of Bageswar
and Someswar', he wrote, 'have always been sympathizers of
Congress'. In Bulandshahr the District Magistrate was evidently
a blusterer. In 'pungent terms he set forth his view of the similarities between Banias and Jews. 'The connection of this caste',
he wrote, 'with Congress activity is well-known, and it has been
suggested that most of the political agitation is a tremendous
ramp to enable the Brahman to regain and strengthen his old
social and religious power and to enable the Bania to make even
larger profits than he does at present'. The Deputy Commissioner
from Sitapur was rather more measured. 'In the urban area', he
found 'the attitude of the Hindus difficult to gauge'. Yet (he added)
'I should say that a large majority of them are really in sympathy
with the Congress and what it stands for. In this city there have
been constant *hartals*.... I have reason to believe that most of
the Hindu shopkeepers and traders are still subscribing secretly
to Congress funds'. His colleague, the Deputy Commissioner
in Rohilkhand, was inclined to think 'the Hindu shopkeeper

element' were not always 'whole hoggers'. All the same he included them in a now all but conventional list of likely 'Congressites'. For his part the Commissioner of Allahabad had no such hesitations: 'the Hindu of the city', so he intoned, 'be he trader or an ordinary professional man'—and we may note the recurring conjunction—'is in sympathy with the Congress aims which includes the creation of the Hindu *raj*, and his sympathy with the aims of Congress is stronger than his dislike of Congress methods'.

And so it was upon similar lines that virtually all the UP returns reported. 'Traders, moneylenders and the moneyed classes generally', came the refrain from the Commissioner of Fyzabad, 'includes many who sympathize with Congress, notably among town dwelling Hindus'. To the District Magistrate of Muttra it was clear that a principal

class sympathetic with the movement is the small shopkeeper class of the Vaish and Kayastha communities. This class is always resentful of taxation, and hopes to obtain remission of taxation through the Congress.... He feels that a Congress *raj* with Mr Gandhi at the head will be favourably disposed to the Vaish community...the Vaish community appreciate immensely the glamour with which Mr Gandhi has surrounded himself as the Mahatma. He is the first Vaish to come into prominence, and the community is proud of this.

This emphasis upon Gandhi's particular importance to the merchant communities figures as well in the other cache of provincial returns which is readily available, more particularly since this comes from Bombay presidency. Hardly surprisingly, in view of Gandhi's long association with the city and the region, the District Magistrate from Ahmedabad reported that there 'the influence of Mr Gandhi is very great indeed amongst the urban population of the District. Large numbers of almost all communities regard him as little less than a deity and would be unwilling to oppose actively any programme he might sponsor, even though it were opposed to their business interests.' And from Thana there came the corresponding report that 'the younger generation...seems convinced that Mr Gandhi's is the only method for achieving political freedom within the shortest possible time...the younger generation which includes professional as well as business men is generally in favour of it.'

The message from the Southern Division was more genera-lized: Congress' supporters included there, so the return ran, 'a proportion of the well-to-do trading class'. And from Ahmednagar came a similar report: the sympathizers with Congress here included 'most of the trading classes', Gujaratis and Marwaris in particular. The same was reiterated from West Khandesh: 'amongst the Hindus themselves in the mercantile community, which consist very largely of the Gujarathis and Marwadis sympathy with the Congress propaganda and methods is very widespread'. Whilst the 'hard-hearted Deccanies' might be more hesitant, 'the logic of the mercantile community at the present time', so the district officer averred, 'is very muddled and there seems no possibility of producing in their minds anything like an intellectual conviction of the soundness of the Government position in the present struggle'. So it was in Poona too: 'in Cantonment', the District Magistrate remarked, 'the Gujarathi trader class are still sympathetic with Congress and in City I believe many of the shopkeepers support Congress demonstra-tions with money subscriptions. In the District Gujar trading classes are in one or two places notably Paud and Saswad conti-nuing to support Congress'. And from Sholapur came a similar account: 'practically all Gujarathis (who are of course immigrants in the Deccan)', so the district officer expressed it, 'are either openly or secretly in favour of the movement'. The same was said of Bijapur, and of Kolaba too. The Collector of Ratnagiri seemed to sum up the case. Along with the usual array of 'educa-ted' supporters 'those sympathetic to the C.D. movement' were, he said, the 'Wanis: who are usually small merchants and money-lenders. They believe they would be better off with swadeshi trade, and with greater opportunities for more profitable money lending under Congress auspices. They also think that their casteman Mr Gandhi cannot do without their assistance in his movement against Government.'

Yet it was the Commissioner of Police from Bombay who penned the most perturbed report. He was in no doubt that Bombay had emerged from the situation a year previously when 'Congress activities were allowed such license ... that the impression grew that Congress was a mightier force than Government'. But now in April 1932, after four months of emergency rule, it was, he bemoaned, 'my opinion that Congress still has greater power in certain parts of the City than Government has'. Whilst there were some signs of business interests revolting against it, nonetheless

where these business men are Gujeratis their sympathies naturally are with Mr Gandhi and Congress, and if they are beginning to smart under the tyranny of Congress, as I believe they are, their opposition to the Ordinances must grow colder and colder until finally they may be glad to seek their protection. But this is not going to happen rapidly. Congress is still powerful, and men who have posed as staunch patriots cannot easily turn for protection to the very power that Congress is seeking to destroy.

In the face of all this evidence of how it appeared to the British—each officer writing quite independently of his colleagues—it seems essential to grant the merchant communities of India a principal position in the front ranks of India's nationalists in a way that does not seem to have been sufficiently allowed to them hitherto. Whilst in the longer run the more prosperous peasant communities were to be perhaps of even greater importance to the Congress, the merchant communities more generally seem to have been earlier upon the scene. In 1936 even Rajendra Prasad underestimated their importance—though perhaps inadvertently.

What lay behind this development by 1932 of such strong and extensive support for the Congress from the Hindu merchant communities of India has still to be explored with the specificity historians have accorded to the other adherences to the Congress. All that can be attempted here are one or two pointers. We should begin by recalling that there is now a strongly argued case that especially in the eighteenth century India's merchant communities grew in strength, cohesion and wealth. At the same time they were always strong in their adherence to their Hindu religious values and practices, and in particular gave very freely of their wealth to religious and charitable foundations. They then became closely associated with the British conquests of India, not only by providing the finance and the provisions the British needed, but through the benefits the y themselves obtained, from, for example, greater security for their trade.[46] Thereafter some of these trading communities much extended their reach, sometimes outside India, but not least within India itself, the Marwaris above all, and into Calcutta especially.[47]

Superimposed upon the peasant economy of India which centred about agricultural production and weekly and bi-weekly markets and periodic fairs, these merchant communities conducted the very much wider 'bazaar' market which came to spread throughout the subcontinent. They rarely exercised very much direct control over peasant production itself. Rather, they managed the seasonality of Indian agricultural production by means of loans to and purchases from peasants; stored the grain, oil seeds, fruits, etc. which this produced; and then marketed these not only locally but sometimes to quite distant places as well. Within the networks all this entailed they traded gold and silver, and increasingly piece goods and other retail items also. In these connections many of their members acted as bankers and commission agents, and not infrequently conducted trade upon a large and extensive scale, using in particular the long established system of credit notes, *hundis*. By 1930, 35 out of the 38 million tons of rice, wheat and linseed produced in India were being marketed in this manner, and goods of this kind that were being carried by rail within India itself comprised nine times the amount exported overseas.[48]

In the cities and towns of India leading members of these merchant communities were always closely involved in urban politics, and not least during the latter part of the nineteenth century.[49] They soon became variously represented as well at the Congress' annual meetings.[50] But characteristically they were much more cautious in its early years in giving vent to strong nationalist aspirations than the more actively nationalist 'western educated'. Many of them were wary, it seems, of breaking their links with their British rulers, with whom they had long been associated, and from whom they continued to derive a number of benefits. Whilst the Banias, Aroras and Khatris

of the Punjab fell into conflict with the British at the turn of the
century over the Punjab Land Alienation Act, and men like
Lala Lajpat Rai figured very largely thereafter in the Congress
movement, even here the adherence of the merchant communities
to the Congress continued to be highly problematic, at all events
until around the end of the First World War.[51]

It would seem to have been very largely the effects of that War
which brought about the crucial change, since thereafter large
numbers of the merchant communities across the length and
breadth of India did throw in their lot with the Congress, often
indeed extremely vigorously. Here contradictory processes had a
mutually reinforcing effect. In some places the huge rise in War and
post-War profits seems to have triggered one change of considerable dimensions. For some of the more successful of these merchant
communities now felt themselves to be fully capable of generating
considerable wealth without having to hold on to their former
British connections—and indeed were now finding that British
policies were curbing rather than assisting their activities.[52]
Elsewhere, however, it was commercial failure that more often
turned members of merchant communities against the British. For
simultaneously many other members of these communities
were being very seriously afflicted, by inordinate government
interference in their trade during the War, by the inflation that
occurred during and after the War, and by the disastrous slumps,
for example in the cloth trade, that accompanied these.[53]

All this was then compounded by the heavy increases in
taxation which the British imposed upon those they thought
could afford to help finance the War. Not merely did these give
rise to significantly enhanced customs and excise duties, but
more especially to a much more burdensome income tax and
even super tax. Each of these fell particularly heavily upon the
merchant communities. They were then especially affronted by
the culturally abhorrent intrusion into their personal affairs
which the newly enlarged income-tax collection entailed. And
in this and other connections many of them became particularly
concerned at the moves by the Government of India to extend
the extraordinary judicial powers it had secured under the Defence
of India Act during the War by means of the so-called Rowlatt

Act of 1919. Gordon and Ferrell have elaborated upon these issues, principally on the basis of the evidence from Bombay and Delhi.[54] A look at some further evidence from an otherwise often quoted source will serve to underscore their points.

In 1919, thanks in part to the deep antipathy towards its urban communities of Sir Michael O'Dwyer, its draconian Governor, the Punjab witnessed the largest urban disturbances in India in the immediate post-War period. Whilst O'Dwyer's government blamed their onset principally upon 'the professional classes', they also set out, in a submission to the Disorders Inquiry Committee their view that 'they [the professional classes] would, however, have achieved little success in the agitation but for the ready support of the shop-keeping and trading classes. It was the adhesion of this class', it declared, 'which secured the success of the agitation. In many cases the hartal of 6th April appears to have owed little to direct organisation of public men; so ready were the trading classes to accept the suggestion for a universal demonstration that the closure of shops appeared to many to be almost spontaneous'.[55]

On one of the major sets of issues which lay behind this ('the new Income-tax Act and the more searching methods of enquiry recently introduced') the Punjab's Financial Commissioner, the very distinguished Sir John Maynard, gave the enquiry a revealing note. 'Ancient Hindu policy', he stated, 'recognized the taxation of traders.... Historical accident and economic theories prevalent in Britain at the time of the annexation of the Punjab led to the condemnation of existing methods of taxing traders.... For years they escaped all direct taxation'. Whilst in due course income and excise taxes did come to be imposed, 'the burden was light,...the system of assessment . . . took the line of least resistance and treated the rich and influential very gently'. But then a new Super Tax in 1917, a new Income Tax in 1918, a new Excess Profits Tax in 1919, and above all a very considerable increase in the numbers and power of the tax collecting staff changed all of that fundamentally. Tax collectors were now empowered to conduct house to house surveys. They were empowered too to use any information they secured to determine an assessee's income. No assessee could object to the rate set unless he himself had made a full return, and any income that escaped tax, or had been assessed at too low a rate, could be reassessed in a following year. As a consequence in 1918–19, so Maynard reported, tax returns in Lahore city went up by 30 per cent, in Amritsar by 55 per cent, and in the other urban areas of the Lahore Division by on average no less than 217 per cent![56] It is scarcely surprising that India's merchant communities were now becoming very seriously alienated from the British when this was only one of the new afflictions being imposed upon them.

There was at the end of the War another consideration. In its aftermath the leadership of the Indian national movement passed into the hands of Mahatma Gandhi, and on at least four related counts that was of major importance for the adherence to it of India's merchant communities. The points are well known, but they warrant underlining. Gandhi himself was a Bania; Indian nationalism's principal figure was thus now one of their own. He was in addition a deeply religious figure. Given the importance of their religious commitments in the culture and values of these merchant communities, adherence to him accordingly involved not only a political but a religious involvement. That proved to be especially important for the powerful, wealthy and now very extensive Marwari community, which was especially influential in Calcutta. Two of its principal leaders, Birla and Bajaj, soon established highly personal associations with him of a quasi-filial and religious character.[57] But this consideration was important for the Gujaratis as well. On his return to India in 1915 Gandhi had made his base amongst them at his Sabarmati Ashram in Ahmedabad, and from there had established very close associations not only with Gujarat's principal commercial figures, but through them with the major Gujarati trading community in Bombay, and elsewhere too. In this and other connections it is perhaps worth stressing that whereas in relation to Congress' growing association with India's well-to-do peasants, the role of link figures (such as Patel, Abdul Ghaffar Khan, Prasad, Rajagopalachari and many a somewhat lesser figure) was often of great importance, so far as the merchant communities were concerned the link with Gandhi was far more direct, and was not shared to anything like the same degree with any other

prominent leader. That was one (sometimes overlooked) reason
for his dominance over the movement as a whole.

The immediate upshot in the post First World War years
was to be found in the heavy involvement of many members of
merchant communities, as in the Punjab, in the Rowlatt satyagraha of 1919, which in these terms marked the major breach in
the hitherto longstanding nexus between so many of the commercial classes and the British.[58] Thereafter there were all manner
of variations in the now largely new association between the
merchant communities and the Congress. Beyond those considerations just mentioned, four others flowed. In the first place
Congress could now ordinarily be assured of having access to
adequate financial resources. Secondly, the extensive, often
intimate, commercial networks across the length and breadth of
India which the merchant communities operated for their
commercial purposes soon began to be used for their new nationalist purposes also. Thirdly, merchant supporters of the Congress,
in the innumerable towns of India, were not only singularly
well placed to organize nationalist activities in them. Their
extensive commercial interactions with the local peasant economy
in their immediate vicinity provided them with a readymade
connection as they and others, under the leadership of Gandhi
and some of his leading lieutenants, sought to respond to the
nationalist impulses of well-to-do peasants and associate them
with the national movement too.

There were thereafter a number of special variations in the
active role played by the merchant communities in the Indian
national movement. These were the more particularly displayed
first in the major thrust they provided to the first Civil Disobedience movement of 1930, and most dramatically in Bombay, and
then in the check their leading spokesmen put upon this in 1931
when its elongation threatened to destroy their trade.[59] A similar
oscillation was exemplified when Civil Disobedience was
renewed in 1932. But, as the British recognized (and as we have
seen), and as subsequent electoral processes soon confirmed, to
a very considerable extent the commercial communities were
now wedded to India's nationalist cause as never before, and the
large majority of Hindus amongst them to the Congress in

particular. Some scattered information is available on these matters—but it would now seem timely to seek for more.[60]

As over a rather longer period and by other means (some of which have been spelt out, but others of which remain to be fully related),[61] well-to-do peasant communities came to adhere in large numbers to the Congress as well, so the alliance was created between the professional classes, the commercial communities, and the richer peasants in so many parts of India that for the rest of this century has so engrossed its life. Whilst that has been sufficiently emphasized, what perhaps has not—and in any event calls for closer comparative consideration—is the apparent unusualness of so large a role being played in the development of a country's anti-colonial nationalism by its merchant communities. Some fleeting examples of this could be found from Africa, especially West Africa (and one thinks of Oginga Odinga in Kenya too).[62] But perhaps the most striking comparison is with Indonesia, where, for a variety of reasons, no similar involvement by its merchant communities in the nationalist cause seems to have occurred, principally no doubt because the counterpart merchant communities there were mainly alien Chinese.[63] At the same time it may be too (as Ray has suggested) that indigenous traders in Indonesia were at this stage little more than peddlers;[64] they did not know the credit note and all which that involved; and thus had none of the expertise and range of connections which their Indian counterparts had to hand. If this is so then it becomes all the more important for historians to probe the more extensively the particularities of the adhesion of the merchant communities to the Indian National Congress. This sketch remains a plea for more study to be made of these matters, by way of a modest contribution to its discussion on the basis of presenting the evidence that many of India's imperial rulers on the ground had clearly come to believe, by 1932, that this was at least as great as that by the longer associated professional classes; and noticeably more so—for the time being at least—than by the majority of India's well-to-do peasants.

NOTES

1. Prasad's draft Mass Contacts Committee's Report, 1936 National Archives of India Prasad papers, IX, 36,4.
2. See below, footnote 45.
3. A welcome exception is S. Sarkar, *Modern India 1885–1947* (Delhi, 1983).
4. A. Seal, *The Emergence of Indian Nationalism: Competition and Collaboration in the Later Nineteenth Century* (Cambridge, 1968); S. R. Mehrotra, *The Emergence of the Indian National Congress* (Delhi, 1971).
5. Ibid; B. Martin, *New India, 1885* (Berkeley, 1969).
6. J. R. Mclane, *Indian Nationalism and the Early Congress* (Princeton, 1977); S. A. Wolpert, *Tilak and Gokhale* (California, 1962); B. Chandra, *Rise and Growth of Economic Nationalism in India. Economic Policies of Indian National Leadership 1881–1915* (Delhi, 1966); B. R. Nanda, *Gokhale, the Indian Moderates, and the British Raj* (Delhi, 1977).
7. J. H. Broomfield, *Elite Conflict in a Plural Society: 20th Century Bengal* (Berkeley, 1968); L. A. Gordon, *Bengal: The Nationalist Movement 1876–1940* (Delhi, 1974); S. Sarkar, *Swadeshi Movement in Bengal 1903–1908* (New Delhi, 1973); R. Ray, *Social Conflict and Political Unrest in Bengal 1875–1925* (Delhi, 1984).
8. G. Johnson, *Provincial Politics and Indian Nationalism. Bombay and the Indian National Congress 1880–1915* (Cambridge, 1973); R. Cashman, *The Myth of the Lokamanya; Tilak and Mass Politics in Maharashtra* (California, 1975).
9. R. Suntharalingam, *Politics and Nationalist Awakening in South India 1852–91* (Arizona, 1974); D. A. Washbrook, *The Emergence of Provincial Politics: Madras Presidency 1870–1920* (Cambridge, 1976).
10. H. F. Owen, 'Towards Nationwide Agitation and Organization: The Home Rule Leagues 1915–1918', in D. A. Low (ed.), *Soundings in Modern South Asian History* (London, 1968).
11. Particularly J. M. Brown, *Gandhi's Rise to Power. Indian Politics 1915–1922* (Cambridge, 1972), and *Gandhi and Civil Disobedience: The Mahatma in Indian Politics* (Cambridge, 1977).
12. E. F. Irshchik, *Politics and Social Conflict in South India: The Non-Brahman Movement and Tamil Separatism 1916–1929* (California, 1969); C. J. Baker, *The Politics of South India 1920–1927* (Cambridge, 1976); D. A. Arnold, *Congress in Tamilnad: Nationalist Politics in*

South India 1919–37 (Delhi, 1977); B. Stoddart, 'The Structure of Congress Politics in Coastal Andhra 1925–37', in D. A. Low, *Congress and the Raj. Facets of the Indian Struggle 1917–1947* (London, 1977).

13. G. Pandey, *The Ascendancy of the Congress in Uttar Pradesh 1926–34. A study in Imperfect Mobilization* (Delhi, 1978); L. Brennan, 'From one Raj to another: Congress politics in Rohilkhand, 1930–50', in Low, *Congress and the Raj.*

14. D. E. U. Baker, *Changing Political Leadership in an Indian Province: the Central Provinces and Berar 1919–39* (Delhi, 1980).

15. G. McDonald, 'Unity on Trial: Congress in Bihar, 1929–39', in Low, *Congress and the Raj.*

16. U. Mahanty, *Oriya Nationalism* (Delhi, 1982).

17. A. Guha, *Planter Raj to Swaraj: Freedom Struggle and Electoral Politics in Assam 1826–1947* (Delhi, 1977).

18. P. Spear, 'A Third Force in India 1920–47: A Study in Political Analysis', in C. H. Philips and M. D. Wainwright, *The Partition of India. Policies and Perspectives 1935–1947* (London, 1970).

19. D. A. Low, *Congress and the Raj, passim.*

20. Brown, *Gandhi's Rise to Power*; J. Pouchepadass, 'Local Leaders and the Intelligentsia in the Champaran Satyagraha (1947): a study in Peasant Mobilization'; *Contributions to Indian Sociology*, no. 8, 1978; S. Henningham, *Peasant Movements in Colonial India: North Bihar, 1917–1942* (Canberra, 1982).

21. D. Hardiman, *Peasant Nationalists of Gujarat; Kheda District 1917–1934* (Delhi, 1981).

22. Dr Hitesranjan Sanyal, Centre for Social Studies, Calcutta, is writing on this subject.

23. See Pandey, Breman.

24. See D. Baker.

25. See Arnold, C. Baker.

26. G. Omvedt, *Cultural Revolt in Colonial Society: The Non-Brahman Movement in Western India 1873–1930* (Bombay, 1976).

27. Prem Choudry, *Punjab Politics. The Role of Sir Chhotu Ram* (Delhi, 1984).

28. J. Manor, *Political Change in an Indian State: Mysore 1917–55* (Delhi, 1977); R. Jeffrey, 'A Sanctified Label—Congress in Travancore Politics, 1938–48', in Low, *Congress and the Raj*; R. Sisson, *The Congress Party in Rajasthan* (Berkeley, 1972).

29. Brown, *Gandhi's Rise to Power*; F. Robinson, *Separatism among Indian Muslims: The Politics of the United Province Muslims 1860–1923* (Cambridge, 1974); A. C. Niemijer, *The Khilafat Movement in*

India, (The Hague, 1972); G. Minault, *The Khilafat Movement, Religious Symbolism and Political Mobilization in India*, (Delhi, 1982); U. Kaura, *Muslims and Indian Nationalism*, (Delhi, 1977).

30. Philips and Wainwright, *Partition, passim*; D. Page, *Prelude to Partition: All-India Muslim Politics 1921–32* (Delhi, 1981).

31. R. Guha (ed.), *Subaltern Studies, Writings on South Asian History and Society*, successive volumes (Delhi 1982—).

32. See Pandey; M. Siddiqi, *Agrarian Unrest in North India. United Provinces 1918–22* (Delhi, 1978).

33. See Henningham; W. Hauser, 'Bihar Provincial Kisan Sabha 1928–1942', Chicago Ph.D. 1961.

34. See Guha, Hardiman, Omvedt, and O'Hanlon; D. Baker, '"A serious time": forest Satyagraha in Madhya Pradesh 1930', *Indian Economic and Social History Review*, 21.1 January–March 1984; S. Sarkar, 'Primitive rebellion and modern nationalism: a note on forest satyagraha in the non-cooperation and civil disobedience movements', in K.N. Panikkar (ed.), *National and Left Movements in India* (Delhi, 1980).

35. R. Jeffrey, 'Peasant Movements and the Communist Party in Kerala 1937–57' (mimeo).

36. R. Kumar 'From Swaraj to Purna Swaraj: Nationalist Politics in the City of Bombay 1920–1932', in Low, *Congress and the Raj*; R. Chandavarkar, 'Workers' Politics and the Mill Districts in Bombay between the Wars', in C. Baker, G. Johnson, A. Seal (eds.) *Power, Profit and Politics; Essays on Imperialism, Nationalism and Change in 20th Century India* (Cambridge, 1981); R. Newman, *Workers and Unions in Bombay 1918–1929* (Canberra, 1981).

37. E. Murphy, *Unions in Conflict; a comparative study of four South Indian textile centres* (Delhi, 1981).

38. V. Pavlov, *Indian Capitalist Class* (Delhi, 1964); B. Chandra, *Nationalism and Colonialism in Modern India* (Delhi, 1979); R. Ray, *Industrialization in India: Growth and Conflict in the Private Corporate Sector 1914–47* (Delhi, 1979); C. Markovits, *Indian Business and Nationalist Politics 1931–39* (Cambridge, 1985).

39. See Spear and Hardiman; S. Sarkar, 'The Logic of Gandhian Nationalism', *Indian Historical Review*, II, July 1976.

40. C. Dobbin, *Urban leadership in Western India: Politics and Communities in Bombay City 1840–85* (London, 1972); J. Masselos, *Towards Nationalism: Public Institutions and Urban Politics in 19th Century Bombay* (Bombay, 1974); C.A. Bayly, *The Local Roots of Indian Politics: Allahabad 1880–1920* (Oxford, 1975); R. Ray, *Urban Roots*

of Indian Nationalism, Pressure Groups and Conflict of Interests in Calcutta City Politics 1875–1939 (Delhi, 1979).

41. A. D. D. Gordon, *Businessmen and Politics: Rising Nationalism and a Modernising Economy in Bombay 1918–1933* (Delhi, 1978).
42. Brown, *Gandhi and Civil Disobedience.*
43. Sarkar, 'Logic of Gandhian Nationalism'; D. A. Low, 'Sir Tej Bahadur Sapru and the First Round Table Conference', in Low (ed.), *Soundings.*
44. D. A. Low, 'Civil Martial Law: the Government of India and the Civil Disobedience Movements 1930–34', in Low, *Congress and the Raj.*
45. The detail in this and the ensuing fifteen or so paragraphs is drawn from National Archives of India, file H. Poll. 4/28/32.
46. C. A. Bayly, *Rulers, Townsmen and Bazaars; North Indian Society in the Age of British Expansion* (Cambridge, 1983).
47. T. A. Timberg, *The Marwaris* (Delhi, 1978).
48. R. Ray, 'The Bazaar' (unpublished monograph).
49. Dobbin, Masselos, Bayly, *Local Roots*; K. Gillion, *Ahmedabad: A study in India's Urban History* (California, 1968); K. Jones, *Arya Dharma: Hindu Consciousness in 19th Century Punjab* (California, 1976).
50. P. C. Ghosh, *The Development of the Indian National Congress 1892–1909* (Calcutta, 1960), p. 24, Chart B.; G. Krishna, 'The Development of the Indian National Congress as a Mass Organisation 1918–1923', *Journal of Asian Studies*, May 1966, 25/3.
51. Jones, *Arya Dharma*; N. G. Barrier, 'The Arya Samaj and Congress Politics in the Punjab, 1894–1908', *Journal of Asian Studies*, XXVI, 3 May 1967.
52. Ray, *Urban Roots*; Gillion, *Ahmedabad.*
53. Gordon, *Businessmen and Politics*; D. W. Ferrell, 'The Rowlatt Satyagraha in Delhi', in R. Kumar, ed., *Essays on Gandhian Politics, The Rowlatt Satyagraha of 1919* (Oxford, 1971).
54. Gordon and Ferrell, ibid.
55. Disorders Inquiry Committee, *Evidence Taken Before the Disorders Inquiry Committee*, vol. IV, pp. 100.
56. Ibid, p. 235.
57. G. D. Birla, *In the Shadow of the Mahatma* (Bombay, 1953); idem, *Bapu—a Unique Association—correspondence 1940–47* (Bombay, 1977); Kaka Kalelkar, *Jamnalal Bajaj Ki Diary* (Allahabad, 1969).
58. Brown, *Gandhi's Rise to Power*; Kumar, *Rowlatt Satyagraha.*
59. Sarkar, 'Logic'.

60. E.g. Gordon, *Businessmen*; Pandey, *Ascendancy*; Sarkar, *Modern India*; Baker, *C. P. and Bihar*; Breman.
61. Low, *Congress and the Raj*.
62. J. S. Coleman, *Nigeria, Background to Nationalism* (Berkeley, 1958); Oginga Odinga, *Not Yet Uhuru* (London, 1967).
63. J. A. C. Mackie, *The Chinese in Indonesia; Five Essays* (Melbourne, 1976).
64. C. Geertz, *Peddlers and Princes. Social Change and Economic Modernization in Two Indonesian Towns* (Chicago, 1963).

IMAGES OF THE CONGRESS: U.P. AND BIHAR IN THE LATE THIRTIES AND EARLY FORTIES

CHANDAN MITRA

In April 1984 I visited some villages in the Masaurhi block of Bihar's Patna district, shortly after Kurmi landlords of the locality had avenged the murder of a kinsman by killing seven Harijans. While probing into the incident I spent some time at a *chamartola* in one of the affected villages and asked the residents who they had voted for in the last elections. 'We were not allowed to vote', said an elderly Harijan, 'These days they dont't let us go near the polling booth. But next time we will vote, come what may', he asserted. For whom? The Congress, naturally. I was surprised because the landlords here also support the Congress and officials claim this to be a 'Naxalite-infested' belt. I do not know if they were allowed to vote during the 1984 parliamentary or the 1985 assembly polls. Significantly, though, the Congress won both with massive margins in this region.

This essay seeks to probe the Congress's image in the Indian countryside, particularly the Hindi heartland of UP and Bihar. I believe that image has something to do with the party's continuing dominance of Indian politics. Of course, 'image' is not an autonomous factor and is related to socio-economic realities, but it undoubtedly supplements the Congress's appeal in the countryside. How do people view the Congress? What are their perceptions of the party that has ruled India since Independence with a brief interruption of thirty-three months (March 1977 to January 1980)?

It is worth keeping in mind that the Congress has been a party of government for over fifty years now. Since 1937, when it was swept into power in six provinces (under the Government of India Act of 1935), it has held office for over half a century in different parts of India, except between 1939 and 1946. But by coming to power in a majority of provinces in 1937 it had established its claim to being the successor government, and to that extent its perception at the popular level underwent a change from that year. In many senses this is a remarkable achievement, for few political parties anywhere, especially in the Third World, have been in power for so long. It is also noteworthy that despite widespread and frequent criticism of its record in office, the Congress's image remains basically favourable.

What are the ingredients of this image? How was it built over the years? To what extent did it suffer once the party of agitation became the party of government in 1937? What are the continuities, if any, between then and now? These are the points this essay seeks to probe.

A perceptive Jayaprakash Narayan was struck by the currency which the Congress's name had gained while campaigning for the 1937 election:

The other night, as I was returning from an election meeting I happened to pass by a smithy. Suddenly I heard the cry *Swatantra Bharat ki jai*, followed by the age-old cry, *Raja Ramchandra ki jai*. Apparently a group of workers was listening to a recitation of the Ramayana, which is periodically punctuated by the most popular of popular cries, *Raja Ramchandra ki jai*, etc. But the thought that a national cry had gained such respectability as to be coupled with this religious and deeply devout cry gripped my mind. It signified nothing short of a great mental revolution among the people. The Revolution has almost matured, I thought.[1]

During the same campaign Nehru, too, remarked on the 'magic' of the Congress name in the villages of UP.[2]

There were two basic factors which contributed to this image. First, the appeal of nationalism had begun to be felt in the countryside and the Congress had come to be identified totally with the concept of 'Swatantra Bharat'. Second, it was also seen as the party of the peasant, many of whom had been enfranchised by the new GOI Act.[3] Not every Congressman would have agreed with Nehru when he said that it was every partyman's 'primary duty' to make the Congress into a 'kisan organization'.[4] But as Swami Sahajanand put it after the 1937 victory, 'the conversion of the elections into a "peasant versus zamindar" or "poor versus rich" issue . . . gave the Congress its marvellous victory'.[5]

This was not too surprising given the attitude of the landlords, particularly in UP. Organized under the banner of the two NAPs (National Agriculturists' Party of Oudh and National Agriculturists' Party of Agra), the UP *taluqdars*, inspired by Governor Harry Haig's unreal assessment of their popularity, assumed that the tenants' votes were theirs for the asking. The Raja of Mallanpur wrote to the British Indian Association in all seriousness:

all the taluqdars should hold a meeting of their tenants in the important places of their estates in the presence of a representative of the BIA and ask the tenants what are their grievances and why they are so easily mislead [*sic*] by an outsider. The ancestral relations and the past and present favours of the landlords should be explained to them. They will say something which will be well-considered, after which they should be asked to sign an agreement that they will not vote for an outsider without the consent of the landlords.[6]

No wonder that 'the big landed magnates who [had] the cruel audacity to seek suffrage of those whom they [had] beaten, badgered and bled white . . . candidates who constitute [d] formidable combines of wealth and borrowed power',[7] were shocked to see 'before their very eyes their own tenants voting against their wishes'.[8]

The 'magic' of the Congress name was to a significant extent connected to the Gandhi myth. As early as in 1921, a CID official in Allahabad had been astonished by the currency Gandhi's name had acquired and the fascinating array of vocations attributed to him:

No one seems to know quite who or what he is. . . . He is a Mahatma, a
Sadhu, a Pandit, a Brahmin who lives in Allahabad, even a devta. One
man said he was a merchant who sells cloth at three annas a yard. The
most intelligent say he is a man who is working for the good of the
country, but the real power of his name is perhaps traced back to the
idea that it was he who got *be-dakhli* (ejections) stopped in Partabgarh.
It is a curious instance of the power of a name.[9]

There is already a great deal of evidence of Gandhi's acquisition
of the status of a legend in eastern UP.[10] Satinath Bhaduri's
remarkable novel *Dhorai Charit Manas* records how 'Ganhi
Bawa' could work miracles. If *bhakats* (disciples, believers) prayed
to him, his image was said to appear on the surface of a pitcher
filled with water. The Bawa was said to have ordered Dhangars
(an untouchable caste engaged in menial work) to give up eating
pork and chicken, and they did.[11] Even Muslims gave up eating
onions after attending one of Gandhi's meetings.[12]

Bhaduri also describes how the Congress's image and Gandhi's
appeal resulted in an upsurge of support for the party during the
1937 elections:

It has come! It has come! What has come? In the white box, what else?
The vote! The vote! Mahatmaji's khadi is white, his box is white too!
White will purify the dirt of men's minds. The zamindars have sucked
your blood white; so the colour of your box is white. You must put it
in, in the white box. . . . This is not a song in praise of the white box, it is a
song that will establish *ramrajya*; it is a song in praise of Ramchandraji's
and Mahatmaji's greatness. When people come to offer bribes on behalf
of the Circle Manager, the urge to lash out at them becomes uncontrollable. On polling day, when the Circle Manager removes the boats
at Kushighat, the same force inspires one to swim across. . . . When
Dhorai entered the voting chamber, the returning officer was scolding
Pitho Santhal. Apparently, Pitho had applied sindur (vermilion powder)
before putting his ballot paper into the box. Dhorai took his slip, bowed
respectfully and put it into the box.[13]

Jayaprakash Narayan corroborated this when he wrote:

On the first day I witnessed polling at two stations. The excitement
is indescribable. The entire prospect before the booths was a sea of
tricolours in which the ensigns of the rival candidates appeared as
specs of dust. National cries and slogans drowned everything else.
Crowds of voters came marching with banners and songs and the

raucous thudding of drums.... The response and enthusiasm of the people have been a revelation to us. And such touching faith in the Congress! Simple peasants, they enter the booth as if it were a place of worship, drop their cards in 'Gandhiji's box', and joining their hands devoutly, make their salutation.[14]

By the mid thirties the image of the Congress had come to acquire tangible proportions: it was reflected in folk-songs and ballads, among other things. Poets in the Bhojpur region composed songs glorifying Gandhi, Civil Disobedience and voluntary incarceration. Two examples of this innovativeness may not be out of place here:

> Gandhi ka aail jamana
> Devar jailkhana ab gaile
> Jab se tape sarkar bahadur
> Bharat mare binu dana re ...[15]

> (The age of Gandhi has come and my brother-in-law has gone to jail. Since this government's reign began, India has gone without food)

Another song, also sung by a woman, tried to capture a Bhojpuri wife's plea to her husband not to go away to a distant place in search of work:

> Ab hum katbi charkha, piya mati jahu bideswa
> Hum katbi charkha sajan tuhu lao
> Mili ehi se surajwa
> Piya mati jahu bideswa
> Deswa ke laaj rahe charka se
> Ganhi ke mano saneswa
> Piya mati jahu bideswa....[16]

> (Now my beloved I will spin the charkha, please do not leave me
> Bring me a charkha so that I may spin
> That is how swaraj will come
> The country's prestige depends on the charkha
> That is Gandhi's message
> Beloved please do not leave me....)

The role of the printed word in spreading the message of swaraj and the Congress, too, cannot be underestimated. A large number of pamphlets, amateurishly but forcefully written, conveying the nationalist message, emanated from the urban centres, notably Benares. Authors of these writings often stood on the roadside or personally distributed them at *melas* (fairs). The impact of such activity sustained over a long period was considerable.

The nationalist press also played an increasingly important role in the dissemination of this message. After Baburao Vishnu Pararkar, a Maharashtrian became editor of *Aaj*, the paper rapidly became an important vehicle of nationalist propaganda. With a readership that was probably ten times its circulation, *Aaj* influenced political opinion to a significant extent in the region around Benares.

By the late thirties, therefore, Congressmen had been able to create almost an institutional support base. With wealthy benefactors like Raja Shiv Prasad Gupta helping to establish Kashi Vidyapeeth (of which Acharya Narendra Dev was the principal), and men like Pararkar converting *Aaj* into a dynamic spokesman for the Congress, the party steadily acquired a degree of legitimacy which proved to be crucial in its years in power.

All these factors contributed to the Congress's magnificent victory in the 1937 elections. In UP it won 134 seats in the 228-member assembly, polling approximately 65 per cent of the popular vote. In the 152-member Bihar assembly, the corresponding figures were 98 and 75 per cent respectively.

A point that needs to be borne in mind here is that in a sense the Congress's image formed a collage: it was amenable to different, even rival, interpretations. The situation in UP was such that the Congress was seen primarily as a nationalist party which was simultaneously opposed to the landlords and committed to protect the interests of the tenants. In Bihar, matters were not so sharply defined as the Congress drew its support from many landlords too. But the Kisan Sabha's unstinted support to the Congress during the campaign and the conduct of a Congress Kisan Inquiry (whose report was never published, despite repeated pleas by Swami Sahajanand) helped to swing the enfranchised peasants fully behind the Congress.

Within the Congress there were groups in favour of and opposed to office-acceptance. The lively debate between them, widely reported in the press, also helped to sustain the Congress's split image. While Rajagopalachari and his supporters like Satyamurti pleaded for immediate acceptance of ministerial responsibilities so that relief could be provided to the people, the Congress 'left', particularly Jayaprakash Narayan, retorted:

Mr Satyamurti and certain others have spoken of benefits and ameliorative measures; of clothing the services in khadi; of flying the national flag over government buildings and so on. A rather doubtful fare. The Congress which has stood for large measures cannot forsake them and seek to appeal to the electorate with a programme of petty reforms.[17]

Although he was then Congress President, Nehru campaigned openly against getting into office: 'Our hands and feet will remain tied. We will not be able to do anything in particular in office', he told a meeting of the Allahabad DCC in February 1937. Opinion was divided down the line. When the AICC asked the PCCs to indicate their views, 13 favoured office-acceptance while 5, including the UPPCC, opposed it.[18] Within the UPPCC, 71 voted for rejection and 49 were in favour of taking office.[19] When the UPPCC asked the DCCs to react, 32 wanted the Congress to form a ministry while 10 opposed it.[20] In Bihar, those favouring office-acceptance outnumbered those opposed to it by 101 to 43 at the PCC.[21]

All this suggests that the notion of the Congress as a broad front encompassing a wide array of political opinion was largely valid. And during its years in office, the Congress was partly successful in sustaining its agitationist image because some sections within the party remained opposed to the ministries or, at least, were critical of many of their actions. The effectiveness of the radical groups within the Congress depended upon their physical strength within the organization. For instance, the large presence of socialists in leadership positions in the UPPCC ensured that the ministerialist and pro-kisan wings of the party did not pull altogether in different directions. In Bihar, on the other hand, the break came quite soon after a ministry headed by Sri Krishna Singh assumed charge in July 1937.

What role did the Congress ministries in UP and Bihar play as landlord-tenant tensions rose in both provinces following the party's assumption of office? Although there was no uniformity of approach, it is difficult to conclude that the ministries always and necessarily backed the forces of 'law and order' so to speak; nor did they inevitably intervene on behalf of the landlords.

In UP's Gorakhpur district, for instance, three Congress MLAs, Shibban Lal Saxena, Baba Raghav Das and Puranmasi Chamar were in the forefront of a major anti-landlord agitation that broke out shortly after the Congress came to power in the province.[22] Significantly, Gobind Ballabh Pant visited Gorakhpur personally after over-zealous officials had arrested the Baba, severely reprimanded the officers, wrote a strong note to Governor Haig, ensured the release of all Congressmen jailed in connection with the anti-landlord agitation and ordered the transfer of some officials.[23] All this reinforced the image of the agitating leaders and Shibban Lal Saxena, in particular, took advantage of this to expand his activities. Shibban Lal, however, was never popular with the party bosses in Lucknow or Allahabad who promoted Harihar Nath Shastri as a rival to him. But since he worked in the name of the Congress, Shibban Lal's agitational activities played a role in keeping alive the Congress's image as a fighting force.

The case of Kalka Prasad in UP's Rae Bareily district can be cited on the other side to show how the Congress leadership clamped down to curb the growth of radicalism within the organization. In Rae Bareily, the Congress was divided in two camps—one headed by the DCC chief, the Lal Sahib of Semri, a taluqdar, and the other by kisan activist Kalka Prasad. The latter's activities compelled the Lal Sahib to mobilize among the peasantry and he organized a big kisan *sammelan* which was addressed by prominent UPCSP leaders.[24] Kalka Prasad, in turn, invited Swami Sahajanand Saraswati, but sensing the division in the DCC, the Swami refused to address a meeting at first, and when finally persuaded only preached homilies.[25] Eventually, the Lal Sahib succeeded in getting the UPPCC Council to censure his rival, and a sulking Kalka Prasad was expelled from the Congress. What is significant here is that a *hartal* called by his supporters in Rae Bareily to protest against the expulsion flopped.[26] Later Kalka Prasad also fell out with Kisan Sabha activists when only 150 persons turned out for a meeting at Fursatganj to commemorate those killed in police firing there in 1919.[27]

Two points emerge from this. First, the pressure of radical activists forced even propertied members of the Congress to mobilize the peasantry with promises of relief in order to retain leadership positions. Thus, even if the radicals were prevented from capturing the Congress organization at the district level, they were partly instrumental in compelling the conservative Congress leadership to adopt agitationist postures. Second, a formal break with the Congress was politically suicidal for the radical leaders. Kalka Prasad's is a small but illustrative case: the fate of Swami Sahajanand Saraswati and the powerful Bihar Provincial Kisan Sabha later demonstrated this more clearly.

The conflict between the Congress ministry in Bihar and Sahajanand's Kisan Sabha is already well-known. A spate of agitations organized and led by the Kisan Sabha broke out all over Bihar shortly after the Congress assumed office. As early as October 1937 Patel had warned:

The Kisan Sabha will give much greater trouble in future and my opinion has always definitely been against their formation. Such rival organizations are bound to destroy the Congress prestige. Congressmen are forced to join these kisan organizations by the atmosphere created by the organizers. They are waiting for a time when they could displace us. That is why I have given them no quarters.[28]

In 1938, during the election of delegates to the Haripura Congress from Bihar, the ministerialist wing guided by Rajendra Prasad and the BPKS, which included the supporters of the CSP, fought a bitter, often violent, struggle.[29] The Kisan Sabha was routed in the unequal battle. Thereafter relations deteriorated sharply and the Kisan Sabha launched several major agitations to which the ministry reacted with full force.[30] By May 1939 the Socialists' Hindi organ, *Janata*, was moved to proclaim:

The poisonous tree planted two years ago by the Congress on its fertile soil has now come of age and begun to bloom. The toxic fumes emanating from it have engulfed every atom of the air that flows around us and is suffocating us. By inhaling these poisonous fumes, the nation is in its death throes.[31]

Clearly, as far as the left wing in the Congress was concerned, the ministries had outlived their utility and were being compared to a toxic plant.

In two years from that date, the Socialists had swung around fully behind the official Congress leadership, while Swami Sahajanand and the Kisan Sabha strayed further away.

When the Swami was released early in 1942 after his virtual conversion to Communism, he was a different leader altogether:

After condemning in his vigorous style his old opponents—the zamindars and the Congress ministry—he [Sahajanand] went on to praise British courage and advised the kisans to emulate it. He appealed for volunteers against Japan and said that without success in the war there could be no Kisan-Mazdoor Raj. He ended his speech with an appeal for money to purchase fighters and bombers. The Swami was also of the opinion that for the present, kisan versus zamindar disputes should be stopped.[32]

In a sense, the Swami was being honest when he said that under war conditions it was unrealistic to pursue agrarian struggles. The Socialists, who had by that time floated a rival BPKS, never said so openly, although they abstained from agitation in practice. But the Swami's solicitude of the British cause was to cost him dearly. And that was evident even before the turbulent events of August–September 1942. Officials who were inclined to be soft towards the Swami in line with the Government's policy reported that the ninth session of Sahajanand's BPKS at Sherghati drew a mere 5000, whereas the Socialists' rival show was estimated to have had an attendance of 70,000.[33]

A disillusioned Swami was later to write plaintively about the desertion of peasants during 1942:

Some of our workers were carried away by the current. . . . Those who have gone astray have done so owing to two reasons. Firstly, they wrongly thought this was freedom's fight and there was nobody to check them. Second, they belonged to the Congress too, and hence they thought it was their duty to obey the call when it came. Their double-loyalty is mainly responsible for their slipping away from our stand.[34]

Even more surprisingly, he subsequently remarked that in reality

few kisans participated in the 1942 movement for they understood more of 'concrete zamindari *zulums* (exploitation) and the
callousness of the banias than of an abstract swaraj.'[35]

The point here is not so much about the Left's failure in 1942:
enough CPI-baiting has been done on this issue, most recently
by journalists like Arun Shourie. Attention needs to be focused
on the Congress's ability to rejuvenate its image from time
to time through mass agitation. There is no doubt that the
stint in office, with its attendant role in the exacerbation of
communal tensions in north India, followed by a long period of
inactivity, had adversely affected the Congress's image; 1942
and mass violence resurrected it to a significant extent. In the
final analysis it did not matter how people interpreted the call to
agitation in 1942: the point was that it was conducted under the
Congress's leadership and when conservative Congress leaders
called a halt (as in Ballia after the district authorities had meekly
surrendered), the movement petered out.[36]

In Bhaduri's *Dhorai Charit Manas* the general disillusionment
with Congress in office is clearly shown. Ladlibabu, younger
brother of the village's oppressive landlord, has left home
to become a Congressman. After the election, however, he is
welcomed back by his brother and it is soon discovered that those
affluent men who had traditionally backed the British authorities
had no difficulty switching sides and rallying behind Ladlibabu.
He soon becomes chairman of the district board, and Mastersahib,
a dedicated Congress worker, is left out in the cold. The Bihar
government's tenancy legislation is also shown inadvertently to
work against the interests of the poor tenants. Interestingly,
however, this does not turn the Koeris and other lower castes
against the Congress. They lament that 'Mahatmaji's Congress'
has been hijacked by the Rajputs and other affluent men. And
when Mahatmaji calls for sacrifice, for the final assault on British
power in 1942, it is the poor peasants who readily join up.
Bhaduri's hero, Dhorai, joins an Azad Dasta, a revolutionary
group of freedom fighters, to work actively for independence.[37]

Is this all rural naivete; is the Congress's success in deceiving
the illiterate masses mere cunning of the Indian bourgeoisie
and its allies the big landlords? Such simplistic explanations do

not hold good for the obvious reason that it is patently absurd to suggest that the Congress has been consistently fooling people for nearly half a century.

And that brings us to certain concluding observations. It would be incorrect to suggest that the Congress worked consciously towards portraying a multi-faceted, split image, of trying to be all things to all men, during its first spell in office. However, as a broad front of diverse nationalist forces, it accommodated all these groups, allowed them to mobilize independently and even challenge the dominant leadership for control of the party machinery. If the challenge became too powerful, however, the dominant leadership determinedly and sometimes ruthlessly stamped it out. But in the years before independence groups that left the Congress risked political oblivion. This essay, as must be apparent, does not take communal mobilization into account.

In some senses the Indian National Congress today retains many of its earlier characteristics. It is not insignificant that the Indian National Trade Union Congress, affiliated to the ruling Congress(I), has the largest membership among central trade unions, far above the CPI-dominated AITUC. Organizations like the INTUC can be quite militant at times, despite the party it supports being in office.

Among the rural poor in most parts of India, except in states like West Bengal, Kerala and Tripura where the Communists have a foothold, the Congress has successfully maintained its dual image. And contrary to the general idea that the Congress has been confused whenever in opposition, it has used periods out of power to refurbish its image. Mrs Gandhi's ride on elephant-back over miles of slush to meet terror-stricken Harijans of Belchi in Bihar in 1979 is well known. In West Bengal today the Congress(I) has built up sizeable support in refugee-dominated slums in Calcutta's suburbs—traditional strongholds of the CPI(M).

My attempt here has been to draw attention to the dynamism of the Congress—a factor that often escapes the attention of historians and political analysts. Too often is the Congress viewed as an organization working towards the betterment of the affluent classes, shrewdly hoodwinking the masses. This, I suggest, may not be the whole truth. I have tried to examine the ingredients of the Congress's image in the 1937–9 ministry period and show why the party succeeded in retaining a dual image, as a party of government and a party of agitation. I have sought to demonstrate that even after independence the Congress has not lost its agitationist image altogether, even if the gloss of the pre-independence years has worn off.

In its centenary year as a political party the Congress faces only one major problem with regard to Indian polity. It has been unable, for various reasons, to come to grips with regionalism in India. Other forces it has successfully absorbed: the Congress can be communal, for instance, if necessary, albeit discreetly. But the failure to come to grips with rising regional aspirations has swept the Congress out of power in many southern states. And, to some extent, the CPI(M)'s domination in West Bengal, too, is not unrelated to regionalism. It seems, however, that under Rajiv Gandhi subtle attempts are being made in this direction. The Punjab and Assam accords are obvious examples.

NOTES

1. Jayaprakash Narayan, 'Political Earthquake in Bihar' in Yusuf Meherally (ed.), *Towards Struggle: Speeches and Writings of Jayaprakash Narayan* (Bombay 1946), pp. 201–2.
2. *Selected Works of Jawaharlal Nehru* (*SWJLN*), vol. 8, p. 21.
3. Compared to a mere 2.75 per cent of the population enfranchised under the 1919 Act, the size of the electorate rose to 13.3 per cent under the 1935 Act. In UP, franchise qualifications were lowered from those paying an annual revenue of Rs 15 to those paying Rs 5 or more and for rent payers from Rs 50 to Rs 100. In Bihar those paying nine annas or more in *chaukidari* tax (five annas for Scheduled Castes) became eligible to vote. Details of the new provisions are given in the 'Report of the Indian Franchise Committee', vol. 1 (London, 1932), pp. 61–2.
4. Congress President's Circulars to the PCCs on Labour and Peasant Organizations, *Indian Annual Register 1937*, pp. 220–1.

5. Swami Sahajanand Saraswati in the *Congress Socialist*, 20 Feb. 1937, Microfilm, Nehru Memorial Museum & Library (NMML), Delhi.
6. Raja of Mallanpur to Secretary, British Indian Association, quoted in P.D. Reeves, 'Landlords and Party Politics in the United Provinces', in D.A. Low (ed.), *Soundings in Modern South Asian History* (London, 1968), p. 275.
7. Jayaprakash Narayan, p. 197.
8. Rai Amar Nath Agarwal, Secretary, UP Zamindars' Association, in a letter to the *Leader*, Lucknow, 23 March 1939, quoted in P.D. Reeves, p. 2.
9. Home (Poll.), File no. 13, Deposit Proceedings, UP CID Report no. 1052 on Kisan Sabha agitation in UP, National Archives of India, Delhi.
10. See Shahid Amin, 'Gandhi as Mahatma: Gorakhpur District, Eastern UP., 1920–21', in Ranajit Guha (ed.), *Subaltern Studies III* (Delhi, 1984).
11. Satinath Bhaduri, *Dhorai Charit Manas* in *Satinath Granthabali*, vol. 2 (second edition, Calcutta, 1977), p. 35.
12. Ibid., p. 121.
13. Ibid., pp. 220–3, *passim*.
14. Jayaprakash Narayan, pp. 197–8.
15. See Krishnadev Upadhyay, *Bhojpuri Lok Geet*, vol. 2 (Allahabad, n.d.), p. 335.
16. Ibid., p. 336.
17. Jayaprakash Narayan, p. 125.
18. AICC Papers, File no. G-39(1) of 1937, NMML, Delhi.
19. Ibid.
20. Ibid.
21. Ibid.
22. For details see Chandan Mitra, 'Political Mobilization and the Nationalist Movement in Eastern Uttar Pradesh and Bihar, 1937–42' (Unpublished D.Phil. thesis, Oxford, 1983), pp. 45–7.
23. IOR, L/P&J/5/264, Haig to Linlithgow, 22 Sept. 1937, IOL, London.
24. Police Abstracts of Intelligence UP, 26 June 1937, CID Record Room, Lucknow.
25. Ibid.
26. PAI, UP, 26 Feb. 1938.
27. PAI, UP, 5 March 1938.
28. Rajendra Prasad Papers, Vallabhbhai Patel to Rajendra Prasad, 2 Oct. 1937, NMML.

29. See AICC Papers. Report of the Committee to Inquire into Violence during the election of delegates to the Haripura Congress, File no. P-6 of 1939–40, NMML.
30. Mitra, pp. 115–27, *passim*.
31. *Janata*, Patna, 18 May 1939, Microfilm, NMML.
32. Fortnightly Report, Bihar, 11 March 1942.
33. FRs, 11 April and 1 June 1942, Bihar.
34. Sahajanand Saraswati Papers, Sahajanand's report on the Quit India Movement to the BPKS executive, n.d., Microfilm, NMML.
35. Ibid.
36. Mitra, chapter 6, 'The Quit India Movement in Ballia'.
37. Bhaduri, *Dhorai Charit Manas*, pp. 224–9, *passim*.

THE CONGRESS AND
HINDU NATIONALISM

B. D. GRAHAM

From its foundation in December 1885 the Indian National Congress sought to involve Indians of all communities in its efforts to bring about social reform and to build a democratic political structure in India. Perhaps inevitably, it found itself treated with some reserve by the Muslims, many of whom felt that democratic government would mean government by Hindus. However it also became involved in an intermittent series of controversies with orthodox Hindus over the question of how the Indian polity should be defined: was it to be an expression of social and religious pluralism or a relatively monolithic entity based primarily on the culture of the majority community? By the turn of the century there were within Congress obvious differences of outlook between Hindus such as Tilak and those of more liberal views, and as time went on groups with varying commitments to Hindu nationalism were formed within the party. This essay aims to give a very brief review of the stages by which this process occurred during the British period, and to examine the circumstances in which a frontier was clearly and firmly established between the Congress and Hindu nationalist parties in the years immediately after independence.

I

Throughout the British period the Congress made fairly consistent efforts to maintain links with Muslim groups and, within its own ranks, to avoid divisions on communal lines, thereby upsetting those Hindu nationalists who wished to see the organization identify itself more explicitly with Hindu values. In December 1888 the Allahabad session of the Congress had adopted a rule excluding from discussion any subject to which the Hindu or Muslim delegates objected, but this was bound to be disregarded whenever a serious issue affecting the communal balance arose.[1] Its first substantial test occurred when regulations issued under the Indian Councils Act of 1909 gave Muslims separate constituencies in the Indian Legislative Council and in several provincial Legislative Councils. Criticizing this provision at the 1909 session in Lahore the Congress President, Madan Mohan Malaviya, blamed the Muslim League for proposing that religion should serve as the basis for representation. He claimed that

a great estrangement has taken place between Hindus and Mahomedans generally all over the country, but particularly in the Punjab and the United Provinces. Under the influence of this feeling, some of my Hindu brethren have been led to think and to advocate that Hindus should abandon the hope of building up a common national life, and should devote themselves to promote the interest of their own community as Mahomedans have tried to promote those of theirs.[2]

A few years later Malaviya was among the Congressmen who objected to the Lucknow Pact, the name commonly given to the proposals for constitutional reform which included recommendations for separate electorates for Muslims, even in those provinces where they formed a majority of the population. This was endorsed by separate sessions of the Muslim League and the Congress in December 1916, in spite of opposition from the All-India Hindu Sabha and Congressmen of Hindu nationalist leanings.[3]

The range of social groups which participated in the satyagraha against the Rowlatt Acts in 1919, in the subsequent Non-Co-operation campaign of 1920–2 and in the Khilafat agitation suggested that it might be possible to create a nationalist movement which cut across communal lines, but this proved not to be the case. In the mid 1920s there was a sharp increase in tension between Hindus and Muslims, brought about by a savage spiral of urban riots, by the *shuddhi* campaign on the Hindu side and by the *tabligh* and *tanzim* movements on the Muslim side, and by the growth of a virulent pamphlet literature expressing extreme communal views.[4] It was at this time that the Hindu Mahasabha, formed in 1915 on the basis of provincial Hindu Sabhas which had been established from 1907 onwards, began to adopt uncompromising attitudes about communal relations and to show an interest in contesting elections as a separate force; its more militant and anti-Muslim phase is usually dated from its Benares conference of August 1923, held under Malaviya's presidency.[5] It was Malaviya, too, who was the prime mover in the formation of an Independent Congress Party to take part in the 1926 general elections. In this venture he was aided by Lala Lajpat Rai of the Punjab and by M. R. Jayakar, the Maharashtrian leader, while in the United Provinces the new party was closely associated with the Hindu Sabhas of Agra and Avadh, where it made telling use of Hindu nationalist themes in its propaganda.[6]

Communal relations again seemed to be improving somewhat in 1927, when leading Congressmen made another effort to unite Hindus and Muslims behind a plan known as the Delhi proposals; this recommended, among other things, that further schemes to provide reserved seats for Muslims and other minorities should envisage joint rather than separate electorates. The essential points were endorsed by the Madras Congress session of December 1927, the principle of joint electorates making it possible for Congressmen such as Malaviya to support the scheme, and for a time the Hindu Mahasabha appeared to be at one with Congress. At a special Mahasabha meeting held during this Congress session, Malaviya told his audience that:

this Hindu Mahasabha was never brought into existence as a communal organization to fight against any community. It is national to the core. Nationalism is as much the creed of the Hindu Mahasabha as Hinduism itself. The main objects of the Sabha are (a) to promote greater union and solidarity among all the section [*sic*] of the Hindu community and to unify them closely as parts of one organic whole and (b) to promote good feelings between the Hindus and other communities in India and to act in a friendly way with them with a view to the attainment of a united self-governing Indian nation.[7]

However, in the following year the hopes for Hindu-Muslim unity were completely shattered: the Muslim League divided into two sections, the one for and the other against the Delhi proposals; the Congress was drawn into an extensive boycott of the Simon Commission and into the preparation of a 'Swaraj constitution' for India; and the Hindu Mahasabha rejected the Delhi proposals.[8] By this stage Hindu nationalist sentiment had become quite widespread in the northern provinces, but Congress leaders hoped that the problem of communalism would disappear once political parties were differentiated by social and economic alignments which cut across communal boundaries.[9]

The prolonged Civil Disobedience movement of 1930–3 again pushed communal issues into the background but the debate about separate representation for religious groups was revived in August 1932, when the British government announced a formula for the reservation of seats for Muslims and other minorities in proposed constitutional reforms. Known as the Communal Award, this formula was bitterly attacked by the Hindu Mahasabha and by Congressmen in the Punjab and Bengal, who feared domination by Muslim majorities. Pressure on the Congress to declare its position on the Award increased early in 1934, when moderate leaders were considering the possibility of contesting the elections for the Central Legislative Assembly which were due to take place at the end of the year. Malaviya was once more at the centre of events, and found himself torn in different directions; he was, according to one observer:

not quite sure what attitude he would take at the time of elections…he holds strong views about the Communal Award, and the Hindu Sabhaites who are eager to go to the Assembly have already begun to exploit him. There is a danger of another party being formed under the leadership of Pandit Malaviya if the situation is not handled tactfully and in time. About the communal question Panditji is sailing between the Congress and the Hindu Sabha. He agrees with none. He would like to have an amicable settlement and yet is not prepared reasonably to satisfy the Mohammadans.[10]

His position became even more difficult when the Congress Working Committee decided in June 1934 that the Congress 'can neither accept nor reject the Communal Award as long as the division of opinion lasts.'[11] Dismayed by the Working Committee's refusal to condemn the Award altogether, Malaviya and M.S. Aney resigned from the Congress Parliamentary Board on 28 July, and Malaviya made overtures to the Hindu Mahasabha. The Mahasabha's President, Bhai Parmananda, told a correspondent of the London *Times* that Malaviya would form a nationalist party to oppose the Congress and that, in constituencies where nationalists were not standing, his supporters would vote for Mahasabha candidates.[12] However, although the new party was formed at a conference in Calcutta in August, it chose to work within the boundaries of the Congress, admitting to its ranks those Congressmen who accepted its creed and generally choosing its candidates from amongst them.[13] Surprisingly, the Congress tolerated such an arrangement, and saw the Congress Nationalists win an important number of seats in the Punjab and Bengal when the Legislative Assembly elections were held in November 1934.[14]

Once again it was the debates on communal issues which, in the mid 1920s and the early 1930s, increased the contrast between two philosophical tendencies that were cutting across much older sectarian and provincial divisions of Hindu opinion within the Congress. The more moderate of these tendencies was Hindu traditionalism, which stressed the need to preserve Hindu religious beliefs and social practices and to foster the study of the Hindi and Sanskrit languages and their literatures. While a Hindu traditionalist might devote much of his public life to cultural associations and institutions dedicated to the promotion of Hinduism, he might well support the Congress as the expression of a purely political nationalism with clearly defined representative and constitutional objectives. On the other hand, the more uncompromising Hindu nationalist was concerned not simply to conserve Hinduism but to develop the latent power of the Hindu community and thus to promote Hindu *sangathan*, the organization of the Hindus, the approach advocated by V.D. Savarkar in his book *Essentials of Hindutva*, published in 1924.

However, at the time of the 1934 elections this differentiation of tendencies had not reached the stage of determining group alignments, and it was still possible for Hindu traditionalists such as Malaviya to form temporary alliances with men such as Bhai Parmananda and Dr B.S. Moonje, who were more inclined than he was to adopt Hindu nationalist positions.

The formation of the Congress Nationalist Party marked the high-point of Hindu nationalist influence within the Congress during the British period. After the 1934 poll the Congress Nationalist Party went into decline, and, although under Savarkar's leadership the Hindu Mahasabha entered another militant phase in 1937, its impact on Congress affairs remained relatively weak. Following the Muslim League's decision in 1940 to work for a separate state, the major division within the nationalist movement became that between the Congress and the League and it was only in the months immediately preceding independence, after the Congress had accepted partition as inevitable, that the Hindu Mahasabha and the Rashtriya Swayamsevak Sangh (RSS) (a volunteer organization which had, since its formation in 1925, built up a following in Maharashtra and the northern provinces) were able to adopt a distinctive position, based upon an uncompromising opposition to the formation of Pakistan. A number of Congressmen sympathized with this stand and the Congress leaders were once more faced with the problem of shoring up the barriers between their organization and the forces of Hindu nationalism.

The communal tensions which accompanied partition and independence further strengthened the position of the Hindu Mahasabha and the RSS, but these two groups were suddenly and dramatically isolated by the public reaction which followed the murder of Mahatma Gandhi on 30 January 1948. His assassin, a young Maharashtrian, was found to belong with his fellow conspirators to an extreme group within the Mahasabha, and the leaders of both the Mahasabha and the RSS were arrested, the latter body being declared an unlawful association. The RSS staged demonstrations against this ban in the winter of 1948–9, but eventually it agreed to adopt a written constitution and to confine itself in the future to 'purely cultural work'.

II

The ban on the RSS was removed on 12 July 1949, and by the autumn of that year both it and the Mahasabha, as well as other Hindu nationalist groups, were trying to re-establish themselves within Indian society. The position of the RSS was a particularly complicated one because although it had been strongly attacked by liberals and social democrats as a potentially fascist body, it was viewed with sympathy by Congressmen with Hindu traditionalist leanings, especially at the provincial and district levels. Under the new RSS constitution, its *swayamsevaks* (volunteers) were free to join any political party (except those which believed in or resorted to 'violent and secret methods to achieve their ends') and there appeared to be no reason why they should not apply to join the Congress.[15] The question of whether they could do so was first raised by the Bihar Provincial Congress Committee and the Congress Working Committee ruled on 5 October 1949 that members of the RSS could indeed enrol themselves as [primary] members of the Congress in terms of the organization's constitution; however, it also stipulated that 'volunteers of any other organisation cannot be enrolled as Congress Volunteers', that is, as members of the Congress Seva Dal.[16]

There can be no doubt that this was a considered decision because, when it came under attack, the Congress President stated unequivocally that the RSS was not 'the enemy of the Congress'. He also claimed that, unlike the Muslim League or the Hindu Mahasabha, the RSS was not a communal political organization: 'It may be and is a communal body but it has repudiated all connexion with politics'.[17] Other Congressmen disagreed with this view and on 17 November the Working Committee effectively reversed the earlier decision; pointing out that all primary members of Congress were subject to rules of discipline and that 'the members of RSS are no exception to these rules even if they choose to become primary members', it cited the rule that no Congressmen should organize or join any volunteer *dal* other than the Congress Seva Dal, which was tantamount to saying that an RSS swayamsevak could not be even a primary member of the Congress so long as he remained attached to the RSS.[18] Jawaharlal Nehru had been absent from the earlier meeting as he was on the point of leaving India for a trip abroad, but he returned on 14 November and his views may well have influenced the change of policy.

From this point onwards Nehru was forced by events to take a much stronger line against those elements in the Congress which were prepared to challenge the party's secular principles. The outbreak of communal violence in East and West Bengal in the winter of 1949–50 placed the Government of India under strong public pressure to deal firmly with Pakistan, on the grounds that the trouble had started in East Bengal and had been caused by the discriminatory policies of the Pakistani authorities. At the end of March 1950 Nehru, who had at one stage seriously considered resigning as Prime Minister,[19] wrote to the Home Minister, Vallabhbhai Patel, proposing that either the Working Committee or the All India Congress Committee (AICC) should meet to settle a clear line of policy. Nehru referred to Gandhi's wish that he and Patel should work together in the government and virtually implied that they were no longer in agreement about basic policies. He complained in particular about criticisms of the government's policies which Patel was alleged to have made at a private meeting with Congress parliamentarians and went on to make a general point:

The whole Bengal problem and the Indo-Pakistan issue have many facets—political, economic, communal, national and international. Of these, the communal aspect has great importance. Indeed the whole problem is in the nature of a communal problem. We have long stood for discouraging and putting an end to communalism. That has been the Congress policy and it has been repeated and affirmed by Parliament. We talk of a secular State. That of course simply means any normal State today, leaving out the abnormality of Pakistan's Islamic State. We adopted our policy regardless of what the Muslim League or Pakistan might say or do, because we thought that was the only policy, both from the idealistic and the practical and opportunist points of view. Any other policy could only lead to disruption and disaster. Certain organisations, notably the Hindu Mahasabha, adopted an exactly contrary policy, that is contrary to ours, though exactly similar, in reverse, to Pakistan's. I find that progressively we are being driven to adopt what is essentially the Pakistan or the Hindu Mahasabha policy in this respect.[20]

Nehru spoke of the insecurity of Indian Muslims and of minorities in general, and came very close to suggesting that Patel did not share his concern: 'In these circumstances, the fact that you and I pull in different directions, and in any event the belief that we do so, is exceedingly harmful.'[21] In a dignified reply, Patel explained how the private meeting had taken place at his house and how the Bengal crisis and other subjects had been raised, but although he agreed that he and Nehru differed in their approach he claimed that there had been no differences:

as regards the secular ideals to which we all subscribe and for which we all stand; in fact I have throughout emphasized the need for full protection of minorities in India and condemned violence. At the same time I have not ignored the basic cause of such violence, namely, what is happening in Pakistan and the bitterness which it engenders in the country. When we consider stern action to deal with trouble on our side we have to take into account this fact, for to ignore it would mean our depending on coercion and suppression to deal with the psychology of deep-seated grievances and prejudices as regards our neighbours which unfortunately has repercussion on the followers of Islam in this country.... I have also laid stress on the fact that our secular ideals impose a responsibility on our Muslim citizens in India—a responsibility to remove the doubts and misgivings entertained by a large section of the people about their loyalty founded largely on their past association with the demand for Pakistan and the unfortunate activities of some of them. It is in this light that to my mind some tangible steps to deal with the present situation become urgent and that is why I have been insisting on a well-considered, firm and determined line of approach.[22]

Shortly aferwards the Prime Minister of Pakistan, Liaquat Ali Khan, accepted Nehru's invitation to visit Delhi and on 8 April 1950 they signed the agreement which became known as the Delhi Pact, which was intended to reassure the minorities and to restore the situation in both West Bengal and East Bengal. However, although the crisis in the eastern region abated from this time onwards, the difference of outlook between Nehru and Patel remained a potential source of conflict within the Congress Party. Many northern Congressmen looked to Patel rather than to Nehru to deal firmly with Pakistan and to uphold the idea that India was a state which reflected the views of the Hindu majority, if not of the Hindu nation. Nehru on the other hand, had attracted the support of those who wanted the conflict between India and Pakistan to be treated as one between independent states rather than as one between rival communal forces. At the heart of Nehru's arguments was the assertion that India could be a secular state only if the Hindu majority refrained from imposing its religious and social values on society as a whole.

These issues complicated the problem of choosing the national president of the Congress when the election for this office came up at the end of August 1950. One of the candidates was Purushottamdas Tandon, a veteran Congressman from the United Provinces who had worked hard in the cause of Hindi, had expressed strong opposition to partition, and had contested the Congress presidential election of 1948 from a Hindu traditionalist position. It was in character that he should have presided over an All-India Refugee Conference at New Delhi on 29–30 July 1950, when he claimed that the main difficulty for the Hindus of East Bengal was that Pakistan was being administered as an Islamic state.[23] Nehru had known Tandon since childhood, but he nevertheless wrote to him expressing disapproval of his candidature and implying that he was an unsuitable nominee because of his links with Hindu traditionalism. Alluding to the need to 'fight against communalism', he wrote:

Unfortunately, you have become to large numbers of people in India some kind of a symbol of this communal and revivalist outlook and the question rises in my mind: Is the Congress going that way also? If so, where do I come into the picture, whether it is the Congress or whether it is the Government run by the Congress? Thus this larger question becomes related to my own activities.

I would have gladly welcomed your election to the Congress presidentship. But when I look at this matter impersonally and from the larger point of view I feel that this election would mean great encouragement to certain forces in India which I consider harmful. Hence my difficulty and my distress.[24]

Nehru also exchanged letters about the impending election with Patel, who told him that he should refer the policy questions to the Congress session which was to be held at Nasik after the completion of the presidential poll. In Patel's view:

A President has either to conform to the settled principles and programme or to quit. If Tandonji is elected, I do not think that the latter
alternative would ever arise. He is too good a disciplinarian himself to
present us with any such problem. It is, therefore, premature to settle
your mind on any particular plan of action in the event of his election.
I think we cannot take it for granted that he would follow a line of policy
and action contrary to Congress ideals and principles. We should wait
and see.[25]

However, Nehru continued to treat the matter as one of the
utmost significance, and informed Patel that he would not serve
on the Working Committee under Tandon whatever the Nasik
session might decide:

That decision was taken for two major reasons: that Tandon had
pursued during the past two years and was still pursuing a policy
which, to my thinking, was utterly wrong and harmful and his election
would undoubtedly give an impetus to this policy, and I must dissociate
myself completely from it. Secondly, because the election was becoming
more and more a [clash] between varying policies and Tandon became a
kind of symbol of one and was as such being supported widely by Hindu
Mahasabha and RSS elements.[26]

Despite Nehru's opposition, Tandon did win the presidential
election and, although the Nasik session then adopted resolutions
on communal questions and relations with Pakistan which
accorded with Nehru's views, the Prime Minister took some
time to join the new Working Committee. However, Patel's
death on 15 December 1950 deprived the Hindu traditionalists of their most effective spokesman in the Congress High
Command and Tandon of his principal ally. From this point
onwards Tandon's opponents forced him onto the defensive; he
finally resigned from office, and at an AICC meeting on 8 September 1951 Nehru was himself elected Congress President.[27]

By this stage the preparations for India's first general elections
under the 1950 Constitution were under way, and in the ensuing
campaign Nehru went to considerable lengths to warn that
the boundary which now separated Congressmen from Hindu
nationalists could not be crossed. He bitterly attacked communalist groups, amongst which he included the Bharatiya Jana

Sangh, a Hindu nationalist party which was being formed under the leadership of the former central minister, Shyama Prasad Mookerjee, with the support of the RSS.[28] In a letter to PCC Presidents on 19 September 1951 he said that:

Recent events have shown that some members of the Congress have functioned almost as if they were members of the Hindu Mahasabha or some like communal organisations. Indeed, some people have actually resigned from the Congress and gone over to the Jana Sangh. This itself is significant because a real Congressman should be as far removed from the communal organizations as anything can be. Our chief opponents in our work and in the elections are the communal organizations.[29]

In a circular of the same date he made a direct comparison between this boundary and another where distinctions were less important:

With the Socialist Party we have some differences, but there is also much in common. But there is almost nothing in common between the Congress approach and the communal approach. Therefore, Congress candidates must be chosen with particular care so that they might represent fully the non-communal character and approach of the Congress. Persons who have been connected with communal organizations should therefore be suspects from this point of view. This is important as there has been a certain infiltration, in the past, of communal elements in the Congress.[30]

Fighting a secular campaign, Congress won a convincing victory in the elections of 1951–2, while for their part the Hindu nationalist parties returned only a very few members to the Lok Sabha and the state Legislative Assemblies. In another letter to PCC Presidents, Nehru spoke warmly of 'our straight fight and success against communalism': 'We have seen at last that we need not be afraid of communalism and we need not compromise with it as many Congressmen did for fear of the consequences. Where we fight it in a straight and honest way, we win. Where we temporize with it, we lose.'[31] In fact, however, the problem was much more complicated than this. By his defeat of Tandon and his allies within the Congress organization, and by his stress on the need to guard against communalism in the selection of candidates and party members, Nehru had redrawn the boundary between the Congress and Hindu political groupings so that the area occupied by Hindu traditionalism became a kind of border zone, dangerous territory for Congressmen and a possible recruiting ground for Hindu nationalist parties. Providing that the right issues could be found, the Jana Sangh and other groups could hope to drain support away from Congress, particularly in the northern states. Shyama Prasad Mookerjee, the leader of the Jana Sangh, had quickly established himself as Nehru's principal opponent in the first Lok Sabha, and the National Democratic Party which he formed in parliament was clearly intended to establish a broad coalition of the non-Communist forces opposed to Congress rule. At that time, one such issue appeared to provide an ideal focus for a Hindu nationalist rally. This was the Kashmir problem, which caused feelings on the subcontinent to run very high during the course of 1952, and by the spring of 1953 the Jana Sangh, the Hindu Mahasabha and the Ram Rajya Parishad had decided to join forces in a campaign of agitation for the integration of the state in the Indian Union. The Congress secularists adopted the view that this campaign was simply a manifestation of communalism: the party's Working Committee claimed in May 1953:

The purpose of this artificial agitation has become increasingly clear and it is evident that it has little to do with the Kashmir issue, which it seeks to exploit and, in effect, harms in many ways. . . . It represents an attempt on the part of the most reactionary, bigoted and communal elements to obstruct the economic and social progress of the country to which the reactionary vested interests represented by these communal organisations are opposed.[32]

However, the agitation did not succeed: not only was the government able to contain it but the sudden death of Mookerjee on 23 June 1953 removed the one person who could have produced an effective Hindu nationalist rally around the issue.

III

By 1954 Nehru had not only succeeded in extending the meaning of 'communalism' to cover both Hindu nationalism and views which were no more than Hindu traditionalist, but he had also attached two distinct meanings to the term 'secularism': so far as minorities were concerned, he defined it as the right to freedom of religious belief and practice, and a corresponding obligation to respect the religious beliefs and practices of others; but so far as the Hindu majority was concerned, he used the term to mean restraint: 'by virtue of numbers as well as in other ways, [the majority community] is the dominant community and it is its responsibility not to use its position in any way which might prejudice our secular ideal.'[33] In the process, he had shifted and hardened the boundaries of Congress in relation to communalism; while he saw Congress as being engaged in its historical task of working for 'the real emotional unity and integration of India', he viewed Hindu nationalism as essentially a disintegrating rather than an integrating force: 'Every communal organisation deliberately seeks the dominance of its own community or special privileges for it. Some Hindu communal organisations talk about a Hindu Rashtra. It is patent that whatever that might be, it is neither nationalism nor democracy. It is a throw-back to some ideas of a medieval period.'[34] Such comparisons between 'secularism' on the one hand and 'communalism' and 'Hindu nationalism' on the other continued to be made frequently by Congress spokesmen in later years, and the party's emphasis on national integration, its extreme hostility to the Jana Sangh and the RSS, and its support for minorities were maintained throughout the 1950s and 1960s and continued by Congress (R) in the 1970s.

IV

In the late 1920s an observer might well have formed the impression that Indian politics were shifting rapidly towards party divisions on communal lines and that Hindu nationalism would become the dominant force in an independent polity. That this did not happen was due to several factors, but perhaps the most important was the ability of the Congress to confront the Muslim League (first in the late 1920s and subsequently in the period 1936–47) without magnifying the conflict between them; although it was under constant pressure from a section of its supporters to portray the struggle between the two parties as the reflection of a deeply-rooted antagonism between the Hindu and Muslim communities, it refused to abandon its secularist and pluralist principles. Its resilience was partly due to the strength of the Hindu traditionalist tendency within its own ranks; in one sense, Hindu traditionalism offered Congressmen a means of affirming their faith in the essentially Hindu character of Indian society while still allowing other religious groups and traditions to find a place in that society.

With the coming of independence in 1947 the conflict between the Muslim League and the Congress was translated from the national to the international plane of politics in the subcontinent. Within India, the League had ceased to exist and the Congress Party's nationalism was directed outwards towards those European powers (France and Portugal) which still possessed colonial enclaves in India, as well as towards Pakistan and, more remotely, China. With this shift in focus came demands to strengthen the Hindu traditionalist tendency within Congress and to give it more content and scope, mainly by converting its anti-Islamic attitudes into hostility towards Pakistan and scepticism regarding the political loyalties of Indian Muslims. Had Congress followed this course, it would quickly have acquired a Hindu nationalist orientation and drawn close to the Hindu Mahasabha and the RSS. That it did not do so was due both to the fact that the public reaction to Gandhi's assassination served to isolate the Mahasabha and the RSS, and to the fact that Nehru, by gaining virtually complete control of the Congress organization in the early 1950s, was able to strengthen the party's secularist tendency and to raise a firm barrier between the Congress and its Hindu nationalist opponents.

NOTES

1. M. V. Ramana Rao, *Development of the Congress Constitution* (New Delhi: All India Congress Committee, 1958), p. 2.
2. Presidential address at the Lahore session of the Congress, December 1909, in *Speeches and Writings of Pandit Madan Mohan Malaviya* (Madras: G. A. Natesan & Co, 1919), p. 116.
3. See Hugh F. Owen, 'Negotiating the Lucknow Pact', *The Journal of Asian Studies*, XXXI, 3 (May 1972), pp. 577–84; Francis Robinson, *Separatism among Indian Muslims: The Politics of the United Provinces' Muslims, 1860–1923* (Delhi: Vikas, 1975), p. 254; Mushirul Hasan,

Nationalism and Communal Politics in India 1916–1928 (Columbia, Mo.: South Asia Books, 1979), pp. 87–8.

4. See N. Gerald Barrier, *Banned: Controversial Literature and Political Control in British India 1907–1947* (Columbia, Mo.: University of Missouri Press, 1974), pp. 92–103.

5. On the origins of the Hindu Mahasabha, see Indra Prakash, *A Review of the History & Work of the Hindu Mahasabha and the Hindu Sanghatan Movement*'(New Delhi: The Akhil Bharatiya Hindu Mahasabha, 1938), pp. 1–31; Richard Gordon, 'The Hindu Mahasabha and the Indian National Congress, 1915 to 1926', *Modern Asian Studies*, IX, 2 (1975), pp. 145–71; Jürgen Lütt, 'Indian Nationalism and Hindu Identity: The beginnings of the Hindu Sabha Movement', Paper read to the 7th International Conference of the Association of Historians of Asia, Bangkok, 22–26 August 1977, pp. 2–9; B. B. Misra, *The Indian Political Parties: An Historical Analysis of Political Behaviour up to 1947* (Delhi: Oxford University Press, 1976), pp. 161–5; Hasan, *Nationalism and Communal Politics*, pp. 254–6.

6. See P. D. Reeves, 'The Landlords' Response to Political Change in the United Provinces of Agra & Oudh, India, 1921–1937': Unpublished D.Phil. dissertation, Australian National University, 1963, pp. 219–24; Gyanendra Pandey, *The Ascendancy of the Congress in Uttar Pradesh 1926–34: A Study in Imperfect Mobilization* (New Delhi: Oxford University Press, 1978), pp. 120–4. See also Gordon, 'The Hindu Mahasabha and the Indian National Congress', pp. 192–201; David Page, *Prelude to Partition: The Indian Muslims and the Imperial System of Control 1920–1932* (Delhi: Oxford University Press, 1982), pp. 73–140.

7. *Indian Quarterly Register*, 1927, II, p. 332.

8. See the account of the Mahasabha's annual session at Jabalpur in April 1928, as reported in ibid., 1928, I, pp. 424–7.

9. For an expression of this theory, see *All Parties Conference 1928, Report of the Committee....* (Allahabad: All India Congress Committee, 1928), p. 49. On the general events of the 1927–8 period, see Page, *Prelude to Partition*, pp. 141–94; Hasan, *Nationalism and Communal Politics*, pp. 263–305; Uma Kaura, *Muslims and Indian Nationalism: The Emergence of the Demand for India's Partition 1928–40* (Columbia, Mo.: South Asia Books, 1977), pp. 29–51.

10. Letter from G. D. Birla to M. K. Gandhi, 14 April 1934, in Birla, *In the Shadow of the Mahatma: A Personal Memoir* (Calcutta: Orient Longmans, 1953), pp. 136–7.

11. For the text, see *Congress and the Problem of Minorities: Resolutions adopted by the Congress . . . since 1885. . . .* (Allahabad: All India Congress Committee, n.d.), pp. 124–5. On the background to this decision, see John Gallagher, 'Congress in Decline: Bengal, 1930 to 1939', in Gallagher, Gordon Johnson and Anil Seal (eds.), *Locality, Province and Nation: Essays on Indian Politics 1870 to 1940: Reprinted from Modern Asian Studies 1973* (Cambridge: Cambridge University Press, 1973) , pp. 298–304; Choudhry Khaliquzzaman, *Pathway to Pakistan* (Lahore: Longmans Green, 1961), pp. 124–5.

12. *Times* (London), 31 July 1934, p. 13 d.

13. Ibid., 20 August 1934, p. 9 c.

14. See *East India (Constitutional Reforms—Elections): Return showing the results of the General Election to the Legislative Assembly in India 1934* (London: HMSO, 1935), Cmd. 4939. For a general account of this episode, see Misra, *Indian Political Parties*, pp. 306–7, and see also an article by Rajendra Prasad on the Communal Award published in the *Hindustan Review* (Patna) in September 1934, reproduced in Valmiki Choudhary (ed.), *Dr. Rajendra Prasad: Correspondence and Select Documents, Volume One (1934–1938)* (New Delhi: Allied Publishers, 1984), pp. 211–16.

15. The text of the preamble and the first five articles of the RSS constitution are given in S. L. Poplai (ed.), *India 1947–50: Volume One, Internal Affairs* (Bombay: Oxford University Press, 1959), pp. 554–5.

16. *Congress Bulletin* (New Delhi: All India Congress Committee) September-October 1949, p. 15.

17. *Statesman* (Calcutta), 11 October 1949, p. 3, reporting Dr Pattabhi Sitaramayya's statements at Kanpur on 10 October.

18. *Congress Bulletin*, November-December 1949, pp. 2–3. For comment, see J. A. Curran, *Militant Hinduism in Indian Politics: A Study of the R.S.S.* (New York: Institute of Pacific Relations, 1951), pp. 65–7.

19. See Sarvepalli Gopal, *Jawaharlal Nehru: a Biography, Volume Two, 1947–1956* (London: Jonathan Cape, 1979), pp. 82–7.

20. Letter from Nehru to Patel, 26 March 1950, in Durga Das (ed.), *Sardar Patel's Correspondence 1945–50*, x (Ahmedabad: Navajivan Publishing House, 1974), pp. 11–12.

21. Ibid., p. 13.

22. Letter from Patel to Nehru, 28 March 1950, in ibid., p. 19.

23. *Statesman* (Delhi), 30 July 1950, pp. 1 and 6.

24. Letter from Nehru to Tandon, 8 August 1950, in Das (ed.), *Sardar Patel's Correspondence 1945–50*, x, p. 198.

25. Letter from Patel to Nehru, 12 August 1950, in ibid., p. 212.
26. Letter from Nehru to Patel, 27/28 August 1950, in ibid., p. 221.
27. The fullest account of the complicated conflict between Nehru and Tandon is given in Stanley A. Kochanek, *The Congress Party of India: The Dynamics of One-Party Democracy* (Princeton: Princeton University Press, 1968), pp. 27–53.
28. On the formation of the Jana Sangh, see Balraj Madhok, *Dr. Syama Prasad Mookerjee: A Biography* (New Delhi: Deepak Prakashan, n.d.), pp. 45–73; Craig Baxter, *The Jana Sangh: A Biography of an Indian Political Party* (Philadelphia: University of Pennsylvania Press, 1969), pp. 54–80.
29. *Congress Bulletin*, September 1951, p. 173.
30. Ibid., p. 176.
31. Letter from Nehru to PCC Presidents, 8 February 1952, ibid., January-February 1952, p. 13.
32. From resolution adopted by Working Committee on 17 May 1953, ibid., May 1953, pp. 158–9.
33. Letter from Nehru to PCC Presidents, 5 August 1954, in Jawaharlal Nehru, *Letters to the PCC Presidents* (New Delhi: All India Congress Committee, 1955), pp. 19–20.
34. Ibid., p. 21.

THE CONGRESS AND THE
HINDU-MUSLIM PROBLEM
1920–1947

ANITA INDER SINGH

The terms 'Hindu-Muslim problem', 'communal problem' and the 'problem of minorities', have all been used to describe and analyse the developments that culminated in another category—the 'partition of India', in August 1947.[1] In each of these categories three factors—political division, the psychological fears of a minority that it will be dominated by the majority community, and social and economic differences—are inextricably interwoven. As this essay proceeds, the difficulties of untangling these threads will become evident; yet it is only by doing so that one can explain the diverse and complex hues that went into the making of communalism and nationalism in India before 1947.

The 'problem of minorities' raises the question why, if the Muslim minority was not able to accept a constitution for a united India in 1947, the same did not apply to Christians, Buddhists and Sikhs. It also reminds us to distinguish between a community as a *religious* minority or majority, and as a *political* minority or majority. The first is demonstrated by census figures. A political majority or minority is dependent on the extent of support a political party gains for its political programme. For example, Muslims were a religious minority in the NWFP in 1937, but the Muslim League was a political minority. This distinction is vital when we discuss Indian nationalism.

The 'communal problem' has usually suggested the different interests of different communities in India but failed to explain why in 1947 the divide occurred only along 'Hindu-Muslim' lines, and not between Hindus and Christians, Christians and Muslims or Hindus and Sikhs.

The 'Hindu-Muslim' problem can be used because a Muslim homeland was created on the subcontinent in August 1947. But is India only the homeland of Hindus? A 'Hindu-Muslim' problem assumes that Hindus and Muslims are homogeneous entities: their religious affiliation marks them off from other groups socially, economically, culturally, and politically. In one sense this is true, for a person may identify himself as a Hindu, Muslim, Sikh, Christian, etc. Merely by doing this he does not create a social or political problem. The problem arises when a unified 'Hindu' or 'Muslim' religious, political and social consciousness is assumed, which leaves no room for political and intellectual differences within a particular community. In this scheme of things we cannot have Congress Hindus, Mahasabha Hindus, Communist Hindus, anti-Congress Hindus; nor can we have League or non-League Muslims. Indeed, as the Muslim League was to claim after 1937, 'Muslims' were only those who supported it.

All this is not to suggest that religious or communal consciousnesses did not exist. They did exist, but they ran alongside, or cut across, divisions of caste, class, province and tribe. The question is why and how the religious division created a political breakdown in August 1947. The long-term answer to this question requires the investigation of the nature of communal consciousness to see how it varied in the contexts of caste and province, or within and outside the spheres of constitutional politics. Such an investigation is beyond the scope of this essay, which only probes the extent to which the Congress approach to the communal problem encompassed these dimensions, and what the results of its strategy were in 1947.

II

The Congress attitude to the Hindu-Muslim problem should be seen in relation to its main political demand—the extension of power to Indians. From 1885 to 1905 the Congress petitioned the British for the expansion of legislative councils and the admission of Indians into the civil service through competitive examinations, and Congressmen professed their loyal allegiance to the British crown. In a century of political and social revolutions these requests appear timid and suppliant, but in the heyday of imperialism they signalled the start of confrontation between Congress and the Raj. As some British officials discerned, the granting of Congress requests would eventually lead to the ousting of all Englishmen from India.[2] This was indeed the logic of the Congress claim. In 1920 the Congress demanded independence, the content of which included, after 1930, the severance of all ties with the British crown. The natural British reaction was to resist the claim for any degree of self-rule for Indians and, if compelled by political pressures, to grant some degree of it, only to preserve and strengthen the empire.[3]

The Congress aim was not only the negative one of wearing down the Raj, but also the constructive one of forging an Indian nation. Congress was aware that existing divisions of caste, class, religion and province were the strongest argument for the British to prolong their Indian empire and weakened the Indian claim to self-government. After 1920 the appeals of Gandhi and Nehru for unity were based on a recognition of these divisions and on the assumption of the separate identities of Hindus and Muslims. But different identities were not considered antagonistic to nation building; Gandhi and Nehru believed that the coming together of people with different historical and religious traditions would strengthen and enrich the foundations of Indian nationalism. Religious division was not synonymous with political division, and it need not stand in the way of nation building. Congress sought to create an entity that had not existed before. This was not unique to India. For example, Theodore Zeldin's account of the variegated hues that went into the making of another, very different nationalism and nation—that of France—serves both as analogy and reminder:

The French nation had to be created. The slogan *Vive la France*! was not just a formal salute but a positive assertion in the virtues of patriotism. . . . One should not indeed unquestioningly assume that the French were a single people, clearly defined by their political boundaries . . . the resistance that patriotism met, the varieties of allegiance that resulted from the clash of innovation and tradition, exactly what was involved in being French and how the sense of belonging to the nation was spread among different groups, all this is usually glossed over, because the division of Europe into nation-states has been regarded as natural and inevitable. But even the ideals that Frenchmen set themselves, the image of themselves that they formed, were not clear or distinct. . . . In political terms, France was one of the first 'nation-states' in Europe, but for long its unity was felt consciously more by its rulers than by its people. . . . Nationalism was an ideal as much as a fact, and it is important to distinguish between the two . . . The idealizers put forward theories as to what France ought to represent, and by force of repetition these theories have sometimes been accepted as the descriptions of what France in fact was.[4]

Nations, quite clearly, are made not born. The main question was how Indians could unite against the Raj and justify their claim to self-government and independence, and Congress strategies, especially after 1920, attempted to carve out the path to achieve this end.

Believing in political advance through negotiations and compromise, Congress was essentially a moderate movement. On the communal problem this meant, to a considerable extent, attempts at settlements with 'leaders' of society or communities whose political status often depended on social or professional background, and, more significantly, on the bestowal of 'leadership' by the British. But this seemingly commonsensical approach lacked content and analysis, and apart from appeals for unity did little to smooth out differences with Muslim politicians. It is worth noting that from 1885 to 1947 agreement between Muslim leaders and the Congress materialized only twice: in the Lucknow Pact of 1916 and for the Khilafat/Non-Co-operation movement of 1920–4. When these 'agreements from the top' broke down, Congress appeared bereft of alternatives to resolve communal discord either at the élite or at the popular level.

The paucity of analysis and the strategy of 'unity from the

top' meant that Congress glossed over the fact that much of the
Muslim opposition to it was based on political conservatism and
social snobbery. Symbolizing this opposition in the late nineteenth
century, Syed Ahmad Khan observed that the aristocracy would
not like decisions affecting their lives and property to be made
by men 'of low caste or insignificant origin, though [they] be a
B.A. or M.A., and have the requisite ability.' In 1906 Muslim
conservatives formed, with British connivance, the All-India
Muslim League, to prevent younger Muslims from joining
Congress. There was also conservative Hindu opposition to
Congress. In the late nineteenth century Hindu landlords thought
representative government was an absurdity and wanted Congressmen to be tried as public criminals; in the 1930s the Hindu
communal organization, the Hindu Mahasabha, felt that the task
of constitution-making 'should be the concern of the Emperor of
India'.[5] But the British ignored conservative Hindu opposition
to Congress, partly because it did not seek to displace the Raj,
partly because they found it expedient to recognize 'Muslim'
opposition to what they labelled variously as the 'Hindu' or
'Bengali' Congress. They thus emphasized the division between
Congress and Muslim conservatives not in terms of ideology
but in terms of religious identity. They introduced separate
electorates in 1909 to ensure that loyalist Muslims, and not
Muslims with 'advanced Hindu inclinations', were elected to the
legislature, and these Muslims would counterpoise Congress
demands for self-government.[6] The British therefore accepted
conservative 'Muslim' demands as representative of *Muslims* as
a *community* and demarcated their interests from those of Hindus
as a community. The 'Hindu' interest was identified with the
'advanced' political stance of the Congress. 'Advanced' in official
parlance generally meant anything that threatened British
influence and power.

In a situation in which the line between ideological and
religious divisions was often obscured, Congress attempts to
conciliate Muslim leaders stemmed from their desire to assuage
the fears of a *religious minority*. This blurred the political division
between Congress and Muslim conservatives—and complicated
the political stance of Congress. Thus, anxious to win over

Muslim leaders, Congress accepted separate electorates in the Lucknow Pact of 1916. There was irony and confusion in the fact that Congress, which claimed to represent all communities, signed the Pact with the Muslim League, which represented only Muslims. Congress leaders generally believed that Hindus, as the majority community, should be generous about accepting Muslim demands and so ease any Muslim fears about being dominated by the majority community. 'Generosity is not only good morals', wrote Nehru in 1929, 'it is often good politics and sound expediency.'[7] Gandhi's reasoning reflects the dilemma of the Congress need to win Muslim support, in its reluctant acquiescence to the Communal Award of 1932, which would institutionalize and perpetuate communal divisions. There was, he wrote to Syed Mahmud in April 1934, 'no escape' from the Award if the Congress was to secure Muslim co-operation and 'if we are to secure any advantage for the nation. The other alternative is retention of the status quo. Then the question of awards does not arise at all. There seems to me to be no via media.'[8]

Congress continually tried to win over Jinnah, one of the architects of the Lucknow Pact, which earned him Sarojini Naidu's epithet, 'Ambassador of Unity'. Congress leaders generally esteemed his political and intellectual calibre and what they regarded as his politically advanced position, in comparison to that of most Muslim politicians. 'So much depends on Jinnah', wrote Motilal Nehru with uncertain hope, just before the All-Parties Convention in 1927. Yet the correspondence between Congress leaders suggests that Jinnah differed with Congress more than with many of their contemporaries, and more than most later historians have cared to note. The Lucknow Pact was signed at a time when Congress was a very moderate organization in terms of aims *and* method, and when it had little interest in mass politics. Gandhi revolutionized Congress by making it a mass-based movement after 1920, and Jinnah totally disapproved of the mass politics of the Khilafat and Non-Co-operation movements. Congress leaders also appear to have been uncertain of Jinnah's stance on important political issues. For example, on 12 August 1929 Gandhi wrote to Motilal Nehru that Jinnah wanted one-third representation for Muslims in the central legislature and separate electorates if the remainder of his Fourteen Points was not accepted. But two days later Motilal Nehru noted that Jinnah was relying on the Fourteen Points to reinstate himself with his followers.[9] Jinnah's political conservatism was evident at the Round Table Conference in 1931, when he suggested that the British should satisfy the aspirations (for Dominion Status) of 'those parties who have checked, held in abeyance the party that stands for complete independence....'.[10] T. B. Sapru, hardly a radical, reported in April 1934 that Jinnah would not denounce the White Paper on Indian constitutional reform as most Muslim politicians had accepted it, and that Jinnah would not risk the new leadership which had been conferred on him.[11] In January 1935 Jinnah wanted Congress to refrain from attacking the White Paper, and in November 1939 he wanted Congress to renounce its anti-imperialist stance. On this occasion both he and British officials admitted that his stand was both anti-national and anti-democratic.[12]

At this point it is worth noting that both Hindu and Muslim communalists, and Jinnah himself, disapproved of the social and economic programmes of the Congress after 1931. Recent scholarship is critical of the moderation, even conservatism, of the Congress. But what of this statement by Muslim communalists at the Round Table Conference? Mixing politics with religion and highly overstating things, they asserted that the alternative to British rule was the 'ubiquitous supremacy of Hindu rule', under which 'there would be heinous strife between the virile and martial Moslem races and those many Hindus in whom the Congress Left-wing has sown the seed of insidious conspiracy and rebellion, blood-lust and lawlessness.'[13] In 1937 Jinnah scoffed at the Congress talk of 'dal-bhat', and for leading India to a communist revolution![14]

Partly because of its own political and social moderation, its preference for political solutions through the conference table and its lack of analysis of the communal problem, Congress never exposed the link between communalism and imperialism, or at least the mistaken and/or the expedient idea of the British and conservative Muslims that the British were protectors of Muslims against 'Hindu' alias Congress domination. Much of the Muslim fear of 'Hindu domination' was grounded in the belief that Muslims were inadequately represented in schools and colleges and in the services.[15] But if the criterion of backwardness is the representation of a community in such institutions in relation to its proportion of the population, most figures belie such a notion. Instead, one might look at figures on Indian and British representation in education and services as a whole. For example, the Simon Commission report of 1930 said that the total percentage of Indians in 'recognized' institutions was 2.96 per cent of the population in 1917, and 4.26 per cent in 1927. As for the services the British, who were less than two per cent of the population, held 58.69 per cent of all ICS posts in January 1937; Hindus had 29.99 per cent and Muslims 6.75 per cent at the same time. In the Indian Police Service the figures were 64.80, 17.6 and 16.7 per cent respectively in January 1940. In January 1946, only eighteen months before the transfer of power, the British held 49.32 per cent of all ICS posts, Hindus 34.54 per cent, Muslims 10.08 per cent. The pattern was repeated in the IPS at the same time: Europeans 60.41, Hindus 20.14 and Muslims 11.05 per cent.[16] So it would appear that Hindus and Muslims were 'backward' while the British made 'progress'. But such facts were not brought before the public by Congress leaders; this was probably one reason why wrong assumptions about the British, Hindus and Muslims persisted.

Like communal organizations, Congress anticipated that constitutional reform and advance would come from the British. The difference was that Congress expected the eventual achievement of Indian independence; Hindu and Muslim communalists were against independence and believed that only the British could safeguard the interests of their communities. This is reflected in the crass servility of Mahasabha leaders in September 1941: 'the Hindus, having no country beyond the frontiers of India to look for help . . . have always to be in association with Great Britain . . . . there is no other ally than Britain for them.'[17] The essential link between imperialism and communalism illustrates why Indian nationalism, represented by Congress, should not be confused with the Hindu nationalism or communalism of the Mahasabha. As Nehru put it in January 1934:

As a matter of fact they [communal organizations] function politically and their demands are political, but calling themselves non-political, they avoid the real issues and only succeed in obstructing the path of others. If they are political organizations then we are entitled to know exactly where they stand. Do they stand for the complete freedom of India or a partial freedom, if such a thing exists? Do they stand for independence or what is called Dominion Status? The best of words are apt to be misleading and many people still think that Dominion Status is something next door to independence. As a matter of fact they are two different types entirely, two roads going in opposite directions.[18]

Lord Templewood's description in January 1935 justified Nehru's suspicion of Dominion Status for India:

if these magiv [sic] words [dominion status] are likely to be of temporary value in pacifying the timid elephant on which the British Raj is riding, why not use them? They may mean little; there will be a British garrison in India; native States will remain under the paramountcy of the Kaisar-i-Hind, etc. . . . . English people don't sufficiently recognize the importance of soothing the invalids of the world. . . .[19]

III

The partial Congress strategy of winning independence through British-sponsored constitutional reforms meant that they negotiated *British* proposals for constitutional advance, which exploited Muslim conservatism as a counterpoise against the Congress demand for independence. Yet Congress hoped to secure the co-operation of the same Muslim leaders who were siding with the Raj and trying to preserve their communal privileges. It is hardly surprising that most negotiations between Congress and Muslim communal organizations proved infructuous.

It must be emphasized that their eagerness to win the support of Muslim communalists never induced Congress leaders to compromise their political stand, whether this was the expansion of legislative councils in the 1880s or independence after 1920. A little known letter from Motilal Nehru to M. S. Aney on 18 August 1928 illustrates the point well:

The recommendations made by [the Nehru Report] may roughly be divided into two classes: (1) Matters of great importance for our national growth and of permanent importance; (2) Minor matters and tentative arrangements designed to bridge the gulf between the communities ... we have not sacrificed any thing which falls under the first category. The one question therefore which presents itself to every true nationalist is: Are the matters falling under the first class to be sacrificed for those which fall under the second? I venture to think that the only possible answer is an emphatic 'no'![20]

But if agreement 'from the top' proved elusive, did Congress conceive any alternative to resolve communal differences? Gandhi's appeal for unity and non-violence was too general to be implemented by any party at any level, for it glossed over traditional structures of exploitation and social envy which sometimes contributed to communal violence. Nehru was one of the few Congress leaders to attempt any analysis of the communal problem. In the early twenties he attributed communal violence to religious bigotry and fatalism among the masses, and opined that education was the best answer to communal hostility. Here he ignored the possibility that communal acrimony sometimes reflected rivalries between upper or middle-class Hindu and Muslim élites. Following the widening of his mental horizons during his European visit in 1927, and influenced to some degree by Marxist philosophy, he started to analyse the communal problem in terms of the demands of communal parties and concluded that it reflected upper and middle-class interests and had no relation to the needs of the masses. Believing that economic issues deserved priority, Nehru suggested in 1930 that political representation should be on an economic basis which would 'automatically do away with the lines of demarcation along communal lines.' He also linked communalism with political reaction and asserted that as the Congress came into greater contact with the masses it would broaden its economic programme, and subsequently leave high and dry both imperialism and the communal reactionaries it buoyed up.[21]

Yet the Congress conception of Hindus and Muslims as separate entities left the field for only Muslim leaders to win Muslim mass support. One such occasion was the Khilafat movement, and the unity it fostered proved fragile and ephemeral, for it stirred religious rather than secular national con-

sciousness among the Muslim masses. At another level it was
the Praja party, led by Muslim politicians, which raised the
demands of upper tenants in Bengal after 1916. Basically the
movement represented agrarian discontent. But in a province
in which the majority of tenants were Muslims, and the majority of zamindars and urban classes Hindus, the Praja wave
eventually contributed to Muslim separatism. Again, because of
its initial distance from the masses, Congress attracted urban
and zamindari classes in Bengal, Punjab and Sind, who were
largely Hindu and regarded by poor Muslim tenants as oppres-
sors. Provincial Congress parties continually failed to organize
the peasantry in these provinces or to support radical agrarian
legislation of non-Congress ministries during the twenties and
thirties. The Congress conception of Muslims as an all-India
minority may have contributed further to this. Provincial
Congress Committees had 'minorities departments' in Muslim-
minority provinces but not in Muslim-majority provinces, in
which the question of Muslim support for the national movement
proved crucial.

It was not before March 1937 that Congress embarked on a
Muslim Mass Contact Campaign. The idea of mass contacts was
not new: Congress had extended its organization and outlined a
programme of social and economic reform to attract mass
support after 1920. What inspired the Muslim mass contact
campaign in 1937 was the dismal performance of communal
organization in the provincial elections of 1936–7. Congress
routed the Hindu Mahasabha in the general constituencies and,
in the words of Nehru, 'disabled it politically'. Nor was the Muslim
League's performance in the Muslim constituencies very credit-
able. The League won 4.8 per cent of the total Muslim vote in
British India in a political system based on separate electorates.
It was not in a position to form a government in any Muslim-
majority province, while Congress assumed office in the NWFP
and six other provinces. So it seemed possible that, even within
the imperialist framework, communal forces could be defeated,
and the British deprived of opportunities to exploit communal
issues.

However, the MMCP never really got under way. It was

poorly organized. As Congress relied on Muslim workers, the campaign could not be carried out where they were not available, and it had more or less fizzled out by the beginning of 1939. It alienated the League by competing with it for Muslim mass support, yet failed to achieve this support. In spite of the campaign Congress did not ignore the League and continued discussions with it between 1937–9, bestowing on it an importance it lacked in terms of popular Muslim support. But such parleys usually broke down because of political differences between the two parties, and the League's insistence that it be recognized as the sole representative of Muslim interests. Here the League assumed a separate and unified Muslim interest, which was unacceptable to a Congress which sought to win support for its political platform from *all* communities. All this meant that Congress had little to show by way of settling communal differences either at the leadership or mass level before the League demanded a separate Muslim homeland in March 1940. Moreover, since most Congress leaders were preoccupied with civil disobedience or were in gaol between 1942–5, Congress was unable to formulate any challenge to resist the call for Pakistan. This was evident in the election campaign of 1945–6, which saw Congress poorly organized (as in 1936–7) in the Muslim constituencies. The underlying explanation lies in the fact that mass contact was part of the strategy to win independence and not an end in itself, and was insufficiently developed even to achieve the primary aim of Congress. So it could hardly have been adequate to carry out the secondary aims, such as defeating communal organizations. The result was that Congress programmes simply did not filter down to Muslims.

IV

Partly because Congress operated within the imperialist framework, it was bound by its limitations. Its participation in elections based on separate electorates meant that it could not escape from making religious appeals or using symbols to win Muslim mass support. For, while they opposed separate electorates and religious divisions in principle, Congressmen could urge that 'no true Muslim' should support any candidate who believed in British beneficence for the realization of his rights. On the occasion of the Bijnor bye-election in October 1937, one of the reasons why Congress reportedly succeeded in avoiding the issue of Hindu versus Muslim being raised was that the Congress candidate pursued his campaign under a green flag similar to that of the Muslim League. Vying with the League in appeals to the religious loyalty of Muslims, the Congress only gave the latter the whip hand in religious propaganda: 'They remembered the prayer, but they forgot the chain of armour donned by the Prophet Muhammad when he went forth to fight the unequal battle with the infidels.... They misled the Muslims to the unworthy tenets of ahimsa.'[22]

V

The broad, catholic outlook of Congress was itself a weakness. In principle, anyone who supported its anti-imperialist platform could join it. But in a situation in which religious affiliation was often the basis of social and political identity, communal feelings could become more complex. The Hindu could claim that his roots lay in India itself; that he was 'more inextricably and more closely bound up with India' than any non-Hindu section. Similarly, turning to his religion for an identity, the Muslim looked beyond India, and here arose the problem of the 'extra-territorial loyalties' of Muslims. Muslims would have to reconcile their love of India with their love of Islam and profess concern over the fate of Turkey during World War I. Muslim loyalty to the Khilafat actually centred on an abstract of the institution: there was no profession of loyalty to the Khalifa himself, nor any great love of Turkey once the Khilafat had been abolished. In a sense it is not surprising that the abolition of the Khilafat should have seen an intensification of communal animosity. A psychological uncertainty about their position in India existed among Muslims even before 1924. Congress contributed to this by the withdrawal of non-co-operation in 1922, which was interpreted by some Muslims as an act of hostility. The abolition of the Khilafat cut the ground, as it were, on which Muslims found an identity, from under their feet, depriving them of a source of emotional sustenance. At a time when they felt that the Congress could not be relied upon to safeguard their interests—as the withdrawal of non-co-operation was followed by a return to the politics of working within the imperialist framework—communal feeling was heightened after 1924. For it was a time when nationalist sentiment was inchoate, and Muslims could have doubts, as Muhammad Ali put it in January 1913, about appeals 'to non-existent patriotism in the name of the nation that is yet to be.'[23]

VI

At another level both the Mahasabha and Congress wanted joint electorates—the first because joint electorates were expected to give upper and middle-class Hindus majorities in the legislatures; the second because they would help to forge a secular Indian nationalism. But because differences in terms of religion were often highlighted more than differences in terms of ideology, the coincidence of Mahasabha and Congress views dismayed most Muslim politicians, although the loyalist communalism of the Mahasabha and the nationalism of the Congress were poles apart.

The frequent fusion of 'Hindu and Congress' worked to the detriment of Congress, especially when Congress made the tactical error of working within the imperialist framework. Nothing illustrates this better than the Congress term in office in seven out of the eleven provinces of British India from July 1937 to October 1939. Acceptance of office made Congress an easy target of League attacks on its discrimination and 'atrocities' against Muslims. The allegations stemmed from the failure of the parties to resolve differences on communal issues. But since ideological differences often took on a communal colouring, the accusations against Congress ministries put Congress leaders very much on the defensive, and they did their best to ease Muslim fears of their intentions and assure the average Muslim voter that their political differences with the League did not imply hostility to Muslims as a community. British officials, hardly sympathizers of Congress, discounted the 'charges of atrocities.'[24] But this very desire to assuage Muslim fears suggests that Congress was far from being 'totalitarian'. Even before the publication of official League charges, Congress leaders themselves were aware of the occasional insenstivity of some local Congressmen. For example on 28 September 1937 Rajendra Prasad wrote to Vallabhbhai Patel that opposition to the hoisting of the national flag and the singing of Bande Mataram was gaining strength because of the 'thoughtlessness and inopportune action of our workers and sympathizers at certain places.' Patel concurred: hoisting the flag on buildings against the wishes of proprietors had no meaning. 'In fact, I regard it as an unseemly demonstration of our intolerance': (*sic*)[25] There is little evidence of what action was taken against such workers or against communal elements within Congress. It was only in December 1938 that the Congress Working Committee defined the Mahasabha and the League as communal organizations and banned its members from belonging to either of them and Congress simultaneously.

VII

'Pakistan' gained currency partly because of the recognition it received from Congress and British after 1940. The Cripps plan of March 1942 offered Pakistan as a real possibility after the Second World War; Rajagopalachari and Gandhi negotiated with Jinnah on the basis of the principle of Pakistan in 1944. The preoccupation of Congress leaders with civil disobedience after November 1939 and their incarceration during much of the War prevented them from formulating any effective challenge to the idea of Pakistan. In the post-War elections of 1945–6 the League's success in Muslim constituencies dispelled Nehru's notion that reactionary parties with medievalistic ideas did not win mass support, although it must be admitted that the League never publicly declared that it desired the prolongation of the Raj for at least another decade.[26]

In the negotiations with the cabinet mission from March to July 1946 Congress was still optimistic about winning an independent united India. The Mission Plan of 16 May 1946 came out against a sovereign Pakistan, and the Plan's grouping scheme was intended as a device to persuade the League into a constituent assembly for a united India. Nehru believed that once the parties entered the constituent assembly they would concentrate on social and economic issues affecting the whole of India and on the task of nation building. In any case, he held that provincial rivalries within the Muslim group of provinces would lead to the collapse of grouping—an assumption shared by the Muslim premiers of Punjab, Sind and the NWFP.[27]

But Congress leaders underestimated or glossed over the League's distrust of the Congress. Given that there had been no agreement between the parties since 1924, what were the chances of their agreeing on the method and results of the transfer of power? Congress leaders thought that their acceptance of the principle of Pakistan would assure the League of their good intentions; perhaps their idealism persuaded them that all Indians would eventually unite against the British. What they overlooked was the force of Jinnah's unwillingness to settle with them. 'But what have you to lose if no agreement is reached?' he had asked Linlithgow in January 1940.[28] When the British conceded the principle of Pakistan in the Cripps plan, he reportedly showed indifference to any rapprochement with the Congress. For, he said, the *British* held and would transfer or confer power, so why should he go out of his way to settle with the Congress'.[29]

The League accepted the Mission plan because it believed that a sovereign Pakistan was inherent in the grouping scheme and because of a British assurance to the League on 16 May 1946 that the British would accept responsibility for the procedure of the constituent assembly. Indeed, Jinnah's talks with Gandhi in September 1944 and his statements at the London Conference in December 1946 also show that he would not settle with Congress unless the *British* were prepared to enforce such a settlement.[30]

This would have been anathema to Congress, which would never have accepted British dictation to the constituent assembly. For their part the British feared widespread civil disobedience in the absence of a settlement and their inability to control mass unrest in 1946-7. They made it clear to Jinnah that they could not or would not assume responsibility for the procedure of the constituent assembly. Feeling betrayed by the British, the League rescinded its acceptance of the cabinet mission plan, and never entered the constituent assembly for a united India.[31]

Sadly, for a movement which had prided itself on the achievement of independence through non-violent secularism, it was the continual outbreaks of communal violence after August 1946, probably the worst in the history of India, and the League's determination to obstruct the working of the interim government for a united India, which brought home to Congress the impossibility of any rapprochement with the League. The Punjab massacres of March 1947 broke the last straw on the camel's back and on 7 March 1947 Congress demanded the partition of Punjab and Bengal. Partition came about because Congress did not achieve total unity, nor did it defeat Hindu or Muslim communal forces. Independence in August 1947 was only the essential first step in the making of the Indian nation.

NOTES

1. For example, the titles of books such as, C. Manshardt, *The Hindu-Muslim Problem in India* (London, 1936); K. B Krishna, *The Problem of Minorities* (London, 1939); A. Mehta and A. Patwardhan, *The Communal Triangle in India* (Allahabad, 1942); C. H. Philips and M. D. Wainwright (eds.), *The Partition of India: Policies and Perspectives 1935–1947* (London, 1970); the titles of my own work—'Nehru and the Communal Problem 1936–1939' (Unpublished M.Phil. thesis, Jawaharlal Nehru University, 1976), and *The Origins of the Partition of India 1936–1947* (Oxford South Asia series, 1987).
2. Crosthwaite to M. Wallace., 17 January 1887, Dufferin papers.
3. For the politics behind the Acts of 1919, 1919, 1935, see M. N. Das, *India Under Morley and Minto* (London, 1964); R. J. Moore, *The Crisis of Indian Unity* (Oxford, 1974); D. Page, *Prelude to Partition* (New Delhi, 1982).
4. R. Kumar, 'Class, Community or Nation', in *Essays in the Social History of Modern India* (New Delhi, 1983), pp. 47–68; T. Zeldin, *France 1848–1945: Intellect and Pride* (Oxford paperback, 1980), pp. 3–6.
5. S. Mohammad, *Sir Syed Ahmad Khan: A Political Biography* (Meerut, 1969), p. 6; and *Writings of Sir Syed Ahmad Khan* (Bombay, 1972), p. 181; M. N. Das, *Morley and Minto*, pp. 166, 175; my 'Nehru and the Communal Problem', pp. 24–5, 39–40; and *Pioneer*, 26 November 1888.
6. Minto to Morley, 31 December 1908, Morley papers, vol. 12, quoted in M. N. Das, *Morley and Minto*.

7. S. Gopal (ed.), *Selected Works of Jawaharlal Nehru* (hereafter referred to as *SW*), vol. 4, p. 187.

8. Gandhi to Syed Mahmud, 7(?) April 1934, Syed Mahmud papers. Congress leaders did not hold the British responsible for creating the communal problem, but for exploiting and so perpetuating it. The distinction is important. See Bipan Chandra, *Communalism in Modern India*, (Delhi, 1984), pp. 237ff. See also this letter from Gandhi to Motilal Nehru, 28 February 1928, Motilal Nehru papers: 'What a sorry exhibition we are making of ourselves.... We are engaged in an unequal duel; on the one hand we are clever whole-timers acting with one mind and with the greatest deliberation; on the other we are part-timers having many irons in the fire and having almost as many minds as our number. [*sic*] My hope however is the justness of our cause.'

9. Gandhi to Motilal Nehru, 12 August 1929, and Motilal Nehru to Gandhi, 14 August 1929, Motilal Nehru papers.

10. *Indian Round Table Conference 12 November 1930–19 January 1931. Proceedings*, Cmd 3778, 1931, p. 146.

11. T. B. Sapru to M. R. Jayakar, 2 April 1934, M. R. Jayakar papers.

12. Nehru to Zakir Husain, 25 November 1939, Nehru papers; Viceroy to Secretary of State, (telegram), 22 and 24 October 1939, Zetland papers, vol. 25; and Linlithgow to Zetland, 16 January 1940, Linlithgow papers, vol. 13.

13. *Indian Annual Register 1932*, vol. 1, p. 317.

14. *Bombay Chronicle*, 4 April 1937.

15. For example, see A. Seal, *The Emergence of Indian Nationalism*, (Cambridge, 1968), pp. 209, 305–6; P. Hardy, *Muslims of British India*, pp. 120–1, 123–4; A. Basu, *The Growth of Education and Political Development in India 1898–1920* (Delhi, 1974), p. 152; and P. Brass, 'Muslim Separatism in the United Provinces', *Economic and Political Weekly*, January 1970.

16. Home Establishments files 42/40 and 30/11/46.

17. B. S. Moonje to Linlithgow, 11 September 1941, B. S. Moonje papers.

18. *SW*, vol. 6, p. 183.

19. Note by Templewood, probably around January 1935, Templewood papers, file VII: 5.

20. Motilal Nehru to M. S. Aney, 18 August 1928, M. S. Aney papers.

21. See my 'Nehru and the Communal Problem', chapter 2.

22. *Morning News*, 28 October 1945. On communal consciousness at the popular level, some interesting insights can be found in the articles by P. Chatterjee, G. Pandey and S. Sarkar, in *Subaltern Studies* (New Delhi), vols. 1, 2, and 3 respectively.

23. *Comrade*, 11 January 1913, quoted in M. Shakir, *From Khilafat to Partition* (New Delhi, 1970), p. 76.
24. See for example, Haig to Linlithgow, 10 May 1939, vol. 6, Haig papers; Linlithgow to Zetland, 28 March 1939, vol. 17, Zetland papers.
25. Rajendra Prasad to Vallabhbhai Patel, 28 September 1937 and Patel to Prasad, 2 October 1937, Rajendra Prasad papers, file II/37.
26. P. Moon (ed.), *Wavell: the Viceroy's Journal* (Oxford, 1973), pp. 206–7.
27. For a fuller discussion of these points see, S. Gopal, *Jawaharlal Nehru: A Biography*, vol. 1 (London, 1975), pp. 326–8; R. J. Moore, *Escape from Empire* (Oxford, 1983); and my *Origins of Partition*, chapters 5 and 6.
28. Linlithgow to Amery, 16 January 1940, Linlithgow papers.
29. Cited in K. B. Sayeed, *Pakistan: the Formative Phase*, 2nd edition (London, 1968), p. 187.
30. Indian Conference in London, 4 December 1946, L/P & J/10/111.
31. See my *Origins of Partition*, chapter 8.

JINNAH AND THE
CONGRESS PARTY

SHARIF AL MUJAHID

In one sense, among the galaxy of INC leaders Quaid-i-Azam Mohammad Ali Jinnah (1876–1948) was unique. Being the first and best organized political party, Congress attracted at one time or another most prominent Indians, whether already established in or aspiring to leadership roles. A great many of these attained prominence in Congress, but a considerable number left it for various reasons and at various times. Such was the hold of Congress over the masses that once they walked out of the Party they generally went into comparative oblivion, their leadership and personal appeal losing much of its lustre. Jinnah was perhaps the only exception to this general rule. Despite walking out of Congress in 1920 he held, with a few others, the centre-stage in Indian politics for most of the subsequent seventeen years (1921–37).

In respect of his attitude towards the INC and vice-versa, Jinnah's political career (1904–48) may be broadly divided into three phases, one merging into the next. During the first phase (1904–20), he was deeply involved with Congress politics and policies and rose high in its echelons. During the second phase (1921–37), despite his alienation from Congress, he kept in close touch with its leadership, striking at times a posture identical or almost identical with Congress postures, and at other times trying to maintain some sort of relationship with Congress. About mid 1937 begins the third phase, when, confronted with and as a riposte to a radical shift in Congress' posture towards him and the All-India Muslim League (AIML), he began a marathon confrontation which ultimately resulted in partition and Pakistan in 1947.

This essay seeks to delineate Jinnah's relationship with Congress during the first two phases, the second more extensively because of its greater consequentiality. For one thing these two phases, as against his confrontation with Congress during the 1937–47 decade, have received scant notice; for another the third phase, being more critical and more crowded, calls for extensive treatment, entailing a longer study.

I

Jinnah had been active in Bombay's Anjuman-i-Islam affairs since 1897, but he formally launched upon a public career in February 1904, when he was elected to the Bombay Corporation. During the next two years he confined his activities to his metro-polis, being active in the Bombay Presidency Association (BPA) and the Bombay branch of the INC, besides the Anjuman and the Corporation. In March 1906 he resigned from the Corporation, and the following December he made his political debut at the all-India level as a delegate to the Calcutta (1906) Congress and Private Secretary to its President, Dadabhoy Naoroji. This was the year of the Simla deputation and of the foundation of the AIML at Dhaka. It is understandable that in the absence of a political organization of Muslims he should have started out with Congress; but why should he have waited seven long years before joining the Muslim League? This question becomes critical in view of the fact that almost all other Muslim leaders joined the League at the time of its foundation or soon after, and that there was no bar to simultaneous membership of the two bodies till much later.

The answer lies in the socialization process Jinnah had under-gone, the sort of personal, professional and social experience that had shaped his political attitude and orientation since the early 1890s. During his student days in England (1892–6) Jinnah had come, as had most Indian students, under the influence of nineteenth-century British liberalism. Indeed one of the little known facts of his early life is that even the change in his career from training in 'business' to law came as a result of his ardent admiration for the British Liberal leaders whose speeches he had listened to with avid attention in parliament during the first few months of his stay in London. 'The Liberalism of Lord Morley', he told Dr K. M. Ashraf years later, 'was then in full sway. I grasped that Liberalism which became part of my life and thrilled me very much.'[1] Jinnah's initial penchant for Liberalism came to be buttressed by his close association with Naoroji, a past Congress president and the foremost Indian Liberal leader in England. Naoroji's decision to stand for the British parliament enthralled Jinnah a good deal since it signified Indians claiming equality with Britons on British soil, and he reportedly worked hard in Naoroji's election campaign.[2] Naoroji thus became the chief formative influence in his life—and his political mentor.

A second formative influence during Jinnah's early life was the BPA, Bombay's foremost political body, which not only worked in concert with Congress but also claimed among its leading lights various Congress stalwarts and past presidents—such as Badruddin Tyabji, Gopal Krishna Gokhale, Sir Pherozeshah Mehta and Sir Dinshaw Edulji Wacha. Jinnah, once he had carved out for himself a place at the bar, became so actively involved in the BPA's activities that early in May 1905 it voted to send him, along with Gokhale, on a Congress deputation to England to plead for self-government for India during the impending British elections.[3]

A third influence was the cosmopolitan milieu and mercantile culture of Bombay which, with its *laissez faire* credo, reflected the ascendancy of liberal thought and put a premium on competition and the survival of the fittest. Metropolitan Bombay, over whose sprawling commercial landscape the tiny Parsi community dominated, provided as it were a living exemplification of the primacy of initiative, enterprise and hard work over numerical inferiority, racial prejudice and communal barriers. Additionally, the Parsis claimed a considerable share in the professions, were pre-eminent in Bombay's public life, and prominent in the INC at both the national and provincial levels. Jinnah himself belonged to the Khoja community (a microscopic minority (1 per cent) within the Muslim minority community) which had also made its mark in Bombay's business and commercial world, as had the Parsis. Given this Khoja legacy Jinnah naturally felt attracted to the Parsis. Early in his professional career he came in close contact with the Mehta group of lawyers, including Bahadurji, and Parsis figure a good deal among his clientele: seven out of the sixteen cases concerning mercantile interests he handled were Parsi, according to entries in his diaries for the years 1897–1903.[4] He also developed personal relations with a number of leading Parsis, which in part explains his later controversial marriage with Rutten Bai, the beautiful teenage daughter of the Parsi baronet Sir Dinshaw Petit.[5] The attributes of initiative, competitiveness, enterprise and hard work which he saw embodied in the Parsis of Bombay thus served as models through his own career. His belief in competitiveness, for instance, impelled him to move an amendment to A. Chaudhuri's resolution on competitive examinations and reforms at the Calcutta (1906) Congress. Jinnah objected to the application of the 'reservation' clause for the 'backwardly educated class' to Muslims and asked that 'the Mohammadan community [be treated] in the same way as the Hindu community';[6] he commended open competition between candidates for civil service posts to the Royal Commission on Public Services in India (1913);[7] and he called upon students to equip themselves in order to carve out a place for themselves in national life.

These beliefs seem to have prompted Jinnah, as they had prompted Tyabji two decades earlier, to join the INC.[8] Fashioned after liberal principles and cast in their mould, the INC was at that time pledged to take India on the road to self-government through constitutional means. The self-government ideal was itself first enunciated at the Calcutta (1906) Congress where Jinnah spoke on two resolutions.

During the years Jinnah was with Congress his allegiance to its creed, policy and programme was unreserved. For instance, much against the mandate of the community he represented in the Imperial Council, he moved at the Allahabad (1910) Congress the resolution deprecating 'the extension ... of the principle of separate communal electorates to ... local bodies'; this he did 'in response to the wishes of a great many leaders of the Congress'.[9] From early 1910, upon his election to the Imperial Council, Jinnah came in close contact with Nadwah, Aligarh and the Muslim League, especially because he was chosen by the League to sponsor the bill on Waqf alal Aulad, a problem of deep concern to Muslims since the time of Syed Ahmad Khan (1817–98). From this time on he strived hard to create an understanding between the Congress and the League, an *entente cordiale* between Hindus and Muslims, arguing that

When England and America think of the Anglo-Saxon race all over the world, when you find the *Entente Cordiale* between England and France an accomplished fact, when you find that Europe consisting of different nationalities and powers can maintain what was known as 'concert of powers' during the recent war, is it too much to ask and appeal to Hindus and Mohomedans, the two great communities in India, to combine in one harmonious union for the common good.... This is the problem of all problems that the statesman in India has to solve before any true advance or real progress can be achieved.[10]

Though not yet a formal member of the League, he was not only in regular correspondence with Wazir Hasan (1874–1947), the Acting Secretary of the League, but was also invited to attend its council meetings during 1910–12.[11] More important, the AIML Secretary sent him draft resolutions, with a request to 'go through them and let me know the result'.[12] An analysis of the discussions at the League Council meeting on 30–31 December 1913[13] clearly indicates Jinnah's singular contribution to the incorporation of the twin ideals of self-government and Hindu-Muslim unity in the League's plank; even the pro-British Mian Mohammad Shafi (1869–1932), the President of the Lucknow (1913) League, declared himself 'in entire accord with' him.[14] Jinnah himself was happy at 'the recent changes in the [League's] thought and feelings', commended their proposed 'earnest endeavours ... for the realization of our common goal', and assured Wazir Hasan of his 'sincere sympathy and co-operation in the noble work your association and yourself specially have set upon'.[15] Thus Jinnah prepared the League and its leadership, step by step, to work for the 'common goal' before he formally signed the League membership form on 10 October 1913.[16]

Having brought the League on par with Congress in terms of its objectives, he brought about Congress and League meetings, at identical venues and over the same dates, with a view to providing an opportunity to their respective leaders to meet each other, exchange views, and work out common solutions to problems confronting the country.[17] This he did despite charges of a 'sell-out', despite the mounting opposition of the League's old guard which finally led to the disruption of the Bombay (1915) League session.[18] Even so, as a result of his efforts Congress and the League met annually at the same time and at the same place from Bombay (1915) to Ahmedabad (1921), and these were the only years when the Congress and League acted in union (Hindu-Muslim collaboration during the Khilafat and Non-Co-operation movements during 1920–2 was chiefly due to the overriding Muslim interest in salvaging the Khilafat.) It was again chiefly due to Jinnah's efforts that the two bodies entered into a pact in 1916, the only one ever signed between them, and put forth a united demand for self-government.[18] Meantime, Jinnah had also got nineteen out of twenty-seven elected members of the Imperial Legislative Council to submit to the Viceroy a memorandum, since known as 'Memorandum of the Nineteen' (November 1916); it put forward proposals identical to those hammered out at a joint meeting of the AICC and the League Council at Calcutta in October 1916, which were later formally approved of by Congress and League sessions at Lucknow. These proposals, which at any rate must have played a large part in inducing HMG into the August 1917 declaration, became the basis of the Montagu-Chelmsford Reforms (1919).[20]

During the 1910s, according to Nehru, Jinnah was 'popular and well known';[21] indeed his was the 'waxing personality' in the Congress.[22] From 1908 to 1920 he was regularly elected a member of the AICC; in 1918 he was elected Vice-Chairman of the Reception Committee of the special Bombay Congress. At the Congress sessions he moved or seconded several important resolutions, mostly bearing on the constitutional framework. In July 1913 he founded the London Indian Association as a forum for Indian students; in May 1914 he was 'the spokesman' of 'the Congress-wallas', as Lord Crewe puts it, for the Congress representation to the Secretary of State on the reform of the India Council.[23] Though considered a moderate, he was in part responsible for the return of the extremists to the Congress fold in 1916, from which they had been hounded out at Surat nine years earlier.[24] Though not a formal member of either Tilak's or Mrs Besant's Home Rule League (HRL) during 1916–17, he yet popularized and pleaded the cause of Home Rule, identifying himself with the movement to an extent that he was invited on several occasions to preside over the combined meetings of the two HRLs at Bombay. On 18 June 1917 he joined Besant's HRL, in protest against her internment. He brought with him 'the entire legal profession', including Bhulabhai Desai, M.R. Jayakar and K.M. Munshi, and also organized 'big public meetings' at Shantaram Chawl in Bombay every fortnight.[25] While Gokhale considered him 'the best ambassador of Hindu-Muslim Unity',[26] Sarojini Naidu hailed him 'not merely as an ambassador, but as an embodied symbol of Hindu-Muslim Unity'.[27]

By 1918 Jinnah was considered important enough for a selection of his speeches and writings (during 1912–17) to be compiled and published, and for Naidu to contribute a pen portrait to the compilation. For his 'remarkable courage' and 'dauntless leadership' in finally defeating in Bombay in December 1918 the move to give the customary farewell to a retiring Governor—Lord Willingdon in this case—the people of Bombay collected a sum of Rs 65,000 within a month and built in his honour the Jinnah Peoples' Hall, in the Congress House compound, and Mrs Besant came all the way from Madras to declare it open.[28] When the draconian Rowlatt Bill passed into law in March 1919 Jinnah resigned his seat in the Imperial Council, accusing the Government of India, in a letter to the Viceroy, of having 'ruthlessly trampled upon the principles' for which Great Britain had 'avowedly fought the war', and of having violated 'the constitutional rights of the people . . . when there is no real danger to the State'.[29]

In the circumstances it was natural for Jinnah to aspire to the

supreme national leadership role.[30] But he was denied the
Congress sceptre. This was rather surprising since he took much
greater interest in the Congress than did Tyabji, Rahimtulla
Mohammad Sayani and Syed Hasan Imam, and since, subsequently, his namesake Mohamed Ali was made president of the
Coconada (1923) Congress, barely three years after his joining
it. But that will not have particularly distressed or disconcerted
him, for, as pointed out by Percival Spear, until 1907 and again
from the early 1920s to 1939, 'the President has been the execu-
tant, but not the initiator of the Congress policy. The dynamic
figures have not usually held the highest office and do not at this
moment [1940].'[31] What, however, did distress him was Gokhale's
premature death in 1915, Besant's loss of charisma during
1919–1920, Tilak's death in 1920, and, above all, the moderates
being 'simply over-powered' and disintegrating at Nagpur (1920)
when confronted with Gandhi's populist slogans, charismatic
charms and 'soul force'. To quote Sitaramayya, 'every one of
the older Congressmen,—seniors, leaders and patriarchs . . .—
[were] aghast, asking themselves and each other, "Who is this
man that speaketh with a tone of authority and whence doth he
come?"'[32]

To illustrate how complete was the rout of the moderates at
the Nagpur Congress, one instance suffices. Chitta Ranjan Das
had been the most outstanding moderate to stand up against
Gandhi at the Calcutta (1920) special Congress. 'There is not a
single argument', he had said in despair, while opposing Gandhi's
Non-Co-operation resolution, 'advanced against my proposition
of any value except one, namely Mr Gandhi—Mahatma Gandhi—
said this and said that. This is not an argument.'[33] But by the
time the Nagpur session, three months later, was half-way
through, he had also succumbed to that 'argument'. How and
why? Because, argues Nehru, Gandhi 'had an amazing knack of
reaching the heart of the people';[34] because 'we felt that we knew
him quite well enough to realize that he was a great and unique
man and a glorious leader, and having put our faith in him we
gave him an almost blank cheque, for the time being at least.'[35]

But Jinnah was not the sort of person to so succumb, being a
much more cold-blooded logician. His arguments at the Calcutta

Congress might be dismissed as 'pompous legalities,' but they are characteristic of his commitment to his own brand of rationalism.[36] This entailed, in this instance, his alienation from Congress.

II

It is usually assumed that when Jinnah walked out of the Nagpur Congress, where he was shouted down and humbled, he severed his connections with Congress for good. However, his attitude during the next three or four years indicates that that was not his intention at the time. First, despite his double discomfiture at the hands of Gandhi within three brief months,[37] he seemed to have harboured no malice or rancour against Gandhi; 'the spendid character' of 'seasoned men' who got routed at Nagpur has been attested to by Sitaramayya.[38] As a man who never refrained from calling a spade a spade, Jinnah would not otherwise have paid the sort of tributes to Gandhi and others he opposed that he did barely two months after Nagpur, in his speech at Gokhale's sixth death anniversary, on 19 February 1921. Here, he voiced 'the greatest respect and reverence for Mr Gandhi and the men who were working with him because he knew of what noble stuff they were made. He worked with them and was firmly convinced of their noble and sacrificing spirit. He was proud of them ...'.[39] Second, he would not have collaborated with Pandit Madan Mohan Malaviya, Jayakar and others to convoke the Bombay Conference in January 1922, to help find a way out of the impasse and devise a solution acceptable to the non-co-operators (headed by Gandhi) and the government, and to prepare the ground for a Round Table Conference (RTC).[40] Along with Malaviya, Jinnah had even attended the Ahmedabad (1921) Congress with a view to 'inducing that body to pass a resolution extending a formal welcome to the idea' for a RTC, but only to be thwarted by Gandhi, who considered it 'undignified for the Congress to pass such a resolution'.[41] Third, Jinnah not only refused to get his name included in the list of politicians and public men opposed to the Non-Co-operation movement, which was being prepared by the government; he also did not stand for election in 1920, nor offered himself for election till the special Delhi (September 1923) Congress had accorded the Swarajists permission to contest the council elections. Fourth, among the non-Congress Muslim leaders he alone put up, more often than not, a nationalist stance till mid 1937, and, as against other erstwhile Congress Muslim leaders (e.g. Maulana Mohamed Ali and Shaukat Ali), he did not resort to name calling.[42] All this tends to indicate that his withdrawal from Congress was meant to be temporary, and that he may well have hoped to return to it, just as the extremists did, when conditions became propitious. The waning of the influence of the moderates in Congress after the death of Gokhale and Mehta in 1915 and the almost simultaneous rise in Tilak's stature and influence (due chiefly to his founding the HRL in April 1916 and the sedition cases against him) had made possible the return of the extremists to the Congress fold; but Jinnah's hope that Gandhi's influence would wane once the Non-Co-operation movement collapsed—leading to the abandonment of extra-constitutional methods by Congress—did not materialize, thereby barring his re-entry into Congress for all time.

The three dominant strands in the first phase of Jinnah's political career were: (i) working for self-government for India; (ii) striving for Hindu-Muslim unity since without this India could not possibly put up a united demand for self-government; and (iii) bringing about unity in disparate Muslim ranks through the Muslim League since he felt that, given their reservations about Congress, there could be no Hindu-Muslim unity without Muslims uniting among themselves first and speaking with one voice. Jinnah had added this last strand to his political programme in 1915. In an appeal to Muslim leaders on 11 November 1915 he urged them to attend the forthcoming Bombay League session in strength, saying that

the success of the sessions of the League this year . . . will show the power of organization, the solidarity of Muslim opinions and their true worth. This will entitle them to claim the rights and privileges of a free people. . . . I urge all the Mohammedan to rally round the flag of the Muslim League and, as true patriots, stand by its Constitution and thus make the community feel proud of the only political organization it possesses at present.[43]

His idea was that once they were united under the League's banner their leaders could speak with authority, effect a settlement with Hindu leaders on their behalf, and join with leaders of other parties to put in a united demand for self-government.

At any rate, these strands continued to dominate his activities during the second phase as well, but with the difference that— with his Congress platform snatched away—he concentrated a good deal on what I have characterized as the third strand. This occurred from 1923 onwards, when he revived the Muslim League after its eclipse during the height of the Khilafat movement (1920–2). While he utilized his position as Permanent President of the League, to which he was re-elected in 1924, to prepare Muslims for co-operation with Hindus in the cause of Indian freedom—in that sense his close association with the League fits in squarely in terms of his involvement in national politics—all through the second phase he worked strenuously for the accomplishment of the first two objectives as strenuously as any Congress or nationalist leader did.

This becomes evident from the time he re-entered the political arena after a two-year (1921–3) period of withdrawal, isolation, and possibly appraisal. He ran for his erstwhile seat in the Assembly as an independent candidate and won in November 1923. Ten months earlier Das had mooted, in a series of meetings with him, the idea of the formation of (what later came to be) the Swaraj Party, but would not agree to Jinnah's suggestion to keep it out of the reach of Gandhi's influence.[44] Since Gandhi passionately believed that the councils would not 'lead to Swaraj', but would only 'tighten the British hold on India', Jinnah felt that no parliamentary programme would have any chance of success if Gandhi were to have any say in it.[45] Hence he could not join the Swaraj Party; instead he formed the Independent Party (1924–37), which claimed a strength of 17 as against 41 members of the Swaraj Party headed by Motilal Nehru, thus holding the balance between the Swarajists and the government in a house of 101 seats. Not only was the Independent Party non-communal, with only two members besides Jinnah being Muslims; but at one time (1929) Jinnah even spurned the offer of the Muslim Centre Party to head a combined Muslim Party 'as he was not prepared to throw over Sir Purshotamdas Thakurdas', one of his closest political associates.[46] Although disagreeing with the Swarajist obstructionist posture, the Independent Party was yet nationalist to the core: it followed a policy and programme similar to the Swarajists', co-operating with them fully to defeat government bills, to press the demand for Dominion Status, and to promote Indian interests. Indeed it was the rapport and understanding Jinnah had established with Motilal that prompted him to formulate the Delhi Muslim Proposals in March 1927.

In May 1924, when Jinnah embarked upon reviving and reorganizing the Muslim League after the abandonment of the Non-Co-operation movement, he laid down that the League would 'not in any way adopt a policy or programme which will, in the least degree . . . be antagonistic to the Indian National Congress'. He also came closer to the Congress after it had suspended non-co-operation and sanctioned council-entry. Not only did he consider attending the Belgaum (1924) Congress, the idea of the AIML holding a joint session with the INC was also mooted;[47] but 'the contemptuous treatment with which the Secretary of the Congress treated the request of the Muslim League constitution committee' prevented its materialization.[48] However, the dates of the Bombay (1924) League were so arranged as to enable 'those belonging to one body . . . to attend the meetings of the other', and several Congress leaders, including Gandhi, Motilal, Jawaharlal, Malaviya, Mrs Besant, Naidu and V. J. Patel, did attend it.[49] While its President, Syed Raza Ali, ruled out a merger with the Congress,[50] Jinnah, while acknowledging communal differences, renewed his plea for a Hindu-Muslim settlement.[51]

During this period Jinnah even mooted with Jayakar the idea of setting up a new nationalist organization with Swaraj as its creed and a membership open to all progressive-minded politicians, irrespective of their party affiliation, to work the legislative and constructive programme—'while working at the same time for the unity of all parties on the Congress platform';[52] but the Swarajists' opposition aborted his plans.[53] On 12 July 1925 he again wrote to Jayakar, suggesting a new strategy to force the

British into appointing 'a Royal Commission with a personnel acceptable to the people'. Here he also called for an RTC to revise and review the constitution so as not to 'allow the blame' for the impasse to be laid at the Swarajists' door.[54] And on the Simon Commission (1927) issue, much to the consternation of Muslim moderates, he aligned himself completely with Congress, called for a total boycott, and took the lead 'in breaking the back of the Simon co-operaters';[55] this posture he stuck to till the last, though it led to a vertical split of the Muslim League into two factions, causing a serious setback to his goal of gathering all Muslims on the League's platform and to his claim to Muslim leadership.

All this he did because the attainment of freedomn was his goal. Since he considered Hindu-Muslim unity as the condition of Indian freedom and 'Swaraj...an almost interchangeable term with Hindu-Muslim Unity', he worked all the while to expand the areas of co-operation and collaboration between the two major political entities.[56] On the constitutional plane, as the January 1925 unity conference and such other efforts had shown over the years, the mode and quantum of Muslim representation had proved to be the most vexatious question, and this he tried to tackle through his four-point Delhi Muslim Proposals (20 March 1927). The most outstanding feature of this formula was that Muslims would waive their right to separate electorates, the most controversial of the Muslim demands from the Hindu viewpoint. Since, however, Muslims could not be expected to surrender this right without getting something which would provide them with a sense of security, the proposals called for a reservation of Muslim seats according to population in the provinces where they were most populous—Punjab and Bengal; the extension of reforms to the NWFP and Baluchistan; the separation of Sind from Bombay; and a one-third Muslim representation at the centre.[57] In providing these conditions Jinnah was guided by the consideration that the

Mussalmans should be made to feel that they are secure and safe-guarded against any act of oppression on the part of the majority and that they need not feel that during the transitional stage towards the fullest development of National Government the majority would be in a position to oppress and tyrannize the minority as majorities are prone to do in other countries.[58]

Jinnah's proposals were considered so reasonable that they were welcomed by the Congress Working Committee on 21 March,[59] accepted by the sub-committee appointed by it to discuss details,[60] approved of with some minor conditions by the AICC at its 15–18 May 1927 meeting at Bombay,[61] endorsed by the Madras (1927) Congress,[62] and applauded by its President M. A. Ansari, who 'recorded the deep appreciation of the Indian National Congress of the spirit of patriotism and statesmanship displayed by the Muslim leaders who rose above prejudice, suspicion and narrow communal outlook and boldly came forward with the proposals which presage a new orientation of Muslim policy in India.'[63]

However, in offering to waive 'the cornerstone' of Muslim demands, Jinnah had staked his credibility as a Muslim leader; by the following December he was not so sure that 'the majority of Musalmans' were 'in favour of' the Delhi Proposals.[64] But the capital concession he was offering was not generally appreciated on the Hindu side (except by Sapru),[65] which failed to realize that even Jinnah could not induce Muslims to give away such an important right without getting something in return. The Mahasabha apart, even Gandhi saw nothing in the proposals except that 'a new door has been opened, on the basis of mixed electorate, for further negotiations'.[66]

Thus, despite previous commitments the Nehru Committee (1928) rejected the two (more basic) of the proposals, modified one and accepted only one.[67] Jinnah was away in Europe when the Nehru Report was published on 12 August 1928, and by the time Jinnah returned on 26 October 1928 the Muslim position had hardened.[68] While remaining non-committal, which in itself was a positive posture from the Nehru Committee's viewpoint, he yet expressed appreciation of the efforts that had gone into its formulation. He also asked Muslims not to be unduly alarmed, saying that the Report was, after all, 'not the final word', and hoping that the communal deadlock would be resolved.[69]

In order to buy off Muslim reservations, and still keen to play a nationalist role, Jinnah presented six demands on behalf of the Muslim League and the Central Khilafat Committee at the All-Parties National Convention on 28 December 1928. Of these, the four basic ones were: (i) a one-third representation for Muslims at the Centre; (ii) the reservation of seats for Muslims on a population basis in the Punjab and Bengal for ten years, in the event of adult suffrage not being introduced; (iii) the vesting of residuary powers with the provinces and a revision of the powers assigned to the centre and the provinces, with a view to ensuring a genuine federation; (iv) that the separation of Sind not be dependent upon the implementation of the Nehru constitution.[70]

Jinnah argued the case for proportional representation in the Punjab and Bengal in some detail since he felt it necessary 'to provide for the contingency' of adult suffrage not being granted.[71] But the Convention paid no heed to Jinnah's arguments, partly because of Hindu and Sikh opposition and partly because of certain conclusions of the Nehru Committee on the joint vs. separate electorates' issue. On the basis of the number of Hindu and Muslim members elected to the District Boards in Bengal in 1927–8 and of the number of Hindu, Sikh and Muslim voters and their members elected in the Punjab, the Committee had concluded that the Muslims had 'nothing to fear from a free electorate without a reservation of seats'.[72] Muslim fears based on the superior economic and educational standard of Hindus and Sikhs, it had contended, were 'largely imaginary', that 'it is one of the tragedies of communal hostility that men shut their eyes to facts and fight against their own best interests'.[73]

This contention was however based on aggregate figures, and aggregate figures by themselves do not tell the whole truth unless worked out and interpreted in terms of certain common basic criteria or denominators—such as, in the present case, population percentage per seat in Bengal, and the population percentage required to yield 1000 voters in the Punjab. This has been done in the two analytical tables included at the end of this essay. They show that the conclusions drawn by the Nehru Committee are misleading. The figures for Bengal (Table I), for instance, show that except for seven (out of twenty-six) districts, the percentage of Muslims per seat was higher— one and a half times in three districts, two times in five, three times in two, five times in three, and six times in one district. Likewise, the Punjab figures (Table II) indicate a great divergence between the population percentages of Hindus and Sikhs on the one hand, and Muslims on the other, required to yield 1000 voters. Was Jinnah, then, too unreasonable, as Jayakar had contended,[74] or 'a spoilt child' as Sapru had claimed,[75] in pressing for proportional representation in case adult franchise was not conceded in the next instalment of reforms? And, as Jinnah visualized it, it was not conceded in the 1935 Act.

However, despite the stout opposition his proposals had evoked, Jinnah made an extremely 'conciliatory' and 'persuasive' speech, appealing to the Convention 'not as a Musalman but as an Indian':[76]

What we want is that Hindus and Muslims should march together until our object is obtained. Therefore, it is essential that you must get not only the Muslim League but the Musalmans of India.... Would you be content if I were to say, I am with you? Do you want or do you not want the Muslim India to go along with you?... Minorities cannot give anything to the majority. It is, therefore, no use asking me not to press for what you call 'these small points....' If they are small points, why not concede? It is up to the majority and minority which alone can give.[77]

But the Convention, dominated as it was by the Mahasabha and the Sikh League, was not open to reason, and negatived Jinnah's 'reasonable' amendments one by one. That these bodies should have put on such a posture is not so surprising; what indeed is inexplicable is that Congress, which had accepted these or similar proposals, and Gandhi, who had offered Muslims proportional representation both in the legislatures and in the services in 1924,[78] should have gone back on their commitments, succumbed to the Mahasabha blackmail,[79] and paid no heed to Jinnah's pleas to accommodate what in the circumstances seem reasonable Muslim demands with a view to making the Nehru Report acceptable to them.[80] And without Muslim acceptance, the fate of the Report was 'sealed', asserted Jinnah.[81] History was to bear him out.

III

Several historians have described the Nehru Report as 'the last straw' so far as the Muslims were concerned, and the Convention's steamrolling of Jinnah's proposals as 'the parting of the ways', so far as he was concerned.[82] But a closer study of future developments controverts these and similar contentions.

Briefly stated, a series of negotiations were held before, during, and after the three RTCs (1930–2) to resolve Hindu-Muslim differences and arrive at a settlement, in which the Aga Khan, Sir Muhammad Shafi, Jinnah, Mohamed Ali, Shaukat Ali, and other accredited Muslim leaders were involved on the Muslim side. Even after the publication of the Communal Award (August 1932), several attempts were made, besides those by Jinnah, to arrive at some sort of formula to replace the Award, or a communal settlement, either at the all-India or at the provincial level. Shaukat Ali, who inherited Mohamed Ali's mantle as the foremost Khilafatist after the death of his younger brother on 4 January 1931, collaborated with Malaviya to call the Allahabad Unity Conference during October-December 1932 and work out a formula to replace the Award on an all-India basis.[83] In the Punjab Sir Sikandar Hayat Khan, along with Chaudhri Shahabuddin and Ahmad Yar Khan Daulatana, hammered out a compromise formula with Sir Jogendra Singh and Sir Gokul Chand in January 1933, which was approved of by Sir Fazl-i-Hussain, the foremost Muslim leader in the province.[84] In Bengal Sir A. H. Ghuznavi concluded, with the consent of the Aga Khan, a three-point 'pact', representing a communal settlement, with the Maharaja of Burdwan, President of the Bengal Anti-Communal Award Committee, in January 1937.[85] That these efforts finally came to naught for various reasons is, however, besides the point; what is important is that these attempts were made despite the Nehru Report, despite the decisions of the National Convention; this belies the contention that the Report or the Convention's decisions represented a 'point of no return' for the Muslims.

More strenuous were Jinnah's efforts for a communal settlement in the post-Nehru Report period. However, he had first to attend to a personal tragedy—the death of his wife—and then to mend his political fences with his co-religionists, badly bruised since the Delhi Proposals. At the National Convention Jayakar had even questioned his credentials to speak for Muslims. Hence his first task was to stabilize his position with them. This he did by patching up with Shafi (despite the taunts and jeers Shafi had hurled out at him at the All Parties Muslim Conference (January) 1929) for his discomfiture at the Convention),[86] and by reuniting the divided League in March 1929; simultaneously, he parleyed at length with various Muslim groups and leaders to evolve a unified response to the Nehru Report.[87] In this he finally succeeded, resulting in the formulation of his Fourteen Points (March 1929). Not only endorsed by the AIML but also accepted by the other Muslim parties—such as the Muslim Conference[88] and Jamiatul Ulama-i-Hind,[89] and above all by the Muslim delegation to the RTC—as the minimum Muslim demands,[90] Jinnah's Fourteen Points were to become the Magna Carta of Muslim India for the next eleven years. Once he had vindicated his right to speak on behalf of the Muslims, he was back in the arena of inter-party politics, playing out the role of an 'arch compromiser'. Along with the Ali brothers, he saw Gandhi in Bombay on 11 August 1929, in a renewed effort to modify the Nehru Report in the light of Muslim reservations. Three months later, after Lord Irwin's 31 October 1929 declaration that Dominion Status was 'the natural issue' of India's constitutional progress, he urged the Viceroy, whom he saw in Bombay, to meet Gandhi and Motilal, along with Sapru and himself, to explore the possibility of Congress co-operation for the RTC idea envisaged in Irwin's declaration.[91] He also conferred with Sapru in Bombay in November 1929 and suggested that he meet Gandhi, Motilal and the Viceroy to prepare them for a meeting to resolve Congress–Government differences. About the same time he told the Viceroy that he was in direct or indirect communication with Gandhi. It took Jinnah almost two months of hard 'negotiating', including a visit to Sabarmati on 30 November, to have 'a long interview' with Gandhi (in the presence of Vallabhbhai and V. J. Patel),[92] and a good deal of correspondence before he could bring Congress leaders and the Viceroy (with Sapru and himself as intermediaries) to a conference table on 23 December.[93] But his efforts foundered on the rock of Gandhi's surprise demand for the immediate acceptance by the Viceroy of two preconditions (i) a declaration that the only purpose of the RTC would be to work out the details of a Dominion Status constitution; and (ii) that 'the establishment of the Dominion Status would be an immediate result of the Conference'.[94] What put Jinnah off completely was not the preconditions but the Congress leaders' failure to take the two intermediaries into confidence before the meeting. Sapru felt equally frustrated, furious and bitter. He complained that they had not 'the least inkling upto the time that we went' into the meeting, and that 'all that came as a surprise to both Jinnah and myself'.[95]

But because of the importance they attached to Congress' participation in the RTC for India to reach its Dominion Status goal, the two intermediaries, despite the rebuff at the 23 December meeting, were back in the arena within seven months, trying to bridge the differences between Congress and the government, the only difference being that this time they were joined by Jayakar.[96] On 6 July 1930 Sapru reported to Irwin that 'Jinnah was understood to have some sort of a formula which was quite definite', assuring the Viceroy that 'there should be no conflict between Jinnah on one side and Jayakar and myself on the other in regard to the assurances that we may be able to give to' Gandhi and others.[97] On the same day Jinnah saw Irwin along with Jayakar at Simla, and on the following day he had 'a long talk' with him about the assurances to be held out by the Viceroy to induce co-operation from Congress and dispel the misunderstanding about the fate of the discussions to be taken at the RTC.[98] Two days later he issued a statement, along with Jayakar and others, urging on the one hand the repeal of emergency measures recently enacted as well as the offering of a general amnesty, and on the other the termination of the Non-Co-operation movement and Congress' participation in the RTC.[99]

Although, as the foregoing discussion indicates, he remained as keen as ever, and moreover encouraged efforts to resolve the deadlock, he yet refused, despite Irwin's urgings, to involve himself personally in carrying on negotiations with Congress leaders.[100] But why? Perhaps he felt, on the basis of his own experience with Gandhi since HRL days, that the latter, while swearing eternal friendship and deep respect, was not averse if it suited him to throwing overboard, or at least putting in an awkward position, those whom he had used to advance his purposes. At any rate, the odium and the series of charges that Sapru and Jayakar earned in nationalist circles (including from those with whom they had negotiated) for their sincere and marathon efforts during July-August 1930 (to bring about an understanding between the Congress and Government) seem to confirm Jinnah's forebodings.[101]

Interestingly, all through the 1925–35 decade Jinnah was gravely suspected in Muslim circles of being ever prepared to give away the separate-electorates' right all too readily, since he had kept the option open even in his Fourteen Points. To counter Jinnah at the RTC, therefore, Fazl-i-Husain got Mohammad Zafrullah Khan and Shafaat Ahmad Khan specifically nominated through Sir Malcolm Hailey.[102] And all through the Conference Husain tried to monitor Jinnah's activities, sending out guidelines to his lieutenants on how to controvert him. 'The only Laodicean', wrote Hailey, 'is Jinnah, who is as usual yielding to the solicitations of his Hindu clients.'[103] He was equally distrusted by the British but for different reasons—his 'aloofness, brittle ability and anti-imperial attitude'.[104]

Of all the Indians I have met [wrote Hoare] I think I have disliked Jinnah the most. Throughout the Round Table discussions he invariably behaved like a snake, and no one seemed to trust him. I greatly hope he is not getting a following among the Muslims.[105]

To quote the *Manchester Guardian*, 'The Hindus thought he was a Muslim communalist, the Muslims took him to be pro-Hindu, the Princes deemed him to be too democratic, the British considered him to be a rabid extremist—with the result that he was everywhere but nowhere. None wanted him'.[106] Such at any rate is the fate of all those who try to play the role of 'compromisers', who try to look for whatever merit or justice there is in each viewpoint and then work out a formula or plan with a view to accommodating, aggregating, processing and harmonizing various, even divergent, interests.

To sum up the argument, then: All this indicates that the Convention's rebuff to Jinnah did not mean a parting of the ways. This was of course to come—but not before he had the rebuff of his lifetime early in 1937. Likewise, the Nehru Report, as against the generally held view, did not prove the last straw for the Muslims as a whole or even for a majority of them; what, however, did, was Congress rule in the Hindu majority provinces during 1937–9.

IV

But this is to anticipate. From early 1934—when Jinnah was summoned back to India from his self-imposed exile (1931–4) in England to head a reunited League—to mid 1937, when the Congress came to power in the provinces, Jinnah set for himself (and the AIML) three goals which, in his perception, were interrelated: (1) the democratization of the constitutional proposals in the White Paper (1933); (ii) Hindu-Muslim unity and co-operation without, however, undermining the Muslim entity in Indian politics; and (iii) the organizing of Muslims on the League's platform.[107] Not only did he concentrate a good deal more on the accomplishment of the first two objectives than on the last one but, even as regards the third objective his aim was to 'produce a patriotic and liberal-minded nationalist bloc' which would be 'able to march hand in hand with the progressive elements in other communities'.[108] And he consistently put up a 'nationalist' posture.[109]

Jinnah's bitter opposition to the White Paper proposals led him to approach the Congress for united action. In January 1934 he invited Naidu, Desai, Nariman, Brelvi, Munshi and Mathurdas Tricumjee twice to his chamber and suggested that they jointly prepare the Indian case against the White Paper. 'Let us', he further suggested, 'accept the communal Award so that even the Muslims will come around.'[110] But the talks aborted because of the Congress leaders' aversion to formally accepting the Award. Interestingly though, Gandhi's stance on the Award in private conversations and correspondence was not much different from Jinnah's. 'I gave it as my opinion [to Dr Syed Mahmud]', he wrote to Malaviya on 7 April 1934, 'that there is no escape from the communal award if we are to secure Mussalman co-operation and if we are to secure any advantage for the nation.'[111] Then why did Congress leaders refuse Jinnah's offer? And why did not Gandhi, on being informed by Munshi about their talks with Jinnah, counsel them to pursue them further to forge a united front? Whatever be the reason, the point worth considering here is that an opportunity was missed for getting the League, if not all Muslims, aligned with Congress on such a critical issue as the White Paper, a document which was to determine the shape of the penultimate constitution that governed India till independence.

About the time Gandhi wrote this letter Malaviya was engaged in protracted negotiations with Jinnah to devise a formula to replace the Award, especially separate electorates by joint electorates. But the talks finally broke down on the quantum of Muslim representation in Bengal and Punjab.[112]

Generally speaking, both the AIML and Jinnah were dissatisfied with the Award, but for different reasons—the League because it fell short of Muslim demands both in quantitative and qualitative terms,[113] while Jinnah because

my self respect will never be satisfied until we produce our own scheme. . . . I accept it, because we have done everything that we could so far to come to a settlement though, so far we have not been able to come to a settlement, and, therefore, whether I like it or . . . not . . ., I accept it because unless I accept that, no scheme of Constitution is possible.[114]

Hence when the Joint Parliamentary Committee's Report was being debated in the Assembly in February 1935, he took the initiative, holding prolonged talks with the Congress President, Babu Rajendra Prasad, and Patel. According to Patel he had confessed,

I have nothing in common with the Aga Khan . . . I am devoted to my old policy and programme . . . If the Congress can support the Muslims on the Communal Award, I would be able to get all the Muslim members except 7 or 8.

. . . As things stand, the practical way would be for just a few leaders of political thought to combine for the purpose of preparing a formula which both communities might accept. The Congress I admit would have to change its attitude in some respects, but looking to the great interests at stake Congress leaders should not flinch. I think that the future is with the Congress Party and not with me or the Aga Khan.[115]

A formula was finally hammered out on 13–14 February 'as a basis for further discussion'.[116] But the stiff attitude of Malaviya—whom the Congress leaders consulted presumably with a view to arriving at a Hindu consensus on the Award—in respect of the quantum of Muslim representation at the centre and of Hindu representation in Bengal wrecked the Jinnah-Prasad efforts. Jinnah's insistence that the formula be countersigned by Malaviya and some other prominent leaders of his Congress Nationalist Party (CNP) was by no means unreasonable because of the Anti-Communal Award Conference at Delhi on 23 February, the Hindu Bengal leaders' memorandum to Secretary of State Lord Zetland,[117] and, above all, the bagging of all seven general seats in Bengal in the autumn (1934) Assembly elections (besides four seats elsewhere) by the CNP on the basis of a one-item anti-Award manifesto. (Significantly though, when the formula was sought to be revived in July 1937 it was immediately repudiated by the Bengal CNP on behalf of Hindu Bengal.)[118]

Despite this setback Jinnah worked hard to establish co-operation with Congress, both inside and outside the Assembly. Inside the Assembly he joined hands with Congress against the government to throw out the Ottawa Trade Agreeement (1935)—recently concluded between Britain and the Indian Government—to reject the Criminal Law Amendment Bill (1935), and to defeat budgets in 1935 and 1936—all of which had to be certified by the Governor-General. Reporting on the Ottawa debate, an enraged Willingdon complained to Zetland—

Jinnah is more Congress than the Congress. He is getting more violent every minute. . . . It was . . . the one purpose of the Congress and of Jinnah and his friends to show their complete independence, and further to make it uncomfortable for Government as a retort to our having smashed civil disobedience movement.[119]

When the Agreement was voted down, he wrote, 'They wanted to down the Government and do something to annoy His

Majesty's Government. Jinnah was the leader of the whole assault
... he is a troublesome person and I shall warn Hopie [Linlithgow]
against him.'[120]

Outside the Assembly, he gave a 'predominantly radical' tone
to the League's policy and programme,[121] got the pro-Congress
Wazir Hasan[122] (as against the pro-British Raja of Salempur, for
whom Shaukat Ali had been lobbying) nominated for the presidentship of the Bombay (1936) League;[123] drew up an election
manifesto (1936) which not only stressed co-operation with like-
minded groups but was almost identical with that of the Congress
in ten out of its thirteen items (three items being designed to
cater to special Muslim interests);[124] and got the pro-Congress
Khilafatists, Ahrars and members of the Muslim Unity Board
included in the League's Parliamentary Board (1936).[125] Indeed
in terms of its policy and programme, as well as in its anti-British
and anti-reforms posture, so close had Jinnah brought the League
to Congress that several Muslim leaders and columnists had
begun accusing him of 'conspiring' to merge the League into
the Congress, or at least of relegating it to a client status.

Jinnah's tilt towards Congress was also reflected in his personal
relations with many of its leaders. Even while he disagreed with
their politics he always maintained the best of relations with
them. On his relations with Jinnah, a confident Motilal soothed
a perturbed Thakurdas, 'Please do not allow yourself to be
disturbed until you come to the end of the chapter. Do not for a
moment think that we are creating an impassable gulf between
ourselves. We can afford to fight like Kilkenny cats and still be
friends.'[126] In March 1934 Satyamurti, Asaf Ali and Malaviya,
among others, welcomed Jinnah's election as President of the
reunited League. Early in April 1936 his inaugural speech in
English at the Jamiatul Ulama Conference at Delhi was translated
for him in Urdu by Asaf Ali. On 29 February 1936 he got the
League Council to pass a condolence resolution on the death of
Kamala Nehru.[127] In May 1936 he reportedly consented to the
inclusion of his name in the Bombay Committee of the Indian
Civil Liberties Union, which was headed by Nehru;[128] on 9 June
1936 he got the League Council to pass a resolution recording
its thanks for Nehru's letter on the Civil Liberties Union, and

'fully sympathizing with and appreciating the principles underlying' it.[129] And in August 1936 he shared with Nehru the same
platform at the All India Students' Conference at Lucknow, 'in
an atmosphere of personal cordiality.'[130]

During 1934–7 Jinnah's stance was similar to the one he took
in 1915: he wanted Muslims to be organized under the League's
banner because 'if they are more organized, they will be all the
more useful for the national struggle'.[131] While on the one hand
he tried to gather all Muslims on the League platform, on the
other he offered an olive branch to other nationalist parties,
especially Congress, and put an extremely conciliatory and
accommodating posture. 'Ours is not a hostile movement', he
told the Calcutta Town Hall meeting on 20 August 1936.[132]
'India's salvation', he told the Calcutta students on 21 August,
'lies in the unity of all communities. . . . If there are differences
and disputes, rise to the occasion and solve them among yourselves as friends, partners and countrymen'.[133] He urged Hindus
and Sikhs, as he did the Muslims, at the Peshawar rally on
19 October 1936, 'to unite to hammer out an advanced nationalist bloc' from amongst themselves to send to the Provincial
Assembly.[134]

Hindus and Muslims should present a united front. We must stand
together and work together . . . for the freedom of our motherland. . . . [We must] produce, by a process of hammering, fine steel and
weed out those who are obstructing our march to freedom [Nagpur, 1
January 1937].[135]

The urgent question facing every nationalist in India to-day is how to
create unity out of diversity and not to fight each other. . . . The
Moslem League is prepared to join hands with any progressive party
in the fight for the country's freedom...[Bombay, 20 January 1937].[136]

The Muslim League stands for full national self-government for the
people of India. Unity and honourable settlement between Hindus,
Moslems and other minorities is the only pivot upon which national
self-government for India . . . can be constructed and maintained
[Bombay, 10 April 1937].[137]

There is no difference between the ideals of the Moslem League and
of the Congress, the idea being complete freedom for India [Simla,
18 September 1937].[138]

Little surprise then, that at this stage in Indian politics the greatest opposition to Jinnah's efforts to organize Muslims on the League's platform came not from the Congress or Congress-oriented groups (such as the Ahrars) but from pro-British leaders and parties. Not only had Jinnah's anti-imperial and anti-1935 Act stance coupled with his continuing efforts to effect a settlement with the Congress alarmed the British; there is also evidence to show that some high British officials encouraged or egged on pro-British elements to organize themselves to give a fight to Jinnah's League at the hustings. Should Jinnah succeed in organizing the Muslims on the League's platform and in evolving a pan-Indian Muslim policy, it was feared, he might line up Muslims with the Congress, as he did on the Simon Commission issue, and help wreck the 1935 reforms to which Congress had pledged itself.

The Aga Khan, who was anxious to get Muslims to work the new reforms,[139] became the chief inspiration and co-ordinator for these leaders and groups, with Fazl-i-Husain serving as his principal deputy in India. From February 1935 onwards the Aga Khan was in regular correspondence with Fazl-i-Husain,[140] urging at the same time the Nawab of Chhatari, Sir Muhammad Yukub, Fazl-i-Rahimullah, Sir Abdullah Haroon and others 'to follow' his 'guidance' and 'organize themselves on similar lines'.[141] Thus Fazl-i-Husain's National Unionist Party became the model for organizing British-oriented parties in other provinces— National Agriculturist Party (NAP) (UP), the Sind United Party, and the United Muslim Nationalist Party (NWFP). Sir Harry Haig, Governor of UP, was directly involved in getting Chhatari to quit the League Parliamentary Board[142] and reorganize the NAP; he coerced Muslim *taluqdars* to join it;[143] he also talked to the Rajas of Salempur[144] and Mahmudabad, ordering the latter to dissociate himself with Jinnah, 'the arch enemy of British Raj', and join the NAP on pain of disinheritance.[145]

In contrast the League was able to establish 'something like a concordat' with the Congress, especially in the UP,[146] 'the key province of Indian politics'[147] (as also in Bombay), with the leaders agreeing on a common platform for election purposes.[148] (This, in part, explains why Congress put up only 58 candidates for the 492 Muslim seats, of which as many as 38 seats were contested in the Frontier because of its special relationship with the Khudai Khidmatgars, and only 30 seats in the rest of India.) Brecher feels that 'notably in the United Provinces...there developed a tacit understanding that a coalition government would be formed'.[149]

Clearly, Jinnah was working towards extending 'the *entente* he had established at the Centre' to the provincial arena.[150] Hence he instructed the League parties in the various assemblies not to join the interim governments set up in April 1937, and the Raja of Salempur was expelled for joining the Chhatari ministry.[151] In Bombay Jinnah instructed A. M. K. Dehlavi, leader of the League Assembly Party, to reject out of hand Governor Brabourne's offer to head the interim ministry;[152] and when the interim ministry under Cooper initially insisted upon a no-confidence resolution being passed in the Assembly before vacating, Jinnah instructed the League members to vote with the Congress and against Cooper.[153]

Thus, till early in 1937 Jinnah had not only taken up a position but had also brought the League very close to Congress. Indeed at this point of time he was the foremost 'nationalist' among Muslim leaders, with a mandate from the community which he claimed to represent.

And yet in the autumn of 1937 the entire situation changed rather dramatically and radically. How and why? Because in the post-election period Congress and its leaders launched upon a series of moves that challenged *a la* Jayakar, Jinnah's right to speak on behalf of the Muslims; these moves, had they succeeded, would have ultimately eroded his representative status. Briefly stated these moves were (i) Nehru's 'two-forces'[154] or 'two-parties' approach,[155] ruling out Muslims as the third party in India's body-politic; (ii) Congress' Muslim mass contact programme, designed to approach and win over the Muslim masses over the heads of their accredited leaders and organization in the name of bread and freedom; this was done in order to make the 'two-forces' claim a *fait accompli*; (iii) the sucking in of the Jamiat-ul-Ulama-i-Hind (which had been consistently aligned with the Muslim League after the Nehru Report)[156] into the Congress on 17 May 1937. This entailed the grim prospect of Congress using Jamiat leaders in its mass contact campaign with a view to ensnaring the peasantry towards itself—the Jamiat leaders did descend in strength in the ensuing Bijnor, Jhansi, Bandhelkund, Amroha, Bulandshaher and Saharanpur by-elections;[157] and (iv) Congress' unitarianism as against Muslim federalism in the formation of ministries, and its 'series of incredible conditions'[158] for sharing power with Muslims, as stipulated in the Azad formula presented to the UP League leaders.[159] This 'amounting to an ultimatum for its [AIML's] self-destruction',[160] envisaged 'absorption' instead of 'partnership'.[161]

Clearly, this posture represented a radical shift in Congress' erstwhile policy. Since 1910 Congress had always treated Jinnah as representing an influential and progressive, if not always a major, segment of Muslims. For over two decades (1915–35/6), whenever Congress negotiated the Hindu-Muslim problem, it was always with Jinnah and the Muslim League. Most commentators have ascribed, if not justified, this radical change to the massive electoral victory of Congress as against the League's poor showing, and to the sudden surge of confidence, if not 'the intoxication of power', this spectacular but unexpected victory endowed it with. It is true that Congress had won 711 out of 1585 seats but it had won barely 26 Muslim seats, 19 of them in the Frontier, 'where Abdul Ghaffar Khan had given the Congress a decisive hold',[162] and none in eight provinces. It is equally true that the League had won only some 112 (about 23 per cent) of 492 Muslim seats, but its score was the highest among the numerous Muslim parties, and more important, it alone could claim to speak on Muslim India's behalf. (For that matter, except for the Khilafat Conference and the Muslim Conference during 1920–3 and 1929–32 respectively, when the League was in eclipse or in the doldrums, no Muslim party had ever contested the League's claim.) The British had tried to prop up various interest groups and breakaway or minor parties as a substitute for, and against, Congress in 1920 and in 1930; now Congress, in bolstering up the Jamiat and the Ahrars against the League, seemed bent upon resorting to the same ploy. From the Congress viewpoint, however, it was convenient to deal with provincial and minor Muslim parties piecemeal and on its own terms, even inducing, humouring or forcing them from its position of strength to walk into its parlour unconditionally. Was not the provincial option tried often during 1928–9 and 1932–3, and with some success? Now that there was a chance of its working better, why deal with the Muslim League or talk to Jinnah, hard bargainer that he was?

For Jinnah, however, who took his representative status rather seriously—not only in the 1930s but as far back as 1913—the new Congress posture meant a challenge, the greatest challenge in his entire political career.[163] His career, it seemed, had reached its nadir: once a serious aspirant to the supreme national leadership role, he was now being perceived as merely heading a group which had 'no real importance' in the 'historic sense', and hence shunned and by-passed.[164] This was the challenge that inexorably drove him, haltingly but finally, to the wall, leaving him with little choice but to take the path of confrontation, if only to validate the Muslim claim to a 'third party' status, and to vindicate himself not merely as a spokesman, but as the sole spokesman, of Muslim India. 'The parting of the ways' had finally come.

TABLE I

*Statement about Elected Members of the District Boards
in Bengal, 1927–1928*[a]

Sr. No.	Name of District	Total No. of Seats	Population Percentage		No. of Members elected		Percentage per seat	
			Hindus	Muslims	Hindus	Muslims	Hindus	Muslims
1	2	3	4	5	6	7	8	9
1.	24 Parganas	20	64.2	34.6	16	4	4.11	8.65
2.	Bogra	15	16.6	82.5	4	11	4.15	7.5
3.	Bakargunj	20	28.7	70.6	5	15	5.74	4.90
4.	Midnapore	22	88.2	6.8	21	1	4.2	6.8
5.	Rajshahi	18	21.3	76.6	7	11	3.4	6.96
6.	Rangpore	18	31.5	68.1	7	11	4.5	6.19
7.	Khulna	16	50.0	49.8	11	5	4.55	9.96
8.	Hooghly	20	81.9	16.0	17	3	4.82	5.33
9.	Darjeeling	20	71.0	3.2	18[b]	2	4.94	1.6
10.	Mymensingh	22	24.3	74.9	Nil	22	—	3.4
11.	Pabna	16	24.1	75.8	3	13	8.03	5.83
12.	Noakhali	16	22.3	77.6	6	10	3.71	7.76
13.	Jalpaiguri	16	55.0	24.8	14	2	3.93	12.4
14.	Tippera	19	25.8	74.1	13[b]	6[b]	1.98	12.35
15.	Nadia	20	39.1	60.2	15	5	2.60	12.04
16.	Burdwan	16	78.0	18.5	14	2	5.57	9.25
17.	Murshidabad	15	45.1	53.6	7	8	6.44	6.7

18.	Faridpur	20	36.3	63.5	8	12	4.54	5.29
19.	Malda	15[b]	40.6	51.6	8	7	5.08	7.37
20.	Howrah	12	79.3	20.3	10	2	7.93	10.15
21.	Beerbhum	16	68.1	25.1	15	1	5.21	25.1
22.	Bankura	10	86.3	4.6	9	1	9.59	4.6
23.	Jessore	16	38.2	61.7	1	15	38.2	4.11
24.	Dacca	22	34.2	65.4	16	6	2.14	10.9
25.	Chittagong	20	22.6	72.8	Nil	20	—	3.64
26.	Dinajpur	18	44.1	49.1	4	14	11.03	3.51

a. Based on *All Parties Conference 1928* (Allahabad: A.I.C.C., 1928), Appendix C, pp. 154–5. Figures in columns 8 and 9 have been arrived at by dividing figures in column 4 by those in column 6 and those in column 5 by dividing those in column 7 respectively.

b. The figure for Hindus elected in Darjeeling has been listed as 'Non-Mohammedan'. In Tippera, 3 Hindus and 2 Muslims were nominated consequent upon the failure of elections in Chandpur subdivision, while all the members in Malda were nominated for the same reason.

TABLE II

Number of Voters, Communitywise and Districtwise, in relation to their Population Percentage in the Punjab, 1927–28

Serial No.	Districts	Population Percentage		No. of Voters		Pop. Percentage per 1000 voters	
		Hindus & Sikhs (Hindus + Sikhs)	Muslims	Hindus & Sikhs (Hindus + Sikhs)	Muslims	Hindus & Sikhs (Hindus + Sikhs)	Muslims
1	2	3	4	5	6	7	8
1.	Hissar	72.71 (67.13 + 5.58)	26.44	7921 (6361 + 1560)	2155	9.179 (10.553; 3.577)	12.269
2.	Rohtak	81.52 (81.52 + —)	16.19	23938 (23938 + —)	1504	3.405 (3.405; —)	10.764
3.	Gurgaon	67.61 (67.47 + 0.14)	31.80	12544 (12446 + 98)	5540	5.390 (5.421; 1.429)	5.740
4.	Karnal	70.65 (67.47 + 1.48)	28.43	15112 (14691 + 421)	3549	4.675 (4.708; 3.515)	8.010
5.	Ambala	68.64 (54.31 + 14.33)	30.19	15850 (12235 + 3615)	3892	4.331 (4.439; 3.964)	7.757
6.	Kangra	94.55 (94.28 + 0.27)	5.00	7198 (7198 + —)	105	13.098	47.619
7.	Hoshiarpur	68.29 (53.95 + 14.34)	31.19	20545 (14725 + 5820)	8047	3.324 (3.663; 2.464)	3.876
8.	Jullundur	54.84 (29.78 + 25.06)	44.57	26598 (5255 + 21343)	11466	2.062 (5.667; 1.174)	3.887
9.	Ludhiana	65.40 (23.87 + 41.53)	34.00	16625 (821 + 15804)	3201	3.934 (29.074; 2.628)	10.622

1	2	3	4	5	6	7	8
10.	Ferozpur	55.46 (27.89+27.57)	43.94	21132 (5977+15155)	5277	2.624 (4.666;1.819)	8.327
11.	Lahore	38.51 (22.60+15.91)	57.24	12445 (1161+11284)	5235	3.094 (19.466;1.410)	10.934
12.	Amritsar	52.88 (22.00+30.88)	45.59	22876 (3928+18948)	8930	2.312 (5.601;1.630)	5.105
13.	Gurdaspur	46.52 (30.37+16.15)	49.62	18045 (7708+10337)	8797	2.024 (3.940;1.562)	5.641
14.	Sialkot	31.23 (23.24+7.99)	61.90	12047 (7566+4481)	11782	2.592 (3.072;1.783)	5.254
15.	Gujranwala	24.44 (16.29+8.15)	71.06	8819 (4349+4470)	12081	2.771 (3.746;1.823)	5.882
16.	Sheikhpura	32.26 (16.40+15.85)	63.25	8603 (1307+7296)	9808	3.750 (12.548;2.174)	6.449
17.	Gujrat	13.59 (7.59+6.00)	86.12	736 (493+243)	15182	18.465 (15.396;24.691)	5.673
18.	Shahpur	15.64 (11.42+4.22)	82.80	4766 (2918+1848)	17286	3.282 (3.913;2.283)	4.790
19.	Jhelum	11.21 (7.30+3.91)	88.66	2931 (1749+1182)	24771	3.825 (4.174;3.308)	3.579
20.	Rawalpindi	15.62 (10.05+5.57)	82.57	2120 (880+1240)	18341	7.368 (11.420;4.492)	4.502
21.	Attock	8.98 (5.11+3.87)	90.91	1821 (1302+519)	15245	4.931 (3.924;7.457)	5.963

1	2	3	4	5	6	7	8
22.	Mianwali	13.67 (12.84 + 0.83)	86.23	1859 (1763 + 96)	3681	7.353 (7.283; 8.646)	23.426
23.	Montgomery	26.66 (13.28 + 13.38)	71.88	7100 (3564 + 3536)	11649	3.755 (3.726; 3.784)	6.170
24.	Layallpur	34.95 (18.53 + 16.42)	60.74	16266 (1352 + 14914)	29842	2.149 (13.706; 1.101)	2.035
25.	Jhang	16.60 (14.96 + 1.64)	83.32	3432 (3205 + 227)	11957	4.837 (4.668; 7.225)	6.968
26.	Multan	17.14 (15.05 + 2.09)	82.18	5033 (4024 + 1009)	12299	3.406 (3.740; 2.071)	6.682
27.	Muzaffargarh	13.15 (12.29 + 0.86)	86.79	2773 (2770 + 3)	4850	4.742 (4.437; —)	17.895
28.	Dera Ghazi Khan	11.59 (11.40 + 0.19)	88.34	1964 (1960 + 3)	2969	5.901 (5.813; 63.333)	29.754

SOURCE: Based on *Census of India, 1921*, vol. XV: *Punjab and Delhi*, part I, ch. IV, Subsidiary Table II (pp. 192–3) and *All Parties Conference; Together with a Summary of the Proceedings of the Conference held at Lucknow* (Allahabad: AICC, September 1928), Appendix, p. 57.

Columns 7 and 8 were constructed by multiplying the figures in cols. 3 & 4 by 1000 and then dividing the resultant figures in these columns by those in cols. 5 & 6 respectively.

NOTES

1. Hector Bolitho, *Jinnah: Creator of Pakistan* (London: John Murray 1954), p. 9. See also S. Qudratullah Fatimi, 'Quaid-i-Azam and Lord Morley', in Ahmad Hasan Dani (ed.), *World Scholars on Quaid-i-Azam Mohammad Ali Jinnah* (Islamabad: Quaid-i-Azam University, 1979), pp. 75–82. Morley was the ideologue of the Liberal Party and the legatee of John Stuart Mill.

2. Fatima Jinnah, 'My Brother', an unpublished personal memoir, National Archives of Pakistan [hereafter NAP], Islamabad.

3. William Wedderburn (1836–1918) and Henry Cotton (1845–1915), on their return to England after attending the Congress session, had stressed the urgency of sending Banerjea, Jinnah, Lajpat Rai and Gokhale as Congress delegates to plead for Indian claims during the impending British elections. Gokhale's departure was blocked by Mehta till September 1905, while Jinnah's nomination by Bal Gangadhar Tilak (1856–1920) was blocked on the plea that he was much too young to be sent as a Congress delegate. Jinnah was only twenty-eight then. See B. R. Nanda, *Gokhale* (Delhi: OUP, 1977), pp. 187–8.

4. Quaid-i-Azam Papers [hereafter QAP], NAP, Islamabad. The diaries' entries are not always complete.

5. Interestingly, Jinnah's Independent Party in the Central Assembly during the 1920s and 1930s included some of the leading Parsi members of the Assembly.

6. *Report of the Proceedings of the Twenty-Second Indian National Congress held at Calcutta on 26th, 27th, 28th, and 29th December 1906* (Calcutta, 1907), p. 120.

7. Jinnah's evidence before the Islington Commission: Minutes of Evidence in Parliamentary Papers, 1914, India Office Library and Records (IOLR).

8. Jinnah had both professional and social relations with Tyabji; see e.g. Jinnah to Tyabji, 5 June 1900, Tyabji Papers, microfilm, London, School of Oriental and African Studies (SOAS).

9. *Report of the Twenty-fifth India.1 National Congress held at Allahabad on the 26th, 27th, 28th, and 29th December, 1910* (Allahabad, 1911), pp. 93–4. Earlier, at the time of the Simla Deputation (1906), he had asked, in a letter to the editor, whether 'the gentlemen... [were] supposed to represent Bombay' since he knew 'of no meeting of the Mahomedan community that appointed these worthies to represent Bombay' on the deputation 'whereever elected'; as to what 'the object of the deputation', was—'nobody

upto now knows what the deputation proposes to do'; and finally he asked whether this was 'the way to speak in the name of millions' since 'nothing has been done to ascertain the real views of the Mohomedans of this city in the matter'. *Gujrati* (Bombay), 7 October 1906, Syed Sharifuddin Pirzada (ed.), *The Collected Works of Quaid-e-Azam Mohammad Ali Jinnah* (Karachi: East and West Publishing Company 1984), vol. I, 1906–21, p. 1; hereafter *CWQAJ*.

10. Speech, Bombay, 20 December 1913, typescript, Archives Freedom Movement [hereafter AFM], University of Karachi Library (hereafter KUL), vol. 119, p. 51.

11. For example see Wazir Hasan to Jinnah, 8 December 1912, ibid., vol. 66, p. 44.

12. Wazir Hasan to Jinnah, 26 February 1913, ibid., vol. 33, p. 37.

13. See *The Pioneer* (Lucknow), 2 January 1913.

14. Syed Sharifuddin Pirzada (ed.), *Foundations of Pakistan* (Karachi: National Publishing House Ltd., 1969), I, p. 272; hereafter *FOP*.

15. Jinnah to Wazir Hasan, 21 May 1913, AFM, vol. 115, p. 56.

16. Ibid., vol. 225, I, p. 37.

17. See his appeal to Muslim leaders, *CWQAJ*, I, pp. 136–7; see extract below, note 45.

18. See his letter to *The Times of India* (Bombay), 10 June 1915, refuting the charges.

19. For an assessment of his role, see Hugh F. Owen, 'Negotiating the Lucknow Pact', *Journal of Asian Studies*, XXXI: 3 (May 1972), pp. 562–87; and Jamnadas Dwarkadas, *Political Memoirs* (Bombay: United India Publications, 1969), pp. 122–3.

20. For October 1916 see B. Pattabhi Sitaramayya, *The History of the Indian National Congress (1885–1935)* (Madras: W.C. of the Congress, 1935), p. 213: text of the Memorandum in ibid., Appendix I, pp. i–iv. For August 1917 see P. G. Robb, *The Government of India and Reforms: Policies towards Politics and the Constitution* (London: OUP, 1976).

21. Jawaharlal Nehru, *An Autobiography* (Bombay: Allied Publishers Private Ltd., 1962), p. 67.

22. Leonard Mosley, *The Last Days of the British Raj* (London: Weidenfeld and Nicolson, 1961), p. 72.

23. Crew to Hardinge, 14 May 1914, Encl., Hardinge Papers, vol. 120, CUL.

24. Kanji Dwarkadas, *India's Fight for Freedom* (Bombay: Popular Prakhasan, 1966), p. 65.

25. Owen, pp. 573, 575.

26. Cited in Sarojini Naidu (ed.), *Mohomed Ali Jinnah: An Ambassador of Unity* (Madras: Ganesh, 1918), p. 1.

27. Ibid., p. 20.

28. For details, *Source Material for A History of the Freedom Movement in India* (Bombay: Suptd., Govt. Printing, 1958), II, pp. 713–24; for Jinnah's role, see pp. 719–22. For an account of a participant in the Town Hall protest, see Kanji Dwarkadas, *Ruttie Jinnah* (Bombay: Bhatkal Books, 1963), pp. 13–14. Willingdon was known to be hostile to Indian aspirations: he was implicated in the controversy on holding Congress and League sessions simultaneously, leading to the break-up of the Bombay League in 1915. Willingdon had also publicly insulted the HRL at the Bombay Provincial War Conference in 1918. See *Source Material* II, pp. 863–88, and D. Tahmankar, *Lokmanya Tilak* (London: John Murray, 1956), p. 216.

29. Matlubul Hasan Saiyid, *Mohammad Ali Jinnah: A Political Study* (Lahore: Shaikh Muhammad Ashraf, 1945), pp. 238–9.

30. Stanley A. Wolpert, 'Congress Leadership in Transition', in B. N. Pandey (ed.), *Leadership in South Asia* (New Delhi: Vikas, 1977), pp. 655–65.

31. Percival Spear, *Memorandum on the Basis and Structure of Indian Government* (1940), p. 18, L/P&J/8/689, IOLR.

32. Sitaramayya, I:348.

33. Cited in Azim Husain, *Fazl-i-Husain: A Political Biography* (Bombay: Longmans, 1946), p. 1240.

34. Nehru, p. 72.

35. Ibid., p. 73. Other Congress leaders had as well and always felt the same way. Thus, Munshi wrote to Gandhi on 20 June 1940, 'So long as you wield the power, it would be a pleasure to follow you even without understanding. That is a matter of faith.' K. M. Munshi, *Indian Constitutional Documents*, vol. I: *Pilgrimage to Freedom* (1902–1950) (Bombay: Bharatiya Vidya Bhawan, 1967), Appendix 48, p. 403.

36. Indulal K. Yajnik, *Gandhi As I Knew Him* (Delhi: Danish Mahal, rev. ed., 1933), p. 154.

37. Jinnah's first discomfiture came at a meeting of the Home Rule League on 4 October 1920 when Gandhi, upon being elected HRL President on Jinnah's proposal, went about changing its constitution and its aims and objects, and renaming it Swarajya Sabha. When his two amendments and Munshi's amendment to Gandhi's original resolution were voted down, Jinnah contended that the constitution could not be changed unless supported by a

three-fourths majority and without proper notice, but Gandhi ruled that a bare majority was competent to change it, adding, 'It was open to any member, be he a life-member or otherwise, to resign his membership if he thought he could not remain a member of the Sabha under its altered constitution'. Whereupon Jinnah, along with Jayakar, Munshi, Jamnadas Dwarkadas, Kanji Dwarkadas and fourteen others, resigned on 27 October 1926, saying that 'the constitution adopted by the League in its general meeting . . . constitutes a fundamental departure from the aims, objects and methods of work hitherto pursued by the League', and that 'these changes in the constitution were made by adopting a procedure contrary to the rules and regulations of the League'. About twenty persons, led by Jinnah, also left the Congress after Nagpur. Munshi feels that Gandhi could not have launched upon the Non-co-operation movement without forcing 'Jinnah and his followers out of the Home Rule League and later the Congress'. Since the Swarajya Sabha was 'killed' soon after getting Jinnah and his supporters out, Dwarkadas sees in Gandhi's move an attempt 'to neutralize Jinnah's political influence'. M. R. Jayakar, *The Story of My Life* (Bombay: Asia Publishing House, 1958), I, pp. 405–6; Dwarkadas, *India's Fight for Freedom*, pp. 153–4; Munshi, pp. 17–18.

38. Sitaramayya, p. 378.

39. Saiyid, p. 273.

40. For details, see Jayakar, I, pp. 517–57. Jinnah, Jayakar and Natarajan to PSV, 28 and 30 January 1922, Sapru Correspondence, 2nd Series, Reel 12, pp. 229, 233. IOLR; see also *The Indian Annual Register* (hereafter IAR) (Calcutta), 1922, I, pp. 353–80; and Sitarammaya, I, pp 388–90.

41. P. C. Bamford, *Histories of the Non-Co-operation and Khilafat Movement* (Delhi: Government of India Press, 1925), pp. 44, 46.

42. While Jinnah never disputed the national character of the INC till the Lucknow (1937) League and often referred to Gandhi as Mahatma Gandhi till the second RTC (1931), Mohamed Ali had this to say in 1930: 'his [Gandhi's] movement is not a movement for complete independence of India but for making the seventy millions of Musalmans dependents of the Hindu Mahasabha'. *The Times of India*, 24 April 1930. In a similar vein Shaukat Ali wrote to Ansari on 19 May 1929: 'For any honourable peace and pact we are always ready but not for the slavery of the Hindus; . . . the Congress . . . has ceased to be National now. It has become an adjunct of the Hindu Mahasabha. . . .' Mushirul Hasan (ed.),

Muslims and the Congress (New Delhi: Manohar, 1979), p. 70; hereafter referred to by the title.

43. *CWQAJ*, I, pp. 136–7.

44. Munshi, I, p. 20.

45. D. G. Tendulkar, *Mahatma: Life of Mohandas Karamchand Gandhi* (Delhi: Ministry of Information and Broadcasting, new rev. edn. 1960–63), II, p. 13.

46. Irwin to Benn, 6 February 1930, Halifax Coll., MSS EUR C152/6, IOLR.

47. David Page, *Prelude to Partition* (Delhi: OUP, 1982), pp. 118, 120. For the preceding quotation by Jinnah, see Saiyid, p. 305.

48. Mushir Hussain Kidwai to Motilal Nehru, 5 December 1924, AICC Papers, 37/1925, cited in ibid., p. 120. Jawaharlal was Secretary of the Congress.

49. *FOP*, II, p. 17.

50. Ibid.

51. *Indian Quarterly Register* (hereafter *IQR*), 1924, II, p. 481.

52. Jinnah to Jayakar, 22 May 1925, Jayakar, II, pp. 558–60.

53. Ibid., II, pp. 560–1.

54. Ibid., II, pp.591.

55. Joachim Alva, *Men and Super Men of Hindustan* (Bombay: Thacker, 1943), p. 212.

56. Cited in Mohammad Noman, *Muslim India* (Allahabad: Kitabistan, 1942), p. 221.

57. The Delhi Muslim Proposals were formulated by a Muslim conference, called and presided over by Jinnah on 20 March 1927. M.A. Jinnah *History of the Origin of 'Fourteen Points'* (Bombay: Shah Bahram Printing Press, n.d.) pp. 3–6. Both Irwin and Bhopal, however, felt that an influential section of Muslims were against abandoning separate electorates. Irwin to Vt. Goschen (Governor of Madras), 19 May 1927, and Bhopal to Irwin, 27 July 1927, Halifax Coll., C152/21.

58. *IQR*, 1927, I, p. 37.

59. *All Parties Conference 1928: Report of the Committee appointed by the Conference to determine the principles of the Constitution of India* (hereafter *APC*) (Allahabad: Hon. Sec., AICC, 1928), pp. 17–18; and *The Civil & Military Gazettee* (hereafter *CMG*) (Lahore), 27 March 1927, p. 11:1.

60. *IQR*, 1927, I, pp. 14–21.

61. Ibid.; *APC*, pp. 18–19.

62. See *Report of the Indian National Congress, Forty-Second session, Madras, 1927*, pp. 61, 75.

63. Ibid., Appendix ɪ, p. 9.
64. Speech, Calcutta (1927) League, *FOP*, ɪɪ, p. 123.
65. For example, see the reaction of Hindu MLA's in the Central Assembly in *CMG*, 26 March 1927, p. 11:1; *Report of the Indian Statutory Commission* (London: HMSO, 1930) ɪᴠ, p. 169. For the Mahasabha, Sikh, and Sindhi Hindus' reactions, see respectively *IQR*, 1927, ɪ, pp. 424–5, *CMG*, 27 March 1927, p. 12:2, and 30 March 1927, p. 8:1. For the general Hindu reaction see the extracts of *The Hindustan Times* (March 1927) in *IQR*, 1927, ɪɪ, pp. 351–2.
66. *CMG*, 25 March 1927, p. 18:2.
67. *APC*, pp. 123–4.
68. *IQR*, 1928, ɪɪ, pp. 421–6.
69. *Tribune*, 8 October 1928.
70. *The Proceedings of the All Parties National Convention* (hereafter *PAPNC*) (Allahabad, APNC, 1928), pp. 76–7.
71. Ibid., pp. 78–82.
72. *APC*, p. 44.
73. Ibid., p. 48.
74. *PAPNC*, pp. 78–82.
75. Ibid., p. 84.
76. Ram Gopal, *Indian Muslims: A Political History (1858–1907)* (Bombay: Asia Publishing House, 1959), p. 214.
77. *PAPNC*, pp. 93–4.
78. GI Home Poll. 37/1925: Hailey to Sir Alexander Muddiman, 11 December 1924, cited in Page, p. 120; and Gandhi to Fazl-i-Husain, 2 March 1925, *The Collected Works of Mahatma Gandhi* (Hereafter CWMG) (New Delhi: Publications Division, 1957) vol. 26, p. 215. Motilal was also committed to 'stand by the Madras resolution'. Motilal to Ansari, 1 May 1928, *Muslims and the Congress*, p. 47.
79. Cf. 'at the Calcutta Convention, it was the Hindu Mahasabha which completely did the work of destruction'. Ansari to Gandhi, 13 February 1930, ibid., p. 96. Uma Kaura feels that 'The failure of the Convention can only be attributed to the inability of the Congress leaders to stand up firmly against the pressures of the Hindu Mahasabha and override its opinions'. *Muslims and Indian Nationalism* (New Delhi: Manohar, 1977), p. 46.
80. M. C. Chagla asserted that 'the delegates whom the League sent to the Convention represented the most advanced section of Muslim thought... and that several of them have fought their own people and broken with their own organization in order to

support the national cause....If these people are going to be dubbed as communalists then perhaps there is not a single Muslim nationalist anywhere in the country.' *Bombay Chronicle*, 1 January 1929, cited in ibid.

81. *CMG*, 3 January 1939, p. 4.

82. See, e.g. Mushirul Hasan, *Nationalism and Communal Politics in India, 1916–1929* (New Delhi: Manohar, 1979), ch. 8; Waheed-uz-Zaman, *Towards Pakistan* (Lahore: Publishers United, 1979), ch. 2; and *Quaid-i-Azam Mohammad Ali Jinnah: Myth and Reality* (Karachi: N.B.F., 1976), p. 70; *The Memoirs of Aga Khan* (London: Cassell & Co., 1954), p. 295; Bolitho, p. 95; and Ram Gopal, pp. 215–16.

83. *IAR*, 1932, II, pp. 308–12.

84. Shahabuddin to Fazl-i-Husain, 30 January 1933; Husain to Jogendra Singh, 31 March 1933; Singh to Husain, 3 April 1933; Shahabuddin to Husain, 7 April 1933; Encl. (Singh to Shahabuddin, 5 April 1933); Husain to Sikander Hayat Khan, 27 April 1933; Sikander to Husain, 1 May 1933; Husain to Singh, 8 May 1933; Husain to Shahabuddin, 11 May 1933; Husain to Zafrullah, 29 May 1933; and Husain to Aga Khan, 26 June 1933; Fazl-i-Husain Coll., MSS EUR E.352/16, 17, 18, 19, 23 IOLR. See also Azim Husain, pp. 279–80.

85. *CMG*, 8 January 1937, p. 1:3; text of correspondence in ibid., 10 January 1937, p. 9:1–2; see also ibid., 9 January 1937, p. 1:5–6, 2:1 and 10 January 1937, p. 5:2.

86. *CMG*, 2 January 1929, p. 15:1–2, and 4 January 1929, p. 13:1.

87. *Hamdard* (Delhi), 5 and 10 March 1929, and *CMG*, 2 April 1929.

88. See Nawab Mohammad Ismail Khan's presidential address, Lucknow, November 1930, K. K. Aziz, *The All India Muslim Conference 1928–1935* (Karachi: National Publishing House Ltd., 1972), p. 65.

89. Ram Gopal, p. 220.

90. See, e.g. Irwin to Geoffrey de Montmorency (Governor of Punjab), 13 May 1930; Hailey to Irwin, 9 December 1930; Halifax Coll., C152/24, 19, Fazl-i-Husain to Shafaat Ahmad Khan, 6 November 1930; Fazl-i-Husain Coll. E352/13; Hailey to Haig, 19 November 1932; Hailey Coll. E.220/18; also the file on Communal Award, Zetland Coll. D609/22, IOLR.

91. Irwin to Sapru, 3 December 1929; Halifax Coll., C152/23.

92. Jinnah to Irwin, 3 December 1929; V. J. Patel to Irwin, 2 December 1929, confidential, ibid.

93. Jinnah to Irwin, 15, 16 December 1929 (tels.); Irwin to Jinnah, 14

December 1929, 15, 19, 20 December 1929 (tels.), ibid.; Jinnah to Sapru, 3, 14 December 1929; Sapru to Jinnah, 5, 13, 19 December 1929. The Sapru Correspondence, 2nd series, Reel 12, microfilm, IOLR.

94. Minutes of the meeting taken by Sir George Cunningham, PSV, QAP, File 15:53–9; Irwin to Benn, 26 December 1929; Irwin to Halifax 25 December 1929; Halifax Coll., C152/5.

95. Sapru to Cunningham, 4 January 1930; Sapru to Irwin, 4 January 1930; Sapru to Jinnah, 5 January 1930, Sapru Correspondence.

96. Jinnah to Irwin, 24 June 1930, Halifax Coll.

97. Sapru to Irwin, 6 July 1930, ibid., C152/25.

98. Irwin to Sapru, 8 July 1930, ibid.

99. Bhopal to Irwin, 9 July 1930, Encl., ibid.

100. Irwin to Sapru, 8 July 1930, Sapru to Irwin, 12/13 July 1930; Jayakar to Sapru, 15 July 1930, Sapru Correspondence.

101. Cf. 'I am only hoping that I may be spared angry demonstrations at Bombay when going to the boat [to sail for England to attend the RTC]. At the moment one who differs from the Congress should be prepared for anything unpleasant and my experience during the last two months have been none too happy or pleasant'. Sapru to Irwin, 6 September 1930; Jayakar to Sapru, 15 August 1930 and 7 September 1930, Sapru Correspondence.

102. See Fazl-i-Husain to Hailey, 20 May 1930 and Hailey to Fazl-i-Husain, 24 May 1930; Hailey Coll., E220/8A.

103. Hailey to Irwin, 20 November 1930; Halifax Coll., C151/19.

104. Sarvepalli Gopal, *Jawaharlal Nehru: A Biography* (London: Jonathan Cape, 1975), i, p. 223.

105. Sir Samuel Hoare to Willingdon, 5 April 1934, Templewood Coll.

106. Cited in William S. Metz, 'The Political Career of Mohammad Ali Jinnah', unpublished Ph.D. thesis, Univ. of Pennsylvania, 1952, p. 10.

107. Speech, Bombay (1936) League, AFM, vol. 168.

108. *CMG*, 20 October 1936, p. 11.

109. Gopal, i, p. 223.

110. Munshi to Gandhi, 27 December 1934, Munshi, i, pp. 360–1 (Appendix 6); see also p. 35.

111. *CWMG*, vol. 57: 390.

112. *The Times of India*, 5–7 April 1934.

113. *IAR*, 1933, ii, pp. 212–13.

114. *Legislative Assembly Debates*, 1935, i, pp. 518–19.

115. 'Summary of conversation between Mr. Jinnah and myself', *circa*

20 January 1935, Vallabhbhai Patel Papers, cited in John Gallagher, 'Congress in Decline: Bengal 1930 to 1939', John Gallagher, Gordon Johnson & Anil Seal (eds.), *Locality, Province and Nation: Essays on Indian Politics 1870 to 1940* (London: CUP, 1973), p. 308.

116. See terms of the formula in Kaura, pp. 102–3, based on Notes on conversation between Jinnah and Rajendra Prasad held on 13–14, February 1935, AICC Papers.

117. Zetland, who was Governor of Bengal prior to his membership of the JPC, was persuaded by the Hindu leaders, including N. N. Sircar (Advocate-General of Bengal, a delegate to JPC and author of *Bengal Under Communal Award and Poona Pact* (Calcutta: The Book Company Ltd., 1933)), into pleading the caste Hindu case in Bengal. Accordingly Zetland sent a secret note on 'Bengal and the Communal Award' to Linlinthgow, the JPC Chairman, suggesting a reopening of the Award in respect of Bengal and amendments to satisfy the Hindus. Zetland to Linlithgow, 5 February 1934; Sircar to Zetland, 18 October 1933, Zetland Coll. D609/22; see also Kaura, pp. 104–5. Zetland also moved an amendment to the Communal Award in respect of Bengal at the JPC meeting when the Chairman's report was taken up para by para. *Joint Committee on Indian Constitutional Reform* (Session, 1933–4), *Proceedings* (1934), pp. 338–46.

118. See statement by Dr Inder Narain Sen Gupta, Secretary, Bengal CNP, *Asr-i-Jadid* (Calcutta), 28 July 1937.

119. 30 March 1936, Zetland Coll., D609/6.

120. Willingdon to Zetland, 6 April 1936, ibid.

121. R. Coupland, *Report on the Constitutional Problem in India* (Madras: OUP, 1944), II, p. 15.

122. Gopal, I, p. 223.

123. Mohammad Yakub (Secretary, AIML) to Wazir Hasan, 1 March 1936, AFM, vol. 168.

124. *All India Muslim League Central Board: Policy and Programme* (Delhi: AIML, n.d.), pp. 9–16; *IAR*, 1936, I, pp. 299–301.

125. See list in Choudhary Khaliquzzaman, *Pathway to Pakistan* (Lahore: Longmans, 1961), Appendix I, pp. 416–17.

126. Motilal Nehru to Thakurdas, 27 April 1925, cited in Page, p. 124.

127. Council Meetings 1936–7, AFM, vol. 222.

128. Jayakar to Sapru, 21 May 1936, Sapru Correspondence.

129. AFM, vol. 222.

130. *CMG*, 14 August 1936, p. 14; Gopal, I, p. 223.

131. *Asr-i-Jadid*, 11 April 1936, p. 1; Saiyid, p. 540.

132. *CMG*, 21 August 1936, p. 7:4.

133. Ibid., 23 August 1936, p. 5:2.
134. Ibid., 20 October 1936, p. 11:3.
135. Ibid., 3 January 1937, p. 8:5.
136. Ibid., 22 January 1937, p. 4:2–5.
137. Cited in Bijoy Prasad Singh, *Parliamentary Government in India* (Calcutta, Thacker, Spink & Co., 1933), p. 367.
138. *CMG*, 21 September 1937, p. 5:1–2.
139. Interview, Karachi, 1 February 1936; ibid., 4 February 1936, p. 9:1.
140. See Aga Khan to Fazl-i-Husain, 22 February, 13 August and 28 December 1935, 14 January,18 and 22 June 1936; and Aga Khan to Fazl-i-Husain, 22 February, 28 December 1935, 14 January 1936, 24 June and 6 July 1936, Fazl-i-Husain Coll., E352/19..
141. Aga Khan to Fazl-i-Husain, 6 July 1936, see also Fazl-i-Husain to Aga Khan, 18, 22 June 1936 and 22 June 1936, ibid.
142. Shafaat Ahmad Khan to Fazl-i-Husain, 27 May 1936, ibid., E352/13; and Azim Husain, p. 310.
143. See, e.g. Linlithgow on Haig's direct involvement in promoting 'the Landlord party in the U.P.', Linlithgow to Zetland, 17 March 1937 (Secret) (handwritten), Zetland Coll., D609/31.
144. Shafaat Ahmad Khan to Fazl-i-Husain, 5 July 1936, Fazl-i-Husain Coll., E352/13.
145. Raja of Mahmudabad, 'Some Memoirs', in C. H. Philips and Mary Doreen Wainwright (eds.), *The Partition of India: Policies and Perspectives 1935–1947* (London: George Allen & Unwin Ltd., 1970), p. 384.
146. Coupland, *Report*, II, p. 15.
147. Francis Robinson, *Separatism Among Indian Muslims: The Politics of the United Provinces, 1860–1923* (London: CUP, 1977), pp. 126, 354.
148. See B. Pattabhi Sitaramayya, *The History of the Indian National Congress* (Bombay: Padma Publications, 1947), II, p. 690; Nehru to Prasad, 21 July 1937, S. Gopal (ed.), *Selected Works of Jawaharlal Nehru* [hereafter SWJN] (New Delhi: Orient Longman, 1976), vol. 8, pp.165–6.
149. Michael Brecher, *Nehru: A Political Biography* (London: OUP, 1969), p. 231.
150. Sir Reginald Coupland, *India: A Re-Statement* (London: OUP, 145), pp. 152, also pp. 152–3, 180.
151. Khaliq-uz-Zaman, p. 167.
152. Dwarkadas, *India's Fight for Freedom*, p. 466.

153. *Asr-i-Jadid*, 13 July 1937.
154. *SWJN.*, vol. 7, p. 468.
155. Ibid., vol. 8, pp. 119, 120–1. Nehru explained his 'two forces' as 'two parties' in his 10 January 1937 statement. Yet some writers (e.g. Nanda) insist that 'Nehru had described the contest as between "two forces" not between "two parties"'. The statement was, of course, primarily 'directed against the Government'; but Nehru's elaboration in his earlier (18 September 1936) statement that 'Intermediate groups, whatever virtue they may possess, fade out and line up with one of the political forces' (ibid., vol. 7, p. 468) does lend itself to the sort of interpretation put on it by Jinnah. In his later (10 January 1937) statement, Nehru further explained, 'All "third parties", middle and undecided groups, etc. have no real importance....' B.R. Nanda, *Gokhale, Gandhi and the Nehrus* (London: George Allen & Unwin, 1974), p. 135.
156. E.g. see editorials, *Al-Jamiat*, the Jamiat's organ, for the following dates: 5 January 1929, 5 April 1929, 13 August 1931, 9 January 1934, 9 and 24 March 1934, 9 April 1934, 5 February 1935, 1 March 1935, and 9 January 1937. The Jamiat invited Jinnah to inaugurate its Conference at Delhi early in April 1936; its leaders issued a *fatwa* in the League's favour and barnstormed the countryside in support of the League's candidates; Maulana Ahmad Saeed was in constant touch with Jinnah; and its organ supported Jinnah's riposte to Nehru's 'two-forces' stance (9 January 1937). For details, see Sharif al Mujahid, *Quaid-i-Azam Jinnah: Studies in interpretation* (Karachi: Quaid-i-Azam Academy, 1981), pp. 430–2.
157. Cf. 'Money and bearded Maulanas were in great demand.' Assistant Secretary, U.P.P.C.C. to Rafi Kidwai, 6 July 1937, AICC File G61/1937, cited in Gopal, I, p. 228.
158. Brecher, p. 95.
159. *The Pioneer* (Allahabad), 30 July 1937; Khaliquzzaman, p. 161.
160. Brecher, p. 95.
161. Penderel Moon, *Divide and Quit* (London: Chatto and Windus, 1964), p. 32.
162. Gopal, I, p. 224.
163. See Jinnah's Speech, Bombay, 20 December 1913, typescript, AFM, 119:51.
164. *SWJN*, 8:121.

CONGRESS AFTER 1967: STRATEGIES OF MOBILIZATION

MEENAKSHI JAIN

When India gained independence the twice-born castes (Brahmins, Kshatriyas and Vaishyas) dominated the Congress party and state governments in most of northern India. Though the agricultural castes (variously called sudras or other 'backward castes') were represented in the party, political leadership remained in the hands of the élite castes. This situation remained largely unaltered up to the mid sixties.

To avoid misunderstanding it needs to be emphasized that this was not the result of any deliberate plan on the part of the Congress leadership, which could not have altered the situation even had it tried. The upper castes were the first to take to western education and therefore to espouse the cause of freedom.[1] Nationalistic activity also helped them meet the challenge of anti-Brahmin movements in various parts of the country. But that too was not part of any deliberate design.

Élite caste domination of the Congress party during the period in question has been amply documented. Angela Burger's study of the 1962 Uttar Pradesh legislative assembly, for example, shows that of all parties Congress was the least representative of backward castes (roughly 40 to 42 per cent of the state's population).[2] Similarly, Ralph Meyer's data reveals that in 1962 almost 63 per cent of all Congress MLAs in UP belonged to élite castes (about 20 to 22 per cent of the population) and only 6.8 per cent to backward castes. Meyer also states that at the time of the first general election in 1952, 28 per cent of all Congress MLAs were Brahmins and 13 per cent Thakurs. In 1962 the figures had risen to 30 and 19 per cent respectively.[3] Paul Brass too has drawn attention to the lack of support for Congress among the middle peasantry in UP, particularly among the other backward castes (OBCs) with land holdings ranging from 2.5 to 30 acres.[4]

Studies by other political scientists highlight the inadequate representation of these groups in the Congress party. Harry Blair's work on Bihar, for example, shows that in that state too Congress was dominated by the upper castes. In the Congress ministry in Bihar in 1962, 58 per cent of the cabinet ministers were from the forward castes (about 13 per cent of the state's population) and eight per cent from the backward castes (about 50 per cent of the population).[5] Nor was the situation different in other states in the north.

Stanley Kochanek's study of the Congress party discloses that 46.4 per cent of the members of the union council of ministers were Brahmins. Brahmins, Kayasthas, Kshatriyas and Vaishyas together constituted 46 per cent of the members of the Congress parliamentary party, though they comprise only about 20 per cent of the population. Sudras, on the other hand, accounted for only 10 per cent of Congress MPs in the Lok Sabha, though Sudras constitute over half the population of India.[6]

This élite-caste-dominated order received vital support from the scheduled castes, tribes and minorities, and these groups were adequately represented in the Congress legislature parties in the states and at the Centre.[7]

Muslim and Harijan support for the Congress after 1947 is not difficult to explain. To put it briefly, traumatized by the consequences of partition, the Muslims were in need of a protector. Jawaharlal Nehru, they felt, could be that protector. Nehru's secular credentials were well established. Moreover, since independent political activity had become 'illegitimate' for the Muslims in view of their support for the demand for Pakistan, they

had to seek cover elsewhere. Congress provided the necessary
umbrella. As for the Harijans, Gandhi had endeared the Congress to them. No other organization reached the villages where
most of them lived, and other political parties were dominated
by land-owning castes that Harijans feared the most.

The position in the south and in Maharashtra was different
from that in the north. By the time of independence, dominant
agricultural castes had displaced the Brahmins in the Congress
party there. Because of their overwhelming superiority over the
twice-born castes, both in terms of numbers and economic
power, the Marathas in Maharashtra, the Reddis and Kammas
in Andhra Pradesh, the Lingayats and Vokkaligas in Mysore,
and the Gounders in Tamil Nadu had emerged as the new political élites. They retained their grip on the party and state governments till the end of the sixties. In the north, however, there
was a struggle for political leadership between the twice-born
and the middle castes. This became a major source of both the
subsequent decline of Congress and of political instability in the
sixties.

The increasing politicization of the other backward castes in
north India posed a serious challenge to Congress. The challenge emerged clearly in 1967 when the Congress party lost
power at the state level in all north-Indian states—from Himachal Pradesh to West Bengal—and middle-caste peasant leaders
took over as chief ministers in Haryana (Rao Birendra Singh),
Uttar Pradesh (Chaudhury Charan Singh), Madhya Pradesh
(G. N. Singh) as a result of defections from Congress. In Bihar
the Yadav leader B. P. Mandal formed a minority Shoshit Dal
ministry in January 1968.

The picture is of course by no means as clear-cut as my formulation might suggest; for among the Hindus political dif-
ferentiations are even less sharp than in other societies; there
are power struggles in each social formation, however defined;
political activities are not necesarily guided by caste considerations, even if politicians use this factor as a political resource; all
in all the position is far more fluid than any attempt at analysis
can provide.

Even so, the defection of Chaudhury Charan Singh from

Congress was symbolic of the nature of the challenge that faced the party. Charan Singh, a Jat by caste, was widely regarded as the spokesman of middle farmers among the other backward castes such as the Ahirs, the Kurmis and the Gujars in Uttar Pradesh. While a member of Congress, he had strongly advocated the cause of individual ownership and opposed proposals for co-operative farming.[8] He had also played an important role in the formulation and implementation of the zamindari abolition laws as a minister in UP. In that capacity he had opposed the imposition of a surcharge on land revenue and favoured a lower ceiling on land. On leaving Congress, Charan Singh became the first member of a non-élite caste to head the UP government. It was from groups which Charan Singh represented that came the main challenge to Congress.

A study of the composition of the SVD governments formed during this period shows a remarkable shift in favour of the backward castes. They, for example, constituted 30 per cent of the ministers in Charan Singh's government[9] and 34 per cent in B. P. Mandal's cabinet in Bihar.[10] In Haryana 45 per cent of the ministers in Rao Birendra Singh's ministry were Jats.[11]

By 1969–70 the SVD governments had collapsed, partly as a result of internal contradictions and partly because of Mrs Gandhi's manipulations through governors.[12] At about the same time Mrs Gandhi made a bid for supremacy in the party. She achieved her objective but at the cost of splitting the Congress. This happened in the latter half of 1969.[13]

The split was not without cost to Mrs Gandhi. About 40 per cent of the organizational strength of the parent body went with her opponents, the party bosses popularly called the syndicate. In a number of states, large sections of the dominant agricultural castes supported what came to be known as the Congress(O), 'O' standing for organization.

A study of the division in the Congress parliamentary party would show that about 77 per cent of the total CPP remained with Mrs Gandhi. Mrs Gandhi's greatest support came from the Hindi heartland: 84 per cent of the Congress MPs from this region sided with her, as against 14 per cent with the syndicate. Mrs Gandhi also won over 77 per cent of the members from eastern

India and 71 per cent of those from the west. In the south over
70 per cent of the legislators remained loyal to Mrs Gandhi.[14] It
is interesting to note that in 1967 the Congress party had suffered its greatest electoral reverses in the two regions where
Mrs Gandhi now obtained the greatest support—in the Hindi
heartland and the east. By contrast the syndicate was dispropor-
tionately strong in south and west India, areas with a high level
of vote for the Congress in 1967.

In terms of caste, the scene was not very different on the two
sides: 51 per cent of Mrs Gandhi's supporters in the CPP were
from the upper castes, 24 per cent from the middle castes and 25
per cent from the scheduled castes. The representation of these
groups among the syndicate supporters was 62, 15 and 23 per
cent respectively.[15]

Following the split in 1969, Mrs Gandhi made a deliberate
attempt to restructure the Congress. She tried to reduce dominant middle-caste representation and raise that of the lower
castes in order to supplement the traditional Congress support
base among the minorities, scheduled castes and tribes.
Populism, in the form of bank nationalization, the abolition of
privy purses, the *garibi hatao* slogan and the 20-point programme served as means of greater mobilization of the lower
castes.

Mrs Gandhi's effort to restructure the party to downgrade the
dominant castes and raise the lower castes is best illustrated by
examples from the south. In Karnataka, as noted earlier, the
Lingayats and Vokkaligas had hitherto dominated the state's
politics. The Vokkaligas, who were the largest single caste in
the old Mysore state, had provided all the chief ministers—
K. C. Reddy, K. Hanumanthaiah and Kadilal Manjappa—till the
reorganization of the state in 1956. Thereafter the chief ministers were all Lingayats—S. Nijalingappa, B. D. Jatti, S. R.
Kanthi and Veerendra Patil.[16]

With the split in the party in 1969 the Mysore unit went
largely to the Congress(O) headed by Nijalingappa. Devraj
Urs was one of the few Karnataka leaders to remain with Mrs
Gandhi. As a result of the weakness of the state unit of the Con-
gress(R) ('R' for ruling), the Congress(O) government headed

by Veerendra Patil continued in office till 1971, when the state was brought under President's Rule.

As a number of scholars have noted, during the 1972 assembly elections the Congress(R) gave tickets to persons belonging to small and backward classes, scheduled castes, tribes and minorities, though it took care not to alienate the dominant castes completely. Instead the Congress(R) sought to break the Lingayat and Vokkaliga hold on power through a skilful exploitation of conflicts among and within these groups. It tried to undermine the importance of Mandya district, the traditional stronghold of the Vokkaligas, and sought Vokkaliga support from areas where they were less well entrenched. At the same time the Congress(R) sought to benefit from divisions within the Lingayat community. Hitherto the small Jangama (priests) and Banajiga (merchants and traders) groups among the Lingayats had prospered much more than the cultivator groups, including the large Sadar Lingayats. The Congress(R) extended its favours to the Sadar Lingayats.[17]

The Congress(R) swept the polls in Karnataka and Devraj Urs was appointed chief minister. Between 1972 and 1980 he adopted a number of programmes to benefit the less privileged groups. To prevent a backlash he also provided some patronage to sections of the old dominant castes, especially to cultivators among the Vokkaligas and to the Lingayats in the northern districts. But his principal concern was for the disadvantaged groups who had now become the main support base of the party.

A study of the composition of the 1972 Urs cabinet shows that Lingayat, Vokkaliga and Brahmin representation declined from 71 per cent in 1967 to 46 per cent, while that of the minority groups increased from 28 to 54 per cent.[18]

Urs in effect forged an alliance between the less prosperous caste Hindus, scheduled castes, tribes and Muslims. The scheduled-caste leader Basavalingappa was appointed revenue minister; a scheduled-caste member was elected speaker of the assembly; scheduled-caste representation in the cabinet more than doubled and the scheduled castes were reassured that reservation for the other backward castes would not reduce

their statutory quotas. Social welfare programmes for the
benefit of the scheduled castes were also launched since these
were less likely to antagonize the cultivating Lingayats of the
northern districts than an attempt to tackle the problem of land-
lessness.[19]

In December 1972 Urs appointed the Karnataka backward
classes commission under the chairmanship of L. G. Havanur to
determine which communities were entitled to preferential
treatment. The commission declared that both the Lingayats
and the Bunts were forward groups. Thus, for the first time, the
Lingayats were deprived of the benefits of reservation. The
Vokkaligas, though formerly dominant, were included among
the backward castes, partly because they were not as advanced
in respect of education as the Lingayats, and partly because it
would have been unwise to alienate both the dominant groups
at the same time. The report recommended 16 per cent reservations for 15 backward castes. The Vokkaligas constituted more
than 50 per cent of these backward castes.[20]

The government broadly accepted the recommendations of
the Havanur Commission but Urs made some important modifications. First, he included Muslims (11 per cent of the population) in the backward classes category and reserved five per
cent of the seats and jobs for the economically backward, irrespective of caste. This was later raised to 15 per cent. And except
for the Lingayats, Bunts and Brahmins, almost every other
group was included in the backward-caste category. However,
an income limit was placed on those eligible for these special
privileges.[21]

In Andhra Pradesh too, after 1969, Mrs Gandhi attempted to
widen the socio-economic base of the party and reduce the
power of the Kammas and Reddis. During the 1972 assembly
elections she selected a large number of candidates from the
non-dominant groups and gave them 173 out of 287 party tickets.[22] As part of her strategy to weaken the dominant castes,
Mrs Gandhi appointed P. V. Narasimha Rao, a Brahmin from
Telangana, chief minister. A study of Rao's 1972 cabinet shows
that representation of the Reddys fell from 28.6 per cent in 1969
to 13.8 per cent, while that of the backward castes increased

from 10.7 to 20.7 per cent. Rao was, however, forced to quit due to violent agitations in the state on the *mulki* rules issue. It was widely believed that the dominant castes had played a key role in the agitation.[23]

Mrs Gandhi then turned to Vengal Rao, who came from the small Valema caste. Vengal Rao too sought to limit the hold of the dominant castes on his government. He also reconstituted party and panchayat committees to prevent these castes from using their socio-economic position to win elections and reassert themselves. The internal emergency proclaimed in June 1975 enabled him to further strengthen his hold on the party.[24]

In 1978 the Congress(I) claimed to have allotted 189 out of the 289 seats it contested to the weaker sections and the remaining 100 to the forward castes.[25] The Congress(R) won 175 seats in the state assembly. Of this the forward castes accounted for 42 per cent and the backward castes 34 per cent. The scheduled castes and tribes won 21 per cent of the seats and the Muslims 3.5 per cent. Clearly the Congress was much more representative of the various communities than in the past.[26]

In Maharashtra Mrs Gandhi made an attempt to reduce Maratha dominance. Here she initially relied on V. P. Naik, a member of the Vanjari tribal community, to do the job for her. Naik too was keen to strengthen his base in Vidarbha and to reduce his dependence on Y. B. Chavan, the unchallenged leader of the Marathas, and compared him to none other than Shivaji. During the 1972 assembly elections Naik recommended a large number of non-Marathas for party tickets. He, however, confined this strategy largely to the Vidarbha region because he was neither strong enough to confront Chavan nor inclined to do so.[27] On the whole he pursued a middle course, keeping both Mrs Gandhi and Chavan reasonably happy. That was the secret of his long tenure in office.

In 1975 Mrs Gandhi appointed S. B. Chavan chief minister in a continuing bid to undermine the support base of Y. B. Chavan, who for her symbolized Maratha power. Hailing as he did from backward Marathwada, formerly part of the Hyderabad Nizam's domain, S. B. Chavan drastically reduced the flow of patronage to western Maharashtra, which was Y. B. Chavan's power base. He stopped subsidies to co-operatives, withdrew some of the concessions to sugar mills and prosecuted loan defaulters. But S. B. Chavan was not an effective enough politician to create a support system for himself. He relied principally on the bureaucracy. As a result he could not make much change in the status quo. Despite the powers the emergency conferred on him, the basic power structure remained largely in Maratha hands. In the 1977 elections Maratha leaders combined to get most of S. B. Chavan's nominees in his native Marathwada defeated.[28]

Maharashtra is unique in this way: No caste in any other state enjoys the dual advantage of numbers and economic power that the Marathas do here. They constitute about 40 per cent of the total population and are the principal landowning-cultivator community. This made it virtually impossible for Mrs Gandhi to build a political structure that did not depend on their support. All that she could attempt was to try and whittle down Maratha domination, and this she achieved. She dispersed the Maratha power which Y. B. Chavan had built and nursed since the mid fifties. She brought a large number of non-Marathas into the party during the seventies. They sided with her at the time of the second split in 1978, whereas most of the Marathas went with Y. B. Chavan.

In Gujarat too an attempt was made to rebuild the Congress(R) between 1975 and 1980 and to reduce the power of the dominant Patidar-Kunbi caste.[29] John Wood's study of the state legislature party, for example, shows that representation of the weaker sections—Kshatriyas, Harijans, Adivasis and Muslims (KHAM)—increased dramatically from 38.7 per cent in 1967 to 68.6 per cent in 1980. Representation of the Kshatriyas (a loosely defined category that included the Rajputs at one extreme and low-caste Kolis at the other) increased even more sharply—from 10.8 to 23.6 per cent. In fact Kshatriyas were the largest single caste group in the Congress(I) in 1980.

Inevitably there was a decline in the proportion of high-caste representation in the Congress. The Brahmins managed to hold on to their position in the Congress(R) and were better represented in this party than in others. But that did not reverse the overall trend in the state. The Brahmins, though high in ritual terms, are not a power to reckon with in Gujarat. The Patidar-Kunbis fill that role and their representation among Congress MLAs declined from 21.5 per cent in 1967 to 10.7 per cent in 1980. Simultaneously their (Patidar-Kunbi) strength in other parties increased from 21.3 to 52.4 per cent. This fact would throw some light on the origins of the crisis in Gujarat in 1985 on the reservation issue. The Patels led and largely manned the anti-reservation agitation, leading to the resignation of Madhavsinh Solanki as chief minister. He had been a key figure in the restructuring of Congress.

In northern India the objectives were different in view of the far higher proportion of twice-born castes in the population in comparison with south and western India. Here, following the Congress split in 1969, Mrs Gandhi made efforts to accommodate backward castes but not to restructure the party to give it a different support base.

In Bihar the Bhumihar and Rajput leaders supported the Congress(O) in 1969, while the Brahmins largely remained with Mrs Gandhi. Unlike in UP, the middle castes did not leave the Congress in Bihar. Here 60 of the 115 Congress MLAs joined the Congress(R), headed at the state level by Daroga Prasad Rai (Yadav); the rest supported the Congress(O), led by Harihar Singh (Rajput). When President's Rule was revoked on 16 February 1970, Rai took over as chief minister.

As in UP, the attempts at adjustment with the middle castes in Bihar received a setback after Mrs Gandhi's victory (though on a minority vote) in the 1972 assembly elections. The Bhumihar and Rajput leaders who had left her in 1969 began to rejoin Mrs Gandhi. Thus the upper-caste representation in the cabinet increased, while that of the backward classes was frozen at the existing level. This was a demonstration of the essentially fluid character of Indian politics.

Thus a study of the composition of the Congress in Bihar over a 13-year period indicates no major change in the party structure. The élite castes constituted 47.8 per cent of the legislature party in 1962 and 41.2 per cent in 1975. In 1962 24.4 per cent of the party MLAs belonged to the backward castes; in

1975 they accounted for 23.6 per cent. The backward castes, it should be noted, constitute about 50 per cent of the state's population. Muslim representation increased marginally from 8.2 to 10.3 per cent while that of the scheduled castes fell from 17.4 to 15.5 per cent. Scheduled tribe representation, however, increased from one to 8.8 per cent.[30]

Also, no effort was made to change the power balance in the state government after the 1969 split. In fact representation of the forward castes in the cabinet increased from 33 per cent in 1970 to 40 per cent in 1975, while that of the backward castes remained stationary at 20 per cent. Similarly, Muslims and Bengalis together constituted 13 per cent of the cabinet in both 1970 and 1975. Significantly, the scheduled caste and scheduled tribe representation declined from 33 to 27 per cent.[31]

The alienation of the backward castes with the state government had widened by 1974, when Charan Singh launched the Bharatiya Lok Dal as a result of the merger of his Bharatiya Kranti Dal (so far confined to UP) with the Samyukta Socialist Party, which was well entrenched in Bihar. The SSP owed its origin to Dr Rammanohar Lohia, who had broken with his erstwhile colleagues, such as Jayaprakash Narayan, Ashoka Mehta and Achyut Patwardhan, in the former Congress Socialist Party (subsequently renamed Socialist Party and then Praja Socialist Party), and propounded the theory that the backward castes would serve the revolutionary role Marx had assigned to the proletariat in Europe. It is an irony of history that the followers of Lohia should have turned to the same J. P. whom they had so bitterly reviled, and that when he launched his 'total revolution' movement in 1974 (aimed essentially at the overthrow of the Bihar government and finally Mrs Gandhi) he should have turned to them. Their troops came from among the backward castes and dissatisfied Bhumihars and Rajputs.)

The backward castes were further alienated from the ruling party during the Emergency, when the Brahmin chief minister Jagannath Mishra opposed the reservations recommended by the state's backward classes commission. In the 1977 elections the Bhumihars, Rajputs and Yadavs supported the conglomeration of opposition parties named the Janata Party, while Congress drew strength mainly from the Brahmins and scheduled castes. In 1977 Muslim support for it was also greatly reduced.

The social composition of the party remained largely unaltered in UP as well. With the split in the party in 1969 the C. B. Gupta group—urban based but linked to important groups in the countryside, especially the Rajputs—left Mrs Gandhi. She then attempted to bring Charan Singh back into the Congress(R) and to that end supported his minority BKD government in UP in 1970. But when Charan Singh failed to reciprocate she withdrew support to him. Her party's massive victory in the 1971 elections reduced the need for an alliance with Charan Singh.[32]

Paul Brass's study shows that after 1971 Mrs Gandhi controlled UP through a rump party organization dominated by Brahmins. The three Congress chief ministers appointed between 1971 and 1977 were all Brahmin (Kamlapati Tripathi, H. N. Bahuguna and Narain Dutt Tiwari). Five of 15 cabinet ministers in the Tripathi ministry (including Tripathi) were Brahmins. In 1973 38 of the 75 district and city Congress committee presidents were Brahmins. Middle castes were greatly under-represented—only two Yadavs and two Kurmis and not a single Jat were presidents of district Congress committees.[33]

Despite the defection of Charan Singh and the Gupta group, popular support for the Congress(R) remained steady at about one-third of the vote in both the 1969 and 1974 assembly elections. Moreover, though the Janata party secured a massive victory in the 1977 elections, when it won 83 per cent of the seats in the assembly, the Congress vote declined marginally from 1974, when it won 50 per cent of the seats against a divided opposition.[34]

Despite loss of support among the middle land-owning castes, the Congress(R) (renamed the Congress(I) after the second split in 1978) was able to retain one-third of the vote partly because of the support of the Brahmins and some Rajput castes. It also won greater support from the rural poor, the landless and the scheduled castes, on the strength of policies designed to favour these groups. As Paul Brass has noted, the

Congress in UP became a party of 'opposite extremes—comprising within its fold the old dominant landlord and leading proprietary communities of Brahmins and Rajputs and the rural poor and landless'.[35]

In Rajasthan an attempt was made to come to terms with Jats. On the eve of the 1967 elections a section of the community under the leadership of Kumbharam Arya had left Congress and formed an alliance with the Rajputs headed by Harish Chandra, the former maharaja of Jhalawar. This was the first Jat-Rajput alliance outside Congress. Mrs Gandhi was clearly anxious to break it. So, in 1972, she allotted over 27 per cent of the party tickets to Jats and Gujjars, as against 19 per cent in 1967.

Simultaneously, she reduced the Brahmin share by as much as seven per cent compared to 1967. The overall Brahmin, Rajput and Vaishya representation among Congress(R) candidates declined from 35 per cent to 26 per cent. In 1972 over 35 per cent of the Congress(R) nominees were from among the scheduled castes and tribes, though only 28 per cent of the assembly seats were reserved for these groups. There was also a slight increase in the number of Muslims allotted Congress tickets.[36]

This brief survey should suffice to establish that Mrs Gandhi was not acting in an *ad hoc* manner and that she was in fact responding to real problems on the ground. She was of course determined to stay in power. Perhaps she had even convinced herself that her continuance in office was necessary in the country's best interests. But that does not detract from the fact that she was pursuing a strategy with long-term implications for the country's politics. In the event the strategy did not work.

In the short term Mrs Gandhi's attempts to rebuild the party on a non-dominant caste basis had met with considerable success in parts of south India and Gujarat, though in the north the old pattern of élite caste domination had remained largely unaltered.

It is not pertinent for my purpose to go into the details of the disintegration of the Janata party, the fall of the Morarji Desai government in the summer of 1979 and the inability of Charan Singh to face Parliament. It will suffice for me to say that all these developments created an atmosphere which facilitated Mrs Indira Gandhi's return to office.

In the elections to Parliament in January 1980 the Congress(I) won 351 of the 525 seats on a popular vote of 42.7 per cent (43.7 in 1971 and 34.5 per cent in 1977). The rump Janata party and the Lok Dal headed by Charan Singh together won 28.3 per cent of the vote as against the Janata's 43.2 per cent in 1977. The Dal was then part of the Janata coalition.

The apparently landslide Congress(I) victory, however, covered up a serious weakness of the party. It won less votes (39 per cent) in the Hindi heartland than its all-India average. The Lok Dal and the Janata combine polled almost seven per cent more votes in this region than the Congress (45.9 per cent). It follows that if the Janata and the Lok Dal had come together the Congress(I) could not have been successful in this area where, as we have noted, Mrs Gandhi had failed to strengthen the party's support base by bringing in the upwardly mobile backward castes.[37] The Congress(I) won more than one-third of its 145 seats in the Hindi heartland because of the Lok Dal–Janata split. Otherwise its tally in this region would have been only 91 seats, whereas the Janata-Lok Dal combine would have annexed 115 constituencies.[38]

The Congress(I) won 50 seats in UP, but a majority of the votes in only three constituencies and an absolute plurality in seven. In the remaining 40 constituencies the Congress(I) won, the Janata-Lok Dal vote exceeded its own.[39] The Congress(I) appeared to have recaptured its traditional Brahmin–Harijan–Muslim support base, whereas the Jats, Kurmis, Yadavs and other intermediate castes voted for the Lok Dal in large numbers.

Though the Congress(I) won 30 of the 54 seats in Bihar, here also the Janata–Lok Dal combined vote was higher than that of the Congress. The Lok Dal performed well in northern Bihar which contains a large proportion of the backward castes. It was believed to have done extremely well among the Yadavs.[40] Congress on the other hand won the support of the upper castes and a large number of Harijans and tribals in south Bihar.

Evidence from Bihar demonstrates the almost total lack of middle-caste support for the Congress(I). In 1971, of the 53 parliamentary constituencies in Bihar, 12 were reserved (as against 13 out of 54 in 1977 and 1980). Mrs Gandhi's party had

then won 31 of the 41 non-reserved seats and as many as 10 of
its elected legislators were from the middle castes. In 1980 however the Congress(I) was able to win only 22 of these 41 constituencies and only two of its winners were from the middle
castes. Even the Janata party had only one legislator from the
middle castes. Not a single upper-caste member was elected to
the Lok Sabha on the Lok Dal or Congress(U) ticket.[41]

In the Jat-dominated Haryana the Congress won five seats
with only 29.3 per cent of the vote, while Charan Singh's Lok
Dal won the highest vote though only 4 seats.[42] Thus it is clear
that the Lok Dal commanded substantial support in Haryana
(33.5 per cent), UP (29 per cent), Orissa (19.5 per cent) and
Bihar (16.5 per cent). It won the highest vote in Haryana and
came second in UP.[43]

The Congress(I) vote in Rajasthan was almost the same as
that of the Lok Dal and the Janata put together, though it won
18 of the 25 seats and all the seven reserve constituencies. The
Muslims, scheduled castes and tribes constitute about 35 per cent
of the population in the state.[44]

The Congress(I) performed better in western India than in
the Hindi heartland. It won 25 of the 26 seats in Gujarat and 29
out of 48 in Maharashtra. It also won a majority of the votes polled in both these states.[45] In south India the party performed as
well as in 1977. It won 92 of the 129 seats in 1977 and 93 in
1980.[46]

According to Myron Weiner's estimate, the Congress(I) won
38.6 per cent of its vote from the minorities as against 26.3 per
cent in 1977. This is indicative of the degree to which the party
depended on minority support to win the elections.[47]

The inability of the Congress(I) under Mrs Gandhi to recapture the parent organization's old position in the Hindi region
meant that its national domination rested on weak foundations.
Mrs Gandhi evidently realized the dangers of the situation. The
available evidence suggests that in the assembly elections that
followed the Lok Sabha poll she made an attempt to recover
ground in this area. Party workers spoke of the major role
played by Sanjay Gandhi in the allocation of tickets for the
assembly elections. They estimated that every second candidate

in Punjab, every fourth in UP, Maharashtra and Rajasthan, every fifth in Bihar and every seventh in Gujarat was actively involved in the Youth Congress(I).[48] For our purposes it is immaterial whether Sanjay Gandhi or Mrs Gandhi herself was the architect of the new strategy. It is possible that the viewpoints of the two converged.

Be that as it may, in the Hindi-speaking areas there was a move away from the traditional Brahmin–Harijan–Minority support base and an attempt made to bring in Rajput–Thakurs (well represented in the Janata) and, to a limited extent, backward castes (well represented in the Lok Dal). In Rajasthan, Rajputs (hitherto associated with the Janata party but disillusioned by the Bhairon Singh Shekhawat government) were promised a substantial share of tickets in the forthcoming elections by the Congress(I) leaders. In Gujarat and Madhya Pradesh Rajputs already occupied top positions in the party. In UP for the first time the Congress allotted the largest number of tickets to Rajputs; 115 of its 334 candidates for general seats came from this caste group. The Brahmins were reduced to second position with 95 tickets. The party also fielded a large number of Yadavs and Kurmis, and also Muslims. In Bihar too an attempt was made to cultivate Rajputs and backward castes.[49] The Congress(I) list for Maharashtra showed the dominance of non-Marathas for the first time. Only 120 of the 288 tickets were believed to have been given to Marathas.[50]

The Congress(I) performed well in all the states except Tamil Nadu, where the AIADMK-led alliance won 162 against 68 by the Congress(I)–DMK. In Gujarat, Madhya Pradesh, Orissa, Maharashtra and Rajasthan the Congress(I) scored major victories. It also won two-thirds of the seats in UP and slightly less in Bihar.[51]

After the elections as many as four states—Uttar Pradesh, Himachal Pradesh, Madhya Pradesh and Gujarat—were placed under Rajput-Thakur chief ministers. This aggressive promotion of the Rajputs was believed to be part of the attempt to counter the influence of the Jats and other backward castes, Mrs Gandhi's formidable opponents in the north. The traditional Brahmin leadership in the states found its wings clipped.

Brahmin leaders like N. D. Tiwari and V. C. Shukla were brought to New Delhi. In Rajasthan too power shifted from the Brahmins who had traditionally dominated the Congress. Here Jagannath Pahadia was appointed chief minister on instructions from the high command. He was the first Harijan to rise to that post.

The Rajputs were believed to have suffered a setback with the death of Sanjay Gandhi in June 1980, soon after the assembly poll. At any rate the struggle between the Rajputs and the Brahmins resumed. While V. P. Singh made way for Sripat Misra in UP, Jagannath Mishra had to yield place to Chandra Shekhar Singh in Bihar.

Meanwhile the support-building strategy Mrs Gandhi had pursued with success in the south began to run into trouble. In 1982 her party lost power in both Andhra Pradesh and Karnataka, which had served as her bastions at the time of her rout in 1977. Forward caste retaliation in Gujarat did not take place in Mrs Gandhi's lifetime but the crisis in that state in 1985 on the reservation issue too exposed the weakness of her strategy of relying on the support of the backward castes. In Maharashtra, though Mrs Gandhi tried to press the attack on the Marathas, she ultimately retreated and conceded the chief ministership of the state to the widely respected Maratha leader, Vasantrao Patil.

Mrs Gandhi herself seemed to have come around to the view that an electoral strategy based on the weaker sections could not prove dependable. Evidence from Andhra Pradesh and Karnataka suggests that she attempted to modify her earlier approach. In Andhra Pradesh the Congress(I) apparently had reason to regard the rise of the Telugu Desam as an upper-caste challenge; 53 per cent of the Telugu Desam candidates for the 1983 assembly elections were from the upper castes. The Congress(I) had to respond to this challenge. So, in sharp contrast to 1978, upper-caste representation among the Congress(I) nominees increased from 34.6 per cent to 62 per cent, while that of the weaker sections and minorities declined from 65 per cent to 32 per cent. But the Telugu Desam party seemed better able to balance the various interests in the state. About 48 per cent of its candidates were from the weaker sections and the minorities.[52]

Mrs Gandhi had been most successful in restructuring the party in Karnataka in the 1970s, thanks to the availability of a highly skilled lieutenant, Devraj Urs. The Congress(I) had won the assembly elections in 1978 despite the Janata wave in the country and Urs had continued as chief minister. In June 1979, however, he broke away from Mrs Gandhi, largely on account of his differences with Sanjay Gandhi, whose leadership style he opposed. Since a majority of party legislators remained loyal to Urs, there was no immediate change in the political set-up in the state. Forty-two MLAs headed by Gundu Rao, however, moved away from Urs to form the Congress(I) party in the assembly. Following Mrs Gandhi's victory in the 1980 parliamentary elections there was a rush of legislators to the Congress(I). Her success in Karnataka was generally attributed to her ability to project herself as the champion of the weaker sections. In the popular mind Urs had merely implemented Indramma's policies. Urs resigned and Gundu Rao was sworn in as the next chief minister.

As James Manor has noted, as a result of these defections the links between political parties and socio-economic groups, which had hitherto been quite clear, became somewhat blurred.[53] Though Gundu Rao won over most of Urs's supporters, a number of defectors from non-Congress parties and independents also joined the Congress(I). Urs founded the Kranti Ranga, a party largely of the weaker sections and minorities, and attempted to come to an understanding with other opposition parties, principally the Janata, which enjoyed strong support among the Lingayats.

It has been stated that under Gundu Rao an 'ephemeral' kind of alliance between the forward groups—the Brahmins, the Bunts and the Lingayats, began to take shape. It is difficult to say how far this is true. Even if such an alliance was sought to be promoted in the early years of Gundu Rao's rule, he was too incompetent a leader to keep any group satisfied for long. M. N. Srinivas and M. N. Panini have drawn attention to the fact that two important movements which originated during his tenure as chief minister—the farmers' movement and the Kannad-linguistic movement—and which ultimately led to his downfall, were led by the upper castes. They have argued that though these movements drew support from large sections of the state's population, irrespective of caste and class, their leadership remained in the hands of the dominant castes. These movements enabled the dominant castes to wield influence through the use of secular, non-caste idioms.[54]

Gundu Rao also alienated traditional Congress support among the scheduled castes and minorities, who felt that his government was incapable of resisting upper-caste pressures to protect their interests.

By the time Congress entered the 1983 assembly elections, it had retreated from its earlier policy of preferment of the weaker sections. Studies by the Christian Institute for the Study of Religion and Society show that Lingayat–Vokkaliga support for the Congress(I) and Janata–Kranti Ranga was almost evenly balanced. The Lingayats and the Vokkaligas accounted for 56.7 per cent of the seats won by the Congress(I) and 57.8 per cent of those won by Janata–Kranti Ranga combine. The OBC's excluding the Vokkaligas constituted only 28.3 per cent of the Congress(I) legislators. Non-Vokkaliga OBC's seemed to have shown a marginal preference for the Janata–Kranti Ranga alliance. The Janata also won 51 per cent of the reserved constituencies.[55]

The Janata chief minister, Ramakrishna Hegde, attempted to provide a good government responsive to all sections of the state's population. He formed his cabinet with great deliberation and saw to it that all interests were more or less balanced. In his initial 24-member ministry the Brahmins, the Lingayats and the Vokkaligas accounted for 10 ministers, the scheduled castes for 4, the Muslims 2 and the other backward castes 5.[56]

In Maharashta too, as Jayant Lele's studies show,[57] it became clear that Mrs Gandhi could at best sustain the conflict between the Marathas and non-Marathas, but could not ignore the Marathas. They could not do without her either. A large number of Marathas who had left Mrs Gandhi at the time of the second party split in 1978 returned to her on the eve of the 1980 poll, when it became clear that she was still a force to reckon with in national politics. The loyalists (mostly non-Marathas who had remained with her after she had lost power in 1977) were, however, determined to prevent the re-establishment of Maratha domination. In this they appeared to have the backing of Mrs Gandhi. That is probably one reason why she entrusted A. R. Antulay with the job of candidate selection for the 1980 assembly elections and finally appointed him chief minister. He gave a large number of tickets to people without much local support.

The appointment of Antulay took the Marathas by surprise. They were in control of most of the co-operatives and zilla parishads. This defined Antulay's principal task—to create alternative channels of patronage for the newly appointed MLAs to enable them to secure lasting support in their constituencies. Towards this end he secured massive donations for a number of trusts he founded from businessmen, industrialists, contractors and co-operatives, including the Maratha-controlled sugar mills. He also appointed loyalists members of committees which decided cases of loans, pensions, cement allocations, etc., and gave money-spinning liquor licences to MLAs.

The Marathas responded to this challenge in two ways—by supporting Sharad Pawar outside the Congress(I) and by launching a major attack on Antulay under Mrs Shalini Patil's leadership inside the party. Antulay was forced to resign, even though largely as a result of adverse judicial pronouncements and newspaper campaigns. Mrs Gandhi appointed Babasaheb Bhosale as his successor. Though an upper-crust Maratha, he was not well regarded by the community. He was a lightweight and had to go. Finally, in January 1983, Mrs Gandhi appointed Vasantrao Patil chief minister. But to curb his powers she insisted on creating the post of deputy chief minister and installed Ramrao Adik, a loyalist from Bombay, in that post, though he had never successfully contested an election and enjoyed a poor reputation for sobriety and uprightness.

As the 1984–5 election approached, Mrs Gandhi was clearly stuck for an electoral strategy. The strategy she had evolved in the seventies had failed on several counts. Nor was it possible for her to go back to the alliance system that had kept the Congress in power in the 50s and 60s. The mobilization of the backward castes put paid to that. Her frequent references to internal and external threats were part of her attempt to provide the Congress a nationalist platform which would cut through caste considerations.

This is not to state that there was no danger to the country; there was. The crisis in Punjab was real and was proving unmanageable. More pertinently, it does not appear that she was able to sell the nationalist platform to the people. The bulk of the intelligentsia just did not trust her. In the event, her assassination set the theme for the 1984 elections, enabling the Congress(I) to avoid the problem of working out a winning caste-community alliance strategy. But the problem has not gone away. It still confronts the Congress party.

NOTES

1. On upper-caste domination of the new education see, among others, Aparna Basu, *The Growth of Education and Political Development in India 1898–1920* (OUP, 1974); Anil Seal, *The Emergence Of Indian Nationalism* (CUP, 1971); B. T. McCully, *English Education and the Origins of Indian Nationalism* (New York, 1940). On the non-Brahman movement see E. F. Irschick, *Politics and Social Conflict in South India: the Non-Brahman Movement and Tamil Separatism, 1916–29* (Berkeley, 1969) Marguerite Ross Barnett, *The Politics of Cultural Nationalism in South India* (Princeton, 1976).

2. Angela S. Burger, *Opposition In A Dominant Party System* (University Of California Press, 1969), p. 54.

3. Ibid., pp. 53–5. The backward castes were more adequately represented in the opposition parties. In 1962 they comprised 19 per cent of the MLAs in the Jan Sangh, 30 per cent in the Praja Socialist Party (PSP) and 27 per cent in the Socialist Party. The Yadavs were the largest single caste in the PSP while the Socialist faction, led by Dr Rammanohar Lohia (The Samyukta Socialist Party, SSP), had the highest percentage of backward caste legislators. See ibid., pp. 54–6.

4. Paul R. Brass, 'The Politicization of the Peasantry in a North Indian State' Parts I & II, in *The Journal of Peasant Studies*, vol. 7, no. 4, July 1980 and vol. 8, no. 1, Sept. 1980.

5. Harry W. Blair, 'Rising Kulaks and Backward Classes in Bihar', *Economic and Political Weekly* (hereafter *EPW*) 12 Jan. 1980.

6. Stanley A. Kochanek, *The Congress Party of India* (Princeton, 1968), p. 386.

7. See Imtiaz Ahmed, 'Indian Muslims and Electoral Politics', in *EPW*, 11 March 1967; Bashiruddin Ahmed, 'Process of Integration', *Seminar*, August 1979; H. A. Gani, *Muslim Political Issues and National Integration* (Sterling Publishing, 1978); R. A. Schermerhorn, *Ethnic Plurality in India* (University of Arizona Press, Tucson, 1978). In 1962, Congress held 80.3 per cent of the Scheduled Caste seats, 58.1 per cent of the Scheduled Tribe seats, and 73.9 per cent of the 'Muslim' seats. The figures for the State Assemblies during this period were 69.2, 50, and 73.5 per cent respectively; See Gopal Krishna, 'One Party Dominance— Development And Trends', in *Party System And Election Studies* (Allied, 1967), p. 55. Congress won 61.3 per cent of the reserved Scheduled Caste and Tribe seats in the fourth Lok Sabha. See Ratna Dutta, 'The Party Representative in Fourth Lok Sabha', *EPW*, IV, nos, 1 & 2, January 1969. Scheduled Caste members comprised 18, 22, 21, and 24 per cent of Congress MPs in the 1st, 2nd, 3rd and 4th Lok Sabha respectively. See S. L. Chopra and D.N.S. Chauhan, 'Emerging Patterns of Political Leadership in India', *Journal of Constitutional and Parliamentary Studies*, IV: 1, 1970.

8. For a detailed account of Charan Singh's activities while in the Congress see, Paul R. Brass, 'Division in the Congress and the Rise of Agrarian Interests and Issues in Uttar Pradesh Politics, 1952–1977', in Paul R. Brass, *Caste, Faction and Party in Indian Politics*, vol. I, *Faction and Party* (Chanakya Publications, 1984).

9. Sarawati Srivastava, 'Uttar Pradesh, Politics of Neglected Development', in Iqbal Narain (ed.), *State Politics in India* (1976), p. 334.

10. Haridwar Rai and Jawaharlal Pandey, 'State Politics in Bihar: A Crisis of Political Institutionalisation' in *Indian Journal of Political Science*, vol. XLII, no. 4 (Oct-Dec. 1981).

11. J. R. Siwach, 'Haryana, Social Dynamics and Politics of Defections', in Iqbal Narain, p. 96.

12. On the role of the governors, see, among others, Bhagwan D. Dua, *Presidential Rule in India, 1950–1974: A Study in Crisis Politics* (S. Chand, 1979); Subhash C. Kashyap, *The Politics Of Power* (Delhi, 1974); J. R. Siwach, *Politics of President's Rule in India* (Indian Institute of Advanced Study, Simla, 1979).

13. On the Congress split, see Atulya Ghosh, *The Split in the Indian National Congress* (Calcutta, 1970); M. P. Singh, *Split In A Predominant Party* (Abhinav Publications, 1981); Vasant Chatterjee,

Congress Splits (S. Chand, 1971); Kuldip Nayar, *India, The Critical Years* (Delhi, 1971).

14. M. P. Singh, pp. 205–6.
15. Ibid., p. 162.
16. Lalitha Nataraj and V. K. Nataraj, 'Limits of Populism: Devraj Urs and Karnataka Politics', *EPW*, 11 Sept. 1982.
17. George Mathew, *Shift In Indian Politics* (Concept, 1984), pp. 47–8.
18. Glynn Wood and Robert Hammond, 'Electoral Politics in A Congress-Dominant State: Mysore, 1956–1972', in John O. Field and Myron Weiner (ed.), *Electoral Politics in the Indian States*, vol. IV (Manohar, 1975), p.151.
19. James Manor, 'Pragmatic Progressives in Regional Politics; The Case of Devraj Urs, *EPW*, Annual No., 1980.
20. Mathew, pp. 49–50.
21. M. N. Srinivas and M. N. Panini, 'Politics and Society in Karnataka', *EPW*, 14 January 1984.
22. K. R. Acharya, *The Critical Elections* (Hyderabad, 1979), p. 30.
23. G. Ram Reddy, 'Politics of Accommodation: The Case of Andhra Pradesh', paper presented at a seminar in America in 1984.
24. James Manor, 'Where Congress Survived: Five States In The Indian General Election Of 1977', *Asian Survey*, 18:8, Aug. 1978.
25. K. R. Acharya, p. 44.
26. Ibid., p. 315.
27. Jayant Lele, 'One-party Dominance In Maharashtra: Resilience And Change', in John R. Wood (ed.), *State Politics in Contemporary India: Crisis of Continuity?* (Westview Press/Boulder and London 1984).
28. See Manor.
29. John R. Wood, 'Congress Restored? The KHAM Strategy and Congress(I) Recruitment in Gujarat', in John R. Wood (ed.), *State Politics in Contemporary India*.
30. See Blair.
31. Ibid.
32. Paul R. Brass, 'Congress, the Lok Dal, and the Middle-Peasant Castes: An Analysis of the 1977 and 1980 Parliamentary Elections in Uttar Pradesh', *Pacific Affairs*, 54, Spring 1981.
33. Paul R. Brass, *Caste, Faction and Party in Indian Politics*.
34. Brass, 'The Politicisation of the Peasantry', part I.
35. Brass, 'Congress, the Lok Dal, and the Middle-Peasant Castes'.
36. H. R. Chaturvedi 'Selection of Congress Candidates—Rajasthan Assembly Elections, 1972', *EPW*, 10 June 1972.

37. H. A. Gould, 'The Second Coming: The 1980 Elections In India's Hindi Belt', *Asian Survey*, vol. xx, no. 6, June 1980.
38. Myron Weiner, *India at the Polls, 1980* (1983), p. 72.
39. See Gould.
40. See Weiner, pp. 85–6.
41. Pradhan H. Prasad, 'Rising Middle Peasantry in North India', *EPW*, Annual No., Feb, 1980.
42. Weiner, p. 87.
43. Ibid, p. 82.
44. Weiner, p. 89.
45. Ibid., p. 91.
46. Ibid., p. 103.
47. Ibid, p. 133. See also Lloyd I. Rudoph and Susanne H. Rudolph, 'Transformation of Congress Party: Why 1980 Was Not a Restoration', *EPW*, 2 May, 1981.
48. *India Today*, 16–31 May 1980.
49. Ibid.
50. *Indian Express*, 1 May 1980.
51. G. G. Mirchandani and K.S.R Murthi, *Massive Mandate for Rajiv Gandhi* (Sterling Publishers, 1985).
52. Mathew, p. 101.
53. James Manor, 'Blurring the Lines Between Parties and Social Bases: Gundu Rao and the Emergence of a Janata Government in Karnataka', in John Wood (ed.), *State Politics in Contemporary India*.
54. See Srinivas and Panini.
55. See Mathew, pp. 55–7.
56. See Manor.
57. See Lele.

THE ARENSBERG LECTURES

SECOND SERIES

FRANCIS BACON

THE ARENSBERG LECTURES

Edited by W. H. Werkmeister

FIRST SERIES: *Facets of the Renaissance*
SECOND SERIES: *Francis Bacon: His Career and His Thought*

FRANCIS BACON

HIS CAREER AND HIS THOUGHT

FULTON H. ANDERSON

Professor of Philosophy, University of Toronto

GREENWOOD PRESS, PUBLISHERS
WESTPORT, CONNECTICUT

Library of Congress Cataloging in Publication Data

Anderson, Fulton Henry, 1895-
    Francis Bacon, his career and his thought.

    Reprint of the ed. published by the University of
Southern California Press, Los Angeles, which was issued
as 1957 of the Arensberg lectures.
    Includes index.
    1. Bacon, Francis, Viscount St. Albans, 1561-1626--
Addresses, essays, lectures. 2. Philosophers--England--
Biography--Addresses, essays, lectures. I. Title.
II. Series: The Arensberg lectures ; 1957.
[B1197.A5 1978]   192 [B]   77-18070
ISBN 0-313-20108-0

ACKNOWLEDGMENTS

DURING THE SPRING SEMESTER of 1957, Fulton H. Anderson was the Arensberg Visiting Professor in the School of Philosophy, University of Southern California. In April of that year he gave three public lectures on "The Philosophy of Francis Bacon." The present book is an expansion of these lectures. Both Dr. Anderson's Visiting Professorship and his public lectures were sponsored by The Francis Bacon Foundation, Inc., Claremont. This foundation has also made possible the publication of the lectures as here presented.

For its interest in, and generous support of, these scholarly activities, I wish to thank The Francis Bacon Foundation on behalf of myself, the School of Philosophy, and the University of Southern California.

W. H. WERKMEISTER, *Director*
School of Philosophy
University of Southern California

PREFACE

THIS STUDY IS AN ENLARGEMENT of a series of lectures delivered at the University of Southern California in the spring of 1957 as part of the Arensberg Lectures sponsored by that institution.

Now printed in book form, on the occasion of the four-hundredth anniversary of Francis Bacon's birth, the study is, in design, an account of that thinker's place within the perspectives of his time. It is hoped that its appearance may mark an advance, however modest, in Baconian exegesis through its attempt to relate certain of Bacon's opinions to traditional and contemporary philosophies; by its emphasis on his originality as a systematic thinker and not merely an exponent of scientific method; by its statement of reasons for his political support of the Royal Prerogative; and by its stress on the place in his thinking of the generic conception of the three kingdoms—of nature, of politics, and of Divine Grace.

This conception, in the writer's opinion, is basic to the pluralistic philosophy which contains within its structure the widely diverse principles of Verulam's thought. Not all, by any means, of his more striking and characteristic undertakings are recorded in the present book—lest, as the saying goes, the reader should fail to see the wood for the trees—but mainly those which have occasioned continuous controversy since that statesman and philosopher first became the subject of biography and commentary.

The writer gratefully acknowledges help received, during the period of years since he first became interested in Bacon's philosophy, from many historians, biographers, commentators, and editors of documents. Among these he would mention James Spedding, E. A. Abbott, R. W. Church, J. G. Crowther, S. R. Gardiner, John Nichol, and Francis Paget. Use has been made freely of such evidence as they, and others, have collected and interpreted. Sometimes, in the present study, particulars stressed in their assembled evidence have been regarded as the more cogent when disagreement with their verdicts has been the more pronounced.

The author thanks three of his colleagues in the University of Toronto for their generous aid in preparing this writing for publication. Professor C. W. Webb drastically reduced the bulk of the manuscript. Professor J. M. O. Wheatley critically examined the typescript and galley prints. Professor William Dray has read the page proof.

F. H. A.

CONTENTS

FRANCIS BACON

I

BACON'S REPUTATION

I N THIS STUDY WE ARE DEALING WITH A PHILOSOPHER and public servant whose life and place in history have occasioned much
dispute among biographers, critics, historians, and expositors
for more than three hundred years. It is our hope that some of
this repetitious conflict may be resolved by the simple device
of recording without presupposition immediate evidence from
Bacon's circumstances, writings, and political undertakings.
We are of the opinion that the reading of this author's character
and the discounting of his endeavor have been reckless, uninformed, even at times malevolent.

Francis Bacon played many roles in the Late English Renaissance: he was courtier, literary artist, Parliamentarian, jurist,
advisor of monarchs, and statesman. But pre-eminently he was
a philosopher. As a philosopher he professed, in addition to a
metaphysics, definite theological, political, and ethical principles.
To these several principles he adhered consistently throughout
his career. The "character studies" which purport to represent
his life abound in philosophical, ethical, theological, and political praecognita which he himself would not have found
tenable or even theoretically congruent. It is mainly through
these presuppositions that Bacon has been represented as a man

3

without principle and a philosopher without a "system of truth," even indeed as a combination of a Judas Iscariot and a Pontius Pilate.

To speak bluntly, Bacon's reputation has been reduced or destroyed through the philosophical naivety of biographers and historians. Those who have passed the severest judgment on his career and his thought have been amateurs in ethics and persons but little acquainted with the sequences and consequences of historical and systematic philosophy. Most of his literary biographers have shown, in what they call "moral" exposition, not the slightest regard to either a system or a hierarchy of virtues. They seem never to assign appropriate places in an ethics to reasoned wisdom, reasoned charity, and reasoned prudence in well-weighed circumstances. Some of their assumptions are ridiculous, and their several conclusions when placed together prove shockingly contradictory. One finds in their writings, for example, the presumption that all the theological and cardinal virtues are to be rendered subsidiary to something called "honor"—especially when dealing with the case of Essex. Readers are told in succession that Bacon failed in virtue because he had no "reasoned ethics"; because he was a "rationalist" in ethics; because his ethics rested on the dogmas of religious faith; because his ethics was "Machiavellian" and without principle.

Those "liberal" clerics among Bacon's critics who regard Christian apologetics as an unbroken journey from natural science to divinity, or in a more sophisticated way from metaphysical being to God, condemn their author as a retrograde thinker for his segregation of the realm of Divine Grace from the areas of natural science and a naturalistic metaphysics. Others, who agree in his rejection of liberal theology and welcome his supplanting of Platonic, Aristotelian, Stoic, Epicurean, and other pagan principles in ethics by the placets of Scripture, turn a deaf ear to his materialistic naturalism. Prepared to accept the teaching that the source of ethics is Divine Revelation, they, like the seventeenth-century "saints," proceed to damn their Elizabethan author for his failure to walk in the byways of what was deemed by Elizabethan churchmen a lawless, obscurely motivated, ever-changing, ever-meandering thing, without philosophically or theologically ordered foundation, the vaguely principled "Nonconformist conscience."

Clerics who habitually associate high thinking with scanty existence and plain fare can rarely abide the supposition that a courtier who lived lavishly, as Bacon undoubtedly did, could ever have been the author of a serious philosophy and ever have put into practice an elevated ethics. Such of their number as can encompass this comprehensive thought will yet have it that Bacon the advisor of monarchs on church affairs, the scholar at Court, the philosopher in politics, the savant on the bench, was but a truant from the academy. In his truancy they discern vices and sins commensurate with great powers wrongly used: inordinate flattery of sovereigns and aggravated vanity; support of the Royal Prerogative in denying the rights of subjects and their Parliament; sycophantic compliance with rulers in the doctrine of the divine right of kings; duplicity, after a shrewd assessment of political circumstances; the sundering of the placets of revealed religion from axioms derived through rational inquiry; illiberal opposition to Sir Edward Coke, the deliverer of the courts of common law from the interference of kings and privy councils; disdain for the "consciences" of Nonconformists; bribery of a judge by litigants; dishonor in the prosecution of the Earl of Essex; and, to end the list of complainings, a literary man's uttering, on his political downfall, a literary and therefore insincere psalm of confession to his Maker.

Those political historians who think that the "common man"

is endowed by nature with "rights" and sovereign "initiative," deplore as retrograde, even iniquitous, Bacon's profession on biblical grounds of the doctrine of divine right. The same historians are commonly prone to treat Bacon's opinions in constitutional law as a besmirched foil for the mediocrities of the politically and juristically ambitious lawyer Edward Coke.

The vicissitudes of Bacon's philosophical reputation are even more striking than those which have beset his "morality." Because of the Platonic and Aristotelian training and attitudes of persons in Court, church, and state, to whom his writings on science were at first addressed, Bacon's philosophy was treated in the beginning with neglect, hostility, or derision. Yet, a generation after his death, his works were accorded a veneration rarely, if ever, given the writings of a naturalistic philosopher. Members of the Royal Society and other investigators with kindred interests hailed Bacon as the sovereign of the kingdom of nature, "the great restorer of physics," "the great architect of experimental history," and the prophet of a "real" philosophy and a "solid" learning. In response to certain entreaties contained in his writings, an unprecedented host of inquirers undertook the collecting and interpreting of scientific data of wide range under the shield of his defending and directing philosophical induction. Impressed by his original classification of the sciences and his institution of a new mode of inquiry, Bacon's followers regarded him as the "modern Aristotle." For his refusal to accept the magisterial impositions of the a priori and the transcendental upon experimental science, they called him "nature's secretary." It was their belief that through the pursuit of a new induction natural philosophy was finally to come into its own. Yet, because their very enthusiasm for their prophet's method led them to the point of disregarding many of his major principles, these early disciples were to detract in perpetuity from his reputation as a systematic philosopher.

Educators of the seventeenth century saw in the scientific regimen of Solomon's House of Wisdom, which Bacon had described in the *New Atlantis*, a new education which would render obsolete many of the disciplines of the past. By this education a new, a truly scientific, humanism would be initiated. Students would turn from the works of Plato and Aristotle to examine the book of nature. Scientists and philosophers of the future would deal with things and not argue about the meaning of terms. Men generally would finally come into their original inheritance, the dominion over nature. Through this reclaimed inheritance would come relief from the miseries which beset the present ignorant, unhappy estate of mankind.

After the political revolution and the regicide (1649) which ended the reign of Charles I, Bacon's countrymen were to remember his unheeded advice to that sovereign's father, James I. Political thinkers would then recall his efforts to establish a liberal government, while upholding the King's sovereignty and confirming the privileges of Parliament and courts. Englishmen were to opine that had Bacon's principles prevailed in the mind of a stubborn Stuart, their nation might have escaped the deprivation of liberty and all the bitterness and misery which were its lot in the days of Charles I, Oliver Cromwell, and another Stuart.

On the Continent, Verulam's name and opinions were invoked in the discussions and the correspondences of scientific "agents" and founders and frequenters of the scientific "cabinets" and academies of the seventeenth century—Samuel de Fermat, Henry Justel, Marin Mersenne, Nicholas-Claude Fabri de Peiresc, members of the Cabinet Dupuy, the Academy of Montmor, and the rest. Bacon was hailed as the scientific progenitor of Robert Boyle, Walter Charleton, John Evelyn, Francis Glisson, Jonathan Goddard, John Wallis, and Thomas Willis. The Solomon's House of the *New Atlantis* (published posthumously in 1627) and the inductive inquiries described in the

Novum organum (1620) and the *De dignitate et augmentis scientiarum* (1623) were treated as models. A French correspondent of Thomas Hobbes wrote in enthusiasm, "If England had only given to science Gilbert, Harvey, and Bacon, she might have disputed the palm with France and with Italy, who have given us Galileo, Descartes, and Gassendi; but Bacon has carried it over all others in grandeur of design." In the opinion of Puffendorf, the jurist, "It was the late Chancellor Bacon who raised the standard, and urged on the march of discovery." To the inquiring Mersenne, René Descartes wrote, "You desire to know how best to make experience useful: On this point I have nothing to add to Verulam." Descartes also expressed the desire that some scientist would undertake an astronomical investigation according to Bacon's method. Pierre Gassendi hoped that the issue of Verulam's *organum* would be a replete natural philosophy.

In later years, Gottfried Wilhelm Leibniz was to say that in the matter of philosophic reach, Descartes, when compared with Bacon, "creeps on the ground." He admonished philosophers "to think highly of Verulam, for his hard sayings have in them a deep meaning," and acknowledged that the study of the *De augmentis* had set his feet on a philosophic path. While developing his own philosophic thought, Leibniz welcomed Bacon's doctrine of figure and motion as one far preferable to that of the matter, form, and change of Aristotle. Leibniz followed Bacon in asserting that "an abstract being is not a principle," and gave his monads those characteristics which Bacon had ascribed to the atom: "a true being, having matter, form, dimension, place, resistance, appetite, motion." One of Leibniz's tracts, written under a pseudonym, is called *Gulielmi Placiti 'Plus Ultra,' sive initia et specimena scientiae generalis, de instauratione et augmentis scientiarum, ac de perficiendâ mente, rerumque inventione ad publicam felicitatem.* In this title every phrase is taken from either a title or common saying of Bacon's. It had been Leibniz's intention to conclude the writing with an exhortation in the manner of Bacon, *"ad viros dignitate doctrinaque egregios de humana foelicitate exiguo tempore, si velemus modo, in immensum augenda."*

Immanuel Kant was of the opinion that the author of the *Novum organum* was "one of the greatest physicists in modern times." Arthur Schopenhauer paid a compliment when he wrote, "beautifully expressed by Verulam: The intellect is not a dry light. . . . Love and hate falsify our judgments entirely." Schopenhauer was probably repeating what he had read in Bacon when he wrote such statements as these: "That which is acted on is always matter, and thus the whole being and essence of matter consists in the orderly changes which one part of it brings about in another part." "To repeat the whole nature of the world . . . and thus to store up a reflected image of it always at the command of reason, this and nothing else is philosophy." Jean D'Alembert saluted Bacon as the most universal of all natural philosophers, and Denis Diderot gave a work a title taken from Bacon—*De interpretatione philosophiae.* They placed his name on the front page of the *Encyclopédie,* and an associate adopted Bacon's classification of the sciences. Charles Darwin wrote in his notebook that he intended, when investigating the problem of the origin of species, to proceed on "true Baconian principles."

All this, however, is but one side of the picture. On the other we see Bacon castigated for his naturalism and his materialism, his exclusion of ontology from philosophy, his refusal to accept any metaphysical account of the nature and being of God. His English contemporaries seized upon his emphasis on "works" and his designing his induction for "operative" ends. They called his philosophy a method for producing mechanics, horticulturists, and apothecaries' clerks. On the Continent, Benedict

Spinoza, too, remarked that Verulam's philosophy was only fitted to use in manufacture and trade. Indeed, from the seventeenth century to the present, contention has continued over Bacon's right to be called a systematic or significant philosopher, an original or originative thinker. Into this controversy have entered both academic prejudice and national rivalry. Frustrated inductionists, ambitious empiricists, outraged rationalists, unrealistic transcendentalists, piqued "liberal" clerics, and ethical tyros have played their several parts. Reliance has been placed on those repetitious "philosophical" causeries which find their way into the "lives" of persons whose systems of thought are never really penetrated by their biographers. There has been obvious ignorance of the author's writings and philosophical environment, misconstruction of his teachings through omission and predisposition, prejudice in the withholding of available reasons for his political and judicial attitudes, and, by no means least in influence, that serpentine venom which can issue from meandering "consciences" led hither and yon by "moral" vagaries masquerading as ethical precepts and disposed to low, and sometimes cunningly contrived, representation of the high motives of intellectually and morally articulate men. By such causes as these, within myriad treatises where his name has been invoked, a great thinker has been reduced, in endless repetition, to a minute philosopher without height, breadth, or profundity; even as, for the part he played in a massive political drama within a politically dramatic age, he has been represented not as a tragic hero but as a moral derelict.

In national rivalry, some of the French will fondly have it that their countryman in exile, Descartes, is the author of all that is modern in modern philosophy. The Germans have gravely suspected a thinker who could write a philosophy in lucid and literary prose. George William Frederick Hegel, whose transcendental habits compelled him to compose an autobiography of the Eternal *Geist*, which he supposed to be immanent within his own deep logic, saw in the case of this characteristic English philosopher no more than a scattering of observations appropriate to greengrocers' assistants. Those of Bacon's own countrymen who have been given to resting their national philosophical reputation on such epistemological writers as John Locke, David Hume, J. S. Mill, and F. H. Bradley, have seen in such of his philosophical writings as they have chosen to read merely the sections of a laboratory manual compiled by a literary man, who had never undertaken a truly scientific experiment. Members of the "Scottish School" of epistemology have been an exception. They have acknowledged Bacon's influence in Locke's elevation of common sense to science, and have found in Bacon's *Novum organum* a more workable and fruitful method for the study of the operations of the knowing mind than that contained within the logical works of Aristotle.

Those philosophers of science who consider all worthwhile speculation since the Renaissance "Galilean and Cartesian" in character condemn Bacon for his failure to discern in the theories of the "new" astronomers and physicists—Nicholaus Copernicus, Galileo Galilei, William Gilbert—the basis of a systematic philosophy. Bacon the philosopher, who rarely, if ever, made a scientific discovery, is on the one hand called the originator of modern "science," and on the other is refused even a prophetic part in the history of science for the reason seemingly that his works are not a reservoir of prior, contemporary, and postmortem discoveries! The philosopher who put Aristotelianism to rout is called a belated Peripatetic. The empirical thinker who saw Plato's induction as a vague, wandering pursuit of "abstractions" within a "divine" realm, beyond the confines of human inquiry, is represented as a proponent of the doctrine of Platonic forms. The philosopher of science who placed the induction of axioms within the province of reason, has, for his mention of "experience," been deemed the founder of modern epistemological empiricism. Because he rarely uses the term hypothesis, and prefers "axiom," Bacon's scientific thought is said to be void of this principle. Bacon's critical interpretation of causation, in which cause and effect are tried by sense (as they are in Hume's doctrine), and in which cause and effect are not sundered in time and act (while in Hume's more naive doctrine they are), is represented by Hume's disciples as an example of philosophical primitivism! Bacon's theory of induction includes J. S. Mill's Instances more critically exemplified, and rectifies, before the fact, Mill's disregard of continuity in nature and failure to describe the nature of objects except in subjective terms. Yet Bacon's scientific endeavor is regarded by those who would place Mill before him in the philosophy of induction as merely an aimless ramble into the realm of real phenomena by an intellect stuffed with traditional book lore!

More drastically yet, Bacon is put beyond the philosophic pale by historians of philosophy and critical philosophers of many sorts. Among the reasons for this are his expulsion of ontology and dialectic from the philosophy of nature, his disregard of what the Scots have sometimes named "the metaphysical," what earlier makers of university curricula have entitled "mental and moral philosophy," and what contemporary writers think epistemology to be. Philosophers of monistic disposition have been offended by Bacon's refusal, for reasons, to bring within a single set of principles the composition of nature, the nature of God, the basis of political sovereignty, the structure of knowledge, and the ethical direction of the creature man. Epistemologists have deplored his failure to cope with the foundations of and the relations between the "subjective" and the "objective," some among them regarding these two things in a Cartesian manner, as "mental and physical substances."

Bacon himself thought that the attempt to "prove" either the reality of natural things or the reality of the knowledge of them a fruitless undertaking, dialectically and not observationally motivated. Bacon's epistemology does not extend beyond a treatment of the respective functions of sense, memory, and reason in the framing and the testing of hypotheses. Human reason as such is, for him, the Image of God and therefore lies within a realm enlightened through Divine Revelation, while the other functions of knowing man belong to the area of experimental physiology. This science, like other natural sciences, requires something more than common sense, hasty abstraction, and verbal definition for its investigation. Its axioms, when established, will become part of a science of nature. They are not to be used—like Platonic forms or Aristotelian principles of analytic or logic—as instruments for the total reconstruction of the whole of reality.

Bacon's philosophical reputation has commonly been made to hang on portions of two of his thirty-odd philosophical pieces, specifically on those parts of the *Advancement of Learning* (1605) and the *Novum organum* which have to do with Idols and a new method of inquiry. Yet his doctrine of Idols extends only to a portion of the *pars destruens* of one section of his philosophic undertaking, and his method is but one of six divisions of the Great Instauration. Bacon's rule of induction is, in design, to furnish eleven "helps to the understanding in the interpretation of nature"; but of these only three are expounded by the author. One who would understand Bacon's philosophy must constantly bear in mind that this embraces much more than his inductive "helps." It includes, as well, a refutation, with reasons, of prevalent philosophies; a distinctive philosophical scheme; a realignment of metaphysics, politics, and theology; a philosophical recognition of an independent kingdom of nature; an emancipation of a "real" and "solid" experimental knowledge from the thraldom of theoretical ontology and theological metaphysics; a specification of the objects of logical demonstration; and a provision for a new regimen of learning. The calculation of the character and the place in history of Bacon's philosophy does not depend, then, on an answer to the question whether the laboratory and extra-laboratory procedures instanced in the second book of the *Novum organum* were ever employed by any investigator, by a Copernicus, say, or a Galileo, a Boyle, a Newton, or a Pasteur. Bacon said in warning that the results reached through these procedures were to be modified as the other eight "helps"—which are not exposed in his writings—were put into employment.

The more philosophically pretentious among Bacon's biographers are given to remarking on his slight knowledge of logic as something indicative of a general philosophical ignorance. Because of their author's summary disposal of deduction as a method of discovery, they surmise that he knew even less traditional logic than a modern university graduate in arts. The fact is obvious, of course, to anyone acquainted with university curricula in the sixteenth century, that a modern college textbook in logic would have seemed a primer for dullards to a disputer who had done the required reading in the complex and abstruse logics employed during Bacon's years at Cambridge. And Bacon was a diligent student with capacity for mastering details.

The same biographers assert, or assume, that their author was little read, if at all, in past and contemporary philosophy, while they themselves can speak of the "breaking down of arid, formal scholasticism" by the "new science," as if either of these were but one thing. Bacon, in fact, explicitly brings under criticism, sometimes in considerable detail—witness his treatment of Aristotle, the Peripatetics, and Telesio—the doctrines of scores of thinkers whom he names, and of varied sects and schools. Actually, the widespread misunderstanding of what is original and nonoriginal in Bacon's thought is in no small measure the result of a disregard on the part of many of his most vigorous critics of the philosophical audience to which he addressed his writings. The Renaissance had not scores but hundreds of philosophers and commentators who put their thoughts into published works, commonly of eclectic sorts, with either a Platonic, or an Aristotelian, or an Augustinian, or a Peripatetic, or a naturalistic emphasis. These works remain largely unread. Scholars, who find their eclecticisms tedious and their repetitions cumbersome, turn away and leave them unexposed. Yet these writers and their readers were the persons to whom Bacon addressed his writings, his later works especially, as one speaking directly, even intimately to an audience. Bacon told his contemporaries that as an author he was none other than "the birth of Time," his philosophy the product of Time and not of an "individual wit."

Historians of philosophy are none too regardful of this off-spring of Time. Such of them as read his works fully find his utterances too distinctive in character to suffer easy adaptation to their continuities. Accordingly, they leave him stranded, so to speak, on Time's shore, while giving lift and transport to his immediate successors Hobbes and Descartes. Transcendentalists of Hegelian or pseudo-Hegelian ilk, who until recently have comprised the greater part of these historians, look upon this author as a kind of stray vagrant lacking desire for settled place or a priori haven. The inductionists who dip into history accord their seminal forbear a polite nod of recognition—although on occasion they can be impertinent. These descendants seem in the main to be over-sensitively wary lest any ancient should appear as a provider for their weak, if sometimes quite turbulent, line. Strangely enough, the naturalists, too, among historians, who could learn a good deal from Bacon's attempts to rid philosophy of the a priori and transcendental and to purge nature of "mind," almost completely neglect his major statements in these regards.

The task confronting the historian of philosophy is not, admittedly, an easy one. He must be selective, and he will be bent on discovering continuities which are more than mere successions. Some of his authors, if only because of spatial exigence, must be treated scantily or overlooked. Thinkers receiving major recognition will be those who sustain in greater degree the historian's continuities. The most usual practice of the historian is to reduce an author to a "moment" or stage in a movement toward one culmination or another. This procedure entails the separating and weakening of the threads of an individual philosopher's design, the more thoroughly when the pattern of his thought is the more distinctive. In effect, the historic thinker's system inevitably undergoes a degree of dialectical reconstruction to accommodate anachronistic and alien principles.

To escape certain of the difficulties inherent in the writing of the story of philosophy there has been brought into use and fashion the history not of philosophers but of "ideas." However, the task of representing an author's thoughts in this sort of history is beset with special difficulties of its own. Strictly speaking, ideas never change, but only the connotations of words and the objects and topics which in denotation terms represent. When the connotation of a word changes, the term's new meaning cannot be understood without the adduction of a new context of reference. This context, in the case of a philosopher, will be found to imply a system of thought in whole or in part. Take, for example, three of Bacon's "ideas": form, matter, atom. Quite unlike Plato's and Aristotle's sorts of form, which require for their understanding two disparate sets of principles in system, Bacon's form is a materiate thing, the constituent law and active cause inherent within a sort of matter which is not recognized either by Plato or by Aristotle. Again, the "matter" of both Plato and Aristotle is unformed, indeterminate, without significant activity of its own, while Bacon's is formed, furnished, and replete with all that issues from it in action. An account of the reality, the operation, and the causation into which matter does or does not enter in the case of any one of these three thinkers necessarily entails an exposition of principles basic to a whole philosophy.

The concept atom, from the days of Leucippus in the fifth century B.C. to the first half of the seventeenth century, carries at least three independent meanings: the primary element in explanation of things whether physical or ontological, the smallest portion of a divided or a compressed body—presumably divided to "infinity" or utterly compressed, and an entity with structural pattern which enters into the composition of bodies. These three meanings cannot be presented in a philosophical succession without a major exposition of metaphysical, physical, and methodological doctrines which involve major parts of three quite different philosophies.

Baconian exposition, in summation, fails to state and to place in perspective those results of the author's thinking which render him a distinctive and original systematic philosopher, and not merely a proponent of a new method of scientific inquiry. These results include a complete reclassification of the sciences; the expulsion of theological ontology, in any guise, from natural philosophy; the removal of ethics and politics from the area of sciences discovered and established by human inquiry; the placing of human ethics under the rule of the placets of Divine Revelation; an all-embracing materialistic naturalism; the disregard in logical and metaphysical inquiry of all that is either a priori or transcendental, including the transcendental "reason"; the removal of "mind," even as "logical" structure or as rationale, from nature; the interpretation of metaphysics as generalized physics; the making of mechanics the operative counterpart of theoretical physics; the regarding of "magic" as generalized mechanics and the operative counterpart of metaphysics; the description of the nature and the place of "axioms," as principles and hypotheses, in inquiry; and, what is most necessary of all for an understanding of Bacon's way of regarding the natural, the religious, and the political events which confronted him as philosopher and statesman, the recognition of three separate kingdoms with three independent jurisdictions, viz., the kingdom of nature under the dominion of man, the Kingdom of God within the disposing of Divine Grace, and the kingdom of politics divinely endowed with a certain judicial and legislative initiative.

II

THE COURT AND LEARNING

ENGLAND IN THE 1560's PRODUCED TWO GENIUSES, William Shakespeare and Francis Bacon. The habitat of the first, by chance and inclination, was the theatre; the habitat of the second, through circumstances of birth and by design, was the Court. The father of the one was uneducated and possessed modest means, and his son went to the grammar school in his native town; the father of the other was learned and wealthy, and his son was sent to Cambridge. The youth who attended the grammar school was taught a little Greek and some more Latin, was exercised in the grammar, rhetoric, and logic which constituted the trivium, and was encouraged to compose pieces by following models taken from great writers. Because genius will out, he was to have sufficient precision in the use of words, feeling for rhythm in verse, awareness of the wisdom contained in historic lore, and sensitive discernment of the humors and motives, comedies, and tragedies of men to write plays such as the world had never before seen. The other youth, after private and thorough schooling in languages and authors, was in his early teens critically to assess academic exercises and the content of university learning. In his early twenties he was to pronounce a judgment against past and present philosophies, a judgment which was an outpouring of gifted precocity. Soon thereafter he would be initiating plans for the supplanting of those philosophies by another, and confronting his political sovereign with a novel philosophical regimen for the promotion of man's rule over nature. If some of the ingredients of his philosophy had been entertained by others before him, even as had the plots of Shakespeare's plays before Shakespeare, their new placing and arrangement, and their amplification and modification in light of a new aim and a new method would mark a departure from all the philosophies that had gone before.

Francis Bacon was born in 1561 and died in 1626. He was junior by almost a century to Copernicus and by half a century to Paracelsus and Telesio; he was senior to Descartes by thirty-five years, and was a contemporary of Bruno, Campanella, Galilei, Gilbert, and Kepler. The circumstances of time, blood, family, and Court which determined Bacon's literary, philosophical, political, and juridical careers were as capacious as the Elizabethan Renaissance itself. Bacon, the product of this Renaissance, was to show the imaginative daring and literary power which characterized the other "great Elizabethans." He was born an Elizabethan and an Elizabethan he remained. If in the days of James I bickering and trading on the part of the king had superseded the majestic acts of a truly regal sovereign, if there was no longer a Drake to voyage round the world and English ships were rotting in untidy ports while Raleigh languished in the Tower for the appeasement of the Spaniards, Bacon could still storm the strongholds of learning and with intellectual daring circumnavigate the realm of nature. When necessary, too, he could call upon the foolish King of England to display the majesty becoming a sovereign and not to bargain with his Commons in the manner of a huckster.

As the "offspring of Time," Bacon's days overlapped those of Edmund Spenser, the "poet's poet"; of Richard Hooker, who in cogent prose set down the basis of a liberal ecclesiastical policy; of Christopher Marlowe, the "wild genius" who died in a brawl; of Philip Sidney, the defender of poetry against contemporary philistines; of Sir Francis Drake, the privateer who swept the Spanish Main and afterwards became Vice-Admiral of the fleet; of Sir Walter Raleigh, adventurer, buccaneer, and literary historian, who was to suffer execution at the dictate of the Spanish ambassador, who under James had for a time become the director of England's foreign policy; and of Shakespeare, the restless forsaker of his hearth for a life with strolling players, who alone among his contemporaries was equal to Bacon in perception of the motives and designs which underlie the actions and promote the prosperities and tragedies of mankind. These—Bacon and the others—were capacious persons in spacious times, whose acts resist computation by measures appropriate to commonplace men. All things, whether real or imaginary, are forgiven all of them save one—Francis Bacon!

Bacon was born within the shadow of the English Court and until his relinquishment of public office, in 1621, five years before his death, never lived beyond the range of its activity and influence. This Court was characterized by magnificence, by learning, by the ambition and intrigue of courtiers, and by belief of sovereigns in their divine right. Bacon's father, Sir Nicholas Bacon (1509-1579), held political posts during three reigns, first during the reign of Edward VI (1547-1553). Although Protestant in outlook and sympathy, he was permitted to continue in office under Mary Tudor (1553-1558), but as one suspect of seeking a closer union between English churchmen and Continental Protestants, he was denied permission to leave England. On Elizabeth's accession (1558) he became Lord Keeper of the Great Seal, receiving the full jurisdiction of Lord Chancellor in 1559. Sir Nicholas presided in the House of Lords at Elizabeth's first meeting with Parliament. For a period he had suffered Elizabeth's disfavor because of her unfounded suspicion that her Lord Keeper was the author of a pamphlet, *A Declaration on the Succession of the Imperial Crown of England*, written in support of the claims of Catherine Grey. She later sought his companionship, listened to his advice, and sometimes visited his estate in Redgrave, where he had, with characteristic generosity, founded a free grammar school. As one who remained aloof from court intrigue, Sir Nicholas was able to tender respected counsel to Elizabeth and her Lord Treasurer —his brother-in-law, William Cecil (1520-1598), Lord Burghley. The Lord Keeper had his friend Matthew Parker made Archbishop of Canterbury (1559). He advised successfully against the taking up of arms against Continental powers. He advocated unsuccessfully a moderating of severe measures against the Nonconformists respecting church discipline and forms of worship.

Francis Bacon's father was a well-informed and greatly respected jurist and it became the ambition of the son to emulate the father. For his formal education the son followed in his father's footsteps. He studied at Cambridge and Gray's Inn. Like his father, he became learned in the law and occupied the offices of Treasurer of this Inn and Lord Keeper of the Great Seal. He enjoyed until the end, despite his removal from office (1621), the reputation of a just judge.

Sir Nicholas had married twice. Three sons by his first wife held political offices, and the oldest, Nicholas, was created premier baronet of England. His second wife was Anne Cooke, who became the mother of two sons, Anthony and Francis. Anthony (1558-1601) was elected a member of Parliament and became an unofficial diplomat in the service of Elizabeth and her favorite Essex. He had entrée to the household of the Queen and communicated to her intelligence on personages and affairs at home and abroad. He was associated with Essex in illegal discussions with James VI of Scotland concerning the succession to the English throne. Anthony Bacon's confidential reporting to Elizabeth, his friendship with Essex, his enjoyment of the high regard of James of Scotland, and his opposition to a bill against Roman Catholic Recusants brought him into the disfavor of Elizabeth's Lord Treasurer, Lord Burghley, and worked to retard the granting of political office to his brother.

Bacon was the nephew by marriage of Lord Burghley. The Cecil family had been associated with royal courts from the days of Henry VII (1485-1509). William Cecil had gone to Cambridge, where he came under the influence of Roger Ascham and John Cheke and acquired skill in Greek learning. On graduation he went to Gray's Inn. He became a member of Parliament and obtained sundry legal and judicial offices. For a short time he was committed to the Tower. He was in a measure responsible for Edward VI's accession to the throne. During Mary's reign, William Cecil overtly acquiesced in her schemes and secretly corresponded with her rival, Elizabeth. After Elizabeth's accession to the throne, he became the most continuously powerful member of her Privy Council. He acted as the Queen's Lord Treasurer, Secretary of State, and first minister. He controlled Elizabeth's caprices, outmaneuvered cabals, was largely responsible for the restoration of the Reformation in its Anglican form, the Queen's foreign policy, and most of the measures instituted by Elizabeth and her Council during the latter part of her reign. Both Burghley and his son Robert (1563-1612), Lord Salisbury, were to have considerable influence on the life of Francis Bacon.

Bacon's mother, Anne Cooke, was a sister of Lady Burghley, and a daughter of Sir Anthony Cooke, the tutor of Edward VI. The two Cooke daughters were extraordinarily well-informed. Roger Ascham described Mildred, Lady Burghley, as one of the two most learned women in the kingdom—the other being Lady Jane Grey. Anne was proficient in Greek, Latin, French, and Italian learning. It was "known" that her father had entrusted her with the tutoring of Edward VI. When twenty-one she translated and published the Italian sermons of Bernardino Ochino (1487-1564), who had become a Reformer, escaped the Inquisition, joined John Calvin (1509-1564) in Geneva, and later became a prebendary of Canterbury under pension from the privy purse of Edward VI. Ochino instructed Elizabeth, to whom he dedicated a written work. Another Continental Reformer, Theodore Beza (1519-1608), a friend of her son Anthony, dedicated to Lady Bacon his *Meditations*. Beza had joined Calvin's church in Geneva. He became professor of Greek at Lausanne, Calvin's assistant in publication, professor in the Geneva Academy, and on Calvin's death his biographer and administrative successor.

From the Latin, Lady Bacon translated and published *An Apology for the Church of England* by Bishop Jewel. John Jewel (1522-1571) was a Zwinglian Reformer, who in a sermon at St. Paul's Cross had challenged "all comers" to prove the Roman case "out of the Scriptures, or the councils or Fathers for the first six hundred years after Christ." His *Apology* was regarded by many as "the first methodical statement of the position of the Church of England against the Church of Rome." In James' reign Richard Bancroft, Archbishop of Canterbury, declared the theology it contained the official statement of the Anglican position.

Anne Bacon was in theology a Calvinist, in disposition a Puritan—more than a little impressed by the writings of Thomas Cartwright (1535-1603) and other "saints"—in temperament a "fanatic," a thinker acquainted with the doctrines of the philosophico-theologians of various schools, and somewhat less than an impartial observer of the contemporary political struggles born of theological disputes. It was she who gave educational direction and dogmas to her mentally robust and physically delicate sons Anthony and Francis before and after they entered the University.

Lady Bacon did not hesitate to berate her brother-in-law, Lord Burghley, for his part in the political measures instituted by John Whitgift, Archbishop of Canterbury (d. 1604), at Burghley's and Elizabeth's bidding, against those who, in conscience, could not subscribe to practices required by the Anglican rule. If this learned and "fanatical" mother would find occasion to remind her son Francis through his brother Anthony that he was holding prayers with his servants less often than he ought, she was also to observe with some satisfaction that the same son, in agreement with the Calvinists, was contending that the forms of worship required by the rulers of the Established Church were not of the essence of religion; in statements replete with learning was separating the placets of revealed truth from man-made ethics, metaphysics, and theology; and was acknowledging in carnal human learning only enough knowledge to confound the atheist and not enough wisdom to redeem the sinner. If her son Francis was to expend a disproportionate amount of effort in the pursuit of political place, to the neglect of "godly offices," he was also to separate explicitly the Kingdom of Saving Grace from both the political kingdoms of this world (under rulers bestowed with initiative and sovereignty by the all-sufficient God) and the realm of nature, whose dominion had been granted unto man by the same Divine Creator.

Bacon's father, his uncle Lord Burghley, his cousin Lord Salisbury, and his own patron and the favorite of Elizabeth, Lord Essex, were all graduates of Cambridge. Attending university was then a relatively new practice among lay members of the Court; colleges were still commonly regarded as hostels for impecunious students destined to be clerics. Members of the families of the minor gentry (of which the English Court was for the greater part composed) who were graduates of Oxford and Cambridge had gone there in a serious pursuit of learning. At Cambridge Sir Nicholas Bacon acquired a desire for learning in the law. Burghley became well-read in Greek; his *Execution of Justice in England for maintenance of Public and Christian Peace* was recognized as a cogent explanation of Elizabeth's religious policy. His son Lord Salisbury composed treatises on politics. George Villiers (1592-1628), James' favorite and chief political agent after Salisbury's death, had not attended Cambridge but had studied in France (where he had gone for training as a courtier) under the tutorship of an Oxford man, Sir John Eliot. He was the author of verses, satires, plays, and a lost work called by Anthony à Wood a *Demonstration of the Deity*.

Queen Elizabeth herself was a woman of unusual learning. She could address the Universities in Greek and in Latin of her own composing and converse fluently with the Italian ambassador in his own tongue. Elizabeth had received instruction from Ascham. He took occasion to remark on her "wisdom and industry," and wrote to the German schoolmaster Sturm:

> She talks French and Italian as well as English: she has often talked to me readily and well in Latin and moderately so in Greek . . . she read with me all of Cicero and the great part of Titus Livius . . . She used to give the morning to the Greek Testament and afterwards read select orations of Isocrates and the tragedies of Sophocles. To these I added St. Cyprian and Melanchthon's Commonplaces.

After Elizabeth's death (1603), when Bacon found reason to write about the attitudes of politicians and monarchs towards learning, he could remind James I that "this lady was endued with learning in her sex singular, and rare even among masculine princes. . . . And unto the very last year of her life she accustomed to appoint set hours for reading, scarcely any young student in a university more daily or more duly."

As for James, who, as Bacon said, spoke "Latin like a scholar," few monarchs had ever been given more severe training in ancient and modern authors. His Scottish guardians had placed him under the instruction of George Buchanan, an accomplished scholar, a great Latinist, and a demanding teacher. Following his preceptor's example, James wrote verses. His first publication was *Essays of a Prentice in the Divine Art of Poesy*. Many others followed: two volumes of *Meditations*, translations from Du Bartas, Lucan, and the Book of Psalms, a book of poems which shows the influence of Buchanan's annotations on Vives, a work on demonology, and several political treatises in exposition and defence of the divine right of kings. His political writings contained doctrines utterly at variance with the principles of his tutor, who published a treatise under the title *De jure regni apud scotos* (1579). So scandalous was this work, ascribing as it did political initiative, even sovereignty, to the sovereign's subjects, that it was twice condemned by acts of Parliament and burned in 1683 by the University of Oxford. Bacon did not exceed the truth when he addressed James I as a sovereign in whom there was "a rare conjunction as well of divine and sacred literature as of profane and human." Nor, again, was he outdoing the ecclesiastical experts when in his *Advancement of Learning* (1605) he contrived the statement, "your Majesty standeth invested of that triplicity which in great veneration was ascribed to the ancient Hermes; the power and fortune of a King, the knowledge and illumination of a Priest, and the learning and universality of a Philosopher." For was not James assured at the Hampton Court Conference (1604) by Bacon's own former Cambridge tutor, Archbishop Whitgift— and Whitgift was no "fanatic"—that "he spoke by the special assistance of God's Spirit"?

These facts considered, there was propriety in Bacon's addressing in his early "devices" praises of learned monarchs to

Elizabeth, along with pleas that the Queen might place at her
subject's disposal means for learning's advancement. There was
literary aptness in his dedicating to Salisbury *De sapientia
veterum* (*Of the Wisdom of the Ancients*, 1609) and to George
Villiers, Duke of Buckingham, the third edition of his *Essays*
(1625). There was fitness in his addressing to James those writings in which he announced his designs for future learning,
The Proficience and Advancement of Learning (1605), *Novum
organum* (*New Organon*, 1620), and *De dignitate et augmentis
scientiarium* (*Of the Dignity and Advancement of Learning*,
1623). Of Bacon's respect for James' erudition there can be no
question. He did not hesitate to cite James' writings, including
Basilicon Doron (1599) and his *True Law of Free Monarchies*
(1598), works which became classical expositions of the doctrine of divine right.

In the year of James' accession (1603) to the English throne,
Bacon began a work which he entitled *Valerius Terminus of
the Interpretation of Nature: with the Annotations of Hermes
Stella*. In the name Hermes Stella was conjoined the powerful,
learned Hermes and a guiding star (*stella*). Both were desig-
nations which Bacon gave elsewhere to his sovereign, and here
he meant none other than King James. It was the author's hope,
in an enthusiasm soon to be dispelled, that the learned Ruler of
the political realm, the Head of the Established Church, and
the Visitor of the Universities, could be prevailed upon to co-
operate with a subject in a publication designed to implement
a new humanism. The way for this humanism would be prepared by Bacon's exposure of certain "false phantoms" of the
human mind and several past and present "impediments of
knowledge," including the traditional methods of inquiry, the
attitudes of politicians and prelates, the "superstitions and errors
of religion," and the manner of the "delivery of knowledge"
within the universities. If Bacon was to decide against the wis-

dom of inviting James in 1603—or 1605—to become a party to this undertaking, seventeen years later he was to find encouragement in the King's writing, on receiving a copy of the *Novum organum*, that he purposed to "read it through with care and attention" and then "give a due commendation to such places as in my opinion shall deserve it." In James' letter to Bacon on this occasion there is the nearest approach on the part of the King to a recognition of Bacon's philosophical enterprise. The *New Organon* probably caused James mild dismay, for it confronted a King with a Lord Chancellor's claim to full authority over a kingdom called Nature and, what was more, with this deputy's request for large financial aid for the inauguration of his philosophic rule from a hard-pressed monarch, who—as Bacon well knew—was finding it increasingly difficult to obtain means to replenish his purse from the Commons with its Puritan burghers, ambitious lawyers, and other sorts of nonconformists, all stubbornly demanding the grants of "privilege" and "right." James, who liked theological jests, indulged himself on this occasion with the remark that the *Novum organum* was "like the peace of God which passeth all understanding!"

Elizabeth, James, and their courtiers were among the learned personages to whom first the youth and then the man Francis Bacon vouchsafed, even while hoping for their support of his philosophical projects, such opinions as the following: The Greek philosophers are prattling schoolboys and their philosophical successors authors of stage plays. All theologies, those of a Calvinistic sort excepted, are heresies through their intertwining the placets of Christian Revelation with the doctrines of the pagan Plato and Aristotle. Learning both within and without the Universities is full of malignancies. The talk of learned men consists of meaningless words about false phantoms. The administrators, professors, fellows, and curricula of the Universities are impediments in the way of learning. And—

here was the important point—a college or school or other foundation supported by public funds should be placed at Francis Bacon's disposal for an instauration of learning on an experimental basis under secular auspices; and, as a consequence of their moral obligation to supply this, sovereigns, personages at Court, and reigns of kings could be esteemed according to a scale of contribution to the reform of learning in prospect.

Bacon's pleas fell on deaf ears. Those of the Court who took note of them undoubtedly reflected, like Bishop (John) Bramhall a generation after Bacon's death, "It is strange to see with what confidence nowadays particular men slight all the Schoolmen, and Philosophers, and Classick Authors of former ages, as if they were not worthy to unloose the shoestrings of some modern Authors." The very learning of the Court itself stood in the way of Bacon's philosophical enterprise. Its clerical and lay members were products of Oxford and Cambridge. Burghley and Salisbury were, in turn, university chancellors. All of them by education, if not by profession, were Platonists and Augustinians or Aristotelians and Peripatetics, or a mixture of these four sorts of philosopher. Elizabeth and James had been schooled in the classics. Elizabeth knew, and no doubt respected, both the Platonic Cicero and the Reformer Philip Melanchthon (1497-1560) who had kept Aristotelianism intact in the theology and the schools of Protestant Germany. She was, as Bacon himself acknowledged, "a great reader" of the "writings of the Fathers, especially those of St. Augustine." James was conversant with traditional doctrines in the fields of logic, physics, ethics, politics, and metaphysics.

Bacon's disciples of a later generation were to have more success than he with a Court far less erudite and literary. Charles II would consort with the virtuosi, look through their telescopes, watch their experiments, become their supporting patron, and grant them a Charter as members of a "philosophical college," now elevated in status to a Royal Society.

III

BACON'S
STUDIES AND AMBITIONS:
HIS EARLY DAYS
IN PARLIAMENT

AFTER RECEIVING INSTRUCTION IN LANGUAGES and authors, and in
biblical theology as well, Bacon entered Cambridge at the age
of thirteen. His tutor was John Whitgift, later chosen by Elizabeth for the archbishopric of Canterbury because of his opposition to any reduction of episcopal authority in church administration, a thing much desired and advocated by those
under the influence of "Genevan reform." Bacon completed his
undergraduate studies in less than three years and earned a
reputation for diligence and proficiency in "the several arts and
sciences."

A major requirement of Cambridge students was *dialectica*:
advanced grammar, rhetoric, and logic. University tutors required the study of books on rhetoric and encouraged the reading of the ethical and other writings of Aristotle, as well as
scholastic commentaries abounding in Platonic, Aristotelian,
Patristic, and Peripatetic references. Public exercises comprised
declamations and formal disputations in Greek and Latin before
university officers. Initial disputations, sometimes called "soph-

isms," were exercises in dialectic preparatory to later "demonstrations of truth." "Truth" in these instances consisted mainly
of theses taken, often out of context, from the ethical, political,
and metaphysical works of Aristotle. Theses were defended by
a respondent arguing in deductive fashion against two or more
opponents. This syllogistic method of demonstration, which
required definition at every stage and turn of argument, was
presumed by university authorities to be the quickest sharpener
of the students' wits and the best way to acquire skill in aligning grounds and consequents within systematic discourse. Contrary to a common assumption by historians, Bacon did not have
opportunity to study mathematics at Cambridge. The subject,
although it was a part of the traditional quadrivium, was not to
be taught there for decades because Peripatetic influence was
against it. During the first third of the seventeenth century
Cambridge was still without tutors who knew mathematics.
John Wallis (1616-1703) and Seth Ward (1617-1689), who
studied there and later became professors of mathematics and
astronomy respectively at Oxford, where they revived these
long defunct studies, could get no tutorial aid in either of these
subjects while undergraduates. Another supposition, incidentally, that soon the fellows and authorities at Cambridge
would be showing themselves receptive of what was to be called
the "new experimental philosophy," is also an error. The main
academic support of the extramural "philosophical college"
which was to become the founding body of the Royal Society,
came from certain men at Oxford, not from their confreres at
Cambridge. Neither university was officially to show any disposition whatever to acknowledge the academic value of this
society's undertakings until very late in the seventeenth century.
Cambridge did not hesitate to elect Bacon as its representative
in the House of Commons and to make him their standing legal
counsel, but its fellows persistently refused to countenance his
philosophy.

When at Cambridge, Bacon seems to have read a considerable part of Aristotle, including his ethics, politics, and rhetoric, and also some of Plato. It was there presumably that he first became aware, through the Stagirite's writings and those of his commentators, of the opinions of Pre-Socratic thinkers. Certainly, he was to find before long in these earliest philosophers what seemed to him a close contact with particulars and operation and, what was even more to his liking, an identification of philosophy with the science of nature and a merging of metaphysical being with formed, furnished, and active matter—not the indeterminate, inert, and deprived thing which Aristotle called by this name. By the time Bacon left the University he had rejected Aristotelianism as a method of demonstration and a system of doctrine. He found it too theoretical in definition and too remote from particulars for science, too contentious for a profession of truth, too speculative for practice and operation. Dr. William Rawley, Bacon's chaplain, early biographer, and editor, tells us that "whilst he was commorant in the university, about sixteen years of age (as his lordship hath been pleased to impart unto myself), he fell into the dislike of the philosophy of Aristotle; not for the worthlessness of the author, to whom he would ever ascribe all high attributes, but for the unfruitfulness of the way; being a philosophy (as his lordship used to say) only strong for disputations and contentions, but barren of the production of works for the benefit of the life of man; in which mind he continued to his dying day."

Bacon, however, learned many things from Aristotle. He saw in the Stagirite an investigator who, during a stay at the Court of Macedon where he was tutor to Alexander the Great, was able to collect, by the help of fowlers, fishermen, and the like, materials for a natural history—even if afterwards this great "wit" was to let the fruits of his early inquiry escape by turning to "abstractions." Aristotle also provided Bacon with the example of a thinker who had the courage to reconstruct philosophy. From the same thinker Bacon learned too that human knowledge can be organized according to a hierarchy of sciences; that logic, as an instrument of all demonstrable proof, is not among the divisions of the sciences; and that there is such a thing as a demonstrated metaphysics. He thought Aristotle wrong in establishing this universal science on the single Principle of Identity—What is, is—and in supposing, in opposition to Plato, that its subject matter could be approached directly rather than through a lesser science. Like the Platonists, who in another regard had identified Plato's Good with the Christian God, Aristotle was mistaken in equating his metaphysics with the natural theology of a First Cause. Aristotle had wisely professed a philosophy of nature and assigned it a method of demonstration, and then had properly concluded that this method was one which could not fully establish knowledge in ethics and politics. If he was to bring confusion into natural science through a division of its subject matter according to basic axioms and by the employment of terms theoretically and not inductively defined, he on principle did at least segregate his physics from theology, ethics, and politics. In addition, he issued something more than a caution against the ambitious schemes of mathematicians, after members of the Academy founded by Plato had interposed nonexistential mathematical entities between particulars and their forms.

On leaving Cambridge Bacon enrolled as a student in the law at Gray's Inn. In 1586 he became a bencher. Twenty years later he was to become, like his father before him, the Inn's Treasurer —equivalent to President; and after his political downfall he was to retire to Gray's Inn and live there "by turns" until his death. Bacon's legal studies were interrupted in 1577, when he joined the staff of Sir Amias Paulet, Ambassador to France. He remained in the Ambassador's service for some three years. On one occasion at least he was entrusted with a diplomatic message to Queen Elizabeth. He also received a commendation to her Majesty. At this period Bacon showed inquisitiveness about "phenomena," including the relations between vibrations and sound, and inventiveness, as evidenced by his new method for diplomatic writing in cipher. His stay in France gave him training in diplomacy and protocol and an opportunity to observe French civil conflicts as well as intrigues against his own country by Portuguese, Spaniards, and papal agents. It was brought to an abrupt end by the death of his father in 1579. Bacon was now left with small financial means. His father, who had already provided for his other children, had been setting aside money for the purchase of considerable land for his youngest and favorite heir—"his father's first choice," as his mother said. When death intervened, the young man inherited only about one-fifth of his father's personal property. At the age of nineteen, Francis Bacon found himself facing the world with great capacities, large ambitions, and little estate.

Bacon's intellectual capacity had become evident at an early age. During his stay in France a painter inscribed on his portrait *Si tabula daretur digna, animum mallem*—"if only I had a canvas worthy to paint his mind." Those who conversed with him were struck by his discernment of principle in circumstance and the aptness of his words. Bacon's way of speaking betokened skill in writing, power in politics, and wisdom on the bench. It impressed and often delighted Elizabeth, and disquieted the Cecils. His manner of writing, like the styles of Shakespeare and Chaucer, had been shaped in the precisions of rhetoric and yet was to soar beyond rhetoric's dimensions. Bacon would become a very learned and, besides, a very observant and reflective man, and would show, as his friend Tobie Matthew said, a "facility and felicity of expressing it all in so elegant, significant, and abundant, and yet so choice . . . a way of words, of metaphors, and allusions, as perhaps the world hath not seen, since it was a world." Soon every word, phrase, and sentence which came from Bacon's pen began to tell. His constructions, now compressed and terse, now open, now prolix, responded in apt rhythm to each nuance of his moving thought. His precise nouns, verbs, and adjectives came in a succession like the inevitable notes of a musical fugue. His prose never weakened into mere rhythmic melody, yet its sentences were to prove as resistant to paraphrase as the songs of a lyrical poet, for no word may be added, changed, or removed without weakening the part and the whole. So original are the springs of Bacon's utterance that his attempted renderings of the language of others, the Psalms of David for example, rise feebly without inspiration. Literary genius does not often, if indeed ever, abide the resaying of what is not its own.

Bacon would become a great speaker in the Commons and courts of law. Ben Jonson would be able to pay him this tribute: "There happened in my time one noble speaker, who was full of gravity in his speaking. . . . No man ever spake more neatly, more pressedly, more weightily, or suffered less emptiness, less idleness, in what he uttered. No member of his speech, but consisted of his own graces. His hearers could not cough, or look aside from him, without loss. He commanded where he spake; and had his judges angry and pleased at his devotion. No man had their affections more in his power. The fear of every man that heard him was, lest he should make an end."

Bacon's tastes—to change the theme—were those befitting one accustomed from birth to houses of splendor and courts of magnificence. His "luxuries" were none other than the necessities of Aristotle's magnanimous citizen who, as a fully actualized and wholly virtuous man, was both a philosopher and a statesman. Aristotle had taught that this virtuous citizen would have at his disposal the products of husbandmen, mechanics, artisans, and artists. Bacon regarded such things as proper means for the elevation of man from savagery to civility and as goods of the kingdom of nature granted to man by God. Bacon would have thought strange indeed an educated biographer's finding signs of moral depravity in the spacious scale of his living. In the *Advancement of Learning* Bacon took note that there were monks who chose poverty for good purposes; but he also deplored those "derogations . . . which grow to learning from the fortune or condition of learned men in respect of scarcity of means." Some years before, he had told Essex in a letter that he "partly" leaned "to Thales' opinion, that a philosopher may be rich if he will." This was an opinion for which Bacon had found specific support in Aristotle, who had used the rich Thales as a model for such householders as had been deprived, by small means, of magnanimous living. Bacon did not associate the acquisition of goods with loose living, idleness, intellectual weakness, or corruption of morals and manners. While he affirmed the necessity of the priceless things of the mind, and while he understood the choice of poverty by monks for religious ends, it was not Bacon's opinion that penurious living as such makes for fuller understanding or greater virtue. He always thought that men of learning were more deserving of financial reward than mechanics, manufacturers, amusement-makers, importers, exporters, and money-changers.

Bacon earned a great deal of money, but his tastes, like his ambitions for science, succeeded always in outstripping his means. He lived lavishly, and the arrangements of his household, which was not well managed, were always in full keeping with what he considered his rôle at Court. On the expectation of a new public appointment he would take the precaution of putting his servants into new cloaks. As he took his seat in Chancery he surpassed all "within living memory" by "the bravery and multitude" of his attendants. While Chancellor (1618-1621) he employed in his household some forty gentleman-waiters, and other servants in proportion. In 1608 his income was nearly £5,000 and some ten years later about £16,000. Yet he was still in debt, paying ten per cent to the money-lenders. At the time of his death (1626), his debts amounted to over £22,000 and his estate to some £7,000. Bacon's thoughts about finance had ever been dominated by the hope, which continued even to the days when he wrote his final will and testament, that financial habilitation would eventually come through James' placing large means at his disposal, as the magnanimous director of an enterprise of experimental inquiry. These grants, he anticipated, might be comparable at least to those bestowed on James' favorite, Robert Carr, Earl of Somerset. They were never forthcoming.

Bacon's career was determined by two ambitions, one political, the other philosophical. From his teens he was sure of his philosophic mission and sanguine about its courtly support. In his scheme of appraisal he placed the attainment and perpetuation of learning above political success. The works on which he relied "to maintain memory and merit of the times succeeding" were not his "advices" to sovereigns, speeches in Parliament, judgments in courts, literary essays, or histories of reigns. They were writings and other efforts on behalf of the advancement of learning. In 1592 Bacon was affirming that "the sovereignty of man lieth hid in knowledge." In 1595, he was reflecting that "the monuments of wit survive the monuments of power." Ten years afterwards, in a temporary despair, he was lamenting to his friend Sir Thomas Bodley his greatest "error": "knowing myself by inward calling to be fitter to hold a book than to play a part, I have led my life in civil causes, for which I was not very fit by nature, and more unfit by the preoccupation of my mind." Two years later, in 1607, after receiving the considerable public appointment of Solicitor-General—earlier he had been made King's Counsel with Patent—he was repining:

"I have found now twice, upon amendment of my fortune, disposition to distaste." In 1617, on taking his seat in Chancery, Bacon told the assembled members of the court that it was his intention to reserve "the depth of the three long vacations . . . in some measure free from business of estate, and for studies, arts and sciences, to which in my nature I am most inclined." In 1620 he wrote in the proem to his *New Organon* that, compared with the instituting of a new philosophy, a new science, and a new learning all other ambitions seemed poor in his eyes. In 1623, now trying desperately to provide written content for some of the six parts of his instauration of the sciences, the author was to reflect on his carriage by destiny, against the inclination of his genius, into political affairs. When overwhelmed politically (1621), deserted by Commons, Lords, and King, the man who still held firm to his philosophy addressed his Maker with a prayer of penitence, worded in keeping with his literary disposition—that prayer which some critics have carpingly called "a public address":

Besides my innumerable sins, I confess before thee, that I am debtor to thee for the gracious talent of thy gifts and graces, which I have neither put into a napkin, nor put it (as I ought) to exchangers, where it might have made best profit; but misspent it in things for which I was least fit; so as I may truly say, my soul hath been a stranger in the course of my pilgrimage.

Never once, however, in any of these statements does Bacon deny, even implicitly, the suitability of political office for a philosopher. In his early *Valerius Terminus* he raised precisely this question, only to give a noncommittal answer. "It is hard to say," he wrote, "whether mixture of contemplations with an active life, or retiring wholly to contemplations, do disable and hinder the mind more." But at the same time he was bringing under censure the "tenderness and want of compliance of some of the most ancient and revered philosophers, who retired too early from civil business that they might avoid indignities and perturbations, and live (as they thought) more pure and saint-like." In his formative years Bacon had been taught by Aristotle, and by Plato too, that philosophers should spend part of their lives in the service of the state. He had found in Aristotle's *Politics* and in Plato's *Republic* portrayals of the most virtuous man as the most fully functioning citizen. The ethical man, according to both these philosophers, would possess both goodness and "universal and methodick knowledge"—something which James I was to acknowledge in Bacon on the occasion of his accepting a copy of the *Novum organum*—and would endure the arduous duties of politics. This conception of the duty of a philosopher became so much a part of Bacon's thinking that he was given to representing threatened retirements from politics, when advancement did not come, as a departure from what was proper and becoming to a full man.

It is hardly appropriate, or even sensible, to call Bacon the politician a "truant from the academy." Bacon never was an academic, and in the scholastic circumstances of his time he could neither have become nor remained one. His views on learning were anathema in the Universities from the beginning, and were to remain so for nearly a century. More than fifty years after his death and a generation after mathematics and astronomy had been revived at Oxford, his philosophy and his disciples in the Royal Society were publicly condemned in the Theatre of the same University, along with "fanatics" and "conventicles," *ad inferos, ad gehennam*. What Bacon proposed for learning could no more have been put into effect by a rebel in academic place than by a seer in solitude. His project entailed the collection of observations and the results of experiments on an enormous scale, in range as vast as "the universe." The natural history on which his philosophy was to rest would have the scope of nature itself. His design could be implemented only at great expense and under great patronage. If, despite these circumstances, Bacon is perforce to be regarded as a truant from the academy—in some strained sense of that phrase—it must be conceded that his truancy took the form of very notable endeavor. Without a nod of encouragement from any learned body—his name was even rejected for enrolment in the Lincei Academy of Florence—and without sympathy on the part of more than a few of his closest friends, this lone thinker prepared a map of the whole territory of human knowledge and then designed in detail a new scheme for its cultivation. He then, as both he and his editor, William Rawley, were to remark, became laborer and workman, dug the clay singlehanded, collected the stubble, and burned the bricks for the philosophical edifice of which he was the architect. The same alleged truant managed to write thirty-odd philosophical pieces. If most of these were composed during vacations between sessions of Parliament, sittings of law courts, and consultations with ministers and monarchs, if many of them were to remain incomplete in pattern and truncated in structure, they proved sufficient to start learning on a new road. It was a road taken at first by only a small band of his countrymen in their "philosophical college," then by an ever-increasing host of inquirers within and without scientific academies at home and abroad, and finally, after a long period of ridicule, doubt, and hesitancy, by fellows and lecturers within the Universities. Bacon, who never was an academician, was to become the propagator of all that is distinctly modern in modern academies. A learning identified with natural philosophy and a natural philosophy identified with experimentally established knowledge were to be his "merit" if not always his "memory" in "times succeeding."

At the age of eighteen Bacon found himself dependent for employment on the influence and goodwill of relatives and

friends of his father at Court. As the son of a former Lord
Keeper and the nephew of Queen Elizabeth's present Lord
Treasurer, Bacon expected that, once he had prepared himself
in the law, political office would be his for the asking. Already,
he had "by birth and education . . . been absorbed with affairs
of state." He had been reared in a politically and juristically
minded family. He was well known to the Queen, who had paid
visits to his father's house, and on one occasion, after receiving
his apt replies to her questions, had jokingly dubbed him her
"young Lord Keeper." Bacon's first request for office seems to
have been addressed in letters to his aunt, Lady Burghley, who
did not look with favor on his suit. For some years she had
thought her nephew too sure of himself. When he was twenty
she told him so, only to become more confirmed in her opinion.
Francis Bacon then assured her, in reply, "My thankful and
serviceable mind shall always be like itself, howsoever it vary
from the common disguising." The nephew next addressed entreaties to his uncle. Burghley, aware of Bacon's capacities of
mind and speech and having at the same time the political
future of his physically deformed son, Robert Cecil, in mind,
was not eager to advance a prospective rival to his heir. Besides,
the uncle considered Bacon presumptuous in his dealings and
arrogant in his nature. Burghley found occasion to tell the
nephew that others had remarked on his arrogancy. Bacon
asked his uncle to believe that "arrogancy and overweening"
were "far" from his nature, explaining that "such persons as are
of a nature bashful (as myself is), whereby they want that
plausible familiarity which others have, are often mistaken for
proud."

In 1584, partly through Burghley's influence, Bacon, at the
age of twenty-three, obtained a seat in the House of Commons.
There he remained, a member of all the ensuing sittings of
Parliament under Elizabeth and James I, until he went to the

House of Lords. In one Parliament he represented two constituencies and in another, three. Five years after his first election, he was made Clerk or Registrar of the Star Chamber, a
court of the Queen in Council. But the clerkship, which carried
a large stipend, was given by reversion, and Bacon was not to
take office until 1608, some nineteen years after its award. A
few years after his nomination to the office, its occupant engaged in irregular practice which could have resulted in his dismissal, and some of Bacon's friends suggested punitive action.
Bacon informed the Lord Keeper, Sir John Puckering—whose
advancement at Court had been dependent on Sir Nicholas
Bacon's influence—that while he had been "incited" to do so he
would not consider "coming in upon a lease by way of for-
feiture" and "would not be thought to supplant any man for
great gain."

In 1592, three years after he had obtained the clerkship in
reversion, Bacon sent a striking letter to Burghley. The outlook
revealed in this communication made it evident that the law,
which he was now practising, had been, in the words of Rawley,
"but as an accessary, and not his principal study." Bacon reminded his uncle of the "meanness" of his estate, professed
"moderate civil ends," and asked for a place to "carry" him. He
wrote:

I have taken all knowledge to be my province; and if I could
purge it of two sorts of rovers (whereof the one with frivolous
disputations, confutations, and verbosities, the other with blind
experiments and auricular traditions and impostures, hath committed so many spoils) I hope I should bring in industrious observations, grounded conclusions, and profitable inventions and
discoveries—the best state of that province. This, whether it be
curiosity, or vainglory, or nature, or (if one take it favourably)
philanthropia, is so fixed in my mind as it cannot be removed. And
I do easily see that place of any reasonable countenance doth
bring commandment of more wits than of a man's own which is
the thing I greatly affect. . . .

And if your Lordship will not carry me on, I will not do as Anaxagoras did, who reduced himself with contemplation into voluntary poverty. But this will I do. I will sell the inheritance that I have, and purchase some lease of quick revenue, or some office of gain that shall be executed by deputy, and so give over all care of service, and become some sorry book-maker, or a true pioneer in that mine of truth which (he said) lay so deep.

In this message Bacon was communicating, somewhat like a prophet, to Elizabeth's Lord Treasurer his twofold ambition: to occupy high office in the manner of Aristotle's virtuous man and, after the example of Aristotle but in his own way, to reconstruct human learning. It was his expectation that if the first of two ambitions were realized, the second would, as a consequence, be attained. But his letter did little more than confirm his uncle in the view that Francis Bacon was highly opinionated, very ambitious, and, by nature, inclined to innovation, which could prove disturbing to settled institutions. How highly opinionated the nephew was, Burghley did not in fact then know. Eight years before (1584), at the age of twenty-three, Bacon had written an unfinished work which he called by no less a title than *Temporis partus maximus* (*The Greatest Birth of Time*). Later, by a change of adjective, this became *Temporis partus masculus* (*The Fertilizing Birth of Time*). In it Bacon had brought under judgment and condemnation, after the manner of a judge in court, all philosophers and all philosophies of the past and the present.

Burghley's earlier opinion of his nephew received further confirmation in a political regard when in 1593 Bacon, who had been granted the privilege of pleading in the courts only some seven years before, assumed that he should be given the Attorney-Generalship. The nephew was not unmindful of his own legal talents or of the fact that his father had been appointed "Solicitor of the Augmentation, (a court of much business) when he had never practised, and was but twenty-seven

years old." Bacon's suit for the place now vacant was supported
by entreaties on the part of Essex; by Bacon's own letters to
the Queen, to the Lord Keeper, and to the Lord Treasurer; and
by his mother's importunity of Burghley. Elizabeth, Burghley,
and others at Court thought Bacon too young and inexperienced for the office. But there was a more personal reason for
Elizabeth's and Burghley's refusing him the Attorneyship.
Earlier in the year the Queen had requested large funds to meet
the danger of Spanish undertakings in prospect against England.
Burghley asked the House of Commons for three subsidies pay-
able at an increased rate; and, because of the largeness of the
sums involved, made the request that the Lower House consult
with the Lords. This procedure was strenuously opposed in
speeches by Bacon, because it violated a "privilege" of the Commons which prevented consultation with the Upper House on
a question of supply. When Bacon's objection was sustained by
the Lower House he was not yet satisfied, and argued against
the proposed rate of collection. "The poor men's rent," he said,
"is such as they are not able to yield it, and the general com-
monalty is not able to pay so much upon the present. The
gentlemen must sell their plate and the farmers their brass pots
ere this will be paid." The Queen showed great indignation at
what she considered an affront to her person by the young man
she had smiled upon from his boyhood and with whom she had
often conversed about serious questions of state. She spoke
bitterly of those who placed the burdens of their constituents
before "the necessity of the time," and banished Bacon from
her presence.

Bacon, who refused to retract what he had said in the Commons, asked the Queen's pardon for his "boldness and plainness"
and told her, "Your Majesty's favour indeed, and access to your
royal person, I did ever, encouraged by your own speeches,
seek and desire; and I would be very glad to be reintegrate in

that." The "exquisite disgrace" he felt on being refused the office he now sought consisted largely in the denial of access to his sovereign. How he regarded such a denial he was to tell in a charge to a jury twenty-odd years later, after he had obtained the office his heart was now set on: "The fountain of honour is the king and his aspect, and the access to his person continueth honour in life, and to be banished from his presence is one of the greatest eclipses of honour that can be."

Bacon told his uncle in a letter, which he hoped the Queen would see, that he "was sorry to find . . . that my last speech in Parliament, delivered in discharge of my conscience and duty to God, her Majesty, and my country was offensive. . . . If my heart be misjudged by imputation of popularity . . . I have great wrong; and the greater, because the manner of my speech did most evidently show that I spake simply and only to satisfy my conscience, and not with any advantage or policy to sway the cause; and my terms carried all signification of duty and zeal towards her Majesty and her service. . . . And therefore I most humbly pray your Lordship, first to continue me in your own good opinion: and then to perform the part of an honest friend . . . in drawing her Majesty to accept of the sincerity and simplicity of my heart, and to bear with the rest, and restore me to her Majesty's favour."

The Queen, who was probably informed of the content of this letter, still refused to see Bacon. To Puckering Bacon wrote of his "grief" and "marvel" at the Queen's "hard conceit" of his speeches in the Commons. "It mought," he told the Lord Keeper, "please her sacred Majesty to think what my end should be in those speeches, if it were not duty, and duty alone. I am not so simple but I know the common beaten way to please. And whereas popularity hath been objected, I muse what care I should take to please many, that taketh a course of life to deal with few."

To Lady Bacon's complaint that her son was being "robbed" through his uncle's denying him office the Lord Treasurer answered that he had "less power to do my friends good than the world thinketh." Throughout a whole year Essex pleaded vehemently with Elizabeth and even begged the Cecils to give Bacon the place that he sought. To Robert Cecil he expressed surprise, which was probably feigned, that the latter's father should prefer a "stranger"—Edward Coke—to a "kinsman," whose "parts and sufficiency" were greater "in any respect." Elizabeth was not to be moved, even after the Earl warned her against losing "the use of the ablest gentleman to do her service of any of your quality whatsoever." When of an evening the favorite talked much of the time of little else besides Bacon's talents and virtues, the Queen would order him to desist. On one occasion she sent him to bed. Finally Elizabeth told Essex that, plead as he might, Bacon would not yet be put into a place where his duties might require access to her person. She reminded the favorite that "if it had been in the King, her father's time, a less offence than that would have made a man be banished from his presence for ever."

In 1594 Sir Edward Coke, Bacon's senior by nine years, an experienced lawyer of considerable repute, became Attorney-General. Bacon then made an effort to obtain the Solicitor-Generalship. Earlier, Cecil had told Essex that his protégé would have been better advised to seek this office instead of the Attorneyship. Burghley recommended the nephew's appointment, but in a half-hearted manner. Robert Cecil presented his cousin's "virtues" in such a way that suspicion of Bacon's political capabilities was spread about the Court. Bacon threatened to retire from law and politics if the office now sought was not to be his. The Queen, through Robert Cecil, who by now was Secretary of State although his appointment had not been made public, made known her decision that, if

Bacon continued to hold the view that either he got the office he now sought "in his own time" or he would regard himself as one denied all office, she would search the whole of England for another candidate rather than give the Solicitor-Generalship to the young man. In November, 1595, Sir Thomas Fleming, Bacon's senior by seventeen years, was appointed to the post.

The following spring Puckering died and Sir Thomas Egerton, Master of the Rolls, was made Lord Keeper and Lord Chancellor (1596-1617), under the title of Lord Ellesmere. Bacon now became a candidate for the Mastership. Essex having twice failed to persuade the Queen to advance his protégé, was not pressed to entreat Elizabeth in his behalf again. Egerton instead was asked to use his influence with her Majesty, who for a third time refused to appoint Bacon to a regular office of state.

The Queen, however, had been keeping an eye on the son of her former Lord Keeper. Her character being what it was, she had probably come to admire his steadfastness during more than three years, while he refused either to apologize or recant. She invited him into the Royal Presence, and made him "Queen's Counsel, Extraordinary"—as Bacon called the office in a letter to James on a later occasion—by her own edict, dispensing with the ordinary Patent. Bacon received no further appointment under Elizabeth, yet he was brought continually into her employment. In retrospect he was to tell King James: "My good old Mistress was wont to call me her watch-candle, because it pleased her to say I did continually burn (and yet she suffered me to waste almost to nothing)." Bacon's first editor, William Rawley, whose opinion in the matter was doubtlessly inspired by the candidate himself, wrote of Bacon's failure to obtain promotion from Elizabeth in his *Life of the Honourable Author*: "His birth and other capacities qualified him above others of his profession to have ordinary accesses at court and to come frequently into the queen's eye, who would often grace him with private and free communication, not only about the matters of his profession or business in law, but also about arduous affairs of estate; from whom she received from time to time great satisfaction. Nevertheless, though she cheered him much with the bounty of her confidence, yet she never cheered him with the bounty of her hand . . . which might be imputed, not so much to Her Majesty's averseness and disaffection towards him, as to the arts and policy of a great statesman then, who laboured by all industrious and secret means to suppress and keep him down; lest if he had risen, he might have obscured his glory." The statesman blamed by Rawley was Bacon's cousin, Robert Cecil, against whose guile and craftiness Lady Bacon had early warned her sons.

Bacon's political undertakings during the reign of Elizabeth were those of a Parliamentarian, a Queen's Counsel "Extraordinary," and a writer of political tracts. His grasp of constitutional questions and his skill in debate gave him a commanding place in the House of Commons. Experienced Parliamentarians, newly elected representatives from the shires, the Secretary of State, and the Queen herself were given the benefit of his advice. In the Commons Bacon's voice was heard in advocacy of the repeal of outmoded laws and in a plea, by implication, for a digest and compilation of legal statutes and precedents. The laws, he said, are "so many in number that neither common people can half practise them, nor the lawyer sufficiently understand them." Bacon asked the Lower House for a rectification of weights and measures in view of the fact that false weighing had become widespread. As the advocate of a strong agricultural population, he argued against any bill on tillage which would further the engrossing of "the wealth of the kingdom . . . in a few pasturers' hands." He opposed a repressive measure of Burghley's against Roman Catholic Recusants, and another affecting procedures in the Council's Court of Star Chamber.

In 1593 Bacon refused to permit Burghley to have the Lords discuss a question of supply, and led a Commons bent on affirming once and for all that its constitutional privileges were to be recognized and sustained. Eight years later Bacon asserted a second constitutional principle of another sort, this time to the Queen's great satisfaction. The Commons had begun to consider the repeal of certain Monopolies with Patents which had been granted by the Queen. Bacon undertook to clarify the general question of Monopolies, which members of the Commons tended to treat in gross. He distinguished among several sorts, arguing that the soundness of any one Monopoly depended on its circumstances and purpose. "If," he said, "any man out of his own wit, industry, or endeavour, find out any thing beneficial to the Commonwealth, or bring any new invention which every subject of this kingdom may use; yet, in regard of his pains and travel therein, her Majesty perhaps is pleased to grant him a privilege to use the same only, by himself or his deputies, for a certain time. This is one kind of Monopoly. Sometimes there is a glut of things, when they be in excessive quantity, as perhaps of corn; and perhaps her Majesty gives licence of transportation to one man. This is another kind of Monopoly. Sometimes there is a scarcity or a small quantity; and the like is granted also." Bacon also made it clear to the Commons that since the granting of Patents lay within the Royal Prerogative, the House could proceed in the matter only by way of petition to the Queen. His speech on this occasion included a statement which was to be recalled in later years by his political enemies: "For the prerogative of the prince, I hope I shall never hear it discussed. The queen hath both enlarging and restraining power; she may set at liberty things restrained by Statute and may restrain things which be at liberty." The Commons concurred in a proposal of petition. On being informed of this proceeding, Elizabeth suspended some of the unpopular Patents in question and revoked others. She granted in unfeigned affection for her subjects what she would have refused a demanding Commons which sought to bring within question her comprehensive Prerogative. It was at this time, near the end of her long reign, that she summoned her Parliament to Whitehall and told them in a farewell, "Though God hath raised me high, yet this I count the glory of my crown, that I have reigned with your loves."

After the defeat of the Irish armies and the rout of a supporting Spanish force in 1601 had terminated a rebellion of eight years' duration, Bacon wrote a letter to the Secretary of State, advising him how to proceed in arranging a settlement of Ireland. He asked Robert Cecil "to embrace the care of reducing that kingdom to civility . . . for . . . sound honour and merit to her majesty and this crown." He counselled his cousin against punitive measures, displanting of ancient "generations," and the opening of wounds in a recrudescence. The reduction of Ireland, he wrote, "as well to civility and justice, as to obedience and peace, which things, as affairs now stand, I hold to be inseparable, consisteth in four points: 1. The extinguishing of the relicks of the war. 2. The recovery of the hearts of the people. 3. The removing of the root and occasions of new troubles. 4. Plantations and buildings."

To further these ends Bacon advised that Irish "weakness" be supplanted by Christianity and Irish "conditions" be replaced by "graces," through such agents as justice, protection, and reward. He asked for a "toleration of religion," "the recontinuing and replenishing of the college begun at Dublin," "versions of bibles and catechisms, and other books of instruction into the Irish language," and "justice . . . as near as may be to the laws and customs of England." He counselled the "carrying of an even course between the English and Irish . . . as if they were one nation," the countenancing of the Irish nobility, the bestowal of knighthood on Irish subjects, and the care and education of their children. He argued that plantations would be better and more economical than a large military force, that persons chosen as "governors and counsellors" must have the affection and esteem of the people, that building and planting should proceed, not haphazardly, but "according to a prescript or formulary," and that an increase of new inhabitants should be encouraged by ample liberties and charters.

Bacon was to make similar representations to James, in 1609, and to Buckingham, in 1616, on the Irish question. His advice on each occasion was the issue of a desire to make Ireland "another Britain." It was characterized by a magnanimity toward a conquered race and by sensitivity to the temperament and the customs of what were called a "wild" people, with their bards, their harps, their contentiousness, their impatience of restraint.

IV

BACON AND ESSEX

WHEN Elizabeth made Bacon Queen's Counsel on her own warrant she intended that his duties should be of an extraordinary sort. She continuously discussed questions of state with him. When in a pamphlet the Jesuit priest Robert Parsons attacked the Queen and her Lord Treasurer for their measures against Roman Catholic Recusants, Bacon was given the task of preparing a reply. He was also called upon to compile a state report on the treason of Robert Devereux (1566-1601), Second Earl of Essex, at whose trial he had been assigned the role of prosecutor, along with Attorney-General Coke. This engagement in what came to be known as "the case of Essex" was to be one of the most distressing episodes of his life. After Bacon had become renowned and his name enduring, few subjects in English history would be dilated upon with more dissolute sentimentality and greater moral confusion than this. The case has been cited, as a biographer, John Nichol, has remarked, "to point half the morals and adorn half the tales against ingratitude for . . . centuries." The Queen's Counsel, who performed a required duty of state, has been presented as a man devoid of "instinct of honor," "ethical sentiment," "moral instincts." Altogether, his conduct "has been the subject of more vituperation than perhaps any other single act of any other single man." One expositor crowns his account of the Earl's trial for treason with this flourish: "Essex was a traitor to the laws which make possible a civilized and organized state, and by those laws he deserved death. Bacon was a traitor to higher laws than these—the laws of honour, of pity, of love; and by those sacred laws he stands condemned." One wonders how the man who composed this statement could ever suppose that any honorable officer of state who loved and pitied the members of the human race could ever prosecute any individual in a court of law. Or should such an officer presume that there is to be one justice for late intimates and benefactors turned political traitors and another for strangers among malefactors? Let us review the circumstances of the case.

About the time when Bacon was imploring his uncle Lord Burghley for an office so that he might pursue his scientific endeavors, he had been extended the patronage of the rising star in the Court, the Earl of Essex. The Earl, five years Bacon's junior, was a man with literary gifts, who had entered Cambridge at the age of ten, and would probably have chosen a "retired course" in study, had he not been brought into the Queen's service. After taking part in a military campaign under the Earl of Leicester, another of Elizabeth's favorites, Esssex was made Master of the Horse, before he was twenty-one. By 1589 he was supplanting Leicester in the affections of an infatuated Queen—almost three times his age. Essex responded with a temperament which always displayed more ardor than caution in the presence of lovers and admirers; he took Elizabeth by storm. She was behaving, once more, like the coquette she was, in demanding the Earl's constant attention. Queen and courtier became jealous one of the other. Anyone who came between Elizabeth and Essex on any matter, in any circumstance, on any business, was deemed a potential rival or enemy by the Earl. Affection for the Queen did not, however, preclude his marrying secretly, and thereby occasioning in Elizabeth great pique and unbounded, uncontrollable rage. The indulgence of the Queen made the Earl unaware of her wariness lest any favorite should presume politically on her sentiment. Jealousy rendered Essex blind to her skill in playing one courtier against another. A romantic temperament made him oblivious to a Queen's capacity to control her affections when confronted with acts or circumstances which might infringe upon her queenly majesty or the welfare of her throne and people.

After a time the new favorite at Court was looked upon as the political rival of Burghley. Essex began to assume that his position was such that he could name the leaders of military expeditions, influence the course of justice by a note to a Lord Keeper, and assign offices of state to persons of his own choosnig. In this assumption he undertook the promotion of Bacon, a candidate to his liking because of his capacity of mind, his conversation, kindliness, reverence of the Queen, and—by no means least—his being denied office by his uncle, Lord Burghley.

Essex became Bacon's patron in the year 1591. For some four years the two men, divergent in temperament, were on very friendly terms. The patron offered "power, might, authority, and amity" to an aspirant for political place at Court, as well as the prospect of advancement for a philosopher's scientific designs. Bacon, long denied what he considered his due recognition by Burghley, became the willing protégé of the Cecils' most powerful opponent at Court. In 1592, Anthony Bacon on his return from travels on the Continent, found his brother "bound and in deep arrearages" to the new patron.

Bacon's early faith in the Earl, even to the extent of entering into the Essex-Burghley rivalry, showed itself in the firmness of his treatment of his uncle on the question of subsidies and other

matters in the House of Commons. When the office of Attorney-General fell vacant Essex was given opportunity to
effect the patronage he had undertaken. The Attorneyship was
a place to which a legally inexperienced man could hardly have
expected promotion. Essex, who had been rapidly advanced at
Court in his twenties, saw no reason why a man of thirty-two
should not be given the post. He had, however, miscalculated
the Queen's character and the influence of her trusted Lord
Treasurer. Bacon's suit, advanced through Essex, failed, despite
the vehemence of his patron's entreaty. In a second suing, for
the Solicitor-Generalship, history repeated itself. Elizabeth may
have secretly admired the young Parliamentarian's standing up
to her "solid" Burghley and his refusal to retreat. Probably, too,
she was unconsciously jealous, as only a coquette could have
been, of the warmth and zeal of her favorite's support of Bacon
in which, as Lady Bacon remarked, "the Earl showed great
affection" and "violent courses." Before many years had gone
by Bacon was to have occasion to remark, when he was entreating the Queen in behalf of the disobedient Essex, "that there are
not only jealousies, but certain revolutions in princes' minds."

While Bacon's political promotion and reconciliation with
the Queen were being pursued, Essex had Bacon prepare devices or masques for Elizabeth's entertainment. In these the
Queen was complimented and praised, Essex was portrayed as
a faithful suitor, and the founding of a new experimental learning under the direction of the author was represented as an
undertaking worthy of a great sovereign. When nothing came
of his efforts to promote Bacon's cause, Essex decided, in 1595,
that he would yet prove himself a worthy patron of an impoverished suitor, gifted beyond any inhabitant of the Court
and denied place because he refused to recant what he had a
right to say in the Commons and because Burghley was intent
on impeding the advancement of any potential rival to his heir.
The Earl presented his protégé with an estate at Twickenham

worth £1,800—the amount obtained by Bacon when he sold the
land to pay creditors. "You fare ill," Essex wrote, "because you
have chosen me for your mean and dependence; you have spent
your times and thoughts in my matter. I die if I do not somewhat towards your fortune. You shall not deny to accept a
piece of land I will bestow on you." Bacon accepted the land
as the gift of a generous patron and friend. On receipt of the
benefaction, which he did not specifically mention in his letter,
because this was intended for the Queen's reading, Bacon
wrote:

TO MY LORD OF ESSEX, it may please your good lordship:

I pray God her Majesty's weighing be not like the weight of a
balance: *gravia deorsum, levia sursum*. But I am as far from
being altered in devotion towards her as I am from distrust that
she will be altered in opinion towards me, when she knoweth me
better. For myself, I have lost some opinion, some time, and
some means. This is my account. But then, for opinion, it is a
blast that cometh and goeth; for time, it is true it goeth and
cometh not; but yet I have learned that it may be redeemed.

For means, I value that most, and the rather because I am purposed not to follow the practice of the law (if her Majesty command me in any particular I shall be ready to do her willing
service), and my reason is, only because it drinketh too much time,
which I have dedicated to better purpose. But even for the point
of estate and means, I partly lean to Thales' opinion, that a philosopher may be rich if he will. Thus your lordship seeth how I
comfort myself; to the increase whereof I would fain please myself to believe that to be true which my Lord Treasurer writeth,
which is, that it is more than a philosopher morally can digest. But
without any such high conceit, I esteem it like the pulling out of
an aching tooth, which I remember when I was a child and had
little philosophy, I was glad of it when it was done.

For your Lordship, I do think myself more beholding to you
than to any man. And I say I reckon myself as a *common* (not
popular, but *common*); and as much as is lawful to be enclosed of
a common so much your Lordship shall be sure to have.

Your Lordship's to obey your honourable commands,

More settled than ever.

This letter, veiled in its wording because intended for the Queen's reading, invites a comment. Bacon now compares himself to a "common," something which, as such, cannot be "enclosed," however much liked, loved, desired, or coveted, with however generous intentions by an individual. His statement in effect amounts to this: he accepts the Earl's gift as one eager to serve the Queen and also to engage in a philosophical enterprise for the common good, and not as one at the disposal of any individual, even an individual to whom, for his efforts to promote a friend and for his financial aid, he is "more beholding . . . than to any man."

The following year, when a vacancy in the Mastership of the Wards occurred, Bacon's candidature for the office was proposed to the Queen and supported by other persons than Essex. The dependence of Bacon on the patronage of the impulsive Essex was about to come to an end. By 1595 Bacon had come to see in clearer perspective, and with more objectivity than before, certain dominant elements in the Earl's mentality and character, and, by way of consequence from these, the Earl's place in the emotions and the thoughts of the Queen. A year later Bacon, having discerned that certain difficulties of his own making were accumulating about the headstrong and temperamental favorite and unable to approve of much of his behavior in the dealings with the Queen, offered the frank advice of a friend to the man who for four years had been his enthusiastic patron.

Bacon and Essex were friends, but there has been a too extravagant playing by biographers upon the "sacred word friend" in their treatment of the Bacon-Essex relationship. By the romanticizing of some of these writers one could be led to suppose that until the time of the trial of Essex for treason, this attachment had been of a Damon and Pythias kind. There had never, in fact, at any time been anything of the sort. Essex was

a vehement, if fond, patron, conscious of his power, his high
estate, and his place in the Court. In keeping with a nature
which could be imperious, the Earl as a patron expected from
his protégé not mere gratitude but submission to "enclosure"
within his personal political service. Bacon's brother Anthony
was at times in this service. A grateful Bacon had to make his
own position clear in this regard and, after he had done so, a
cooling in relations became manifest. It was at this juncture
that Bacon thought it his friendly duty to address some pointed
admonitions to the Earl. In 1596 Essex stood in need of advice,
not because of a failure but because of a success. As the leader
of an expedition, he had made a dashing assault on Cadiz and
destroyed what had remained of the Spanish fleet after the
rout of the great Armada. Overnight Essex became a nation's
hero, and began to behave like a popular figure much aware of
the fact. Elizabeth, who never desired that any person in her
service should hold the centre of the public stage for long, was
displeased, the more now because in this instance, the manners
and the mien of a favorite were being affected. For some time
the Queen had been troubled by the Earl's heady and uncontrollable behavior. Never fully submissive to the Royal will,
and long given to presuming on the Queen's affection, Essex
was becoming increasingly demanding, even sullen and trucu-
lent, when not given his own way.

The burden of the advice which Bacon now tendered the
Earl was: "Win the Queen; if this be not the beginning, of any
other course I see no end." Bacon, as a friend, told his former
patron that, as the Queen's favorite, he could no longer rely on
the mere "favour of affection" but must in the future cultivate
"correspondence and agreeableness" with her wishes. He should
dissipate certain impressions which were fast becoming fixed
opinions in the Queen's mind: that he is "opinionastre and not
rulable," is "of a militar independence," is desirous of a "popu-

lar reputation," is lax in financial matters, and is given to making use of the Queen's sentiment to further his own financial ends. The aptness of the last of these several cautions was later to be confirmed, when Essex had been put under detention for disobeying the Queen's orders. Then Elizabeth was to tell Bacon, in so many words, that the Earl's professions of affection in his letters of entreaty were motivated by the desire to have his Monopoly on sweet wines renewed. None of the warnings of the protégé of earlier years was acted upon by Essex.

The Earl's relationship with the Queen deteriorated the following year. An expedition which he led against the Azores (1597-1598) proved a failure. Its only success was the capture of Fayal, and this minor achievement Essex refused to have recorded because it was the work of Raleigh. In a compounded jealousy the Earl showed so great vexation at the promotion during his absence of Robert Cecil and the raising of the Lord Admiral, Charles Howard of Effingham, to the rank of Earl of Nottingham, that he left the Court and refused to return until he had been made Earl Marshal. This was a position against the seeking or acceptance of which Bacon had cautioned Essex. Never thereafter, until the time of the Earl's detention for disobedience, did Bacon offer Essex specific personal advice. Many letters requested of Bacon by Essex were not written; those sent contained little but polite compliment and general comment on circumstances. To Bacon it had become clear that the man whose place at Court rested on the Queen's affection, was incapable of taking to heart any reasonable advice, no matter how sincerely he might request it. The two men drifted apart. The days of patronage had ended in 1595 when Bacon had declared himself against "enclosure" as a patron's bondsman. The patron's interest in philosophic and scientific causes had evaporated on the presentation of the masques for Elizabeth's entertainment and her favorite's advancement. The independent and irresponsible attitude of Essex to the Queen, seemingly devoid of any discernment of the monarch's circumstances, was not pleasing to the man who in his youth had himself been content to "bear the yoke," as he said, of his Queen's displeasure. So wide had the cleavage between Bacon and his former patron become by 1597 that Bacon dedicated the first edition of his *Essays* not to Essex but to his brother Anthony, a political servant of the Earl. The brother became so perturbed over this act that he begged of Essex "leave to transfer my interest unto your Lordship." Despite the implied reproof in this pointed dedication, the Earl, in the following year, again wrote Bacon, seeking advice. The occasion was an uprising under Hugh O'Neill, Earl of Tyrone in Ireland. Essex was assuming that if forces were sent to quell this rebellion either he himself would be put in command, or, if he decided not to go, the choice of a leader would be his. Bacon withheld detailed advice. Thinking that an admonition to the Earl to remain in England, near the Queen, was best in the circumstances, he gave this, in March, 1598, and added a warning:

> But that your Lordship is too easy in such cases to pass from dissimulation to verity, I think if your Lordship lent your reputation in this case—that is to pretend that, if peace go not on, and the Queen mean not to make a defensive war, as in times past, but a full reconquest of those parts of the country, you would accept the charge—I think it would help to settle Tyrone in his seeking accord, and win you a great deal of honour *gratis*.

The Queen and her Council decided that an expedition should be undertaken. Members of the Privy Council were aware that the man who led the English forces would probably suffer in reputation, for already a soldier of much skill, Sir John Norris, had failed to subdue the rebels. Tyrone was a resourceful leader in guerilla warfare. Essex now began to suspect that the Cecils were bent on sending him to Ireland in order to accomplish his ruin. His reputation had already been damaged by the failure of the expedition to the Azores; it might not survive another defeat. Essex named Sir George Carew, a friend of the Cecils, as the person fitted for the command. The nominee of the Cecils was Sir William Knollys, uncle of Essex. At a stormy meeting of the Council, when Essex acted imperiously, the Queen interposed some observations. These Essex received with a show of contempt—the accumulated contempt of a young man for an old mistress who was in turn demanding, teasing, physically withholding, and irritable. Elizabeth gave Essex a slap on the face and had him removed from the Council-Chamber. The Earl stayed away from the Court, expecting that the Queen would soon show contrition. Had he been a wiser lover, he would have known that one show of public scorn could seal a favorite's fate with a coquette who was still the daughter of Henry VIII. Egerton, the Lord Keeper and Lord Chancellor, who had witnessed the scene in the Council, and was a friend of Essex who had continued on good terms with him even after the favorite had interfered in cases before the courts, wrote the Earl. "Yield," he said, "let policy, duty, and religion enforce you to yield; submit to your sovereign, *between whom and you there can be no proportion of duty*." Essex replied, "In such a case I must appeal from all earthly judges ... I keep my heart from baseness, although I cannot keep my fortune from declining."

Before long, the Earl gave the impression that he himself was ready to lead an expedition into Ireland. Whether he intended to go remained a question; the odds were that he did not. Once more he would act contrary to Bacon's advice; he was about "to pass from dissimulation to verity." Within months he would be disobeying the Queen's orders and then setting out with an armed force to seize her person. If the first of these deeds could ever be excused, the last could never in Bacon's view be condoned. It was the outrageous and treasonable act of an outlaw. If let pass without resort to a court of justice, neither sovereign, constitution, government, nor minister of state could ever be secure in rightful authority.

Meanwhile the Earl's friend Henry Wriothesley, Earl of Southampton—who was to be one of the cooperators in his rebellion—begged him to retrace his steps and not to undertake the Irish assignment. Essex replied: "I am tied in my own reputation to use no tergiversation; the Queen hath irrevocably decreed it, the Council do passionately urge it." Before the expedition had departed Bacon wrote a letter of encouragement to the Earl, whose mind by now was becoming apprehensive and confused. He mentioned the honor and other desirable ends which could be attained by success in the campaign and begged of Essex, now that an opportunity was his for mending his relationship with the Queen, "that your lordship in this whole action, looking forward, would set down this position, that merit is worthier than fame; and looking back hither, would remember this text, that obedience is better than sacrifice."

The Irish campaign was doomed to failure from the start. At the outset Essex declared: "I am defeated in England." The Earl now realized that he had already played into his enemies' hands. To his mortification, Sir Christopher Blount—his stepfather and the third husband of his mother, Letitia Knollys—was refused a seat on the Irish Council. Blount had served under the Earl at Cadiz and in the Azores; he would be going with him to Ireland and would be a fellow conspirator. Essex became more convinced than ever that the Cecil faction was plotting his downfall. The Queen's attitude was uncertain. He refused to embark for Ireland until Elizabeth had granted him permission under seal to return when he so desired.

Essex on setting out in March, 1599, had under his command 16,000 infantry and 1,500 cavalry. By the end of two months' campaigning his forces had been reduced to 4,000. In September he arranged to meet Tyrone, and agreed to a truce whose terms amounted to an English capitulation. The Queen sent two dispatches to the Earl, demanding a written explanation of his conduct. She retracted her former permission for his return, and forbade him to leave Ireland without her express command. Contrary to this order, the Earl landed in England and threw himself at the Queen's feet on the 28th of September, six months and one day after he had embarked on his ill-fated undertaking. So fearful was the Earl's state of mind, and so far had he already gone in contemplating open warfare against real or supposed intriguers at home while he had been in Ireland, that he had intended initially "to carry with him as much of the army as he could conveniently transport." However, he brought only "the main part of his household and a great part of captains and gentlemen."

Essex was put under detention by the Queen's orders and so kept until the following March. After his release he remained under the Queen's "displeasure." This, as the Secretary of State, Robert Cecil, explained, prevented persons from resorting to him, except a few on business and those "that were of his own blood." While Essex was under detention two commissions, one in November, 1599, and another in the following June, had considered two charges against him, disobedience to the Queen and disregard of military orders in the moving of his troops from place to place. Before the second hearing took place, Bacon, in order to present the Earl's acts in as favorable a light as possible, arranged for his employment as one of the Queen's Counsel. Bacon also, when he found himself in the presence of Elizabeth, tried, time after time, to assuage her feelings and moderate her displeasure with the Earl's conduct. The Queen proved unyielding, and finally, having grown weary of Bacon's incessant pleading, told him to cease from speaking on the subject of the Earl.

When Bacon's discussion of Essex with the Queen became

known, it gave rise to ugly rumors. Robert Cecil thought it well to send a caution: "Cousin, I hear it, but I believe it not, that you should do some ill service to my Lord of Essex; for my part I am merely passive and not active in this action, and I follow the Queen, and that heavily, I lead her not ... and the same course I would wish you to take." Fearing that Essex might have heard and been misled by the rumors, Bacon sent the Earl a letter offering his support and stating the conditions under which this could be given. He now affirmed the principle of the order of his duty, as a loyal subject of the Queen, the same principle he had enunciated in correspondence with Burghley twenty years before. In 1580 Bacon had written: "To your lordship ... I can be but a bounden servant. *So much may I safely promise and purpose to be, seeing public and private bonds vary not, but that my service to God, her Majesty, and your Lordship draw in a line.*" Loyalty to God came first, then loyalty to the Queen, then loyalty to minister of state or friend, as Bacon was more than once to tell Essex. Bacon wrote Essex as follows:

No man can better expound my doings than your Lordship, which maketh me say the less. Only I humbly pray you to believe that I aspire to the conscience and commendation of first, *bonus civis*, which with us is a good and true servant to the Queen, and next of *bonus vir*, that is an honest man. I desire your Lordship also to think that, though I confess I love some things much better than I love your Lordship, as the Queen's service, her quiet and contentment, her honour, her favour, the good of my country and the like, yet I love few persons better than yourself, both for gratitude's sake and for your own virtues, which cannot hurt but by accident or abuse. Of which my good affection I was ever and am ready to yield testimony by any good offices, but with such reservations as yourself cannot but allow. For as I was ever sorry that your Lordship should fly with waxen wings, doubting Icarus' fortune, so for the growing up of your own feathers—especially ostrich's or any other save of a bird of prey—no man shall be more glad. And this is the axle-tree whereupon I have turned and shall turn. Which to signify to you, though I think you are of yourself persuaded as much, is the cause of my writing. And so I commend your Lordship to God's goodness. From Gray's Inn, this 20th day of July, 1600.

It was not a mere afterthought, then, which Bacon stated in the year 1604 in an *Apology ... in certain imputations concerning the late Earl of Essex*, where he wrote: "For every honest man that hath his heart well planted, will forsake his king rather than forsake God, and forsake his friend rather than forsake his king; and yet will forsake any earthly commodity, yea, and his own life in some cases, rather than forsake his friend. I hope the world hath not forgotten these degrees, else the heathen saying, '*Amicus usque ad aras*,' shall judge them."

So far was Bacon prepared to go in risking his reputation with the Queen, Privy Council, and public on behalf of the Earl, he even composed pretended letters between his brother Anthony and Essex, writing these in the different styles of the two, for presenting to the Queen as evidence, first, of the Earl's devotion and allegiance to her person and, second, of the common public belief that her displeasure with Essex was the result of the representations of his enemies at Court. To these secret letters Essex was to make allusion at his trial in an attempted defence. There can be no doubt, then, that up to the time of the Earl's engaging in a treasonable act, Bacon still felt "much bound unto him" as a former friend and generous benefactor. Bacon could write excusably to Lord Henry Howard (Northampton) respecting his attitude to Essex, "I have spent more time and more thoughts about his well-doing than ever I did about mine own."

While on campaign in Ireland Essex had become fully convinced that his enemies at home had determined on his destruction. He was of the opinion, too, that Robert Cecil was bent on making the Infanta of Spain the next ruler of England. The Earl began a treasonable correspondence with James VI of Scotland about his assuming the throne of England in succession to Elizabeth. Essex, while still in Ireland, seems to have discussed with his fellow-intriguers the question of obtaining the support of the Roman Catholics in a national uprising, on the promise of their political toleration.

In September, 1600, while the Earl was under the Queen's displeasure, his Monopoly on sweet wines came up for renewal. This was refused by the Queen. Essex, already heavily in debt, faced financial ruin. Thoroughly distraught by now, with a mind inflamed by frightful imaginings, the Earl railed against Elizabeth for her inconstancy, against Cecil for a supposed design to put the Infanta on the throne, and against members of the Privy Council as enemies seeking his life. He determined on the physical seizure of Elizabeth and her segregation from her ministers. Plans to this end had been discussed in a vague manner by Essex and his military intimates while he was still in Ireland. As early as August, the Earl's followers began to hold secret meetings in Essex House. A plot was taking definite shape. First the Queen was to be taken captive, and then the City was to be aroused to the support of the rebels. Elizabeth would be held under restraint until new officers of government, of the Earl's own choosing, were appointed. The uprising was to be much more than part of a "private quarrel." The conspirators had political designs and meant business. "Now I see too late," confessed the convicted Blount on the scaffold, "that rather we should have failed of our purpose, it would have cost much blood, and perhaps drawn some from her Majesty's own person."

On February 7th, 1601, some eight months after Bacon had joined a commission in order to promote the Earl's defence on a charge of disobedience—still knowing nothing of the former patron's treasonable intent—Essex was summoned to appear before the Privy Council and provide an explanation of meetings in his residence. He declined to attend, pleading illness. That night some three hundred armed followers gathered at his house. The next day the Lord Keeper, Egerton, accompanied by three other peers, came officially to demand an explanation of the assembly. They were confronted with a blustering crew. Of those surrounding the Earl some shouted, "Kill them"; others, "Nay, but shop them up, keep them as pledges, cast the Great Seal out of the window." The general cry was, "To the Court! To the Court!" The Lord Keeper and his company were held as hostages. Essex was sure that the inhabitants of the City would respond in support, once an uprising had begun. The Earl was thinking of himself as a romantically popular hero. Many influential persons in the City had displayed great anger and indignation at the findings of the Queen's ecclesiastical commissions and her grants of Monopolies. There was precedent for the success of the present undertaking—precedent to which Bacon was to point, when as Queen's Counsel he addressed Essex at his trial for treason. "It was not," Bacon was then to say to Essex, "the company you carried with you, but the assistance which you hoped for in the City, which you trusted unto. The Duke of Guise thrust himself into the streets of Paris on the day of the Barricadoes, in his doublet and hose, attended only with eight gentlemen, and found that help in the City which (thanks be to God) you failed of here. And what followed? The King was forced to put himself into a pilgrim's weeds, and in that disguise to steal away to scape their fury. Even such was my Lord's confidence too; and his pretence the same—an all-hail and a kiss to the City. But the end was treason, as hath been sufficiently proved."

The armed conspirators set out on their undertaking. Word was brought them that the Queen's guard had already been doubled and made ready for action. Essex thereupon directed his men towards the City to sound an alarm. This alarm fell on deaf ears. The revolt was over before it had begun. After a brief skirmish with some loyal troops, the rebels retreated. The Earl managed to make his way back to his house to destroy incriminating papers. That night he was a prisoner in the Tower.

Essex was brought to trial before twenty-five of his peers—

"a greater number than hath been called in any former precedent." Bacon was required to take part in the proceedings as Queen's Counsel, as one of a commission earlier involved in the examination of the Earl's disobedience, and as assistant to the Crown-Attorney, Edward Coke, whose competence in handling constitutional cases was not great. In this trial, as in many others, Coke let questions become confused by unessentials, and the proceeding returned to the main charges only after Bacon had intervened. Whether Bacon would have withdrawn from the case, had he been permitted, is impossible to say. "The precedence of personal over political ties," as a historian has observed, was "hardly applicable to a state of affairs in which anarchy, with its attendant miseries, would inevitably follow on the violent overthrow of the Queen's right to select her ministers, even if her person for a time continued to be outwardly respected; and it is, at all events, one which Bacon studiously renounced from the very beginning of his connection with Essex."

Bacon thought Essex guilty of treason with intent. He discovered that the Earl's conspiracy against the Queen was being hatched even while he had been making representations to the Queen of the Earl's affectionate and loyal devotion. After the trial had begun he was informed of some of the Earl's treasonable acts and intentions while in Ireland. Bacon could not in honesty entertain the Earl's defence that his actions were part of a "private quarrel," and that he was intent only on supplication to the Queen by way of petition. Said Bacon to the court, "Now put the case that the Earl of Essex's intent were, as he would have it believed, to go only as a suppliant to her Majesty. Shall their petitions be presented by armed petitioners? This must needs bring loss of liberty to the prince. Neither is it any point of law, as my Lord of Southampton would have it believed, that condemns them of treason, but it is apparent in common sense. To take secret counsel, to execute it, to run together in numbers armed with weapons—what can be the excuse?

Warned by the Lord Keeper, by a herald, and yet persist. Will any simple man take this to be less than treason?"

Essex was found guilty, and seventeen days after his abortive rebellion was executed for the crime. During the trial Bacon had performed a public duty in defence of the Queen's honor and person, with temperance, courage, wisdom, and justice. He had acted in accordance with his own studied views respecting honor and morality. To contend that these were overlooked or repudiated by him in or out of court is nonsense. Certainly, he would have considered the invoking of the word "honor" in criticism of his taking part in the trial as a perversity. It was Bacon's definite and explicit opinion, as he told a jury in a later case respecting duelling, that "the fountain of honour is the king and his aspect." Those who upheld the aspect of the sovereign could be deemed men of honor; those who defaced it must be treated as dishonorable. The sort of "honor" which promoters of "moral sentiment" were to invoke was regarded by Bacon, in explicit statements before courts of law, as something "no better than a sorcery, that enchanteth the spirits of young men, that bear great minds, with a false shew, *species falsa;* and a kind of satanical illusion and apparition of honour against religion, against law, against moral virtue, and against the precedents and examples of the best times and valiantest nations."

The trial of Essex, as Bacon saw it, was a proceeding within justice. Justice, in Bacon's view, was a "royal" virtue, "which doth employ the other three cardinal virtues in her service: wisdom to discover, and discern nocent and innocent; fortitude to prosecute and execute; temperance, so as to carry justice as it be not passionate in the pursuit, nor confused in involving persons upon light suspicion, nor precipitate in time."

V

BACON'S RELIGIOUS WRITINGS IN THE REIGN OF ELIZABETH

During the reign of Elizabeth, Bacon composed three political pieces: first, a *Letter of Advice* in 1584, the year in which Bacon was first elected to Parliament; second, *On the Controversies of the Church of England* in 1589; and third, *Observations Upon a Libel Published This Present Year, 1592* (1593 according to the modern calendar). The first and second were addressed to the Queen; the third was written in defence of her policies. The first dealt with the Puritans and Roman Catholics, the second with the Puritans and the Anglican episcopate, the third mainly with the Roman Catholics and incidentally with the Puritans generally and lesser religious sects. In order to comprehend the tenor, purpose, and implications of these three writings of Bacon, his later *Pacification and Edification of the Church of England*, written for James, and his still later *Advice to Villiers*, certain aspects of the earlier stages of the Puritan movement in England must be kept in mind. These entered into the author's thought while his opinions on questions of religion and politics were in process of formation. They were among the immediate concerns of Bacon's father, as Lord Keeper; of his mother, as a politico-religious contender; of his uncle, as the Queen's chief advisor; of Whitgift, his tutor at Cambridge, and later Archbishop of Canterbury; of his University, where two of the chief Puritan contenders were, for a time, respectively a professor and a fellow.

Some of Bacon's commentators seem to be under the impression that the Puritans in the reigns of Elizabeth and James were gentle, quiet, tolerant, and charitable individuals who sought only freedom to engage in a private and personal worship required by their biblically informed consciences. Few opinions, of course, could be more opposed to the facts. The Puritans were a severe, clamorous, intolerant, uncharitable band, ever bent on putting out of countenance and sometimes given to consigning to punishment in this world and to Hell in the next those who refused to accept their tenets. Members of the English clergy who had fled to the Continent during the persecutions of the Protestants under Mary Tudor (1553-1558) acquired in Geneva a doctrine of salvation, and saw in operation a fully regimented "godly discipline" under the rule of a Consistory. They returned home with very definite opinions on Saving Faith and church discipline. It was their belief that the Church in England had never really undergone reformation; that its prescribed ritual, clerical orders, and canonic laws were still Roman in character. Now that England had a Protestant sovereign, the time had come, they believed, for the bringing of the Church of England—or rather the Church *in* England—within the true Reformation; they would provide this Church with a new rule and a new theology, both founded on Scripture and on Scripture alone. The Church of Geneva would be their model. These English Calvinists found encouragement in the success of John Knox (1505-1572) with the Scots to the north. The Church in Scotland had accepted his directions for the rule of elders, Presbytery, and a General Consistory or Assembly. One sovereign, Mary of Scotland, had been cashiered for her ungodliness, and another ruler, James VI, was being kept under spiritual duress by a General Assembly. The Word of the Lord, as interpreted by Geneva, was beginning to prevail. The English Calvinists, however, were confronted with three difficult obstacles: the Act of Supremacy, the Act of Uniformity, and the Court of High Commission. Through the use of these Queen Elizabeth and her Privy Council were bent on enforcing uniformity in a church far removed in organization and rule from that of Geneva. The Sovereign of England had determined on having both a unified state and a unified church. The civil organization of the nation included several estates; so did the Established Church, with its bishops, priests, deacons, and laity. In this church, as it now stood, there could be no "democratic" rule by elders and a Genevan Consistory of laymen and ministers.

In theology the Calvinists professed the doctrine of the utter efficacy of God's Free Grace for the saving and the continued redemption of fallen man, without regard to natural knowledge, the exercise of the human will, or "works." In the organization of the Church, according to the Genevan understanding, con-gregations were assemblages of persons elected by God unto sal-vation, who submitted themselves to the rule and care of men chosen for their superior "wisdom" within the area of Divine Grace. Over all was a Consistory composed of six ministers who continued in office more or less permanently and twelve laymen elected annually. In Geneva the permanent members controlled policy, and the most influential among them came to be re-garded as the source of ecclesiastical wisdom. Bishop Bancroft observed that in Genevan practice the laymen of the Consistory had been "not only over-ruled by the said six ministers; but like-wise all the ministers over-topped by Maister *Calvin*, as that in effect he was *Domine fac totum*." "In show," said Richard Hooker, "a marvellous indifferently composed senate ecclesias-tical was to govern, but in effect only one man should."

After a study of the opinions of the English Calvinists, Archbishop Parker reported to Burghley: "All that these men tend towards is the overthrow of all honourable quality and the setting afoot a Commonwealth, or a popularity." The Queen wrote to James in Scotland: "There is risen a sect of perilous consequences, who would have no kings but a presbytery.... Suppose you I can tolerate such scandals." James, before he left Scotland to assume the throne of England, thought it well to tell his son Henry (1594-1612, Prince of Wales in 1610):

> Some fiery spirited men in the Ministry got such a guiding of the people in the time of confusion that, finding the gust of government sweet, they began to fancy a democratic form.... I was calumniated in their sermons not for any vice in me but because I was a king, which they thought the highest evil. For they told their flocks that kings ... were naturally enemies to the Church.

Bancroft in his *Dangerous Positions* (1593) warned of the peril to the Established Church in the professions and undertakings of the new sect: "Hereby," he wrote, "it shall appear to our posterity if ... mischiefs shall happen, they were suffciently warned."

Under the Act of Supremacy, the Court of High Commission was empowered "to visit, reform, redress, order, correct and amend all such heresies, errors, schisms, abuses, offences, contempts and enormities whatsoever which by any manner of spiritual or ecclesiastical power, authority or jurisdiction can or may lawfully be reformed, ordered, redressed, corrected, restrained or amended." By the Act of Uniformity, "any manner of parson, vicar or other whatsoever minister" who should wilfully "use any other rite, ceremony, order, form or manner" of service than that set forth in the Prayer Book of 1559, or who should "preach, declare or speak anything in the derogation or depraving of the said book" would render himself liable to punishment and, in case of repeated offence, to life imprisonment.

Yet these Acts were far less comprehensive in scope and far less drastic in penalty than the regimen advocated by persons under the influence of Geneva. To the Genevan Consistory, a "standing ecclesiastical court," was committed—in Hooker's words—"the care of all men's manners, power of determining all kind of ecclesiastical causes, and authority to convent, to control, to punish, as far as with excommunication, whomsoever they should think worthy, none either small or great excepted." In Genevan teaching it was the duty of the secular power to uphold the Consistory in its decisions. A Christian magistrate, as a person obedient to the "spiritual powers," could do nothing less. The Calvinist John Knox, in a reference to the Book of Deuteronomy 13: 6-10, and in full compliance with its primitive severity, found it righteous to say, "Of these words of Moses are two things appertaining to one purpose, to be noted. Former, that such as solicitate only to idolatry ought to be punished to death without favour or respect of person." "I say," he also wrote, in characteristic vein, "if any go about to erect and set up idolatry or to teach defection from God, after that the verity hath been received and approved, that then not only the Magistrates, to whom the sword is committed, but also the people are bound by that oath, which they have made to God, to revenge to the uttermost of their power the injury done against his Majesty."

Thomas Cartwright, the leader of the English Calvinists, a disputer against Whitgift, and the professor of a faith that "purifieth the heart," was not to be outdone by the Scottish Knox. He held that "the same severity of punishment that was used against false prophets then under the Mosaic law ought to be used now under the gospel against false teachers comparing one person and circumstance with another. As he that hath fallen away from God and gone about to draw others away; to be handled according to the law prescribed in that Ch. 13 of Deuteronomy. If this be bloody and extreme I am content to be so counted with the Holy Ghost." "In this case of willing sliding back and moving others to the same, and other some cases which are expressed in the law, as of open and horrid blasphemy of the Name of God, I deny that upon repentence there ought to follow any pardon of death, which the Judicial law doth require."

When Bacon intimated in his *Controversies of the Church of England* that "profane scoffing" had proceeded out of the Universities he undoubtedly had in mind Thomas Cartwright and a disciple Walter Travers. Cartwright had been Lady Margaret Professor of Divinity and Travers a fellow of Trinity College in the University of Cambridge. In Travers' eyes the Universities were "the skulking places of drones, monasteries of yawning, snoring monks, trees not only barren but baneful with their poisonous shade to all plants that grow up under them." Cartwright called the clergy of the Established Church "bastards" and "boys and senseless asses"; non-Calvinist Christians, "swine"; the Universities, "dens of many-thievish non-residents"; benefices, so many bestowals "to the greedy use of many cormorant masters of Colleges at their wicked pleasure"; bishops, "a remnant of Antichrist's brood" for their corruption, arrogance, tyranny, and "flat heresy in the sacrament." One of the writers of what came to be known as "the First Admonition to Parliament" (probably Cartwright) deemed cathedral churches "the dens ... of all loitering lubbers," the Archbishop's Court "the filthy quagmire and poisoned plash of all the abominations that do infect the whole realm," and the Court of Commission "but a petty little stinking ditch."

Those adherents of Geneva who refused to accept the Anglican rule and rite on principle, even when they yielded in passive obedience, were given the name of Puritans or Precisians about 1564—three years after Bacon's birth. "The English Bishops," Thomas Fuller (1608-1661) says, "conceiving themselves impowered by their Canons, began to show their authority in urging the Clergy ... to subscribe to the Liturgy, Ceremonies and Discipline of the Church, and such as refused the same were branded with the odious name of Puritans." "This name Puritan," said Whitgift, "is very aptly given to these men, not because they be pure no more than were the Heretics called Cathari, but because they think themselves to be *mundiores caeteris,* more pure than others, as Cathari did, and separate themselves from all other Churches and congregations as spotted and defiled. Because also they suppose the Church which they have devised, to be without all impurity."

At the beginning of their endeavor the English Puritans put their request in words like these: "That we may altogether teach and practise that true knowledge of God's Word, which we have learned in this our banishment, and by God's merciful providence seen in the best reformed Churches." Before long they made a specific entreaty for the discontinuance in the services of the Established Church of what they called "Popish remnants," such as the wearing of the surplice, the making of the Sign of the Cross in baptism, kneeling at Communion, use of the ring in marriage, proceeding according to the Prayer Book, and the regarding of the Communion table as an altar. Certain of these practices soon became more than subjects of petition; in many instances, they became rejections in fact. In 1564 Burghley compiled a list, in manuscript, of *Varieties in the Services of the Church of precisians.* In this Burghley repeatedly mentions the failure on the part of clergy to wear the surplice. He notes discrepancies in the saying of service and prayers, in the position of the Communion table, in the administration and receiving of Communion, and in baptizing. "Some," he records, "say the service and prayers in the chancel; others in the body of the Church." The Communion table "standeth in the body of the Church in some places; in others it standeth in the chancel. In some places the Table standeth Altarlike, distant from the wall a yard." Some administer the Communion "with chalice, some with a Communion Cup, others with a Common Cup. Some with unleavened bread, some with leavened.... Some receive kneeling, others standing, others sitting." "Some baptize in a Font, some in a Basin. Some signed with the sign of the Cross; others not signed."

Burghley asked the Queen to bring these discrepancies to Archbishop Parker's attention. Parker summoned two Nonconformists, Thomas Sampson and Lawrence Humphrey, from Oxford and commanded them "to wear the cap appointed by Injunction, to wear no hats in their long gowns, to wear a surplice with a non-regent hood in their quires at their Colleges, according to the ancient manner there, to communicate kneeling in wafer-bread." Sampson, Dean of Christ Church, could not agree in "conscience" and was removed from his place. Humphrey, Regius Professor of Divinity and President of Magdalen, "for his usefulness in the University" was treated with leniency. Later he complied. At Cambridge the situation had become equally irregular. One George Withers, who refused to wear the square cap, had "stirred up a racket for the reformation of the University Windows" on the ground that their subjects smacked of superstition; "whereupon followed a great destruction of them." On a festival day, when the master of St. John's College was conveniently absent, "the most part of the College-Company," about three hundred in number, came to chapel without their surplices. Burghley, the Chancellor of the University, was shocked. Comparable happenings were becoming frequent in London.

Early in 1566, the Queen found it necessary to promulgate *Advertisements* for the bringing of order into the service of the Church. From that time the Puritan struggle entered upon a new phase. Some of the deprived clergy decided that "since they could not have the word of God preached, nor the Sacraments administered without idolatrous gear . . . it was their duty . . . to break off from the publick Churches, and to assemble, as they had opportunity, in private houses, or elsewhere, to worship God in a manner that might not offend against the light of their consciences." There was to be secrecy in meeting.

Edmund Grindal, Bishop of London, wrote to Henry Bullinger, in 1568:

Some London citizens of the lowest order, together with four or five ministers, remarkable neither for their judgment nor learning, have openly separated from us; and sometimes in private houses, sometimes in the fields, and occasionally even in ships, they have held their meetings and administered the Sacraments. Besides this, they have ordained ministers, elders, and deacons, after their own way, and have even excommunicated some who had seceded from their Church. And because masters Lawrence Humphrey, Sampson, Lever, and others, who have suffered so much to obtain liberty in respect of things indifferent, will not unite with them, they now regard them as semi-papists, and will not allow their followers to attend their preaching.

Within eight years after the publishing of the *Advertisements*, there appeared signs of the politico-religious revolution that was to become openly manifest in England after the Civil War in the reign of Charles I. In 1573 a number of Puritan leaders resolved on the secret formation of a Presbytery at Wandsworth. Eleven elders were chosen and their offices stated in a register called "The Orders of Wandsworth." About the same time another sort of assembly, the "Protestation of the Puritans," was organized. Each member swore to "come not back again to the Preaching of them that have received . . . marks of the Romish Beast," and took the following vow: "I have now joined myself to the Church of Christ. Wherein I have yielded myself subject to the Discipline of God's Word, as I promised at my Baptism. Which if I should now again forsake, and join myself with their Traditions, I should forsake the Union, wherein I am knit to the Body of Christ, and join myself to the Discipline of Antichrist." Persons who took this vow or made a similar assent came to rely increasingly on the immediate vouchsafing to the believer of the presence and the "wisdom" of God. The more this "wisdom" was exalted and proclaimed in "prophesying," the less place was given to the "carnal" knowledge acquired from university or other secular learning as part of the training of preachers. One culmination of the belief in the immediate presence of God appeared in the "conspiracy" of William Hacket, who had been "called," through the influence of Puritan preaching, to take "a strange and extraordinary course." On July 16th, 1591, two of his followers went through the streets of London proclaiming that Jesus Christ in the person of Hacket had come to judge the earth, to separate saints from sinners, and as King of Kings to establish the Throne of God and his gospel in Europe. Hacket was hanged. One disciple starved himself to death in prison; the other repented a year later, made a submission, and turned to the writing of poetry.

Puritanism now embraced, first, those who connived at the rule of Presbytery within the Established Church and hoped that this rule would ultimately be imposed on the whole ecclesiastical system; second, those who awaited the day, in passive conformity to what the law required, when a Presbyterian body independent of the national church would be countenanced; and third, those who, placing their trust in the "wisdom of God" immediately vouchsafed to them as "prophets," disapproved of all rule in matters of religion. These last persons came to be known as Enthusiasts.

The Puritans began to have energetic spokesmen and organizers. The former prepared contentious "admonitions" for Parliament and the public, as well as "loyal petitions" to the Queen and the Commons. The organizers promoted conventions, or *classes*, throughout the nation on a provincial and a national scale. In these *classes* instructions were to be given to ministers for the purpose of spreading the New Discipline within their parishes. Sympathetic clergymen were told that "those ceremonies in the Book of Common Prayer, which being taken from popery are in controversy, ought to be omitted, if it may be done without danger of being put from the ministry; but if there be imminent danger of being deprived, then let the matter be communicated to the *classis* in which that Church is, to be determined by them." Puritan ministers were to look about parishes for prospective "elders" and "deacons." The elders were to be made church wardens for the present and the deacons assigned the task of collecting and distributing monies for the poor—their proper office according to the Puritan understanding of the practice of the Church of the Apostles. Clergymen were to encourage any who felt called to the ministry to appear for approval before *classes*. For the increase of "true religion" and progress in "true reform" there was to be continuous prophesying, in covert and open meetings, by resident clergymen and gifted laymen, by itinerant ministers, and indeed by any who could profess a "call" from the Lord. Needless to say, prophesyings became a cause of alarm among the bishops and even for the Queen herself. Archbishop Parker made attempts to suppress them. They were "put down" in 1577, two years after Parker's death; but down they would not remain.

Of the publicists, controversialists, and pamphleteers within the ranks of the Puritans, the most impressive were Thomas Cartwright and Walter Travers. The latter—one of the promoters of the Wandsworth Presbytery—had been Reader at the Temple Church. After Archbishop Whitgift appointed Hooker to the Mastership of the Temple, then, as Fuller said, "the pulpit spake pure Canterbury in the morning, and Geneva in the afternoon." Travers, who was removed from the Readership, was strong on church discipline. He contended that discipline and dogma were like the twins mentioned by Hippocrates, who always fell ill at the same time. In Travers' opinion, it was futile to reform doctrine without prescribing, at the same time, a "polity of the Church of Christ ordained and appointed by God." Cartwright, of whom Travers was a disciple, instigated one Admonition to the Parliament and was author of another.

The first of these was published in 1572 without the name of either author or publisher. So widely was it read, four printings were called for in the same year. The First Admonition brought under condemnation "Romanist" survivals within the Church of England: the regarding of the Apocrypha as Scripture, saints' days, kneeling to receive Communion, private Communion, the title "priest," private baptism, baptism by women, the Sign of the Cross, questions to sponsors in the rite of baptism, the use of the ring in marriage, confirmation, prayers for the dead, prayers that all men might be saved, "organs and curious singing," the orders of bishops, archbishops, archdeacons, and chancellors, canon law, episcopal authority, cathedral churches, and bishops' courts. Cartwright in the Second Admonition, as did Travers in his writings, argued against all of the foregoing practices as "innovations" lacking the sanction of Scripture and the approval of the Early Church. Both authors demanded that every remnant and reminder of the Roman mass be discarded, that every Romanist court and discipline be abolished; priests ordained in the reign of Mary Tudor must be removed from office. In the Church of the Apostles bishops were pastors, and these they must again become. All ministers are to be equal in status and of two sorts, pastors and teachers. The rule of the Church is to be under local Consistories, Provincial Councils and, perhaps, a National Council. These bodies will control the ceremonies of congregations and the lives of their members. Excommunication is to be exercised, but only with great care and for great offences, since the punishment of excommunication is so dreadful there is nothing like it on earth, "but only hell eternally." The Consistory, according to Cartwright, will "excommunicate the stubborn . . . yet ever so must they excommunicate, and receive the excommunicate in again, that they require the assent of their whole congregation . . . Nevertheless, what they do well, the congregation cannot alter, neither shall the congregation put them, or any of them out, but upon just cause proved, either in that Consistory or in some one of the Councils, and the cause accepted for sufficient." "The civil magistrate, the nurse and foster father of the Church, shall do well to provide some sharp punishment for those that contemn this censure and discipline of the Church." The Queen will defend in righteousness this Church government, founded as it is on Scriptural authority; for although the rule of the Church be taken from the Book of God, "yet it is her majesty that by her princely authority should see every of these things put into practice, and punish those that neglect them."

The efforts of the Puritans produced a very great effect on the English public. Their stress on the Scriptures, as God's Revealed Word and wisdom, their opposition to Rome, their professed return to the practices of the original Church, their theology, which depended utterly on God's grace without the interposition of "sinful priests," the strictness of their self-sacrificing lives, their endurance of suffering at the hands of prelates and magistrates, all these things won them compassion and support throughout the kingdom. Complementary to this general sympathy was the common knowledge that nearly all of the ablest clergy in the Established Church were Calvinist in dogmatic theology at least—a fact that Elizabeth had to bear in mind when seeking appointees for archbishoprics. If in 1598 George Cranmer, a friend of Hooker, could discern some subsidence in public sympathy for the Genevan discipline, a few years before he had found that "the greatest part of the learned in the land were either eagerly affected, or favorably inclined. Many which impugned the Discipline yet so impugned it, not as not being the better form of government, but as not so convenient for our state." As time went on, the House of Commons included among its popularly elected representatives an increasingly large number of Puritans, engaging in "godless politics" for necessary, worldly ends.

In his *Letter of Advice* (1584) to Queen Elizabeth, Bacon at the age of twenty-three shows as much assurance in his political thinking as he does in the philosophical judgment which he delivers in his *Greatest Birth of Time* of the same year. In the *Letter of Advice* he undertakes a review of the Queen's political policies generally and more specifically of her dealing with Puritan preachers and her "strong factious subjects and foreign enemies," the Papists and the Spaniards. Bacon's concern here, as he informs the readers of his later *Observations Upon a Libel* (1593), is with "two extremities in state concerning the causes of faith and religion," the "dangerous indulgence and toleration" of permitting a number of religions and "the entering and sifting into men's consciences when no overt scandal is given." At this stage of his thinking, the author, as a Calvinist reared in a loyal household, sees no real danger to the unity of the state in the claims and contentions of the Puritans, notwithstanding the fact that they have won many sympathizers. Having made it clear to the Queen that he himself is "not given over, nor so much as addicted, to their preciseness," Bacon tells her that the Puritans are not heretical, nor do they purpose sedition, while the persecution they suffer at home creates the impression abroad of a disunity in the kingdom. Bacon also tells the experienced Queen, with a show of modesty, *"till I think that you think otherwise,* I am bold to think that the Bishops, in this dangerous time, take a very evil and unadvised course in driving them from their cures." The ecclesiastical authorities are overlooking the fact that the Puritans' "careful catechizing and diligent preaching" are producing the "fruit" of "the lessening and diminution of the Papistical number." The state might well consider the members of this sect its allies in the struggle with Rome, and extend them at least the trust which Frederick II gave the infidel Saracen soldiers whom he employed "against the Pope because he . . . knew they would not spare his sanctity." As for fears of what the Puritans might do were they to get authority in the Church, this is a remote and uncertain evil whose consideration must give way in the face of closer and more certain perils. As to meeting the danger of the present from Rome and her agent Spain, Bacon advises the cultivation of the friendship of France, the promotion of an alliance among the Dutch and northern princes, such aid to the Low Countries as may be advanced without precipitating a Spanish war, the weakening of Spain by attacks on her possessions in the Indies, and the seeking of aid from Florence, Ferrara, and Venice.

Of the Roman Catholics at home, none should be admitted to any office of government, Bacon warns, "from the highest counsellor to the lowest constable." All must be excluded from active military forces, and none is to be "trained up in the musters except his parishioners would answer for him that he orderly and duly received the Communion." No Roman Catholic is "to have in his house so much as a halbert without the same condition." Since punitive measures, even death, have proved ineffectual for the reduction of the number of Recusants—they are like the Hydra which grows several heads when one is removed—recourse should be had in the future to education as a means to bring them into a condition of loyalty.

Bacon now raises the second question, of "entering and sifting into men's consciences." In this regard, he thinks, Roman Catholic subjects have an honest cause for grievance. The Oath of Allegiance, as now framed, requires the subject to swear "that which, without the special grace of God, he cannot think." This makes him a perjurer. If for honesty's sake he refuses to take the oath, he becomes a traitor, "which, before some act done, seems somewhat hard." The proper course would be to change the oath to a form which required "that whosoever would not bear arms against all foreign princes, and, namely, the Pope, that should invade your Majesty's dominions, he should be a traitor." A subject who refused the amended oath could no longer be regarded as a martyr for his religion, but only as a deserving sufferer for his political stubbornness. The new oath would also serve to undermine the present confidence between the Pope and religious Roman Catholics disposed to loyalty towards the English throne.

After five years of further observation, reflection, and Parliamentary experience, Bacon feels called upon to prepare a second advice for the Queen, *An Advertisement, Touching the Controversies of the Church of England* (1589). In this he examines the occasions and causes of those religious controversies which are at present troubling the state. The writing is confined to the bishops of the Established Church and the Puritans—without use of the latter title and the name "Precisians," which are greatly disliked by those on whom they have been fastened by their opponents. Both parties to the controversies are brought under censure. The Puritans are now regarded by the author as "the enemy of unity, sobriety and peace" in the Church and the kingdom. Their "irreverent and violent impugning of the government of bishops" has become, in Bacon's thinking, "a suspected forerunner of a more general contempt." The Church, as an institution which has survived attacks from without by the Pope and his agents, is now faced with an internal commotion in which "truth itself" is "challenged and pretended."

The Puritans, says the author, have sought truth in "the conventicles and conciliables of heretics and sectaries, "their critics and condemners in the "external face and representation of the Church." Both parties have been seduced. There has been "forbidden" writing on the one side and "authorized" pamphlets on the other; both are deserving of suppression. If the Puritans have defamed the governors of the Church, the bishops by their attacks on Puritan preachers have disgraced religion. Through controversies kept alive by the two parties, an exaggerated report of faction and disorder in the kingdom has gone abroad, as if civil government in England "were ready to enter into some convulsion." While "sympathy" between the civil and ecclesiastical estates must be conceded, and while it is true "that . . . 'there will be kept no unity in believing, except it be entertained in worshipping,' "—as the Queen's Lord Treasurer and others contend, there is as yet in England "no such matter in the civil policy, as deserveth so dishonourable a taxation."

Unlike the disputes between the Eastern and Western churches touching images, and those in the West over the adoration of the Sacrament, current religious contentions in England are about "things indifferent," such as ceremonials and the government of the Church. "If we would but remember," reflects the author, "that the ancient and true bonds of unity are 'one faith, one baptism,' and not one ceremony, one policy; if we would observe the league amongst Christians that is penned by our Saviour, 'he that is not against us is with us'; if we could but comprehend that . . . religion hath parts which belong to eternity, and parts which pertain to time; and if we did but know the virtue of silence and slowness to speak, commended by St. James, our controversies of themselves would close up and grow together."

In the "immodest and deformed" writing of these times, the "matter of religion is handled in the stile of the stage"; a notable exception being "a challenge . . . Mr. [John] Jewel made to confute the pretended Catholics by the Fathers." "To turn religion into a comedy or satire; to search and rip up wounds with a laughing countenance, to intermix Scripture and scurrility sometimes in one sentence, is a thing far from the devout reverence of a Christian, and scant beseeming the honest regard of a sober man. . . . There is no greater confusion than the confounding of jest and earnest. The majesty of religion, and the contempt and deformity of things ridiculous, are things as distant as things may be. Two principal causes have I ever known of atheism; curious controversies, and profane scoffing: now that these two are joined in one, no doubt that sect [the Puritans] will make no small progression."

The state of mind which these violations of sobriety signalize is nothing short of a disease of which the Universities are "the seat or the continent." In these institutions, immature youths "skip from ignorance to a prejudicate opinion, and never take a sound judgment in their way." When their reasons have ripened, they are already so obsessed with prejudice that the exercise of judgment has been forever forestalled.

The occasions of present controversy are in the main four. The first is "the conversation and government of those which have chief place in the Church." The bishops, on the whole, are men of knowledge and good works. Some of their number, however, have dimmed the light of virtue and become worldly—lovers of themselves and pleasers of men. The laity in consequence have begun to doubt their leaders' succession from the Apostles, grope for religion "as in the dark," and show a readiness "to depart from the Church upon every voice." A second cause of contention is the seeker of pre-eminence. "The Church never wanteth a kind of person, which love the salutation of Rabbi, master; not in ceremony or compliment, but in an inward authority which they seek over men's minds." In the third place, the Puritan sect is obsessed with "the opinion that anything is good which differs widely from the Church of Rome, and necessarily polluted if it does not." From this conceit has stemmed the demand for the reordaining of priests and the re-baptizing of children. And fourthly, comes the "affectation and imitation of foreign churches." "God forbid," says the author, "that lawful kingdoms should be tied to innovate and make alterations." Bacon desires the removal of "some abuses" from the Established Church, but he will not countenance the ecclesiastical republicanism extolled by the Puritans. Equality of ministers and government by synods can only, he thinks, be the source of "wonderful great confusion."

The Puritans, recounts Bacon, concentrated at first on their dislike of certain abuses, such as "Romanist" ceremonies and the idleness of some among the Universities' clergy. Next, they condemned the government of the Established Church, both on "scriptural grounds," as they admitted, and also out of a desire which they did not admit, to have, even as "mercenary bands . . . the spoil of . . . endowments and livings." Next the aim of the sect became nothing less than the establishment by the magistrate of "an only and perpetual form of policy in the Church" to their liking. On this ground the majority of the Puritans now take their stand, with the consequence that there exists an open breach between their body and the Established Church. It should be said in fairness, however, that the excesses of a part, however proportionately large, must not be charged against the whole side.

The Puritans, in a misguided zeal, have gone to great extremes. They profess a reliance on Scripture, and yet ignore the precept of the apostle that the weak are not to be admitted to questions and controversies; for they entitle ignorant people to join discussions which involve abstruse questions of doctrine—a point of great peril to religion. They encourage "prophecy," not only on the part of clergy, as in the earlier practice of the Church, but by all who profess "faith," however lacking these modern "prophets" may be in Scriptual knowledge and a coherent theology. To the minimizing of worship, the sect makes preaching and the hearing of sermons essential to church services. With their "embasing" of the Church Fathers and their resort to "naked examples, conceited inferences, and forced allusions," Puritan preachers, through "an addicted respect to their own opinions," have become the entrenchers of "errors and misproceeding." The leaders of the sect are too ready to make general pronouncements on what is unlawful. They prescribe restraints and prohibitions, but fail to instruct their followers in the use of lawful liberty.

Bacon, with an emphasis on godly "works," detaches himself doctrinally from the Calvinist contention that ethical criteria have nothing to do with the wisdom or the rating of the merits of a Christian. For the strict Calvinist, a redeemed elect soul cannot himself attain or depart from a state of salvation. His condition and belief are utterly remote from humanly derived ethical principles, things which belong to the realm of "carnal" knowledge. The knowledge which saves is the "wisdom" given immediately through Divine Revelation to the redeemed soul. While Bacon agrees in the opinion that Christian conduct is not ultimately to be governed by knowledge attained through human powers, but by what is given in Revelation through faith, he rates the life of a Christian by a practical subscription in deeds and works to those moral principles which through natural human knowledge are derived from the placets given in Revelation. Bacon thinks that the views of the Calvinists in these regards are contrary to the Scriptures, which teach us "to judge and denominate men religious according to their works of the second table; because they of the first are often counterfeit, and practised in hypocrisy. So St. John saith, that 'a man doth vainly boast of loving God whom he never saw, if he love not his brother whom he hath seen.' And St. James saith, 'This is true religion, to visit the fatherless and the widow.' So as that which is with them but philosophical and moral, is, in the apostle's phrase, 'true religion and Christianity.' "

Like the Puritans, the bishops who govern the Established Church have in late times followed a dubious road. For a time they answered their critics with an admission that some of the ceremonies to which the Nonconformists objected were "indifferent" things. They acknowledged certain imperfections in the Church, which, like tares among the corn, as they said, "were not with strife to be pulled up, lest it might spoil and supplant the good corn." But of late the ecclesiastical authorities have been regarding every critic of the Established Church as an infamous outlaw. Some of their bishops have even defamed from their pulpits the Protestant churches abroad, and declared that clerics ordained by these churches are no lawful ministers.

The present bishops deserve censure for their "standing so precisely upon altering nothing," because laws, wherever found, when not refreshed with new laws wax sour. Like the good husbandman who is ever pruning his vineyard, the Church should be diligent in correcting such abuses as have issued from their proceedings; but the bishops offer no measures of reform in Parliament. "A contentious retaining of custom is a turbulent thing, as well as innovation."

The Church authorities speak and act as though their Puritan brethren were criminals, lumping the whole sect with such an infamous group as the Family of Love. They accept any accusation by persons piqued by Puritan denunciations of their sins and their vices. In their inquisitions, they make men swear to "blanks and generalities." Their requiring subscription to articles word by word have irritated sores which would otherwise have cured themselves. Such petty molestations as are rumored, such as the charging of a minister for saying in baptism, "Do you believe?" instead of "Dost thou believe?" are only to be lamented. As for the excommunication which they employ: can any man defend this, "as a base process to lackey up and down for duties and fees; it being a precursory judgment of the latter day?" While it is certainly better to live under laws than not, surely "the wrath of man worketh not the righteousness of God."

Bacon's third political writing, *Observations Upon a Libel* (1593) is a reply to a pamphlet of the Jesuit Robert Parsons, called *Responsio ad edictum reginae angliae*. In this tract Parsons assailed Elizabeth's Lord Treasurer, Burghley, and ascribed what he said were the failures and ills of England to the Queen's measures against her Roman Catholic subjects and the agents of Rome within her kingdom. Bacon's reply is enlightening for its remarks on the prosperous state of England, on Burghley's public service and character, on Elizabeth's treatment of Roman Catholics, and on the distinction which it draws between the main

body of Puritans and such minor sects as the Brownists, Barrowists, and the Family of Love. By the time the *Observations Upon a
Libel* is written, Burghley's nephew has had reasons to be angered
by the refusal of the Cecils to promote a potential rival of his
cousin Robert. The author at this juncture is relying for advancement on the patronage of Essex, the competitor of the
Cecil faction at Court. Yet Bacon makes a thoroughly objective
and just statement of his uncle's service to the Queen. "It is
rather true," he writes, "that his lordship, out of the greatness
of his experience and wisdom, and out of the coldness of his
nature, hath qualified generally all hard and extreme courses, as
far as the service of her majesty, and the safety of the state,
and the making himself compatible with those with whom he
served, would permit."

"Assuredly many princes have had many servants of trust,
name, and sufficiency: but where there have been great parts,
there hath often wanted temper of affection; where there have
been both ability and moderation, there have wanted diligence
and love of travail; where all three have been, there have sometimes wanted faith and sincerity; where some few have had all
these four, yet they have wanted time and experience: but where
there is a concurrence of all these, there is no marvel, though a
prince of judgment be constant in the employment and trust of
such a servant."

In a statesmanlike review of the affairs of the kingdom, the
author mentions several grounds for the conclusion that "if a
man weigh well all the parts of state and religion, laws, administration of justice, policy of government, manners, civility,
learning and liberal sciences, industry and manual arts, arms and
provisions of wars for sea and land, treasure, traffic, improvement of the soil, population, honour and reputation, it will
appear that, taking one part with another, the state of this
nation was never so flourishing."

The greater part of Bacon's reply to Parsons concerns Elizabeth's dealings with the Roman Catholics and her protective measures against papal designs on her kingdom. Of these designs some had been covert, some overt. The Pope had excommunicated Elizabeth (1570) and absolved the faithful of obedience. Mary Stuart (1542-1587) had been made Rome's instrument, under the direction first of France and then of Spain, for the bringing of the British Isles under papal control. Reared in France as a Roman Catholic, Mary came to Scotland in 1561 with a court bent on gay pleasures, and found herself in the midst of a dour people professing a rigorous Calvinistic theology. Her hasty marriage (1567) to Bothwell, the murderer of her second husband, Lord Darnley (the father of James VI of Scotland) was too much even for her most loyal chieftains. She suffered suspension from authority "for the preservation of the Commonwealth and for that her sins appeared incurable." After her flight to England in 1568 Mary Stuart became the centre of Roman Catholic intrigue. Elizabeth was to be destroyed; English heretics were to be reconverted to the Roman faith; revolts were to be engineered; Spanish forces were to support rebellion in Ireland; and the Spanish Armada was to set sail for the subjugation of England. Jesuit agents in disguise roamed over the country and persuaded subjects, who earlier had been the religious adherents of Rome under Mary Tudor, against the acceptance of the English Prayer Book and the rule of the Established Church. Roman Catholic nobles in the north of England rose in rebellion (1569-1570). Crusaders marched under the banner of the "Five Wounds of Christ" and tore up the Bible and the English Prayer Book. The insurgents had expected help from their fellow religionists in Scotland, but those of the Scots who would have come to their aid were prevented by their government from crossing the border. The uprising was crushed and eight hundred insurgents were executed. Papal agents throughout the country were hanged. One notorious Jesuit among them, Parsons, escaped to the Continent to help engineer the Spanish invasion. In expectation of the conquest of England, this Jesuit had pondered the question, "What form or manner of Inquisition to bring in, whether that of Spain (whose rigour is misliked by some) or that which is used in divers parts of Italy (where coldness is reprehended by more)."

When word had gone abroad that a definite plot was under way to assassinate Elizabeth and place Mary of Scotland on the throne, the Queen was finally prevailed upon to accept a parliamentary resolve and petition of fifteen years' standing: Mary was beheaded (1587). The invasion of England by Spain was repulsed by the defeat of the Great Armada in 1588. Spanish forces aiding the Irish in revolt were repelled. England was no longer in danger of attack by arms from without, but her sovereign had still to contend with the undermining from within of the unity and stability of the kingdom by determined and resourceful papal agents.

In his *Observations Upon a Libel*, Bacon describes Elizabeth's way of proceeding against the Roman Catholics. The Queen's acts, he explains, have from the beginning been grounded in two principles: that consciences are not to be forced, and that contempt and faction are to be punished even if "coloured with the pretences of conscience and religion." Although on coming to the throne, Elizabeth had despised the inquisitorial tyranny of the Church of Rome, she had treated members of that body with great lenience. While "as a prince of great wisdom . . . she suffered but the exercise of one religion," she did not attempt to coerce belief, but merely outlawed manifest disobedience and treason. In the face of this toleration, the Queen was excommunicated; her subjects were rendered disobedient under threat of damnation; and rebellion was promoted in the northern part of her kingdom. Spain was encouraged by Rome to invade England, and "a principal point of the plot was to prepare a party within the realm that might adhere to the foreigner." As the "poison" spread, most Roman Catholics "were no more papists in custom, but papists in treasonable faction." It therefore became necessary to make laws for the punishment of renunciations of obedience, renunciations even "more insinuative into the conscience" than the papal bull which declared Elizabeth a heretic had been, since these were now joined with an absolution from mortal sin in the rite of confession. The Queen's new laws prescribed a pecuniary punishment, "not to enforce consciences" but to discover treason. Only when the secrecy of the implanted evil made it a growth extremely difficult to stamp out did the Queen stop its source and nurture. Then, "seditious priests... were exiled; and those that were at that time within the land shipped over, and so commanded to keep hence upon pain of treason."

Among the calamities of England which Parsons instances is "the great and wonderful confusion, which he saith, is in the state of the Church." Parsons distinguishes two factions within the English Calvinists: one with professions of "purity" and the other filled with idolatry and heresies. He mentions the Brownists and their direction by "the unholy ghost." He holds it to be the Protestant belief in England—we quote Bacon—"that if the prince or magistrate do refuse or defer to reform the Church, the people may ... take the reformation into their own hands: and hitherto he addeth the fanatical pageant of Hacket."

In comment and reply, Bacon remarks that the Church in every age is beset by schisms and contentions, since there are never tares except where the wheat has been planted before. He dissociates the Brownists, the Barrowists, Hacket, the Family of Love, and other fanatics among the Puritans (in 1616 he separates specifically the Anabaptists also) from the main body of Nonconformists. The Brownists, he describes as "a very small number of very silly and base people, here and there in corners dispersed ... now, thanks be to God ... suppressed and worn out; so that there is scarce any news of them." Among their number he places Henry Barrow (d. 1593). This man Bacon describes as a "gentleman of a good house" with agreeable "table-talk" who "made a leap from a vain and libertine youth, to a preciseness in the highest degree; the strangeness of which alteration made him very much spoken of." The Family of Love, which Parsons does not explicitly mention by name, is, Bacon remarks, "banished and extinct." As for the "phrenetical and fanatical . . . Hacket": he obtained but two disciples out of the whole population of London, and his so-called uprising was "rather laughed at as a may-game."

Of the main body of Puritans or Precisians Bacon, as a loyal English Protestant replying to a traitor abroad and at the same time cautioning Nonconformists at home, speaks leniently. Some persons, he says, "with an inconsiderate detestation of all cere-monies or orders, which were in use in the time of the Roman religion, as if they were without difference superstitious or polluted, and led with an affectionate imitation of the govern-ment of some protestant churches in foreign states; have sought by books and preaching, indiscreetly, and sometimes undutifully, to bring in an alteration in the external rites and policy of the Church; but in neither have the grounds of the controversies extended unto any point of faith; neither hath the pressing and prosecution exceeded, in the generality, the nature of some inferior contempts: so as they have been far from heresy and sedition, and therefore rather offensive than dangerous to the Church or state."

Parts of *Observations Upon a Libel* amount to a panegyric on the motives and deeds of the Queen. This praise is unquestion-ably sincere, for in a continuing devotion to Elizabeth Bacon is to write in 1608, five years after James has ascended the throne, another panegyric equally laudatory of this beloved sovereign. The second eulogy is called *In felicem memoriam elizabethae* (*On the Fortunate Memory of Elizabeth*). In it Bacon remarks on Elizabeth's having been brought up in a hard school of fortune, her passing "from the prison to the throne" without "a mind embittered and swelling with the sense of misfortune"; her courage and constancy, strength and serenity in face of dangers from within and without her kingdom; her skill in maintaining peace at home and abroad; her controlling "at the beck of a woman" a nation "fierce and warlike"; and her sustaining the reputation of her people for military prowess.

A passage or two of this writing will serve to indicate the tone of the whole: "In a kingdom labouring with intestine faction on account of religion, and standing as a shield and stronghold of defence against the then formidable and over-bearing ambition of Spain . . . it was she who by her forces and her counsels combined kept it under; as was proved by an event the most memorable in respect of felicity of all the actions of our time. For when that Spanish fleet, got up with such travail and ferment, waited upon with the terror and expectation of all Europe, inspired with such confidence of victory, came plough-ing into our channels, it never took so much as a cockboat at sea, never fired so much as a cottage on the land, never even touched the shore; but was first beaten in a battle and then dispersed and wasted in a miserable flight with many shipwrecks; while on the ground and territories of England peace remained undisturbed and unshaken."

"As for those lighter points of character,—as that she allowed herself to be wooed and courted, and even to have love made to her; and liked it; and continued it beyond the natural age for such vanities;—if any of the sadder sort of persons be disposed to make a great matter of this, it may be observed that there is something to admire in these very things, which ever way you take them. For if viewed indulgently, they are much like the accounts we find in romances, of the Queen in the blessed islands, and her court and institutions, who allows of amorous ad-miration but prohibits desire. But if you take them seriously, they challenge admiration of another kind and of a very high order; for certain it is that these dalliances detracted but little from her fame and nothing at all from her majesty, and neither weakened her power nor sensibly hindered her business:—whereas such things are not unfrequently allowed to interfere with the public fortune. But to conclude, she was no doubt a good and moral Queen; and such too she wished to appear. Vices she hated, and it was by honest arts that she desired to shine."

This sincere memorial, written as it was some years after Elizabeth's death, should in itself be sufficient to dissipate the charge commonly brought by guileless biographers that Bacon's attitude to the Queen was one of sychophantic flattery. Everyone, of course, flattered Elizabeth somehow; sometimes in plain speech and sometimes in poetry. When the man of prose flattered the Queen he felt somehow poetic in the act. No mere sprite, Elizabeth became England's "fairy-queen." She was Belphoebe, Britomartis in arms, and Gloriana, the defender of truth against religious "superstition." There had been doubt about the legitimacy of her birth. She had spent a period in the Tower (1554). For years the Papists had sought her undoing and the Spaniards had hoped for her execution. She had endured. She could act as her own prime minister and hold Parliament, and her Council too, at bay with a shake of her head. While she performed her religious exercises duly, read her books daily like a student, addressed the Universities in Greek or in Latin of her own composing, she could swear like a trooper, box Essex on the ears at a Privy Council meeting, and declare with conviction that she could fill any high or low place in the kingdom. A woman of great passion, Elizabeth never married because, while she loved men unevenly in succession, she loved England steadily always, and most of all. When the years had taken their toll and the Queen, with all her feminine finery about her, gazed sadly into her mirror and at the end was consoled with the truth of her address to the people, "I have reigned with your loves," she was then, as she always had been, the daughter of her mother, Anne Boleyn—a coquette—and the offspring of her father, Henry VIII —a Queen.

VI

BACON AND JAMES: THE
EARLY PERIOD

WHEN IT BECAME EVIDENT THAT ELIZABETH'S REIGN was drawing
to a close and that James of Scotland would be assuming England's throne, Bacon contemplated his future with both apprehension and hope. Of his capacity to play a part in the settlement of political questions he had not the slightest doubt. He
knew that there were certain questions of magnitude which
Parliament and the Privy Council had avoided in Elizabeth's
lifetime, through a respect for both her person and her temperament and out of a regard for her successes without and within
the kingdom. "For Queen Elizabeth," as Bacon was to write
later in his *Beginning of the History of Great Britain*, "though
she had the use of many both virtues and demonstrations that
mought draw and knit unto her the heart of her people, yet
nevertheless carrying a hand, restrained in gift and strained in
points of prerogative, could not answer the votes either of
servants or subjects to a full contentment; especially in her
latter days, when the continuance of her reign (which extended
to five and forty years) mought discover in people their natural
desire and inclination towards change."

In the same writing Bacon remarked that "those that had made their way with the King or offered their service in the time of the former Queen, thought now the time was come for which they had prepared: and generally all such as had any dependance upon the late Earl of Essex ... made account their cause was amended." Both Papists and the supporters of Presbytery felt their brethren had fared better in Scotland under James VI than they had in England. His mother had been a Roman Catholic. James had accepted religious rule by Presbytery and the General Assembly.

Bacon's immediate objective was the obtaining of a place in political administration. He had still to bear in mind the attitude of Robert Cecil. Yet, although the cousin had carried on the negotiations, begun by Essex, which assured James of the English throne, there was no certainty that he would continue as Secretary of State under the new king. Henry Percy, Earl of Northumberland, another promoter of James' accession, was a strong rival for the post. Promisingly for Bacon, Northumberland had been an intimate of Anthony Bacon and shared a kinship of mind with Francis Bacon himself, for he was a scientific inquirer, inclined to "experiments," and the patron of the mathematician Thomas Harriot. The new king would remember Anthony Bacon as an agent of the Earl of Essex in his early negotiations; on the other hand, he might recall with displeasure that Anthony's brother had been a prosecutor at the trial of Essex. James of Scotland, however, while stubborn and mindful of past friends and foes, could nevertheless show magnanimity in personal dealings. More important, he was proud of his learning and professed a respect for literary men. He might regard with favor a man who showed respect for his erudition. He might even be the sort of sovereign who, if told in apt writing what was expected of Majesty per se, would answer by appropriate deeds.

Bacon undertook to cope with present circumstances by a correspondence with persons who were likely to have influence with the King. A few days before the Queen's death he had already written to Michael Hickes, Robert Cecil's confidential agent: "The apprehension of this threatened judgment of God ... if it work in other as it worketh in me, knitteth every man's heart more unto his true and approved friend. . . . And as I ever used your means to cherish the truth of my inclination towards Mr. Secretary, so now again I pray, as you find time, let him know that he is the personage in this State which I love most." There were grounds for the writing of this letter. Through Bacon's days in Parliament and in Elizabeth's service as Queen's Counsel Extraordinary, his cousin had treated him with great civility; he had written a friendly caution when gossip arose from Bacon's misinterpreted conversations with the Queen on behalf of Essex. Bacon for his part had grown more politically mature, and could look back with less heat on the Cecils' earlier preference of Coke and other men more experienced for senior offices in the kingdom.

Bacon also wrote to Northumberland, recalling Anthony's association with him, and likewise to the Abbot of Kinloss. To Thomas Challoner, a creditor who had been introduced by Anthony into the service of Essex, Bacon expressed the hope that in view of "the openness of the time, caused by this blessed consent and peace," the debtor's financial means could be increased, and that "our agreement, according to our time ... observed." He assumed, in a confidence, that Challoner would become an acceptable servant of the King, and requested him to "further his Majesty's good conceit and inclination" towards the debtor. Bacon even wrote to Southampton—whom James had released from the Tower immediately on his coming to the throne of England—assuring him of his goodwill and saying that, although he would gladly have waited on his Lordship in person, he chose to write him rather than risk any possible displeasure in a personal meeting over his part, as Queen's Counsel, in the Essex trial. In a letter to another conspirator with Essex,

Sir John Davies, he asked the author of the philosophical poem *Nosce Teipsum* (1599) "to be good to *concealed poets.*"

The phrase "concealed poets" has often been cited in argument for Bacon's secret authorship of poetry, more especially of the works of Shakespeare. The works of Shakespeare are not in the usual literary style of Francis Bacon, yet without touching on the Bacon-Shakespeare controversy, it may be observed that Bacon could write in many styles. When trying to bring Essex back into Elizabeth's favor, he had successfully composed a feigned correspondence in the two styles of the Earl and his brother Anthony. He had written letters to Elizabeth at the bidding of Essex in exact imitation of the Earl. His versatility in this regard is again exemplified by a communication which he now addresses to the King, where the statement moves ponderously as in James' own writings. This missive begins, for the complimenting of the learned King, with a quotation from the Vulgate and ends with another from Ovid. Part of the letter proceeds as follows:

> ...further and more nearly I was not a little encouraged, not only upon a supposal that unto your Majesty's sacred ears (open to the air of all virtues) there might perhaps have come small breath of the good memory of my father, so long a principal counsellor in this your kingdom; but also by the particular knowledge of the infinite devotion and incessant endeavours (beyond the strength of his body and the nature of the times) which appeared in my good brother towards your Majesty's service; and were, on your Majesty's part, through your singular benignity by many most gracious and lively significations and favours accepted and acknowledged, beyond the merit of anything he could effect. All which endeavours and duties for the most part were common to myself with him, though by design (as between brethren) dissembled.
>
> And therefore most high and mighty King, my most dear and dread sovereign lord, since now the corner-stone is laid of the mightiest monarchy in Europe; and that God above (who is noted to have a mighty hand in bridling the floods and fluctuations of

the seas and of people's hearts) hath by the miraculous and universal consent (the more strange because it proceedeth from such
diversity of causes) in your coming in, given a sign and token
what he intendeth in the continuance; I think there is no subject
of your Majesty's who loveth this island, and is not hollow and
unworthy, whose heart is not set on fire, not only to bring you
peace-offerings to make you propitious, but to sacrifice himself a
burnt-offering to your Majesty's service; amongst which number
no man's fire shall be more pure and fervent than mine.

In this letter we have an early instance of what was to become
a habit of "obsequiousness" on Bacon's part, and indeed on the
part of every person at James' Court. Bacon's address here is not,
of course, the spontaneous, affectionate flattery which he and
others freely accorded to Elizabeth. Nor is it servile writing,
nor indeed praise at all, but rather the studied abasement in
address which James expected of all persons who corresponded
with him. There was no more conviction behind it than there
was sincerity in James' own salutation to Bacon himself, as a
Lord Keeper temporarily out of favor: "Right trusty and well
beloved counsellor, we greet you well." It is an example of the
manner of approach required of "suppliants" by a king who
regarded every subject, in or out of Court, as an inferior creature
dependent on the prerogative power of an anointed, divinely
endowed ruler.

Bacon had definite opinions about "praises" of sovereigns and
the "pains" and "indignities" to be endured while in their service.
These things he deemed necessary means to definite ends. In the
case of a worthy public servant these ends included just government and the common good. "By indignities," Bacon wrote in
his *Essays*, "men come to dignities"; it is "the solecism of power,
to think to command the end, and yet not to endure the
means. . . . Some praises come of good wishes and respects, which
is a form due in civility to kings . . . when by telling men what
they are, they represent to them what they should be." This last
maxim Bacon was always to keep in mind when addressing

James in private letters and publicly describing his character and deeds; when confronting the King with the grievances of the Commons, when advising the Sovereign as Solicitor-General, Attorney-General, Lord Keeper, and Lord Chancellor. In reflection on the whole question as a problem confronting a philosopher, Bacon made some observations in his *Advancement of Learning* (1605). "I have no purpose," he wrote, "to give allowance to some conditions and courses base and unworthy, wherein divers professors of learning have wronged themselves and gone too far; such as were those trencher philosophers, which in the later ages of the Roman state were usually in the houses of great persons, being little better than solemn parasites." But philosophers in pursuit of becoming ends, he believed, should not be condemned for cultivating rich men in high place. Aristippus, for example, when reproved for grovelling at the feet of Dionysius, suitably answered that it was not his fault, but it was the fault of Dionysius, for he had "his ears in his feet." "The like applications and stooping to points of necessity and convenience cannot be disallowed," Bacon continued, "for though they may have some outward baseness, yet in a judgment truly made they are to be accounted submissions to the occasion and not to the person." By 1605, Bacon had prepared himself to "endure" the obsequiousness and other conditions imposed by the new sovereign of England as incidents to the pursuit of an unwavering justice, the public good, and the instauration of a new scientific learning.

Two months after James had reached Whitehall (1603), Bacon wrote optimistically of his own prospects to Tobie Matthew: "I have many comforts and assurances: but in mine own opinion the chief is, that the canvassing world is gone and the deserving world is come. And withal I find myself as one awaked out of sleep." Within three months more Bacon had been disillusioned. He had received no recognition from either the King or the Secretary of State. Even his name, to which no formal Patent had been attached in the former reign, had been omitted from the list of those reappointed as King's Counsel. Bacon wrote to Robert Cecil:

For my purpose or course, I desire to meddle as little as I can in the King's causes—his Majesty now abounding in counsel—and to follow my thrift and practice, and to marry with some convenient advancement. For as for any ambition, I do assure your Honour mine is quenched. In the Queen's my excellent Mistress's time, the *quorum* was small; her service was a kind of freehold and it was a more solemn time. All those points agreed with my nature and judgment. My ambition now I shall only put upon my pen, whereby I shall be able to maintain memory and merit of the times succeeding.

Lastly, for this divulged and almost prostituted title of knighthood, I could without charge, by your Honour's means, be content to have it, both because of this late disgrace, and because I have three new knights in my mess in Gray's Inn commons, and because I have found out an alderman's daughter, an handsome maiden, to my liking. So as, if your Honour will find the time, I will come to the Court from Gorhambury upon any warning.

Two weeks later, Bacon wrote again to his cousin:

For my knighthood, I wish the manner might be such as might grace me, since the matter will not; I mean, that I might not be merely gregarious in a troop. The coronation is at hand. It may please your Lordship to let me hear from you speedily. So I continue your Lordship's ever much bounden. . . .

A week thereafter Bacon was dubbed knight by the King, along with some three hundred others—judges, serjeants-at-law, gentlemen ushers, doctors of civil law, and other persons of diverse sorts. Soon he was made a King's Counsel with Patent, and was given an annual pension in perpetuity of £60 "in consideration of the services" of his brother Anthony. No other award came his way. Now in a condition of despair over his failure to receive an administrative post, Bacon sought the consolation of philosophy. He penned an *apologia pro vita sua*, calling it *De interpretatione naturae prœmium (Of the Inter-*

pretation of Nature: a Proem, 1603). In this writing Bacon appears as one ready to abandon politics and to devote himself entirely to the pursuit of scientific inquiry. He assumes that by the time the work is ready for publication his method of discovery—a new "formula of interpretation" which nearly twenty years before he had called "the greatest birth of Time"—will have been made ready and put to use.

Mature reflection has convinced him, Bacon now writes, that "nothing is of as much benefit to the human race as the discovery of and devotion to new truths and arts by which the life of men is cultivated.... And above all if a man should bring forth no particular invention... but were to kindle a light in nature which from its very beginning would illuminate the confines which hold within their grasp facts already discovered, and once raised aloft would straightway lay open and bring into view the most hidden things, that man seemed to me to be the propagator of man's empire over the universe, the protector of liberty, and the conqueror of necessities."

The author has reached the conclusion that, although by birth and education he had seemed committed, at an earlier stage in his life, to affairs of state, he is actually by nature more fitted to the contemplation of truth. He possesses "a mind agile enough to recognize the resemblance of things... and sufficiently steadfast and eager to observe the refinements of their diversity." He has desire to seek, patience to ponder, fondness to meditate, slowness to assert, readiness to reconsider, carefulness to set in order, in short, a nature with "an intimacy and kinship with truth." Until recently, he had hoped to be the better able to foster the advancement of science by obtaining place in government. He had, accordingly, learned the civil arts and sought the favor of powerful friends—yet ever mindful that "these things... do not penetrate beneath the circumstances and attainments of this mortal life." But his "zeal" was "taken for ambition," and his impaired health had warned him of his "tardiness." Duty now forbids further neglect of his proper task. In future he will devote himself entirely to scientific endeavors.

The science on which he is intent will be secured by "utility and works," however much the old science, with its school learning and contemplations, may suffer in consequence. Should someone demand an immediate production of works, the author will reply that he, as a man of weak health faced by "the most obscure of all subjects without guide or light," has made sufficient advance by constructing the machinery of inquiry without setting the same in motion. The restraining of all precipitous desire for "works," until some general principles of the new science are discovered, will be the wiser course for all concerned. Those who would demand specimen certainties should bear in mind that in the prevailing science men are not able even to hope for such assurances. In any event, the new science cannot be judged by recourse to precedent, "for the matter is without precedent." As for publication, those matters which "conduce to the capturing of the correspondence of men of wit and the cleansing of the threshing-floor of minds" may better be publicized by word of mouth. Scientific information should be disseminated with discretion, for both its "formula of interpretation" and discoveries are properly confined to persons of select capabilities. Finally, Bacon assures the reader that he has at heart "nothing which is dependent on externals." He is not seeking fame; he is not attempting to found a sect; nor is he moved by a desire for private gain, but only by "the consciousness of well-deserving and the effecting of things with which fortune itself cannot interfere."

Before this *Proem* can be completed, Bacon discovers that he has already made an impression on the King, an impression far from scientific in character. His written advices to James on the political union of England and Scotland and on problems of church government have been well received. His skill in mediating between the Lords and Commons and his capacity for dominating the Lower House and putting ambitious lawyers—the *literae vocales* of this House—in their place, has not gone unnoticed by the new King. Bacon's prospects are greatly on the mend. In 1607 he is made Solicitor-General. In 1608 the Clerkship of the Star Chamber becomes vacant, and Bacon takes over the office which he had held in reversion for nearly nineteen years.

In 1603 Bacon had watched the new King's "progress" from Scotland to Whitehall and, like many others, he had learned with dismay and disquiet that during a stop at Newark, James had ordered the hanging of a cutpurse caught in the act, without even the semblance of a trial. Clearly, the new king would have to learn that England was not Scotland, nor Scotland England; that the English courts were extremely jealous of their authority; that in England even thieves were tried according to due processes of law; that there were Englishmen who thought even kings were subject to law; that some thought that the Courts of the King, as they were styled, might better be called Courts of England. James would have to learn, too, that in England Parliament was not a mere court of record, as in Scotland, and that many among his new subjects, including Parliamentarians, placed less trust in the rule of bishops in the Church of England than did their new monarch. By the English constitution, King James possessed an extensive Prerogative; but by the same unwritten constitution, Parliament, courts of law, and even the humblest subjects had their acquired privileges. Further, there were ambitions abroad in the kingdom—ambitions held under restraint in the days of Elizabeth—of acquiring more assured rights, independent of what any monarch might or might not choose to grant as graces. A wise king would decrease the area of his Prerogative and gradually increase the range of his subjects' "privileges." For some sixteen years, Bacon would be trying to make James aware of these things; but the King would prove neither wise nor teachable.

Bacon soon became aware that, as he told Northumberland, the King "hasteneth to a mixture of both kingdoms and nations faster perhaps than policy will conveniently bear." He addressed the new sovereign in the first year of his reign with an advice, a *Brief Discourse of the Happy Union of the Kingdoms of England and Scotland* (1603). This writing was prepared for the perusal of a king very much aware of his philosophical erudition, by a counsellor who just then was writing his *Advancement of Learning* for address to the same monarch. In the latter work Bacon was calling the metaphysics of physical nature—the only metaphysics he recognized—"magic," after the title of the wisdom of the Persian Maji. Bacon hoped that the *Brief Discourse* would serve two purposes: first, to remind the philosophically erudite James that "sudden mutations as well in state as in nature, are rarely without violence and perturbation," and, second, to prepare the mind of this learned sovereign for the reception of a work on a new sort of learning.

The *Brief Discourse* opens with the statement that the author does not find it strange that a certain book by Heraclitus, now lost, should have been regarded by some readers as a discourse on nature and by others as a treatise on politics, because "there is a great affinity and consent between the rules of nature, and the rules of policy." It was for this reason, that the education of the kings of Persia was called "magic," since this science was none other than "an application of the contemplations and observations of nature unto a sense politic; taking the fundamental laws of nature, and the branches and passages of them, as an original or first model, whence to take and describe a copy and imitation for government."

James has been in the habit of regarding his judges and other political servants after Aristotle's manner of treating the celestial spheres. It is the opinion of James, who has derived his analogy from Aristotle's theory of the heavens, that the King, as the *Primum Mobile* or "First Moved" by the First Mover or God, imparts his "motion" to his subordinates. With this view of James in mind, Bacon makes a plea for "the cherishing of inferior bodies." He tells the King that even as the planets fulfil their perpetual office of motion, constant and regular in imitation of the movement of the *Primum Mobile*, so should the activities of the officers of government proceed. He also reminds James that, while the heavens enrich themselves at the expense of the earth, "whatsoever moisture they do levy and take . . . they do spend and turn back again in showers."

Continuing the analogy of "congruity between the principles of nature and policy," Bacon in Peripatetic vein distinguishes *compositio* from *mistio* (putting together from mingling), "the one being a conjunction of bodies in place, the other in quality and consent." The former is exemplified in the mixing of water and oil, where fusion is never successful, and the latter in the union of earth, water, and oil in vegetable growths, where the "mingling" is so complete that the contributing "simple" bodies cannot be separated. In a *compositio* there is a lack of a new integrating form; in a *mistio* this factor proves a *commune vinculum*. Without this, the old forms of bodies conjoined remain in strife and discord. Natural philosophers say for good reasons that "composition" is the work of man and "mingling" the work of nature and of time, which "perfect fermentation and incorporation."

Having cautioned the King against a hasty uniting of his two kingdoms, Bacon specifies five of the components of a united nation: sovereignty, name, language, laws, and employments. Sovereignty and language, allowing for local dialects in both England and Scotland, are already one in the Island of Britain. Employments are "indifferent" things. "Name, though it seem but a superficial and outward matter, yet it carrieth much impression and enchantment: the general and common name . . . always apt to unite." Within laws, "the principal sinews of government," Bacon includes *jura*, or "abilities and freedoms";

leges, or laws proper; and *mores,* or customs. Of abilities he instances "kinds, or rather degrees" which are recognized by the Roman jurists: naturalization, voice in Parliament, place in council or office. As for specific laws, those of England and Scotland are so many, various, and disparate, that there is no possibility of bringing them together in one system. All that can be hoped for in the beginning is some uniformity in the principal and fundamental laws, both ecclesiastical and civil. When the time comes for a consideration of such of these laws as pertain to the Church, it will be well to call to mind that Christ's coat, while without seam, was of many shades and colors. As "for manners: a consent in them is to be sought industriously, but not to be enforced: for nothing amongst people breedeth more pertinency in holding their customs, as sudden and violent offer to remove them."

The *Brief Discourse* made an impression on the King. The Commons elected Bacon to a committee designed to make James' two kingdoms one. He prepared another writing for the King's guidance, *Certain Articles or Considerations Touching the Union of the Kingdoms of England and Scotland* (1604). This dealt with the union under many headings: sovereignty, subjection, territory, statutes, naturalization of Scottish subjects, customs, the Churches and their disciplines and doctrines, commissions, councils of state, Parliaments, offices of the Crown, nobilities, courts, trials and processes, finances, garrisons and navies, freedoms and liberties, merchandisings, taxes, and fitting title for the Sovereign. The author reminds the King that "for the sovereignty, the union is absolute in your majesty and generation." In his discussion of naturalizaton Bacon set down for James' consideration the principle "that all Scotsmen from the very instant your majesty's reign begun are become denizens," but not as yet "subjects." The *post-nati,* however, like the inhabitants of Ireland, are "for the time forwards" natural subjects of the Crown of England, "not by any statute or act of parliament, but merely by the common law, and the reason thereof."

Bacon suggested and James took "the stile and title of King of Great Britany." The Crowns of England and Scotland were now united, but their Parliaments and Churches were to remain separate. The coalescence of the former was not to take place for a century; the union of the latter was to be indefinitely deferred. James decisively refused to accept Bacon's opinion that Scottish "denizens" required naturalization, after Bacon had all but succeeded in bringing into agreement the commissioners appointed to deal with the union. A majority of the members of the Commons showed a readiness to entertain the naturalization of every subject of James VI of Scotland, who was now James I of England, when the King indicated that he was not of a mind to have his people in Scotland created subjects either by act of the elected representatives of other subjects or through the operation of English law. He himself would be the *Primum Mobile*, God's first agent in the creation of subjects. His Prerogative alone would be the source of their being. Members of Parliament then began to exercise unrestrainedly the right of free speech. James' Scots were called, in turn, a horde of savages intent on a foray into a civilized land, beggars eager to feast at the well-laden English board, impoverished cattle from the north about to be turned loose on the rich pastures of the south. Some members of the Commons opposed the union, in a more reasonable manner, on the ground of competition in business and trade. Bacon, who had composed a *Preparation toward the Union of the Laws of England and Scotland* for the King and, in expectation of a successful outcome of negotiations, had made ready for presentation to Parliament a *Certificate or Return of the Commissioners of England and Scotland* (1604), raised his voice in the Commons. There has been, he admitted, "some inequality in the fortunes of these two nations, England and Scotland, by the commixture whereof there may ensue advantage to them and loss to us," but these differences have consisted only in "the external goods of fortune." As for the goods

of mind and body, the Scots are *"alteri nos,* other ourselves."
They are ingenious, valiant, industrious, strong and active in
body, and so much like us generally that "we are participant
both of their virtues and vices." If they seem less than tractable
in government, we ourselves are not free of this fault, it "being
a thing indeed incident to all martial people." "I hope, Mr.
Speaker," said Bacon, "I may speak it without offence, that if we
did hold ourselves worthy, whensoever just cause should be
given, either to recover our ancient rights, or to revenge our late
wrongs, or to attain the honour of our ancestors, or to enlarge
the patrimony of our posterity, we would never in this manner
forget considerations of amplitude and greatness, and fall at
variance about profit and reckonings; fitter a great deal for
private persons than for parliaments and kingdoms."

While engaged with the problem of political union, Bacon
was also concerned with other constitutional questions. Sir
Francis Goodwin's election in 1604 to Parliament had been
declared illegal, but the House of Commons had ordered him to
take his seat, and asserted the principle that it alone had the right
to pronounce upon the legality of its membership. King James,
however, insisted that the question be settled in Chancery.
Bacon was called upon to mediate the case, which involved
Parliament, courts of law, and the sovereign. He managed to
find a solution whereby a writ would be issued for a new election
in the present instance, and the King and other disputants in the
case would undertake to see that hereafter the Commons would
possess the right it now vocally asserted. Goodwin's case was
probably the one which provided James with the occasion, as
James Spedding surmises, for uttering the opinion in a case on
the use of the Royal Prerogative—as Bacon was to report in his
De augmentis (1623)—"That kings ruled by the laws of their
kingdoms, as God did by the laws of Nature, and ought as rarely
to put in use their supreme prerogative, as God does his Power
of working miracles."

In the same year the question of the King's Purveyance was

brought before the Commons. Bacon, being one of those members who held the opinion that Purveyance was now being carried on illegally, was nominated by the Lower House to present a case to the King. He prepared an address in the form of a *Petition Touching Purveyors* and delivered this to James in "the withdrawing-chamber" at Whitehall. In it he wrote: "In the course of remedy which we desire, we pretend not, nor intend not, in any sort, to derogate from your majesty's prerogative. . . . For we seek nothing but the reformation of abuses, and the execution of former laws whereunto we are born." The present grievance is this: the King's purveyors are taking what they ought not to take, and may appropriately be called taxers. They demand the poor man's hay, wood, or poultry, which he has reserved as provision for his family; and then tax him on the money he is given in return. The purveyors put their axes to trees, "which are the beauty, countenance, and shelter of men's houses; that men have long spared from their own purse and profit." If the possessor is too difficult to deal with while he is at home, purveyors strike while he is away. When the representatives of the Crown are asked to reimburse for goods illegally taken, a fee of twelve pence per pound is exacted. Incredibly, such poundage is sometimes taken twice over on the same transaction.

To compound their wrong the purveyors take much more than ever comes to the King's use. For every pound's worth of goods that the King receives, it is affirmed on good authority that three pounds of damage is inflicted on the populace. Purveyors conceal their thievery by failing to register their exactions as the law provides. Illegally they set their own prices. They cheat in appraising goods. By law they are required to procure only in the daytime, but now they are abroad in twilight and at night. By law they are required to show their commission, but this they refuse. "A number of other particulars there are," Bacon adds, "whereof as I have given your majesty a taste, so the chief of them upon deliberate advice are set down in writing by the labour of some committees, and approbation of the whole house, more particularly and lively than I can express them, myself having them at the second hand by reason of my abode."

About this time the courts, the Privy Council, and the King were deliberating the constitutional question, whether the Council of the Marches lay beyond the jurisdiction of the ordinary courts of law. The Council of the Marches had been set up in an effort to reduce the power of the nobles in outlying districts, notably the frontier areas of Wales and Yorkshire. Because of the manner in which the King had empowered local magistrates, these areas had become veritable crown colonies as far as the dispensing of justice was concerned. The motives behind the present agitation for a change were not unmixed. There were representations against the efficiency of magistrates by noblemen who deemed the inhabitants of these regions their special "care." There was a preference on the part of inhabitants for trial by jury, because jurors could be brought under local influence. There were arguments by lawyers greedy for costs. And there was another opportunity for Edward Coke—who never missed one—to make a case against the King's holding within his power any court which could establish new law by precedent. The question was brought before a series of tribunals and then sent back to the King. The matter was settled, for the time being, by James with the declaration, in keeping with his own political doctrine and according to Bacon's constitutional advice, that the empowering and the continuance of the Court of the Marches lay within the Prerogative of the King.

It was the opinion of Bacon that in this instance, at least, the poor could obtain better justice at less expense from the King's courts than from "lawyers' courts," that the "power of the gentry is the chief fear and danger of the good subject." Bacon also thought that an unconstitutional assault on the sovereign's

Prerogative in any instance could be more dangerous in the long run to subjects' liberties than the retaining within the Prerogative of what was assumed by certain judges and lawyers bent on constitutional changes to lie within subjects' so-called "rights." A debate in the Commons on the question of the Marches called forth one of Bacon's most notable constitutional utterances. In this he affirmed by legal argument, with citation of precedents established in the days of King Alfred, William the Conqueror, Henry III, Edward III, Edward IV, and Henry VIII, that the King acting on his Prerogative could establish courts by a power of initiative divinely bestowed upon rulers *qua* rulers. Bacon's speech on that occasion would not be forgotten by some of those who were to try him before the High Court of Parliament in 1621.

The King, argued Bacon, "holdeth not his Prerogatives of this kind mediately from the Law, but immediately from God, as he holdeth his Crown; and though other Prerogatives by which he claimeth any matter of revenue or other right pleadable in his ordinary courts of justice, may be there disputed, yet his Sovereign Power, which no Judge can censure, is not that of nature; and therefore whatever pertaineth or dependeth thereon, being matter of government, and not of law, must be left to his managing by his Council of State. And that this is necessary to the end of all government, which is preservation of the public, may in this particular appear. For no doubt but these grave and worthy ministers of justice have in all this proceeding no respect but their oaths and the duties of their places, as they have often and deeply protested; and in truth it belongeth not to them to look any higher, because they have charge but of particular rights. But the State, whose proper duty and eye is to the general good, and in that regard to the balancing of all degrees . . . will happily consider this point above Law, that monarchies, in name, do often degenerate into Aristocracies, or rather Oligarchies, in nature, by two insensible degrees." These degrees are the making of the Sovereign's Prerogative subject to the constructions of law and the affixing of law to some office, where it can be overruled or inspired by a judge, to the enablement of magistracy to stand independent by itself. "God forbid," said Bacon, "that we should be governed by men's discretions and not by the Law; 'for certainly a King that governs not thereby,' as his Majesty has written, 'can neither be comptable to God for his administration, nor have a happy and established reign.' But God forbid also, upon pretence of liberties or Laws, Government should have any head but the King. . . .

"We say that in the King's Prerogative, there is a double power: one which is delegate to his ordinary judges in Chancery or Common Law; another which is inherent in his own person, whereby he is the supreme judge both in Parliament and all other Courts; and hath power to stay suits at the Common Law." Acts of Parliament may be suspended by the King's sole authority. The inherent power of the Sovereign is exempt from control by any court of law.

James, while making his initial "progress" from Edinburgh to London (1603), had been presented with a petition from the Nonconformist clergy. This document came to be known as "the Millenary Petition" because of its supposed one thousand signatures—it actually contained some eight hundred. The petitioners described themselves as not "factious" men nor "schismatics," but as faithful ministers of Christ, who humbly desired redress of certain abuses. As one who had surveyed the Established Church of England from a distance, James had thought of this as a communion which could countenance a sufficient variety of doctrines and modes of worship to satisfy all reasonable men. He was inclined to listen, however, to the complaints of any worthy Nonconformists who, because of troubled "consciences," were finding it difficult to conform to the letter of some of the ecclesiastical laws. On meeting with his first Parliament, the King and Head of the Church stressed his re-

luctance to persecute or threaten his subjects "in matters of
conscience," referred to Puritans as persons "impatient of any
superiority," and reminded his hearers that he had been born a
Roman Catholic. He affirmed that he had ever been considerate
of persons of that faith, but added in warning that priests who
contended that the Bishop of Rome could exercise political
power over the subjects of other lawful sovereigns, or held that
excommunicated kings could be lawfully assassinated, would
not be permitted to enter or remain within his kingdom. There
would be no condoning, moreover, of attempts on the part of
Roman Catholic laymen to convert other subjects either by
argument or coercion.

James advised the Universities that he intended to make provision for preaching ministers who would travel from one
vacant parish to another, as need required, by such impropriate
tithes as he was able to set aside for this purpose. This project,
however, was abandoned when Whitgift remonstrated that it
would amount to a capitulation to Puritans bent on the undermining of the rule of bishops by spreading through the agency
of itinerant "prophesying" clergy the doctrine of rule by Presbytery. It soon became apparent to Bacon that the King, while
aware of the threat of the Recusants to the unity and independence of his kingdom, was not fully informed of the demands and the connivings of the Puritans, the extent of their
following throughout England, and the influence of the sect
within Parliament.

His advice on the union of England and Scotland had been
well received; the King might entertain *Certain Considerations touching the better Pacification and the Edification of
the Church of England* (1603). In this latter advice Bacon introduces the subject with this statement: "The unity of your
Church, excellent Sovereign, is a thing no less precious than
the union of your kingdoms; being both works wherein your
happiness may contend with your worthiness. Having therefore

presumed, not without your majesty's gracious acceptation, to say somewhat on the one, I am the more encouraged not to be silent in the other: the rather, because it is an argument I have travelled in heretofore." Bacon then sets down three premises: first, that "all actual and full obedience is to be given to ecclesiastical jurisdiction as it now standeth"; second, that "mutation" in church affairs, for the "taking away abuses," will not necessarily "undermine the stability . . . of that which is sound and good"; and third, that there is not "one form of discipline in all churches, and that imposed by necessity of a commandment and prescript out of the word of God." He tells James that he can find nothing in Scripture contrary to the view that "God had left the like liberty to the Church government, as he had done to the civil government," so that the forms of the former can befit the time, as Divine Providence may order and dispose. It is his opinion, nevertheless, that government by bishops, which is warranted by the practice of the ancient Church, is "much more convenient for kingdoms, than parity of ministers and government by synods." The "sympathy" between the state ecclesiastical and the state civil is of such a nature that it is not possible to alter the government of the one without endangering the stability of the other.

There are, however, two features of the present administration by bishops in the Established Church which might well be changed; the first is their "sole exercise" of rule, and the second their deputation of certain parts of their authority to chancellors, commissaries, and other officers. As for the first: there were in the original government of the Church Presbyters and Consistories who, with the bishops, had to do not only with endowments and revenues but also with general ecclesiastical jurisdiction. It would seem fitting, therefore, that in ordaining, suspending, or depriving ministers, and in judging cases of blasphemy and the like, bishops should not proceed "sole and unassisted." This is a point in which present-day bishops might concede without perturbation to the Church and to their own strengthening and better proceeding in causes. Yet, while this is so, the bishop as bishop cannot properly put his authority from him by means of deputation, as a civil sovereign may. The imitation of kings by bishops, through their having chancellors and judges, is not contained in their "original grant." The bishop's "trust and confidence . . . is personal and inherent: and cannot, nor ought not to be transposed."

Turning to the liturgy and the ceremonies of the Church, Bacon finds the emphasis on preaching so extreme that reverence in worship is declining and "superstition" is in prospect. "As the extolling of the sacrament bred the superstition of the mass; the extolling of the liturgy and prayers bred the superstition of the monastical orders and oraisons: and so no doubt preaching likewise may be magnified and extolled superstitiously, as if all the whole body of God's worship should be turned into an ear." The Puritans "inveigh against a dumb ministry," but make too "promiscuous an allowance" for those of their number whom they account prophets. Many of their preachers have no acquaintance with learning or regard for the arts and sciences which are the handmaidens of theology, nor indeed respect for the true gift of preaching, which in many cases among them is no gift at all. While it must be acknowledged that there is a great variety in auditories and congregations, there is surely some level below which preaching ought not to descend. As for prophesying, an exercise which because of abuses has been put down by an order of the Church, the question might profitably be considered whether this should be revived by having the clergy within a precinct meet upon a weekday, with an "ancient grave minister" presiding, for the exposition by those who attend of a selected and previously announced text of Scripture. Such an exercise, an earlier custom of the Church, would prove an excellent means for the training of preachers in the proper handling of the Word of God.

In the remainder of *Certain Considerations* Bacon grants several concessions to the Puritans. He advises that bishops act in council with Presbyters and Consistories. "The word, priest," he says, "should not be continued, especially with offence, the word, minister, being already made familiar." When dealing with the cap and surplice, Bacon asks whether the Church should insist more on what belongs to the unity of the Christian faith in articles of doctrine, and less on a common conformity with outward rites and ceremonies. Cap and surplice, in Bacon's opinion, are among things "in their nature indifferent." In the conflict between those who do and those who do not wear them, Bacon would have the Church obey "the apostle's rule, which is: 'that the stronger do descend and yield to the weaker.'" This would make for toleration, bring about liberty within the law, and discourage that connivance which encourages disobedience. As part of church worship there should be "singing of psalms and spiritual songs," but no employment of "figures of music" which "have no affinity with the reasonable service of God, but were added in the more pompous times." The ceremony of the ring should be dropped from the marriage service; even vulgar persons think it not "grave" or an "essential part."

Having, next, considered the rites of confirmation and of absolution, the latter of which he thinks was "first allowed in a kind of spiritual discretion," Bacon turns to "the abuse" of excommunication. This, in his opinion, is a punishment too indiscriminately prescribed by bishops for persons who fail to conform with "indifferent" practices. "Excommunication," he writes, "is the greatest judgment upon earth; being that which is ratified in heaven; and being a precursory or prelusory judgment of the great judgment of Christ in the end of the world. And therefore for this to be made an ordinary process ... how can it be without derogation to God's honour, and making the power of the keys contemptible?"

After touching on the questions of nonresident clergy and the placing of several parishes under one minister, Bacon makes a brief reference to penal measures against Roman Catholics. "I am persuaded," he writes, "that the papists themselves should not need so much the severity of penal laws, if the sword of the Spirit were better edged, by strengthening the authority, and suppressing the abuses in the Church."

Certain Considerations was written to prepare the mind of the King for a conference in prospect between the ecclesiastical authorities and representative Puritans. Whether James gave any thought to Bacon's advice, in whole or in part, it is impossible to say. Certainly, any effect it might have had on his thinking was soon dissipated by the behaviour of both Puritans and bishops at this meeting. The conference was convened at Hampton Court in 1604: nine bishops and nine other dignitaries represented the Church; there were four Puritans present. The Puritans moved to have the doctrine of the Church of England made so extremely Genevan in character that John Whitgift, who was sufficiently Calvinist in theology to believe that "it is not placed in the will and power of every man to be saved," could not even consider their proposals. It occurred to the bishops that the Puritans hoped that by their first precipitating an involved and lengthy doctrinal debate, in which they would undoubtedly make a good showing, their later propositions of reform in church government might be the more readily entertained, as having to do with "less essential" matters. The Puritans requested that a pastor be provided for every parish and that pluralities be abolished. This proposal was, in the surmise of the bishops, shrewdly motivated by a twofold desire, to bring to an end the silencing of Puritan preachers by ecclesiastical courts and to have vacancies in parishes about the country filled with untrained pastors of a "prophesying" sort. Archbishop Whitgift thought the motives of the Puritans in every discussion serpentine. In a letter to Robert Cecil he called the "contentious brethren" so many "vipers" who "have made petitions and motions correspondent to their natures." Bishop Bancroft countered a Puritan proposal for democratic church government with an assertion of the doctrine of the divine right of the King and Head of the Church. He called for a more rigid statement of Articles. When the question of rituals was raised the Puritans repeated their familiar charge that all the "forms" of the Established Church, from the surplice to the Sign of the Cross in baptism, were "relics of Popery, and had been abused to idolatry, and therefore ought to be abolished." Their leader, John Reynolds, taking hold of the Archbishop's sleeve, told him mockingly that he was clad in the "rags of Popery." In a brief on discipline the Puritans asked that in the case of grave decisions the bishops be required to consult with Presbyters. James, on hearing this request and remembering what he had suffered at the hands of the Presbyterians in Scotland, flew into a rage and exclaimed that its proposers were aiming at a Scotch Presbytery which, he said, "agreeth as well with a monarchy as God with the devil. Then Jack and Tom, and Will and Dick shall meet and at their pleasure censure me and my council and all our proceedings." The King told the Conference plainly: "I will have one doctrine, one discipline, one religion, in substance and ceremony." To the Puritans he addressed the threat: "If this be all your party have to say I will make them conform, or I will harry them out of this land, or else worse."

The Conference produced nothing of consequence for theology or ritual except a few minor changes in the catechism and the service of worship. It had, however, one issue of great consequence, the authorized translation of the Bible—what was to be the King James Version—long to continue as a standard work. This translation would be read or heard by Protestants ·everywhere, and was to do more for the furtherance of principles on which the Puritans stood than any concession which could conceivably have been obtained through debate or by any other strategy from any bishops at any conference in the seventeenth century.

As a result of the Hampton Court Conference, "many cripples in conformity were cured of their former halting therein; and . . . for the future quietly digested the Ceremonies of the Church." More robust persons among the Puritans, however, were to become stronger in conviction and bolder in speech. In the thinking of many of these, repugnance against the severe rule of bishops was to be associated with aversion for the exercise of the Royal Prerogative in secular acts by the King. The disappointment, and fear too, of the Recusants, who had been awaiting the results of the Conference, and then learned of the King's announcement respecting "one doctrine, one discipline," was great.

The strong sense of frustration in some of their number showed itself vehemently the following year in the unsuccessful Gunpowder Plot (1605). The design of this "Powder Treason" was to kill the King, members of the Privy Council, the Lords, and Commons all at one blow. The conspiracy made a great impression on the mind of Bacon. He was to recall it in his writings time after time. Two years after the "Powder Treason" was hatched, Bacon in a letter to his friend Tobie Matthew, who earlier had become a Roman Catholic, described the conspiracy as "the extreme effects of Superstition . . . fit to be tabled and pictured in the chambers of meditation, as another hell above the ground; and well justifying the censure of the heathen that superstition is far worse than atheism."

VII

BACON AS SOLICITOR-GENERAL

Bacon assumed his first administrative post in government, that of Solicitor-General, in 1607. So many and exacting were the duties attached to this office, that he came to regard it as one of the "painfullest places in the Kingdom." Bacon was now required to consult with the King, the Privy Council, the judges, the Lords, and the Commons. He prepared proclamations for the Star Chamber, cases for the courts, and measures for presentation to Parliament. Because, as Henry Howard, Earl of Northampton (d. 1614), Lord Privy Seal, said, the present Solicitor was "a person very apt . . . to apprehend," Bacon was assigned duties which ordinarily would have been performed by the Attorney-General. Bacon gave advice on the continuing case of Court of the Marches, the pacification of unquiet Ireland, the amelioration of laws which were harsh and the repeal of those which were obsolete, the abuses of those who made it their business to be "informers" against others, the duties and dignities of the juror's office, and the practice of duelling. In addition, he undertook heavy tasks in the Commons, wrote twelve philosophical pieces, and became a judge and the President of the new Court of the Verge. The high regard in which James held Bacon's services became very evident when, in 1611, on establishing by Patent the Court of the

Verge, he decided to appoint the Solicitor to its Presidency. The King's intention was that the new tribunal, which he was establishing on his own warrant, should supersede the old Court of the Marshalsea. The range of the latter had been too narrow and uncertain. The new court's jurisdiction would extend to all offences, except breach of private contract, committed by any subject within the Verge of the King's House, an area with a radius of twelve miles. James still retained vivid memories of the Gunpowder Plot. He was apprehensive of the Recusants, who were ever plotting, and of conniving Puritans, who were becoming increasingly bolder in their demands. He had been reflecting of late, too, on the assassination of Henry IV of France (1610). He had also been taking advice from his Solicitor-General.

In his address on the occasion of the opening of the new court, his first speech as a judge, Bacon describes the Verge as a "carpet spread about the king's chair of estate," and declares that "where the king cometh, there should come peace and order, and an awe and reverence in men's hearts." The newly appointed judge does not overlook a reminder to the court of the privileges of the King's subjects. "It is," he says, "the happy estate and condition of the subject of this realm of England, that he is not to be impeached in his life, lands, or goods, by flying rumours, or wandering fames and reports, or secret and privy inquisitions; but by the oath and presentment of men of honest condition, in the face of justice." Sections of his address present evidence of a change in Bacon's attitude towards the Roman Catholics after the Gunpowder Plot, and towards the Puritans after the Hampton Court Conference. The toleration manifest in his *Letter of Advice* (1584) to Elizabeth and in his more recent *Certain Considerations* (1603) is now modified. He bluntly asserts that there are to be no "contempts" of "the service of Almighty God," and illustrates what he means by his words: "For contempts of our church and service," he says, "they are comprehended in that known name ... recusancy; which offence hath many branches and dependencies; the wife-recusant, she tempts; the church papist, he feeds and relieves; the corrupt schoolmaster, he soweth tares; the dissembler, he conformeth and doth not communicate." In a second reference, this to the Puritans, Bacon reminds the jurors that "because the vulgar people are sometimes led with vain and fond prophecies; if any such shall be published, to the end to move stirs or tumults, this is ... punished by a year's imprisonment and loss of goods; and of this also shall you inquire." The judge further instructs the jury on a question which concerns both Puritans and Roman Catholics: "If any minister refuse to use the book of Common-prayer, or wilfully swerveth in divine service from that book; or if any person whatsoever do scandalize that book, and speak openly and maliciously in derogation of it; such men do but make a rent in the garment, and such are by you to be inquired of."

Bacon's speech on this occasion contains some of his early reflections on the subject of duelling. He observes that, with the increase in this practice, life has grown so cheap that it is "set at the price of words, and every petty scorn and disgrace can have no other reparation." Through duelling "the very life of the law is almost taken away." English law makes many distinctions in the question of the taking of life, "but yet no such difference as the wanton humours and braveries of men have under a reverend name of honour and reputation invented." In a later speech when, as Attorney-General, he argues a case of duelling before the Star Chamber, Bacon finds occasion to remark that if this practice continues and prevails, English legal yearbooks and statute books must give way to French and Italian pamphlets. Already it is being said, sometimes in scorn, that the law of England makes "no difference between foul murder and the killing of a man upon fair terms as they now call it." The seed of the mischief is being nourished by "vain

discourses, and green and unripe conceits." As by a kind of be-
witching or sorcery, which enchants immature minds, the evil
has so grown that "the stream of vulgar opinion" makes it
necessary to attempt the life of another, "or else there is no
living or looking upon men's faces." The growth of duelling is
a consequence of a misunderstanding and wrong conception of
fortitude and valor. "For fortitude distinguisheth of the
grounds of quarrels whether they be just; and not only so, but
whether they be worthy; and setteth a better price upon men's
lives than to bestow them idly; nay it is weakness and dis-
esteem of a man's self, to put a man's life upon such liedger
performances: a man's life is not to be trifled away; it is to be
offered up and sacrificed to honourable services, public merits,
good causes, and noble adventures." The notion underlying
what are deemed affairs of honor is a "fond and false disguise
or puppetry of honour" which is set up in defiance of the
"honour of religion, law, and the king." In English tradition
"the fountain of honour is the king and his aspect." From these
flow justice to the courts of law. When revenge for wrong is
taken out of the magistrates' hands, contrary to God's ordi-
nance, "and every man shall bear the sword, not to defend, but
to assail; and private men begin once to presume to give law to
themselves, and to right their own wrongs . . . the state by this
means shall be like to a distempered and imperfect body, continually subject to inflammations and convulsions."

During the years of his Solicitorship other matters besides
those of Recusants, Puritans, and duellists were disturbing
Bacon's mind. There was no support in sight for his projected
instauration of the sciences. The *Advancement of Learning* had
failed to make an impact on the King, to whom it was addressed,
or on members of the Court, who ignored it. Political promotion had been slow; Bacon, already in his late forties, was
still only Solicitor-General, a subsidiary officer at the beck and
call of every official in authority. Hobart, the present Attorney-

General, was, in Bacon's opinion, seriously lacking in the capacities required for this office. Robert Cecil, Lord Salisbury, the Secretary of State was transacting the nation's business by covert negotiations at home and abroad. He was playing England's enemies, the French and the Spaniards, one against the other, while secretly collecting pensions from both parties. His allowances from the state and the perquisites which he was collecting from office holders and agents, who sought his goodwill and support, were making the Secretary financially rich, but by his deplorable trading, this cousin was gradually bringing the King to poverty and the constitutional affairs of the kingdom to an impasse.

For the impasse in prospect, not only Cecil but the King, certain judges, and the Commons also were partly to blame. James could better have refrained from interfering continuously with the operation of the established institutions of state and have left the Council, the courts, and the Commons to work out their own problems. His incessant assertion of the Sovereign's Prerogative, sometimes for the maintaining of his own dignity but mainly in justification of questionable Impositions, burdensome Monopolies, improper Purveyance, and outmoded Tenures and Wardships, was bringing that Prerogative under regrettable discussion, even indeed into disrepute.

There was no doubt in Bacon's mind about the historical and continuing priority of the Sovereign's Prerogative in the unwritten constitution of England. The Prerogative, as Bacon often affirmed, was as old as the law itself. Such curbs as had been put upon it had been slowly accumulated by the establishment of precedents from reign to reign, as in the case of the privileges of the Houses of Parliament and the assured jurisdictions of the courts of law. Yet the sovereign himself, in Bacon's opinion, had never been brought under the rule of Parliament or the law. The courts, despite what some lawyers might think and some judges might say, were still King's Courts.

The source of political initiative and of justice as well, no matter how fervently some members of the Commons might contend to the contrary, was still the Throne.

In English history, the initiator and dispenser of law was the King. From early times the King had had his *curia*, or court, and his councillors, but he himself had always remained the source of legislative and judicial power. The King in Council—privy to himself—was in early days a judiciary and parliament combined. Gradually, definite modes of procedure and precedents in judging took shape to form the basis of a law applicable to like cases, common to the whole of England. In the sorting of precedents judges and lawyers, as counsel, had played a part. Parliament, or "parley," had its beginnings in a feudal assembly of knights, summoned for consultation with the King and his Council on such questions as territory, taxes, internal and external policies, and arrangement of governmental offices. While the early "parley," whose members often responded but grudgingly to the King's call, discussed these matters, it never, as a Parliament, assumed the power or right of final judgment or settlement. This lay with the King in Council. Under the Edwards, Parliament was enlarged to include representatives of King and Church, barons, knights, and burgesses. Edward I (1272-1307) invited the enactment of statute after statute by this body. In consequence, the offices of Parliament and King's Council became more or less distinct. Petitions addressed directly to the King were sometimes presented to Parliament for discussion. Gradually it became an assumption that Parliament's consent was proper for the passing of certain statutes, as distinct from judicial precedents, Council's proclamations, and levies of extraordinary taxes. Gradually two Houses of Parliament emerged, one of Commons and another of Lords. Each body became increasingly jealous of its own privileges. Yet, before the days of the present King, it had never been seriously assumed that either House derived its power of "initiative" from any source but the King.

Each court had been established permissively by the King in Council for purposes. The presumption continued that the sovereign remained the final source of right, of law, of justice. The courts remained King's Courts, their advocates King's Counsel. When, in the present reign, Edward Coke called himself "Lord Chief Justice of England" and not "Lord Chief Justice of the King's Bench," he had already made himself a party to far-reaching constitutional change. Probably this fact was not fully comprehended by this judge, who never showed much discernment of constitutional matters. His failure in comprehension was to make him an unwitting precursor of political revolution.

The Court of Common Pleas was a bench of judges, sanctioned by the King and set up at Westminster in King John's reign (1199-1216) for the convenience of subjects who would find it difficult or impossible to follow about the country a king who might be given to journeying. The Court of Chancery was designed by the King in Council as a means to redress miscarriages of justice in courts where the common law, based on precedents, largely prevailed. And so it was in the case of the origins of other courts. Yet early in James' reign the two Houses of Parliament and a variety of courts were advancing definite claims for their respective jurisdictions without any reference, in some instances, to the King's power of initiative.

Constitutional advancement from privilege to privilege, from precedent to precedent, was, in Bacon's opinion, sound and desirable, provided there was no attempt on the part of Parliament, courts of law, or any commission to destroy continuity in constitutional development or to dissipate unity in constitutional administration. A comprehending king would take care to grant more and more political authority to subjects and developing courts of law and to the Commons—which contained the elected representatives of loyal and desiring subjects. Wise kings in the past had done so. If the present occupant of the throne would not so concede, then, in Bacon's mind, two things had firmly to be kept in mind: first, there was to be no giving way on the concessions already won by courts and by Parliament. Second, the continuity of the constitution, according to which the Throne retained powers never conceded to any other institution, was to be guarded against inroads by judges or by members of Parliament who might attempt to set up, as Coke and some lawyers undoubtedly would, *imperium in imperio*.

Time after time in the reign of the present sovereign the Commons had already undertaken to debate what it constitutionally could not question, namely, the King's power within his Prerogative to impose Impositions, grant Monopolies, to establish and continue the Court of the Marches. The chief promoters of unconstitutional debates in the Commons had been the lawyers. The judges of the common law courts had gone so far in their boldness as to warn the Council of the Marches, which had been set up by the King, that if it went beyond certain jurisdictional limits, a Prohibition would be issued to restrain it. They had declared that cases arising in four specified English counties were not to be kept within these limits. The judges, too, had been interfering in increasing degree with the proceedings of the Commissions of the Privy Council and ecclesiastical courts, by issuing Prohibitions for their inhibition until they proved their own right to proceed in cases. When Archbishop Bancroft claimed that the King had "power to take what causes he pleased out of the Judge's hands and to determine them himself," Coke, now Chief Justice of the King's Bench, issused a flat denial. "Then," exclaimed James, "I shall be under the Law, which is treason to affirm." Coke, in comment, quoting Henry de Bracton, replied that "the King ought not to be under any man but under God and the Law."

While pondering these several problems in 1608, Bacon set down in a private notebook called *Commentarius solutus* (*Casual Commentary*) some reflections on current perils to the state, on the King's conduct, the Royal Prerogative, the Secretary of State, the Attorney-General, recent foreign policy, law and judges, lawyers in Parliament. The diarist also made notes on ways and means to promote his scientific projects, and on his private and personal difficulties, such as monetary affairs and certain aspects of his temperament which might be preventing his political promotion. Some of Bacon's "ethical" biographers have raised a great to-do over certain of the personal items in his *Casual Commentary*. Their revulsion, in a display of "moral sensibility," has ranged from indignation to horror. Yet when approached simply, as they should be, those jottings in a diary appear as artless memoranda, largely in self-criticism. As directions for future conduct, they portend nothing sinister; they are but self-helps to a man seeking promotion in public office when he is not of a "politic" nature, as such a nature is regarded in his time. Bacon from his youth had shown shyness, formality in speech, and alternating timorousness and self-assurance, qualities commonly found together in a reserved person of capacity. He had in his make-up some of the stiffness of manner and the censoriousness of speech which belonged to persons reared under Calvinist influence. To his complaining uncle, Lord Burghley, he had found it necessary to explain, in his youth, some of these qualities as the characteristics of a student who lived *in umbra*. Bacon from the beginning had been certain of his gifts of reflection, tongue, and pen. His assurance in these regards had enabled him to give political advice of consequence to sovereigns and the members of the three estates, Lords Spiritual, Lords Temporal, and Commons. It had carried him from success to success in Parliament. Yet even after these achievements and his demonstration of administrative efficiency in the Solicitor-General's office, he was still being looked upon and treated as a person theoretically remote, a man not quite fitted to high public office. On such facts as these Bacon had been ruminating before he jotted down the items of his diary. It had dawned upon his thought that if his political and scientific ends were to be achieved some incidental difficulties would have to be overcome.

In the *Casual Commentary* the diarist reckons that his current income is £4,975, his present debts in sum £4,481, and the monetary worth of his property and offices £24,155. Turning from personal finance to public matters, he notes, among present perils to the state, the King's "poverty and empty coffers," an irresolute Privy Council, daring judges, a hostile Commons, religious unrest, a devious Secretary of State, possible invasion from Scotland, foreign wars, and James' interference with institutions of government. Through the diarist's mind there pass, during the few days in which the *Casual Commentary* is written, some thoughts on ways to obviate these perils: the fixing of the respective jurisdictions of the political and the legal offices in the kingdom; the restoring of the Church to its true limits of authority; the putting into office of "persons *act(ive)* and in their nature *stir(ring)*"; the making use of the Presbytery and nobility of Scotland; the practice by the King of what is majestic and not of a meddling and bargaining sort; "new laws to be compounded and collected"; persuasion of the King to be "lawgiver perpetuus princeps" after a compilation of laws has been made by his present Solicitor-General; "confederacy and more straight amity with the Low Countries"; means for providing the King with funds.

In a note Bacon reveals his own immediate political ambition. He will "succ(eed) Salisbury and amuse the K(ing) and P(rince) [Henry] with pastime and glory." The cousin is, in Bacon's opinion, not fitted in capacity or by motive to be the King's first minister, and James, Bacon thinks, could do much to further the affairs of the kingdom by giving more time to his esteemed amusements and less to attempts to bring under his personal direction settled offices of government. (Bacon's opinion in this regard was to be one of the causes for his optimism when the King's second "favorite," George Villiers, began to undertake the King's tasks in the administration of state.) Three months before the *Casual Commentary* is written, Salisbury has assumed the office of Lord Treasurer; and Bacon includes a reference to means employed by his cousin for replenishing the King's Treasury without recourse to Parliament: "My L(ord) of Salisbury is to be remembered of the great expectation wherewith he enters that he will *moderate new Impositions.*"

On the capacity and performance of Hobart, the Attorney-General, Bacon sets down the jotting, "Solemn goose ... they have made him believe he is wondrous wy (wise). He never beats down unfit suits with law. In persons as in people, some shew more wise than they are." "He will alter a thing, but not mend." "Nibbling solemnly, he distinguisheth, but not apprehendeth." On the subject of judges, lawyers, Prohibitions, and the Royal Prerogative the Solicitor-General records the following reflections:

"The K(ing) assembled his Judges—not all, but certain of them—before their Circuits, and found fault with multitudes of Prohibitions. ... The K(ing) was vehement, and said that more had been granted in four years of his Reign than in forty of former time; and that no kingdom had more honourable Courts of Justice; but, again, none was more cursed with confusion and contention of Prohibitions. Seemed to apprehend the distribution of justice after the French manner was better for the people and fitter for his greatness, saying that this course, to draw all things to Westminster was to make him K(ing) as it were of the Isle of France. ... Warned a surceance of granting Prohibitions for the vacation following."

"Judges to consult with King as well as the King with Judges. ... Query, of making use of my Lord of Canterbury his opposition to the la(wyers), in point of reforming the laws and disprizing mere lawyers."

"To prepare either collect(ions), or at least advice, touching the equalling of laws."

"Rem(inder); to advise the K(ing) ... to keep the lawyers in awe."

"Summary justice belongeth to the King's prerogative. The fountain must run, where the conduits are stopped."

"Being prepared in the matter of Prohibitions. Putting in a claim for the K(ing). The 4 necessities, (1) time, as of war; (2) place, as frontiers remote; (3) person, as [for example] poor [persons] that have no means to sue those that come in by safe-conduct; (4) matter, mixed with State."

As helps to his demeanor, Bacon mentions in advice to himself "struggling against shyness, hurry in speech, brusqueness or formality," and the suppression of "panting and labour of breath and voice" when speaking. Hereafter he will try "not to fall upon the main too sudden; but to induce and intermingle speech of good fashion," and also to "free myself at once from payment of formality and compliment, though with some shew of careless-ness, pride, and rudeness." He intends also, "To set foot and maintain access with his Majesty.... To attend some time his repasts and to fall into a course of familiar discourses. To find means to win a conc(eit), not open but private, of being af-fectionate and assured to the Sco(tch) and fit to succeed Sa(lis-bury).... To have ever in readiness matter to minister talk with every of the great counsellors *respective*, both to induce familiarity and for countenance in public place.... Insinuate myself to become privy to my L(ord) of Salisb(ury's) estate.... To correspond [i.e., conform] with Salisbury in a habit of natural but no way's perilous boldness, and in vivacity, invention, care to cast and enterprise, but with due caution ... to listen how the King is affected in respect of the Prince, and to make use of my industry in it towards the Pr(ince).... To make them [the Lord Chancellor and Lord Treasurer] think they shall find an alteration to their contentment over that [Attorney] which now is.... To furnish my Lord of Suffolk with ornaments for public speeches; to make him think how he should be reverenced by a L(ord) Chancellor, if I were:—princelike.... To take notes, in tables, when I attend the Council; and sometimes to move out of a memorial, shewed and seen. To have particular occasions, fit and grateful and continual, to maintain private speech with every the great persons, and sometimes drawing more than one of them together, *ex imitatione* Att(orney). This especially in public places and without care or affectation."

In the optimistic mood of a dreamer Bacon sets down some thoughts about his instauration of the sciences. He thinks of "a place to command wits and pens, Westminster, Eton, Winchester, specially Trinity College in Cambridge, St. John's in Cambridge, Magdalene College in Oxford, and bespeaking this betimes with the King, my Lord Archbishop, my Lord Treasurer." It occurs to him that either Salisbury or Bancroft, the respective chancellors of Cambridge and Oxford, may be induced to influence one or the other of the Universities towards the granting of a college for the promotion of a new knowledge. He entertains the hope that the junior scholars of the Universities will prove receptive of a new kind of fruitful inquiry in replacement of frustrating Peripatetic argumentation. Possible backers of his plan would include his friend Bishop Andrewes, "single, rich, sickly, a professor to some experiments," and the Earl of Northumberland—who was his late brother's friend and is now the patron of Thomas Harriot, the mathematician—and perhaps Harriot himself. He also thinks of the imaginative Sir Walter Raleigh "in the tower," the court physicians Leonard Poe and John Hammond, and one of the Scottish Murrays who is treasurer to Prince Henry. If an already established college could be put to new use, or a new foundation obtained, it will be provided with "laborities and engines, vaults and furnaces, terraces for insulation," and the like, for the carrying on of experiments and observations and the compiling of histories of operations in nature and the mechanical arts. Investigations in all sorts of phenomena, including those of motion, will be pursued. There will be scientific correspondence with members of foreign societies. The diarist thinks of "giving pensions to four, for search to compile the two histories"; of marvels and the mechanical arts; of providing facilities for inventors; of having "two galleries with statuas for Inventors past, and spaces, or bases, for Inventors to come. And a library and an Inginary." These practices will, in his opinion, further a scientific advance, since "marvels" or monsters, the manual arts, and "works" in practical operation—which inventions are—have no sanctioned place, strictly speaking, in traditional histories of natural science.

The *Casual Commentary* continues with more notes on the institute of science: "Query, of the order and discipline, to be mixed with some points popular to invite many to contribute and join. Query, of the rules and prescripts of their studies and inquiries. Allowance for travelling. Allowance for experiments. Intelligence and correspondence with the Universities abroad. Query, of the manner and prescripts touching secrecy, tradition, and publication. Query, of removes and expulsions in case, within a time, some invention worthy be not produced. And likewise query of the honours and rewards for inventions."

As for the diarist's own philosophical writings: the *Advancement of Learning* will be translated into Latin; a new piece, *Cogitata et visa (Thoughts and Impressions)*, will be circulated privately; the Aphorisms on scientific method will be added to; and the Tables of Heat, Cold, and Sound, on which some work has been done, will be completed. In pieces to be prepared the author will "discuss scornfully of the Grecians, with some better respect to ... the utmost antiquities and the mysteries of the poets," and perhaps make an "oration '*ad filios*' " to prospective disciples. The issue of the last of these musings are *Redargutio philosophiarum (Refutation of Philosophies,* 1608) and *Sapientia veterum (Wisdom of the Ancients,* 1609).

In 1610, two years after he made a note in his *Casual Commentary* on Salisbury's management of the King's Treasury, Bacon was to see the Sovereign of the Realm turned into a bargainer without kingly majesty—as Bacon later told James—under the leading of this Lord Treasurer. When Salisbury took over the office of Lord Treasurer, in 1608, he found a disparity of £83,000 a year between the King's ordinary revenue and his ordinary expenditure. There was, besides, an accumulated debt of £1,000,000, half as much as Elizabeth had been voted in supply during her whole reign. (Elizabeth had left James with debts.) To relieve the situation, Salisbury had been relying on the King's Prerogative for the levying of Impositions on exports and imports, and by these unpopular means had acquired an additional annual revenue of £60,000. He had also collected £10,000 by a tax on alehouses. Early in 1610 the Lord Treasurer presented the House of Commons with a detailed statement of the King's revenues and his necessary expenditures. He then made an intimation of a "retribution" in prospect from James, as a response to a desired "contribution" from the Commons. The "retribution," Salisbury indicated, would be conditional upon the receipt of a requested "contribution." In plain words, the Lord Treasurer, who was also the Secretary of State, was undertaking to arrange with the Commons a straight business deal, in which a portion of the King's Prerogative—the historically originating source of justice and rights—would be negotiated away at a price.

On announcing his plan, Salisbury found the mood of the Lower House far less pliant and conciliatory than he had hoped for. Members of the Commons were conscious of too many accumulated grievances. In 1604, the first year of his first English Parliament, James, whose Parliament in Scotland had been but a court of record, had provoked the Lower House into making the Remonstrance that "The privilege of our House, and therein the liberties and stability of the whole Kingdom, hath been more universally and dangerously impugned than ever, as we suppose, since the beginning of Parliaments." The Commons was now of the opinion that in the mind of the King its "privileges" did not exist. Ever since the Remonstrance had been presented, James had been acting as if this petition of grievance had never been. His Lord Treasurer had been using dubious means to obtain what it was the Common's office to supply. After petition by the Lower House only the lesser of many offensive Monopolies, granted by the King, had been suppressed. The rest had been left intact, to the continued constraint of manufacture and trade, and to the increasing of the wealth of the rich and the decreasing of the means of the poor. There was still the continuance of the abuse of power by ecclesiastical commissions, and of legislative arbitrariness on the part of the King's Privy Council in dealings with Wardships, Feudal Tenure, and the Council of the Marches. These three outmoded institutions, despite complaints and entreaties in and by Parliament, were still being retained, as institutions within the King's Prerogative. The evils of Purveyance still flourished after a petition, on proven legal grounds, had been presented to the Sovereign. Clergy who could not meet the requirements of the ruling bishops were still undergoing persecution for opinions on which God alone, and no prelate, could pass judgment. The silencing, depriving, and excommunicating of Puritan clergy for relatively minor offences was increasing the number of parishes without resident ministers.

In the opinion of many members of the Commons the inhabitants of the Marches were subjects who deserved availability to courts similar to those within cities, where ordinary judges made their circuits and employed the common law. As for Wardship and Tenure: there had been a time when minors were conveniently made wards of the Crown and parts of the revenues from their estates sequestered because they could not be enrolled in the King's forces; when knights who held their lands in tenure were fittingly required to render an equivalence if they themselves could not do battle for their sovereign. But this time was long past. The occasions of present exactions from wards and knights had little relation to original military reasons and circumstances.

The Commons had already advanced a proposition of grievances over Tenure and Wardships. The King, through Salisbury, had indicated a "gracious construction of their proposition," but had added the observation that it was their duty to "attend his Majesty's times at his good pleasure." On that occasion Bacon had been chosen as the representative of the Commons "to treat of compounding for tenures" with the King. On commission from the Commons he had addressed the Lords, "moving and persuading" them to join with the members of the Lower House in petition to the King, "to obtain liberty to treat of a composition with his Majesty for Wards and Tenures." In his speech he had said: "We have grave professors of the common law, who will define unto us that those are parts of sovereignty, and of the regal prerogative, which cannot be communicated with subjects: but for tenures in substance, there is none of your lordships but have them, and few of us but have them .... the subject is capable of tenures; which shews that they are not regal, nor any point of sovereignty. . . . So have we many deputy lieutenants to your lordships, and many commissioners that have been for musters and levies, that can tell us, that the service and defence of the realm hath in these days little dependence upon tenures. So then we perceive that it is no bond or ligament of government; no spur of honour, no bridle of obedience. Time was when it had other uses, and the name of knight's service imports it: but *vocabula manent, res fugiunt.*"

Despite such representations and earlier petitions on other grievances, the King's Lord Treasurer was offering no more than a "retribution" for a monetary "contribution." Once more the House of Commons was being treated as if it were a mere source of financial supply, devoid of political power and even of political sense. What was more, the Lord Treasurer was confronting the House, not with a proper supplication for supply, or even with a request, but simply with a business offer, a mere "contract," with "consideration"—which is the essence of contract—attached. Some two weeks after Salisbury had announced

what came to be known as the "Great Contract," he began his
bargaining in earnest. His first request was for a payment to the
King of £600,000 down and £200,000 annually. The Commons,
after four weeks' consideration of this, offered the King £100,000
annually on condition that he make the services of knights, as
King's tenants, a matter of tenure of land with fixed and determinate, and not arbitrary, equivalence. A month later the Commons repeated their counteroffer. But the day before they did
this, the King had obtained a loan of £100,000 from the City of
London. Immediately his Treasurer became a more difficult
party to negotiation.

Salisbury now raised the price of a royal concession. The
King, he said, while not intending to diminish his Prerogative,
would meet the known wishes of the Commons on the question
of Wardships, provided that they paid him £200,000 annually
and made a grant of £600,000 immediately, and in addition reim-
bursed him with a sum equivalent to the worth of the Wardships. The Commons replied by withdrawing their counteroffer.
Salisbury, now resorting to intimidation, warned the Lower
House that to engage in any discusssion of the King's right to
levy any Impositions his Majesty thought fit "were to bark
against the moon." The Privy Council also sent an order to the
Speaker of the House to make a statement, "as from the King,"
warning its members that any question "as to his right to impose
duties upon merchandise exported and imported had been settled
judicially, and was not to be disputed in the House." The Commons took note that this message was not from the King himself, but from the Council, and then declared "that the same
message, coming not immediately from his Majesty, should not
be received as a message; and that in all messages from his
Majesty, the Speaker, before he delivered them, should first ask
leave of the House, according as had anciently been accustomed."

Bacon, who regarded this declaration as a constitutional

affront to the King—which it was intended to be—took the opportunity to remind both parties to the controversy of their places in the government of the kingdom. "The King's sovereignty," he said, "and the liberty of parliament, are as the two elements and principles of this estate; which, though the one be more active, the other more passive, yet they do not cross or destroy the one the other; but they strengthen and maintain the one the other. Take away liberty of parliament, the griefs of the subject will bleed inwards: sharp and eager humours will not evaporate; and then they must exulcerate; and so may endanger the sovereignty itself. On the other side, if the king's sovereignty receive diminution, or any degree of contempt with us that are born under an hereditary monarchy, so as the motions of our estate cannot work in any other frame or engine, it must follow, that we shall be a meteor, or *corpus imperfecte mistum;* which kind of bodies come speedily to confusion and dissolution."

Soon the King appeared in person to address the two Houses of Parliament. He declared that he had the right to levy any Impositions he thought proper, implying that he had the right not only to make levies on exports and imports but to impose taxes on merchandise and all other properties. The next morning the Commons, thus affronted with what they regarded as a threat to "liberties" and "privileges," appointed a committee "to devise upon some course to be taken to inform his Majesty how much the liberties of the subject and the privileges of the Parliament were impeached by this inhibition to debate his Prerogative."

Bacon advised the House not to press for, or even to assume, the right to question the King's Prerogative, but to proceed by petition, since the matter had been so determined within the Commons itself in the reign of Elizabeth—on Bacon's own advice. The Commons, this caution notwithstanding, sent a message to the King with a Petition of Right to discuss Impositions. James informed them that the House had misinterpreted the Council's intention. Bacon again advised the Commons, on constitutional grounds, not to press explicitly for a right. Accordingly a petition was framed "by way of grievance, implying the right, though not in express terms." In response to this, some Impositions were removed, and the King, in a great concession, declared his willingness to assent to an Act whereby his power would be suspended to levy further Impositions upon merchandise without consent of Parliament. Three days after James had granted these concessions, the Commons decided to supply him with £180,000 a year. Salisbury, however, now quoting a letter from the King, said his bargaining price was £200,000, and added the warning that if this offer was not accepted, it would never again be repeated and Parliament would be immediately dissolved. The Commons agreed to pay the Lord Treasurer his price, but only on condition that some eight specified concessions would be granted by the King in return. Parliament was then prorogued for three months.

The Privy Council, meanwhile, became apprehensive of the temper of the Commons and began to question whether their forbidding of certain actions, under penalties, by Proclamation was not presumptive of a power to legislate which they did not possess. The Lord Chancellor, Egerton, expressed the opinion that this power lay within their disposing, as a power of the King, and that, if there was no precedent in law to justify the exercise of the power, then the courts should establish one which would. When the Chief Justice of the Common Pleas, Edward Coke, was invited to state his view on this question, he asked for time to consult with the other judges. Bacon, aware that Coke would be put into a state of confusion when confronted with this constitutional problem, reminded him of the fact that he had already sanctioned the King's power to legislate, when as a judge in the Court of Common Pleas he had in "divers cases" given sentence in keeping with a Proclamation against building in or about London. Coke, who did not want the King's power mentioned in any discussion of the law courts, replied that "it was better to go back than to go on in the wrong way." After consultation, the judges reported their opinion that "the King by his Proclamation cannot create any offence which was not an offence before." With this James intimated his agreement.

James, after Parliament was again convened, asked the Commons for a "resolute and speedy answer whether they would proceed with the Contract, yea, or no." The Lower House, suspicious that Salisbury was up to some new mischief, demanded the inclusion of certain provisory clauses within what the King now called "the Contract." The Commons asked for the guarantee, first, that hereafter Parliament would be regularly summoned; secondly, that the £200,000 granted annually would go into the kingdom's Treasury and not be alienated to other purposes—such as gifts to the King's favorites—and, thirdly, "that this £200,000 be not doubled or trebled by enhancing of the coin by the King." When faced with these stipulations, the King became enraged and, perhaps with the intention of bringing a shameless negotiation to an end, countered the demands of the Commons by mentioning an exorbitant sum in price. James in the end had probably recoiled from his Treasurer's putting his regal Majesty up for sale. The King dissolved Parliament on February 29th, 1611. Three months before, November 25th, 1610, Salisbury had received a letter filled with rage and fury from James. In this the King reminded his Treasurer that the Privy Council had "parted irresolute" after a meeting, and, as for Parliament, he had suffered with forbearance "this assembly these seven years, and from them received more disgraces, censures, and ignominies than ever Prince did endure." The Council had advised patience on his part, and this he had already exercised; but he could not "have asinine patience."

The Lord Treasurer was now reaping the fruits of a policy

begun and continued without regard to political principle. He had been squeezed by King and Commons in a deal which had turned a sovereign ruler of a kingdom into a huckster. The Sovereign was showing something more than annoyance. Salisbury became ill. Failure in dealing with Parliament and resultant cares, including a failing confidence on the part of the King, were increasing his infirmities.

Bacon had long been aware that Salisbury had kept him out of political office, yet he had always been on civil terms with his cousin. Bacon had not forgotten their family kinship. He had been meticulous in his service to Robert Cecil; had gone to him after he had been bullied as a counsel in court by Coke; had appealed to him on occasions for help when hard presssed by debtors, and had received aid. Salisbury had arranged for the dedication of the *Advancement of Learning* to the King, after getting its author a knighthood. Before that, he had warned him about rumors arising from his discussing with the Queen the conduct of Essex. Bacon had dedicated *De sapientia veterum* to his cousin. After Salisbury had been ailing for several months, Bacon wrote his cousin a New Year's letter, in January, 1612:

It may please your good Lordship,
I would entreat the new year to answer for the old, in my humble thanks to your Lordship . . . for many your favours . . . *though I find age and decay grow upon me*—yet I may have a flash or two of spirit left to do you service. And I do protest before God, without compliment or any light vein of mind, that if I knew in what course of life to do you best service, I could take it, and make my thoughts, which now fly to many pieces, be reduced to that centre. But all this is no more than I am, which is not much, but yet the entire of him that is.

Salisbury died on May 24th, 1612. The King was now without an experienced Secretary of State. His Privy Council was ineffectual. There was no Parliament in fact or in prospect. The Treasury was empty. Accumulated debts could be paid only by what might be raised through Impositions, Monopolies,

Feudal Tenure, Wardships, and other means within the Prerogative. Until 1621 there would be no Parliament in England,
except one of two months' duration, which Bacon would
arrange. This would be summoned on April 5th and dissolved on
June 7th, 1614. The destiny of the kingdom for a period of nine
years was to be in the hands of the King, his Council, his judges,
two of James' rascally favorites, Robert Carr (created Earl of
Somerset in 1613) and George Villiers (created Duke of Buckingham in 1617)—and Francis Bacon. During these years, rule
in England, so far as James was concerned, might have reverted
to a primitive form, but for certain institutions which the King
could neither decimate nor reduce: the courts with their rights,
the law with its statutes and precedents, and the hard-won
"privileges" of subjects. Parliament was in abeyance because
the Commons would neither surrender their privileges, nor
allow the King to take them captive through threat or specious
promises. Throughout the kingdom there was dissatisfaction
with the exercise of the Royal Prerogative and disquiet over
the operations of the commissions and courts of the Privy
Council. The times, in Bacon's opinion, were dangerous in the
extreme for the unwritten constitution of England. Even the
common law judges, under the leadership of Coke, were far
from certain of what was and what was not proper constitutional procedure. The courts and the constitution were to be
preserved in a continuity through great trials and hazards by
one man and one man alone, Francis Bacon. In this regard he
became for a period the axial officer of the kingdom. He
managed, without ill-deserving, to keep the constitution intact
and in operation, to maintain the law and liberty of subjects,
and to preserve "the King's honour," through wise, skilful, and
just resorts.

VIII

BACON AS ATTORNEY-GENERAL

Bacon's humane regard of his cousin notwithstanding, it was definitely his opinion that the King should not appoint another of Robert Cecil's sort to the office of Secretary of State. The Solicitor-General made no attempt to conceal from James this opinion or his desire to obtain the place for himself. Long denied promotion by Salisbury, Bacon believed, for good reasons, that he was the one subject of the King who could prove successful in mitigating James' financial, Parliamentary, and general constitutional circumstances. Bacon had been dismayed by the manner of Cecil's bringing of the Throne into disrepute with members of the Commons and their constituencies. He was distressed at the lack of a Commons, the proper, constitutional source of the King's supply. He deplored the prospect of seeing the coffers of the King filled through means which depended solely on the use of the Prerogative. He began a draft of a frank, unfinished letter to James with these words:

If I shall seem in these few lines to write *majora quam pro fortuna*, it may please your Majesty to take it to be an effect not of presumption but of affection. For of the one I was never noted; and for the other I could never shew it hitherto to the full; having been as a hawk tied to another's fist [Salisbury's], that mought sometimes bate [i.e., flutter] and proffer, but could never fly.

In a completed letter (May 31st, 1612), Bacon wrote the King:

Your Majesty hath lost a great subject and a great servant. But if I should praise him in propriety, I should say that he was a fit man to keep things from growing worse, but no very fit man to reduce things to be much better. For he loved to have the eyes of all Israel a little too much upon himself, and to have all business still under the hammer, and like clay in the hands of the potter, to mould it as he thought good; so that he was more *in operatione* than *in opere*. And though he had fine passages of action, yet the real conclusions came slowly on. So that although your Majesty hath grave counsellors and worthy persons left, yet you do as it were turn a leaf, wherein if your Majesty shall give a frame and constitution to matters, before you place the persons, in my simple opinion it were not amiss. But the great matter and most instant for the present, is the consideration of a Parliament, for two effects: the one for the supply of your estate, the other for the better knitting of the hearts of your subjects unto your Majesty . . . for both which, Parliaments have been and are the antient and honourable remedy.

Now because I take myself to have a little skill in that region . . . though no man can say but I was a perfect and peremptory royalist, yet every man makes me believe that I was never one hour out of credit with the lower house; my desire is to know, whether your Majesty will give me leave to meditate and propound unto you some preparative remembrances touching the future Parliament.

In another letter Bacon entreated the King to employ his services. He wrote:

My principal end being to do your Majesty service, I crave leave to make at this time to your Majesty this most humble oblation of myself. . . . Your Majesty may have heard somewhat that my father was an honest man, and somewhat you may have seen of myself, though not to make any true judgment by, because I have hitherto had only *potestatem verborum*, nor that neither. I was three of my young years bred with an ambassador in France; and since, I have been an old truant in the school-house of your council-chamber, though on the second form; yet longer than any that now sitteth hath been upon the head form. If your Majesty find any aptness in me, or if you find any scarcity in others, whereby you may think it fit for your service to remove me to business of State; although I have a fair way before me for profit (and by your Majesty's grace and favour for honour and advancement), and in a course less exposed to the blasts of fortune, yet . . . I will be ready as a chessman to be wherever your Majesty's royal hand shall set me.

In the last of the sentences quoted from this letter Bacon employs an analogy from the game of chess. The same analogy, whose meaning would be immediately clear to James, is to be found in Bacon's statement of the relationship between the placets of Revelation and ethical modes of conduct, which are derived, as "inferences," from these. Chessmen are moved on a chequered board according to prescribed rules. Similarly, specific modes of ethical action are governed by rules, or placets, which are declared and given in Divine Revelation, and not made by those who perform or contrive these actions. In the present use of the analogy, Bacon is regarding kingship as a Divine bestowal of sovereignty and political initiative. The sovereign by virtue of this bestowal is the source of political justice. Legal precedents, statutes, and judicial "mercies" are but derivations from the King's sovereign justice. The makers and administrators of these derivations are to be "moved" in accordance with the Sovereign's supreme justice, which is not originated by persons subject to it or engaged in dispensing it, whether they be members of the Privy Council, judges, Attorneys, Solicitors, Parliamentarians, or ordinary voters. Political legislation and legal dispensing are, so far as initiating sovereignty is concerned, always permissions on the part of the King.

Bacon, despite his entreaties to the King, was given neither the Secretaryship of State, which he greatly desired, nor the Mastership of the Wards, which he also sought—although he felt so sure of obtaining the latter that, as William Rawley later reported, he "put most of his men into new cloaks" for the occasion of its assumption. For almost two years, James refused to entrust any person with the Secretaryship. Finally, in 1614, he gave the office to Sir Ralph Winwood, a diplomat in the foreign service, a man without Parliamentary experience and —what was more to the point in James' thinking—with no Parliamentary ties.

However, in 1613 Bacon was granted the office on which he had set his heart twenty years before, the Attorney-Generalship. To make this accommodation, the occupant, Sir Henry Hobart, was moved into the Court of Common Pleas and Sir Edward Coke, one of the judges in this court, was promoted to the office of Chief Justice of the King's Bench. On his being thus promoted, Coke was made a member of the Privy Council. Three years later, Bacon, too, became a member of the Council. In 1617 Bacon was promoted to Lord Keeper; one year thereafter he was made Lord Chancellor and Baron Verulam, and in 1621 Viscount St. Albans.

Chief among the causes for Bacon's failure to obtain the Secretaryship in 1612 was the belief, shared by the King and the Council, that the Solicitor-General, despite his defences of the Royal Prerogative against assaults by Commons and common law judges, was a Parliamentary man. Risking and suffering Elizabeth's displeasure, Bacon had supported the claims of the Lower House. More than once he had been chosen by the Commons as their delegate in dealings with the Lords, the Council, and the King. Bacon was undoubtedly bent on allowing only so much to remain within the Prerogative as could not be taken away by appeal to precedent. On more than one occasion his arguments, filled with historical erudition and framed with great resource, had been employed to this end. His speeches were full of deferences to the King, but his deeds, when he acted as the spokesman of the Commons, spoke louder than his words. Those who held this opinion of the Solicitor-General were to have their belief confirmed by the Commons' treatment of the Parliamentarian they still trusted in the short-lived Parliament of 1614. Then, with a new sense of authority, members of the Lower House were to question the propriety of an Attorney-General's occupying a seat in the Commons. Yet they would make an exception in Bacon's case. After enacting the rule that no Attorney-General should frequent the Lower House, the Commons would indeed make Bacon their spokesman in a proposed dealing with the House of Lords.

Although denied the office of Secretary of State, Bacon was immediately called upon for advice by the frustrated, suspicious, and somewhat fearful James. While still Solicitor, Bacon found himself confronted with great problems. There was the question of the King's debts, of the emptiness of the Treasury, of James' conflicts with Parliament, and his proneness to interfere in the administration of the offices of government. The courts of law required attention. The law itself required study, especially because Coke had been making digests of cases according to his own formulas and under the assumption that the common law contained all that was essential in legal justice. Not to be overlooked were the problems occasioned by the agents of Rome and by the Puritans, both parties bent on overthrowing the presumably settled principles and practices of the Established Church. In dealing with each of these difficult matters, in whatever capacity, Bacon would feel required to see that the Sovereign's honor was kept intact while the liberty and rights of his subjects were sustained. There was one complicated puzzle which could not be evaded, or seemingly solved: this concerned the King's Scottish "favorite," Robert Carr, a physically vigorous, morose, and sly individual, who once had served as James' personal page, and was now, as Viscount Rochester (1611), distributing public offices according to the amounts of the perquisites he could exact, and advising the King on questions of domestic and foreign policies in the secrecy of his closet.

Bacon made a successful attempt to lessen the influence of

the King and his favorite on the ordinary administration of state by suggesting the restriction of the sovereign's own signature to documents of unusual importance and requesting permission from James to have the Council certify the others. At the King's behest the Solicitor examined such means as might serve for the replenishment of the Treasury: revenues from crown lands, customs, taxes, Monopolies, and industries which, in an opinion of James, could be aided through loans from a bank established to this end. Bacon successfully advised against the establishment of the bank in question and reported on inefficiency and fraud in the administration of customs and taxes. The Solicitor, who held that Parliament was the rightful source of the King's main revenue, warned James against expecting too much from the sources he had examined. He wrote James in caution, employing references which might make an impression on the learned recipient: "Generally upon this subject of the repair of your Majesty's means, I beseech your Majesty to give me leave to make this judgment: that your Majesty's recovery must be by the medicine of the Galenists and Arabians, and not of the Chemists and Paracelsians. For it will not be wrought by any one fine extract or strong water, but by a skilful compound of a number of ingredients, and those by just weight and proportion. . . . And secondly, that as your Majesty's growing behindhand hath been the work of time, so must likewise your Majesty's coming forth and making even." Bacon then added the pointed warning: "I forsee that if your Majesty shall propound to yourself to do it *per saltum*, it can hardly be without accidents of prejudice to your honour, safety, or profit."

Bacon gave the King some comfort in his present misery by observing that financial debts do not necessarily bring diminution to the greatness of persons; and that the Divine Majesty sometimes prefers uncertainties to certainties for those dependent on Him, because the former teach "a more immediate dependence on his providence." The Solicitor also made the entreaty "that your Majesty, in respect of the hasty freeing of your State, would not descend to any means, or degree of means, which carrieth not a symmetry with your majesty and greatness. . . . To have your wants and necessities, in particular, as it were hanged up in two tablets before the eyes of your Lords and Commons, to be talked of for four months together. . . . To have such worms of Aldermen to lend for ten in the hundred upon good assurance. . . . To pretend even carriage between your Majesty's rights and the ease of the people and to satisfy neither—these courses and the like I hope are gone with the deviser of them: which have turned your Majesty to inestimable prejudice."

It was Bacon's hope that the King, in order to speed both his financial and his political recovery, could be persuaded to summon a Parliament, "the ancient and royal way of providing the King with treasure." He expressed the desire that "this Parliament may be a little reduced to the more ancient form . . . which was to voice the Parliament to be for some other business of state, and not merely for money." Bacon was aware that any subsidy voted by any conceivable Parliament would be far from enough to supply the Treasury; there would still have to be taxes and duties. It had long been so with the exchequers of sovereigns. The twelve subsidies granted to Elizabeth by Parliament during her whole reign had not amounted to more than £2,000,000. In consequence, she had been hard-pressed to pay her ministers abroad and officers at home. To make ends meet, her household staff had been driven to exacting bribes and her political officers to collecting perquisites. The Queen had been thought parsimonious when she was in fact poor. Elizabeth, however, had enjoyed certain advantages over James: she was beset by threatening enemies, and Parliament would never seriously question any subsidy required for the protection of their Queen and her kingdom against the designs of Spain and France.

Moreover, as a queen, Elizabeth was regarded with awe, as a person partaking in the divinity which in Tudor times had still been accorded without question to sovereigns. But in this later reign, the Commons was refusing to support a king who had thought it wise to buttress popular belief with reasoned argument. The doctrine of the divine right of rulers had been expounded by James in theologico-philosophical treatises, and yet his very Prerogative was being questioned—in confirmation of Bacon's opinion that there are abstruse questions whose solutions should not be submitted to the general public for a verdict.

The Privy Council, when confronted with the fact that the King could not meet his pressing debts or pay his officers, bestirred themselves. They appointed a committee to consider ways and means to curtail expenditures and to tap such legal sources of supply as might be available. This committee's proposals, however, promised but little increase in revenue. Bacon, now Attorney-General, strenuously advised that a Parliament be called, pointing out that "few actions of Estate that are harsh, have been in agitation or rumour of late; and the old grievances, having been long broached, wax dead and flat." He argued that "if any man dissuade a Parliament, he is exposed to the imputation of creating or nourishing diffidence between the King and his people; he draweth upon himself the charge of the consequences of the King's wants; and he is subject to interpretation that he doth it for private doubts and ends." Bacon also uttered another caution, saying, "I conceive the sequel of good or evil not so much to depend upon Parliament, or not Parliament, as upon the course which the King shall hold with his Parliament." The Council decided, in February, 1614, that a Parliament should be summoned. In preparation for its meeting, Bacon compiled various notes and prepared a letter of advice for the King. He asked James to "put off the person of a merchant and a contractor," and said in warning: "Until your Majesty have tuned your instrument you will have no harmony. I for my part think it a thing inestimable to your Majesty's safety and service that you for once part with Parliament with love and reverence." He advised that Impositions by the Council be *"buried and silenced,"* and asked for a consideration of "gracious and plausible laws" designed for the "comfort and contentment" of the people. He mentioned, as one of many matters of serious concern, "the winning or bridling of the Lawyers (which are the *literae vocales* of the House) that they may further the King's causes or at least fear to oppose them."

Lawyers had become prominent in the Commons after the relaxing of a rule which required that a member reside in the constituency which he represented. The solicitors of London and other large centres offered themselves as candidates, and were elected in considerable proportion to the Commons. Many of them, skilled in speech, were prone, for obvious reasons, to accommodate their rhetoric to the opinions of an ever-increasing body of elected Nonconformists from the shires. "Law and pulpit," to use a phrase of John Chamberlain, became a combined means for giving a bad "colour" to the reputation of the King, his Council, and the Council's courts and ecclesiastical commissions. Not a few of the lawyers, under the influence of Coke, became promoters of a legal *imperium in imperio*.

Parliament was summoned and met on the fifth of April, 1614. It was to be known as the Addled Parliament. The King addressed the two Houses and professed his affection for both, and for all his subjects as well. Some members of the Commons immediately charged that the Lower House had been "packed" by "small undertakers," persons pledged by varied means as individuals, and not as proper representatives of constituencies, to support the King's cause. The House demanded their expulsion. Bacon, who was fearful lest Parliament again "be dissolved, as gamesters use to call for new cards when they distrust a pack," argued against any attempt at an impossible sifting of rumors to discover "deputies" suspected of betraying "the people" to the defeat of the "public good." As one long associated with courts of law, he knew "how far men will ingenuously confess, how far they will politically deny, and what we can make and gather upon their confession, and how we shall prove against their denial; it is an endless piece of work." "For protestations, and professions, and apologies," he told the House, "I never found them very fortunate; they rather increase suspicion than clear it." Keeping in mind the Lords, the Council, and the King—whom he had warned against using "undertakers"—Bacon exclaimed: "That private men should undertake for the Commons of England! Why, a man mought as well undertake for the four elements. It is a thing so giddy, and so vast, as cannot enter into the brain of a sober man."

Winwood, the inexperienced Secretary of State, tried at the beginning—contrary to established Parliamentary procedure—to have a measure for supply considered immediately. The Commons began to debate whether hereafter an Attorney-General, as the King's officer, should be admitted to the House, and determined in the negative. Bacon they would, however, allow to remain for the present sitting. A member offered a bill against Impositions, and another a bill against ecclesiastical courts. The House asked for a meeting with the Lords on the question of Impositions, and appointed Bacon their spokesman. The discovery had been made that since the meeting of the last Parliament, whose protest had led to the removal of many Impositions, there had come into operation three or four hundred more, some of which were of greater profit to the King. Worse still, certain of these Impositions were for the benefit not only of the present sovereign, but of his "generation" as well, his heirs in perpetuity. Bacon, who on more than one occasion had told the Commons that the power to institute Impositions lay within the Royal Prerogative, was now, as he always had been, jealous of maintaining whatever had by precedent restricted the employment of this Prerogative. The present case was one in which the Royal Prerogative was not running in what Bacon regarded as "the ancient channels and banks." An ominous feature of the King's grant of the Monopolies now under discussion was the undermining for all time of a privilege of the House of Commons, the constitutionally sanctioned providing of the sovereign with supply. Impositions had been recognized as necessities of the time, but their present granting was being associated, on an assumed principle, with sovereignty forever. The profits were being assigned not to the King in present circumstances, but to his "generation," the royal line, in perpetuity. For the conference in prospect Bacon prepared a pointed introduction to the "business" to be discussed between the two Houses. It ran as follows:

An Introduction, briefly declaring the matter in fact and state of the question. Direction to him in three things, wherein we conceive the King, to have, by misinformation, done other than any of his ancestors.

1. *The time:* for now by letters patent, and in print, these Impositions set for him and his heirs for ever: which never done before; which strange; because no proclamation bindeth longer than the King's life; so could not impose but during his own life.

2. *Multitude of Impositions:* Queen Mary—gascoigne wines and clothes, Queen Eliz. added only one, of sweet wines. From Ed. III to Queen M. none. In Ed. III, Ed. II, Ed. I, but five in all. —That upon a petition last Parliament divers hundredths of these taken away; so now not remaining above 300 or 400; yet that those remaining far more worth than those abolished.

3. *The Claim:* for none of his ancestors ever did so, but pretended [i.e., alleged] wars, needs, &c.: prayed continuance, but for a time.

The proposed conference with the Lower House was debated, and then rejected, by the Lords. One of the members, Richard Neile, a bishop, insulted the Commons by declaring that their present proposal was both seditious and mutinous. Neile's remarks were resented especially by many members of the Commons because the Cecils, father and son, had been his patrons, and he had served as chaplain to Burghley and Salisbury in turn. An outraged Lower House demanded satisfaction. The King interposed and told the Commons to proceed with their business, which was the problem of supply. Thereupon the Lower House resolved that no business would be done until such time as explanation and satisfaction from the Lords were forthcoming. Nor were they pacified when the offending bishop undertook to have them believe, "with many tears" and "sorrow" on his part, that his words had been misconstrued. There had been no indication that his peers intended to censure the culprit. It was the belief of many angry members of the Lower House that what the bishop had uttered in contempt of the Commons was the settled opinion of more than a few of the Lords. James became impatient with these goings-on, and by Friday, the third of June, threatened the Commons with dissolution on Thursday the ninth if they refused to vote on his Secretary's motion of supply. The Commons called for a committee of the House to compose an answer to the King. Thereupon James dissolved Parliament, two days before the date named in his threat. Bacon's efforts to have the Commons function again had come to naught.

After James' dissolving, for a second time, of Parliament, the Council was again faced with the acute problem of providing the King with funds. Now at their wits' end, its members decided to ask for a "benevolence," from corporations, counties, noblemen, bishops, and individuals of all ranks. Circulars were sent out, recommending bountiful giving and intimating that contributions could not "without discredit and note fall too low." Soon there was widespread complaining that the Benevolence was an illegal tax. The contributions received were not great, only some £66,000 over a two-year period. Bacon at the outset had advised the Council against the use of the term "benevolence." In the reign of Richard III a law had been passed to the effect "that the subjects and commons of this realm from henceforth should in no wise be charged *by any charge or imposition called a Benevolence, or any such like charge, and that such exactions called a Benevolence* shall be damned or annulled forever."

A "principal person" of Marlborough, Mr. Oliver St. John, when asked to support an appeal for the Benevolence, made the charge that in calling for this exaction the King had performed an illegal act, had violated the Magna Charta, and was indeed "a Prince perjured in the great and solemn oath of his coronation." St. John also claimed that Parliament was being currently slandered by a rumor to the effect that the Commons had refused to supply the King with necessary funds. St. John was summoned before the Star Chamber, the Council's court. In the absence of the Lord Chancellor, Bacon was assigned the prosecution. The Attorney-General took this opportunity to call the court's attention to what he considered a too hasty dissolution of the late Parliament. He told members of the Council plainly that he "never could perceive but that there was in that house a general disposition to give, and to give largely. The clocks in the house perchance might differ; some went too fast, some went too slow; but the disposition to give was general." (The Secretary of State, Winwood, had introduced his measure of supply too soon, at the beginning of the proceedings, contrary to recognized procedure; and the business of the House had been slowed and, finally, stopped through altercation with the Lords.) For the benefit of Anti-Parliamentarians among his hearers Bacon described Parliament as "the great intercourse and main current of graces and donatives from the king to the people, from the people to the king." For the informing of the King's subjects generally, he pointed out that the call for a free benevolence was made after the summoning and the dissolving of a Parliament which "made profession to give, and was interrupted." The Benevolence, then, could be considered an "after-child" of this Parliament. In justice to the King in Council, Bacon explained that the present Benevolence was not to be confused with that earlier sort of Benevolence which had been made illegal by statute, because there is "a great difference between a Benevolence and an exaction called a Benevolence." The present Benevolence was of the former kind. In its case every man could exercise "a prince's Prerogative, a negative voice." It was not compulsory, and no rate of giving had been set down. There was no certifying by name of any who refused. The accused, therefore, was not being tried for his declining to give, but for his assault upon the King. If St. John had been satisfied with refusing a donation, no case would or could have been made against him.

Before the accused was sentenced to a short imprisonment and a heavy fine—this was remitted on the prisoner's making an abject apology—Bacon took occasion to say some things about the office of the sovereign within the constitution of England. In his address to the court, Bacon had already, by implication, criticized James for his having gotten rid of the late Parliament; now he praised him, not to declare what the King did in practice, but rather to make clear to the King and his Council what the duty of the sovereign *qua* sovereign was. "Is it so," Bacon asked, "that king James shall be said to be a violator of the liberties, laws, and customs of his kingdoms? Or is he not rather a noble and constant protector and conservator of them all? I conceive this consisteth in maintaining religion and the true Church; in maintaining the laws of the kingdom, which is the subject's birth-right: in temperate use of the prerogative; in due and free administration of justice, and conservation of the peace of the land.

"For the maintaining of the laws, which is the hedge and fence about the liberty of the subject, I may truly affirm it was never in better repair. . . . Neither doth the universality of his own knowledge carry him to neglect or pass over the very forms of the laws of the land. Neither was there ever king, as I am persuaded, that did consult so oft with his judges, as my lords that sit here know well. . . .

"As for the use of the prerogative, it runs within the ancient channels and banks: some things that were conceived to be in some proclamations, commissions, and patents, as overflows, have been by his wisdom and care reduced; whereby, no doubt, the main channel of his prerogative is so much the stronger. For evermore overflows do hurt the channel."

As the Attorney- or Procurator-General of the Crown, Bacon at this period was continuously in the courts, where he took the more difficult cases, especially those with constitutional involvements. In two notable instances the accused persons were Roman Catholics, and in a third, a Puritan minister. William Talbot, an Irish member of Parliament, had asserted the opinion—which he credited to the Jesuit philosopher Francisco Suarez (1548-1617)—that tyrannicide was legally justified in the case of heretics, including the Protestant sovereigns of England. When brought before the Court of Star Chamber, Talbot claimed that for him the doctrine of Suarez concerned a matter of "faith," and that on all questions respecting faith he submitted his opinion to the judgment of the Roman Catholic Church. In his plea he said, "*And for matter concerning my loyalty, I do acknowledge my Sovereign Liege Lord King James, to be lawful and undoubted King of all the kingdoms of England, Scotland, and Ireland; and I will bear true faith and allegiance to his Highness during my life.*" The Attorney-General regarded this submission as the going "backward and forward," the "repenting and relapsing" of a coward. Bacon was less concerned with the prosecution of the offender than with the branding of the crime, which in his view had arisen out of "the swelling pride and usurpation of the see of Rome *in temporalibus*, tending altogether to anarchy and confusion." Talbot was fined as a formality and then discharged from custody, his four months' earlier incarceration in the Tower having been deemed a sufficient punishment.

Bacon's address to the court on this occasion is informative of his political thought, for in it he expressly puts political sovereignty within the "prerogatives of God." "The Pope of Rome," argues Bacon, has pretended "by cartels to make sovereign princes as the banditti, and to proscribe their lives, and to expose their kingdoms to prey. . . . Surely I had thought they had been the prerogatives of God alone, and of his secret judgments: '*Solvam cingula regum*, I will loosen the girdles of Kings'; or again, 'He poureth contempt upon princes'; or, 'I will give a king in my wrath, and take him away again in my displeasure'; and the like: but if these be the claims of a mortal man, certainly they are but the mysteries of that person which 'exalts himself above all that is called God, *supra omne quod dicitur Deus*.' Note it well, not above God, though that in a sense be true, but above all that is called God; that is, lawful kings and magistrates."

A second case concerned John Owen. The accused was a Roman Catholic who had spent some time in Spain. On his return to England, Owen made "divers most vile and traitorous speeches confessed and subscribed with his own hand; as, among others, that it was as lawful for any man to kill a king excommunicated, as for the hangman to execute a condemned person." He was not an Irishman with the usual grievances, like William Talbot, nor had he been convinced of a doctrine, as Talbot had been, through theological speculation. Owen, in Bacon's opinion, had simply imbibed the political "poison" which had long been spread about the southern part of Europe in talk about the rulers of England. Owen was brought before the Court of Star Chamber and charged with treason. The Attorney-General informed the court that the accused was not being indicted according to any statute against the Pope's supremacy or with any religious implication, but on a law made when the Pope was "received" in England, to the effect that the "compassing and imagining" of the King's death is treason. Owen's defence was that, while he meant kings generally in his utterances, he did not intend specifically the King of England. Bacon, who understandably could not accept this distinction, charged Owen with maintaining that "it is lawful to kill the king, but conditionally; that if the king be excommunicated, it is lawful to kill him: which maketh little difference either in law or peril."

In his address to the court Bacon argued that were the Bishop of Rome able to absolve a subject from allegiance to his king, any English bishop could free any person from his duty, say, a son from his duty to his father. An opinion which allowed the killing of a sovereign excommunicated by a high Romanist official would also permit the slaughtering of any individual on his excommunication by a bishop. Surely this is putting the bishops, whether in Rome or in any other see, above the commandments of God Himself. The words of Owen remind one, Bacon continued, of the teaching of the Anabaptists, for they too advocate the "pulling down of magistrates: and they can chaunt the psalm, 'To bind their kings in chains, and their nobles in fetters of iron.'" Taking unto themselves "the glory of the saints," these sectaries maintain that their teaching is of a "spiritual" order and for the salvation of souls, even when they make God Himself "in the likeness of the prince of darkness." "What is there" of evil, asked Bacon, "that may not be made spiritual by consequence: especially when he that giveth the sentence may make the case?" Owen was found guilty of treason and sentenced to death. After three years' imprisonment he was permitted to leave the country.

A third case concerned Edmond Peacham, a Puritan minister in Somersetshire. Peacham, on becoming disgruntled over some acts of his bishop, made accusations against his ecclesiastical superiors. For these he was brought before the Court of High Commission. When the house of the accused was being searched for evidence, among his papers was found a sermon, not yet publicly preached, in which the King and his family were threatened with the fates of Ananias and Nabal, and reference was made to the assassination of the King's heir at such time as he should come to the throne. The King and members of the Council suspected that behind this particular sermon lay something more universal within a not untypical shire. In their opinion the unpublished statements of an individual Puritan portended a general disloyalty to the Sovereign and clandestine agitation in contempt of the acts of ecclesiastical commissions and the use of the Royal Prerogative. James himself had been made so nervously apprehensive by the attitude of Parliament, the scheming of the Puritans, and the intrigues of the Recusants that he could sleep at night only when his bed was surrounded by a barricade of other beds.

Peacham was summoned before the court of the Privy Council. The warrant for his trial, which was formally addressed to the Secretary of State and *ex officio* to the Attorney-General and the Solicitor-General, carried the signatures of the Archbishop of Canterbury, the Lord Treasurer, the Lord Steward, the Secretary of State, the Chancellor of the Exchequer, the Master of the Rolls, and a representative of the Lords. Because the offence in question was regarded as treasonable, the accused, when he failed to explain the reasons for his statements, was put on the rack and "stretched" for discovery of the circumstances of the writing of his sermon, including probable instigators, but not for evidence against himself—for, "by the law of England"—as Bacon had written—"no man is bound to accuse himself." Bacon was not, of course, responsible for Peacham's torture, although as Procurator-General he was required to sign, with others, the official report. The accused confessed and denied his guilt by turns. Sometimes he refused to recognize his own handwriting. No evidence of specific consequence could be got from his utterances.

Lest the public should think the indicting of Peacham before the Council was designed to make an example for the terrorizing into submission of Puritans and other malcontents, his case was submitted to the judgment of the Court of the King's Bench. Edward Coke, the Chief Justice, refused to consider a charge of treason against the accused on other grounds than his having impugned the King's title. Scandal, defamation, and even contention that the King was an unworthy sovereign did not, in the opinion of the present Chief Justice, constitute treason. The several judges of the King's Bench were unable to agree in a judgment on the case. Peacham was then tried in Somersetshire before a jury composed of seven knights, "taken from the bench," and found guilty of high treason. The prisoner was left to languish in the Taunton jail for the remainder of his life. When he died he left behind "a most wicked and desperate writing, worse than that he was convicted for."

IX

BACON, COKE, AND THE LAW

IT HAD LONG BEEN THE AMBITION OF EDWARD COKE to bring the Sovereign of England "under the law." That fact had become very evident in the protracted negotiation over the Council of the Marches and was seen more recently in the case of Peacham. In the former instance, a conflict arose when Coke required a resort to a conference of the judges before answering the King's questions concerning this council's jurisdiction. Some members of the Commons had been given to understand that, on that occasion, the opinion of the company of judges under Coke, which was delivered in writing and not published, was opposed to that of the Crown. Soon thereafter, Coke and the other judges in the court which he controlled began to issue a series of Prohibitions designed to obstruct and inhibit the proceedings of the Court of the King's Council. When the case of Peacham was referred to the Court of the King's Bench, James proposed that the judges should be asked to state their opinions severally "to put Coke in doubt that he shall be left alone." To this Coke, as Chief Justice, objected on the ground, as Bacon found necessary to report to the King, that "particular and . . . auricular taking of opinions was not according to the custom of this realm." A contest between the Chief Justice and the King in Council now began to take definite shape. In this conflict Bacon was to be on the side of the Sovereign because of a constitutional principle. For other reasons the contest was to his liking.

A rivalry between Bacon and Coke had begun when the latter was preferred before Bacon for the office of Attorney-General. Following this defeat, Bacon lost out to his rival for the hand of Lady Hatton, a wife who subsequently did not make Coke's life "comfortable," and who refused to use his name. Bacon, while recognizing Coke's very considerable acquaintance with the law, came to have sufficient reasons for regarding him as an indifferent scholar, who invented law when his memory or information failed him; a poor legal thinker, who thought of law as a body of "almost infinite particulars"; and a crude performer at trials. When the two rivals were required to act together in the prosecution of Essex, Coke had allowed the introduction of irrelevant matters and brought confusion into the case. Then Bacon was made to appear as a punitive agent against a former benefactor because he had stressed apt points and made sharp distinctions in fact and in law. When Coke became a judge, a lack of capacity to clarify causes left him open to impression by doubtful evidence. In his behavior in court while Attorney-General, Coke showed the disposition of a bully. When presiding as a judge he intimidated accused persons, browbeat witnesses, and insulted counsel. At the trial of Sir Walter Raleigh, he behaved like an executioner before the fact. Bacon during his early days in the courts had found it necessary to send a report on Coke's conduct to the Secretary of State, Robert Cecil. In one incident this Attorney-General, as Bacon complained, had introduced into court proceedings the personal matter of Bacon's having been charged for indebtedness and had made derogatory remarks about his acting as Counsel without Patent, when the Queen herself had not deemed the usual warrant necessary.

Bacon, in due time, found an opportunity to take a verbal revenge on Coke, but not in court. When Judge Coke had been elevated, to his disliking, from the Common Pleas to the King's Bench, he told the new Attorney-General, "This is all your doing." Then Bacon made the retort: "Ah, my lord, your lordship has all this time grown in breadth; you must needs now grow in height, else you will become a monster."

One of Coke's major shortcomings, in Bacon's view, was his failure to recognize the commanding place of the King's Prerogative in the constitution of England. This failure was manifest in his subscribing himself Chief Justice of England and not of the King's Bench, his habitual dissatisfaction with proceedings in all courts where the common law did not suffice, his misconstruction of cases in his *Reports* for the confirmation of his own prejudices, his proneness to make justice the business of lawyers, his encouragement of lawyers to inveigh against ecclesiastical courts and thereby to bring comfort to Nonconformist members of Parliament, and his presumption that in the common law, as interpreted by a judge with little capacity to discern principle within particulars and the spirit beneath the letter, was to be found the beginning and the end of justice.

Coke had great influence over lawyers and judges. His admirers within the Commons were many. He continued in unabated judicial power after he had inhibited the Council's commissions and courts and presumed that the Court of Chancery could not review judgments pronounced in lower courts. Coke was beginning to regard himself as the ruler of a kingdom of justice within the Kingdom of England. Indeed, he had begun to subdivide the latter kingdom in a judicial way when he and the judges under his sway told the Council which shires should and which should not be placed under the jurisdiction of the Court of the Marches. When Coke refused consultation by the judges with the King, he had in effect told James that the Throne was no longer—if, in his opinion, it ever had been—the source of justice. James had met these affronts to his person and Council with unusual forbearance. The time was at hand, however, when Coke was to go too far in a pursuit of legal victories.

The events which led to Coke's downfall involved three cases. In one of these the Chief Justice achieved a partial triumph, and in the others ignominious defeat. The first of the three was occasioned by the King's granting Mr. John Murray of his Majesty's Bedchamber a Patent for making writs in the Court of Common Pleas. A prothonotary whose profits were threatened with decrease by this appointment brought an action, probably at Coke's prompting, for the denial of the legality of the Patent. The Patent was annulled in Coke's court. Thereupon Bacon and other Crown Counsel made a strong protest, and a compromise was arranged whereby the King's present appointee should take office, but no successor should similarly be issued a Patent. Encouraged by this partial success, and at the same time suffering pique at being forced to retrace a step, Coke was to overplay his hand. He was to demonstrate what Bacon called his "over-ruling nature." Two fraudulent debtors had been granted judgments in their favor by the King's Bench, and these findings had then been reversed in the Court of Chancery. Coke thereupon persuaded the culprits to ask for indictments of *praemunire* in his own court against the several persons involved in the proceedings in Chancery, against the plaintiffs, the counsel, the Solicitor, even the Master of Chancery himself. So determined was the Chief Justice of the King's Bench to make a case that the action which he had promoted, over a matter of debt, was grounded on a statute of Edward III which had been designed to deal with persons given to appealing to Rome in ecclesiastical cases adjudged in England! A grand jury threw out the bill, despite remonstrances and threats by Coke and the other judges of the King's Bench.

Bacon told the King that something should be done "for the settling of your authority and strengthening of your Prerogative according to the true rules of Monarchy." Bacon thought this " a just and fit occasion to *make some example against the*

presumption of a Judge in causes that concern your Majesty,
whereby the whole body of those magistrates may be contained
in better awe; and it may be this will light upon no unfit subject
of a person that is rude and that no man cares for"—meaning, of
course, Judge Coke. Bacon advised also that each of the several
courts be required to keep within its own limits and precedents,
and that in "these high causes that touch upon State and Monarchy, your Majesty give [the judges] strait charge that upon
any occasions intervenient hereafter they do not make the
vulgar party to their contestations by public handling them before they have consulted your Majesty, to whom the reglement
of those things only appertaineth."

Meanwhile, another significant case was taking shape.
Richard Neile, Bishop of Lincoln—the bishop who had pre-
cipitated a tumult in the late short-lived Parliament by insulting
the Commons—had been granted a benefice temporarily *in com-
mendam* by the King. A claimant who thought he should have
the place brought action against the bishop of the diocese concerned. The bishop was asked by the King to provide a full
report of the circumstances. James, on receiving this, instructed
Bacon, as Crown-Attorney, to inform Coke and the other
judges that they should not proceed with the case until they
had consulted with the King, who would know the conditions
surrounding the appointment. This command the judges refused to obey. They went on with the action, and sent a letter
to the King stating that they were bound by oath "in case any
letters come unto us contrary to law that we go forth to do the
law." James called a meeting of the Privy Council and summoned the judges of the King's Bench—twelve in number—to
attend. He informed the assembled gathering of a letter he had
already written the judges to the following effect:

"You might very well have spared your labour in informing
us of the nature of your oath; for although we never studied
the Common Law of England, yet are we not ignorant of any

points which belong to a king to know: we are therefore to inform you hereby, that we are far from crossing or delaying any thing which may belong to the interest of any private party in this case; but we cannot be contented to suffer the prerogative royal of our crown to be wounded through the sides of a private person: we have no care at all which of the parties shall win this process in this case, so that right prevail, and that justice be truly administered. But on the other side, we have reason to foresee that nothing be done in this case which may wound our prerogative in general; and therefore so that we may be sure that nothing shall be debated amongst you which may concern our general power of giving Commendams, we desire not the parties to have one hour's delay of justice: but that our prerogative should not be wounded in that regard for all times hereafter, upon pretext of private persons' interest, we sent you that direction; which we account as well to be wounded if it be publicly disputed upon, as if any sentence were given against it: we are therefore to admonish you, that since the prerogative of our crown hath been more boldly dealt withal in Westminster-Hall, during the time of our reign, than ever it was before in the reigns of divers princes immediately preceding us, that we will no longer endure that popular and unlawful liberty; and therefore we were justly moved to send you that direction to forbear to meddle in a cause of so tender a nature, till we had farther thought upon it."

After this statement had been read, the King went on to speak of what he deemed the errors of the judges in their dealings with this and other cases. He said that "it was a fault in the judges, that when they heard a counsellor at the bar presume to argue against his majesty's prerogative, which in this case was in effect his supremacy, they did not interrupt and reprove sharply that base and bold course of defaming or impeaching things of so high a nature by discourse; especially since his majesty hath observed, that ever since his coming to the crown, the popular sort of lawyers have been the men that most affrontedly in all parliaments have trodden upon his prerogative: which being most contrary to their vocation of any men, since the law or lawyers can never be respected, if the king be not reverenced; it doth therefore best become the judges of any, to check and bridle such impudent lawyers, and in their several benches to disgrace them that bear so little respect to their king's authority and prerogative: that his majesty had a double prerogative, whereof the one was ordinary and had relation to his private interest, which might be, and was every day, disputed in Westminster-Hall; the other was of an higher nature, referring to his supreme and imperial power and sovereignty, which ought not to be disputed or handled in vulgar argument: the courts of the common law are grown so vast and transcendent, as they did both meddle with the king's prerogative, and had incroached upon all other courts of justice; as the high commission, the councils established in Wales and at York, the court of requests."

The sovereign in this instance had desired "to know of the judges how his calling them to consult was contrary to law, which they could never answer unto," for it was "no bare supposition or surmise, that this cause concerned the king's prerogative," and that a delay of the consultation requested by the King was not for an "infinite nor long time, but grounded upon his majesty's weighty occasions, which were notorious . . . and that there was a certain expectation of his majesty's return at Whitsuntide: and likewise that the cause . . . would not receive judgment by Easter term next, as the judges themselves afterwards confessed."

The King further told his Council and the judges of his Bench that "it was a new thing, and very indecent and unfit for subjects to disobey the kings commandment, but most of all to proceed in the mean time, and to return him a bare certificate; whereas they ought to have concluded with the laying down and representing of their reasons modestly to his majesty, why they should proceed; and so to have submitted the same to his princely judgment, expecting to hear from him whether they had given him satisfaction."

Thereupon Coke and the other judges fell on their knees, and acknowledged "their error for matter and form, craving his majesty's gracious favour and pardon for the same." Coke, however, put in the remark that the King's request through the Attorney for a delay in the recent action "mentioned no day certain, and that an adjournment must always be to a day certain." James replied that this "conceit . . . was mere sophistry, for that they might in their discretions have prefixed a convenient day."

The King now asked the Lord Chancellor for his opinion on the question whether he had acted illegally in making his request for a delay to the judges. The Chancellor suggested that James invite the opinion of his "Learned Counsel." Bacon, as Crown-Attorney, then said that "the putting off of the day in manner as was required by his majesty, to his understanding was without all scruple no delay of justice, nor danger of the judges' oath." To this he added the remark that the judges should "consider seriously with themselves, whether they were not in greater danger of breach of their oaths . . . to counsel his majesty when they are called." Coke immediately took exception to this statement, saying it was the duty of the King's Counsel to "plead before judges, and not to dispute with them." To this opinion Bacon replied that he found the "exception strange," because the King's Counsel, by oath, office, and the King's express command, were "without fear of any man's face, to proceed or declare against any the greatest peer or subject of the kingdom; and not only any subject in particular, but any body of subjects or persons, were they judges, or were they of an upper or lower house of parliament, in case they exceed the limits of their authority, or took any thing from his majesty's royal power or prerogative."

The Lord Chancellor then declared himself in agreement with the Attorney's opinion, and requested that the oath pertaining to judges be read out of the statute. This was done by the Solicitor. At this point James and the Lords thought it proper to ask the judges severally their opinion on the question now at issue, whether they would or would not stay particular court proceedings at the request of the King. In reply, all the judges present, with the exception of Coke, said that they would, and acknowledged it their duty to do so. The Chief Justice of the King's Bench made, for his answer, the statement that "when the case should be, he would do that which should be fit for a judge to do."

The King had been annoyed at Coke's behavior over a period of several years. When Chief Justice Coke had enunciated the thesis that there can be "no appeal from the King's Bench to any court except the High Court of Parliament," the outraged James had called this statement "treason" and "blasphemy." The King on one occasion had become so enraged with Coke's criticism of proceedings within the ecclesiastical courts that he "clenched his fists as if to strike the Chief Justice." When the Chief Justice of the King's Bench had called himself Lord Chief Justice of England, he had been guilty of sufficient misdemeanor in the eyes of James to warrant his dismissal from office. James' view of the Sovereign's relation to law and judicature was definite and positive. He had written shortly after his accession to the throne of England, in his *True Law of Free Monarchies*, "Although a good King will frame all his actions to be according to the law, yet he is not bound thereto, but of his own will and for example-giving to his subjects." The King had repeated the same theme in a speech in the Star Chamber after becoming angered at what Archbishop Bancroft called Coke's "contempt of the command of the King." James had then told his listeners: "Kings are properly Judges, and judgment properly belongs to them from God, and thence all judgment is derived. It is atheism and blasphemy to dispute what God can do; so it is presumption and high contempt in a subject to dispute what a King can do, or say that a King cannot do this or that."

Bacon, the King's chief advisor during his late dealings with Coke, had previously written in his *View of the Differences in Question betwixt the King's Bench and the Council of the Marches* (1606): "We say that in the King's Prerogative there is a double power: one, which is delegate to his ordinary judges in Chancery or Common Law; another, which is inherent in his own person, whereby he is the supreme judge both in Parliament and all other Courts; and hath power to stay suits at the Common Law; yea, *pro bono publico,* to temper, change, and control the same; as Edward III did, when, for increase of traffic, he granted juries to strangers *de medietate linguae,* against the Common Law. Nay, our Acts of Parliament by his sole authority may be mitigated or suspended upon causes to him known. And this inherent power of his, and what participateth thereof, is therefore exempt from controlment by any Court of Law."

Bacon had ever been of the opinion that the source of justice was the Throne itself; that the sure friend of the wronged subject seeking justice, of the penitent criminal begging mercy, of the litigant under the pressure of book-lawyers and even common law judges, was the King himself. As for the conferring of judges with kings, now in sharp dispute: this practice had been sanctioned by time immemorial. Bacon's opinion on this matter was to be succinctly stated in his essay "Of Judicature": "Judges ought, above all, to remember the conclusions of the Roman Twelve Tables; *Salus populi suprema lex*; and to know that laws, except they be in order to that end, are but things captious, and oracles not well inspired. Therefore it is an happy thing in a state when kings and states do often consult with judges; and again when judges do often consult with the king and state: the one, when there is matter of law, intervenient in business of state; the other, when there is some consideration of state intervenient in matter of law. For many times the things deduced to judgment may be *meum* and *tuum*, when the reason and consequence thereof may trench to point of estate: I call matter of estate, not only the parts of sovereignty, but whatsoever introduceth any great alterations or dangerous precedent; or concerneth manifestly any great portion of people. And let no man weakly conceive that just laws and true policy have any antipathy; for they are like the spirits and sinews, that one moves with the other. Let judges also remember, that Salomon's throne was supported by lions on both sides: let them be lions, but yet lions under the throne; being circumspect that they do not check or oppose any points of sovereignty." Then Bacon was to add, characteristically: "Let not judges also be so ignorant of their own right, as to think there is not left to them, as a principal part of their office, a wise use and application of laws."

Three weeks after the meeting with the judges and the Privy Council, the King directed the latter to inform Coke that he was not for the present to sit either at the Council Table or on the Bench. Instead, he was to employ his leisure time in correcting his *Reports* and the "many exorbitant and extravagant opinions set down and published for positive and good law ... and having corrected what in his discretion he found meet in these Reports, his Majesty's pleasure was that he should bring the same privately to himself that he might consider thereof, as in his princely judgment should be found expedient." After a period of three months Coke reported that he had gone over eleven volumes of some six hundred reported cases and had found only five examples of questionable statements on his part, and these of no consequence. When told that certain of his interpretations, now cited by Bacon and Sir Henry Yelverton, the Solicitor-General, cast doubt on the Royal Prerogative, Coke stubbornly affirmed that this was not so.

James finally decided that Coke must be removed from office. Bacon, as both Attorney-General and a member of the Privy Council—a combination with rare precedent in English history—

was invited to prepare an advice on what the King should declare in explanation of the dismissal of his Chief Justice. In this document Bacon mentioned Coke's "perpetual turbulent carriage" towards the liberties of the Church and its ecclesiastical commissions; towards the "prerogative royal, and the branches thereof; and likewise towards all the settled jurisdictions of all his other courts . . . in all which he had raised troubles and new questions." The Attorney reminded the King in a reference to the trial of Peacham, that there had been "turbulent carriage" also in what might concern the safety of the Sovereign, namely, the interpretation of the law in cases of high treason. James was invited to recall that Coke in his dealings had been "neither civil, nor affable, nor magnificent," that he "made himself popular by design only, in pulling down government . . . that whereas his majesty might have expected a change in him, when he made him his own, by taking him to be of his council, it made no change at all, but to the worse, he holding on all his former channel, and running separate courses from the rest of his council; and rather busying himself in casting fears before his council, concerning what they could not do, than joining his advice what they should do." The Attorney requested the King to keep in mind how he had given Coke a vacation "to reform his 'Reports' wherein there be many dangerous conceits of his own uttered for law, to the prejudice of his crown, parliament, and subjects; and to see, whether by this he would in any part redeem his fault," but that "after three months time and consideration, he had offered his majesty only five animadversions, being rather a scorn, than a satisfaction to his majesty."

Shortly after preparing this advice, Bacon found great satisfaction in being able to send the King a letter which read:

May it please your excellent Majesty,
I send your majesty a form of discharge for my lord Coke from his place of chief justice of your bench.
I send also a warrant to the lord chancellor, for making forth

a writ for a new chief justice, leaving a blank for the name to be supplied by your majesty's presence.

Bacon's motives in his dealings with Coke were not, of course, merely personal. As one learned in the law, Bacon had not been greatly impressed by Coke's *Reports*. He was aware that his rival in the law had distorted records of cases through his own legal propensities; that his digests were neither accurate in citation nor properly informative by induction of rules; that Coke had been given to exalting the common law beyond what it could bear; that he had undertaken the impossible task "to reduce the common laws of England to a text-book as the statutes are." Bacon himself had two legal Propositions in an early stage of preparation for the King's consideration, one the making of a "Digest . . . of the Laws of England," and the other "the Compiling and Amendment of the Laws of England." The first Proposition Bacon was calling, in the very words he had employed when he described his instauration of the sciences, "means to perpetuate . . . memory and merits." The second Proposition had been in its author's mind for years. As early as 1592, in a digression within a Parliamentary speech—an aside which made an impression on Elizabeth—Bacon had intimated the need for a compilation and a reform of the laws. Ever since then he had maintained a scholarly interest in the development of English law, which he found "as mixt as our language, compounded of British, Saxon, Danish, Norman customs." Bacon believed that even as the language of England was richer for an intermingling of native and foreign roots and idioms, so were her laws the more complete because of their past drawing on the resources of many peoples.

In the first Proposition, Bacon, in words which contain a moral for sovereigns, tells the King: "Certain it is, that good laws are some bridle to bad princes, and as a very wall about government. And if tyrants sometimes make a breach into them, yet they mollify even tyranny itself, as Solon's laws did the tyranny of Pisistratus: and then commonly they get up again, upon the first advantage of better time." Bacon instances among "the better works of perpetuity in princes" colleges, learned lectures, the education of the young, the founding of noble orders, and the like. Such things are, however, "but like plantations of orchards and gardens, in plots and spots of ground here and there; they do not till over the whole kingdom, and make it fruitful, as doth the establishing of good laws and ordinances; which makes a whole nation to be as a well-ordered college or foundation." Here Bacon has in mind a projected *New Atlantis,* a writing in which he hopes to delineate the practices and regulations of an ideal kingdom with informed learning and ideal laws. In a mildly veiled reference to the constitutional struggles of the present and the part he himself could play as an English Justinian, the author makes the observation that in former times, after the days of Augustus and the rest, "there was such a race of wit and authority, between the commentaries and decisions of the lawyers, and the edicts of the emperors, as both law and lawyers were out of breath." It was Justinian who in the end compiled a system of laws, an "edifice or structure of a sacred temple of justice, built indeed out of the former ruins of books, as materials, and some novel constitutions of his own."

Bacon introduces his second Proposition, which concerns the "compiling and amendment" of laws, by saying that he will be a "workman" under his "master," the King. He tells James: "Your majesty hath set me in an eminent place, whereby in a work, which must be the work of many, I may the better have coadjutors." Here, one is immediately reminded of the author's plea to the King, on several occasions, for helpers to collect a natural history for the instauration of a new learning and science.

Bacon informs James that it is not his intention to bring charges against the law of England generally; he is bent only on perfecting English laws that already exist, giving them "rather light than any new nature." In the beginning he will mention, and meet, some objections which may be raised against this undertaking. It will be said that English law, as it stands, "is in good estate comparable to any foreign law"; whereas in fact, the laws of England and their administration are subject to delays, evasions, and great uncertainties which include fluctuating opinions. There is multiplicity of suits and endless litigation. "The contentious person is armed, and the honest subject wearied and oppressed." The judge becomes the more absolute, since in doubtful cases he has the "greater stroke and liberty." Chancery is filled to overflowing because the law is often obscure. Lawyers cover their ignorance by arguing what is doubtful. Many legal transactions hang on hollow questions.

It will be objected by some, again, that in purging the common laws and statutes much that is sound may be taken away. To this, Bacon replies that "in all purging, some good humours may pass away; but that is largely recompensed by lightening the body of much bad." In face of any remonstrance to the effect that the labor required for the undertaking in prospect could be better employed in "bringing the common laws of England to a text law, as the statutes are," the common law, as it stands, deserves a defence. Certainly in legal practice more doubts arise over statutes, which are text law, than over the common law, which is not.

Turning from objections to the particulars of his Proposition, Bacon recommends a proper "digest or recompiling," first of the common laws, and, then, of the statutes. In the case of the common laws, three things, he says, are required:

1. The compiling of a book *De antiquitatibus juris*. This will involve a sifting of ancient legal records and a selecting of the most informing of these for summary and chronological arrangement. Cases thus compiled will serve "for reverend precedents, but not for binding authorities."

2. The reducing and "perfecting" of the course or, if you will, the body of common law. This may be done by compiling year-

books from the time of Edward I to the present. Here five directions will help. First, cases "which are at this day clearly no law, but constantly ruled to the contrary," are to be omitted, while cases whose legal points are not now questioned may be entered as judgments simply, without arguments "which are now become but frivolous." Second, repetitious cases are to be purged away. Third, cases which show contradictions among judgments rendered should be noted in a special manner, so that the doubts to which they give rise may be settled either by Parliament or by assembly of judges. Fourth, idle queries should be omitted; and fifth, cases reported with too great prolixity are to be shortened in statement by the omission of "tautologies and impertinences."

3. The preparation of certain auxiliary books which can both further the study and develop the science of law. These books will be of three sorts, in keeping with three subjects: legal institutions, the rules of law, and legal terms. A work on legal institutions generally will serve as a general preparative to the reading of a course of law. This book should be perspicuous, clear in method, and comprehensive, like "a model towards a great building." A work which dealt properly with the second subject, the rules of law, would be "of all other things the most important to the health . . . and good institutions of any laws . . . like the ballast of a ship, to keep all upright and stable; but I have," says Bacon, "seen little in this kind, either in our law or other laws, that satisfieth me. The naked rule or maxim doth not the effect: It must be made useful by good differences, ampliations, and limitations, warranted by good authorities; and this not by raising up of quotations and references, but by discourse and deducement in a just tractate. In this I have travelled myself, at the first more cursorily, since with more diligence, and will go on with it, if God and your majesty will give me leave. And I do assure your majesty, I am in good hope, that when Sir Edward Coke's Reports, and my rules and decisions shall come to

posterity, there will be, whatsoever is now thought, question, who was the greater lawyer?" Yet "to give every man his due . . . Sir Edward Coke's Reports . . . though they may have errors, and some peremptory and extrajudicial resolutions more than are warranted," do nevertheless contain "good decisions and rulings of cases." They, too, may be compared to the "ballast" of which we speak.

In the case of statute law, recompiling and reforming will require four undertakings: 1. The clearing of statute books of obsolete laws and of enactments long since expired and clearly repealed. Where the repeal of any of these is in doubt recourse should be had to Parliament. 2. The repeal of all statutes which "are sleeping and not of use, but yet snaring and in force: in some of those it will perhaps be requisite to substitute some more reasonable law, instead of them, agreeable to the time; in others a simple repeal may suffice." 3. The mitigation of harsh penalties attached to many statutes. 4. The reducing of concurrent statutes, heaped one upon another, to one clear and uniform law. "Towards this," Bacon writes, there "hath been already, upon my motion, and your majesty's direction, a great deal of good pains taken by Lord Hobart, myself," and others. The work is already considerably advanced.

Finally, Bacon tells the King, in a reminder both of the legislative capacity of the Houses of Parliament and of his own work on the Commission for the Union of the Kingdoms of England and Scotland, that "because this part of the work, which concerneth the statute laws, must of necessity come to parliament, and the houses will best like that which themselves guide, and the persons that themselves employ," the best procedure will be to follow Parliamentary precedents, such, for example, as the arranging of the union of England and Scotland, when the commissioners were named by both Houses.

Needless to say, had James placed at his Attorney-General's disposal time and means for the effecting of his Propositions,

English law would have been freed of much obscurity and conflict, for Bacon had a skill which amounted to genius in the mastering of legal details and in the induction and enunciation of principle. Undoubtedly, he would have ordered and brought consistency into the main body of English law without destroying its structure and function, its principles and capacity for growth.

X

BACON AND JAMES' FAVORITES

W<small>E HAVE HAD OCCASION TO MENTION</small> J<small>AMES'</small> "<small>FAVORITES</small>." There were two of these, Robert Carr and George Villiers. Bacon had been given the Attorney-Generalship by the King himself, yet, as he said, one of the favorites sought to "thrust himself into the business for a fee." This was Carr, Viscount Rochester. Bacon became a member of the Privy Council (1616) partly through the goodwill of the succeeding favorite, Villiers, and from him received the promise of the Lord Chancellorship. There was accuracy in the statement made in 1613 concerning Carr: "The Viscount Rochester sheweth much temper and modesty without seeming to press or sway anything; but afterwards the King resolveth all business with him alone." Three years later it was said in equal truth of Villiers: "This is now the man by whom all things do and must pass."

Among the causes for the King's cultivation of favorites were a complete lack of sympathy between him and his Parliament and the opposition which he encountered from judges, lawyers, Puritan gentry, Roman Catholic Recusants, and subjects commonly opposed to his Impositions and Monopolies. The King sought in the company of favorites escape from difficulties of state, which were compounded by conflicts within his Privy Council and between Commons and Lords, Sovereign and Parliament, Crown and courts of law, and upholders of the common law and members of the Privy Council. There could be no composure or unity of purpose in a Council which included the anti-Romanist, Calvinist George Abbot, Archbishop of Canterbury; Lancelot Andrewes, a bishop who detested Calvinism; Sir John Digby, the favorer of Spain; Sir Ralph Winwood, the Puritan Secretary of State and desirer of a Spanish war; Sir Thomas Edmondes, who sought an alliance with France; the Earl of Suffolk, the chief promoter of the large Howard interests; and the Earl of Arundel, the heir of the Roman Catholic Norfolks.

The first of the two favorites, Robert Carr, was a physically robust Scot who had been a personal page to the King in Scotland. When James came to England, Carr had been left behind. But in three years he appeared at the English Court; and while taking part in a contest on the tilting field, in James' presence, broke a leg. The sympathetic King, impressed by Carr's continuing physical exuberance and his present misfortune, again took him under his personal care. Soon the former page was knighted (1611). He had previously been provided, too, with an estate (1609), after Salisbury found a flaw in the deed of Sherborne Manor and dispossessed Sir Walter Raleigh's wife and children. Soon Carr, who was far from stupid, became the King's personal political minister. He was permitted to dispose of public offices, both high and low, for perquisites in return. When Bacon sought the Mastership of the Wards, he found it necessary, as much as he deplored the agency, to negotiate his request through the favorite. So successful was Carr in the business of selling offices, that he was eventually able to accumulate, for his personal spending, as much as £90,000 a year.

In 1613, Carr, who two years before had become Viscount Rochester, was created Earl of Somerset. The new honor was bestowed in order to provide him with a fitting title to offer in marriage to Frances Howard, after this lady had obtained a "disgraceful" divorce from the third Earl of Essex, the son of the Essex who had been Queen Elizabeth's favorite. Sir Thomas Overbury, an intimate friend of Somerset, became displeased with the divorce proceedings, and gave Somerset some plain advice against his forthcoming marriage. Before long, Frances Howard, now Lady Somerset, and Carr too, partly because he had previously communicated secrets of state—secrets which, as Bacon said, had never been brought to the Council Table— to Overbury, was anxious to have him put out of the way. The Somersets plotted his arrest on a technical charge. Overbury was put into the Tower (1613). The Countess then arranged a plan whereby her agents were made his keepers. After experiments had been made on animals with noxious drugs, Overbury was poisoned, and the rumor was circulated that he had died of a loathsome disease. When charged with the murder (1615), the Countess confessed her guilt. Somerset, who was later (in 1616) found guilty of a part in the crime, maintained his innocence. Actually, his guilt was never finally established in the court where he was tried. Coke determined the case on doubtful evidence. The chief agent in the murder, Weston, was hanged, but the lives of the Somersets were spared. Soon the Countess was pardoned (1616), as one who was not "a principal, but an accessory before the fact." Carr was confined to the Tower. Bacon, whatever he thought of the legal proceedings, was "far from the opinion that the re-integration or resuscitation of Somerset's fortune can ever stand with his Majesty's honour or safety." The succeeding favorite of James, Villiers, kept Carr incarcerated for six years, trying unsuccessfully all the while to exact from the prisoner, as the price of his freedom, the "gift" of Sherborne Manor. James, shortly before his death, issued a pardon for Somerset.

George Villiers had come to James' notice in 1614. A year thereafter he was knighted and, to Carr's great annoyance, made a Gentleman of the Bedchamber. An opportunity now presented itself to those about the Court to displace the morose, cunning, feared, and despised Carr. Villiers had been trained in France as a courtier under the guidance of no less a person than Sir John Eliot. He was intelligent, approachable, affable, diplomatic, literary, and appreciative of things of the mind. Archbishop Abbot and lay members of the Privy Council, including Bacon, the Attorney-General, commended Villiers to James. Bacon in a letter to the King in 1616 described Villiers as a man of "a safe nature, a capable mind, an honest will, generous and noble affections, and a courage well lodged; and one that I know loveth your Majesty unfeignedly, and admireth you as much as it is in a man to admire his Sovereign upon earth."

Villiers' advancement at Court was exceedingly rapid. Knighted in 1615, he was made a Viscount, Master of the Horse, and a Knight of the Garter in 1616. In 1617 he was given the rank of Earl and in 1618 that of Marquis. In 1621 he assumed the office of Lord High Admiral. In 1623 he was created Duke of Buckingham. Within a very short period this perceptive and resourceful courtier took over the political will of an arbitrary king. James was happy in the fact; his dealings with the Council, Parliament, judges, and Secretaries of State had been very troublesome. So complete was James' attachment to Villiers by 1617 that the King put himself on record with this statement: "I James am neither a god nor an angel, but a man like any other. . . . I wish to speak in my own behalf and not to have it thought to be a defect; for Jesus Christ did the same, and therefore I cannot be blamed. Christ *had his John and I have my George*."

After Villiers had read the letter in which Bacon commended him to the King—James had showed it to him—the new favorite displayed an affectionate regard for the writer, like the esteem of a devoted son for a benignant and discerning parent. Villiers sought the older and politically experienced man's advice, and

Bacon in return assumed a paternal role. When, as Attorney-General, he sent Villiers his Patent of creation as Viscount, he enclosed with the document a letter of personal advice. Remembering what had happened in Carr's case, Bacon gave a frank warning to the new favorite against some of the besetting temptations of his position. He wrote to Villiers:

After that the King shall have watered your new dignities with his bounty of the lands which he intends you, and that some other things concerning your means which are now in intention shall be settled upon you, I do not see but you may think your private fortunes established; and therefore it is now time that you should refer your actions chiefly to the good of your Sovereign and your country. It is the life of an ox or beast always to eat, and never to exercise; but men are born (and especially Christian men) not to cram in their fortunes but to exercise their virtues; and yet the other hath been the unworthy and (thanks be to God) sometimes the unlucky humour of great persons in our times. Neither will your further fortune be the further off; for assure yourself that fortune is of a woman's nature, that will sooner follow you by slighting than by too much wooing.

Having offered this admonition, Bacon made the request to the new favorite that he do something "which was never done since I was born, and which, not done, hath bred almost a wilderness and solitude in the King's service." He asked that men of capacity and merit be placed in offices. The filling of places, said Bacon, still depends too much on "money and turn-serving and cunning canvasses and importunity." Far from being piqued by this frank counsel, Villiers expressed a desire for more. Bacon thereupon prepared a comprehensive *Advice*. Two drafts or versions of this have survived. One of these, the longer, may have been put in shape at a later period, perhaps in 1619, to serve as a record of what Bacon regarded as proper opinions on certain questions of state and offices of government. There is no discrepancy between the two documents, and it is not improbable that the parts of the second which are omitted from the first draft were orally, and in a more casual way, communicated to Villiers.

In the shorter and first version of the *Advice* (1616), which Bacon sent in written form to Villiers, the Attorney-General first admonishes the new favorite on his relations with the King: "Remember well," says Bacon, "the great trust you have undertaken; you are as a continual sentinel, always to stand upon your watch to give him true intelligence. If you flatter him, you betray him; if you conceal the truth of those things from him which concern his justice or his honour, although not the safety of his person, you are as dangerous a traitor to his state, as he that riseth in arms against him. . . . Kings must be answerable to God Almighty, to whom they are but vassals, for their actions, and for their negligent omissions: but the ministers to kings, whose eyes, ears, and hands they are, must be answerable to God and man for the breach of their duties, in violation of their trusts, whereby they betray them."

Turning to matters of religion and the Established Church, Bacon tells the favorite: "If any question be moved concerning the doctrine of the Church of England expressed in the thirty-nine articles, give not the least ear to the movers thereof: that is soundly and so orthodoxly settled, as cannot be questioned without extreme danger to the honour and stability of our religion; which hath been sealed with the blood of so many martyrs and confessors, as are famous throughout the Christian world. The enemies and underminers thereof are the Romish Catholic, so stiling themselves, on the one hand, whose tenets are inconsistent with the truth of religion professed and protested by the Church of England, whence we are called protestants; and the anabaptists, and separatists, and sectaries on the other hand, whose tenets are full of schism, and inconsistent with monarchy: for the regulating of either, there needs no other coercion than the due execution of the laws already established by parliament.

"If any attempt be made to alter the discipline of our Church, although it be not an essential part of our religion, yet it is so necessary not to be rashly altered, as the very substance of religion will be interested in it . . . it is dangerous to give the least ear to . . . innovators; but it is desperate to be misled by them."

"If any transplant themselves into plantations abroad, who are known schismatics . . . they [should] be sent for back upon the first notice; such persons are not fit to lay the foundation of a new colony."

Bacon's present disposition of mind towards Roman Catholics and Nonconformists shows the effect on his thinking of not only the Hampton Court Conference and the Gunpowder Plot, but the regicidal theories of some Papists, the attitude of the Puritan gentry towards the King's ecclesiastical courts and the use of his Prerogative, the aims of the Presbyterians, who seem determined on setting up a Genevan church government, and the contempt for law and magistrates by the Brownists, Anabaptists, and other fanatical sects. Thirteen years before, Bacon, as one who "lived more than two centuries ahead of his time," had advised the King to grant a greater religious toleration to his subjects than would be found in England for more than two hundred and fifty years. But events of the last dozen years have convinced him that such a toleration is not yet feasible. He no longer speaks as a theoretical Calvinist, still under the spell of his "fanatical" mother (d. 1610), but as a statesman taking a considerable part and about to take a greater part in the government of a kingdom. He thinks that the unity of the Established Church must be maintained, if grave political conflicts are to be averted. In the next reign these conflicts would come, as Bacon now knows they could; and after the downfall of King Charles I—the present Prince—Genevan ecclesiastical rule would be established in the Church of England. In succession to that, in the days of the Protector, Oliver Cromwell, there would be ecclesiastical chaos throughout the kingdom under the dispensation of disagreeing sects and a variety of self-designated

"Saints." Bacon's present task was the averting of such happenings.

The remainder of the first draft of the *Advice* contains admonitions respecting plantations or colonies. These remind one of the contents of the humanitarian letter of advice on Ireland which Bacon had sent, years before, to Robert Cecil. Bacon still wants "no extirpation of the natives under pretence of planting religion." The inhabitants of colonies are to "be governed according to the laws of this realm." Care is to be taken that "some few merchants and tradesmen, under colour of furnishing the colony with necessaries, may not grind them, so as shall always keep them in poverty." There are to be "such governors as may be qualified in such manner as may . . . lay the foundation of a new kingdom."

The second and longer draft of the *Advice* shows the range and variety of matters under the control of Villiers, who, Bacon says, is not merely a King's courtier, but a person "in his bosom also . . . for kings and great princes, even the wisest of them, have had their friends, their favourites, their privadoes in all ages." In this version Bacon brings under review the many institutions and offices of state, from the sovereign to embassies abroad. He lists the subjects on which Villiers will be receiving "petitions" and "petitioners" under eight headings:

I. Matters that concern religion, and the Church and churchmen.
II. Matters concerning justice, and the laws, and the professors thereof.
III. Councillors, and the council table, and the great offices and officers of the kingdom.
IV. Foreign negociations and embassies.
V. Peace and war, both foreign and civil, and in that the navy and forts, and what belongs to them.
VI. Trade at home and abroad.
VII. Colonies, or foreign plantations.
VIII. The court and curiality.

This second version of the *Advice* is a lengthy document.

Mention of some of its salient points will serve our present purpose. We shall continue to quote Bacon's own writing as definite evidence against misrepresentation, in "probabilities," of his understanding of the place and function of certain offices of government. At the beginning, Bacon tells Villiers, some of whose family connections have Roman Catholic inclinations, to be "rightly persuaded and settled in the true Protestant religion, professed by the Church of England, which doubtless is as sound and orthodox in the doctrine thereof, as any Christian church in the world." Of this church's discipline, "I will not positively say, as some do, that it is *jure divino*; but this I say and think *ex animo*, that it is the nearest to apostolical truth; and confidently I shall say, it is the fittest for monarchy of all others."

After warning the favourite against his being made "an instrument of Rome," Bacon tells him that "besides the Romish catholics, there is a generation of sectaries . . . they have been several times very busy in this kingdom, under the colour of zeal for reformation of religion: the king your master knows their disposition very well; a small touch will put him in mind of them; he had experience of them in Scotland, I hope he will beware of them in England; a little countenance or connivency sets them on fire . . . the true Protestant religion is seated in the golden mean; the enemies unto her are the extremes on either hand."

Bacon proceeds next to make clear his views respecting the place of laws, courts, and Parliament in the kingdom. "Let the rule of justice," he writes, "be the laws of the land, an impartial arbiter between the king and his people, and between one subject and another: I shall not speak superlatively of them, lest I be suspected of partiality, in regard of my own profession; but this I may truly say, they are second to none in the Christian world. . . ."

"And as far as it may lie in you, let no arbitrary power be

intruded: the people of this kingdom love the laws thereof, and nothing will oblige them more, than a confidence of the free enjoying of them."

"The execution of justice is committed to [the King's] judges, which seemeth to be the severer part; but the milder part, which is mercy, is wholly left in the king's immediate hand: and justice and mercy are the true supporters of his royal throne."

"By no means be you persuaded," Bacon warns the favorite, "to interpose yourself, either by word or letter, in any cause depending, or like to be depending in any court of justice, nor suffer any other great man to do it where you can hinder it, and by all means dissuade the king himself from it, upon the importunity of any for themselves or their friends."

Since the administration of justice has, in the Attorney's view, suffered from the interference of one court with the jurisdiction of another, he writes in admonition, "There are many courts . . . some superior, some provincial, and some of a lower orb: it were to be wished, and is fit to be so ordered, that every of them keep themselves within their proper spheres. The harmony of justice is then the sweetest."

Treating next of the two Houses of "the high court of parliament in England, which is superlative," Bacon affirms that "no new laws can be made, nor old laws abrogated or altered, but by common consent in parliament . . . but nothing is concluded but by the king's royal assent; they are but embryos, it is he giveth life unto them."

"But the house of commons have only power to censure the members of their own house, in point of election, or misdemeanours in or towards that house; and have not, nor ever had, power so much as to administer an oath to prepare a judgment."

"Yet the house of peers hath a power of judicature in some cases: properly to examine, and then to affirm; or, if there be cause, to reverse the judgments which have been given in the court of king's bench, which is the court of highest jurisdiction in the kingdom for ordinary judicature." However, when the House of Lords acts as a court of justice its office is not to make new laws but to determine causes "according to the known laws of the land."

Bacon would have occasion to recall these statements about the Houses of Parliament when, a few years hence, the Commons would be sending his own case on to the Lords. Now almost prophetically—when one thinks of the treatment of holders of Monopolies with Patents by the Commons in 1621 and of ensuing events in the reign of Charles I and during the Commonwealth—Bacon remarks that the "true use of parliaments in this kingdom is very excellent . . . but if they should be unjustly enlarged beyond their true bounds, they might lessen the just power of the Crown, it borders so near upon popularity."

There can be no doubt that the elder statesman's advice exercised for a number of years a restraining influence on Villiers. The favorite, however, was not to live up for long to the monitor's early hopes in several regards. The temptations which surrounded his place and his power were to prove too great for his nature. As Villiers' political experience and authority increased, he yielded to an ever-increasing desire to accumulate wealth. To this end he sold political offices, reputations—indeed, everything that could be rendered a subject of bargaining. In his financial negotiations, Villiers did not hesitate to use his mother, his brother, any relative. He even bought Coke's daughter for his worthless brother John at a large monetary price. Villiers would probably have sold justice itself, the law, and the constitution, had Bacon, as a mentor and a holder of high office, not stood in his way. Yet when Bacon had undergone an undeserved political trial before the court of the Lords and had been found guilty on a technical count, Villiers alone, of all his peers, refused to give his word of assent, and uttered Nay.

In 1616, the year in which Bacon presented the first draft of his *Advice* to Villiers, he became a Privy Councillor. The year after he was made Lord Keeper. So great a conception did Bacon have of the Lord Keeper's office, he even supposed that he should convey to the King's favorite the thought that its present incumbent could take over the government of the king-dom—under the advice of the Monarchy, of course, through correspondence by letter—while the King was absent in Scot-land. Bacon wrote to Villiers: "I had a conference with some Judges (not all, but such as I did choose), touching the High Commission and the extending of the same in some points; which I see I shall be able to despatch by consent, without his Majesty's further trouble. . . . And I see now that his Majesty is as well able by his letters to govern England from Scotland, as he was to govern Scotland from England." Bacon also told the judges, who were proceeding to their summer circuits, that "at this present [they] ought to make the people know and consider the King's blessed care and providence in governing this realm in his absence; so that sitting at the helm of another kingdom, not without great affairs and business; yet he governs all things here by his letters and directions, as punctually and perfectly as if he were present."

A month before writing this letter to Villiers, the Lord Keeper had assumed that he, as the Sovereign's deputy, could exercise his discretion by withholding a King's Proclamation to the Privy Council which commanded the nobles to absent them-selves from London during his Majesty's "progress" in Scot-land. (Bacon had either known or assumed that most of the nobility had already left the city.) James, on learning of the disregard of his order, made his displeasure known and re-minded the members of his Council that "obedience is better than sacrifice, and that he knoweth he is King of England."

Having made it evident to Villiers and the judges that he regarded himself as the Sovereign's deputy, both in form and in fact, and having disobeyed an order of the King, the Lord Keeper overstepped discretion a third time while both James and Villiers were in the north. At this period, Edward Coke was engaged in improving his political lot, to "make a faction," as Bacon thought, by ingratiating himself with Villiers. Some time before, the favorite's brother, Sir John Villiers, had begun to look with favor on Coke's daughter, whose father and mother both had considerable means. After the favorite began a negotiation for a marriage between the two, and then demanded a large dowry, the transaction was suspended. The favorite had asked for an immediate payment by Coke of £10,000 with an annual gratuity of £1,000, but Coke had offered only £6,666 all told. The girl's father, after being dismissed from office and "disgraced," renewed the bargaining. He finally settled for £30,000. Coke's wife, Lady Hatton, a woman of character and spirit, had been far from pleased from the first with the negotiation between her husband and Villiers. She claimed that her daughter was not of a mind to marry Sir John, having another admirer—real or fictitious—in view and desire. Lady Hatton removed her daughter, without the father's knowledge, to a place near Oatlands, and afterwards hid her in a house of the Lord of Argyle near Hampton Court. Coke, who discovered the place of the daughter's seclusion, asked Villiers' mother to obtain a warrant from the Lord Keeper for her recovery. When this was refused by Bacon, another writ was sought and obtained from Winwood, the Secretary of State. Then with a troop of retainers, including a pugilist, Coke went to the house where the daughter was secreted, "but indeed went farther than his warrant, and brake open divers doors before he got her." Bacon meanwhile—still remembering, no doubt, that he once had wooed Lady Hatton and lost her to his rival in both love and the law—helped the mother to obtain a warrant for the custody of her child, who by this writ was now brought within the care of the Privy Council. Lady Hatton had received promise of his aid in this regard after she had affrighted Bacon by entering his private quarters and bouncing against the door of his bedroom during one of his periodic illnesses. She had acted, as she admitted when begging the Lord Keeper's pardon, with the fury of "a cow that had lost its calf." Coke, for his violent rescue of the daughter, was summoned before the Privy Council where an order was made to charge him in the Court of Star Chamber with "force and riot." Winwood, however, when requested to explain to the Privy Councillors his part in the proceedings, as one threatened with a *praemunire* by the Lord Keeper, produced a letter from James which approved of the Attorney-General's action. Thereupon the Council made a retraction and sent information to this effect to the King.

Bacon had meddled earlier in the nuptial business by sending Villiers a letter which reflected on the favorite's judgment, his friends, and his place in the King's service. Bacon had also written the King, mentioning the "humbled Sir Edward Coke" and warning James that if Coke were restored to the Council— an eventuality which Bacon surmised might be the result of the present business—division in that body would inevitably follow. To Villiers he had written respecting the match in prospect as follows:

I hold it very inconvenient both for your brother and yourself. First, he shall marry into a disgraced house. . . . Next, he shall marry into a troubled house of man and wife, which in Christian discretion is disliked. . . . Thirdly, your lordship will go near to lose all such your friends as are adverse to Sir Edward Coke. . . . Lastly, it will greatly weaken and distract the King's service. . . . Therefore my advice is . . . your lordship will signify unto my lady, your mother, that your desire is the marriage be not pressed or proceeded in without the consent of both parents . . . the rather for that it hath been carried so harshly and inconsiderately by Secretary Winwood; as, for doubt that the father should take away the maiden by force, the mother, to get the start, hath conveyed her away secretly. . . . Hoping your lordship will not only accept well, but believe my faithful advice, who, by my great experience of the world, must needs see further than your lordship can.

When Bacon came to realize that he had gone much too far in pursuing something which was in truth not his legitimate concern, he wrote the King a letter by which, he knew, he could provide only an extremely lame excuse. This letter was, in fact, one of the few halting, disjointed, and irrelative statements Bacon ever carefully penned. Even the scriptural references, put in for James' appeasing, carried no point. In the missive Bacon admitted that in his recent advice to Villiers he had been "a little too parent-like, this being no other term, than his lordship hath heretofore vouchsafed to my counsels. . . . But yet I was afraid, that the height of his fortune might make him too secure; and as the proverb is, a looker-on sometimes seeth more than a gamester." Bacon acknowledged, too, that at the Council Table he had sometimes been "sharp, it may be too much," in statements where Sir Edward Coke was concerned. This admission was followed, however, by a reference to Coke's "riot or violence." Bacon brought his "explanation" to an end with an unfortunate reference to Solomon, to whom he had often before compared the King, saying, "Solomon were no true man, if in matter of malice the woman should not be superior."

Sir Henry Yelverton, Bacon's successor in both the Solicitor-Generalship and the Attorney-Generalship, who also had incurred the King's displeasure for his opposition to the Villiers-Coke negotiations, found it politic to make a journey to Coventry to meet James in an attempt to bring himself and the Lord Keeper into the King's good graces. He was accompanied on his journey by none other than Coke. Yelverton reported to Bacon by letter that "Sir Edward Coke hath not forborne by any engine to heave both at your Honour and at myself." The Attorney said that he had "seen the face of . . . the King . . . more clouded towards me than I looked for," and, when he had been given the royal hand to kiss, he had been told by James that he "deserved not that favour, if three or four things were true." In his letter Yelverton advised Bacon to present himself to the King "bravely and confidently, wherein you can excel all subjects." The Attorney also thought it well to incite the Lord Keeper to heroic action on the present occasion by intimating some things touching the latter's reputation. He mentioned his belief that "it is too common in every man's mouth in court, that your greatness shall be abated; and as your tongue hath been as a razor to some, so shall theirs be to you." He also warned the Lord Keeper that "there are laid up for you, to make your burden the more grievous, many petitions to his majesty against you."

The King, before he reached London, during his progress homeward, put Bacon in his place by a letter which contained "some observations" on the Lord Keeper's conduct in the present affair. James had suffered on more than one occasion from Bacon's barbed comments on his handling of the nation's business. Even Bacon's high praises had been lessons in regal conduct. Now an opportunity had come to return this treatment. The King censured his Lord Keeper for his official legal proceeding—a very touchy point. James wrote:

And was not the thefteous stealing away of the daughter from her own father the first ground whereupon all this great noise hath since proceeded? For the ground of her getting again came upon a lawful and ordinary warrant, subscribed by one of our council, for redress of the former violence: and except the father of a child might be proved to be either lunatic, or idiot, we never read in any law, that either it could be lawful for any creature to steal his child from him; or that it was a matter of noise and streperous carriage for him to hunt for the recovery of his child again. . . .

[In] your opposition to this business . . . you either do, or at least would seem to, mistake us a little. For first, whereas you excuse yourself of the oppositions you made against Sir Edward Coke at the council-table, both for that, and other causes; we never took upon us such a patrociny of Sir Edward Coke, as if he were a man not to be meddled withal in any case.

James also reproached Bacon for the unfriendliness and bad manners he had displayed throughout his recent treatment of Villiers, and continued:

We will not speak of obligation; for surely we think, even in good manners, you had reason not to have crossed any thing, wherein you had heard his name used, till you had heard from him. For if you had willingly given your consent and hand to the recovery of the young gentlewoman; and then written both to us and to him what inconvenience appeared to you to be in such a match; that had been the part indeed of a true servant to us, and a true friend to him. But first to make an opposition; and then to give advice by way of friendship, is to make the plow go before the horse.

The King charged Bacon with suspicion and jealousy and wrote:

You say, that you were afraid that the height of his fortune might make him too secure; and so, as a looker-on, you might sometime see more than a gamester. Now we know not how to interpret this in plain English otherwise, than that you were afraid, that the height of his fortune might make him misknow himself. And surely, if that be your 'parent-like affection' toward him, he hath no obligation to you for it. And, for our part, besides our own proof, that we find him farthest from that vice of any courtier, than ever we had so near about us: so do we fear, that you shall prove the only phenix in that jealousy of all the kingdom.

In an attempt to retreat from the perilous position in which his persistent dislike for Coke had landed him, Bacon made an oral "submission" to Villiers, who turned this into a plea for forgiveness to the King. Villiers wrote a reply in pencil:

I do freely confess that *your offer of submission unto me, and in writing (if so I would have it)*, battered so the unkindness that

I had conceived in my heart for your behaviour towards me in my absence, as out of the sparks of my old affection toward you I went to sound his Majesty's intention how he means to behave himself toward you, specially in any public meeting; where I found on the one part his Majesty so little satisfied with your late answer unto him, which he counted (for I protest I use his own terms) *confused and childish,* and his vigorous resolution on the other part so fixed, that he would put some public exemplary mark upon you, as I protest the sight of his deep-conceived indignation quenched my passion, making me upon the instant change from the person of a party into a peacemaker; so I was forced upon my knees to beg of his Majesty that he would put no public act of disgrace upon you, and, as I dare say, no other person would have been patiently heard in this suit by his Majesty but myself, so did I (though not without difficulty) obtain thus much: —that he would not so far disable you from the merit of your future service, as to put any particular mark of disgrace upon your person.

Villiers added, as a solicitous observer writing in portent:

I protest all this time past it was no small grief unto me to hear the mouth of so many upon this occasion open to load you with innumerable malicious and detracting speeches, as if no music were more pleasing to my ears than to rail of you: which made me rather regret the ill-nature of mankind, that like dogs love to set upon him that they see once snatched at.

A relieved Bacon wrote in reply:

My ever best Lord, now better than yourself, your Lordship's pen, or rather pencil, hath portrayed towards me such magnanimity and nobleness and true kindness, as methinketh I see the image of some ancient virtue and not anything of these times. It is the line of my life and not the lines of my letter that must express my thankfulness; wherein, if I fail, then God fail me, and make me as miserable as I think myself at this time happy by this reviver through his Majesty's clemency and your incomparable love and favour.

The now chastened Lord Keeper, who had been soaring too high, knew that he was never again to presume that he might be the deputed ruler of England; that his jurisdiction was to be confined to the courts of law; that in his dealings with the favorite, whose will was one with that of James, he could no longer play the part of one *in loco parentis*. Lady Hatton's daughter became Lady Villiers. Coke paid his £30,000 and again became a member of the Council. The Villiers family took another step forward on the road to riches. The Lord Keeper of the Great Seal, having been reminded of his place, and having acknowledged this, was restored to royal favor. The next year (1618) he was made Lord Chancellor and Baron Verulam of Verulam.

Villiers was fast becoming a very wealthy man, the wealthiest, it was said, of all save one in England. With the accumulating of a monetary fortune he was not, however, satisfied. The favorite would also establish in perpetuity the Villiers family as the foremost in the land. To the disposition of the Scottish King, this ambition was quite agreeable. "Of myself," said James, "I have no doubt, for I live to that end; and I hope that my posterity will so far regard their father's commandments and instructions so as to advance that house above all others whatever." In order to effect the desire for such eminence on the part of the Villiers family, one other clan would have to be reduced, namely, the powerful Howards. Its members and dependents were in occupancy of most of the commanding places in government: the offices of Lord Treasurer, Lord High Admiral, Master of the Wards, Secretary of State, and Attorney-General. The holders of the first and second of these offices were Howards, of the third the son-in-law of a Howard, of the fourth and fifth dependents of the Howard family. It occurred to the favorite that if it became necessary to pay present holders for the relinquishment of one or two of these offices, the filling of enforced vacancies in the others would provide more than compensating perquisites. In any event, no matter what the immediate profit or loss might be, the occupants of all five places must be ousted by whatever means.

Villiers himself was already Master of the Horse (1616); he

would assume the office of Lord High Admiral as well (1621). Charles Howard, Earl of Nottingham, the present occupant, was old and incompetent. As luck would have it, he had resisted an inquiry by a Naval commission, whose report had in the end showed many abuses in administration. The suggestion was conveyed to Nottingham that he should give up the office. To this he agreed as a return for a pension from the King and other compensation from the favorite. The Master of the Wards, Viscount Wallingford, the son-in-law of Thomas Howard, Earl of Suffolk, surrendered easily after an offer of compensation had been made, and after he had been told, among other things, of the King's displeasure at his wife's lampooning the Villiers faction.

In the reduction of other members of the Howard connection, Bacon's duties as judge rendered him an agent in furthering Villiers' family designs, because these holders of office had either left or would leave themselves open to attack through legal causes. The Secretary of State, Sir Thomas Lake, despite his offering the favorite a bribe of £15,000—which probably found its way into the purse of Villiers' mother—was charged with malfeasance, found guilty, sentenced to fine and imprisonment, and put out of office. The Lord Treasurer, Thomas Howard, Earl of Suffolk, was put out of his place for malpractice, and brought to trial along with his wife for embezzlement. The sentence imposed on the guilty parties was a fine of £30,000. Coke had wanted to make the penalty £100,000. Bacon was to have occasion to remember this sentence, when Suffolk was his accuser and a party to his sentencing in the court of the House of Lords.

The Attorney-General, Yelverton, came to grief through his self-assurance, a quality which characterized members of the Howard family and faction, even the most irresolute among them. This characteristic was displayed when Yelverton failed to obey an order of the King in cases involving a Monopoly, and when afterwards he amended on his own authority the clauses of a Royal Charter. The Monopoly concerned had been granted to a company in which Sir Edward Villiers, the favorite's brother, had invested £4,000. The reason advanced by the patentees to the certifying judges for its granting was the furtherance of national prosperity by keeping the goldsmiths from melting down the gold coin of the realm. Under the Monopoly only imported gold was to be used in the manufacture of thread and laces, two articles in wide demand for uniforms and elegant clothes. The goldsmiths put up a strong resistance and, as opponents of a Monopoly, received large support from London manufacturers generally.

Violators of the Patent were charged, but cases brought against them in the Court of Exchequer were abandoned. The King then wrote to Yelverton as Attorney-General, telling him to have offenders detained. Yelverton failed to act, presuming, as he explained, that the King, who had been in the north, was not aware of the extent of the current opposition to the Monopoly and to the arrest of its violators. Bacon, as Lord Chancellor, and as one of those responsible for passing on the Patent, argued that by an Act of Henry VII goldsmiths had been forbidden to melt gold and silver except for the making of certain objects; the Monopoly was, therefore, good in precedent. As violations of the Patent increased, a commission was appointed to undertake the discovery of offenders; this included a kinsman of Buckingham, Sir Giles Mompesson, who himself held the Patent for Inns. The commissioners were instructed to bring persons charged before the Star Chamber, but the cases they brought there were abandoned one after another. The patentees then appealed to the Attorney-General to maintain the Monopoly as a grant good in law. Yelverton, for answer, resorted to the questionable device of simply putting offenders into prison and then throwing the onus of their continued confinement, or disposal otherwise, upon the Lord Chancellor.

When the Attorney-General refused to keep arrested persons under further restraint, the Lord Chancellor promptly had them recommitted. An uproar arose in the City, where bail in the amount of £100,000 was raised. A deputation was sent to the King and the prisoners were released. The outlawed goldsmiths were now the victors in what was a skirmish against the Royal Prerogative, within which the Monopoly had been granted. This skirmish was to prove but an incident in a constitutional battle which was now taking shape. A breach, however small, had been made in a constitution sustained by the Prerogative. Coke and his judges had made earlier breaches. These had been repaired, but only temporarily. There would come a time, even in the next reign, when the traditional line of constitution would be broken and its holding forces put to rout.

Yelverton now began to feel a little too sure of himself after his success in refusing an order of the King and then throwing a legal onus, which he himself should have dealt with, on the shoulders of the Lord Chancellor. He was even growing "pert" with the Chancellor, as Bacon had occasion to note. When, as Attorney-General, Yelverton was called upon to draw up the Charter recently granted to the City of London, he proceeded to insert nonauthorized clauses of his own, clauses "not agreeable to his Majesty's warrant, and derogatory to his honour." For this act he was brought before the Star Chamber. On the accused's making a submission, denying "corruption" and acknowledging only "error" in "mistaking" the King's directive, a majority of the councillors voted to stay proceedings until James had been informed of the submission. The reason for this course of action was doubtless the fact that Yelverton had paid James £4,000 for his office! (The King had used the money to buy needed dishes for the Palace.) Bacon wrote to Villiers: "I do not like of this course, in respect that it puts the King in a strait; for either the note of severity must rest upon his Majesty if he go on; or the thanks of clemency is in some part taken away, if his Majesty do not go on." James did not interfere, and the case continued.

The Lord Chancellor, in an address to the court, remarked on his past association with the accused: how he had lived with him in Gray's Inn; had served with him when he had been the Crown Attorney; had joined with him in legal endeavors; how the accused had been one who gave him "more attributes in public" than he "deserved," and was "a man of very good parts." Yet, as a judge, Bacon found himself compelled to regard the offence of the present Attorney-General as a very great one, for if officers of the Crown, entrusted with warrants, "shall practise the art of multiplication upon their warrants, the crown will be destroyed in small time. The great seal, the privy seal, signet, are solemn things." Bacon was far from satisfied with the statement in defence that the Attorney-General's "mistaking" was a mere error in judgment; rather, he was of the opinion that the "error" amounted to both a contempt and an excess of authority. He concluded his brief speech by recalling "the wisdom of the law of England, which termeth the highest contempts and excesses of authority, 'misprisions'; which, if you take the sound and derivation of the words, is but 'mistaken.' " Mistaking, in this sense, "is ever joined with contempt; for he, that reveres, will not easily mistake; but he, that slights, and thinks more of the greatness of his place than of the duty of his place, will soon commit misprisions." The accused was found guilty. Coke proposed a fine of £6,000, but the court reduced this amount. Yelverton was fined £4,000, given a nominal sentence to the Tower, and discharged from office.

Bacon's decision in the case, was, of course, both informed and just. There is no reason for supposing that Bacon on this, or any other, occasion "perverted justice." One instance, however, has been cited by E. A. Abbott, a biographer who pursues Bacon through every incident of his life, both private and public, with a "moral" guile that sometimes appears malignant, to prove that Bacon could subvert justice. Abbott calls this "the one case in which the Chancellor is apparently shown . . . to have been guilty of a deliberate perversion of justice." The action concerned a minor, eight years of age, who had been left a legacy of £800 and a share in his parents' property. The rents were to be collected by the executors, two uncles, a Dr. Steward and his brother, until the boy became twenty years of age. In the ensuing years the rents and profits, if any, became mixed with the uncles' own incomes and outlays. When the youth was twenty, in 1617, he filed a suit for the recovery of the money with profits. The uncles were unable to say whether they had "made any commodity out of the estate or not."

Bacon, having heard argument in the case, gave a formal order that the defendants "answer over to the point of the legacy," to show whether or not there had been profit on the estate. Indignant over what they considered an injustice in the circumstances, the defendants refused to answer for several months, claiming that they could not provide the particulars demanded. When half a year had gone by, the uncles made a statement of the amount of the estate due the heir, without providing an account of profit, this "being a thing by law not due to the plaintiff nor yet in equity, as these defendants verily believe any man will think that shall be truly informed of this case." The court's order was confirmed, but the defendants still refused to make further response. Dr. Steward could have asked for a rehearing before the decree was made final, but had failed to do so, either through ignorance of judicial practice or on the presumption that a further hearing would but lead to an accumulation of court costs.

After several new orders, of increasing severity, had been issued to force the defendants to comply with the court's decision, Dr. Steward made an appeal to Villiers as the accessible agent of the King. There was, of course, nothing unusual about a petitioning of the King through his immediate agent in a matter "concerning justice." Bacon in his second *Advice* to Villiers had mentioned this as one of the subjects on which he would receive "petitions."

Villiers first sent a letter to Bacon, saying, "I owe Dr. Steward a good turn which I know not how to perform but this way." This was the sort of note by which the approachable Villiers would terminate, so far as he was concerned, the solicitations of petitioners. On giving second thought to the case, however, Villiers began to suspect there might have been a miscarriage of justice through the Chancellor's being misinformed of circumstances by officers of court, who sometimes were not above withholding information which might prolong actions. The present case was complicated by the young plaintiff's "infirmity"; and during the proceedings the Solicitor-General had thought it just and proper to oppose the order being made. Villiers dispatched a second, less casual letter to the Chancellor, with a description of Dr. Steward—whom he called "a man of very good reputation, and a stout man that will not yield to anything wherein he conceiveth any hard course against him"—and the request: "If you can advise of any course how you may be eased of that burden and freed from his complaint, without shew of any fear of him or anything he can say, I will be ready to join with you for the accomplishment thereof." Villiers seemed to be of the opinion that, however correct the formalities of the case may have been, justice and equity had not prevailed.

On receiving Villiers' second letter, Bacon heard Dr. Steward *in camera*, had the litigants in the case brought together, ordered the defendants to pay £800—the amount of the original legacy— into court, and appointed a commission to investigate the conditions and circumstances surrounding any profits. There was nothing unconstitutional in Bacon's thinking about such a reopening after judgment had been made. He had addressed Chancery on first taking his seat there with these words: "I will say, that the opinion, not to relieve any case after judgment, would be a guilty opinion: guilty of the ruin, and naufrage, and perishing of infinite subjects." On the same occasion the Lord Chancellor had said that, in certain cases respecting "revenue, or treasure, or profit": "If . . . I do forsee inconvenience to ensue . . . in respect of the King's honour, or discontent, and murmur of the people; I will not trust mine own judgment, but I will either acquaint his majesty with it, or the council table, or some such of my lords as I shall think fit."

Abbott goes too far when he assumes that contemporary practice precluded the reference of a "closed" case to an advisory commission. The range of matters dealt with by committees of the Privy Council in Bacon's day was very wide. Abbott is also guilty of wrong judgment when he assumes that Bacon's professions respecting justice were not consistent with his practice. The weight of biographical opinion, both critical and sympathetic, is in favor of Bacon and against Abbott. More than one biographer has pointed out that had Bacon been guilty of a perversion of justice in this case, which had on several occasions been before the courts, his wrongdoing would have been discovered and published before and during his trial when his enemies—among them the energetic Edward Coke—resorted to an examination of the proceedings in cases over which he had presided.

England's affairs were now in the hands of Bacon, the Lord Chancellor, Villiers, the favorite, and Sir Lionel Cranfield, a "born financier." Through the skill of Cranfield the financial worries of the King and Council had been abated. He was "a London prentice," with a natural aptitude for casting accounts, who had got his first start in the world by marrying his master's daughter. Despite his lowly origin he had become Master of the Wards. Cranfield introduced economies into the management of the King's Household, the Wardrobe, the Admiralty, and the Treasury, and increased the annual revenues from Customs and wine duties from £90,000 to £156,000. He had impressed the King and Council as early as 1615 with his economic policy of decreasing levies on exports and increasing duties on imports. At that time Bacon had expressed his concurrence in this policy, and added a statement which he was to have cause to remember during his political tribulations in 1621. "I do allow well," he had said, "the proposition of Sir Lionel Cranfield, being more indeed than I could have looked for from a man of his breeding."

While the "base fellow" Cranfield—as Bacon called him because of his origin—was providing a bulwark for the Treasury, Bacon was sustaining the Royal Prerogative and all that this implied for the continuity of the unwritten constitution of England. In an address in the Court of Exchequer, Bacon told Sir John Denham, who had been called to be one of the barons of the Exchequer, that "above all you ought to maintain the King's prerogative, and to set down with yourself, that the King's prerogative and the law are not two things; but the King's prerogative is law, and the principal part of the law, the first-born or *pars prima* of the law; and therefore in conserving or maintaining that, you conserve and maintain the law. There is not in the body of man one law of the head, and another of the body, but all is one entire law."

In a speech in the Star Chamber, Bacon went even further when he admonished the judges before they set forth on their summer circuits. On this occasion he told his listeners: "You that are the judges of circuits are, as it were, the planets of the kingdom, I do you no dishonor in giving you that name, and no doubt you have a great stroke in the frame of this government, as the other have in the great frame of the world. Do therefore as they do, move always, and be carried with the motion of your first mover, which is your Sovereign. A popular judge is a deformed thing; and 'plaudites' are fitter for players than for magistrates." Bacon was now depicting the King, the primary source of law and justice, after the manner of James himself, as the *Primum Mobile*, the First Moved by God. In the Aristotelian cosmology the planet which is first moved, because closest of all to the Prime Mover, communicates its motion to the other spheres, to each according to its position in the planetary scheme; even as in the case of the political kingdom the initiative divinely bestowed upon the sovereign is passed on to each judge in turn according to his place in the judicial system. Bacon as Lord Chancellor naturally took great satisfaction in regarding himself as the planet nearest of all to the *Primum Mobile*!

XI

BACON'S POLITICAL DOWNFALL

O N JANUARY 22nd, 1621, FRANCIS BACON celebrated his sixtieth birthday in the house of his birth, York House in the Strand. His guests included Ben Jonson who poeticized "the fire, the wine, the men," and sang of

> England's High Chancellor, the destin'd heir
> In his soft cradle of his father's chair,
> Whose even thread the Fates spin round and full
> Out of their choicest and their whitest wool.

Already a peer of the realm, the host was five days later to be created Viscount St. Albans, "with all the ceremonies of robes and coronet." This would be his "eighth rise or reach, or diapason in music," he told the King in his letter of thanks. Bacon could have been forgiven for any reflection of his on his extraordinarily good fortune: how he had risen in Court from "Learned Counsel, Extraordinary without patent" to Chancellor of the Realm; how he had been made a Privy Counsellor even while Attorney-General, a "kind of miracle," as he said, "that had not been in many ages." Now he had a court of his own at Gorhambury near St. Albans. His London mansion, York House in the Strand, was a dwelling fit for a king. He could still remember that occasion when, in 1618, he first took his seat in the

213

Court of Chancery. Then a reporter of news had been able to write that "to the Hall, besides his own retinue, did accompany him all the Lords of his Majesty's Council and others, with all knights and gentleman that could get horses and footcloths." "He was accompanied," as John Chamberlain said, "by most of the nobility, with other gallants, to the number of more than 200 horses, besides the Judges and the Inns of Court. There was a great deal more bravery and better show of horse than was expected in the King's absence; but both Queen [Anne] and Prince [Charles] sent all their followers and his other friends did their best to honour him."

This had happened three years before. Since then Bacon had been able to publish, only some months earlier, his *New Organon*, a nonpolitical and nonlegal writing in which he had been able to assert a dominion over nature. Bacon might have been excused, therefore, if he was now regarding himself (in Abraham Cowley's later words) as the one

> Whom a wise king and nature chose
> The Chancellor of both their laws.

Parliament would soon be assembled, because the Spaniards had invaded the Palatinate, of which the King's son-in-law, who had married James' daughter Elizabeth, was the "rightful prince." The King would be asking for money with the plea that Protestants on the Continent must be supported. Funds would be granted without opposition from the Nonconformists, because Frederick of the Palatinate was the leading Calvinist Prince of Germany. The Commons would again be voting supply. All the institutions of government would be in function. The Lord Chancellor was contemplating with great satisfaction the meeting of a new Parliament. He had always been a Parliamentary man. Recognition of his political capacity and the political trust of his peers had first been given him by the Lower House. At Parliament's next meeting he would not be in the Commons; yet he would address both Houses at the opening. His speech would follow upon that of the King. Already he had made notes of an address "intended to be spoken after the King's speech." It would include an admonition, in keeping with what he had said on earlier occasions, against meddling with *Arcana Imperii*. After Parliament had got under way he would be able to relax for study and recreation in the summerhouse which he had built near the fish ponds at Gorhambury. There he would meditate on problems in science and the law.

But nemesis in its ancient guise, as politico-social disapproval and pressure, was to intervene. Within four months the High Court of Parliament, having tried the Lord Chancellor on a charge of bribery, would adjudge:

1. That the Lord Viscount St. Alban, Lord Chancellor of England, shall undergo fine and ransom for forty thousand pounds.
2. That he shall be imprisoned in the Tower during the King's pleasure.
3. That he shall for ever be incapable of an office, place, or employment in the State or Commonwealth.
4. That he shall never sit in Parliament, nor come within the verge of the Court.

"There had been," as a biographer, R. W. Church, has said, "and were still to be, plenty of instances of the downfall of power, as ruinous and even more tragic. . . . But it is hard to find one of which so little warning was given, the causes of which are in part so clear and in part so obscure. . . . Every public man, in the England of the Tudors and the Stewarts, entered on his career with the perfectly familiar expectation of possibly closing it . . . in the Tower and on the scaffold. . . . So that when disaster came, though it might be unexpected as death is unexpected, it was a turn of things which ought not to take a man by surprise. But some premonitory symptoms usually gave warning. There was nothing to warn Bacon that the work which he believed he was doing so well would be interrupted."

This statement is not completely apt. There had been some "premonitory symptoms." Both Villiers and Yelverton had told Bacon of petitions against him to the King, and James himself had given intimation that this was so. There had been widespread discontent over Monopolies—whose warrants Bacon, as a certifying referee, had sanctioned—and over Proclamations, presumed to have the force of law, on the part of the Privy Council, of which Bacon had for several years been a member. The nation, said John Chamberlain in a correspondence, is already "much terrified with the Star Chamber, there being not so little an offence against any Proclamation but is liable and subject to the censure of that Court; and, for Proclamations and Patents, they are become so ordinary that there is no end, every day bringing forth some new project or other. In truth the world doth even groan under the burthen of these perpetual Patents; which are become so frequent that whereas, at the King's coming in, there were complaints of some eight or nine Monopolies then in being, they are now said to be multiplied by so many scores."

As early as October, 1620, a committee, with Bacon presiding, had been appointed by the Council for the perusing of Monopolies and other "grievances." This committee had selected for consideration some "that are most in speech, and do most tend either to the vexation of the common people, or the discontenting of the gentlemen and Justices." It had noted that there were "many more, of like nature but not of like weight, nor so much rumoured; which to take away now in a blaze, will give more scandal that such things were granted, than cause thanks that they be now revoked." The selected grievances were reported to the King and Villiers, who left their disposition to the Council. Members of the Council, still "irresolute," were not in agreement over what should be done. Coke, an opponent of the granting of Monopolies, as something which lay within the King's Prerogative, probably knew at this time what was in store for Bacon and therefore was not eager to mitigate circumstances by helping the Council decide on a course of action. The Lord Chancellor was inclined to think that some of the Patents should be cancelled, but he did not press the matter. He believed, of course, that if criticism were directed against him, or any of the other judges who had sanctioned the Patents, he would be able to make a good defence by showing that in certifying the Monopolies the referees had acted in the public interest. Monopolies had long been employed successfully as devices for strengthening the kingdom's economy. They had promoted invention through assuring discoverers of rewards for their ingenuity and labor. When the upholding of quality had been required of importers with Patents, the public had been protected from the sale of inferior foreign goods. Monopolies had served to encourage native manufacture by assuring sales until such time as English products were able to compete with those from abroad. When services had become lax and inferior, as in the case of inns, for example, these, it could be presumed, were improved through granting a Patent which entailed the meeting of a standard.

Parliament met on January 30th, 1621. In the Commons were Sir Edward Coke, Bacon's enemy of old, and Sir Lionel Cranfield, mindful of slights from the Lord Chancellor. In the Lords were Southampton, formerly a conspirator with Essex, and one whose imprisonment Bacon had helped secure; Suffolk, whom Bacon had recently fined and sentenced to the Tower; and Suffolk's son, another Howard. Members generally of the two Houses were already acquainted with or would soon be made aware of certain things which in recent years the Lord Chancellor had condoned, defended, or advocated: the Benevolence, to which most of those present had been called upon to contribute; Monopolies whose discussion in Parliament had been inhibited; the rendering of the courts consonant with what the King desired through his consultation with the judges. Other practices which Bacon had expressly opposed in "advices," in speeches in

Parliament, and in addresses to courts of law, would be wrongly associated with his name, as one given to defending the Royal Prerogative: the depriving of a people of their Parliament when it would not come to heel; the provision of supply for the Treasury without recourse to the Commons; the invasion of the consciences of subjects through the requirement of "one doctrine, one discipline, one religion," always the same "in substance and ceremony"; the excommunication and depriving of worthy ministers by prelates; the continuance of illegal Purveyance and outmoded Wardships and Tenures; the King's acting as if he thought that of all the inhabitants of the realm he alone possessed and would ever retain the power of political initiative, and that all the privileges of settled institutions and lawful subjects were revocable by him.

These many matters for grievance were not made the ground of an indictment or a move for impeachment against the Lord Chancellor; yet they were inherent within that political nemesis which had chosen him as the victim of its fury. If these matters had been made reasons for legal causes, Bacon could have answered them on grounds of fact or constitutional principle. Had the charge against Bacon been his part in the declaring of Proclamations, in that case Coke, as a member of the Council, would have been equally responsible with the Lord Chancellor, as would also several members of the House of Lords—the court before which Bacon was eventually to be tried. If the nature of Monopolies granted had been the reason for proceeding against the Lord Chancellor, then all the referees who passed on the Patents would have been equally involved. If the members of the King's ecclesiastical courts had been brought to trial, the accused would have included Lords Spiritual within the Upper House. If issues from the Prerogative had been made causes in law, then the King himself would have been tried by what he considered his own courts and his own Parliament. (This was to happen in the next reign.) Events, however, did not proceed in any of these ways. Punitive action was taken against one member of the Privy Council, one judge, one member of Parliament, one subject alone—Francis Bacon. He was to be fined, imprisoned, and put forever out of public life for having taken gifts from litigants in cases pending, when his judges knew that the giving and receiving of such presents was a conventional practice and, in Bacon's case, had never occasioned a departure from justice or legal rectitude.

By February 5th a committee on grievances had been set up by the Commons. A member of the House, Noy, moved, and Coke seconded, a resolution that Monopolies should be investigated. Coke, again a member of the Commons after his expulsion from the office of Lord Chief Justice, was an experienced Parliamentarian, and knew a great deal about courts of law. He would tell the Commons just when the court of the Lords was to be approached, and would meanwhile permit the Commons to act as arbitrarily as he himself had done in the ordinary courts over which he had earlier presided and in the Star Chamber, of which, as one of the Privy Council, he was also a member. The Monopoly on Alehouses was brought up for consideration. The committee discovered that, instead of curbing drunkenness, many licensed proprietors were encouraging violation of laws against this offense by collecting their own private penalties from the transgressors whom they harbored. Sir Francis Michell, who had administered the Patent, was summarily and arbitrarily condemned without any entertainment of a defence. Another Patent (for Inns) was held by Sir Giles Mompesson. After an investigation, it was found that this patentee had demanded perquisites before he issued licenses, and that of inns he had licensed in one shire alone some sixty had been closed as disorderly houses. Mompesson admitted in a petition that "so general a Patent cannot but be a great grievance to the subject." The committee at first decided, with Coke agreeing, that this Patent was good in law but not in execution, but later reported through Coke that it

was bad both in execution and in law—without an apposite defining of terms. Mompesson fled to the Continent and was
sentenced *in absentia* by the Lords to imprisonment for life.

The Monopoly for the manufacture of gold thread and laces
presented a special problem and in consequence occasioned a
resourceful tactic on the part of Coke and a denunciation by
James. In 1619, Bacon, in order to relieve the courts of law, had
this Monopoly put under the direct jurisdiction of the King,
who since then, along with the two Villiers—as former patentees
and now pensioners—had been receiving whatever profits the
Monopoly brought. It was no longer an ordinary Monopoly.
James took occasion to inform Parliament that in his opinion
any inquiry into such a "Monopoly" as this, and indeed into any
Patent granted by the King, was a presumption of a right which
Parliament did not possess. The Lower House was now, in effect,
attempting to revive an old and long-unused principle of Impeachment by Parliament, whose employment had had precedent only in former times of political anarchy. The Commons,
none the less, insisted on a discussion with the Lords on the
question of Patents. At the meeting which followed, when the
representatives of the Commons presented their case, the Lord
Chancellor was refused admission to reply to their charges.

Up to this point Bacon had regarded the recent conduct of
the members of the Lower House in a purely constitutional light.
He had not looked with favor on their debating the Monopolies
granted by the King and he had been appalled by their high-
handed action in the case of Michell. The latter was an indication
of what might follow from an assumption by Parliament of
sovereign power. By now, because of his treatment during the
conference between the two Houses, and from indications on
the part of Coke and Cranfield that the Commons were casting
their gaze in the direction of the Chancery—but not of the Star
Chamber, to which Coke belonged—Bacon began to realize that
not all of the members of the Privy Council nor all of the
judges who had certified the Monopolies, but only *one* council-

lor and *one* judge, the Lord Chancellor, would soon be called upon to bear the brunt of an attack. Bacon warned James that "those that will strike at your Chancellor, it is much feared will strike at your Crown."

Soon the committee of the Commons began an inquiry into the proceedings of the Chancery. Bacon who, as an upholder of the King's Prerogative, had been distressed by their attitude towards the whole question of Monopolies and their treatment of Michell, welcomed this turn of events. He was willing "that any man might speak freely anything concerning his court." However, at this juncture, to the Lord Chancellor's disquiet, a former Deputy Registrar of the Chancery, John Churchill, who some time before had been cashiered for exacting fees for forging documents, came upon the scene, bearing "revelations." Before long, the investigating committee was reporting that it had also received "divers petitions, many frivolous and clamorous," but also "many of weight and consequence," against practices in the Chancellor's court. So far, the petitions seemed to be complaints against real or imagined incivilities and inattentions by court officials. But by the middle of March, information was received and evidence provided of two cases in which the Chancellor had accepted gifts from suitors while their causes were still pending in his court. Bacon, on being informed of a report on the first of these, wrote to Villiers that he was in "Purgatory"; "but," he added, "I know I have clean hands and a clean heart. . . . And if this be to be a Chancellor, I think if the great seal lay upon Hounslow Heath, nobody would take it up." A third complaint was advanced by a habitual litigant, Lady Wharton, who had had three husbands and was now having trouble in her attempt to prove the deed of the property of the second of these. She had lost a case—as had the others—after she had presented the Chancellor with a purse of gold. Earlier, Lady Wharton had successfully bribed an official—John Churchill, who had been dismissed—to change a court record.

The inquiry into the actions of the Lord Chancellor was now

transferred to the House of Lords, on the assumption that the Viscount St. Albans should be tried for his crimes by his peers. Bacon, now ill, wrote the Lords to regard his absence from the Upper House rightly, and to allow him, when his present indisposition had passed, to examine witnesses. He also wrote to James:

> When I enter into myself, I find not the materials of such a tempest as is comen upon me. I have been (as your Majesty knoweth best) never author of any immoderate counsel, but always desired to have things carried *suavibus modis*. I have been no avaricious oppressor of the people. I have been no haughty, or intolerable, or hateful man, in my conversation or carriage. I have inherited no hatred from my father, but am a good patriot born. Whence should this be?

The King had already attempted, and failed, to have the pending case brought before a select body of commissioners, twelve from the Commons and six from the Lords. The day after he received Bacon's letter, James went in person to Parliament. He acknowledged the authority of the Lords as a criminal court, undertook to impress the Upper House with the seriousness of their present undertaking, and promised the Commons that he would "strike dead" obnoxious Monopolies in return for grants in equivalence and a cessation of the present attack on his judges. Villiers urged the King to dissolve Parliament and thus bring the present commotion to an end. The Scottish King, fool as he often showed himself to be in his constitutionl dealings with the English, was sufficiently wise to reject Villiers' advice. The favorite then wavered in his loyalty to Bacon, and for a time seemed to take the side of the Lord Chancellor's accusers. He remarked that "with so bad a case he could have no sympathy." The King was aware that members of the Commons were now assuming an authority over things which they never before had dared debate, except as subjects for petition. One of their number, Coke, had even introduced a bill to the effect that all things which had previously lain under the King's grant of Monopoly were henceforth to be placed within the disposing of the Lower House. Things were on the march, and no one could say what the end would be. The present Parliament wanted a greater sacrifice than Mompesson in exile, and had chosen as a scapegoat none less than the King's Chancellor. James, who wept over Bacon's plight, knew that Parliament was now seeking something more than the punishment of "bribery." He had already been apprised (through the rejection of his request for a commission of judges) of the fact that the case of his Lord Chancellor would be one in which the trying court would definitely not subscribe to his strongly affirmed principle that judges should consult with their King.

While definite charges were being prepared against him, Bacon remained at Gorhambury in a state of great physical depression. For many years far from robust, he now feared that death was at hand. On April 10th he prepared a draft of a will, beginning with the words:

I bequeath my soul to God above, by the oblation of my Saviour. My body to be buried obscurely. My name to the next ages and to foreign nations.

In this will he left a symbolic token to Prince Charles (1600-1649, Prince of Wales in 1616) as one of a succeeding age. The Prince was to have the offer of Gorhambury. It was at this time that Bacon wrote the prayer or psalm which, according to Joseph Addison, is composed in the style of an archangel, and which, in the view of another critic, is "rather like a passage for a nation's liturgy than the outpouring of a broken spirit." The prayer or psalm ran—to quote a part of it:

The state and bread of the poor and oppressed have been precious in mine eyes: I have hated all cruelty and hardness of heart: I have (though in a despised weed) procured the good of all men.... Besides my innumerable sins, I confess before thee, that I am debtor to thee for the gracious talent of thy gifts and graces, which

I have neither put into a napkin, nor put it (as I ought) to exchangers, where it might have made best profit; but misspent it in things for which I was least fit; so as I may truly say, my soul hath been a stranger in the course of my pilgrimage.

Within a week the Lords had prepared a list of specific charges. The Lord Chancellor, in the meantime, had been examining law and precedents in "cases of bribery," in preparation for a meeting with the King. He set down in writing the following conclusion:

There be three degrees or cases of bribery charged or supposed in a judge:—

1. The first, of bargain or contract for reward to pervert justice, *pendente lite*.

2. The second, where the judge conceives the cause to be at an end by the information of the party, or otherwise, and useth not such diligence as he ought to inquire of it.

3. And the third, when the cause is really ended, and it is *sine fraude* without relation to any precedent promise.

For the first of them I take myself to be as innocent as any born upon St. Innocent's Day, in my heart.

For the second, I doubt, in some particulars, I may be faulty.

And for the last, I conceived it to be no fault, but therein I desire to be better informed, that I may be twice penitent, once for the fact, and again for the error. For I had rather be a briber than a defender of bribes.

I must likewise confess to your Majesty, that at New Year's tides, and likewise at my first coming in (which was as it were my wedding), I did not so precisely, as perhaps I ought, examine whether those that presented me had causes before me, yea or no.

And this is simply all I can say for the present concerning my charge, until I may receive it more particularly. And all this while I do not fly to that, as to say that these things are *vitia temporis*, and not *vitia hominis*.

On April 21st, four days after the charges had been formally presented by the Lords, Bacon wrote to the King that he hoped his accusers would be satisfied with a "submission" and his surrender of the Great Seal, for "if it be reformation that is sought, the very taking away the Seal upon my general submission, will be as much an example, for those 400 years, as any further severity." The following day he sent a "humble submission and supplication" to the Lords, where this was presented by Prince Charles. The Lord Chancellor acknowledged technical guilt of some of the charges, and continued with this statement:

For after the clear submission and confession which I shall now make unto your Lordships, I hope I may say and justify with Job in these words; *I have not hid my sin as did Adam, nor concealed my faults in my bosom.* This is the only justification which I will use.

It resteth therefore, that, without fig-leaves, I do ingenuously confess and acknowledge that, having understood the particulars of the charge, not formally from the House, but enough to inform my conscience and memory, I find matter sufficient and full, both to move me to desert the defence, and to move your Lordships to condemn and censure me.

Neither will I trouble your Lordships by singling those particulars which I think may fall off.

As a reason for his decision not to defend his case, the accused said, "In the midst of a state of as great affliction as mortal men can endure, honour being above life," he would "take no small comfort in the thought that, hereafter, the greatness of a judge or magistrate shall be no sanctuary of guiltiness, which in few words is the beginning of a golden world." He also reminded the Lords that he was confessing conformity to a general practice among judges, which would now be made judicially culpable. He wrote:

Neither will your Lordships forget that there are *vitia temporis* as well as *vitia hominis,* and that the beginning of reformations hath the contrary power of the pool of Bethesda; for that had strength to cure only him that was first cast in, and this hath commonly strength to hurt him only that is first cast in. And for my part I wish it may stay there and go no further. . . .

And therefore my humble suit to your Lordships is, that my penitent submission may be my sentence and the loss of the Seal my punishment; and that your Lordships will spare any further sentence, but recommend me to his Majesty's grace and pardon for all that is past. God's Holy Spirit be amongst you.

This statement was read in the House of Lords on April 24th and "no Lord spoke to it, after it was read, for a long time." The silence was broken by the Lord Chamberlain, who inquired "whether this submission be sufficient to ground your Lordships' judgment for a censure, without further examination." Suffolk demanded that the accused be required to appear in person before the bar of the House. Villiers and Prince Charles favored the acceptance of the submission as sufficient. Southampton, of a different mind in the matter, moved that "the House could not proceed without particular confession" from the accused. "He is charged by the Commons with corruption," said this former conspirator in treason and rebellion, "and no word of confession of any corruption in his submission. It stands, with the justice and honour of this House not to proceed, without the parties' particular confession; or to have the parties to hear the charge, and we to hear the parties' answer."

The court determined that since the accused was not entering a defence he should be permitted an expeditious answer to particulars without personal appearance. This Bacon provided by letter on April 30th. He admitted twenty-eight charges. Six of these had to do with the acceptance of monies from suitors with cases pending. To the twenty-eighth charge—that "The Lord Chancellor hath given way to great exactions by his servants, both in respect of private seals, and otherwise for sealing of Injunctions"—the Lord Chancellor, who had issued two thousand orders a year, replied, "I confess it was a great fault of neglect in me that I looked no better to my servants." On May 3rd, after Southampton had suggested banishment and Suffolk's son had moved unsuccessfully for degradation of title, sentence was passed, Villiers alone dissenting.

The cause for Bacon's trial was not the perversion of justice;

that was never seriously entertained, even by his most ardent accusers. The charge against the Lord Chancellor was aimed at an official *persona*, a destructible representative and symbol of a regime. Constitutionally speaking, the trial was the first major assault against a position to which Bacon, acting on principle, had given his support. It had been Bacon's firm belief that in the political circumstances of his time there could be no middle ground between that position and anarchy. James, had he been a wise monarch, could have brought about a constitutional development which would have met the reasonable desires of his people. But since this development could not be brought within the orbit of a Stuart king's mind, a dedicated public servant, whose political endeavor had extended over two reigns, had to take the consequences. The action taken by Parliament had meant disgrace for the Lord Chancellor, but it had also brought defeat to the King. There had been a free debate in Parliament of the whole question of Monopolies; James had been forced to capitulate to the Commons in an offer for their discontinuance so far as the Prerogative was concerned. The Sovereign had found himself in a condition of duress; for once he had not dared to dismiss Parliament. He had been denied a commission of selected judges who could have been persuaded to consult with their King before and during the hearing of the case. There had been a final trial before the High Court of Parliament, which Coke had long been maintaining was the highest court of the kingdom, and James had been unable to interfere. Even the Chancellor's expressing the hope that his trial might mark the ushering-in of a golden age of justice had been a reflection on James' management of his kingdom. Bacon had accepted bribes; but so had every other officer in the kingdom, including many who tried him. Those who received bribes ranged from servants in the royal household, through administrative officers and favorites, up to the King himself. James once told the Spanish Ambassador that if he dismissed all those in his service who took bribes, there would be no one left to carry on the work of the kingdom. James himself sold public offices; but the bribes involved in the transactions of the King, his Secretary of State, and his favorites were not comparable in character to those "gifts" which since the days of the Magi had been offered in homage to great persons in high office, including judges and Lord Chancellors. The complaining litigants whom Coke and Cranfield had employed as witnesses during Bacon's trial had mistaken traditional homage for contractual "consideration" in a business deal. Even the dull Coke, as well as the bishops and other members of the Lords, was aware that such was the case. There could be *vitia temporis* even among the Lords Spiritual. The most vocal of those among the Lords Temporal who tried the case had been criminals earlier sentenced, for proper reasons, to the Tower.

Of the three persons against whom Parliament's action had been directed—James, Villiers, and Bacon—only the third was named in an indictment. He only, as things were, could have been brought before the court of Parliament—and Bacon had an Achilles' heel, a conformity with an accepted practice among judges. James would never have permitted a trial or an impeachment of Villiers. The time was not yet when Parliament would undertake the destruction of a king. His accusers could only strike at his deputy. James kept his throne and lived out his natural life. But his son Charles would be beheaded. In the same Charles' reign it would be the fate of the favorite, James' beloved George, to be declared in a Remonstrance by the Commons "the cause of all our miseries." King Charles I (1625-1649) would thereupon prorogue Parliament, and one John Felton would quote the Remonstrance, and then use an assassin's knife to terminate the career of George Villiers.

After a verdict had been rendered at his trial, Bacon's sentence proved to be light in effect. Having asserted its right to sit in judgment without consultation with the King and to move within areas of government which James and his Lord Chancellor had reserved to the Royal Prerogative, Parliament was not interested in punitive measures against one of its most notable and memorable members. (What Coke, Cranfield, Southampton, Suffolk, and Howard felt in this regard was another matter.) Bacon's fine was remitted to trustees named by himself. By this disposing of the fine, which was never exacted, and whose payment took precedence over the discharge of all other debts, Bacon was given a relief from creditors he had never since the days of his youth enjoyed. After two days in the Tower he was released through Villiers' intervention. At the end of two years (1623) he was permitted to dwell in London, and given a full pardon. The King ordered the payment of arrears in his pension of £1,200. For his part in easing the lot of the condemned Chancellor—at least, so it seemed for a time to Bacon—Villiers exacted the price of the conveyance, if not to himself, then to Cranfield, of York House, Bacon's mansion by the Thames. By this act the favorite, whether intentionally or unintentionally, did his old friend, who complained bitterly over the transfer, a favor. Bacon's failure to compute his financial assets and expenditures had long been notorious. With his now greatly reduced income —from pensions from the state and rents at Gorhambury—he might still have attempted to keep up both his country estate and his elegant establishment in the Strand.

In Bacon's opinion the verdict of the Lords and his own sentence to the Tower had not been tantamount to future political disablement. Elizabeth herself, and Burghley too, had been confined in the Tower. Coke had been disgraced, and then brought back to the Privy Council. Persons whom he had fined and sentenced to the Tower, when a judge, were among his triers in the Lords. The sting had been removed from the charge of bribery through the awareness on the part of those who had judged him that the accused was speaking the truth when he affirmed that he had no "bribe or reward in his eye or thought

when he pronounced any sentence or order." His peers had
discerned his sincerity when he called his conviction "the beginning of reformations." They could understand what he meant
when he told Villiers in a letter that he had been "(howsoever I
acknowledge the sentence just, and for reformation sake fit) the
justest Chancellor that hath been in the five changes since Sir
Nicholas Bacon's time."

Soon Bacon was contemplating a return to the King's confidence and service. He wrote to James and to persons of influence, seeking political offices. None was forthcoming, yet for
a time the King thought of employing his former Chancellor as
advisor on the reform of the courts of the realm. When approached in the matter, Bacon, always a Parliamentarian and a
defender of Parliament's privileges, told the King to "pursue the
reformation which the Parliament hath begun." In enforced
retirement from politics, Bacon pursued his literary and scientific
works for the remaining five years of his life. With these he
soon became content—although he tried unsuccessfully to obtain
the provostship of Eton. It seemed now that politics had been an
intrusion into the main current of his thought and desire. Within
five months he completed his *History of Henry VII*. He began
the writing of a history of the reign of Henry VIII and the
preparation of parts of a "Digest of the Laws of England." The
political histories were designed for the instruction of Prince
Charles, the King-to-be. By 1622, Bacon had presented the
Prince with the first part of a *Natural and Experimental History
for the Foundation of Philosophy*, and promised a "particular
history" each month thereafter. He was now hoping that his
philosophic design might be looked upon with favor by a succeeding sovereign and the members of a succeeding Court. Before long the author was forced to admit that the furnishing
of an "experimental" history in sufficient variety and detail for
the instauration of the sciences would be an impossibility during
his lifetime. In feverish haste he compiled a thousand short his-

tories from whatever sources he could lay his hands on—largely from ancient and modern books—and assembled the components of a very inadequate *Sylva Sylvarum* (*Forest of Materials*). These, he thought, would at least help to indicate the range of the materials required for the third of the six parts of his Great Instauration. In 1625, now ill, Bacon wrote to the Venetian Father Fulgentio saying he could not complete his natural history; and, as if consigning the task to others in the future, he described it as clearly the work for a king, a pope, or some college or religious order. Most of his last days were given over to labor on the *Sylva Sylvarum*.

Bacon came to his death through an experiment in refrigeration. On a sunny day he set out for Highgate to dine with the King's physician. There was snow on the ground and, according to Thomas Hobbes—who for a period had been a secretary to Bacon—it occurred to him that flesh might be preserved in snow as well as in salt. Bacon alighted from his coach and "went into a poor woman's house at the bottom of Highgate Hill, and bought a hen, and made the woman exenterate it, and then stuffed the body with snow, and my Lord did help to do it himself." He became suddenly ill with a chill and, unable to return to Gray's Inn where he was now living, he "went to the Earl of Arundel's house at Highgate"; there "they put him into a good bed warmed with a pan, but it was a damp bed that had not been lain in about a year before, which gave him such a cold that in two or three days he died of suffocation."

Not knowing that he was on his deathbed Bacon wrote a note of apology to Arundel for the enforced visit to his house, and remarked, "I was likely to have had the fortune of Caius Plinius the elder, who lost his life by trying an experiment about the burning of the mountain Vesuvius."

Verulam was buried, as he had desired, near his mother, in the Church of St. Michael in St. Albans. In his last will he remembered his servants generously, left a legacy to Lady Hatton, and designated sums for endowment of two lectureships in either of the Universities and twenty-five scholarships for needy students. Although he had lived at the rate of £12,000 a year while Lord Chancellor, Bacon's liabilities at his death amounted to £22,371 and the assessed value of his estate to £7,000. The Universities were not to reap the profit of his good intent. For "just and great causes," as he said, he left nothing beyond her legal "right" to his wife, an alderman's daughter with a modest income, whom he had married in 1606. Lady Bacon's mien and manner of living had not kept pace with her husband's rise in station. She had never been at ease in the miniature court at Gorhambury and could not cope with York House, the mansion in the Strand. She had sought her company, some of it more physically masculine than her husband, outside her home and Court circles. She had not been content in the days of her husband's prosperity and had made his life miserable by incessant complaining after the reduction of his circumstances. A clause in the will was her husband's reminder that it would be appropriate for Lady Bacon to return to her earlier station.

Regarded as an event in Stuart history, Bacon's downfall was the climax of a tragedy within a greater political drama of heroic dimensions, which would reach its climax in the beheading of Charles I. Of Bacon it could be said: "If ever a man was fitted by nature and study to be the leader of a great nation it was he," for he "was not one man as a thinker and another as a politician." This thinker had postponed a revolution through his sway over Parliament and his informed and authoritative ordering of the juridical affairs of a kingdom. Now tragedy had come. If soon a greatness of mind and character was to reassert itself in full endeavor without repining, still there had been tragedy, personal as well as political. The motion of the political planet nearest the First Moved by God had been brought to an absolute stop. The most active agent in the constitutional life of the kingdom had been rendered completely inert. The King's deputy, devoid of injustice in motive or deed, had been put out of place as a disgraced creature. The undaunted Parliamentarian whose effort and pride had been the preserving of Parliament's privileges had been sent to the political scaffold through the self-deception of Parliament's members. The man of the age who had placed his memory and merit in the keeping of "times succeeding" was entreating the King "to the end that blot of ignominy may be removed from . . . my memory with posterity." Magnificence had been reduced to straits. The victim now "cast for means" was being forced to sell his furniture to "spread," as he said, "upon poor men unto whom I owed, scarce leaving myself bread." A fallen Lord Chancellor was imploring his peers in words—as E. A. Abbott remarks—King Lear himself might have uttered: "I am old, weak, ruined, a very subject of pity." He was writing in lamentation to a correspondent, "I do not think any except a Turk or a Tartar would wish to have another chop out of me."

The scenes of Bacon's political life were thronged with characters, plots, and subplots which sustained a single dramatic action. In the midst of these was a man whose "immensity" of "genius" was, as S. R. Gardiner has said, to be "a sore trouble to his biographers"—as all heroes of great tragedy are bound to be. The cause of the hero's downfall had not been the acceptance of "bribes"—that had merely provided the tragic occasion—but his belief that what the Greeks had called *arche*, political initiative, issued from the King as *persona*. In this tragedy Nemesis was comprised of the opinions and actions of men less constitutionally informed than he, and less forbearing towards a determined monarch intent on keeping everything political, including all privileges and power, within his own disposing.

Bacon's trial by his peers as a legal cause ended in 1621; his trial by biographers and commentators on grounds of political philosophy and ethics has continued ever since. It has not uncommonly been maintained, in a late-seventeenth-century manner, that Bacon, when he thought politically, disregarded the Law of Nature on which were founded the "rights" and the "liberty" of subjects. E. A. Abbott, who usually goes further in condemnation of Bacon than any of his other critics, says that this Parliamentarian and administrative officer "deliberately espoused the cause of despotism." The reason for this extreme accusing on Abbott's part is Bacon's upholding of the Royal Prerogative in conflicts between the King on the one side and his Parliament and courts of law on the other. With this much misunderstood constitutional problem on the part of "ethical" commentators we have already dealt. As for the conception of natural rights, as stated by John Locke (1632-1704): this was not current in Bacon's time, nor was the doctrine of natural law conjoined with that of an historical state of nature on which the liberty of subjects was premised in the manner of late-seventeenth-century thinking. Whether the concepts employed in enunciating a doctrine of natural rights and a universal law of nature are philosophically sound, or merely so many "fictions," is a question which need not concern us here. Bacon's political principles were derived initially from his interpretation of Scripture. He separated three kingdoms: the kingdom of Saving Grace, whose works God keeps within the "mystery" of his own dispensing; the political kingdom established within the same "mystery" by God on the giving of power, initiative, and rule to temporal monarchs; and the kingdom of nature, created by God and placed under the dominion of man. These three kingdoms were not united by the bond of natural law. As a participant in each of the three kingdoms, man had, according to Bacon, specific stations and duties. In his religious, political, and moral thinking, faith and its issue of charity belonged to God, and justice flowed from the King, as an agent divinely endowed with sovereign initiative. Man's first duty was to God; then came his obedience to the sovereign; and from these followed his just dealings with his fellow men and fellow subjects.

The divine endowment of kings remained for Bacon as great a "mystery" as the salvation of man through Divine Grace. Kings were "ordained" by God's "secret providence." This ordination was certified by Scripture—not to mention its attestation by acceptance and use in English history. According to the statements of Scripture, political sovereignty lies within the prerogatives of God alone: "*Solvam cingula regum;* I will loosen the girdles of Kings," says the Scripture; "He poureth contempt upon princes"; "I will give a king in my wrath, and take him away again in my displeasure"; and the like. When such prerogatives as these were made the claims of mere men they became, in Bacon's opinion, the iniquities of mortal creatures who now placed themselves on an equality with God. Bacon read Scriptural statement quite literally. It was his opinion that "as wines which flow gently from the first treading of the grape are sweeter than those which are squeezed out by the wine-press; because these last have some taste of the stones and skin of the grape; so those doctrines are very sweet and healthy, which flow from a gentle pressure of the Scriptures, and are not wrested to controversies or commonplaces."

The alternative "pagan" theories of sovereignty, which did not impress Bacon, were several. One, which went back to the ancient Sophists, was to the effect that selfish subjects created a sovereign for their protection, one against the other, by entering into a contract mutually to abstain from lawlessness. This was obviously fanciful history. Establishment by contract is not in keeping with sovereign majesty, power, rule, and justice. No one in his senses could imagine how justice could issue from non-justice, rule from lawlessness, sovereignty from subjection, and God's-anointed from creatures without power to anoint. After the Sophists in time, Plato and Aristotle had founded the state on the basis of human needs, desires, and powers. The former, in a refutation of the proposition of contract, made some men deserving of rule through their recognition of forms in a non-accessible domain; while the latter made men politically capable through a desire for an abstract being equally remote. Plato and Aristotle gave men a dialectic when they needed a Creator. The Stoics, in turn, propounded a law of nature which, with Cicero, became the natural light of reason, a reason within the whole of man, within nature, and within human judgment. On this, the theologians seized, making it a binding principle on the mind and will of God, kings, bishops in council, judges in court and legislators in assemblies, and ethical agents. These thinkers were, of course, wise in at least one regard: rulers must respect reason as the ruling part—but far from all—of their nature and the nature of their subjects, if they would escape monstrosity and barbarism. But escape from such evils is not the establishment of sovereignty. To hold with Stoically inspired philosophers that the source of human justice, the sanctity of human law, the authority of the ruler, and the rights of subjects are consequent on an impersonal law and not upon the will of a Creator, is, especially when regarded in the light of God's Revealed Word, to promote wrong opinion, superstition, and great presumption. Such a contravention and theoretical enfeeblement of Scriptural truth through philosophical argument is an example of the principle that "the more you recede from your grounds the weaker do you conclude." The operation of this principle is found in natural philosophy, where "the more you remove yourself from particulars the greater peril of error do you incur, so much more in divinity the more you recede from the Scriptures by inferences and consequences, the more weak and dilute are your positions." Bacon, without a doubt, looked upon the king under whom he served as a weak vessel of divine power. But James was still, as king, such a vessel. In the case of the sovereign, as in the case of bishops, Bacon believed that it was not the person of an incumbent that determined kingly rule as such, but the *persona* of the office. This had been so from the beginning of the human race: "Neither," said Bacon, "did Adam's sin, or the curse upon it, deprive him of his rule."

What Gardiner calls the "immensity" of Bacon has far too often been reduced and dissipated by the embroidering on the main theme of his tragedy pointless and formless moralistic cacophonies. In saying this, we are not now contending—after Aristotle—that there are better ways of interpreting tragedy than through ethical precepts; nor are we merely maintaining that there are more things in life's drama than moral consequences; rather, we are affirming that, when judged by principles fit for reasoned ethical criticism, Francis Bacon's character is one of the most virtuous to be found among men of great political renown. Bacon was eminently virtuous in that distinctive part of man which is called the human reason, and in that distinctive virtue which is called charity and said by moralists and, certainly, by theologians to be best of all moral attributes. Bacon displayed in his life Aristotelian magnanimity, Plato's four cardinal virtues, justice, wisdom, fortitude, and temperance, and the three theological virtues, faith, hope, and charity, not to mention the attribute of honor whose source, in tradition, was the King. For these virtues Bacon provided a foundation in his philosophical thinking. Surely all this should be enough to satisfy any ethically critical biographer. Certainly, no devious interpretation of motive, no malignancy of minds filled with "vapours and fumes," no sentimental rhapsodizing on pseudo-honorable themes, no assumption by clerics of man's right, and not God's, to judge the secrets of the human heart, should ever be allowed to dissipate or impair the political consistency, moral vigor, and ethical virtue of a man of Bacon's stature.

Even such a highly censorious biographer as E. A. Abbott has had to admit that Bacon was held in reverence by his chaplain, friends, and servants. Persons who knew him best saw in him a temperate, religious, charitable man, no "less gracious with the subject than with his sovereign," consistent through good and ill fortune. Bacon's secretary and domestic apothecary, Peter

Boener, hoped that a statue might be put up not only in cele-
bration of his master's learning—which time could never efface—
but "as a memorable example to all, of virtue, kindness, peace-
fulness, and patience." Dr. William Rawley, his chaplain,
rendered Bacon the following tribute, among many other
praises, after his death: "When his office called him, as he was of
the king's counsel learned, to charge any offenders, either in
criminals or capitals, he was never of an insulting and domineer-
ing nature over them, but always tender-hearted, and carrying
himself decently towards the parties (though it was his duty to
charge them home), but yet as one that looked upon the *example*
with the eye of severity, but upon the *person* with the eye of
pity and compassion." Tobie Matthew could write of the man
he had known intimately for years: "I never saw any trace in
him of a vindictive mind, whatever injury were done him, nor
ever heard him utter a word to any man's disadvantage which
seemed to proceed from personal feelings. . . . It is not his greatness that I admire, but his virtue. It is not the favours I have
received of him . . . that have thus enthralled and enchained my
heart, but his whole life and character; which are such that, if
he were of an inferior condition, I could not honour him the less,
and if he were my enemy, I should not the less love and endeavour to serve him." Ben Jonson said in sincerity of the fallen
Lord Chancellor: "What I feel for his person has never been
augmented by his place. I hope his disgraces will only serve to
show his virtue in a clearer light . . . greatness could never fail
him."

With the "theological" and the four "cardinal" virtues in
mind, consider for a moment Bacon's conduct. Of his faith and
Christian hope there can be no doubt. These, acquired early, he
never relinquished throughout his life. Bacon was "God-
conscious" in doctrine and in practice. Reared a Calvinist, he
yet became Arminian enough to believe that faith would manifest itself in moral endeavor. From the days when he first sought
aid for scientific means to relieve mankind, until the end of his

life, the love of man and desire for his relief pervaded Bacon's thoughts and deeds. His instauration of knowledge was conceived and nurtured for the easing of human misery and the cure of human ills. His legal reforms, attempts to repeal "snaring" statutes and reduce penalties for minor offenses, his readiness to reconsider legal cases already determined when considerations of equity required, his pleas for the joining of mercy to justice, these were all the outward guarantees of an inner charity. The same was true of his designs for religious toleration, frustrated by the parties who might have reaped benefits therefrom; his efforts with the Queen on behalf of the unfortunate Essex; his loyal endurance of his cousin, Robert Cecil; his patient forbearance with King James and George Villiers to the end of maintaining constitutional continuity; his acceptance of many things as they were because nothing better could then conceivably have been attained in the circumstances of what Bacon himself called Time.

Never strong in body, Bacon was almost abstemious in his habits. His deportment in and out of office, in gatherings with his friends, in courts of law and Parliament, when presenting Remonstrances of the Commons to the Lords and King, throughout magnificent living—as Aristotle had understood the term—on a scale which befitted his station, was seasonable, appropriate, and apt—as Plato would have said—always within the bounds required by what Plato found "temperance" to be. Bacon's courage became manifest when he opposed Burghley in Parliament and endured the Queen's displeasure while refusing to retract or retreat. It continued when he told a contending Commons time after time what they could and could not constitutionally debate; when he acted as the spokesman of a remonstrating Lower House in compounding matters with the Lords and with the King; when he pointedly told James to cease trading and put on Majesty, and many things in like vein; when he faced the days of his political disgrace.

Bacon's exercise of legal justice can never be seriously

questioned. It was continual from the time he entered the Commons and the courts of law as a young man, through years on the Bench, to the day when he heard the verdict of the Lords on his own case. He accepted this verdict as just, even as he had thought just the judgments pronounced upon Essex, Suffolk, Yelverton, and lesser persons who had appeared before the tribunals over which he had presided. Bacon left the precedents of the law and the courts of England without any of the "vapours and fumes of law, which are extracted out of men's inventions and conceits." As for the fourth cardinal virtue, wisdom: Bacon's "immense" mind encompassed the principles of theological, philosophical, scientific, legal, and literary knowledge. By the age of forty his learning was vast in detail, and to the end of his days it continued to increase. He could justly be called the most universally informed man in the England of his time. He was, as Rawley said, "the glory of his age and nation, the adorner and ornament of learning."

XII

EARLY PHILOSOPHICAL
WRITINGS

Francis Bacon was by nature and nurture a reformer. Always he desired to make things "better," as he said. In his parents' home he had imbibed religious "reform" from the time of his birth. As a constitutional lawyer, he had taken a firm stand in upholding the Royal Prerogative; yet, had circumstances permitted, he would have enlarged the power of Parliament as a legislative body and made the courts of law independent of the King's will. Had the Puritans not made the government and rituals of the Church matters of faith, and of politics as well, Bacon might have succeeded in moderating the contemporary rule of the bishops in the Established Church. Had James provided his Solicitor and Attorney with leisure and means for the purpose, outmoded statutes and conflicting precedents would have been removed from English law. In these several conjunctions political conditions had worked against Bacon. There was one area of endeavor, however, in which, as he said himself, circumstance could not interfere. This was the realm of philosophy. Nothing short of an Inquisition could militate here and, thanks to the defeat of the Spanish Armada, there was no longer any possibility of an English Inquisition.

Bacon's bent towards philosophical reform showed itself before the age of sixteen. While at Cambridge he rebelled against Aristotelian doctrines and Peripatetic instruction, as "unfruitful" things. After he had left the University and continued with his reading in modern as well as ancient authors, his opinions, as the thoughts of one who would rebuild, became firmly set in an opposition to all the philosophical systems of past and present. A piece written in his middle twenties showed a predisposition towards the experimental investigation of nature. This unfinished treatise was designed to promote a new "formula" or method of scientific discovery. The young author called the writing in which this method was announced *Temporis partus maximus* (*The Greatest Birth of Time*). Later on he changed the title to *Temporis partus masculus* (*The Fertilizing Birth of Time*).

This, Bacon's first philosophical treatise, takes the form of a trial in court of a number of past and present philosophers, who are known to the presiding judge as "phrenetics"—persons out of their senses in more ways than one—and of their followers, whom the court regards as a company of professional hirelings. Of these phrenetics, commands the author in juristic fashion, let Aristotle be summoned first, because of all those now accused he is probably in the worst condition, having a mind utterly confused with useless subtleties—a laughingstock of words. Aristotle is the person who, when the human mind had arrived, as by chance, at some truth, put the intellect under an insane logic, and thus delivered it over to verbiage. He then became the sire of many artful babblers who, on their cessation from Peripatetic ramblings, make up, through the agitation of their own wits, from the stuff of his foolish precepts and propositions, the endless trash of the schools. Aristotle, as their progenitor and instructor, is more deserving of accusation than they. At one stage of his life this founder of a contentious line was able to face the open facts of nature; but he was not satisfied with the observation of these. He would weave constructions on the histories of particulars like a spider spinning a web. These fabrications he would then take as actual causes—such make-shifts, indeed, as one, Jerome Cardan, in our own age produces. But, Bacon continues, now addressing his remarks to a pro-spective disciple among the listeners in his court, do not divine that we are in agreement with that modern rebel against Aristotle's teachings, Peter Ramus by name. We will have no traffic with that producer of handbooks. Ramus binds together empty and arid trifles. Aquinas, Scotus, and their associates were given to fashioning a variety of things out of nonexistent objects, but this rhetorician produces the nonexistent out of what actually is. He is indeed worse than a sophist.

Let Plato be called next—Plato the cultivated scoffer, the elated poet, the theologian out of his natural wits. When this writer merged popular opinions in a system and at the same time loosened and stirred men's minds by use of some vague inductions, he might well have been content with providing grace and charm for the *noctes* of literary persons. Instead, he must go on to disguise facts. Plato turned the human under-standing inward, upon itself, and made it ponder, in the guise of a contemplator of things, blind Idols or phantoms of the mind. Plato's disciples, under the spell of their master's verbal subtlety, have occupied themselves with that pleasant ruminat-ing upon delicate notions which brings to ruin the severe in-vestigation of truth. Among Plato's followers are Cicero, Seneca, Plutarch of Chaeronea, and many others of lesser stature.

Let the court deal next with the physicians. Galen is here, narrow in mind, the vainest of pretenders, the deserter of ex-perience. He has composed a complete system, and by this he banishes all ignorance from medicine, puts its practitioners into a place of false security, and brings their art to a standstill. By pronouncing incurable all diseases which do not conform to his rules, Galen dooms mankind to suffer endless ills and casts a malignant blight on human capacity.

Let us not overlook old Hippocrates, whose disconnected utterances all physicians still quote—because once upon a time he set down some narratives of cases of diseases. Hippocrates still seems to be taking in particulars through his senses; but actually his gaze is wandering. His mind is obsessed by the phantoms of theory, and when he is under their influence he behaves as if he considered himself an oracle.

Over there is a troop of chemists, and one of them, Theophrastus Paracelsus, is vaunting himself. This physician and chemist, for his very impudence, deserves correction separately from the rest. Let him be summoned. You, Paracelsus, charges the judge, by putting together your false images, have turned man into a mummer. We can more easily endure Galen weighing his so-called elements than you when you embellish your fantasies. By mixing the divine with the natural, the profane with the sacred, the heretical with the fabulous, you have corrupted truth, both human and divine. The light of nature, whose sacred name you often appropriate to your impure speech, you have not concealed, as have the Sophists, but have quenched. They have been the deserters of experience, you its betrayer. Among your disciples is a man of capacity, Peter Severinus. He deserves a better occupation than the translation of your falsehoods into fables, however delightful to the ear his tales may be.

Unlike Paracelsus, the empirical chemists occasionally do hit upon, as by chance, some useful things. But, alas, these burners of charcoal will attempt to build a whole philosophy on a few experiments in distillation. Speaking of the fabrication of systems from meagre materials, Telesio has recently been holding the stage with a new philosophic play of no sound argument and, we may add, without any reward of applause. In astronomy, where system-building has long been a vogue, the contrivers of eccentrics and epicycles, on the one side, and the modern wagoners who move the earth about, on the other, are employing exactly the same evidence to support diametrically opposed theories. There is something wrong there, for quarrels among scientists betoken not truth but error.

At this stage of our proceedings someone may think it appropriate to ask the question, whether among all those who have thought and written in mankind's past about nature, have there not been some persons who have discovered some truth. Is it not possible that the river Time, which has brought down many light and inflated imaginings, has carried beneath its surface some solid and weighty things? What of the ancient Heraclitus, Democritus, Anaxagoras, and Empedocles, whose records have disappeared but whose doctrines are still available in the writings of others? Our opinion, replies the judge to his own question, is that in the surviving fragments of some of these early philosophers there is evidence of diligence and ingenuity, and of an auspicious scientific beginning. The number theory of Pythagoras, too, is of good omen. At this point, however, we must utter a caution—and this is intended for investigators in prospect: any inquirer who desires to bring benefits to mankind had better seek truth by the light of nature, and not in the darkness of antiquity. What the past has done will be seen to matter little when this is placed in a comparison with what the future may achieve through the employment of a new method of inquiry. Fortuitous discovery, which has characterized the past, is not science. To use a rustic metaphor, it is not unlike the chance upturning by a digging animal—say, a sow. If by empirical chance such a creature, endowed with senses as it is, were to form the letter *A* by its uprooting, one would not suppose that it could by the same token compose a whole literary tragedy! An empirical item in discovery is solitary and not germinous. Only a procreative activity, in which sense and reason are united and in which one discovered item is conjoined with another, will produce a family of scientific works. Certainly a single finding or several unrelated discoveries, even when upheld by observation and experiment, can never serve as sufficient means for the founding of a philosophy of nature. The thinker who attempts to make a philosophy out of such meagre materials must either have recourse to the Idols of the Marketplace, mere words, or rely on the Idols of the Theatre, stageplays. As things now are, an immense sea flows around the island of truth, and everywhere are to be found scatterings of systems strewn about by the winds of Idols.

We have entertained charges against past and present thinkers, including some of the tallest scions of the theoretical sects. Their indictments have been more moderate in statement than their deeds warrant. While we condemn them, we would not act like Vellius, that literary rhetorician who touches hastily on the opinions of Cicero merely to cast them away; nor like the modern Agrippa, that trivial buffoon, who in reviewing the opinions of Aristotle and others distorts for purpose of mere ridicule. O miserable me! who, because I have taken it upon myself to condemn the follies of the past, am compelled to compare myself with the jackasses of the present!

This early statement by Bacon, which reads like the animadversions of a very censorious judge in court, is a rhetorical preamble to a major philosophical undertaking. The nature of this enterprise is indicated by its author in 1592. Then Bacon asks Burghley for an office to "carry" him because, he says, "I have taken all knowledge to be my province, and if I could purge it of two sorts of rovers (whereof the one with frivolous disputations, confutations, and verbosities, the other with blind experiments and auricular traditions and impostures hath committed so many spoils) I hope I should bring in industrious observations, grounded conclusions, and profitable inventions and discoveries." The two "rovers" are, on the one hand, the rationalists in a tradition from Plato to Bruno and, on the other, the contemporary experimenters and their empirical kind.

Two years later (1594), in a masque presented at Gray's Inn for the entertainment of Elizabeth, Bacon, in the person of "The Second Counsellor, Advising the Study of Philosophy," addresses the Queen as follows: "I . . . will wish unto your Highness the exercise of the best and purest part of the mind, and the most innocent and meriting conquest, being the conquest of the works of nature; making this proposition, that you bend the excellency of your spirits to the searching out, inventing, and discovering of all whatsoever is hid and secret in the world. . . .

"And to this purpose I will commend to your Highness four principal works and monuments of yourself. First, the collecting of a most perfect and general library. . . . Next, a spacious, wonderful garden, wherein whatsoever plant the sun of divers climates . . . either wild or by the culture of man, brought forth, may be, with that care that appertaineth to the good prospering thereof, set and cherished; this garden to be built about with rooms to stable in all rare beasts and to cage in all rare birds, with two lakes adjoining, the one of fresh water, the other of salt, for like variety of fishes. And so you may have in small compass a model of universal nature made private. The third, a goodly huge cabinet, wherein whatsoever the hand of man by exquisite art or engine hath made rare in stuff, form, or motion; whatsoever singularity, chance, and the shuffle of things hath produced; whatsoever nature hath wrought in things that want life and may be kept, shall be sorted and included. The fourth, such a still-house, so furnished with mills, instruments, furnaces, and vessels as may be a palace fit for a philosopher's stone. Thus, when your Excellency shall have added depth of knowledge to the fineness of your spirits and greatness of your power, then . . . when all other miracles and wonders shall cease, by reason that you shall have discovered their natural causes, yourself shall be left the only miracle and wonder of the world."

After a lapse of eleven years these early attempts to obtain aid from the Court for the founding of a new sort of learning are to be followed by another, when Bacon addresses to James, as a learned Sovereign and Visitor to the Universities, a full work called *Of the Proficience and Advancement of Learning* (1605). By this writing Bacon hopes to bring about a change in university practices or, failing in this, to have the ruler of the kingdom provide helpers and means for a suppliant who would collect natural histories and labor industriously in the sciences and arts of nature—even as another king, the father of Alexander the Great, gave similar aid to Aristotle. The author brings under review the uncultivated areas of knowledge; provides a new classification of the sciences—which is to supersede that of Aristotle; announces a new instauration of learning with a new method of inquiry; and finds great fault with the exercises, anciently begun and still continued, within the Universities.

About the same time, partly before and partly after the preparation of the *Advancement of Learning*, Bacon prepares some chapters of an unfinished work in which he treats of certain aspects of his new philosophy which are not stressed or mentioned in the completed work. This treatise he calls *Valerius Terminus of the Interpretation of Nature: with the Annotations of Hermes Stella*. The latter half of the title is a memento of Bacon's early hope that the scholarly King would join with an enterprising subject in a publication dealing with a new learning. Another work of Bacon's written a little later (1606-7), *Partis instaurationis secundae delineatio et argumentum (Outline and Argument of the Second Part of the Instauration)*, exhibits in a preliminary way a new scheme of scientific inquiry. These three pieces and, probably, two sets of jottings, *Cogitationes de scientia humana (Thoughts on Human Knowledge)* and *Cogitationes de natura rerum (Thoughts on the Nature of Things)*, are written before the author is made Solicitor-General (June, 1607). While holding the Solicitor's office, Bacon produces twelve more philosophical writings. Of the seventeen pieces written by the time he becomes Attorney-General, only two are completed and published: the *Advancement of Learning* and *De sapientia veterum (Concerning the Wisdom of the Ancients)*. In the remainder of this chapter we shall indicate some of the contents of the *Advancement of Learning* and the *Valerius Terminus* and sketch the *Outline and Argument of the Second Part of the Instauration*.

The first part of the *Advancement of Learning* is an exposure of what the author calls the "vanities and errors" of present learning. His attack is directed in the main against the Universities, which, the author says, are not reservoirs of truth but houses of relics. Learning, contends Bacon, lies in the keeping of grammarians who render it bookish, of editors who make it textual, and of logicians who reduce it to disputation. Its professors are aspirants for "second prizes," such as befit the commentator, compounder, abridger, and adder of glosses—all scholarly debasers of generative thinking. The disputers, who include all persons within the Universities, assume that tumbling up and down in intellectual conceits produces sublime philosophers. These arguers equate scientific inquiry and proof with the art of deductive logic. By this art they have hedged every division of learning with a set of determining, yet unproven, axioms, and then have put the several parts into a system complete in structure and detail. To demonstrate a truth, they cite a text, define the terms of their citation, add objections, and finally frame solutions which prove on examination to be no more than additional verbal distinctions. Disputation, with its adduction of authorities and its citation of their theses, with its cavillings, its "breeding" of many questions for the solution of one, is practised by schoolmen of several persuasions. But, in the main, peripateticism, as a method, prevails. The earlier schoolmen undoubtedly possessed "sharp and strong wits, and abundance of leisure, and small variety of reading; but their wits being shut up in the cells of a few authors (chiefly Aristotle, their dictator) ... and knowing little history, either of nature or time; did out of no great quantity of matter, and infinite agitation of wit, spin out unto us those laborious webs of learning which are extant in their books. For the wit and mind of man, if it work upon matter, which is the contemplation of the creatures of God, worketh according to the stuff, and is limited thereby; but if it work upon itself, as the spider worketh his web, then it is endless, and brings forth indeed cobwebs of learning, admirable for the fineness of thread and work, but of no substance or profit."

Science and philosophy, despite the immense speculation of schoolmen, have undergone but slight advance since the days of the ancient Greeks, while the arts, through mere chance discovery, have progressed—witness modern printing, instruments of navigation, and gunpowder. The names of the great innovators of antiquity, Plato, Aristotle, Hippocrates, Euclid, and Archimedes, are still being invoked, not so much to promote inquiry as to provide cause for doubt that anything not already discovered can ever be found out. Aristotle's divisions and descriptions of the sciences are presumed to be established forever, as if no new branch or kind of science could ever again be developed. Such provisions by the Universities as might conduce to observation and experiment—small botanical gardens, some anatomical dissection, globes, spheres, and astrolabes— even these are designed not for scientific discovery, but as aids to immediate practice in the professions.

Having made a protracted attack on the Universities in the above vein, Bacon goes on to announce plans for a new learning. These include a reclassification of the sciences and a reorganization of such knowledge as may be discovered through the use of the natural faculties. Excluded from Bacon's new classification of the sciences and reserved to that wisdom which is given in the inspired Scriptures are the knowledge of the truths of revealed theology, the derivation of a supreme rule of ethical conduct and of the discovery of the "nature and state" of the part of man which is made in the Divine Image. "The soul in the creation," writes Bacon, "was not extracted out of the mass of heaven and earth by the benediction of a *producat*, but was immediately inspired from God; so it is not possible that it should be (otherwise than by accident) subject to *the laws of heaven* [i.e., heavenly bodies] *and earth*, which are the *subject of philosophy*; and therefore the true knowledge of the nature and state of the soul must come by the same inspiration that gave the substance."

Bacon classifies the parts of natural knowledge initially according to the dominant faculties concerned—for the reason functions in all three parts. History depends on memory, poetry on imagination, philosophy on reason. History and poetry treat of particulars circumscribed by place and time, while natural philosophy—which is generalized physics—dismisses or discards individuals and operates by means of general notions and general axioms. History is of two main sorts, natural and civil. Natural history comprises the history of generations, of pretergenerations, and of the arts; that is to say, it is a record of nature in "ordinary" course, of nature when it "strays" from this and produces what are called "monsters" or "marvels," and of nature when "vexed" by the hand of man for the production of works of art. The main function of natural history is to provide materials for the inductions of natural philosophy.

Philosophy has three objects: God, nature, and man. It accordingly has three main branches, but like a tree, which has a trunk, natural philosophy includes a universal part which nourishes and sustains the several parts. Bacon calls this *philosophia prima*. This "first philosophy" is concerned with such axioms as are common to several sciences. It also, according to the later Latin version of the *Advancement of Learning*, brings under reckoning "adventitious" or accidental "conditions of essences," such as much and little, like and unlike, possible and impossible, being and not-being. Bacon's *philosophia prima*, he informs us, is quite distinct in conception from traditional "first philosophy," or metaphysics, called by Aristotle theology. It is not based, like Aristotle's "first philosophy," on the abstract Principle of Identity—What is, is; it is not concerned with being as such; and it is not independent of all lesser sciences. Its axioms, common to several sciences, are derived through inductive inquiry into particulars in such fields as physics, ethics, and politics. It operates in the area of the adventitious—or what may or may not be—and not in the realm of the necessary. It does not include a doctrine of a "first cause." It provides no knowledge of the being, mind, or operation of God.

Philosophy, concerned with nature, is divisible into a speculative part, the inquiry into causes, and an operative part, the production of effects. The speculative part is to be further divided, according to the causes investigated, into physics, which deals with "material" and "efficient" causes, and metaphysics, which inquires into "formal" and "final" causes. While making these distinctions Bacon is aware that he is using old terms in new senses. In the Latin translation of the *Advancement of Learning*, the *De augmentis*, the author criticizes Aristotle for his "undertaking . . . to coin new words of science at pleasure," and then goes on to say: "But to one on the other side . . . it seems best . . . to retain the ancient terms, though I often alter their sense and definitions; according to the moderate and approved course of innovation in civil matters, by which, when the state of things is changed, yet the forms of the words are kept." Soon, in his dealing with causes Bacon will, in effect, discard the four traditional sorts, except one, the material, which for him will become also an efficient cause.

Physics investigates what is more relative and variable—the same fire, for example, can produce opposite effects on diverse materials—while metaphysics studies what is more general and determined. Conjoined with these two divisions of speculative natural philosophy are two operative parts: mechanics, which is accordant with physics; and "magic," in its early sense of "wisdom," which is accordant with metaphysics. Mathematics, dignified by Aristotle as an independent "theoretical" science along with physics and metaphysics, Bacon classifies as an agent of metaphysics and an appendix to physics. "Knowledges," writes the author, "are as pyramides, whereof history is the basis: so of Natural Philosophy the basis is Natural History; the stage next the basis is Physic; the stage next the vertical point is Metaphysic. As for the vertical point, *Opus quod operatur Deus a principio usque ad finem* [the work which God worketh from the beginning to the end], the Summary Law of Nature, we know not whether man's inquiry can attain unto it. But these three be the true *stages* of knowledge; and are to them that are depraved no better than the giants' hills [Pelion, Ossa, and Olympus, piled upon each other] . . . but to those which refer all things to the glory of God, they are as the three acclamations, *Sancte, sancte, sancte* [Holy, Holy, Holy]; holy in the description or dilatation of his works, holy in the connexion or concatenation of them and holy in the union of them in a perpetual and uniform law. And therefore the speculation was excellent in Parmenides and Plato, although but a speculation in them, That all things by scale did ascend to unity. So then always that knowledge is worthiest which is charged with least multiplicity; which appeareth to be Metaphysic; as that which considereth the Simple Forms or Differences of things, which are few in number, and the degrees and co-ordinations whereof make all this variety."

Human philosophy, concerned with man, Bacon divides into two parts: the study of "man segregate" and the study of "man congregate" in society. The first part he subdivides into three more studies; one treating of man's body, another of his mind, and a third of human nature as a whole. The study of "man congregate," or civil science, includes three parts which deal respectively with three activities of society: "conversation," or the dealings of individual with individual; "negotiation," or business; and government.

The *Valerius Terminus*—a compiled set of papers—is less erudite in presentation and more strictly philosophical in character than the *Advancement of Learning*. It contains an early statement of the major principles and concepts of the author's systematic philosophy. There is definite indication in this writing that Bacon's philosophical scheme is to be both naturalistic and materialistic in character.

The "troublesome" title of the present writing, *Valerius Terminus of the Interpretation of Nature: with the Annotations of Hermes Stella*, applies specifically to the first, the only full chapter of the treatise, which has been assembled from fragments of writing. In this chapter the author contends that the province of natural philosophy does not include divine "mysteries," since God "is only self-like, having nothing in common with any creature," and no "light for the revealing of the nature of God" can be obtained by "inquiry into . . . sensible and material things." The name "Valerius" is one which belongs to ancient Roman consuls or highest magistrates or to praetors or senior magistrates during consulates; as in the case, for example, of P. Valerius Publicola, consul, 508 B.C.; L. Valerius Flaccus, consul—with Marius, 100 B.C.; L. Valerius Flaccus, praetor during Cicero's consulate, 63 B.C. Bacon observes that "the names of the Roman magistrates are the same" even "when the status of things changes." "Terminus" in the title means boundary or limit; "Valerius," here employed as an adjective, means authoritative; hence, the first part of the title of the work, when translated, becomes "the authoritative limit of [natural science, or] the interpretation of nature." Of the words in the second part of the title, "stella" (star) is a symbol employed by the author to designate the sovereign, as in his early device, or masque, for Elizabeth's entertaining—the *Gesta Grayorum* in the

Advancement of Learning, and in the *De augmentis.* As for "Hermes": in the *Advancement of Learning* the author compares James with this ancient god to whom, he says, was ascribed in veneration "the power and fortune of a King, the knowledge and illumination of a Priest, and the learning and universality of a Philosopher." Apparently during the period in which Bacon assembles the *Valerius Terminus* he is entertaining the hope that James, who long has been drinking at the "fountains of learning," may be prevailed upon to annotate a subject's writing. But on reflection, he thinks it imprudent to make such a request, for the present at least, of this learned sovereign and very considerable author. He writes on the title page of the compiled document, "None of the Annotations by Stella are set down in these fragments."

In the compiled work, especially in the first chapter, whose content occasions the title of the whole, a sharp distinction is drawn between the respective areas of revealed theology and philosophy. The former of the two is not to encroach in any degree upon the province of the latter, which is to be pursued through inductive inquiry by natural human powers. While philosophy is to be limited by religion, the scientist, as a religious man, will put his natural philosophy, with whose findings revealed theology is never to interefere, into the service of a charity prescribed through Divine Revelation. Natural science is not to provide a bridge—like the natural theology of the Peripatetics—for the making of an ascent from the causes, operations, and structures of nature to God, as First Cause, Prime Mover, or Being *qua* Being. Indeed, for Bacon these three modes of description of God, either in metaphysics or in theology, are gratuitous and inept.

The subject matter of the philosophy which Bacon sketches in the *Valerius Terminus,* and develops in his later works, is to be limited to physical nature. Between this philosophy and revealed theology a definite boundary is fixed. Physical nature, as one body, is to be understod within one limited system of truth. In the investigation of nature there is to be no enfranchisement of independent, mutually exclusive sciences to the weakening of all, in the manner of Aristotle, through the use of mutually exclusive basic axioms. All axioms, whether newly proposed or in process of establishment, will, as investigation proceeds, receive their authority and draw their strength from a unified body of physical science, within which they are to be intimately conjoined. "Without this intercourse the axioms of sciences will fall out to be neither full nor true; but will be such opinions as Aristotle in some places doth wisely censure, when he saith, *These are the opinions of persons that have respect but to a few things.*" "I mean," writes Bacon, "not that use which one science hath of another for ornament or help in practice, as the orator hath of knowledge of affections for moving, or as military science may have use of geometry for fortifications; but I mean it directly of that use by way of supply of light and information which the particulars and instances of one science do yield and present for the framing or correcting of the axioms of another science in their very truth and notion ... for sciences distinguished have a dependence upon universal knowledge to be augmented and rectified by the superior light thereof, as well as the parts and members of a science have upon the *Maxims* of the same science, and the mutual light and consent which one part receiveth of another. And therefore the opinion of Copernicus in astronomy, which astronomy itself cannot correct because it is not repugnant to any of the appearances, yet natural philosophy doth correct. On the other side if some of the ancient philosophers had been perfect in the observations of astronomy, and had called them to counsel when they made their principles and first axioms, they would never have divided their philosophy as the Cosmographers do their descriptions by globes, making one philosophy for heaven and another for under heaven, as in effect they do."

Care must be taken, however, to make certain that, through a desire for immediate unity, the results of investigation in limited areas do not dominate all other divisions of knowledge. With such an unfortunate consequence, Plato mingled his whole philosophy with theology, Aristotle his with logic, and Plato's followers of the Second Academy theirs with mathematics. At present the alchemists are prone to produce a full philosophy out of the results of a few chemical experiments, while Gilbert makes a whole universe from his observations of the loadstone. These are examples of thinkers who elevate what actually applies to "a few things" into something which supposedly pertains to all.

Bacon now names some of the objects which are to be investigated by a new inductive method. These are the "natures," "motions," and "appetites" of bodies. The "natures," "few and permanent," are "as the alphabet or simple letters, whereof the variety of things consisteth; or as the colours mingled in the painter's shell, wherewith he is able to make infinite variety of faces or shapes." As for "motions" and "appetites": philosophers of the past have written too much and badly about the first "beginnings or principles" of things and have neglected to inquire into the "motions, inclinations, and applications" of matter here and now. Actually there can be no "beginnings" in a philosophy of nature. Doctrines respecting a First Cause are groundless and invalid, "impertinent and vain." Among other "conceits" and "mere nugations," which have appeared in past interpretations of motion, Bacon lists the views of Aristotle, certain Platonists, Parmenides, Anaxagoras, Empedocles, Leucippus, Democritus, and Epicurus: "shift or appetite of matter to privation; the spirit of the world working in matter according to platform; the preceeding or fructifying of distinct kinds according to their proprieties; the intercourse of the elements by mediation of their common qualities; the appetite of like portions to unite themselves; amity and discord, or sympathy and antipathy; motion to the centre, with motion of stripe or press; the casual agitation, aggregation, and essays of the solid portions in the void space." Of the three best known of the thinkers who have treated of the subject motion Democritus is to be preferred to Aristotle and Plato. "There is no great doubt," he says, "but he that did put the beginnings of things to be *solid, void, and motion to the centre,* was in better earnest than he that put *matter, form, and shift*; or he that put the *mind, motion, and matter.*"

The author inveighs against the deference which is being paid by investigators to "antiquity and authority; common and confessed notions; the natural and yielding consent of the mind; the harmony and coherence of a knowledge in itself; the establishing of principles with the touch and reduction of other propositions unto them; inductions without instances contradictory; and the report of the senses." Such things as these fall within sorts of "idols" or "false appearances that offer themselves to the understanding in the inquisition of knowledge." Bacon has already mentioned Idols in the *Fertilizing Birth of Time* and the *Advancement of Learning.* Here they are specifically named and their number stated as four: "the Idols of the *Tribe,* the Idols of the *Palace,* the Idols of the *Cave,* and the Idols of the *Theatre.*" (The word "Palace" is, presumably, the result of a scribe's slip, the original having been "Place," or "Market Place.")

In the *Valerius Terminus,* unjustified conclusions in science, over-hastily arrived at, are called "anticipations," as opposed to "interpretations," of nature. The necessity of a natural history for the founding of philosophy is reasserted and stress is laid on particulars, especially those of a "vulgar and ignoble" sort which, the author observes, are at present being put to use mainly by "persons of mean observation." Definite indication is now given of the role of the senses, the reason, and the axiom —occasionally called "hypothesis" by Bacon—in philosophic inquiry. The senses are said to have their own distinctive "sufficiency," not because they do not err, but because of their contribution—which is not, for the most part, "immediate"—to knowledge. "It is the work, effect, or instance," says Bacon, "that trieth the Axiom, and the sense doth but try the work done or not done." Scientific truths are general in character; their objects are universals available to reason. Particulars are infinite and transitory. Truths are to be sought through reducing particulars "by exclusions and inclusions to a definite point." Reason provides the axiom; sense tries the exemplification of the axiom in the operation of the particular which the axiom governs. After particulars have served in the establishing of the axiom, "the axiom found out" by reason "discovereth and designeth new particulars." The axiom, through intercourse with other axioms, also begets axioms of a more general character. These begotten axioms are either established or disproved by the evidence of particulars in causal operation within works available to sense. "In deciding and determining the truth of knowledge ... the discovery of new works and active directions not known before, is the only trial to be accepted of ... you may always conclude that the Axiom which discovereth new instances is true, but contrariwise you may safely conclude that if it discover not any new instance it is in vain and untrue." Here, the active direction is the axiom in operation. "The fulness of direction to work and produce any effect consisteth in two conditions, certainty and liberty. Certainty is when the direction is ... infallible. Liberty is when the direction ... comprehendeth all the means and ways possible. . . . If therefore your direction be certain, it must refer you and point you to somewhat which, if it be present, the effect you seek will of necessity follow, else you may perform and not obtain. If it be free, then must it refer you to somewhat which if it be absent the effect you seek will of necessity withdraw, else you may have power and not obtain." These things are so because the nature—or cause, or form—which the axiom defines is convertible, through identity, with the object in operation.

Most of what Bacon writes in the *Valerius Terminus* will be incorporated in some form or other within his *Novum organum* (*New Organon*, 1620). Much of the author's next philosophical treatise is so similar to portions of the *New Organon* that it may be regarded as an attempt to produce a draft of the later work. The main subject of the present, unfinished treatise, *The Outline and Argument of the Second Part of the Instauration*, is a new logic or method of investigation. This is to constitute the second of six parts of Bacon's Great Instauration of the sciences, which will be formally announced in the *New Organon*. In the *Outline and Argument* the author mentions five "books," which, he says, belong to the instauration of the sciences. The second of these is concerned with method, and the third, fourth, and sixth with the "interpretation of nature." The fifth book deals with "anticipations" of nature, findings not yet attested by the requirements of the new method. These, after subjection to full inquiry, may, if not then rejected, be incorporated in the sixth book. Nothing is said about a first book because, presumably, the author has not yet decided on the specific character of its content.

The purpose of the second book of the instauration, says the author, is to expose a use of reason more thorough than any hitherto known to man, to the end of exalting the human understanding as far as "this mortal state permits" and thus enabling man to assert his rightful dominion over nature. To achieve this aim, the surface of the mind must, first of all, be levelled and cleared of those impediments which have hitherto encumbered it. Next, the mind must be turned in the direction of the proper subject for investigation. Finally, information is to be imparted to the understanding, now rendered capable and ready to receive it.

The obstructive—and scientifically destructive—part of the human understanding is multiplex, in keeping with the several sorts of Idol which frequent the mind. Some Idols are old inhabitants, "settlers" long in occupancy, of the intellect. These include notions which have been received from the systems and sects of philosophers, who derived them originally through use of false rules and wrong methods of demonstration. Other Idols are native to the mind itself, inherent within its very constitution. Even as an uneven mirror distorts the real shape of objects, according to the curvature of its surface, so the understanding on receiving impressions through the senses mingles its own nature with what comes before it. The first task, then, is the dispersal and banishment of the host of theories which have been argued in the schools. Next will follow the job of freeing the intellect from the bondage of perverse methods of demonstration. Then will come a third undertaking, the holding of the mind's own seductive influence in check, either by uprooting its native Idols or, if this is not feasible, by indicating what these are, so that they may be recognized and, where possible, controlled. It will be fruitless, even harmful, to demolish and destroy prevailing errors in philosophy if new offshoots of error, conceivably worse than those which they supplant, are encouraged to proliferate.

Some readers, continues the author, will perhaps object to the delay we are inflicting on scientists by the tedious experimentation we are about to invite. Others may argue that by the entertainment of the immense number of particulars which we require for observation and study, the intellect will be thrown into a "*tartarus*," or hell, of confusion, far removed from the high serenity and calm of abstract wisdom—as if the latter were a godlike state. Those who, having abandoned themselves to a passion for contemplation, find our constant reference to "practical" achievements harsh and offensive, as something appropriate to mechanics, will now be shown how, in fact, they are working against the attainment of their own desire; because clarity in theoretical reflection on nature and the invention of practical works can only be achieved together, and by a common dependence on the same means. If someone demurs, because in his caution he regards our scheme for the regeneration of the sciences as a proceeding without any finality, we tell him with assurance that our instauration will mark the end of prevailing error and desolation. We hope to make it evident to all that a full and proper investigation of particulars and the concepts derived from these will amount to something more finished, manageable, intelligible, sure of itself, and better informed than any number of abstract speculations and meditations, such as at present prevail in science and philosophy.

Some sober critic—as he may think himself—will perhaps regard our whole undertaking with a reserve befitting a prudent man of affairs, and say that our statements are but "prayers"— and overly optimistic prayers at that. He may form the opinion that our transformation of philosophy will effect nothing but a change in dogma, by which the human situation would be improved in no way whatever. In that case, we shall persuade this critic that we are doing anything but establishing a dogmatic system or sect; that our method differs completely from any hitherto employed in philosophy and the sciences; and that a harvest of practical results is quite certainly assured, that is, if "practical" men do not in their hurry and haste attempt to reap the crop while it is still green, or grasp with childish impatience at what can be but promises of results to follow. The true interpretation of nature, the project in which we are engaged, is, of course, an arduous undertaking, but the greatest part of its difficulty does not depend upon anything that is placed beyond our capacities, but rather on what lies within our own power, and can therefore be overcome. One thing we would have our readers believe at the outset: we are not starting on a journey into a wilderness without reconnaissance. Our strategy is devised according to a formulated method or art.

The art of discovery which we are now introducing belongs

to the same family as ordinary logic, for that too prepares aids and constructs defences for the understanding. But ours differs from the common logic in various respects, and in three especially: the starting point of investigation, the order of demonstration, and the end and nature of proof. Our inquiry starts at a deeper level, by subjecting to examination things which the ordinary logic takes on trust, such as first principles, the basic axioms of the several sciences, and the evidence of the senses. Our method departs utterly from the old order of demonstration. It develops and elicits propositions and axioms cautiously, moving in a gradual ascent from recorded observations of particulars, as both positive and negative instances, to general truths, instead of jumping immediately from what is given in sense to "first" principles and large generalities, and from these speculatively deducing intermediate propositions. The end of the logic we profess is not the invention of arguments but the discovery of the natures of real things, a discovery which will be established by operations within particulars.

The new logic is an instrument which controls and, at the same time, aids human faculties or powers. Aristotle, whose teachings still prevail, acknowledges sense, memory, and reason as three instruments of knowledge. But he provides no assistance for the first of the three and disregards the particulars to which they are exposed. His account of the second is indefinite. He permits the third to range and soar at will. The new logic, on the contrary, both controls and supplies aids for the senses, aids for memory, and aids for reason.

In presenting helps for the senses, we shall attempt to show how a good notion (comparable to what the Peripatetics in the context of their logic call the middle term) may be elicited and established, and how the senses, whose testimony is ever proportionate to man, may be brought into adjustment through axioms with the scale of the universe of nature. Actually, we do not attach great weight to the senses when operating by themselves, however necessary they may prove themselves to be in the trying of experiments which establish axioms. In cases where things escape the faculty of sense because of the small-ness of their bodies or of their parts, or through their distance, the slowness or quickness of their movements, or in other ways, we shall show how such objects may be brought within the scope of sense. We shall also indicate what may be done where objects cannot be presented immediately to sense. To this end we shall emphasize, for example, the employment of instru-ments, the skilled observation of gradual processes, and the drawing of such evidence from what is perceptible in bodies of size and character proportionate to the senses as may be re-lated to bodies or parts of bodies which cannot be made avail-able for immediate observation. Finally, we shall examine the question of natural history, including experiments, and shall designate the sort of history which can be made to serve as a foundation for philosophy. We shall also indicate what kind of experimentation should be made when other natural history is not available. At this point we shall introduce remarks on the stimulating and the retaining of attention, for many things which belong to natural history and scientific experiment have long been within the field of our vision, and yet have never be-come part of our scientific experience.

Our second sort of aids, those to memory, will further the extraction of a specific set or sort of observations from the mass of particulars, the accumulation of serviceable natural history in general, and the arrangement of this material of philosophy in a manner which permits the understanding to make use of it. The capacity of the understanding does not allow a ranging over the infinity of nature. Memory, too, can embrace only a limited number of objects. When unaided, the memory is not fitted to select matters relevant to definite inquiry. The best means, generally speaking, of overcoming its incapability in these two regards is a single, simple remedy: the rule that no result of investigation is to be accepted unless presented in a written record with properly ordered tables. To pursue the interpretation of nature in any field by relying upon memory unaided by such tables is like trying to retain and recite the content of an astronomer's almanac.

The selective function of memory requires special attention. Once the subject for research has been decided upon and placed within limits, so that it stands isolated from other matters and freed from any confusion with them, aids to memory can provide three services. To illustrate these we shall first indicate the kind of questions which are to be asked when the natural history of the subject concerned has been accumulated and considered —here we are reminded of what the logicians call "topic." Secondly, we shall explain in what order particular histories are to be marshalled into tables. We do not expect, of course, at this stage of investigation to hit the actual "veins" of the subject under study; all we can hope for is its tentative partitioning. We shall bear in mind, too, that truth emerges more readily from error than from confusion, and that reason can rectify a wrong division more easily than it can penetrate a heap of jumbled evidence. Thirdly, we shall show how and when an investigation should be started afresh; when the charts of previously compiled tables are to be transformed, and how often the inquiry should be repeated, as the case may require. We think that the first series of charts or results should be mounted upon adjustable axes, because they can represent only trial phases of investigation. The senses and the memory by themselves cannot, of course, establish axioms, but only simple notions and ordered histories for their placing at reason's disposal.

When considering our third group of helps, those to the reason, we must bear in mind the fact that, while the scientific reason is essentially a single thing, its aim is twofold: knowledge and contemplation on the one hand, and action and achievement on the other. Accordingly, we shall have regard for both the understanding of causes and the ability through means to produce effects. These two objectives, on close examination, will prove, like the reason itself, to be one thing. They can be separated only for the purpose of separate inquiry. What in reflection counts for a cause is in operation a means. If every means required for any purposes were available to man at his wish, there would be little or no point in treating theory and practice separately. But man finds that his action is confined within much narrower limits than his knowledge and that sometimes he can act experimentally in works without employing a scientifically established axiom. These are among the reasons why we treat the theoretical and practical aspects of reason separately. So far as the theoretical part is concerned, everything turns upon a single problem, that of establishing true notions and axioms. The established axiom contains a solid portion of truth, while a plain motion is, so to speak, only truth's surface.

There are three procedures which can especially further investigation in its theoretical aspect: the maintenance, the adaptation, and the abridgement of investigation. When we come to describe the first of these we shall have to explain how axioms may be used to suggest and to establish other axioms of a higher order and of greater generality, so that by a firm and unbroken ascent the investigator may eventually arrive at a unity of system. We shall also find it necessary to provide a way for testing and verifying these higher axioms by natural history and experiments, so that the user of our method may not lapse at any stage of inquiry into conjecture and mere probability.

The adaptation of investigation depends on the sort of cause being sought and the nature of the subject under investigation. Setting aside final causes, which have thoroughly corrupted natural philosophy, our search may be restricted to formal, efficient, and material causes. When we speak of efficient or of material causes, we do not mean "ultimate" agents or indeterminate matter—common topics in scholastic disputations—but proximate agents and formed matter. Lest the search for these be pursued through pointless refinements, we shall annex a method of discovering what may be called hidden processes. This is the name we give to the series and successions of change which result from the actions of efficient causes and the fluctuations of materials affected by them.

As for the abridgement of inquiry: this can help in two ways, to blaze a trail through trackless areas and to make a short cut across paths already worn. In these regards a certain kind of experiment and a certain kind of question have prerogative power. We shall accordingly indicate questions of a definite and comprehensive sort, queries by which an inquirer can early "take the auspices" of an investigation. Such questions, when placed in the vanguard will bear a torch, so to speak, for those which are to follow. We shall also indicate some experiments which can furnish more information than a multitude of others less outstanding and less enlightening. (A large section of the *New Organon* is given over to the illustration of "prerogative instances.")

Reason's second office, which has to do with operation in works, may be disposed of with a threefold thesis. As a preparative to this thesis, we must make an observation or two. When inquiry is conducted according to the requirements of our new induction, whatever is found to concern the practical reason should be interspersed with considerations which relate to the theoretical. Again, the fact should be borne in mind that in practical inquiry the procedure is by a ladder of *descent*, for here operations involve particular matters, which occupy the bottom of the scale of investigation—whose top is the most universal axiom—and must therefore be descended to, step by step, from general axioms.

The threefold thesis itself is, in effect, a prescription of three special parts or rules of method. One of these is appropriate to investigation where the desideratum is not so much a cause or an axiom as a practical achievement. Another concerns the compilation of such records as may further and hasten the production of works; and a third, an admittedly imperfect part of inquiry—an appendix as it were to scientific method—provides aid for the disclosing of operative possibilities by proceeding from experiment to experiment without the establishment of an axiom.

Having given this outline of what he intends to provide as principles and specific rules for a new method of inductive investigation, Bacon expresses the hope that he has prepared the way for the marriage of the "Human Mind and the Universe, if divine goodness will be their bridesmaid." It is his trust that the supplication of the "prayer of their nuptial hymn" will be for the begetting from their union of a line of heroes who may, in some degree at least, conquer and subdue man's necessities.

XIII

PHILOSOPHICAL WRITINGS
WHILE SOLICITOR-GENERAL

Between 1607 and 1612—the year in which he was called upon to assume heavy responsibilities of state—Bacon wrote some twelve philosophical pieces. Many of these were brief, some were of considerable length, some had hardly been begun; only one, *De sapientia veterum (Concerning the Wisdom of the Ancients)*, was completed. One can hardly imagine what the results would have been had this thinker been denied public office in the reign of James I. This much is sure: a stream of impressive writings would have flowed from his pen. The implications for philosophy of the doctrine of the three separate kingdoms (of nature, politics, and Divine Grace), of a new classification of the sciences, of the concepts and principles of a new naturalistic philosophy, of an inductive metaphysics hitherto unknown, and of a new method of inquiry, would have been worked out. There would have been exposition of the eight aids to investigation which are merely announced in the *New Organon*. A man of genius would have illuminated the field of induction which has remained to this day an area of philosophic obscurity. As it was, Bacon wrote more fully and more impressively on this subject than any other philosopher was to write for more than three hundred succeeding years.

269

Bacon's philosophic writings while Solicitor-General include: *Filum labyrinthi, sive formula inquisitionis (Thread of the Labyrinth, or Rule of Inquiry); Cogitata et visa: de interpretatione naturae, sive de scientia operativa (Thoughts and Impressions: Concerning the Interpretation of Nature, or Concerning Operative Science); Redargutio philosophiarum (The Refutation of Philosophies); De sapientia veterum (Concerning the Wisdom of the Ancients); Phaenomena universi (Phenomena of the Universe); Filum labyrinthi; sive inquisitio legitima de motu (Thread of the Labyrinth; or the Legitimate Investigation of Motion); Calor et frigus (Heat and Cold); Historia et inquisitio prima de sono et auditu, et de forma soni, et latente processu soni; sive sylva soni et auditus (History and First Investigation of Sound and Hearing, and Concerning the Form of Sound, and the Latent Process of Sound; or the Material of Sound and Hearing); Descriptio globi intellectualis (Description of the Intellectual Globe);* and *Thema coeli (Theory of the Heaven).* Either in this period or soon thereafter he wrote *Scala intellectus sive filum labyrinthi (Ladder of the Understanding or Thread of the Labyrinth)* and *Prodromi sive anticipationes philosophiae secundae (Forerunners or Anticipations of the New Philosophy).*

Bacon's publication of the *Advancement of Learning* (1605) had not produced the effect which its author had desired it to have on the King, the Court, Universities, clergy, and laymen of consequence. James and the frequenters of his Court had showed no interest in the establishment of either a new learning or a new science. Members of the Universities were resentful of the author's attack on their opinions and practices, and regarded his alternative for traditional logic as an unworthy thing, fit only for the training of mechanics and apothecaries' clerks. Clerics who read the book were appalled by its identification of metaphysics with universalized physics. The author's separating the principles of ontology from the placets of revealed theology did not appeal to those among the reading public who were sure that they knew what they intended when they thought that "truth is one and not many."

In 1608, Bacon, now intent on making a stronger and a better impression on his readers, conceived the plan of writing "scornfully" of the pagan Greek philosophers and respectfully of the "ancient poets"—as authors whose sayings contained in the form of parables some of his own most cherished opinions. Bacon began to prepare the *Redargutio philosophiarum (Refutation of Philosophies)*, two other similar pieces, and the *De sapientia veterum (Concerning the Wisdom of the Ancients)*. In the following year he was able to send a copy of the first of these to Tobie Matthew. Within an accompanying letter he included the statement, "I send you at this time the only part which hath any harshness. . . . it doth more fully lay open that the question between me and the ancients is not of the virtue of the race, but of the rightness of the way." He also sent, about the same time, a copy of another writing, *Cogitata et visa (Thoughts and Impressions)*, to his friend Bishop Andrewes. This piece had been composed for distribution to a few persons so as to invite comment and criticism before the author embarked on his large undertaking, the preparation of the *New Organon*. In *Thoughts and Impressions* Bacon repeats with increased emphasis arguments he has already employed in earlier treatises, and introduces topics which are to become prominent in writings to come. The piece is an enlargement of another written in English under the Latin title *Filum labyrinthi, sive formula inquisitionis (Thread of the Labyrinth, or Rule of Inquiry)*. This *Filum labyrinthi*—the author composes another on Motion—is one of the very few philosophical pieces which Bacon writes, or leaves, in English; the *Advancement of Learning* and the *Valerius Terminus* are two others. At the top of the last page of its incomplete manuscript is written, in Bacon's hand, "The English as much as was parfited." In the same hand is added to the first page *"ad filios,"* as if the author were communicating with an audience of disciples in prospect. The writing is probably the preliminary draft of the Latin *Cogitata et visa (Thoughts and Impressions)*.

There is, says Bacon in the *Thread of the Labyrinth, or Rule of Inquiry*, neither magnitude nor certainty in the knowledge now possessed and professed. Men strive by argument to save the credit of ignorance and to make themselves satisfied with their poverty. The good opinion of their store is the cause of their want. The physician has his set rules of practice and pronounces diseases incurable which are not encompassed by his prescribed art. The alchemist makes his experiments according to the recipes of auricular tradition, and explains his failures as the misunderstanding or misuse of the same. The aspiring magician is bent on finding what he deems to be breaches in the operations of nature. The mechanic refines what has been come upon by chance. The learned man regards the sciences as bodies of truth forever settled, and not as pursuits of examination and discovery. The succession of knowledge is from master to disciple, and not from discoverer to advancer.

In the course of learning, since the days of the ancient Greeks, natural science has been given the least attention of any part of philosophy. After Socrates taught, Grecian thinkers became concerned with moral instruction, as a sort of applied philosophical divinity. Able men among the Romans, because of the large problems posed by the extent and complexity of their Empire, confined their reflections to political and legal questions. Among the Greeks natural philosophy flourished but a very short time, for soon it became disputation among competing sects. Never since has science possessed a man wholly, except a rare monk in a cloister or an unusual gentleman at his country estate. At present it receives only casual recognition in the Universities, and that by raw wits in passage to professional studies.

Whenever the investigation of physical nature showed signs of producing results, religious authorities intervened. Greek thinkers who gave a naturalistic explanation of thunder were condemned for impiety. Fathers of the Church censured cosmographers who had discovered and described the roundness of the earth and told of the Antipodes. After scholastic philosophers "almost incorporated the contentious philosophy of Aristotle into the body of Christian religion," learning became a matter of texts, glosses, and disputations. The level of knowledge could go no higher than the source of its flow, the works of the defining, determining, magisterial Stagirite. In addition to a continuing authoritarianism which issues ultimately from Aristotle, other hindrances to science have appeared in a religious guise. Clerics argue that the desire to probe the secrets of nature is akin to the temptation of Adam which—as they understand it—brought about man's original sin and fall; that the more men know of second causes, the less they depend upon the First Cause; that innovation in philosophy leads to the subversion of orthodox theology. Such contentions are, of course, foolish and unsound. The occasion of the Fall was not a knowledge of the creation which is nature, but the assumption of a moral knowledge of God's will and intention and a refusal to obey His commands. Natural inquiry, which has nothing to do with a First Cause, is both sanctioned and required by God of men for the exercise of their dominion over the lower creatures, a dominion granted them by the Creator at Creation. Adam, accordingly, gave a name to every living creature, and Solomon wrote "a natural history of all verdor, from the cedar to the moss, and of all that breatheth." True Religion, so far from restraining natural inquiry and promoting submission to ignorance, requires diligent investigation of such of God's works as are put under man's dominion, works which show the Creator's power, but not His essential nature and will. This dominion will never be reclaimed by means of theological studies or through a continuance of the past and present practices of learned Christians.

In *Thoughts and Impressions* the author repeats several of his earlier observations. The science of the present possesses no certainty, magnitude, or promise of increase. Medicine, alchemy, and magic are filled with impostures. Mechanics is not sustained by a general philosophy of nature. Chance, and not design, is the discoverer and inventor. The preoccupation of thinkers with theology and ethics, the devotion of the Universities to narrow and retrograde studies, the despair of would-be inquirers, the contempt by the learned of "works" and of the "vulgar" things in nature, the common reliance on the opinions of the ancients—these have served to bring science to a standstill. There are, however, some grounds for hope. Age is wiser than youth and, opinion to the contrary notwithstanding, to the modern and not to the ancient times belongs the adulthood of the human race. There is a general weariness of religious controversy. The discovery of the new world has occasioned some expectation that the intellectual globe may be correspondingly enlarged. Recent inventions, acquired through groping and chance, have led men to expect greater discoveries from planned inquiry. Some investigators are professing a reliance on observation and experiment, if still continuing in the persistent vice of system-building.

From the contemporary builders of systems we can expect nothing of consequence for science. Like the ancient Greeks, the modern Bernardino Telesio, Giordano Bruno, Thomas Campanella, Jerome Cardan, and even William Gilbert have constructed large fictions, like so many stageplays, out of a few observations. Certain of these thinkers have discovered through experimentation some limited causes extending to limited observable effects. But with patient inquiry they cannot be satisfied. They must turn from this and assert axioms which imply great causes generally operative; yet causes, alas, of which no one can discern commensurable and corresponding effects. Their more general principles are not accordant with observable or proved operations in nature, as inductively established comprehensive axioms must be.

Science should make a new beginning. Natural philosophy must be purged of those methods and theories which have traduced it. Inquirers must again become like little children and approach nature with wonder and awe and without prejudice. Through experience and induction, they can learn its alphabet. A strict method of induction would bring guidance and furnish helps for the senses and the understanding. As the human hand by itself fails when it attempts to draw an exact circle without a compass, so the human mind wavers and wanders when without proper direction it would discover and comprehend the system of natural causes. Science must be provided with a new method. If renown accrues, as it does, to the maker of a discovery of a single cause in nature, how much more deserving of honor would be the discoverer of the method of all discovery of all causes. The immediate consequences of his invention would be nothing less than the purification and control of the human faculties. From this would issue the recapture of man's dominion over the kingdom of nature. Such a discovery would be so productive of results that it might well be called the "Fertilizing Birth of Time." Such a discovery would surely be more worthy of recognition than any deed of any conqueror, lawgiver, or founder of empire, since it would make man the ruler over the whole realm of nature.

The new method of science (the Second Part of the Great Instauration) is not to be confused with the modes of demonstration employed and taught by Aristotle, namely, induction and deduction. Aristotle's induction consists of a simple enumeration of agreeing particulars without the salutary employment of any negative instance, which might invalidate the principle asserted. In his deduction, the middle axioms are obtained not through observation of particulars but through derivation from more general propositions previously established by initial precluding definitions. Whatever fits these definitions is by the definitions determined; what fits them not is from demonstration excluded. This traditional method when compared with what is now proposed is as water to wine. As a vintage of discovery, the principles of the new science will not be a raw product rudely and hastily fermented, but a yield slowly produced from select particulars carefully gathered, mildly pressed, and well-purified.

In addition to a method, the new science requires an accumulation of a "forest" of particulars, the material on which the method may operate (the Third Part of the Great Instauration). In this collection particulars will not be thrown together as in a heap, but arranged and tabulated. When the material thus ordered will have been interpreted according to the rules of the new method, Tables of Discovery will be prepared in exemplification of the preliminary results of induction (the Fourth Part of the Great Instauration). Next, a scale or ladder of ascent to more general comprehensions must be undertaken. At this stage the investigator will be assailed by the temptation to proceed without inductive warrant to the enunciation of most general comprehensions—after the manner of Cardan, William Gilbert, and Telesio. Care must now be taken to make certain that at every step of ascension no instance contrary to an asserted axiom is overlooked.

For its scientific ratification, an axiom at any stage of inquiry must submit to two tests. First, it must meet the basic requirement of induction: proof by observable positive instances and disproof by observable negative instances. The latter sort of instance is not to be accommodated, in the manner of Aristotle, by the introduction of new verbal definitions to meet their cases. Secondly, no general principle is to be made a party to intellectual negotiation or let at large unless it give earnest, or bail—to use a figure from the courts—by indicating new particulars, and not merely principles, beyond those from which it has itself been derived. At this point of his exposition, Bacon is about to enter upon the Sixth Part of his Great Instauration.

The writing, which is said by its author in the quoted statement to Tobie Matthew to contain "harshness," is called by Bacon *Redargutio philosophiarum (Refutation of Philosophies,* 1608). This takes the form of an address to disciples in prospect by a wise man who bears on his countenance—like the Head of Solomon's House in the *New Atlantis* (1627)—a look of kindly pity for mankind. He speaks not from a pulpit or dais, but on a level with his hearers. His address is, in dramatic supposition, reported verbatim to the author, who is engaged in a discussion of his philosophic plans with a friend in Paris. The speech has been delivered in that city before an audience of some fifty persons eminent in church and state. The address in substance is as follows:

God has made you, my sons, not beasts in subjection but free men capable both of receiving by faith a knowledge of your Creator and also of attaining through your own faculties an understanding of the material world which the Creator has placed under your dominion. In what you consider your knowledge of nature, you think yourselves very rich, while in fact you are extremely poor. All your income of the present and the prospective future consists of reduced revenues from the labors of some six of your intellectual forebears, Aristotle, Plato, Hippocrates, Galen, Euclid, and Ptolemy. Yet your Maker requires, in addition to your allegiance to Himself, your own effort and toil in the study of His created works. The God who has endowed you with trustworthy faculties for search into the nature of His creation will hardly be satisfied with a blind faith in the opinions of six men. The conversion of your minds to what I am about to say will not be an easy undertaking, because all your theological and political treatises assume the sufficiency of the thought of the aforementioned persons. Your language and literature have been set in their terms and maxims. Their thoughts have been confirmed within you by the training received at colleges, by your social inheritance, and, one may almost say, by your national endeavor.

I am not asking you to surrender your learning; keep that for your dealing with those who speak and think in its terms. Have one way of communicating with the public, but employ another for dealing with nature. Give yourselves to the ignorant for a time, but beware lest they hold you captive forever. If you would understand and control nature you must first acquire a new method of inquiry, one hitherto untaught and unused. This you will not be ready to employ, or even to entertain, until your minds are prepared through a deliverance from much that is false. It is to make a beginning in the effecting of this deliverance that we are assembled today.

The people from which the old philosophy has come belonged to the boyhood of the race. The Egyptian priest in Herodotus wisely said, "You Greeks are ever children," for those whom he censured were like boys, given to much talking but incapable of generation. In the matter of time, the Greeks had not even a thousand years of history to look back upon. In the matter of place, they knew only a small portion of the world; their travels, in comparison with the voyages of modern discoverers, were merely suburban jaunts. Their foremost teachers, Plato and Aristotle, were men of capacious, and in a way sublime, intellect; yet by pretension to authority in everything, they became contending sophists, ignorant of most things. If Aristotle, who was to draw into his train men of learning in every age, is still regarded as chief among teachers, his continued eminence is the token of the indolence and pride of those who follow him; of indolence that retards the search for truth, of pride that conceals ignorance. So far is the com-

mon consent which prevails among Aristotle's disciples from
the betokening of truth, it is the worst of all signs where the
intellect is concerned. Nothing wins universal consent unless it
is either commonplace, ostentatious, or superstitious. Phocion,
when he was applauded by all the Athenian populace, properly
suspected his past conduct, and asked, "What error have I
committed?"

In the new philosophy there is to be no dictator; he who is
least in the new kingdom of learning will be greater than the
greatest in the old. Eminence will be measured according to the
fruitfulness of inductive inquiry. The produce from former
philosophical tillage has consisted of idle disputations, without
a single discovery. While the mechanical arts have progressed,
the sciences have remained stationary, lifeless images to be
adored in idle contemplation. The chief defect of the philosophy of the past, the one which has dominated all the rest, has
been the lack of a valid method. In this regard, let no one be
misled by the common assumption that Aristotle employed
induction and relied on experience. His so-called induction was
an imposture. So opposed was Aristotle to consulting with experience, he dragged her along as a captive chained to the
wheel of his chariot.

Train yourselves then, my sons, to study the ways of God's
creation, and not the behavior of Aristotle. Pursue the subtleties
of things themselves and not those of the Peripatetics. And be
not like the empirical ant, who only collects, or like the weaving
spider, who fills the air with the cobwebs of theory; rather use
your senses and your reason in the manner of the bee, who first
collects and then produces means for life and growth. Do not
fear the "nothing beyond" which has been written on the
Pillars of Hercules to mark the boundary of the charted Medi-
terranean Sea. Let your own cry be "further yet." Dare to pit
your strength against imaginary perils. With Jove's ancient
"non-imitable thunder" match a greater thunder of your own,

devised by art. Let the voyages of daring men who discovered unimagined places and areas be your encouragement to chart the whole intellectual globe, ever bearing in mind the words of the prophet, "Many shall run to and fro, and knowledge shall be increased."

The philosophical work which Bacon publishes while Solicitor-General, *De sapientia veterum* (*Concerning the Wisdom of the Ancients*, 1609), contains two dedications, one to Robert Cecil, Lord Salisbury, Chancellor of the University of Cambridge, the other to the University of Cambridge itself, in the "hope," as the author writes, "that the inventions of the learned may receive some accession by these labours of mine." The work, written in Latin, proves to be popular, and is reprinted and translated into English and Italian. The *Wisdom of the Ancients* presents a philosophy both naturalistic and materialistic, and yet in such a manner that not even a member of the Spanish Inquisition, as the author says, could find fault with any of its contents. Bacon in this writing interprets pagan parables only, yet in all his thinking he never finds reason to distinguish a "Christian" natural philosophy—something quite independent of revealed theology—from a "heathen" philosophy of nature. Here he presents in a disarming manner some of those major principles of his naturalism which most of the clergy and laity consider an erroneous or a disturbing philosophy.

In the Preface, Bacon affirms the opinion that the ancient fables have "hidden and involved meaning." He tells Salisbury in a dedication that "parable has ever been a kind of arc, in which the most precious portions of the sciences were deposited." The author has already esteemed the fable, as a vehicle of philosophic thought, sufficiently to incorporate in a short writing, *Cogitationes de scientia humana* (*Thoughts on Human Knowledge*), the myths of the Sisters of the Giants or Fame,

Coelum or the Origin of Things, Proteus or Matter, and Metis or Counsel. Later, in his *De augmentis*, he will employ for philosophical purposes the fables of Pan, or Nature; Perseus, or War; and Dionysus, or Desire. One of his last writings, *De principiis atque originibus (Concerning Principles and Origins)*, will include a treatment of the myths of Cupid, or Eros, and Coelum, or Uranus.

The *Wisdom of the Ancients* contains philosophical readings of thirty-one fables. Some of these interpretations are as follows. Pentheus, according to poetic myth, climbed a tree in order to observe the secret mysteries of Bacchus. In punishment, he became frenzied and saw everything double. Then, as he journeyed to the city of Thebes, he saw in his madness one Thebes in front of him and one behind, and knew not whither to proceed. The calamity of Pentheus, says Bacon, is a poetic representation of that perplexed, vacillating state of mind which is to be found in those who have aspired to penetrate what God keeps within his own curtain, through mistaking the light of nature for divine wisdom. Similarly, the punishment of Prometheus for his attempt on the chastity of Minerva signifies the plight of those who, having failed to keep faith free from incursions by human sense and reason, are doomed to perpetual struggle with fictional philosophies and heretical religions.

Another story concerning Prometheus singles out man's creation from other events, because the intellectual part of man, as the poets teach, is not the product of matter and is not brought forth by natural generation. The fable of Proteus makes clear that matter, and not man, is the oldest of created things. Matter spans the past, the present, and the future. Like Proteus, matter assumes all shapes, from fire and water to organic bodies. While Proteus himself represents matter, his flock represents the species of animals, plants, and minerals. Proteus may be put in chains and can be made, as matter can be made by art, to assume more shapes than those found in the recognized species of things. Proteus is also a knowing prophet. If one were to understand, as Proteus does, the "sum and general issue" of nature one would also comprehend both the composition of the whole world and the constitutive forms of individual things.

Coelum, according to poetic story, was the most ancient of the gods. His generative parts were removed with a scythe by his own son, Saturn. This son also devoured his own children, of whom only one, Jupiter, escaped. Jupiter in turn overpowered Saturn, cast him into Tartarus, and removed his generative parts. The teaching of this fable, says Bacon, is in agreement with the philosophy of Democritus, which asserts the eternity of matter and denies the eternity of the world. The deprivation of further power to create indicates allegorically that the totality of matter remains fixed and the *quantum* of nature undergoes neither increase nor decrease. The devouring by Saturn and his treatment by Jupiter represent the shaping and reshaping of the fabric of nature, and its perturbations and changes.

The fable of Pan has to do with the universal frame of things. To Pan are ascribed horns, broad at the base and narrow at the tip. The teaching in this case is clear: nature, when understood, is seen to be like a pyramid. At its base are infinite particulars, farther up numerous species, higher still genera, and at the top a single principle. Pan's horns ascend to heaven, but only touch it, because what is beyond nature pertains to God and is reserved to God's own Revelation. Pan is also given a biform nature, brute in the lower part and human in the upper. By this is signified the mixed nature of natural species. Strictly speaking, there are no simple species in nature. Man has in him something of the brute, the brute something of the vegetable, the vegetable something of the mineral. Again, the imputing of but few amours to Pan is not without meaning. Pan, who represents the natural universe, married Echo. Echo, who represents science, reflects nature as it is.

The story of Vulcan's forced attentions on Minerva shows how art, here figuratively portrayed by Vulcan, cannot subdue nature except through an understanding of her ways through patient and diligent research. Atalanta, who represents art, lost her race by turning aside to seize the fruit—in her case an apple —before the full course of her trial was undergone. The Sphinx's riddle and its solving in the myth which bears her name, makes a similar point. Those who attempt a hasty solution of the riddle of nature are certain to end with nothing more than false promises and pretensions.

Many of the stories associated with the name of Prometheus contain good counsel for scientific inquirers. In the contests held in his honor, when the light of a torch went out its bearer stepped aside to let the one who came after proceed in pursuit of the victory. The application of this fable to scientific endeavor is obvious. Aristotle, Euclid, Ptolemy, and some others made lively beginnings, but their successors were not to carry the torch.

Prometheus is said to have stolen fire from heaven and given it to mankind. Men, far from grateful for the gift, arraigned the giver before Jupiter. Jupiter in return rewarded the human race with the present of perpetual youth. Man put this gift on the back of an ass. The ass became thirsty on his way home and sought relief at a spring guarded by a serpent, which demanded as the price of the water the object the ass was carrying on his back. The price was paid, and mankind lost its gift of perpetual youth. In this parable perpetual youth signifies man's achievement in medicine and other arts and sciences. The slow pace of the ass, his turning aside on his way, and his surrendering of a precious gift for an immediate satisfaction all shadow forth those events which are to be found in the history of human inquiry.

The accounts given by the poets of Cupid, or Love, involve not one person but two, the elder Cupid, the oldest of the gods, and the younger Cupid, the son of Venus and youngest of the gods. The elder Cupid is said to be without parents. Both are represented as blind, naked, given to archery, and perpetually in a state of infancy. The infancy of Cupid represents "the appetite or instinct of primal matter; or to speak more plainly, *the natural motion of the atom*; which is indeed the original and unique force that constitutes and fashions all things out of matter." One Cupid's lack of parentage signifies the fact that matter, which contains causal agents, cannot be regarded philosophically as having any cause outside itself. There can be no First Cause in natural philosophy, Bacon argues, because if there were, the line of causes would be broken, and causation as such rendered incomprehensible through the adduction of an uncaused cause. The blindness of Cupid is a poetic representation of the the truth that God's created works are not to be interpreted as so many continued acts of Providence but as the operations of the parts of matter in motion.

Bacon now interrupts his reading of the parable, and turns to history. The investigation of motion, "wherein lies all vigour of operation," has, he says, been "negligent and languid." There are those who take a leap beyond nature and ascribe all motion to the immediate operation of God. Another account, by the Peripatetics, in terms of privation is the naming of a problem and not the explanation of a fact. The Epicurean opinion that motion is a fortuitous agitation of atoms is an example of trifling and ignorance. Democritus does better than the others, because having attributed to the atom dimension and shape, he assigns it two motions: a primary motion to the centre, where all atoms gravitate; and a secondary motion engendered in conflict whereby that which has less matter is forced away from the center by what has more. This limited doctrine of Democritus will not, however, explain either the movements of the celestial bodies or the phenomena of rarefaction and condensation.

To return to the parable: Cupid is described as an infant always, for the reason that the atoms, of which all things are composed, remain eternally what they are. He is said to be naked because only atoms can, in the last analysis, be so described. Cupid's skill in archery represents the action of matter through distance in space, for any doctrine of atoms and the void, or vacuum, must imply the action of the atom at a distance. The younger Cupid is called the youngest of the gods because he cannot operate until the species of things have been brought into existence, when he brings the appetition within matter to bear on particular objects. His mother, Venus, appropriately represents the general "appetite" of things for production and conjunction through locally contiguous causes.

The rest of Bacon's philosophical writings between 1607 and 1612 are mainly of two sorts, drafts of parts of the *New Organon* and pieces having to do with local motion, as the dominant factor in the explanation of the operations of nature and art—as befits a materialistic philosophy. Motion is the subject of the author's first attempt, presaged in his *Commentarius solutus* (1608), to furnish a "table" of inductively discovered knowledge. His second *Thread of the Labyrinth*, in which the author undertakes to provide a clue to the maze which is nature, includes within its title "the legitimate inquiry concerning motion." This short writing treats of variants of local motion. The several types of change, or "motion," traditionally recognized in the schools as generation and decay, increase and decrease, alteration in quality, and transference in place are all regarded by Bacon, a materialistic naturalist, as variants of local motion, the contiguous operation of the constituents of matter. Causation is not allowed a teleological pattern. There are to be no final causes in natural philosophy. Local causation is to prevail in the sphere of art, which, contrary to what Peripatetics teach, is not to be sundered from nature. In the *Descriptio globi intellectualis* (*Description of the Intellectual Globe*), a work concerned mainly with the motions of the heavens, Bacon declares that "things artificial differ from things natural, not in form or essence but only in the efficient; that man has in truth no power over nature except that of motion—the power, I say, of putting natural bodies together or separating them—and that the rest is done by nature working within. Whenever, therefore, there is a possibility of moving natural bodies towards one another or away from one another, man and art can do everything; where there is no such possibility, they can do nothing."

XIV

THE <u>NEW</u> <u>ORGANON</u>

During the years between Salisbury's death, in 1612, and the end of his own political career, in 1621, while he carries heavy burdens of state, Bacon's philosophical writings are few. Between 1614 and 1617 he composes the first draft of the *New Atlantis*. This work in design is to include two constitutions, one for an ideal commonwealth and another for a scientific brotherhood, or order. Only the second is written, however, and that merely in outline. During the same period, Bacon prepares one scientific history, *De fluxu et refluxu maris* (*Of the Ebb and Flow of the Sea*), and before 1620 draws up a set of rules for the collecting and sorting of observations and experiments. The latter he calls *Parasceve ad historiam naturalem et experimentalem* (*Preparative toward a Natural and Experimental History*). The author is also working between 1613 and 1619 on several pieces obviously intended for incorporation in some manner within his *New Organon*. These include *De interpretatione naturae, sententiae XII* (*On the Interpretation of Nature, XII Judgments*) and *Aphorismi et consilia, de auxiliis mentis et accensione luminis naturalis* (*Aphorisms and Counsels, concerning the Mind's Aids and the Kindling of Natural Light*).

In 1620, Bacon is in his sixtieth year, and he has not yet published any work in representation of his instauration, as he now conceives it to be. There is still no lessening of his public labors. Now, in order to put some parts of the instauration "out of peril," he decides to publish his *Novum organum sive indicia de interpretatione naturae (The New Organon or True Directions concerning the Interpretation of Nature)*. This is the most philosophically comprehensive of all his writings to date; to its preparation all of his previous philosophical pieces have, in one way or another, been either preparatory or contributory. As a book on scientific direction it is far from complete. Readers will be made to understand that the cause of his haste in publishing it now, is "not ambition for himself, but solicitude for the work; that in case of his death there might remain some outline and project of that which he had conceived, and some evidence of his . . . inclination towards the benefit of the human race." The author calls the work the Second Part of the Great Instauration. To this major treatise he adds a proem; an epistle dedicatory to the King, saying that its contents are "totally new in their very kind"; a preface to the Great Instauration; the plan of the Great Instauration; and the argument of its six parts. The author attaches to it in publication the *Parasceve ad historiam naturalem et experimentalem* and also *Catalogus historiarum particularium secondum capita (A Catalogue of Particular Histories by Title)*. This catalogue lists one hundred and thirty topics for investigation. The *Preparative* will serve to show something of the Third Part of the instauration, as will certain experiments included within the Second Book of the *New Organon;* the *Catalogue* will indicate the range of subjects requiring investigation. The First Book of the *New Organon* will present, too, something of the First Part of the instauration, which is now to include an account of Idols, in a partial "refutation" of the doctrines and the methods of past and present philosophies. The deficiencies of these old and new systems and the mode of their support and continuance by learned men and institutions have already been exposed in another manner in the *Advancement of*

Learning (1605). A Latin translation of this early work can be prepared, with some textual additions and deletions to make the whole more palatable to Continental readers. The amended and translated treatise will not be fully adequate for the purpose, but since there is no other appropriate writing at hand or in prospect, it will have to do as a representation of the First Part of the instauration. The translation will be published, as soon as it has been made ready (in 1623), under the title *De dignitate et augmentis scientiarum* (*Of the Dignity and Advancement of Learning*).

In the Proem, attached to the *New Organon*, Bacon states that by this treatise he intends to inaugurate "a total reconstruction of sciences, arts, and all human knowledge, raised upon the proper foundations." By the method which it contains he hopes to restore "to its perfect and original condition, or if that may not be . . . to a better condition" than at present, "that commerce between the mind of man and the nature of things, which is more precious than anything on earth, or at least than anything which is of the earth." In the Plan of the Work, the author explains that the Great Instauration consists of six parts:

1. The Divisions of the Sciences.
2. The New Organon, or Directions concerning the Interpretation of Nature.
3. The Phenomena of the Universe, or a Natural and Experimental History for the foundation of Philosophy.
4. The Ladder of the Intellect.
5. The Forerunners, or Anticipation, of the New Philosophy.
6. The New Philosophy, or Active Science.

The First Part of the instauration exhibits the knowledge at present in possession of the human race and indicates those areas of the intellectual globe which still remain unknown and uncultivated. The scientific cultivation of the latter will proceed, the author says, within those newly transformed and newly classified sciences which have been described already in the *Ad-*

vancement of Learning. A new classification of the sciences is
required for the present instauration because "in adding to the
sum total you necessarily alter the parts and sections; and the
received divisions of the sciences are fitted only to the received
sum of them as it stands now." The Second Part of the instauration is given over to a new method. This method differs from
the old logic in end, order of demonstration, and point of departure. Its aim is the invention not of arguments but of arts,
not the bringing of things into agreement with principles and
definitions already assumed by the inquirer but the discovering
of axioms which conform to nature's operations. The starting
point of the new logic is not, then, a fixed position of argument,
seized upon after a hasty flight of the intellect to a first notion
or principle. Its demonstration proceeds from particulars, ordered according to their agreements and disagreements as affirmative and negative instances, to lesser axioms, and then gradually
through middle axioms of greater generality to the highest
axioms of the greatest possible comprehension. Each axiom, of
whatever degree of generality, will be tried by the observation
of the particulars which it presumes to include within its range.
There is to be no setting down at the outset of certain axioms as
so many determining principles, things which, according to the
thinking of members of the traditional schools, underlie and
separate the several sciences. The foundations of knowledge
must be sunk deeper than these, into things themselves, where
no such separation can be found.

The Third Part of the instauration will consist of a large body
of natural history. This history, which is to be collected and
ordered to meet the requirements of the method of the Second
Part, is indispensable to scientific investigation. "What I have
often said," Bacon writes in the *Preparative*, "I must here em-
phatically repeat, that if all the wits of all the ages had met or
shall hereafter meet together; if the whole human race had
applied or shall hereafter apply themselves to philosophy, and

the whole earth had been or shall be nothing but academies and colleges and schools of learned men; still without such a natural and experimental history, such as I am going to prescribe, no progress worthy of the human race could have been made or can be made in philosophy and the sciences."

The Fourth Part of the instauration will consist of exemplary results obtained through the employment of the new inductive process, while the Fifth Part, which is only for temporary use, will embrace conclusions reached through incomplete observation and experiment not as yet under the control of a rigorous induction. Such inferences, somewhat like the inventions of chance, will serve as wayside inns for temporary rest. To vary the metaphor, they will be like interest given before the principal is returned. Eventually, as many of their number as can be proved will be incorporated within a system of axioms. The Sixth Part of the instauration, to which all the rest is subservient and ministrant, is a philosophy to be established according to the rules of a severe, legitimate, inductive interpretation of natural history.

In the First Book of the *New Organon* proper, discussions of questions contained in the author's earlier published and unpublished writings reappear in aphoristic summary. Criticisms of past and present philosophers become, in the main, examples of the Idols of the human mind. Bacon has entertained a doctrine of Idols for some thirty-seven years, ever since he began to write the *Fertilizing Birth of Time*. He has derived the meaning of the term Idol, as false phantom or image, from a statement of Democritus to the effect that in the act of perception *eidola*, or images, on entering the human soul, produce conventional, and not true or genuine, opinions. Idols, Bacon now explains, are either adventitious, coming from without the mind, or innate, within the mind's constitution. The sources of the adventitious sort are the doctrines of sects of philosophers and traditional methods of demonstration. These Idols may be eradicated with difficulty. The inherent kind can only be controlled.

Idols may be classified according to four kinds: those of the Tribe, of the Cave, of the Market Place, of the Theatre. The Idols of the Tribe have their foundation in human nature itself. The human understanding is like an uneven mirror which distorts and discolors objects by mingling its own nature with what it receives. The understanding is prone, for example, to find in the world an order and a regularity not in keeping with facts. It sees "parallels and conjugates and relatives" which do not exist; hence the fictional opinions of Aristotle and his followers that the motion of the heavenly bodies, as "perfect," is circular, and that a fourth element, "fire," must be added to three others, the cold, the moist, and the dry, to make a quaternion.

Once the human understanding has adopted an opinion agreeable to itself, it tends to bring everything it can muster to this belief's support. Negative instances of particulars which might prove embarrassing are disregarded, or taken care of by a new definition, or set aside as so many "monsters"—as the writings of Aristotle and his followers make manifest. The human understanding, again, cannot rest in what it comprehends; it must press on to what it cannot know. The treatment of causes is a case in point. Thinkers who deal with natural causes will have it that beyond these lies a further cause which itself cannot be part of a causal order, but must be an uncaused cause, or "first cause." After unsuccessful attempts to describe this agent remotely, the rationalists fall back on what is closest to hand, their desires and volitions, and crown their thinking with a doctrine of final causation.

The human understanding is not a "dry light," but ever "receives an infusion from the will and affections." What a man prefers, that he takes to be true. He shrinks from difficult questions because of his own impatience and their narrowing of his hope. He avoids the deeper problems of nature because of religious superstition; neglects the examination of mean and vulgar things because of pride; and refuses to entertain new opinions from fear of public disapproval. The intellect and the senses, man's enabling faculties in inquiry, can both produce grave misrepresentations of fact. The senses can be dull, incompetent, and deceptive. The inner workings of organisms, subtle changes in inorganic bodies, very slow and very fast motions, and comparable phenomena lie beyond their range. Instruments such as microscopes and telescopes, devised for their help, are not sufficient to overcome their inherent weakness. In the interpretation of nature the evidence they supply may be taken as crucial only in the trial of experiment; it is never sufficient for the establishment of an axiom. The intellect, for its part, is given to reliance on abstractions of its own making. It confers reality and stability on things which are nonexistent. In its speculation, without stopping for investigation, tedious or otherwise, it will soar, like a bird in flight, to "first" notions of the mind and what it takes to be the first or most general principles of things.

The second sort of Idols, those of the Cave, are several and varied. Their sources, which are many, include the mental and bodily constitutions, the habits, the trainings, and the accidental circumstances of the individuals concerned. Some investigators become attached to certain studies, more especially those with which they have taken great pains, or in which they deem themselves authorities, or of which they consider themselves the authors. Such inquirers adjust their findings to their special preoccupations. Aristotle, for example, puts his natural science under the rule of his logic of abstractions, and Gilbert makes the philosophy of nature accord with his theory of magnetism. Some inquirers are given to the admiration of antiquity, others to a desire for novelty. Some are strong on differences, distinctions, and minutiae; others find resemblances everywhere and readily compose comprehensive systems. The atomists, like

Leucippus and Democritus, are so absorbed with particles that they forget the structure of things; other philosophers of many sorts are so lost in admiration of nature's complexities that they fail to regard her simplicities.

Of all Idols, those of the Market Place are the most troublesome. These have to do with words. It is a common supposition that the reason controls words; but the truth is that words, having been put into commerce, lay hold on the understanding and place it in bondage. When an honest observer would alter his thoughts to bring them into conformity with the structures of investigated things, resistant words stand in his way. Definition does not ease the situation, as some philosophers suppose—except, of course, in mathematics, where the beginning and the end lie in definition of terms—because definitions consist of words, and beget new words. This fact accounts for the disputations among philosophical sects, which are concerned, not with things, but with the meanings of terms. The Idols which words set up and perpetuate are either names for things which do not exist or false names for things which do. Among the former sort are Fortune, Prime Mover, Planetary Orbits, Element of Fire. False names, which are commonly the result of hasty and confused abstracting, differ in degrees of error. The names of common substances, such as chalk and mud, are the least faulty. Examples of greater confusion and error are the Peripatetic Generation, Corruption, Alteration, Augmentation, and Diminution. Perhaps the most faulty of all terms in natural philosophy are those which stand for the so-called qualities of terrestrial bodies, Heavy, Light, Rare, Dense.

The Idols of the Theatre consist of philosophical systems which, like the fictions of the stage, are more elegant and compact than things themselves are. To produce these, some philosophers make a great deal out of a few things, and other philosophers take a little out of each of many things. The productions of the empirical schools are as mixed and disordered in content as their experiments are aimless and dark in conception. The combining of pieces taken from disparate things is most evident, however, in the corrupting of philosophy by mixing it with theology. This has been going on since the time of Pythagoras. In recent years it has shown itself in the raising of a natural philosophy on the first chapter of Genesis and the Book of Job, to the production of fictional philosophy and heretical religion. The ambition to draw too much out of a few things, however diligently and laboriously examined in the beginning, as in Gilbert's case, say, and perhaps that of Telesio, too, has in age after age brought science and philosophy to a standstill, sometimes to ruin.

"To what purpose are these brain-creations and idle displays of power?" Bacon is to ask in his *Historia naturalis et experimentalis* (*Natural and Experimental History*, 1622). "In ancient times there were philosophical doctrines in plenty; doctrines of Pythagoras, Philolaus, Xenophanes, Heraclitus, Empedocles, Parmenides, Anaxagoras, Leucippus, Democritus, Plato, Aristotle, Zeno, and others. All these invented systems of the universe, each according to his own fancy, like so many arguments of plays. . . . Nor in our age, though by reason of the institutions of schools and colleges, wits are more restrained, has the practice entirely ceased; for Patricius, Telesius, Brunus, Severinus the Dane, Gilbert the Englishman, and Campanella have come upon the stage with fresh stories, neither honoured by approbation nor elegant in argument. . . . There is not and never will be an end or limit to this; one catches at one thing, another at another; each has his own favourite fancy; pure and open light there is none; every one philosophizes out of the cells of his own imagination, as out of Plato's cave; the higher wits with more acuteness and felicity, the duller, less happily but with equal pertinacity. And now of late by the regulation of some learned and (as things now are) excellent men (the former variety and licence having, I suppose, became wearisome), the sciences are confined to certain and prescribed authors and, thus restrained, are imposed upon the old and instilled into the young; so that now (to use the sarcasm of Cicero concerning Caesar's year), the constellation of Lyra rises by edict, and authority is taken for truth, not truth for authority. Which kind of institution and discipline is excellent for present use, but precludes all prospect of improvement. . . . I know not whether we more distort the facts of nature or our own wits; but we clearly impress the stamp of our own image on the creatures and works of God, instead of carefully examining and recognizing in them the stamp of the Creator Himself. Wherefore our dominion over creatures is a second time forfeited, not undeservedly; and whereas after the fall of man some power over the resistance of creatures was still left to him—the power of subduing and managing them by true and solid arts—yet this too through our insolence, and because we desire to be like God and to follow the dictates of our own reason, we in great part lose. If therefore there be any humility towards the Creator, any reverence for or disposition to magnify His works, any charity for man and anxiety to relieve his sorrows and necessities, any love of truth in nature, any hatred of darkness, any desire for the purification of the understanding, we must entreat men again and again to discard, or at least set apart for a while, these volatile and preposterous philosophies, which have preferred theses to hypotheses, led experience captive, and triumphed over the works of God; and to approach with humility and veneration to unroll the volume of Creation, to linger and meditate therein, and with minds washed clean from opinions to study it in purity and integrity. For this is that sound and language which went forth into all lands, and did not incur the confusion of Babel; this should men study to be perfect in, and becoming again as little children condescend to take the alphabet of it into their hands, and spare no pains to search and unravel the interpretation thereof, but pursue it strenuously and persevere even unto death."

Portions of the First Book of the *New Organon* and the first part of the Second Book are given over to an account of the present state of scientific inquiry and to arguments for its reform. These are mainly amplifications of statements already made by the author in other writings. The remainder of the present work deals with a new method of induction. This, Bacon again takes pains to inform his readers, is not to be confused with mere empiricism, or with the practices of the past which are said to be inductive. The author is not an empiric who collects a heap of observations and experiments without a definite cause, nature, or form in mind. He does not rely merely on senses and particulars for his hypotheses or his proof. He begins with a nature, a form, or a cause, to be defined through an examination of agreeing and disagreeing instances of particulars under observation and experiment. The senses, to which these particulars are for the most part available, can try the experiment, but only operation can establish the axiom which scientific definition becomes.

Bacon does not attempt to explain knowing in terms of its "logical" content, like Plato; or as process initiated by the organism's contact with external objects and ending with the "informing" of the rational soul, like Aristotle; or as physical impact, like Democritus. He does not say where sense, reason, forms, and axioms "come from." He finds these four factors available like the planets in the heavens and like verdure and heat on the earth. He does not "make" them in the manner in which an epistemologist makes them to be what an epistemologist wants them to be for an explanation. Bacon is aware that the attempts in philosophy to explain the origin of concepts and axioms and the acts of sense or reason have resulted in one or other several unsatisfactory things: the scepticism of persons like Pyrrho, the "image" theory of Democritus, the assignment by Plato, Aristotle, and the Stoics of a rationale to nature—a device for putting "mind" into material things. In any event, Bacon's own placing of reason within the province of revealed theology precludes a turning from the method of science and its employment in physical inquiry into the byways of an epistemology of sense or of reason, or of a mixture of the two. Bacon thinks that by his new method he has brought about "a true and lawful marriage between the empirical and the rational faculty, the unfortunate separations ... of which" by those who have advanced theories of knowledge "have thrown into confusion all the affairs of the human family." Having done this, Bacon draws the curtain on their bedchamber and refuses to interrupt or impede their nuptial activities by epistemological descant.

Bacon asserts that his method of inquiry is not to be confused with a "wandering" Socratic induction which in Plato's case becomes the definition of essences unavailable to sense and removed from particulars. Nor is it to be identified with the induction discussed by Aristotle. Aristotle in the beginning recognized two sorts of induction. The first of these was a "perfect" kind which imposed an impossible task on the inquirer by requiring the examination of every particular of the species of thing under investigation. This was soon put aside by the author, who proceeded to employ induction by definition, which made every object that failed to conform to his own definitions an exception. Some of these exceptions Aristotle was able to accomodate by shifts of definition; the others remained for him "monsters." Aristotle also cut off his sciences, one from the others, through axioms which defined several independent and mutually exclusive areas of inquiry. After doing this he made deduction by syllogism the method of demonstrating whatever lay within each separate science. This deduction was based on the first notions of the mind, gained by intuition; on first principles, or axioms, of the several sciences, gained by intuition and secured by definition; and on the middle terms of demonstrating syllogisms, secured by definition. Aristotle provided no satisfactory means for establishing the middle term of the syllogism on which his deduction depended. The main objection, then, to the whole business of Aristotle's deduction—still regarded as the proper method of scientific discovery and proof by learned persons within and without the Universities—is the obvious fact that his syllogism did not apply to the "first notions" of the mind nor to the "axioms" of the sciences, and consequently could never establish a lesser proposition with a true middle term, except in a purely formal and, as far as scientific discovery is concerned, a fruitless way.

In academic demonstrations of "truth," argument by syllogism hangs on the defined middle term. Here, this term is "elected at the liberty of every man's invention." Such a practice will not serve, however, in the investigation of nature, whose end is not the defeat of an opponent in verbal argument but the discovery of actual forms, causes, or laws. Aristotle, after he had discarded his "perfect" induction, which involved the examination and enumeration of every particular instance of the form under examination, and therefore was not feasible, attempted to compensate himself for his loss by bringing induction under syllogism. His classic statement in the matter, which Bacon most likely knew first- or second-hand, is this: "Man, horse, and mule [i] are long-lived animals [ii]; man, horse, and mule [i] are bileless animals [iii]; therefore all bileless animals [iii] are long-lived animals [ii]." In this case the validity of the argument obviously rests on the assumption that [iii] is no wider than [i]. Such a demonstration as this exemplifies three of what Bacon regards as great defects in Peripatetic proof: first, induction by simple enumeration of particulars or species; second, induction by positive instances only; and third, the too hasty and arbitrary definition of terms, without a full citing, sifting, and aligning of instances. Proof with these defects leaves the conclusion in the realm of extreme probability or, if you would have it, of mere improbability.

There can be, reflects Bacon, but two ways of philosophizing about nature. The first of these is to fly speculatively from sense and particulars to the most general axioms—with all that this practice entails—and, after taking these as settled truths, to deduce from them "middle" axioms. This is the proceeding now in fashion. In the other way, as yet untried and untrodden, axioms are derived from sense and particulars by gradual ascent until the most general axioms are reached. Here the senses are guarded and made subject to rule and correction; that mental operation which is said by Aristotle to follow upon the perception of sense is for the greatest part discarded; and the intellect will be controlled at every step. If the rules of a new sort of logic do not intervene from the beginning, and the intellect is allowed to soar suddenly to high abstractions and great generalities, as the old logic permits and encourages, then no logic will ever be able to set matters right again. Certainly, if the syllogism is to enter the picture at either an early or a late stage in inductive progression, it will probably do nothing more than confirm error. The new inquiry will proceed by gradual stages—except, of course, in purely mathematical thinking—and at every stage will bring such universalities as the intellect may provide back to particulars for proving. Thus, it will always both ascend and descend.

The new induction begins with experience duly sifted, prepared and digested, and from this educes axioms. These axioms suggest more universal axioms and, in turn and consequence, new experiments. At every stage of the procedure the axiom must descend to particulars for verification, in order to show that whatever it asserts as principle is operative as cause in nature. No axiom is worthy of the name unless its representation of the schematisms and the processes of nature can be established by the operations it elicits from nature when bodies are put together according to its formula. Nothing obscure, then, nothing occult, nothing general that cannot be shown through particulars directly or indirectly available to the senses, will do at any stage of search for the truth of nature. Care must be taken, therefore, to see that each axiom proposed by the intellect is framed to the measure of the sort of instance it is presumed to cover. As it goes beyond these in hypothesis, suggesting other experiments and axioms, both it and the axioms which it suggests must be brought back to particulars for proving and demonstration by operative causes. A wider hypothesis, when it has been proved, will manifest the possibility of great "clusters" of discoveries. If such an hypothesis transcends the boundaries of any one of the traditional sciences, so much the better. It has already put that science on the way to drawing sustenance from a larger body of scientific truth than its own. Any "profound and radical alteration" of nature will depend on general axioms. The same is true of the knowledge of things on which man cannot experiment as, for example, the heavenly bodies. A full knowledge of these bodies can result only from comprehensive discoveries respecting motion and such "natures" as magnetism, attraction, and "spontaneous" rotation.

The tasks confronting the scientific investigator are of two sorts, one speculative and the other operative. "Of a given nature to discover the form, or true specific difference, or nature-engendering nature, or source of emanation (for these are the terms which come nearest to a description of the thing), is the work and aim of Human Knowledge." "On a given body to generate and superinduce a new nature or new natures is the work and aim of Human Power." The form of which we speak may be regarded as a nature, a cause, a law. These four terms are all convertible, one with the others. The choice of a term in a particular instance is determined by use in context. "The form of a thing is the very thing itself." "Forms are the laws of pure act." "When I speak of forms," Bacon writes, "I mean nothing more than those laws and determinations of absolute actuality which govern and constitute any simple nature, as heat, light,

weight, in every kind of matter and subject which is susceptible
of them." The forms of the new philosophy, then, are not to be
confused with Plato's Ideas, which are not materiate or within
particulars, nor with Aristotle's abstract forms, nor with the
atoms of Democritus. Democritus does affirm, however, something of great worth and consequence when he asserts that
formed matter and its configurations and changes are the proper
objects of inquiry, because "forms are figments of the human
mind" unless they be regarded as "laws of action." Aristotle, on
the other hand, employs one of his abstract forms to mark
wherefrom the operation of his formless matter proceeds and
another to mark *whereto* this proceeds, but he fails to provide an
explanation of the process itself which is brought about by cause
within formed matter.

Aristotle is content with the supposition, which readily follows the slight observation of things, that nature contains primary forms which she seeks to educe as species. He separates
the members of these natural species, not only from "monsters"
—so-called because his ordinary definitions cannot accommodate
them—but also from works of art. He maintains that in the case
of the last an artificial "form" is added to one already in nature.
Bacon cannot countenance Aristotle's segregation of species,
monsters, and works of art, each from the others, nor his separation of matter and form even in conception. Matter, for
Bacon, is not something deprived, formless, indeterminate, and
inert, but a formed and active entity. It has within it causes and
laws of lesser and greater generality, from which issue, as components of one body or system, without segregation of parts,
all the particulars in nature, all so-called "marvels," and all
works of art. The form is the law of actual operation in matter.
Even as a civil measure has its clauses, so the more general laws
of nature have subsidiary laws confined to lesser areas of natural
things. By the same token, some forms are more inclusive in
operation than others. Here the reader should be cautioned, says

Bacon, lest he imagine that a greater form—which is always the very nature of the object concerned—is composed of lesser forms. Such is not the case. The more general form has a more general authority in operation, and this authority cannot be divided, any more than one law, one nature, one cause can be divided into part laws, part natures, or part causes. "Every body contains within itself many forms of natures." These natures, which constitute bodies, are to be regarded—to use terms from the old logic—as predicates of which complex bodies are subjects. In the new logic, however, the "predicates" are fully explanatory of the subjects, and themselves come under more general forms or laws or causes. To take an example: motion in the case of the nature of heat is one thing; motion in the case of the nature of celestial bodies is another thing; yet, and as science progresses, we may hope to have an account of the nature of motion which includes a nature common to the motion of heat and the motion of the heavens. Then we shall have knowledge of a higher law, a more inclusive cause, a greater form.

The object pursued in science is not, then, the form of what the Peripatetics call a substance, but the forms, or laws, of matter. "To inquire the form of a lion, or of an oak, of gold," writes the author, "nay, even of water or air, is a vain pursuit; but to inquire the form of dense, rare, hot, cold, heavy, light, tangible, pneumatic, volatile, fixed, and the like ... which (like the letters of the alphabet) are not many and yet make up and sustain the essences and forms of all substances:—this, I say, it is which I am attempting." The subject matter of inquiry becomes the more "disentangled ... the nearer it approaches to simple natures ... the business being transferred from the complicated to the simple; from the incommensurable to the commensurable; from surds to rational quantities; from the infinite and vague to the finite and certain, as in the case of the letters of the alphabet and the notes of music. And inquiries into nature have the best result when they begin with physics and end in mathematics."

Here Bacon is showing the influence of Plato's *Philebus*. Among the four "concauses" of the intelligible world, Plato lists the infinite, or indeterminate, and the finite, or determinate—the other two being the "mixture" of these and the *nous*, or Reason. Knowing, according to Plato in this dialogue, proceeds by bringing what is indeterminate under determination.

When an object undergoes change, a form previously present is superseded by another form—a doctrine in Plato's *Phaedo*. The object changes; the form does not. Forms, however general, remain simple and fixed. They are not transient or efficient causes in the old meaning of these terms. The cause does not precede the effect in time, for it is the object in actual operation. The form is the "very thing itself" within operative, material nature. Forms are materiate, and not abstract, or separate, or separable from matter. Matter is subject to inherent causation, but the cause itself is not caused. The only authority beyond any cause is a more general cause; to this it stands not in the relation of effect but as a species to a genus.

Having dealt with these general questions, Bacon proceeds in the remainder of the Second Book of the *New Organon* to provide specific examples of induction in use. These examples prove disappointing for several reasons. In the first place, they are lacking in full and precisely detailed and determined experiment and observation, because natural history of a "new kind" collected according to a "new principle" is simply not available in sufficient quantity or variety for the author's purpose. Secondly, Bacon pursues his investigation only as far as the preliminary stages of induction. Thirdly, of the eleven aids to the understanding which are promised, the author expounds by example only three. The other eight are presumably not ready for description and exemplification in 1620—nor will Bacon ever have or find time to make them ready.

The chief example of induction, in its preliminary stages, which the author now employs concerns the form of heat. For the investigation of this—and any other form—there should, says Bacon, be mustered from a natural history, assembled and sorted, particular instances which agree in possessing the nature in question. The author lists some twenty-seven instances of heat and indicates that others may be added. These instances include the rays of the sun—especially at noon in midsummer, rays of the sun when "condensed"—as on walls and in burning-glasses, eruptions of flames in volcanoes, ignited solids, boiling liquids, substances rubbed violently, quicklime sprinkled with water, natural baths, animal bodies, and so on. Such affirmative instances will constitute a Table of Essence and Presence. Next, a Table of Deviation or Absence in Proximity is to be prepared. This will contain examples from which the nature under investigation is absent. Such cases, Bacon observes, are of the greatest consequence, because even one contradictory example can render nugatory an axiom founded only on positive instances. The instances chosen for this second Table should be those which agree in as many ways as possible with those in the first, and yet disagree in one regard, the absence of the nature under investigation. Of such cases the author provides some thirty-two examples, among them the rays of the moon, the rays of the sun in the middle air, unheated liquids, oil mixed with quicklime. A third Table, Degrees of Comparison, will exhibit recorded observations of the increase and decrease of heat in the same subjects, and also in different subjects under comparison. There can be more or less heat in an object at one time than at another, because the operation of this species of form, or cause, may at times be restrained in degree by the operations of other forms or causes. Bacon provides some forty-one examples for use in the third Table: increase of heat in animals by motion and exercise, striking repeatedly on anvils, fires progressing against a strong wind, the sun's approaching the zenith, alternating coldness and heat in persons with intermittent fevers, air in process of losing heat, and so on.

After a lengthy examination of the instances presented in the three Tables, with special emphasis on negative instances, Bacon states the conclusion that the form, cause, or nature of heat is motion of a sort. That is not to say, he warns the reader, that heat generates motion, because heat itself, its quiddity, its essence, its nature, is motion. The motion which is heat is a species within the genus motion, set apart from other species of motion by certain differences. These differences are part of the definition of heat which, as the First Vintage or Commencement of Interpretation, may be stated thus: *"Heat is a motion, expansive, restrained, and acting in its strife upon the smaller particles of bodies."* However, expansiveness must be further qualified within the definition, because heat's motion, *"while it expands all ways, it has at the same time an inclination upwards."* Strife upon particles also must be qualified; in the case of heat this *"is not sluggish, but hurried and with violence."* Since the definition we are concerned with belongs to the operative part of physics as well as to the theoretical, it may be stated as a direction thus: *"If in any natural body you can excite a dilating or expanding motion, and can so repress this motion and turn it back upon itself, that the dilation shall not proceed equably, but have its way in one part and be counteracted in another, you will undoubtedly generate heat."*

Having provided the foregoing example of what he calls the Presentation of Instances to the Understanding and the Commencement of Interpretation, Bacon goes on to list nine more aids to the understanding. These are, Prerogative Instances, the Supports of Induction, the Rectification of Induction, the Variation of Inquiry according to the Nature of the Subject, Nature's Prerogative with Respect to Investigation—what should be investigated first and what afterwards, the Limits of Investigation or the Synopsis of All Natures in the Universe, the Bringing Down to Practice, the Preparations for Investigations, and the Ascending and Descending Scale of Axioms.

Prerogative Instances are so named because they deserve priority for their outstanding assistance to the senses and reason and their striking promotion of operative works. The author lists twenty-seven kinds. Of these, five sorts of Instances of the Lamp serve especially to enlighten the senses. Solitary Instances aid the reason by hastening the exclusion of the form; Migratory, Striking, Companionship, and Subjunctive Instances by indicating more clearly than others the affirmative of the form; Clandestine, Singular, Constitutive, Conformable, Alliance, and Bordering Instances by leading the intellect more immediately to genera. Other instances help to guard the reason against false forms and causes, to indicate aims for practice, to measure operation, and generally to facilitate the production of works by which axioms must ultimately be tried.

After an exposition in considerable detail of his twenty-seven sorts of Prerogative Instance, Bacon brings the *Novum organum* abruptly to a close. No account of the eight remaining aids to induction is given. The *Novum organum* of 1620 is incomplete, and destined to remain so. In the remaining years of his life, the author's philosophical writing is to consist almost wholly of works in representation of the Third Part of his Great Instauration.

XV

BACON AND NATURAL HISTORY

Between 1621 and 1626, the year of his death, Bacon composes an almost unbelievable number of works. Among these are a *History of the Reign of King Henry the Seventh;* in dialogue form, an *Advertisement touching an Holy War;* a *Preface to a Digest of the Laws of England;* the *Beginning of the History of the Reign of King Henry the Eighth;* a third edition of the *Essays;* the *Translation of Certain Psalms into English Verse.* The philosophical writings of this period include a revision of the *New Atlantis; De principiis atque originibus, secundum fabulas cupidinis et coeli: etc. (Concerning Principles and Origins, according to the Fables of Cupid and Coelum: etc.); Historia naturalis et experimentalis ad condendam philosophiam; sive phenomena universi (Natural and Experimental History for the Foundation of Philosophy; or Phenomena of the Universe); Abcedarium naturae (The Alphabet of Nature); Historia vitae et mortis (History of Life and Death); Historia gravis et levis (History of Heavy and Light); Historia sympathiae et antipathiae rerum (History of the Sympathy and Antipathy of Things*—preface only); *Historia sulphuris, mercurii, et salis (History of Sulphur, Mercury, and Salt*—preface only); *Sylva Sylvarum (A Forest of Materials); Historia densi*

et rari: necnon coitionis et expansionis materiae per spatia (History of Dense and Rare: or the Contraction and Expansion of Matter in Space); Topica inquisitionis de luce et lumine (A Topic of Inquiry Concerning Light and Illumination).

By 1621 Bacon has become rather desperate over the problem of supplying a natural history sufficient in scope and variety for the illustration of the Third Part of his instauration. Ever since he began to entertain a philosophy of his own he had always thought of its foundation in terms of natural history. When this philosophy became definite in design the author engaged himself in entreaty to members of the Court for aid towards the collecting and ordering, under his own direction, of a record of nature on a large scale. By the time he composes his *Outline and Argument* (1606 or 1607), Bacon's thinking has become certain about the characteristics of this natural history. Some six years thereafter he wrote in his *Description of the Intellectual Globe*: "I consider myself bound not to leave the completion of this history which I pronounce deficient to others, but to take it upon myself; because the more it may seem a thing open to every man's industry, the greater fear there is that they will go astray from my design; and I have therefore marked it out as the third part of my instauration." In the same vein he will write in the introductory part of his *Natural and Experimental History* of 1622: "It has occurred to me . . . that there are doubtless many wits scattered over Europe, capacious, open, lofty, subtle, solid, and constant. What if one of them were to enter into the plan of my Organum and try to use it? He yet knows not what to do, nor how to prepare and address himself to the work of philosophy. If indeed it were a thing that could be accomplished by the reading of philosophical books, or discussion, or meditation, he might be equal to the work, whoever he be, and discharge it well." The author will, therefore, provide examples of the sort of history required. He will tell Prince Charles, to whom the present history is addressed: "I have bound myself as by a vow every month that the goodness of God (whose glory is sung as in a new song) shall add to my life, to complete and set forth one or more parts of [natural history]. . . . It may be also that others will be stirred by my example to a like industry; especially when they shall fully understand what it is that we are about."

Bacon's entreaty for aid actually began in 1592 with the request to Elizabeth's Lord Treasurer for a place to "carry" him, so that he might have more "wits" than his own for the pursuit of "industrious observations." It was continued in a request of a similar sort to Elizabeth within a "device" for her entertainment, the *Gesta Grayorum* of 1594. Eleven years later Bacon reminded another sovereign of the support given to Aristotle by the ruler of Macedon for the compiling of "an History of Nature," and told James, after reviewing learning's defects, that the improvement in prospect were *opera basilica*, works for a king. What is now required, he then said, "may be done by many, though not by any one . . . may be done by public designation, though not by private endeavour." In 1608, James' Solicitor-General conceived the plan of acquiring a "place to command wits and pens, Westminster, Eton, Winchester, especially Trinity College in Cambridge, St. John's in Cambridge, Magdalene College in Oxford, and bespeaking this betimes with the King, my Lord Archbishop, my Lord Treasurer."

Within a few years Bacon began to prepare a constitution, under the title *New Atlantis*, for a scientific foundation which he called Solomon's House. This college or brotherhood of benign, beneficent, assiduous inquiries would be dedicated to the "interpreting of Nature and the producing of great and marvellous works" for the benefit of mankind. This college Bacon described as "the noblest . . . upon the earth." It was to contain among many other resources for scientific inquiry, a mathematical house, with instruments for the study of the planets; horticultural gardens for the examination of soils, trees, shrubs, and herbs; enclosures for the observation of beasts, birds, insects, and fishes; theatres for anatomical dissections; laboratories for the study of diseases, medicines, foodstuffs, refrigeration, minerals, gems, the effects of natural and artificial baths, motions of sounds, tempests, earthquakes; houses for the production of new species of animals, birds, and plants; facilities for producing magnifying glasses, telescopes, gunpowder, instruments of war, silks, dyes, wines, boats which might travel under the seas and others which might fly in the air. Certain Fellows of the House would engage in experiments; others would travel abroad to obtain scientific information; others would concentrate on the production of operative works; some would draw experiments into "titles and tables"; still others would direct such new inquiries as might be indicated by earlier experiments, observations, and axioms; and some would raise discoveries by experiments "unto greater observations, axioms, and aphorisms." All members of the House would praise God daily for His marvellous works, and pray for His blessing on labors designed for "good and holy uses."

On presenting a copy of the *New Organon* to James, in 1620, the Lord Chancellor told his sovereign, in language befitting an address to this monarch, that one part of the instauration, "namely the compiling of a Natural and Experimental History . . . is but a new body of clay, whereinto your Majesty, by your countenance and protection, may breathe life." In simpler speech, he called upon his readers "to come forward and take part in what work is to be done." In the *Preparative Toward a Natural and Experimental History*, Bacon again reminded the King of what he had "said elsewhere," that the history, which "cannot be executed without great labour and expense; requiring as it does many people to help . . . is a kind of royal work." "My own strength," he continued, "is hardly equal to such a province"; the materials "on which the intellect has to work are so widely spread, that one must employ factors and merchants

to go everywhere in search of them and to bring them in."
After three more years had gone by, in 1623, Bacon, in the *De
augmentis* (the Latin translation of the *Advancement of Learning*), was again addressing James, in complaint, with the words:
"I often advisedly and deliberately throw away the dignity of
my name and wit (if such be) while I serve human interests;
and being one who should properly perhaps be an architect in
philosophy and the sciences, I turn common labourer, hod man,
anything that is wanted; taking upon myself the burden and
execution of many things which must needs be done, and which
others shun through an inborn pride."

Two years later, in 1625, Bacon would write Father Fulgentio that the Third Part of the instauration, the *Natural
History*, "is plainly a work for a King or a Pope, or for some
college or order, and it cannot be done as it should be by a private man's industry." In 1627, a year after Bacon died, Rawley,
in preparing the *Sylva Sylvarum* for publication, would include
in an epistle to the reader the following note: "I have . . . heard
his lordship discourse that men (no doubt) will think many of
the experiments contained in this collection to be vulgar and
trivial, mean and sordid, curious and fruitless. . . . I have heard
his lordship speak complainingly, that his lordship (who thinketh he deserveth to be an architect in this building) should be
forced to be a workman and a labourer, and to dig clay and
burn the brick; and more than that (according to the hard condition of the Israelites at the latter end), to gather the straw
and stubble over all the fields to burn the brick withal. For he
knoweth, that except he do it, nothing will be done; men are so
set to despise the means of their own good."

In the *Preparative* of 1620, Bacon calls natural history "the
nursing-mother" of active science or philosophy. Two years
later, he writes in the preface to his *Natural and Experimental
History*: "My Organum, even if it were completed, it would
not without the Natural History much advance the Instauration

of the Sciences, whereas the Natural History would advance it
not a little. And therefore, I have thought it better and wiser
by all means and above all things to apply myself to this work."
The histories of the past, Bacon observes, are filled with fabulous experiments, fabricated "secrets," and frivolous records.
No author except Pliny has dealt with nature in her threefold
manifestation, that is, in her ordinary courses, her constraint by
art, and her production of prodigies through her so-called
"erring." Extant natural history is bulky, pleasingly varied, and
often diligently prepared, yet when its fables, antiquities, quotations, "reported" opinions, controversies, philology, and ornaments are removed, it shrinks into very small compass. As a
record, it fails almost entirely to meet the requirements of a
"legitimate interpretation" of nature. Its content is better fitted
to table talk than to the foundation of a philosophy. A new
natural history, collected and arranged according to the rules
of the new inductive method, must therefore be compiled.

In the *Preparative*, Bacon calls for a natural history free of
mere antiquities, citations by doubtful authors, everything
purely philological and ornamental, all superstitions, and tales
by old wives and empirics. He invites histories of the arts, of
those, in the first instance, which "exhibit, alter, and prepare"
materials, such as cookery, agriculture, freezing, and the making
of commodities, including glass, enamel, gunpowder, fires, and
clocks, because these can provide needed information about
nature's motions. The collecting of these and other natural
histories is not to be a haphazard business because, when properly done, it involves the bringing of the infinity of particulars
within determinate investigation. To this latter end, topics or
points of inquiry should be noted, and tabulations and written
records of the results of observation and experiment set down
with exactitude. All natural history is to be carefully, even
reverently, compiled, since it is the record of God's works and,
therefore, is a second kind of Scripture. As such, it will include

within its scope the movements of every sort of thing, including objects which learned men of the present think too "illiberal" and commonplace for inquiry, even childish, base, or filthy. Let the motions and virtues of all bodies, then, says Bacon, from the largest planet to the smallest terrestrial object, be determined; and let these be numbered and measured, so far as circumstances permit, because the combination of physics with mathematics engenders the most fruitful knowledge of causes, a knowledge which leads directly to the production of operative works.

Bacon's precipitancy in turning out "histories" of his own compiling resulted inevitably in a failure to produce any that were worthy of a place in his Great Instauration. Those written between 1608 and 1612 were definitely excluded by the author from the Third Part. Their contents were too "mixed" with general philosophical problems. Of the several histories prepared betwen 1622 and 1626, that of *Dense and Rare* is especially interesting because it contains the only extant record of the author's considerable application of mathematical quantity to experiment. This work includes some tentative hypotheses respecting rarefaction, condensation, and the vacuum. The *History of Winds* and the *History of Life and Death* are comprised of topics, observations, and provisional or hypothetical conclusions *(canones mobiles)*. The *Sylva Sylvarum* consists of a thousand paragraphs dealing with phenomena in the fields of inquiry even more varied than those indicated in the *New Atlantis*. The work contains some observations and results of experiments of the author's own, but, taken as a whole, the compilation is "bookish." The author has drawn, in great haste, on the writings of authors from Aristotle to the contemporary George Sandys. No one writer or investigator, nor even a thousand, could have prepared within a period of five years adequate histories of the subjects specified in the *Sylva Sylvarum*.

One can hardly avoid the question why the author, who was to produce a "Bacon-faced generation" less than two scores of years after his death, failed to acquire during his lifetime support and help for his inductive enterprise. An answer would include many factors. Burghley looked upon his nephew's philosophical preoccupation as a weakness in an aspirant for political place. Elizabeth took Bacon's mention of scientific gardens and the like as a compliment rather than a request. The learned James, whose mind was full of theology and learning of traditional sorts, thought little of the proposed philosophy of nature. The Universities disdained the "new learning." The author, notwithstanding his public career as Parliamentarian, judge, and administrator of state, was by nature an individualist —as, no doubt, every genius is. Bacon's political, legal, literary, historical, and philosophical concerns left him little time to frequent the company of others. What he did in these several regards he could in the main do too well to require, or to suffer, cooperation with others. Bacon had devoted friends, but their interests were chiefly political or literary. While he conceived his Great Instauration as a common effort under the principle of universal charity, he always looked upon himself as its one sufficient intellect, its architect, and its supreme director. When he sought aid from the Court, he saw himself either as the magnanimous superior of a foundation, or the employer of a large number of secretaries and factors who would carry out his benign bidding.

Bacon's instauration of knowledge and learning had inherent within its philosophy a great difficulty—the education, learning, and habitual mentality of his contemporaries considered. Its metaphysics was naturalistic and materialistic, nothing more or less than a generalized physics. The author had asserted that Democritus should be set above Plato, Aristotle, the Augustinians, and the Peripatetics; and required that philosophy, as something attained by the use of natural faculties, be completely

sundered in source and establishment from the truths of revealed theology. Had Bacon been less of a systematic thinker
and, as a scientific naturalist and not a philosophical materialist,
more of a recorder of nature, his enterprise might have fared
better from the beginning. His systematic philosophizing became a warning to his followers in the philosophical college
which became the Royal Society. They prudently excluded
questions of theology and metaphysics from their transactions,
and found a supporter in Charles II, who granted them a Royal
Charter.

Bacon, as an exponent of a materialistic metaphysics, enjoyed,
of course, one great advantage over contemporary Continental
thinkers: he could not be condemned before an Inquisition of
either a Romanist or a Genevan sort. He could not be sent to
the stake, like Giordano Bruno. The Reformation in England
had engendered ecclesiastical conflict, but it had produced a
considerable tolerance for theologico-philosophical speculation. James, to his discomfort, knew that his kingdom had
within its borders, his Church among its clergy, and his Privy
Council among its members, Aristotelians disposed toward and
Calvinists opposed to the mingling of philosophy and theology,
High Churchmen who were Aristotelians or Platonists and yet
maintained a belief in the Real Presence, and Puritans who professed no philosophy at all and thought the High Churchman's
belief idolatrous. But Bacon's scheme of reform was very extreme. The author was supplanting the prevailing Platonic and
Aristotelian ontologies with a universalized physics and was
seeking to transform academies of learning into laboratories designed for the production of "works." It was with such aims as
these that Bacon confronted a sovereign schooled in traditional
learning, prelates of Platonic and Aristotelian training, clergy
and laity who regarded a materialistic metaphysics as the work
of the devil, and heads, fellows, and graduates of the Universities whose exercises were based on the medieval trivium, and

whose books of study were largely the works of classical authors or writings derived from these. It can hardly be a subject for wonder, then, that Bacon's philosophical undertaking was to receive its initial support not from the Head of the Established Church, nor from members of the King's Council, nor from the clergy, nor from the Universities, but from a detached band of independent thinkers and experimenters.

Within a generation after his death, experimenters and Nonconformists of the Enthusiastic persuasion, who completely separated the revelation of saving faith from natural and "depraved" knowledge, were to disregard Bacon's materialistic metaphysics and to accept his inductive inquiry. That scientific regimen which promised best to promote "useful" knowledge and attendant prosperity in the temporal world was acceptable to Puritan Enthusiasts, whose "carnal" thought and business affairs did not impinge on their Revealed Wisdom. Oliver Cromwell, one of their number, prompted by such Baconian agitators as John Webster and Samuel Hartlib, showed a readiness, at one stage, to convert the Universities into scientific academies. After the Restoration, when the rule of the "Saints" was over and done with, Bacon's philosophy would be associated with Enthusiasm, Cromwell, Puritans, and Nonconformists generally, in a public damnation and consignment to Hell by a senior Oxford divine in the Oxford Theatre. The association would be accurate, if the condemnation would be excessive.

XVI

BACON'S ORIGINALITY

Bacon is an original and originating philosopher. He propounds, in the first place, a distinctive pluralistic philosophy by which the science of nature is rendered free from overt invasions by revealed theology and from covert incursions by the same in the guise of theologico-metaphysics. Secondly, Bacon puts "mind" out of metaphysics. Thirdly, he reorganizes natural knowledge by assigning its recognized divisions new places and functions in a new classification of the sciences. Fourthly, he sets down the principles of a distinctive metaphysical naturalism, materialistic in character. Fifthly, he undertakes to establish metaphysics through a purely inductive procedure. Sixthly, he attempts to do for induction what Aristotle did for deduction, namely, to describe in detail its principles and to exemplify its operation. Seventhly, he regards logic, not as reason in operation, not as the alignment of terms in propositions, but as a "machine" for controlling the human faculties, including both sense and reason—an instrument which operates in exacting fashion between the empirical collecting of particulars and the asserting of general axioms. Eighthly, without a lapse into deduction, he makes the observation of induced causal processes in nature, that is, of operative works, including those of art, the test of every axiom or scientific principle, from the highest—erroneously called "first" in traditional logic—to the lowest.

Let us consider, partly by way of review, some of these achievements, omitting what has already been elaborated in detail. It is Bacon's opinion that the "Prerogative of God comprehends the whole man." Man's lot, under God's dispensing, lies within the three kingdoms: the Kingdom of God—known through Revelation—in which through Divine Grace man is saved from his sin and receives his moral rule of charity; the civil kingdom, where God—as the Scriptures teach—bestows political initiative upon rulers, who are the creatures of His own making; and the kingdom of nature—known through inductive science—whose dominion has been given to man by the Creator. These three areas of knowledge are not brought by Bacon under a single classification of sciences. They have no common categories. They cannot become parts or aspects of one integrated system. Bacon's philosophical thinking—to use this phrase in a most comprehensive sense—remains pluralistic in character. The author will not permit the weakening of the placets of Revelation by any accommodation to a "unity of truth" in which the several truths of theology, metaphysics, politics, ethics, and natural philosophy are made components of a system organized either according to a principle of equality or to a scale of ascent in a hierarchy.

Attempts by thinkers of the past to bring differing kinds of truths into a single system have, in Bacon's opinion, resulted in the reduction of all. Plato made knowledge and virtue dependent on the contemplation of abstract forms divorced, beyond reconciliation, from the world of particulars. As these abstract entities became the more removed from matter and actualities, they became for this author, in an absurdity, the objects of inquiry in natural philosophy, the ends of dehumanized human desire in ethics, the foundation of rule and sovereignty in politics, the components of a dialectically constructed universe in metaphysics, and in theology the mind and power of God, now reduced to a dialectical entity.

Aristotle, in turn, laid some stress on actual particulars, but not for long. He was not content to dissect these, but must abstract them. Then he went on to define his abstractions, and not physical nature as it is, nor ethical and political motives as they are, nor metaphysical operations of specified scientific significance, nor God as Creator, for the so-called First Cause of what Aristotle calls nature is but the crowning abstraction in a system of abstractions. Aristotle's philosophical system was supposedly held together by a teleological principle, which pervaded all things from the "first bodies" to the highest and first cause. But as a comprehending, unifying principle, governing all areas of being and operation, Aristotle's teleology was of a questionable sort: for it contained a contradiction, because by definition the Stagirite had already rendered completely segregate the several regions over which it was to prevail, his metaphysics or theology, physics, ethics and politics, and the poietical sciences or arts.

Later writers under Stoic influence made an attempt to overcome Aristotle's discontinuities by bringing the operations of physical nature, human conduct, political rule, even the mind of God, within the orbit of an all-comprehending Law of Reason. However, as the extension of this principle increased, and the attempt was made to tie physical nature and God together as subjects under one law and rule, the terms and clauses became the more incomprehensible and illusory. The distinctions and exclusions required in such a case as this must of necessity dissipate any unity and authority within a law.

Bacon is a pluralist. Of philosophical opinions which make for pluralism Bacon recognizes three sorts. One of these, of which Aristotle is a supporter, affirms that nature is composed of individual substances, or entities. In this opinion Bacon agrees, but only up to the point where he argues that the objects of philosophical investigation are not particular substances, but common forms, or natures. In the *New Organon* he writes, "Though in nature nothing really exists beside individual bodies, performing pure individual acts according to a fixed law, yet in philosophy this very law, and the investigation, discovery, and explanation of it, is the foundation as well of knowledge as of operation. And it is this law, with its clauses, that I mean when I speak of *Forms*; a name which I rather adopt because it has grown into use and become familiar." It is Bacon's contention that philosophy is not concerned with particulars or individuals as such, but moves in the realm of universals. The universals which the investigator of nature seeks are forms or laws or causes, constitutive of and operative within material bodies.

A second kind of philosophical pluralism, which is also to be found in Aristotle, rests on a plurality of segregate sciences, each with distinctive principles and concepts, notions, terms, whose only bond of union is a rationale called analytic, or logic. With this, Bacon disagrees. It is his opinion that the natural sciences can be brought together through informing general axioms which are inherent within the subject matter of each and all of them. These principles are to be established inductively by a method not hitherto employed, a method which is not "logical" in character, and which operates only after the rejection of what hitherto have been received as the "first" and commanding principles of reason and the founding and segregating axioms of independent sciences.

A third sort of pluralism issues from a regard for the distinctive sources and appropriately distinctive knowledges of truly different subject matters. This is Bacon's kind of pluralism. His theology treats of the nature and will of God, the knowledge of which is given to man by Divine Revelation—a knowledge unto which man by use of his own faculties cannot attain. Bacon's political doctrine is premised on the principle of divinely bestowed sovereignty and initiative which comprehends rule by justice and law. This principle he finds in the repeated affirmations of Holy Writ, which are not to be weakened or reduced by any philosophical reconstruction of their placets. Bacon's philosophy of nature is discovered through natural inquiry. In this there is no legitimate place for a doctrine of a First Cause, which Aristotle accommodates through the services of a teleological metaphysics. The principles of nature as a body, or system, are not to be confused with what in tradition are taken to be the subjects of metaphysics, such as the four causes and matter and form. They belong only to the physics of materiate things. They are the very axioms of nature itself, and do not apply to God, nor to political sovereignty and subjection of political subjects under sovereign rule.

In the next place, Bacon rejects mind as a metaphysical principle, or entity. Mind has been made inherent within the intelligible world by Plato. In one of his latest dialogues, the *Philebus*, Plato assigns four "concauses" to the objects of inquiry: the indeterminate, the determinate, the "mixture" of these two, and *nous*, or reason—the determining principle within whatever is knowable. Plato also, in his last dialogue, the *Laws*, finds *nous*, or reason, within the elements, laws, and the cosmos generally. Aristotle, in turn, makes *nous* a kind of divine reason which actualizes in intelligence logical forms; he also makes logic a rational thing, the normal function of reason in demonstration; and he finds a *logos*, or rational principle, as something pervasive within each area of science. The Stoics identify the *nous* with their *logos*, and make this *logos* a reason within nature, man, and God. This reason they employ as an explanatory principle in three conjunctions, as the judgment of the knower, as the formal statement of judgment in the scientific proposition, and as the objective counterpart of judgment in the rational structure of the universe. With the theological Platonists, the *logoi*—the *logos* pluralized—become both ideas in the mind of God and seminal principles in nature. Causes are now reasons, and the world, as intelligible order, contains the rational principles of the Creator's mind. These several meanings of the *nous* and the *logos* and varied offices of reason are put into employment by a succession of Platonists, Peripatetics, and eclectic philosophers.

In the *Advancement of Learning* (1605), a work written when the author is embarking on his "voyage of discovery"— to use his own metaphor—and mentioning doctrines which he will later amend, he includes the statement that metaphysics handles "that which supposeth . . . in nature a reason, understanding, and platform." Then, almost immediately, Bacon goes on to say that "the natural philosophy of Democritus and some others, who did not suppose a mind or reason in the frame of things . . . seemeth to me . . . in particularities of physical causes more real and better enquired into than that of Aristotle and Plato." This qualifying of the earlier statement is what we should expect, if we bear in mind that metaphysics is being regarded by the author as universalized physics. In the Latin translation of the *Advancement of Learning*, the *De augmentis*, of 1623, Bacon lays stress on the greater "penetration" into nature by Democritus, the philosopher who "removed God and Mind from the structure of things, and attributed the form thereof to infinite essays and proofs of nature . . . and assigned the causes of particular things to the necessity of matter." In the same reference the author maintains that God in his wisdom has not "communicated to all natural figures and motions the characters and impressions of His providence [or knowledge]." In the early *Valerius Terminus* (1603-5) the author states that "God hath framed the mind of man as a glass capable of the image of the universal world, joying to receive the signature thereof"—"signature" and not mind of nature or of God. In the *New Organon* (1620), which contains his mature philosophy, Bacon states explicitly that what are sometimes taken to be the ideas of God in nature are properly to be regarded as the Creator's "seals" or "signets" on His creation. These are not, in manner or degree, divine ideas. The seals of nature are not reasons. The laws, processes, and structures of nature are not "logical" in the traditional meaning of the term. What is logical for Bacon belongs to a method which, he says, is a "machine" to control reason as a human faculty, and not to show a rationale inherent within nature. Bacon holds that the forms, or causes, or natures of philosophy are materiate, subject to the materiate laws of matter in motion. The structures and processes which scientific axioms embody are not of a rational or a mental, let alone a divine, order. The Creator has not put into nature His own mind, or any other sort of mind.

Bacon is so impressed by the greatness and majesty of God that he cannot entertain the opinion that the forms of matter are in any manner or degree participant in or even "imitative" of the ideas of the Creator. In the *Valerius Terminus* he writes: "If any man shall think by view and inquiry into . . . sensible and material things, to attain to any light for the revealing of the nature or will of God, he shall dangerously abuse himself. . . . God is only self-like, having nothing in common with any creature, otherwise than as in shadow and trope. Therefore attend His will as Himself openeth it, and give unto faith that which unto faith belongeth." Man at his creation "being a spirit newly inclosed in a body of earth, he was fitted to be allured with appetite of light and liberty of knowledge," yet, through his "intruding" by natural faculties "into God's secrets and mysteries," through his "presuming to come within the oracle of [Divine] knowledge, man transgressed and fell."

For Bacon there can be no "similitude" between man and God in the matter of knowledge, but only in goodness or charity, which "is nothing else but goodness put into action or applied." The rule of charity, which "comprehends and fastens all virtues together," is given in Revelation for the governing of that part of man which is made in the Divine Image. In the *De augmentis* Bacon explains: "We are bound to obey the divine law though we find a reluctation in our will, so are we to believe His word though we find a reluctation in our reason. . . .

"And this holds not only in those great mysteries which concern the Deity, the Creation, and the Redemption; but it pertains likewise to a more perfect interpretation of the moral law, 'Love your enemies'; 'do good to them that hate you,' and so on. . . . To which words this applause may well be applied, 'that they do not sound human'; since it is a voice beyond the light of nature."

"The use of human reason in matters of religion is of two sorts; the former in the explanation of the mystery, the latter in the inferences derived from it. With regard to the explanation of the mysteries, we see that God vouchsafes to descend to the weakness of our apprehension, by so expressing his mysteries that they may be most sensible to us. . . .

"But with regard to inferences . . . after the articles and principles of religion have been set in their true place, so as to be completely exempted from the examination of reason, it is then permitted us to derive and deduce inferences from them. . . . the first propositions are not only self-existent and self-supporting; but likewise unamenable to that reason which deduces consequent propositions. Nor yet does this hold in religion alone. . . . we see in games, as chess or the like, that the first rules and laws are merely positive, and at will; and that they must be received as they are, and not disputed; but how to play a skilful and winning game is scientific and rational. . . .

"But as the use of the human reason in things divine is of two kinds, so likewise in the use there are two kinds of excess; the one when it inquires too curiously into the manner of the mystery; the other when the same authority is attached to inferences as to principles."

When we bear in mind that Bacon has put reason, even as rationale, out of nature as system and has placed questions respecting the supreme rule of ethical conduct, the basis of political sovereignty, and the being, knowledge, and providence of God within revealed theology, we can the more readily comprehend some of the naturalistic implications of his classification of the parts of human knowledge obtainable by the exercise of human powers. This classification, which we have already stated in outline, is undoubtedly modelled on that of Aristotle. But Bacon's originality becomes immediately evident when we consider his radical modifications of the traditionally accepted Peripatetic system. According to Aristotle, there are three main sorts of science, the theoretical, the practical, and the "poietical" —the third having to do with the making of things. Each science, of whatever sort, has its own distinctive determining axioms, by which it is rendered separate from and independent of all the others. The sciences of the theoretical group include metaphysics, mathematics, and physics; these manifest several degrees of abstraction. Metaphysics is the most abstract and most universal of all the sciences, having to do with being *qua* being, which may be regarded, in several contexts of explanation in turn, as Pure Form, the First Cause, the First Mover, and God—the object of whose thought is Himself. This supreme science is founded on the metaphysical—as distinct from the logical—principle of identity: What is, is. From this principle is derived both being and unity, the latter convertible with being, as is also goodness which is being in act. The second of the theoretical sciences, mathematics, treats of quantity in abstraction from motion and matter, while the subject matter of the third, physics, consists of materiate things in motion. The motions of physics may be classified in a general way as generation and decay, augmentation, change in character, and local motion. Of the practical sciences, Aristotle names two, ethics and politics—in which ethics attains its end. While in the theoretical sciences the objects concerned cannot be other than they are, in those called practical the subject matter includes adventitious factors, such as choice and deliberate willing on the part of human agents. The third general sort of science includes the arts: medicine, cooking, architecture, husbandry, navigation, poetry, rhetoric, and so on. When describing these "poietical" sciences—those which have to do with making—Aristotle draws a distinction between nature and art. In the case of the latter, a secondary form is imposed on a primary, natural form—the form of a table, for example, or of a house, or the form of a tree. Some of the Peripatetics divide the arts into those of a higher, an "intellectual," sort, such as poetry and music, and those which are "manual," and lower, such as cooking, shoemaking, and husbandry. Aristotle recognized a science or art, namely analytic, later called logic, with its induction and deduction, which he did not place in any one of the divisions of his sciences because, in his view, it was assumed by all.

Aristotle's universe consists of fifty-five concentric spheres, with the earth at the centre. The outermost sphere is the *Primum Mobile*—the First Moved by the Prime Mover. This transmits motion to the remaining spheres in turn. The earth and terrestrial bodies are composed of four elements: fire, earth, air, and water. Terrestrial motion is rectilinear in character. Through this, the elements or "first bodies" tend to take up their respective appropriate places. Actually, the "first bodies" are never found in isolation, and the motions of earthly bodies are always combinations of several rectilinear motions. The element assigned by Aristotle to celestial bodies is a fifth essence, or quintessence, the "ether." Celestial motion is circular, without end or variation, as befits spheres near the First Mover. Their motions may appropriately be regarded as "imitations" of the motion of the *Primum Mobile*, the First Moved by God.

Materate things are composed of matter and form. Matter in and by itself is formless, indeterminate, meaningless, deprived, potential. It is made significant when activated through the agency of form. In the motion of materiate bodies, four causes are to be distinguished: the material, that out of which something becomes; the formal, which brings what becomes out of privation into existence and significance; the efficient, which brings into act what without its operation remains potential; and the final, which is the actuality achieved when something becomes what it had had in it to become. Because the form is the activating agent upon matter, and also marks the end achieved through passage from potency to act, Aristotle sometimes reduces his four causes to two: the formal and the material.

Such is the system in part which Bacon learned at Cambridge. He was not taken with it. Soon he began to regard its logic, in ways already noted, as fruitless, and became unhappy over its divisions, its abstractions, and its interpretations of natural processes and causation. In a rebellion against the teaching of the Peripatetics, Bacon turned to Plato and the Pre-Socratics. He also began to acquaint himself with some more immediate predecessors and contemporaries. In Plato he found to his liking a system of truth wherein things ascended from multiplicity to unity, and also a principle of determination by which infinite particulars were brought within intelligible bounds. But to his disliking he also found in Plato a doctrine by which forms were set in opposition to an indeterminate matter. Going back beyond Plato, Bacon discovered that "almost all the ancients, as Empedocles, Anaxagoras, Anaximenes, Heraclitus, and Democritus, though in other respects they differed about the first matter, agreed in this, that they set down matter as active, as having some form, as dispensing that form, and as having the principle of motion in itself." Of these early thinkers, Democritus impressed him most of all. "The philosophy of Democritus," he said, "seems worthy to be rescued," both because of its freedom from final causes and its assertion of a formed and determinate matter, causal in its motion.

By the time Bacon prepares his first philosophical publication, the *Advancement of Learning*, he has rejected from his thinking the main parts and principles of the Peripatetic philosophy and has chosen alternatives of his own conceiving. These he cultivates during the next fifteen years. He will have nothing to do with any metaphysics or other natural science which professes to deal with the nature and the mind of God, with abstract being as such, with a First Cause or with a Prime Mover. Metaphysics is for him generalized physics, the science of formed matter in motion.

Bacon will not agree in the separation of fields of inquiry by means of axioms. He regards the principle of abstraction, on which the Peripatetics rely in aligning the sciences, as the source of "infinite error" and as one of the impediments in the way of scientific advancement. Aristotle's several motions are reduced by Bacon, as a philosophical materialist, to one, local motion. He will not countenance a separation of matter from form. Rejecting Aristotle's formal and final causes, he recognizes one efficient materiate cause active within formed matter. Bacon dismisses as useless things the four terrestrial elements and also the fifth element, the celestial quintessence. He regards the separation of the respective elements and motions of celestial and terrestrial bodies as a calamity in the history of astronomy. He notes that this separation is still being retained by some of those who profess a "new," heliocentric, theory.

In Bacon's classification of the sciences, mathematics is reduced in status from an independent science to an instrument of metaphysics and physics. The "poietical" sciences are merged with physics. Art and nature become one, both the products of the operation of common material causes. The practical sciences are put within "the Prerogative" of revealed theology. Political initiative and sovereignty are divine bestowals on rulers; the source of the governing principle and rule of ethics is Divine Revelation; all so-called principles of ethics are but "inferences" from this rule.

Bacon is extremely critical of Aristotle's teaching on the subject of ethics. It does not, in his opinion, touch the springs of human action. "We may," Bacon says, "discourse as much as we please," after the manner of Aristotle, "that the moral virtues are in the mind of man by habit, and not by nature, and we may make a formal distinction that generous spirits are won by doctrines and persuasions, and the vulgar sort by reward and punishment; or we may give it in precept that the mind like a crooked stick must be straightened by bending it the contrary way, and the like scattered glances and touches; but they would be very far from supplying the place of that which we require."

For an understanding of human motives, we could find more wisdom, says Bacon, if we turned from the philosophy of Aristotle to poetry and history. Machiavelli also has written informatively in this regard. In the works of poets and historians "we find painted forth with great life and dissected, how affections are kindled and excited, and how pacified and restrained, and how again contained from act and further degree; how they disclose themselves, though repressed and concealed; how they work; how they vary; how they are enwrapped one within another; how they fight and encounter one with another; and many other particularities of this kind amongst which this last is of special use in moral and civil matters."

Bacon has been attacking the Universities continuously for their employment in instruction of the Peripatetic logic and the doctrines and writings of Aristotle. His pleas for alternatives to these were often addressed directly to James and sometimes to Prince Charles. These entreaties produced no discernible effect in the reign of either of these sovereigns. However, during the days of the Commonwealth, Bacon's scheme for learning became the subject of common and vigorous debate. University curricula and exercises were made the objects of attack by pamphleteers and others who repeated what Bacon had written, often in the very words of the *Advancement of Learning*, the

New Organon, and the *New Atlantis*. No less a person than a renowned Oxford professor, Seth Ward—a member of the experimental "philosophical college" which became the Royal Society—found it necessary to publish a vindication of university practices in answer to the writings of William Dell and John Webster, who had stated in vehement language what others again had presented, in keeping with Bacon's criticism of learning, as "humble advices" to the Universities and Petitions to Parliament. Before long, plans for a new sort of institution of learning, which would give effect to Bacon's principles, were drawn up by such men as William Petty, Abraham Cowley, John Evelyn, and Robert Hooke. These innovators were one in thinking what Evelyn said, that "Solomon's House ... however lofty, and to appearance Romantic, hath yet in it nothing impossible to be effected." John Amos Comenius was invited to England mainly for the purpose of reforming the schools of the kingdom according to Bacon's design. Oliver Cromwell warned the Universities that unless they adopted Baconian methods they would be closed. Plans were made to sequester cathedral funds for a "new" public education. Cromwell tried to place the Baconian Samuel Hartlib in the headship of an Oxford College. None of these plans came to fruition. Cromwell's attention was diverted by troubles in Ireland and at Westminster. The Universities refused to provide Hartlib with a post or to bring their curricula into conformity with what was now generally known as the "new learning."

Seth Ward, in his defence of the attitude of the Universities, had the following to say in his *Vindicae Academiarum*, a reply to Webster's *Academiarum Examen, or the Examination of Academies, Wherein is discussed and examined the Matter, Method, and Customs of Academick and Scolastick Learning, and the insufficiency thereof discovered and laid open* (1654): "There is one thing which this sort of pamphleteers insist on, which as it is pursued by my L. Verulam, so it carries weight with it, but it is very impertinently applied, either as an exception against us, or as a general rule to be imposed upon us in our academical institution. It is, that instead of verbal exercises, we should set upon experiments and observations, that we should lay aside our disputations, declamations, and public lectures, and betake ourselves to agriculture, mechanics, chemistry, and the like.

"It cannot be denied that this is the way, and the only way to perfect natural philosophy and medicine: so that whosoever intend to profess the one or the other, are to take that course, and I have not neglected occasionally to tell the world, that this way is pursued amongst us. But our academies are of a more general and comprehensive institution, and as there is a provision here made, that whosoever will be excellent in any kind, in any art, science, or language, may here receive assistance, and be led by the hand, till he come to be excellent; so is there a provision likewise, that men be not forced into particular ways, but may receive an institution, variously answerable to their genius and design.

"Of those very great numbers of youth, which come to our universities, how few are there, whose design is to be absolute in natural philosophy? Which of the nobility or gentry, desire when they send their sons hither, that they should be set to chemistry, or agriculture, or mechanics? Their removal is from hence commonly in two or three years, to the Inns of Court, and the desire of their friends is not, that they be engaged in those experimental things, but that their reason, and fancy, and carriage, be improved by lighter institutions and exercises, that they may become ... graceful speakers, and be of an acceptable behaviour in their countries.

"I am persuaded, that all of these, who come hither for institution there is not one of many hundreds, who if they may have their option, will give themselves to be accomplished natural philosophers (such as will, ought certainly to follow this course). The pain is great, the reward but slender, unless we reckon in the pleasure of contemplation; that indeed is great and high, but therefore to draw all men that way, by reason of the pleasure, were to present a feast for all of custard or tart, and not to consult the variety of tastes, and tempers of our guests."

Although a member of the experimental "philosophical college," which for a period held extramural meetings at Oxford, Ward in the middle of the seventeenth century defended the use of Aristotle's works in ethics and politics and of manuals of traditional logic for pedagogical purposes within the University. In the pamphlet now quoted in part Ward states definitely that the logical works of Aristotle which comprise his "organon" were no longer being read at Oxford. He also expresses the doubt whether any appreciable number of fellows and tutors subscribe to the principles of Peripatetic physics and metaphysics. By the end of the century the opinion was general that, largely through the influence of Bacon and his disciples, the physical and metaphysical doctrines of Aristotle were no longer entertained by learned men in England. Nevertheless, Peripatetic teaching continued in the Universities, not as dogma, but as training in definition, organization of thought, and apt and clear speech; and as means, to acquaint students with the content of historic learning. The authorities of Oxford were not disposed to have their Greek and Latin communications polluted by the recipes and the vernacular, vulgar conversation of "burners of charcoal"—called chemists, apothecaries, farmers, and mechanics, however earnest and diligent these mixers of concoctions, tillers, and assemblers of machines might show themselves to be.

The scientific search which Bacon had begun was to be carried forward outside the Universities from the middle of the century. Members of the Royal Society undertook a "work," as their first historian said, "becoming the largeness of Bacon's wit to devise." These inquirers, at the bidding of the author whom their President, Robert Boyle, called "that profound naturalist . . . Verulam," took for their ambitious aim the investigation of every area of nature available to human observation and experiment. John Locke, whose scientific environment as a member of the Royal Society and whose study of the works of his philosophical progenitor made him one of the most thoroughly Baconian writers of the seventeenth century—specifically in doctrine, illustration, problem, and method—undertook the "historical" recording of the operations and structures of the human mind. Locke became, in turn, the progenitor of an ambitious family of epistemologists of a "psychologically" historical sort.

Not a few historians of philosophy would undoubtedly take issue with our placing of Locke in the Baconian tradition. Because of Locke's concern with "ideas" and "intuition" and his attempt to cope with the body-mind problem, he is often regarded as a disciple of Descartes (1596-1650), and his philosophy as a part of "Cartesianism." This is one of the causes of the contention that Descartes is the source of everything that is distinctively modern in the questions and the methods of modern philosophy. Let us pause, then, to look at some of the differences and similarities in outlook, doctrine, and issue between the two original philosophers of the Late Renaissance, René Descartes and Francis Bacon.

Both these thinkers are products of learning and remain critically aware of the fact. Both have been exposed in university discipline and instruction to practices and problems which had entered the schools of philosophy through successive revivals in learning: of verbal dialectic in the ninth century, of Platonic Augustinianism in the eleventh, of Arabian Aristotelianism in the twelfth, of Christian Aristotelianism in the thirteenth, and of Stoic eclecticism in a succession of ages from the time of Cicero. Neither thinks philosophically fertile the contendings among Scotists, Thomists, Occamists, and the followers of Bonaventure. Both turn from the study of books to consider what is involved in knowledge—in this case, of "nature"—Descartes to determine the character of the things which compose the mind's content and Bacon to control the mind's activities after its purge from "malignancies." Either rejects the main conceptions of the Peripatetics, Descartes after examining his own doubts and Bacon after condemning dialectical modes of thinking. Either is denied an explanation of the epistemological conjunction of subject and object, Descartes because of his absolute separation by definition of mind and body, and Bacon because of his placing the part of man made in the image of God within the domain of Revelation. Both find the Peripatetic logic an unsatisfactory method of inquiry, Descartes advancing an alternative logic of mathematical implication and Bacon providing an inductive directive. Both reject the Aristotelian alignment of the sciences through a doctrine of multiple axioms. Either, like Aristotle, professes a metaphysics. While the Peripatetics in the schools give the ontology of being *qua* being ascendancy over mathematics and physics, Descartes identifies the metaphysics of nature which he professes with mathematical continuities, and Bacon his with the physics of materiate forms. Both reduce Aristotle's varied sorts of motion—including generation, movement from place to place, change in character—to one sort, local, spatial motion. Neither considers contemporary astronomical hypotheses either sufficient for or essential to the formulating of a general philosophy. Neither thinker is, of course, wholly original in what he has to say; no philosopher since Thales, perhaps not even Thales, had ever been that. Descartes revives certain Augustinian conceptions, acquired at La Flèche. Bacon avowedly attempts a return to Pre-Socratic methods and conceptions, and draws, too—perhaps more than he would care to acknowledge—from Plato and the Platonists. Descartes and Bacon are both to prove themselves generative thinkers, yet not so much by the making of specific scientific discoveries, as through something more continuously seminal.

The progeny of Descartes is a succession from generation to

generation of a priori rationalists. Descartes, after entertaining doubt about the offices of sense and reason, takes refuge in mathematically clear and determined ideas. Having applied quantity to geometric forms, he rests his case on an ontology dialectically established. His philosophy emerges as a sort of Stoical, Augustinian Platonism. Its structures are not the products of the activities of a knowing *anima*, or soul, but the noetic content of a nonorganic *mens*, or mind. This content, so far as it serves science, is composed of innate ideas, mathematically coördinated. This content Descartes divides according to two categories, *res cogitans* and *res extensa*, thinking "substance" and extended "substance," by a defining which forbids intercourse between the two things defined. And while he states the former of his two "substances" in the form of the active participle, this "thinking" thing actually performs no operation; its "acts" are specified in terms of its structure—as in the later case of Kant's transcendental mind. By his establishment of a noetic content, Descartes solves to his own satisfaction the problem—a concern of Augustine and Francisco Suarez before him—of making available to human comprehension the *logoi* inherent within the principle of divine omiscience. Descartes' treatment of this question, we may add, is motivated not by an epistemological requirement, but rather by a theological preoccupation.

Thought's content, having been elevated by Descartes into the structure of the "universe," is bequeathed in this form to his philosophical heirs, the Continental rationalists. By them it is specified in such terms as divine attributes, transcendental ideas, transcendental categories, schemata of thought, all of which they find innate, as it were, certainly inherent, within a transcendental mind. Descartes, therefore, may properly be regarded as a "modern" who introduces into inquiry that epistemological puzzle whose solution is said to lie, by the Spinozists, the Kantians, and the logical idealists respectively, in the intellectual

knowledge of God, the identification of human thought-struc-
tures with a transcendental understanding, the possession within
human logic, in "degree" at least, of the Eternal Mind.

Bacon, following a thoroughly different line of thought, denies that man has capacity by natural inquiry to know in range
or degree what God thinks or is. The assumption that man could
do so is for Bacon the presumption and sin whereby Adam fell
and forfeited his rule over the kingdom of nature. Bacon banishes from philosophy the *logos* and *logoi* of the Stoics and the
Augustinians. He sees in philosophical objects only the structures and motions of formed matter. He reduces the transcendental status assigned by Plato and some sorts of Platonist to
mathematics, making it an instrument in physical discovery. He
relegates ontology to the verbal limbo of dialectic, and expels
metaphysical theology from science achieved through human
faculties. He puts distinctively human powers to work on the
investigation of the created world for the recapturing of man's
dominion over Nature.

After rejecting the dialectic procedures of the rationalists
Bacon calls for "a true and lawful marriage between the empirical and the rational faculty," whose ill-starred divorce and separation have brought "confusion" into the philosophical life of
mankind. He asks for a new sort of philosophy, whose "end,
scope, office" will lie not in plausible, resolved, and admired discourse and argument, but in the understanding of particulars
and the production of operative works for "the better endowment and help of man's life." The new philosopher will recognize that the subtlety of nature is greater than the subtlety of
subtle words and arguments. His discoveries will not "float in
air," but will "rest on the solid foundation of experience of every
kind, and the same well examined and weighed." He will be
satisfied with the recapture of that "parcel of the world . . .
fitted to the comprehension of man's mind." His aim will be "the

restitution and reinvesting (in great part) of man to the sovereignty and power [over Nature] which he had in his first state of creation."

The descendants of Descartes, because of the recognition by academics of the continuity of their thinking with *philosophia perennis*, were readily assimilated by learned institutions. Bacon's progeny, when looked at by academics in the "old way," were regarded as little more than mechanics. They were long to be denied admittance to the Universities. Their laboring faithfully, fearlessly, and fruitfully beyond the walls of learning, their industrious example, and the report of undeniable discoveries, eventually caused learned academics to relent. Finally the Baconians were reluctantly invited to enter the portals of the Universities. They arrived with vigor and authority. Step by step they brought about a great modification of university studies. The scientific curricula of modern universities—and modern research foundations; the varieties of and the relations among scientific subject matters; the sciences which employ induction and not simply speculation, experimentally and not verbally defined terms; the philosophies which hang upon the methods and discoveries of the inductive science; the adjusting of new means to new ends for the betterment of the lot of man as an inhabitant of the kingdom of nature with the status of ruler, but not yet in full control—these were to be some of the offspring of the greatest thinker of the English Renaissance. No Telesio, no Campanella, Descartes, Spinoza, Hume, Kant, Schopenhauer, or Hegel has ever produced, or ever could have produced, a like progeny. The more these philosophers, and their kinds, have meditated and have contemplated their concepts and definitions, the less, according to the disciples of Bacon, have they furthered the understanding and the conquest of nature. The more some of them have attempted to elevate to the realm of the a priori and transcendental what, the Baconians say, does not there belong, the more have they hindered man's exercise of his original birthright and his religious duty, the rule over the kingdom of nature.

Bacon's indebtedness to the ancients, notably to Democritus, Plato, and Aristotle is obviously great. His debt to the "philosophers of nature" among his more immediate predecessors and contemporaries is considerable—greater, perhaps, than is commonly supposed. While we know that Bacon was acquainted with their doctrines, in whole or in part, the questions of their influence upon him and his borrowing from them must remain in degree problematical. Certain facts, however, are evident: Bacon philosophizes in the manner of these "moderns," even if he rejects most of their elaborate terminologies. From them he has learned ways of approaching philosophy, problems to be considered by a "modern" philosopher, and some solutions of these problems. Generally speaking, Bacon ignores the Platonico-Aristotelian eclectics, John Pico, Pietro Pompanazzi, Juan Luis Vives, and the rest. He discerns in the "reports" of the observations and experiments of Roger Bacon of the thirteenth century a "good beginning" of inductive inquiry. He is aware of that author's doctrine of Idols, which is different from his own, and his stress on the offices of mathematics and language. Bacon acknowledges, too, that some recent chemists and alchemists have hit upon useful discoveries. As experimenters, he finds them comparable to the sons of a farmer who were told by their father to search in a field for hidden gold. After much digging the laborers failed to discover the object of their search, but by their tillage they did unwittingly cause an increase in the grain crop. Bacon praises William Gilbert (1571-1630) for his diligent, laborious, and fruitful observations of the loadstone, but he thinks that no scientist or philosopher as such would undertake to build a complete universe on the principle of magnetism. Like Descartes after him, Bacon entertains an enlightened scepticism of the "new" astronomy and its philosophical import. Even as Descartes would never have undertaken to propound a theory of the whole of nature on the results of his study of nerve structures, so neither he nor Bacon could suppose that a complete natural philosophy might be founded on some observations of the motions of the heavens. The "new" helio-centric theory, propounded by Nicolaus Copernicus (1473-1543), Galileo Galilei (1564-1642), and their disciples, is, Bacon observes, in fact not new. It was proposed by Pythagoras and has since been advocated by others. It is now being advanced again, but only as an hypothesis which can explain in simpler manner what the Ptolemaic hypothesis can also explain. There still re-main in the minds of some of its late advocates the queries whether the planets contain celestial intelligences, as Aristotle seemed to think they did, and whether they are composed of the same elements as the earth. Bacon notes with approval Galilei's rejection of the traditional opinion that the planets move in perfect circles, and he remarks in jest that in the Ptolemaic com-piling of cycles and epicycles, wheels many miles in circuit are required to carry a ball the size of a palm! Bacon disapproves of Galilei's account of the cause of tides: the incapacity of water to keep up with the velocities of the earth. Bacon's own views on this subject are transmitted by others to Gallilei, who in turn sends reasons for his explanation. Bacon hails Galilei's improve-ment and use of the telescope. This invention marks, in Bacon's opinion, one of the greatest advances in the history of astronomy. The telescope has provided evidence of the fact that the Milky Way is a collection of stars; has enabled an observer to descry the dances of the smaller stars about the greater planets; and has provided the grounds for new hypotheses about centres of mo-tions in the heavens.

Bacon is sympathetic to the appeal by contemporary astron-omers to the axiom of simplicity as a cause for choosing be-tween two opposing theories which both "save" phenomena. Now going beyond what these astronomers in general say, Bacon expresses the opinion that the "passions and desires" of matter are the same in both terrestrial and heavenly bodies, because there is evidence of an expansion of matter, its collection into masses, its contraction, cession, and attraction both on the surface and in the inner parts of the heavens and at their summit as well. His advice to astronomers—advice which is to be acted on by one member of the Royal Society, Isaac Newton (1642-1727)—is to the effect that they should pursue the hypothesis which suggests that there is a common matter with "common passions and desires" in both the earth and the heavens. The investigation of this problem, which is now made feasible by a "new commerce with the phenomena of the heavens," will entail, in Bacon's opinion, two things: the collecting of a massive natural history of phenomena and a doctrine of matter. Let there be arranged, then, pleads Bacon, a valid alliance between the new astronomy and a new philosophy of matter in such a manner that the former will not prejudice the facts, and the latter will affirm only what is explicable and demonstrable through the observation of phenomena in both heaven and earth.

Theophrastus Paracelsus (1493-1541), a physician, has attacked the philosophy of Aristotle and the medical systems of Galen and Avicenna, and condemned the methods of the three authors. Paracelsus professes a reliance on experiments and the histories of diseases. For the humors of the traditionalists among physicians and the four elements of the Peripatetics he substitutes three chemical elements: salt, sulphur, and mercury. Paracelsus also separates, initially but not ultimately, the operations of nature from divine acts in the Kingdom of Grace. Philosophy and science, he says, come from the light of nature, theology and wisdom from the revelation of faith. Philosophy and science by origin are ancient and pagan; they become Christian only by the end to which they are employed. The aim of a Christian philosophy is to bring to completion unfinished nature, which is under the dominion of man. This it can do by use of the applied science of medicine, the most comprehensive of all disciplines.

The creation, according to Paracelsus, contains an invisible astral body, or *spiritus,* and also a *limus terrae,* out of which the elements and all natural things, including man, issue. From created nature issue, too, the nutrition of organisms, sense, desire, and natural reason. Each work in nature displays an *archeus,* which is both an organizing and a transforming agent, the source of the virtues or functions in things; this is shown, for example, in the making of bread and wine and in the assimilation of food. Beyond the realm of nature lies soul, or the non-natural reason, which is the Breath of God, breathed into man by his Maker. This reason is the source and agent of man's moral virtue.

Man is a microcosm in whom are represented all the works of nature; and he is also a participant in what is divine. In the former conjunction, man is nourished through assimilation of metals, herbs, and animals; in the latter he becomes by faith the agent of divine goodness. The task of the physician is to make the ill man whole through the two great healers, nature and God, by drawing upon minerals, herbs, and animal substances on the one hand, and on divine goodness on the other.

Bacon, of course, is very critical of Paracelsus' statement of "medical" therapy, because if its mixing of the human and the divine. He finds the doctrine of the *limus terrae* very obscure. He rejects the new elements, salt, sulphur, and mercury. Like the four Peripatetic "first bodies" which they would supplant, these appear initially as things immediately available to sense but, on further inquiry, they prove to be mere terms of definition, things which never can by either direct or indirect observation, or by experimentation, be made available to sense. Bacon, however, has been struck by the attack of Paracelsus on Aristotle and the Peripatetic methods of demonstration, and by his separation of natural philosophy from the wisdom and the rule of virtue received in revelation by faith. He has been impressed with Paracelsus' regarding the rational part of man as the Breath of God, and his opinion that man can exercise dominion over nature by the employment of applied science. Bacon is sympathetic to Paracelsus' view that natural philosophy as such is neither pagan nor Christian. He has become interested in the Paracelsan kinship between man and the whole of nature. He proposes a doctrine of universal "perception," whereby man and nature "take hold" of each other in nutrition, in sensation, in knowledge, and in the act of producing operative works. Bacon, too, makes use of the *archeus*, calling it *spiritus*, and regarding it as a governing and integrative agent in the composing of material bodies.

Jerome Cardan (1501-1576), another recent thinker, is a systematic physician, very different from Paracelsus in outlook. He is an exponent of traditional medical systems, notably that of Galen. Cardan separates philosophy from theology, taking the aim of the former to be the understanding of nature, and the purpose of the latter the salvation of human souls. He considers both philosophy and theology extremely difficult undertakings, entailing abstruse inquiries; consequently, he thinks that their problems are not suited to the comprehension of the vulgar. As esoteric disciplines, these two studies should not be set forth in vernacular languages to the raising of uninformed disputes about ill-comprehended questions. Of sciences, Cardan regards mathematics as the chief, nothing less than the instrument of the Creator's wisdom in nature. Its prominence in the scheme of things is made evident by the amenability of the motions of the planets to quantitative calculation. Nature is regarded by Cardan as a system of parts related by sympathy and antipathy. Nature is possessed of a common, pervasive soul which manifests itself in heat at the level of sense. Set in opposition to heat, which may also be regarded as light, is cold, which belongs to passive, inert matter. Through the conjunction of these two opposites arise those mixtures which are natural things, possessing in varying degrees warmth, activity, and soul. The highest entity among natural things is man, who contains within him all that is found in minerals, plants, and animals. Man as a part of nature has both body and soul. As a creature capable of faith, likeness to God, and immortality, man is also in possession of *mens*, or mind.

Bacon disapproves of Cardan's dependence on traditional medical systems and his doctrine of sympathy and antipathy. He rejects outright his theories of passive matter and a world-soul. Yet Bacon probably learns several things from this predecessor. Certainly he is taken with the latter's manner of separating theology from natural philosophy and with his rejection of Aristotle's elements. He is in agreement with Cardan's separation of *mens* from those parts of man which belong to a science whose subjects include minerals, plants, and animals. He is impressed by the view in which *mens* is the recipient of what faith bestows. He thinks well of the assigning of a central place to mathematics in an explanation of nature. To the influence of Cardan's emphasis on the abstruse and esoteric character of scientific and theological questions may, perhaps, be attributed Bacon's disdain of the vernacular languages as vehicles of learning, his addressing some of his pieces *ad filios*, and his indicating in his early *Proem* to an interpretation of nature that his new induction should, in discretion, be revealed to but a capable few.

Of all the "novelists," the most impressive in Bacon's view is Bernardino Telesio (1508-1588). Telesio separates philosophy from theology, and contends that the office of the former is to understand the nature of the creation and not to expose the nature of the Creator. Philosophy, Telesio claims, must rely on the observation of particulars and not on "first principles." Even mathematical definitions must have objects of sense for their basis. The scientist should seek through experimentation the simplest explanations which will serve; his hypothesis should never go beyond what may be tried by observation and experiment. Such notions as a general sympathy and antipathy in nature and the four causes of Aristotle must always be held in suspicion. The doctrine of formal and final causes assumes in the beginning what cannot be demonstrated in the end. In place of Aristotle's four elements, or "first bodies," and their severally assigned motions, Telesio offers the principles of Heat and Cold as elements which act upon a motionless, characterless matter. Heat, for Telesio, is neither a first body nor the consequence of motion through activation of matter by form; it is motion itself, with a visible aspect of light. Cold is the principle of inertness, and, in contrast to heat, which has light, it may be regarded under the aspect of darkness. Matter is indifferently susceptible to either agent. Both agents are manifest in the condition of bodies; density is the effect of cold, rarity the effect of heat. Heat through rarity excites motion, and cold through density subdues it. Heat, rarity, light, and mobility are found in greater degree in celestial bodies, most of all in the sun; coldness, density, darkness, and immobility exist in degrees proportionate to distances from what is most hot. In the middle regions cold and heat compete, the latter trying to subdue the former. The things of nature produced in this conflict are each united through the agency of *spiritus,* which governs physical organization.

According to Bacon's interpretation of Telesio and his pupil Donius, these thinkers have "in part... maintained" that the "sensible soul" of man is—to quote Bacon's statement—a "corporeal substance, attenuated and made invisible by heat; a breath... compounded of the natures of flame and air, having the softness of air to receive impressions, and the vigour of fire to propagate its action; nourished partly by oily and partly by watery substances; clothed with the body, and in perfect animals residing chiefly in the head, running along the nerves, and refreshed and repaired by the spirituous blood of the arteries."

Bacon accepts Telesio's account of the soul as valid for that part of it which is produced in natural generation. He praises Telesio as an inquirer who initially undertakes the founding of an inductive philosophy on observation and experiment. Telesio's stress on density and rarity is, likely, the reason for

Bacon's emphasis on condensation and rarefaction among subjects for inductive inquiry. Bacon, however, deplores Telesio's
failure to think through the nature of induction, and his tendency, in consequence, to rely, as his investigation proceeds, on
principles theoretically derived. Telesio, explains Bacon, seizes
upon the factors Heat and Cold because he recognizes them as
major instruments of operation in nature and in art. Heat is
essential to the growth, maturing, and propagation of organisms;
it is indispensable in the arts and in the making of experiments
in the laboratory. Bacon himself chooses the form of heat as the
object of investigation when he provides his most detailed exemplification of inductive process. He incurs his fatal illness
through experimenting on the use of cold in preserving flesh.
Telesio, in Bacon's opinion, goes too far when he assumes, in
keeping with his unproved principles, axioms not established by
observation and experiment: that all celestial bodies are hot and
all earthly bodies cold. Telesio is too intent on regarding heat,
brightness, rarity, and mobility as inseparable "messmates"; because while air has rarity and mobility, it is not necessarily hot.
The moon, while bright, is not heated; boiling water, while hot,
is opaque. An opaque, cold, dense needle on a pivot in a compass
can display quick motion. Telesio also fails to see that there are
many operations in nature and art which show indifference to
heat and cold. But the gravest of all mistakes on his part is the
assumption of an inert matter. Telesio has failed to observe that
even the most minute portion of actual, and not theoretical,
matter possesses an inherent active virtue whereby it resists separation from its kind and refuses to be annihilated. We must
turn away, then, says Bacon, from Telesio's imaginary inert and
formless matter "to the atom; which is a true being," with
formed matter, "dimension, place, resistance, appetite, motion,
and emanations."

Another philosopher who, like Telesio, undertakes in the beginning to base a natural philosophy on what he calls "sense"

and "history" is Thomas Campanella (1568-1639). He separates philosophy from theology, maintaining that theological truths cannot be established on the principles of physics, nor those of a philosophy of nature through appeals to Scripture. As a thinker, Campanella is faced with two "codices," the codex, or manuscript, of Holy Writ and the codex of writing on nature. These two codices, according to Campanella, require separate interpretations. Campanella professedly undertakes to complete that interpretation of the book of nature which Telesio has begun. To this end he, unlike Telesio, interposes between experimental philosophy and revealed theology a metaphysics which possesses its own principle of certainty and also contains certain "proprincipia," or primary principles, which Campanella finds basic to the physical sciences. Metaphysical certitude Campanella founds on the certainty of the existence of the thinking self. *Ens* (being) having been thus attested, *non-ens* (not-being), or *nihil*, follows from the limitation of this *ens*, a limitation attested by the finite character of the self's capacity in thinking and willing. *Ens* (being) contains the proprincipia potentiality, wisdom, and love. The proprincipia of *non-ens* (not-being) are impotency, ignorance, and hate, which mark the limits of the negation inherent within it. *Ens* contains eminently all that comes to be. Nature is the *ens* of the Creator operating under self-imposed negation. *Ens* includes within its essence an archetypal world which contains all possible creations, the world-soul, immortal human souls, or *mentes* (minds), and physical things. Each of these has within it the three proprincipia of both being and of not-being; they consequently possess capacity, knowledge, and desire, but only in limited degree. No object, not even the passive matter of Telesio, is completely inert. The planets, as physical bodies, are, according to Campanella, to be brought along with other bodies in nature under common proprincipia and not left segregate as the so-called heavenly intelligences of the Peripatetics are. While the other planets move around the

sun, as their *centrum amoris* (centre of love, or desire), the sun
as the most fiery, and therefore the most active, of all moves
around the earth as its *centrum odii* (centre of hate, or repugnance). Thus does Campanella attempt to merge the old and
new astronomical theories.

Bacon is greatly taken with Campanella's doctrine of the two
"codices." He thinks of nature as a "second scripture," requiring
a reverent approach by the interpreter. He is impressed also by
Campanella's stress on sense and natural history, which is its
product; but he regards the extension of the doctrines of Telesio
by Campanella as a continuation of the disposition to assert principles which are not inductively established by such a history,
nor rendered through induced operations available to sense as a
faculty which proves particular works. Bacon does not agree, of
course, in Campanella's establishing *ens*—as Descartes does afterwards—through reflection on the self as a thinking being. Bacon
is struck, however, by Campanella's attempt to find in physical
things evidence of a universal science and by his bringing celestial and earthly bodies within one system of matter and motion.
So great a regard has he for Campanella's use of proprincipia
that he incorporates within his own "first philosophy" being and
not-being and the possible and the not-possible. At times, Bacon
seems to agree with Campanella in regarding bodies as desiring
things, for he speaks of their "appetites," but, unlike Campanella,
he denies bodies knowledge, in any degree, and potentiality—as
distinct from possibility—as well. When Bacon adopts, and
adapts, Campanella's proprincipia he prefers the term "the possible" to "the potential" because of the association of the latter
term with Peripatetic doctrine. Bacon is firm in asserting that
everything which happens in nature is actual and never potential.
There are, of course, possibilities which are not yet actual in
nature; but the statement that these somehow exist as potentiali-
ties amounts, for Bacon, to a contradiction in terms. They may
be made actualities only through the operation of what is actual,
and not of what is potential and deprived.

Bacon is in agreement with Campanella when he regards mathematics as an "instrumental science." He takes note that Campanella's *Compendium of Physiology* (or *Natural Philosophy*) is published under the title *Prodromus totius philosophiae Campanellae* (*Forerunner of the Complete Philosophy of Campanella*). Bacon, in turn, calls the introductory fragment which he writes in representation of the Fifth Part of his Great Instauration *Prodromi sive anticipationes philosophiae secundae* (*Forerunners or Anticipations of the New Philosophy*).

Another novel philosopher is Giordano Bruno (1548-1600). He has associations with England. He gave lectures at Oxford on the principles of the Copernican astronomy, interpreting them through the teachings of Nicholas of Cusa (1401-1464). If these lectures were proscribed, Sir Philip Sidney was his patron, and he was favorably regarded by Queen Elizabeth. Bruno has attacked all philosophers, ancient, medieval, and recent; and while he considers the so-called reform of the Aristotelian logic by Peter Ramus (1517-1572) as pretentious and fruitless rhetoric, he finds the formal logic of Raymond Lully (1235-1315) helpful to memory and a useful means for organizing established principles. Bruno has discovered ethical teachings in the ancient poets and from their fables has acquired incentive for condemning the deduction of philosophical principles from the dogmas of revealed theology.

For Bruno, the subject matter of philosophy is nature. Nature is a unity, and this unity is the God of philosophy. Nature is divine through the presence of the One. God is in all things. The whole of nature is both materiate and besouled. The soul of nature is an all-pervasive inner cause. Matter in possession of soul and cause fills infinite space. Nature, or the universe, is a congruence of "atoms," which are the minima of matter. Each atom of matter possesses a unity analogous to the mathematical point. Such a point is not to be regarded as abstract, but as a minimal *prima pars* which contains within it the possible dimensions which become actualized in line and figure. Material entities are actualizations of possibilities within minimal monads. God, as *monas monadum*, the monad of monads, is the supreme philosophical unity, cause, principle, and the final explanation of all things in their attainment of possibilities.

Bacon looks upon the "natural theology" of Bruno as verbal artistry, but he nonetheless learns several things from the artist. Like Bruno, Bacon seeks and finds philosophical teaching in the ancient poets, including grounds for the separation of natural philosophy from revealed theology. He agrees with Bruno in a respect for Lully and a disdain of Ramus. It is probable that through Bruno's influence Bacon is led to treat Lully's logical scheme as a worthy instrument for aligning truths already discovered. Bacon does not, of course, think that Lully's representation of truths by chosen letters of the alphabet and pigments, and the manipulation of these in an elaborately constructed logical mechanism, can lead to any new discovery. Bacon is in agreement with Bruno's contention that nature when spatially regarded is seen to be a system of causes in motion. Bruno provides grounds for the elevation by Bacon of the Democritean theory of atoms into a doctrine of the form as entity with inherent law, cause, and activity.

From these several foregoing thinkers Bacon undoubtedly learns more than we have indicated; yet, taken either singly or together, their philosophical doctrines are never quite equivalent to Bacon's own. Bacon is neither an eclectic philosopher nor a detached historian of thought. Whatever he accepts is transformed by his own thinking in accord with his own distinctive principles. Bacon's main criticism of systematic philosophers generally, from Plato to Bruno, is advanced on the ground of their departure from induction. Bacon considers himself the author of a philosophy unique in its kind. This is a naturalism established from beginning to end through the employment of a specific inductive method, which never lapses into, nor takes refuge within, deduction. Whatever it asserts must be verified experimentally by sense in conjunction with reason. Sense tries the experiment which proves the axiom provided by reason. The axiom is not, then, a sense datum, nor is it composed of sense data; it is a universal definition demonstrable in most instances by particular processes in nature available to sense. If the definition as a direction can show an identical operation in fact, then that definition is a true axiom of science. If the definition is said to pertain to effecting causes which cannot be so demonstrated, as in the case of the principles of Telesio, say, the truth of the axiom is not demonstrated. In this regard, the more comprehensive and general axioms of science, which can suggest yet more comprehensive axioms, require special watching, for the aim of an inductive natural philosophy is the certification in the above manner, until the very end, of those most general principles which are presumed to command the widest causal operation in nature. It is Bacon's opinion that such general principles can be inductively proved and a full philosophy of nature thereby established.

Bacon, of course, never succeeds in providing a full inductive philosophy of nature; but he does, at every stage of his endeavor, resist the temptation to invent a speculative alternative which might pass for such a philosophy. Bacon does not succeed in preparing works in representation of the Fourth Part of the Great Instauration, which is to consist of exemplary Tables of axioms inductively discovered, and consequently can provide nothing of the Sixth Part, which is to contain a systematic philosophy. What this philosophy is to be, and not to be, the author of the *New Organon* can do no more than indicate, because inquiry has only begun. Its subject matter will, he says, comprehend all the structures and processes of nature. Its aim is to discover the forms, causes, and laws of natural operation and, having established these, to control nature in the production of operative works. This philosophy will not become a reality until the immense history on which it must be founded has been fully gathered, and until the axioms—whether lowest, middle, or highest—which sustain it have been inductively secured. No matter how properly its general axioms may be established, these are not at any stage to be considered an all-comprehensive and complete statement of the operations of God's whole natural creation. Nature can never be fully known until inductive inquiry is finally complete. There is to be no premature constructing of a theoretical system.

"God forbid," says Bacon, "that we should give out a dream of our own imagination for a pattern of the world; rather may He graciously grant to us to write an apocalypse or true vision of the footsteps of the Creator imprinted on His creatures." Care must be taken to see that the universe of nature is not endowed by investigators with final causes or with mind. There is in nature no mind or reason, logical, universal, or divine. Such appellations can properly mean nothing more than the "seals" or "signets" which the Creator has stamped upon his material creation, where they appear as material, and not rational, forms. The material universe is not divine in nature, but only in origin. Only from the placets of Divine Revelation—and not through inductive philosophy—does man learn that God is nature's Creator and that nature as a kingdom lies under man's dominion. Inductive science provides no basic rule for human conduct. Human rules for the use of nature's operative works are but inferences from a divinely originated and divinely imposed rule of charity, which is the foundation and the supreme principle of all human virtue.

INDEX

INDEX